CAPTAIN JOHN'S
Fishing Tackle

PRICE GUIDE
SECOND EDITION

John A. Kolbeck
(aka capt. john)

COLLECTOR BOOKS
A Division of Schroeder Publishing Co., Inc.

On the front cover:
South Bend, Nip-L-Diddee, $27.00.
Lex Baits, Kentucky Leader, $18.00.
Rinehart, Musky Jinx, $53.00.
Ness, Nifty Minnie box, $3,742.00.
Pico, Peppy, $145.00.
Heddon, Tiny Punkinseed, $41.00.
Vom Hofe/Conroy, Silver King reel, $310.00.
Haskell, Musky Minnow, photo courtesy of Lang's, $101, 200.00.
CCBC, Pikie, Baby, $189.00.
Makinen, Merry Widow, $13.00.

On the back cover:
Abbey & Imbrie, Crawdad, $21.00.
Hawk, Walleye, $36.00.
South Bend, Bass Obite, $25.00.
CCBC, Midget Pikie, $321.00.
Paw Paw, Pikie type for Sears Roebuck, $34.00.
Pfluger, Palomine, $33.00.
Martin, Salmon lure, $43.00.

Cover design by Beth Summers
Book design by Allan Ramsey

COLLECTOR BOOKS
P.O. Box 3009
Paducah, Kentucky 42002-3009

www.collectorbooks.com

Copyright © 2006 John A. Kolbeck

The current values in this book should be used only as a guide. They are not
intended to set prices, which vary from one section of the country to another. Auction prices as well as dealer prices vary greatly and are affected by condition as well
as demand. Neither the author nor the publisher assumes responsibility for any
losses that might be incurred as a result of consulting this guide.

Searching for a Publisher?

We are always looking for people knowledgeable within their fields. If you feel
that there is a real need for a book on your collectible subject and have a large
comprehensive collection, contact Collector Books.

*Proudly printed and bound in the
United States of America*

Contents

Dedication

I would like to dedicate this edition to my wife, Jackie, and my son, James. Without their help and understanding, I would never have finished!

Acknowledgments

Thanks to Debbie and John Ganung, who provided prices realized and some great photos from recent Lang's Sporting Collectables Inc. sales. I also must thank Bill McVeigh and Larry Sundall for providing actual prices of many items they sold off their mailing lists.

Introduction

"What's it worth?" How many times have I heard that question!

If old tackle were like stocks and bonds, the answer would be much easier. But unlike shares of stock, every old piece of tackle is unique. Value depends on the exact model, color, type of hardware, packaging, condition, and many other factors.

One could check asking prices at shows, on price lists, or on the Internet. But unless somebody actually buys the item at the asking price, it is not a reliable indicator. Sellers often ask far more than what the market will bear. After all, you can always lower your price if nobody buys, but it is hard to raise it once it is sold. Likewise you could check prices being offered by buyers — but these offers are much harder to find than asking prices. And again, the person posting a "Wanted to Buy" price may be making a very low offer.

So what's a swab to do? Well, you have the answer in your hands!

While no price guide is ever perfect, I think prices of actual transactions are much closer to the truth than anything else. Now, I have heard the argument that auction prices are too high because folks often get carried away and bid too much. Or even that auction prices are too low because of outside events. But I contend that they are still a whole lot better than somebody's estimate. At least with a completed transaction, the buyer and seller were both happy with the price at the time the deal occurred. The time of transaction is another crucial ingredient. That is why I include the date of the transaction in this book.

The prices contained in here are real prices. They come from auctions (both live and electronic) as well as private deals (including price lists). They are not wishful thinking on my part because I want to sell you my lures (too high) or because I want to buy your lures for my collection (too low).

A key ingredient for these prices is the date of the transaction. This is missing from nearly all other guides. Since prices do change, a price without a date is not of much use. Prices for many lures are lower now than when I wrote the first edition. Many of these prices from 1999 to 2003 are still included. By comparing them to more recent entries, you can get an idea of the way things are changing.

Many times auctions end with a reserve not met (arrrgh!). Much as I hate reserve auctions, they still are valuable sources of information. They let you know how much someone was willing to pay for an item, even though the seller wasn't willing to accept it. Such auctions are noted with "NOT MET" in the description area.

I have tried to sort things into a logical order. There are many entries for more popular items. This is something missing from most other guides. Now you can actually look up what a bluegill Heddon Punkinseed sold for or one in any of several other colors. I have tried to squeeze as much information as possible into the description area. I have used standard company abbreviations plus a few of my own. Hopefully you will able to figure out my shorthand.

I have tried to make every effort to be sure that the information contained in this book is accurate. But with so many entries, no doubt a few errors will creep in. Before you spend all your doubloons on a deal that sounds too good to be true, best double check. Too easy for a decimal point to be misplaced! I won't be held responsible for any errors — but if you find some, please let me know and I'll fix them in a future edition.

State of the Market

As I write this during the summer of 2005, lure prices are down. Good news if you are a buyer, but not so good if you are liquidating your collection. While some areas continue to show unbelievable prices, other things, like underwater minnows, continue to bring less at auction.

Why? Too many folks have never been in the collectibles market before. They think of purchases as investments — in my opinion, nothing could be further from the truth. Whether it is a Picasso or a Heddon, it is not an investment. Old lures should only be purchased because you enjoy looking, touching, and researching them. It drives me to drink (well at least some good comes of it — har!) when I see auctions with reserves that say "I have placed a reserve on this item to protect my investment." I have seen it all before in coin collecting and baseball card collecting. Once investors show up, prices rise rapidly. Then prices crash when these speculators try to sell the items for even higher prices to new investors. At some point, fresh money is no longer coming into the market. Throw in a bad stock market and some terrorist attacks and you have investors panicking when they finally realize they will have to sell at a loss. By the time this is in print, even more changes are likely to have taken place!

Japanese collectors seem to be getting back into the market. This should cause prices to rise, at least for the items they are buying. Less expensive items seem to be holding their own. Unlike the stock market, high-end lures are very thinly traded. Not many folks are willing to plunk down five-figures for a fishing lure. If several collectors with major collections liquidated at the same time, prices would drop. Not only would the supply increase, but in this scenario, there would now be fewer buyers. Course, the opposite is also true. If few are selling high-end lures and a dozen Baby Boomers suddenly decide to collect Heddon musky minnows, you can bet prices will climb.

Another thing that always lowers prices of genuine old items (for a time, anyway) is the appearance of fakes, altered items, and authorized reproductions. Once an item is made and marketed as a "collectible" rather than as a usable item, I start to worry. The most sought-after collectibles are those that were made to be used – not saved up to sell at a higher price down the road. "Limited Editions" are usually only limited by how many the manufacturer can sell. But there is no use complaining about reproductions that come right from the factory. After all, the factory is in business to make a profit and has every right to make more lures. You do need to learn how to tell the originals from the authorized reproductions. All the complaining by collectors will have little effect eliminating factory reproductions.

Fakes and unmarked repaints are another matter, and those making them should be rooted out and prosecuted. Sadly, fakes and repaints are starting to show up more and more in antique tackle. Experienced collectors are rarely fooled by fakes, but the new collector is often fleeced. Once cheated, the new collector is likely to leave the hobby for good. But this same thing happens in every collecting area. Once prices get high enough, the con artists show up. Knowledge is your only real defense. Joining a tackle club such as the National Fishing Lure Collectors Club (NFLCC) is a great first step in learning about old tackle before you plunk down lots of money.

My best advice is to buy only what you like and want to keep. Do your homework before you buy. Join a club. I will be glad to help you join the NFLCC. Attend shows and find someone you can trust. When in doubt, get several opinions. Avoid any collectable that is hyped as a "great investment." Authorized reproductions are here to stay. I know many hate repros, but better to learn to live with 'em than waste time complaining.

I am always looking to buy lures for my collection. I also take them on consignment and get you the best possible price. Email or call me if you have any old tackle you want to sell.

Email: jakolbeck@charter.net
Telephone: (715) 341-5687

How to Use This Book

The easiest way to use this book is to note the column headings. Each item is arranged alphabetically by column. If you have a Heddon 210 in frog spot that you want to look up, first find the lure section. All the lures are grouped together. Now look down the first column ("Brand") until you find the Heddon lures. Again, these are all clustered together. Finally, find the 210 lures by looking in the second column, "Model."

You should note several Heddon 210 lures all grouped together. Shift over another column to "Description" and look for a frog spot. It might be listed as 210BF, which is the manufacturer's code. It might also be "frog spot" or just "frog." Try to find one that closely matches your lure, as there might be several frog 210s listed. Many details are listed in the description column, including type of eyes, hardware, type of box if included, and much more. I tried to squeeze in as much info as possible — especially critical details that can make a huge difference in price.

If you find more than one match, check the grade to see if it is close to your example. Lastly, check the price and when the item sold (last two columns). The date of the transaction can be crucial, as prices have been changing rapidly the past five years. But even if the date of the transaction is old, it still is useful. By comparing similar lures in this guide, you can get an idea which specific colors or models are rare in relation to others. In the case of the Heddon frog 210, you will note this color has some of the lowest prices of all 210s. This is your tipoff that frog is a common color on this lure.

Many prices have been rounded off to the nearest dollar.

Author Abbreviations

Abbrev.	Definition	Abbrev.	Definition
2pc	Heddon two-piece hardware	NIP	new in pouch
2PCCB	two-piece cardboard box	NIT	new in tube
2PPTB	two-piece plastic top box	NMIB	near mint in box
3-hk	three-hook lure (two side hooks)	NNOP	no name on prop
3-scr	three-screw	NOC	new on card
4-scr	four-screw	NOP	name on prop
5-hk	five-hook lure (four side hooks)	NOT MET	reserve not met in an auction
alum	aluminum	NR	non-resident
avg	average	NSOB	name stenciled on back
Banner	Heddon Banner box	NSOS	name stenciled on side
BBE	bead eyes	o	orange
blk	black	pat	patent
BW	belly weight	PE	painted eyes or pressed eyes
bx	box	PGE	painted glass eyes
DBB	Down Bass Box	POBW	paint off belly weight
DLB	Down Leaping Bass Box	PTCB	plastic top cardboard box
DLT	double line tie	RB	rainbow
Down	Heddon Down Bass box	rf	rough
EX	excellent	RH	red/white or red head
EX-	excellent minus	ROBW	ring (crack) around paint
EXIB	excellent in correct box		on belly weight
EXIT	excellent in tube	r/w	red/white or red head
FS	free spool	SD	star drag
G	good	SLT	single line tie
GE	glass eyes	sm	small
goodies	extra stuff with a reel	SR	surface rig hardware
gs	German silver	TE	tack eyes
g. silver	German silver	toilet	Heddon toilet seat hardware
HD	heavy duty	un	unmarked
HPGM	hand painted gill marks	Up	Heddon Up Bass box
IC	in case	VG	very good
lg	large	VG-	very good minus
MO	molded on hardware	VG+	very good plus
MR	mint restored	w	white
NIB	new in correct box	y	yellow

Manufacturers' codes are used extensively when known. These are too numerous to explain in this key.

Ads

BRAND	MODEL	SERIES / MFG. CODE / DESCRIPTION	GRADE	PRICE	DATE yy/mm
Heddon	Lone Eagle Reel	12" x 18"	VG	$2,027.00	00-11
South Bend	Stand-up Display	3' x 5', "Fish & Feel Fit"	EX	$2,150.00	99-10

Award Pins

BRAND	MODEL	SERIES / MFG. CODE / DESCRIPTION	GRADE	PRICE	DATE yy/mm
Field & Stream	?	30 lb., not sure of fish	EX	$61.00	99-08
Field & Stream	Arctic Grayling	round award badge with "Grayling"	EX	$205.00	04-02
Field & Stream	Bass	4 lb., 4 oz.	EX	$66.00	99-02
Field & Stream	Pike	26½ lb.	EX	$37.00	04-11
Field & Stream	Smallmouth	4 lb. 11 oz.	EX	$67.00	99-01
Field & Stream	Smallmouth Bass	5 lb. 13 oz.	EX	$35.00	04-11
Field & Stream	Walleye	9 lb. 5 oz.	EX	$169.35	00-03
Toronto Star	Birks Sterling	¾" round, leaping fish unknown vintage	EX	$164.00	05-07

Bait Tins

BRAND	MODEL	SERIES / MFG. CODE / DESCRIPTION	GRADE	PRICE	DATE yy/mm
Winchester	Belt Worm Can	a few letters left of "WINCHESTER"	avg	$190.00	05-02

Bobbers

BRAND	MODEL	SERIES / MFG. CODE / DESCRIPTION	GRADE	PRICE	DATE yy/mm
Bait Life		Mass. item	NIB	$12.00	02-12
Childress	6 Different	nice paint, c. 1950	EX	$102.50	99-07
Glo Lite	Electric Bobber	green, nice box & crisp papers EX	NIB	$55.00	05-07
Hagen	Rotor Bobber	papers included	NIB	$41.00	01-08
Mermaid Bait Co	Novelty	black hair	EX	$25.77	99-07
Mid-North Tackle	Kroker	12 bobbers on stand-up counter display, NOT MET	NIB	$99.00	05-07
Montague	Automatic Casting Float	great picture box, still in original cellophane	EX-NIB	$137.00	04-11
Olsen, Nels	Bobber	1901 patent, papers, unmarked box, IA item	NIB	$301.00	01-10
Pequea	Display	19 floats (15" wood box)	EX	$550.00	04-11
Pequea	Display	59 floats in folding box 18" x 29", one of only two known	EX	$10,450.00	04-11
Smith, Charles	Wood	1881 patent paper copy, unmarked, 2⅜", 60% paint	VG	$330.00	04-11
Stamdie Products	Nibble Nabber	auto strike	mint	$510.00	00-08

Books

BRAND	MODEL	SERIES / MFG. CODE / DESCRIPTION	GRADE	PRICE	DATE yy/mm
Heddon	Bee Culture	128 pages, 1885, very plain looking	VG	$772.00	03-12
Helin	1953	48 pages, promo from factory	EX	$31.00	05-05
Orvis Marbury	Favorite Flies	1896 original, first 5 pages loose, not too bad otherwise	VG	$129.00	05-07
Rhead, L.	American Trout Stream Insects	177 pages, 1916, spine repaired, 13-Apr		$550.00	04-11
Taylor, Samuel	Angling in All Its Branches	1800, 1st edition, 298 pages	VG	$280.00	99-11
Wells, Henry	Fly Rods & Fly Tackle	1885, 357 pages	VG+	$143.00	04-11

Bottle Openers

BRAND	MODEL	SERIES / MFG. CODE / DESCRIPTION	GRADE	PRICE	DATE yy/mm
Philadelphia	Metal Fish	1911 patent Philadelphia Gun & Fishing Club	EX	$27.00	05-01

Boxes

BRAND	MODEL	SERIES / MFG. CODE / DESCRIPTION	GRADE	PRICE	DATE yy/mm
4 Brothers	#3167	minnow, 3⅝"	VG	$546.00	99-074
4 Brothers	Underwater Minnow	white label, NOT MET!	ugly	$143.00	00-08
Abbey & Imbrie	Go-Getter	colorful 2PCCB	EX-	$32.75	99-11
Abbey & Imbrie	Go-Getter	1PCCB window style	EX-	$16.00	02-08
Abbey & Imbrie	Weedless Surface Minnow	yellow dolphin label over S. Bend box, NOT MET	EX-	$294.99	99-07
ABU	5000DLX	wood with goodies	mint	$152.50	99-01
ABU	Ambassadeur	black imitation leather for C reels	EX	$25.16	99-06
AL&W	Up Bass	red beaver logo, bass with fly	VG	$250.00	99-03
Bass A Lure	BO 2 Special	bottom missing	VG	$34.85	99-08
Bauman	Minnow Cage Bait	all corners split	VG	$1,280.00	00-10
Biff	Godevil & Whoopee	2 very nice early pic boxes	EX	$130.00	01-05
Bomber Bait Co.	3 Different	2PCCB boxes	VG	$10.00	99-01
Bomber Bait Co.	7 Different	4 2PCCB, 3 CBPT	EX	$23.00	99-01
Bomber Bait Co.	Mfg. Co.	no number	avg	$56.00	00-09
Buel, J.T.	Minnow Gang	plain looking	EX-	$585.00	01-01
Carter/Dunks	Bestever	pic box	VG+	$61.00	99-12
CCBC	12-pack	empty for Baby Crawdad 4000	EX-	$300.00	99-11
CCBC	7000 12-pack	fish pictures, grease pencil	EX	$255.00	00-04
CCBC	Crawdad intro	lure & papers, box VG-	VG-	$421.00	02-07
CCBC	Creek Crab Wiggler	white intro box w/lure, NO BIDS	avg	$2,250.00	99-10
CCBC	Delux Six Assortment	beater box with lures	VG+IB	$710.00	00-08
CCBC	F50	red edges, pike & bass normal box	vg	$262.00	03-01
CCBC	Fly Rod Froggie	fly rod pic box	EX	$3,217.00	01-02
CCBC	Fly Rod Froggie	F-80 with picture of lure on top	EX-	$2,025.00	05-07
CCBC	Hum Bird	F300 fly rod pic box	EX	$3,251.00	01-02

BRAND	MODEL	SERIES / MFG. CODE / DESCRIPTION	GRADE	PRICE	DATE yy/mm
CCBC	Injured Minnow Husky	3500 label	EX-	$67.00	99-11
CCBC	Large	unmarked	EX-	$40.00	99-10
CCBC	Pikie	12-pack, graphic! NOT MET	VG-	$153.51	99-05
CCBC	Pikie 700 Picture Box	y, comes with lure (VG+), pocket catalog EX-	EX-	$2,500.00	01-12
CCBC	Sarasota	3308, stencil, papers	EX	$153.50	00-04
CCBC	V344	Baby Dingbat in pearl chub	VG	$107.00	00-10
CCBC	Wiggler	picture intro box with papers	VG	$635.00	99-01
CCBC	Wiggler	yellow intro pic box	VG	$325.00	99-01
CCBC	Wiggler intro	early version? not in Smith's book	VG-	$409.00	02-02
CCBC	337	ALW box with stencil 337	EX	$28.01	99-11
CCBC	732	stencil	EX-	$37.00	01-10
CCBC	1524	Injured Minnow, redwing blackbird label	EX-	$140.00	04-02
CCBC	1619	stencil	EX-	$49.00	04-02
CCBC	2000	darter, insert	EX	$7.00	01-02
CCBC	2201		VG	$26.00	99-08
CCBC	2631	Rainbow Fire jointed pikie, stamp	EX	$42.00	99-05
CCBC	2632	Fireplug jointed pikie, stamp	EX	$42.31	99-05
CCBC	3000	SOLD	EX-	$28.00	99-10
CCBC	3401	Snook pikie, end label	VG+	$14.00	03-01
CCBC	4002	big green box	EX-	$45.00	03-02
CCBC	5113	label, "Black Ding Bat"	EX	$76.00	02-03
CCBC	5119	label, "Frog Ding Bat"	EX	$75.00	02-03
CCBC	5404	Golden S. Surface Dingbat	VG	$37.00	98-12
CCBC	5419	Surface Dingbat label, papers	EX	$53.00	00-08
CCBC	6701	Big Bomber Musky lure box	EX	$49.99	99-12
CCBC	6913	corners split	avg	$20.00	01-02
Eger	Nature's Lures	real frog skin bait, pic of frog	G	$1,852.00	02-10
Eger x 5	Fish Logo	blue/white, 5 diff	VG	$84.00	99-08
Etchen	Helga Devil	nice cartoon box	EX	$16.00	01-08
Expert	Wooden Minnow	wood box, paper label, unknown mfg.	VG	$535.00	04-12
Foss, Al	#13	2PCCB, True Temper	EX+	$50.00	05-06
Foss, Al	#15	2PCCB, red mouse	VG+	$25.00	05-06
Foss, Al	#16	2PCCB, r&w Minnie the Moocher	EX	$75.00	05-06
Foss, Al	#4	green hinged	VG+	$35.00	05-06
Foss, Al	Little Egypt	intro picture box top nice, sides rf white pasteboard	VG+??	$201.00	04-03
Foss, Al	Pork Rind Fly	tin	VG-	$32.51	99-01
Foss, Al	Tin	blue, unmarked	VG+	$25.00	05-06
Frost	Senate	wood, paper label ratty, NY lure	VG	$484.00	00-08
Frost, H.J.	Otter 2WT	maroon picture box	EX-	$426.00	99-12
Garland	Cork-Head A4	red box, text only, FL lure	EX	$355.00	01-02
Gateway	CR-24	green	VG+	$76.00	01-01
Harkauf	Plug Bait	picture box white label, maroon 2PCCB, "Hooks 1 doz"	VG-	$711.00	05-07
Heddon	0 Minnow	white pasteboard	avg	$887.50	99-11
Heddon	00	Down Bass, can barely see number	avg	$281.00	00-04
Heddon	100 Wood	Fancy Back 2-way slide	EX	$1,080.00	99-09
Heddon	100 Wood	NOT MET	EX-	$650.00	00-10

BRAND	MODEL	SERIES / MFG. CODE / DESCRIPTION	GRADE	PRICE	DATE yy/mm
Heddon	103 Aluminum	wood	EX-	$1,675.00	00-09
Heddon	103 Wood	alum, papers!	EX-	$850.90	00-01
Heddon	109A	white Down Bass, VG- with lure	VG-	$1,000.00	99-10
Heddon	109A	wood box type V, yellow perch nice	EX	$1,000.00	05-06
Heddon	109D	Down Bass crisp, avg lure	avgIB	$471.99	00-02
Heddon	109D	Up Bass	EX	$180.00	00-10
Heddon	109L	Down Bass, red border, tall box	EX-	$330.00	00-05
Heddon	109L	Up Bass	EX	$128.00	01-05
Heddon	149P	Up Bass, flipper, very faint	VG+	$170.00	00-12
Heddon	150 Wood	rough papers	VG	$712.00	00-03
Heddon	150 Wood	very faded	avg	$227.00	00-12
Heddon	150FG	wood, NOT MET	VG	$531.00	99-06
Heddon	152 White	wood, sm corner chip	VG+	$711.51	99-06
Heddon	154 Wood	faded some but nice	VG+	$885.52	00-02
Heddon	154 Wood	c. 1905, "Hung!"	EX-	$1,576.51	99-07
Heddon	154 Wood		VG+	$800.00	00-01
Heddon	159BP	Up Bass	VG-	$100.00	00-08
Heddon	159H	red scale, top only tall box	VG+	$200.00	01-01
Heddon	159L	Up Bass	avg	$36.00	02-01
Heddon	1600S	extra tall Down Bass, c. 1915	EX	$303.00	05-07
Heddon	179M	Up Bass EX-, dace L-rig lure	avgIB	$93.00	01-02
Heddon	1809B	Down Bass nice	EX	$340.00	00-07
Heddon	1809C	Down Bass, papers	VG+	$86.00	00-08
Heddon	1909L	Baby Crab, Down Bass	EX	$92.00	01-05
Heddon	190-NP	Banner	EX	$22.00	01-02
Heddon	2 Up, 1 Brush	7502 LUM R, 9109P, 9332XS	avg	$56.01	99-08
Heddon	2100XBW	WBH lure in EX, S-rig	EX	$101.51	99-06
Heddon	2100XRS	Banner	VG	$11.50	99-02
Heddon	210BM	Brush	EX	$75.00	99-08
Heddon	212 LUM	Brush + paper	EX-	$35.00	05-06
Heddon	2120BWH	Brush	VG	$15.00	05-06
Heddon	2120XRW	Brush	VG	$15.50	99-08
Heddon	2150 BF	Banner box	EX	$79.00	05-07
Heddon	2150YRH	Banner	EX	$97.00	01-04
Heddon	229D	Brush	VG+	$20.00	05-06
Heddon	2509M	Down Bass	EX	$70.00	01-05
Heddon	290CP	Down Bass with catalog	EX-	$90.00	04-11
Heddon	34	Trout-size Wilder Dilg #34 Up Bass box	EX	$165.00	05-06
Heddon	3409BB	Up Bass Little Luny frog	VG-	$57.00	01-08
Heddon	5009D	intro Tadpolly box, top decent/ends rough	avg	$138.00	02-12
Heddon	5009L	Down, pat 1902	VG	$113.50	99-08
Heddon	53	Bass Bug Down Bass	EX	$173.00	01-10
Heddon	5509D	Down Bass	EX	$123.51	99-12
Heddon	5509M	Up Bass, UM or JM	VG	$139.50	99-02
Heddon	589XPLB	Brush small (BX-6) Wee Willy	EX	$200.00	01-09
Heddon	7050RH	Brush large	VG+	$26.00	00-11
Heddon	709R	Down Bass, oversized	?	$250.00	01-02
Heddon	730 XBW	Banner box!	VG+	$64.00	05-07

BRAND	MODEL	SERIES / MFG. CODE / DESCRIPTION	GRADE	PRICE	DATE yy/mm
Heddon	7300S	Banner box	EX	$21.00	99-01
Heddon	7309M	Down Bass	EX	$135.75	99-04
Heddon	7309N	Brush 7309N jointed Vamp	VG	$78.00	99-01
Heddon	730BGL	Brush	VG	$76.00	99-02
Heddon	730BGL	Brush, "Improved" Punkinseed paper	EX-	$104.00	02-03
Heddon	7359L		EX-	$91.00	01-03
Heddon	740 SHA	Punkinseed, Brush box with pocket catalog	mint	$211.00	03-05
Heddon	740ROB	Brush	EX+	$281.00	01-12
Heddon	740ROB	Brush box for Punkinseed	EX	$157.00	05-07
Heddon	7500S	Up Bass, L-rig hook, patent sides	VG+	$30.00	05-06
Heddon	7509D	Down Bass, ugly big tear on top	avg	$46.00	01-05
Heddon	7509D	Down Bass, Game Fish nice	EX-	$178.51	99-05
Heddon	7509L	Vamp, Down Bass	EX-	$128.49	99-07
Heddon	7509M	Up Bass	EX-	$66.55	99-12
Heddon	7509P	Down Bass	VG+	$75.00	05-06
Heddon	8509PRH	Up Bass	EX	$47.00	00-02
Heddon	9109P	Fish Flesh	EX-	$27.50	00-04
Heddon	9109XRY	Brush for Super Dowagiac Spook	EX	$57.00	05-07
Heddon	9110RH	minty Runt box & pocket cat	EX+	$22.49	99-04
Heddon	9119GW	Brush	EX-	$63.00	02-03
Heddon	9140XRYF	2PCCB	G	$9.99	98-12
Heddon	9149L	Brush	VG+	$15.00	05-06
Heddon	9339XRS	Brush	VG+	$15.00	05-06
Heddon	9339XRY	Brush + paper	VG+	$15.00	05-06
Heddon	9400GFR	Runt box	EX-	$17.00	04-03
Heddon	9400SR-XRW	River Runt box & papers	EX	$41.00	04-02
Heddon	9400XRY	Runt Box with color pocket catlog	EX-	$10.00	04-03
Heddon	9402LUM	River Runt "wall eyes"	VG+	$76.00	01-08
Heddon	9409GW	Brush box	EX	$32.31	99-04
Heddon	9409SS	Brush	VG+	$20.00	05-06
Heddon	9409XRG	Brush	VG+	$15.00	05-06
Heddon	9409XRG	Brush box with new version color catalog	EX-	$13.00	05-03
Heddon	9509M	Up Bass	VG+	$30.00	05-06
Heddon	9630Sun	PTCB	EX	$29.00	03-01
Heddon	B110P	Brush	EX-	$20.00	00-11
Heddon	B112	Brush, Midget Digit	VG-	$36.57	99-09
Heddon	Bass Bug	#52, red/white letter box	EX	$227.51	99-08
Heddon	Bass Bug	#61, red/white letter box	EX	$260.01	99-08
Heddon	Basser	8502 Brush	EX+	$64.55	99-09
Heddon	Basser	Down Bass 8509M	G	$36.00	99-01
Heddon	C9859P	Flesh Basser Spook, NOT MET	EX	$70.00	01-03
Heddon	Chugger	9542 Brush, cat	EX	$29.00	99-04
Heddon	Crab	9909NC Brush	VG	$16.55	99-03
Heddon	Crab Wiggler	Down Bass un	VG++	$78.00	01-02
Heddon	Crazy Crawler	2100XRS, Banner, catalog	EX-	$46.00	99-07
Heddon	Crazy Crawler	2120BWH Banner box	mint	$41.00	99-03
Heddon	D9110S	Runt box with color pocket catalog	VG+	$21.00	04-03
Heddon	Deep-O-Diver	white box	fair	$280.00	99-04

BRAND	MODEL	SERIES / MFG. CODE / DESCRIPTION	GRADE	PRICE	DATE yy/mm
Heddon	Deep-O-Diver	intro box with VG+ lure	VG	$224.00	03-12
Heddon	Deep-O-Diver	white intro box, lightly soiled	EX	$503.00	02-03
Heddon	Deep-O-Diver	white pasteboard	EX-	$450.00	99-12
Heddon	Down Bass	white border	poor	$55.00	00-04
Heddon	Down Leaping Bass Box	Marked "No. 1," c. 1912, general wear flyer and 4 loose dummy double hooks	G?	$412.50	05-04
Heddon	Fish Flesh	large size	VG+	$55.00	99-11
Heddon	Gamefish	Down Bass, tall box	VG	$105.00	01-02
Heddon	Gamefisher	5509D	VG+	$127.00	01-03
Heddon	ICE L	Down Bass for decoy, comes with a pike scale (M color)	VGIB	$1,243.00	04-01
Heddon	Killer 450	white, NOT MET, sm notches, b/w pic	VG	$2,282.00	01-06
Heddon	Musky Vamp	Down Bass, no stamp, 8¾" x 3" and 1¾"	EX-	$2,183.00	02-06
Heddon	N9119GW	Brush box, end stencil little rough	VG	$77.00	03-04
Heddon	N9119L	with pocket cat & intro paper	VG+	$46.00	99-04
Heddon	N9119XGF	Brush + paper	VG+	$45.00	05-06
Heddon	No. 156	wood box	VG+	$385.00	05-07
Heddon	Punkinseed	740BGL Brush	avg	$31.00	99-03
Heddon	Punkinseed	740ROB	mint	$162.50	99-01
Heddon	Punkinseed	740SUN	VG	$36.00	99-01
Heddon	Punkinseed	740SUN, Brush	VG+	$67.00	00-04
Heddon	Punkinseed	740XRY	VG	$59.00	99-01
Heddon	Punkinseed	9630BGL, Banner, 3 Runt boxes	EX – fair	$51.00	99-05
Heddon	Punkinseed Tiny	stand up card for 6 tinys, 3 included	NOC	$550.00	00-08
Heddon	River Runt	9010SFWBS with catalog	EX	$53.00	04-11
Heddon	River Runt	9119XRY, wall-eye	EX-	$8.00	99-01
Heddon	River Runt	9330S	EX	$29.00	00-03
Heddon	River Runt	9439P, Brush	EX	$42.00	99-04
Heddon	River Runt	W9119P, No-Snag GW, Brush	VG	$79.00	99-01
Heddon	River Runt Deep Diver	D9110RH, square lip	NIB	$26.00	04-03
Heddon	River Runt No-Snag x 2	N9112, N9119M	EX-	$71.00	02-07
Heddon	Sliding Lid Wood Box.	Dowagiac Minnow box, fancy back No.100	GD	$104.50	04-11
Heddon	Spoony Frog	lg display box, NOT MET	EX	$2,025.00	99-03
Heddon	Spoony Frog box	display box with 5 – 6 compartments	EX-	$577.50	05-07
Heddon	Surface Wiggler	1602, tall Down Bass box	VG	$167.50	99-03
Heddon	Tadpolly	intro box	VG	$200.00	04-03
Heddon	Tiger	circus wagon promo box, in Daisy mailer	mint	$228.00	04-11
Heddon	Up Bass	no code, punch-through top, OK	VG-	$57.50	00-01
Heddon	Up Bass		EX-	$75.00	01-02
Heddon	Vamp	7500 S, Down Bass	EX	$126.55	99-11
Heddon	Vamp	Down Bass, not numbered	EX-	$69.00	01-05
Heddon	Vampire	shiner scale, GE, L-rig, Down Bass EX, paper	EXIB	$147.00	05-07
Heddon	Walton Feather Tail	#42, Down Bass	EX	$86.00	99-08
Heddon	White No. 102	wood very nice	VG+	$688.88	99-01
Heddon	Wiggle King	intro box	EX	$621.00	02-03
Heddon	Wiggle King	intro	VG	$455.00	00-07
Heddon	Wilder-Dilg #33	red letter/white box, trout size	EX	$102.51	99-08
Heddon	Wilder-Dilg Trout	intro box, "PAT.APP'D FOR" on end	EX-	$500.00	05-06

BRAND	MODEL	SERIES / MFG. CODE / DESCRIPTION	GRADE	PRICE	DATE yy/mm
Heddon	Wilder-Dilg	Irvin Cobb pic box	EX-	$432.00	02-08
Heddon	Wood	Heddon/Daisy	EX	$85.00	99-02
Heddon	Wood #2	"Hung!"	EX	$1,712.00	00-01
Heddon	11	white intro box, casting minnow lure	VG-	$1,500.00	99-10
Heddon	100	Down Bass	EX-	$352.00	00-08
Heddon	100	Up Bass	EX-	$96.01	99-06
Heddon	100	wood box type IV, comes with lure with huge crack in wood	EX+	$900.00	05-07
Heddon	101	Down Bass later	EX	$230.00	01-02
Heddon	101	tall Down Bass box	EX-	$211.00	05-07
Heddon	101	white pasteboard & papers	VG-	$758.00	04-01
Heddon	101	white pasteboard with VG+ lure	VG	$1,785.00	00-06
Heddon	101	white with newer lure (VG+), NOT MET	VG-	$761.00	01-10
Heddon	102	Brush	EX-	$75.00	01-02
Heddon	102	Down Bass	EX-	$307.00	02-12
Heddon	102	Down, tall box, red border	VG+	$204.00	00-05
Heddon	103	with red 100 cup VG+, papers, "Hung!"	mint	$1,540.00	00-02
Heddon	104	Down Bass, "On the metal"	EX-	$185.00	01-02
Heddon	105	wood, top badly faded, 4-side bold	VG	$861.00	00-11
Heddon	150	white early, a pig	poor	$238.37	00-03
Heddon	150	wood, dirty, "HUNG!" 150 paper	VG	$848.00	04-05
Heddon	150	wood, top faded, "Hung," eye-end cut-out notch	VG-	$414.00	03-11
Heddon	151	wood, newest, super clean	EX+	$780.00	00-10
Heddon	152	Down Bass, c. 1912	EX-	$283.00	05-07
Heddon	154	wood	VG-	$535.00	99-05
Heddon	158	Down Bass, 1 end flap missing	EX-	$26.00	99-04
Heddon	162	Up Bass	EX+	$70.00	99-01
Heddon	200	Down Bass, blue border	VG+	$1,257.00	02-02
Heddon	700	large Down Bass	EX	$375.00	00-02
Heddon	1604	Down Bass, Deep Diving Wiggler box, NOT MET	VG-	$58.00	05-07
Heddon	1705	Down Bass, papers	VG	$152.50	99-07
Heddon	1902	Crab Wiggler	VG	$90.00	00-05
Heddon	1902	Down Bass	VG-	$51.00	00-05
Heddon	1902	Down	VG	$151.99	99-08
Heddon	1951	Baby Crab Wiggler, rainbow	EX	$100.99	99-04
Heddon	2402	Down Bass	EX-	$80.00	05-06
Heddon	2502	Up Bass	VG-	$32.51	99-04
Heddon	5002	Brush	VG+	$15.00	05-06
Heddon	5009	Tadpolly intro	VG-	$200.00	99-08
Heddon	7501	Up Bass, L-rig hook, patent sides	VG+	$35.00	05-06
Heddon	9112	Brush + paper	EX+	$30.00	05-06
Heddon	9402	Brush	EX-	$15.00	05-06
Heddon	Killer	silver box/white, blue label, 1902 pat	VG	$4,050.00	01-09
Holzwarth	Expert	wood box, long paper label	EX-	$2,550.00	00-10
Howe's	Vacuum Bait	black tin box gold lettering	VG+	$159.00	05-07
Hurd	Supercaster	leather case	VG	$78.77	99-04
Hurd	Supercaster Reel	tube shaped box	EX	$100.00	99-04
Immell	Chippewa P-66	fancy green back, NOT MET	EX	$1,402.00	02-09

BRAND	MODEL	SERIES / MFG. CODE / DESCRIPTION	GRADE	PRICE	DATE yy/mm
Jamison	Fly Rod Wiggler	3" x 1", one end torn	VG	$157.00	01-03
Johnson	Auto Striker	rough edges, pic OK	VG-	$261.00	01-01
Kalamazoo	Bal Cli No 20	reel	EX	$12.00	99-04
Kazoo	33RW	box says nothing about Shakespeare, white	EX-	$2,125.00	04-12
Keeling	Red/white Babytom Pictured		avg	$71.50	04-11
Keeling	Tom Thumb	red on white	EX-	$178.50	99-08
Keeling	Unmarked	common style	VG	$77.00	00-02
L & S	Bassmaster	2PCCB, 12-pack, gold/black	EX-	$46.00	01-05
Meek	Wood	$1800 NOT MET	VG+	$1,252.97	99-05
Meisselbach	Takeapart 481	2PCCB, black with dark blue label/ white printing, nice!	EX	$130.00	05-07
Midwest Co.	Ypsilanti	picture box with repainted lure	VG	$141.00	05-07
Miller	Reversable Minnow	picture label	VG	$13,099.00	02-05
Millsite	203BB	Floating Beetle Bug Natural 2PCCB	EX-	$42.00	04-02
Millsite	214 Sinker	rainbow 2PCCB	VG	$9.95	99-03
mixed	9 Different	nice picture boxes	EX	$104.00	98-12
Moonlight	Jumping Bass	night screen, bass on left	EX	$237.00	05-07
Moonlight	2905		EX	$308.00	00-11
Moonlight Bait Co.	Jumping Bass Box	Box No. 2004 (joined Pikaroon red & white)	EX	$324.50	05-04
Ness	Nifty Minne	white picture box (tape), paper included	VG-	$3,742.00	05-01
Nieboer Flies		pic box 2" x 2"	VG-	$108.50	99-10
North Channel	3-hooker	wrong lure (Shakespeare?), box not awful	avg	$602.00	00-07
Paw Paw	4W	orange/white	VG	$49.00	01-03
Paw Paw	3804	Lucky Lure blue box, "R&W" handwritten	EX	$56.00	03-01
Pflueger	3970 Luminous	blue canoe, Surprise paper	VG+	$391.00	00-08
Pflueger	4 Brothers	3169, large lettering rare	VG	$350.00	99-10
Pflueger	4 Brothers	maroon for 5-hooker, unmarked	VG	$500.00	99-10
Pflueger	4 Brothers	maroon unmarked, "target"	EX-	$775.00	99-10
Pflueger	4 Brothers	maroon unmarked, large lettering rare	EX-	$600.00	99-10
Pflueger	4 Brothers	3181	EX	$700.00	99-10
Pflueger	5-hooker	3105, 3⅝", nat frog scale, paper	VG+	$152.50	99-11
Pflueger	7606 Nat. Perch	3-hooker	EX-	$56.00	00-01
Pflueger	Canoe	blue border, no code numbers	EX-	$32.00	02-02
Pflueger	Globe	maroon target logo	EX	$725.00	01-08
Pflueger	Monarch	2171, wood box for 5-hooker	EX	$1,800.00	99-10
Pflueger	Monarch	3181, wood box for 3-hooker	EX-	$1,200.00	99-10
Pflueger	Monarch	wood, rail damage, NOT MET	VG+	$670.00	00-01
Pflueger	Musky Tandem Spin	maroon box, lure, card	EX-	$78.00	99-06
Pflueger	Neverfail	4 Brothers, maroon	EX-	$350.00	00-01
Pflueger	Neverfail	maroon target, un, NOT MET	VG+	$350.00	00-01
Pflueger	Neverfail 3-hk	4 Brothers, maroon, size 3	avg	$106.50	00-01
Pflueger	Neverfail 2¼	wood, badly stained paper label over nice label	VG	$480.00	05-01
Pflueger	Neverfail 3196	blue border canoe	EX-	$100.95	99-05
Pflueger	Neverfail 5-hk	4 Brothers, maroon, size 3⅝	EX-	$350.00	00-01
Pflueger	Neverfail Wood Minnow	wood box for 3-hk, paper label, unmarked	VG+	$920.00	99-10
Pflueger	New Winner	9006, wood box in very nice shape, rough lure	EX	$735.00	05-07
Pflueger	Sterling Wood Minnow	wood box, partial label	rough	$200.00	99-10
Pflueger	Surprise Minnow	3901, Golden Shiner, canoe	VG	$67.00	99-08

BRAND	MODEL	SERIES / MFG. CODE / DESCRIPTION	GRADE	PRICE	DATE yy/mm
Pflueger	3184	target maroon box	EX-	$820.00	99-10
Pflueger	5004	Canoe, Pal-O-Mine, nice paper	EX	$23.00	02-03
Rhodes	Frog	wood faded, repaired	avg	$850.00	00-05
Rhodes, Roy	Rhodes Minnow	small picture box, Martinsburg, PA	VG	$64.00	05-07
Shakespeare	03FG	gray	VG+	$227.50	00-01
Shakespeare	03YP	gray with oval in yellow? w fish	EX	$273.00	01-05
Shakespeare	172 Floater (br/white) 2-hk	2-hk, white picture intro box, wowser	EX	$3,000.00	01-06
Shakespeare	44 SW	white lable picture, 5-hk, end lable "Size 2"	VG+	$3,700.00	05-04
Shakespeare	54FBJ	gray box, label poor, NOT MET	VG	$120.00	00-01
Shakespeare	590FG	Kazoo, fancy green scale	VG+	$38.00	00-04
Shakespeare	5-hooker	1632 pic, c. 1905, SOLD	VG	$3,400.00	99-10
Shakespeare	Featherweight Reel	white pasteboard, wrong reel color EX-	VG+	$289.00	03-05
Shakespeare	Hydroplane	709GW, label, SOLD	EX-	$220.00	99-10
Shakespeare	Kazoo Wooden Minnow	with avg lure, SOLD	EX-	$2,500.00	99-10
Shakespeare	Musky Revolution	black pic box, 6½", top only, SOLD	VG-	$1,900.00	99-10
Shakespeare	Rhodes Frog	wood, top faded	VG	$1,426.00	02-03
Shakespeare	Rhodes Mechanical Frog	wood box, seller bid on OWN item!	EX	$2,276.00	03-09
Shakespeare	Sure Lure	intro pic box, silver/black	VG	$3,500.00	01-08
Shakespeare	Whirlwind	intro box, with EX- lure, SOLD	VG	$2,500.00	99-10
Shakespeare	Wood	#1 type, SOLD	EX	$650.00	99-10
Shakespeare	Wood	#2 type, SOLD, faded, cleaned	VG	$350.00	99-10
Shakespeare	Wood	#3 type, SOLD	EX-	$500.00	99-10
Shakespeare	Yellow Spinner	wood	VG	$300.00	01-02
Shakespeare	44	wood end label, stamped top, c. 1910	EX-	$1,000.00	01-06
Shakespeare	546	Dalton Special, checkerboard	EX-	$10.00	01-02
Shakespeare	1632	white back & belly, 2PCCB, left side picture	VG-	$2,400.00	04-11
Shapleigh	SD103	for ball-bearing reel	EX	$20.00	05-07
Shur Strike	0-5	yellow/red nice	EX	$57.00	01-08
Shur Strike	3563G1	green/white	EX	$21.00	00-06
Shur Strike	3563X2	red/blue nice	EX-	$26.25	99-03
Shur Strike	A2	yellow/green box	EX	$122.00	04-03
Shur Strike	B2	yellow/green fish/red	EX	$52.00	01-05
Shur Strike	BBO-6	green/white	EX	$27.00	00-02
Shur Strike	BO-0	green	EX-	$23.00	01-04
Shur Strike	FHR -5	blue/orange	EX	$35.00	01-01
Shur Strike	Guardian Brand	blue, shield, neat	VG	$31.00	99-08
Shur Strike	HRT-O	blue/red	VG-	$12.30	99-10
Shur Strike	P6	red/yellow, NRA box, plus RH lure	EX	$100.18	99-12
Shur Strike	Pikie Type	y/r, NRA box nice, lure poor	EX	$155.50	99-04
Shur Strike	RR14	yellow/red, NRA stamp	avg	$68.89	00-01
Shur Strike	RR-2	yellow/red, NRA box	mint	$78.00	04-01
Skinner	12-pak	yellow, black lettering	EX	$27.00	04-11
South Bend	2090R	Bass Oreno, distributed by Shakespeare	EX	$331.00	00-04
South Bend	903RSF	South Bend Minnow, 3-hooker	EX-	$79.00	00-03
South Bend	929RH	Plunk Oreno, script	EX-	$25.00	02-04
South Bend	929YP	for tack eye, Plunk Oreno	EX-	$39.00	04-02
South Bend	949GM	Mouse Oreno	EX	$51.00	02-03
South Bend	972 12-pack	2PCCB x 12, in large 2PCCB, no lures	EX	$380.00	99-10

BOXES

BRAND	MODEL	SERIES / MFG. CODE / DESCRIPTION	GRADE	PRICE	DATE yy/mm
South Bend	973 Rain	red sky, pocket catalog	EX-	$70.00	03-04
South Bend	Bass Oreno	intro box, pat pending	EX+	$150.00	03-07
South Bend	Calamac Bub	unusual box with flyfish papers	EX	$304.75	99-04
South Bend	Calmac Bass Bug #7	No.7 Chadwick's	avg	$91.00	00-11
South Bend	Fish Oreno	Guarantee with paper	EX	$71.00	00-11
South Bend	Gulf Oreno	982RHS, old style 2PCCB	EX	$382.77	99-09
South Bend	Gulf Oreno	Yellow intro 2PCCB for 983 (no color)	EX+	$200.00	05-05
South Bend	Pike Oreno	intro box 975 RH	EX-	$31.00	04-05
South Bend	RH920	intro box	EX-	$265.00	99-01
South Bend	Truck Oreno	936 very faint, plain yellow box	VG-	$153.50	99-08
South Bend	Wiz Oreno	967RH, intro type box	EX	$28.00	04-11
Supplee-Biddle Congress	5-hooker	box VG, lure by PF crackle	EXIB	$1,407.00	99-12
Tango, Rush	$50 Gold	$50 prize nice box + lure	GIB	$75.00	01-03
Wallsten	Cisco Kid	lg 6-pack 2PCCB, pic of 2 lures with 4 sm 2PCCB crisp boxes	EX-	$169.00	05-07
Weber	Spiderweb	2 windows, trout nice	EX	$26.00	01-05
Winchester	Minnow	with papers, little rough	G	$437.00	99-01
Woods	Deep R Doodle	803	EX	$5.50	99-01
Wright McGill	Flapper Crab	#10, NOT MET	VG	$51.00	99-08
Wright McGill	Wiggling Minnow	blue box (R.M. No. 3), white paper	EX-	$150.00	00-07
Yawman & Erbe	No. 1	automatic fly reel box	EX-	$310.00	05-07

Bugs

BRAND	MODEL	SERIES / MFG. CODE / DESCRIPTION	GRADE	PRICE	DATE
Bickmore	Repellent	8 tins	NIB	$92.00	99-06

Catalogs

BRAND	MODEL	SERIES / MFG. CODE / DESCRIPTION	GRADE	PRICE	DATE
A L&W	1920s	63 pages	VG-	$214.73	99-09
A L&W	1933	115 pages, Spring	EX-	$93.00	01-03
Abbey & Imbrie	1897	100+ pages	VG-	$330.00	99-03
Abbey & Imbrie	1908	supplement to 1907	VG+	$152.00	01-05
Abbey & Imbrie	1910	super fisherman cover	EX-	$157.00	01-05
Abbey & Imbrie	1914	cover rough	VG	$127.00	01-05
Abbey & Imbrie	1920	160 pages, 6" x 9"	EX-	$120.50	99-10
Abbey & Imbrie	1929	127 pages, 8" x 5½"	VG	$101.00	05-07
Abbey & Imbrie	1929	binding torn, SOLD?	G	$75.00	99-10
Abbey & Imbrie	1929	red cover	EX-	$77.00	01-05
Abbey & Imbrie	1930	128 pages	EX	$78.00	03-02
Abbott, W.W.	1884	Philadelphia, 40 pages	EX	$271.52	99-08
Abercrombie & Fitch	1909	cover poor, inside decent	rough	$44.00	05-02

BRAND	MODEL	SERIES / MFG. CODE / DESCRIPTION	GRADE	PRICE	DATE yy/mm
Abercrombie & Fitch	1910	456 pages	G	$235.00	99-10
Abercrombie & Fitch	1934	64 pages	VG	$60.07	99-01
Abercrowbie & Fitch	1910	456 pages	VG+	$125.00	01-03
Airex	1940s?	in envelope	NIE	$78.00	99-05
Allcocks	1921	165 pages hardbound	EX	$305.00	01-09
Bristol	1934	32 pages	mint	$45.51	99-12
Camp Outfits & Fishing Tackle	1916	196 pages, color Heddon, NOT MET	EX	$128.00	00-09
CCBC	1927-28	44 pages	EX	$719.00	05-06
CCBC	1952-53	31 pages	EX	$297.50	99-04
CCBC	1918	8 pages fold out, 7 lures, "New Pikie Minnow"	EX-	$330.00	04-11
CCBC	1919		EX	$750.00	01-12
CCBC	1924	48 pages, NOT MET	VG	$618.00	03-04
CCBC	1925	47 pages	EX-	$546.00	05-07
CCBC	1931	48 pages, NOT MET	mint	$316.00	01-05
CCBC	1931	mailer & order form	EXIE	$622.00	00-10
CCBC	1931	wade angler & bass/musky	EX	$315.00	04-03
CCBC	1936	31 pages	EX-	$460.71	99-06
CCBC	1936	31 pages	EX	$306.99	99-07
CCBC	1936	31 pages	VG	$204.00	01-12
CCBC	1936	nice!	EX	$280.00	99-11
CCBC	1938	35 pages	mint	$370.00	01-05
CCBC	1938	envelope, order form, return envelope	NIE	$338.00	02-01
CCBC	1938		EX	$280.88	99-12
CCBC	1939	35 pages	EX-	$350.00	01-04
CCBC	1940	pic letter, envelope only	EX	$71.00	99-06
CCBC	1940	with mailing envelope	Mint	$310.00	00-01
CCBC	1942	35 pages	EX	$227.00	01-05
CCBC	1942	35 pages, NOT MET	EX	$198.00	00-04
CCBC	1942	36 pages, crease down center	VG+	$100.00	02-11
CCBC	1942		rough	$31.00	00-05
CCBC	1945	NOT MET	EX	$300.00	99-08
CCBC	1947		EX	$150.00	03-12
CCBC	1949	1949 sticker over 1948	EX	$152.00	00-10
CCBC	1950	24 pages	EX	$202.50	99-11
CCBC	1950	some water on pages	VG	$140.36	99-05
CCBC	1950		VG	$350.00	99-05
CCBC	1951	24 pages	mint	$338.00	02-03
CCBC	1951	NOT MET	EX+	$200.00	99-09
CCBC	1951	with price sheet	EX+	$300.00	99-03
Chubb	1909	122 pages	MINT	$361.00	00-11
Coxe	1951	color pages	EX	$81.00	03-12
Enterprise Mfg. Co.	1916	Pflueger, No. 37, 394 pages	EX	$550.00	04-11
Eppinger	1934?	no date, but approximate	mint	$128.00	03-04
Eppinger	1934	a beauty plus flyer	EX+	$92.00	00-01
Fin Nor	1950s	8 pages	EX	$51.63	99-03

BRAND	MODEL	SERIES / MFG. CODE / DESCRIPTION	GRADE	PRICE	DATE yy/mm
Frost, H.J.	1910	14 pages	mint	$41.00	99-04
Garcia	c. 1965	not the annual	VG-	$31.00	99-05
Garcia	1959		VG	$18.75	99-06
Garcia	1963	annual	EX	$11.55	99-02
Garcia	1964	annual	EX	$57.06	99-02
Garcia	1972	annual	EX	$28.00	00-11
Hardy	1926	Feb. 1926, some color plates	rough	$155.00	03-06
Hardy	1934	445 pages	EX	$66.00	01-03
Heddon	1920-21	#19 cover poor	EX-	$535.00	02-07
Heddon	1936	nice shape	EX-	$137.50	05-07
Heddon	1942-43	dealer edition	EX-	$333.78	99-01
Heddon	1952 DLX	trout pic, envelope	NIE	$152.00	99-05
Heddon	1965, 1970	2 diff	VG	$35.75	99-04
Heddon	1911	38 pages (some loose), with fragile sleeve	EX-	$2,500.00	05-02
Heddon	1912	pencil writing at top, white cover w/printing	EX-	$12,100.00	03-02
Heddon	1913	#11, NOT MET	EX	$2,176.00	03-04
Heddon	1916	#14, spine shot, cover creased, ugly	avg	$1,075.00	02-02
Heddon	1922	NOT MET	VG	$162.50	00-01
Heddon	1924	16 pages, 6¾" x 9¾", Tackle Science, NOT MET	EX	$365.00	03-06
Heddon	1924	original mailer	NIE	$650.00	01-02
Heddon	1924	with mailer	EX	$950.00	99-10
Heddon	1924		EX-	$650.00	00-11
Heddon	1926	22 pages, 8" x 11", tiny spine tear	EX	$412.00	04-11
Heddon	1926	23 pages, "Trade" catalog	EX	$873.00	00-12
Heddon	1926	24 bids, NOT MET	EX-	$454.12	99-03
Heddon	1926	color plates, 5 inserts, SUPER	EX-	$461.00	01-03
Heddon	1926	poster cat, corner missing	VG	$267.00	99-06
Heddon	1926	sold	EX	$850.00	99-10
Heddon	1928	all inserts	mint	$350.00	01-02
Heddon	1928	cover rough, nice brochure & order form	VG	$182.00	04-02
Heddon	1928		EX	$339.00	01-10
Heddon	1929	binding some seperation, NOT MET	EX-	$158.00	02-11
Heddon	1930	SOLD	EX	$400.00	99-10
Heddon	1931	36 pages	EX-	$326.00	03-02
Heddon	1931	36 pages	EX	$372.01	99-04
Heddon	1931	36 pages, factory envelope, order blank	NIE	$363.00	05-07
Heddon	1931	stains on cover, still not bad	VG+	$129.00	03-02
Heddon	1931		EX	$357.00	01-05
Heddon	1932	31 pages	EX	$500.00	00-12
Heddon	1932	cover rough, inside EX	VG	$275.00	99-10
Heddon	1933		EX+	$237.00	01-09
Heddon	1934	31 pages	VG	$276.89	99-04
Heddon	1934	31 pages	EX	$230.00	02-03
Heddon	1934	31 pages, NOT MET	VG+	$250.01	99-05
Heddon	1934	dealer catalog, 31 pages	EX	$202.00	01-10
Heddon	1934		EX-	$255.00	03-04
Heddon	1935		VG+	$255.50	00-01
Heddon	1936	37 pages	EX	$270.00	99-07

BRAND	MODEL	SERIES / MFG. CODE / DESCRIPTION	GRADE	PRICE	DATE yy/mm
Heddon	1936	mailer, extra mail-ins	NIE	$356.00	01-05
Heddon	1936		EX	$340.00	99-10
Heddon	1937	40 pages, 7" x 10"	EX	$160.00	04-11
Heddon	1937	lg size, 40 pages	EX	$203.50	99-04
Heddon	1937		EX	$250.00	01-02
Heddon	1937		EX	$300.00	99-10
Heddon	1938	40 pages	EX	$216.00	00-05
Heddon	1938	42 pages	EX	$202.00	01-03
Heddon	1939		VG+	$300.00	99-03
Heddon	1939		mint	$331.35	99-11
Heddon	1941		mint	$204.00	01-01
Heddon	1941		EX-	$275.00	99-03
Heddon	1941		mint	$610.00	01-03
Heddon	1948	vest pocket	EX	$41.00	99-02
Heddon	1949	80 pages	mint	$153.00	01-05
Heddon	1951	30 pages	EX	$131.38	00-03
Heddon	1951	79 pages	EX	$70.99	99-06
Heddon	1952	31 pages, large	VG	$50.66	99-04
Heddon	1952	deluxe	EX	$60.00	05-06
Heddon	1952	small size	EX-	$56.00	99-04
Heddon	1952		VG	$25.00	99-10
Heddon	1953	deluxe, 76 pages	EX	$43.95	99-03
Heddon	1953	small size	EX	$36.00	99-05
Heddon	1954	deluxe	EX+	$60.00	05-06
Heddon	1954	DLX	EX	$102.51	99-02
Heddon	1958	deluxe, NOT MET	mint	$87.00	01-05
Heddon	1959	31 pages	EX-	$42.19	99-05
Heddon	1960	nice	EX	$51.00	98-12
Heddon	1960		EX	$39.25	99-02
Heddon	1962	31 pages	EX	$32.01	99-07
Heddon	1962		EX+	$50.00	05-06
Heddon	1963	55 pages	EX	$45.00	99-04
Heddon	1964	63 pages, dealer trade copy	EX	$73.00	99-01
Heddon	1964	63 pages	mint	$57.60	99-11
Heddon	1964		VG+	$43.00	99-04
Heddon	1965	63 pages	VG	$91.00	99-06
Heddon	1965	this is the old and new tradition cover	EX	$40.00	05-06
Heddon	1966	63 pages	EX	$36.00	99-07
Heddon	1966		EX	$37.00	02-09
Heddon	1968	68 pages	EX-	$40.00	00-02
Heddon	1968		EX	$37.00	02-09
Heddon	1969		EX	$38.00	00-07
Heddon	1970	63 pages	VG	$41.00	99-06
Heddon	1972	cover small dog-ears	VG+	$52.00	05-02
Heddon	1974	32 pages	mint	$56.00	02-11
Heddon	1975	32 pages	EX	$49.00	04-02
Heddon	1985		EX	$15.50	99-04
Helin	1945		EX	$32.00	01-05

BRAND	MODEL	SERIES / MFG. CODE / DESCRIPTION	GRADE	PRICE	DATE yy/mm
Helin	1952	48 pages	EX	$17.00	98-12
Helin	1962		EX	$26.00	99-01
Hendryx	1910	175 pages	VG+	$263.00	04-03
Horton	c. 1919	Bristol rods & Meek reels, great cover	EX-	$255.00	99-08
Jamison	c. 1923	27 pages	EX	$190.00	99-10
Johnson	1885	16 pages, Flying Helgrimite ad	VG+	$787.75	99-04
Johnson, Ivar	1913	207 pages, 5" x 7"	EX	$77.00	04-11
Kiffe	1895	167 pages	EX	$177.50	99-03
Kiffe	1905	174 pages, 6" x 9"	EX	$132.00	04-11
Kiffe	1925	72 pages	EX	$62.00	01-05
Lazy Ike	1970s	color charts, Sail Shark & more	mint	$12.00	01-08
Marshall Fields	1917	144 pages	EX	$145.00	99-10
Meisselbach	?	9" x 11½", color cover with trout, 13 pages each with one reel nice	EX	$275.00	05-07
Mills	1909	pamphlet, advice & rods only	EX-	$75.00	99-03
Mills & Son	1925	80 pages	EX-	$77.00	99-06
Mills & Son	1928	160+ pages	EX-	$87.00	99-03
Mills & Son	1929	154 pages	EX	$156.00	99-01
Mills & Son	1929	156 pages	EX	$70.00	99-10
Mills & Son	1931	No. 131	EX	$48.25	00-01
Mills & Son	1933	144 pages	VG	$65.00	99-04
Mills & Son	1934	144 pages	EX-	$75.00	99-10
Mills & Son	1934		EX	$57.00	99-09
Mills & Son	1940	NOT MET	EX	$41.25	99-06
Montague City Rod Co.	c. 1890s	136 pages, 6½" x 10", cover loose	EX-	$110.00	04-11
Moonlight	1923	#11, 16 pages, NOT MET	EX-	$328.00	99-11
Ocean City	1941	#41A	EX-	$26.00	99-05
Olivers	1989	32690	EX	$38.89	99-03
Orchard Ind.	1962	13 pages	EX	$16.00	00-07
Orvis	c. 1896	16 pages, 3½" x 6"	EX+	$154.00	04-11
Orvis	c. 1891	4 pages, 3" x 6", glass minnow trap brochure	G	$55.00	04-11
Orvis	1889	No. 16, 114 pages, 6" x 8"	VG	$1,980.00	04-11
Orvis	1894	86 pages, 6" x 8"	EX	$1,320.00	04-11
Orvis	1908	114 pages, 6" x 8"	VG	$907.00	04-11
Orvis	1957	64 pages	EX	$33.00	99-01
Orvis	1960		EX	$47.00	99-02
P & K	1946	32 pages	EX	$33.00	00-07
Payne	1940s	mint with envelope	mint	$170.00	99-03
Peck	No. 46	nice	EX	$102.00	98-12
Penn	1936	#4, 4 pages, intro for Senator line	VG+	$279.00	04-11
Penn	1941	#9	avg	$37.00	04-11
Pflueger	1959	#196, 49 pages	EX	$48.00	99-04
Pflueger	1916	394 pages	VG	$660.00	00-08
Pflueger	1919	"Tips on Tackle," 112 pages	EX	$261.00	00-08
Pflueger	1926	#146	EX	$148.00	00-11
Pflueger	1926	133 pages	VG-	$102.50	99-04
Pflueger	1927	#247	EX	$46.99	99-07

BRAND	MODEL	SERIES / MFG. CODE / DESCRIPTION	GRADE	PRICE	DATE yy/mm
Pflueger	1928	#148, 125 pages	EX	$85.00	02-08
Pflueger	1928	#148, 130 pages, NOT MET	EX-	$78.00	00-01
Pflueger	1928	#148, NOT MET	EX-	$102.50	99-08
Pflueger	1928	128 pages, color	mint	$202.50	99-04
Pflueger	1928	128 pages	EX-	$134.00	00-05
Pflueger	1928	128	EX-	$113.00	00-09
Pflueger	1929	#149, 152 pages, SOLD	EX	$225.00	99-10
Pflueger	1929	152 pages, NOT MET	VG	$55.25	99-05
Pflueger	1929	280 pages, distributor cat, nice	EX	$280.00	00-03
Pflueger	1931	#151	EX	$125.00	99-01
Pflueger	1931	#151	EX	$224.00	99-01
Pflueger	1931		EX	$105.00	01-05
Pflueger	1931		EX-	$128.50	99-03
Pflueger	1934	128 pages	EX	$127.00	00-07
Pflueger	1934	154 pages	EX	$90.50	99-12
Pflueger	1934	dealer, extra price lists, letter, nice	EX+	$128.50	99-03
Pflueger	1934		EX	$132.00	01-05
Pflueger	1935	128 pages	EX	$67.00	99-12
Pflueger	1935	No. (1)55, cover & binding torn	G	$40.00	99-10
Pflueger	1936	5 x 8", 130 pages	EX	$132.50	99-03
Pflueger	1936		EX	$162.00	99-01
Pflueger	1937	#157, 128 pages, SOLD	EX	$100.00	99-10
Pflueger	1938	#158	EX	$65.00	99-12
Pflueger	1938	125 pages	EX	$76.00	99-04
Pflueger	1938	128 pages	EX	$83.33	99-04
Pflueger	1938	130 pages	EX	$201.00	00-01
Pflueger	1938			$75.00	99-03
Pflueger	1938		EX	$125.00	99-03
Pflueger	1940	#160	VG+	$56.00	99-05
Pflueger	1940	128 pages	EX	$167.50	99-04
Pflueger	1940	nice	near mint	$107.50	99-03
Pflueger	1943	#161	EX-	$80.00	99-10
Pflueger	1952	#88 Trade, NOT MET	EX-	$44.75	99-06
Pflueger	1967		EX	$30.00	03-02
Pflueger	1968		EX	$20.00	03-02
Pflueger	1931	5" x 8", color cover, rest is b&w, light wear, 136 pages	EX-	$85.00	05-05
Philipson Rod	1960s	12 pages	mint	$75.00	00-03
Read, Wm. & Sons	1912	94 pages, 9" x 12"	G	$82.00	04-11
Richardson	1936	16 page foldout, color	EX	$12.00	99-03
Rummel Arms	1909	146 pages, mostly fishing stuff	G	$139.00	03-11
Shakespeare	1912	"Art of Baitcasting"	VG	$104.56	99-02
Shakespeare	1916	#20, 288 pages, contains Heddon & others	EX	$750.00	01-12
Shakespeare	1919	112 pages, NOT MET	EX-	$305.00	99-11
Shakespeare	1924	30 pages	EX	$290.00	99-10
Shakespeare	1925	39 pages, 8 color	EX-	$355.00	00-02
Shakespeare	1925		EX+	$264.89	99-12
Shakespeare	1926	88 pages, spine rough	VG	$157.00	00-04
Shakespeare	1926	88 pages, NOT MET	VG+	$103.50	99-08

BRAND	MODEL	SERIES / MFG. CODE / DESCRIPTION	GRADE	PRICE	DATE yy/mm
Shakespeare	1926	88 pages	EX	$430.51	00-01
Shakespeare	1927	folded down center	VG+	$99.00	03-02
Shakespeare	1934	80 pages, 5¼" x 7¼"	EX	$88.00	05-07
Shakespeare	1937	100 pages	EX	$105.00	00-07
Shakespeare	1939		EX	$51.00	03-04
Shakespeare	1940	92 pages	EX	$44.09	99-04
Shakespeare	1941		mint	$87.50	99-03
Shakespeare	1949	36 pages	EX	$43.00	01-04
Shakespeare	1949		EX-	$18.00	99-11
Shakespeare	1950		EX	$41.50	99-02
Shakespeare	1951	44 pages	EX	$36.58	99-05
Shakespeare	1951		EX-	$16.00	99-11
Shakespeare	1952		EX	$24.76	99-04
Shakespeare	1952		EX	$29.00	00-01
Shakespeare	1970	with mail envelope	EX	$22.00	99-04
Shoverling	1911	144 pages	EX	$99.99	99-09
Shoverling	c. 1900	lures, reels, 158 pages	EX-	$262.00	99-02
Shoverling, Daly	1925	161 pages, great pics	EX	$291.00	00-04
Silaflex	1956	16 pages	EX	$21.50	99-11
Skinner	c. 1890s	24 pages	EX-	$158.00	99-01
Skinner	c. 1920s	nice with illustrations	VG	$66.00	99-05
Skinner	1895	24 pages, 5" x 9", string bound, envelope	EX	$203.00	04-11
South Bend	1917-18	48 pages, 5½" x 12", page supplement, color, center cover stain	EX-	$275.00	04-11
South Bend	1922-23	trade cat, 73 pages, cover torn, SOLD	EX-	$425.00	99-10
South Bend	193?	136 pages	EX	$70.00	99-10
South Bend	1931	some color, one of best covers	EX	$65.00	05-05
South Bend	1940s	48 pages	EX-	$35.00	99-10
South Bend	1848	52 pages	EX	$36.00	99-01
South Bend	1920	NOT MET	EX	$493.00	00-09
South Bend	1922	40 pages, NOT MET	EX	$272.00	02-10
South Bend	1922	40 pages, NOT MET	EX	$144.52	99-11
South Bend	1922	fly rod lures!	EX	$354.00	99-06
South Bend	1922	NOT MET	EX+	$227.50	99-06
South Bend	1924	a beauty	EX	$115.00	04-03
South Bend	1924	nice envelope	NIE	$415.00	00-10
South Bend	1925		EX	$173.49	99-05
South Bend	1926	116 pages, NOT MET	VG+	$102.50	00-01
South Bend	1926	118 pages	EX	$79.00	04-12
South Bend	1926		VG+	$59.99	99-12
South Bend	1930	96 pages	EX	$191.94	99-11
South Bend	1931	79 pages, "What & When"	NIE	$180.27	99-03
South Bend	1931	79 pages	EX-	$100.00	99-10
South Bend	1931		EX	$48.00	03-04
South Bend	1932	83 pages	VG	$52.00	00-01
South Bend	1932	88 pages, #83, boy & muskies	EX	$204.50	00-01
South Bend	1932	boy and pole, 81 pages	VG	$122.50	99-05
South Bend	1932	few mouse chews	VG	$32.50	99-09

BRAND	MODEL	SERIES / MFG. CODE / DESCRIPTION	GRADE	PRICE	DATE yy/mm
South Bend	1932	full line	EX-	$63.00	00-05
South Bend	1932	sm	EX	$95.00	99-03
South Bend	1933		EX-	$129.25	00-01
South Bend	1934	92 pages	VG+	$43.00	01-08
South Bend	1934	92 pages	EX	$49.99	99-10
South Bend	1934		EX-	$56.00	99-05
South Bend	1934		EX	$60.00	99-03
South Bend	1935	full line	EX	$51.00	00-05
South Bend	1936	112 pages, "Fish and Feel Fit"	VG	$36.32	99-07
South Bend	1936	114 pages, "Fish & Feel Fit"	EX	$65.00	99-06
South Bend	1937	112 pages	EX	$95.00	99-10
South Bend	1937	full line	EX	$52.00	00-05
South Bend	1939	128 pages	EX	$46.00	98-12
South Bend	1939	128 pages	VG	$51.00	99-04
South Bend	1939	128 pages, "Fish & Feel Fit"	EX	$41.99	99-07
South Bend	1939	full line	EX-	$31.00	00-05
South Bend	1939		EX	$60.00	99-03
South Bend	1941	136 pages	EX	$56.00	99-05
South Bend	1941	full line	EX	$47.00	00-05
South Bend	1941	super graphics envelope	NIE	$72.00	01-05
South Bend	1942	cover poor, rest EX	?	$37.50	99-02
South Bend	1942		EX	$55.00	99-01
South Bend	1945	46 pages	EX	$66.00	99-01
South Bend	1947	44 pages	EX+	$51.00	99-05
South Bend	1947		EX-	$39.00	99-04
South Bend	1948	48 pages, boys & bluegills	EX-	$51.00	99-05
South Bend	1949	72 pages	EX	$45.00	99-10
South Bend	1949		EX	$59.00	99-01
South Bend	1949		EX	$78.00	99-02
South Bend	1950	89 pages, trout	EX	$50.00	99-06
South Bend	1951	104 pages	EX	$28.00	99-04
South Bend	1952	112 pages	EX	$51.51	99-05
South Bend	1953	full line	EX	$36.00	00-05
South Bend	1959		EX-	$42.51	99-06
South Bend	1970	72 pages	EX	$42.50	99-01
South Bend	1937, 1941	covers poor	G	$32.00	99-02
Squires, Henry C.	1890	164 pages, 9½" x 12", cover separated, some loose pages	VG-	$330.00	04-11
Tryon, Edw. K	1937	311 pages	EX-	$115.00	04-11
Tryon, Edw. K	1939	340 pages, 9" x 12", Kingfisher cover	EX-	$220.00	04-11
Tyron	1934	Kingfisher cover, 536 pages, 8½" x 11", 200 pages, dealer's catalog	EX	$79.00	05-07
V L & A	1925	154 pages	EX	$100.00	99-03
V L & A	1932		EX	$100.00	99-03
VLA	1927		EX	$61.00	00-02
Vom Hofe	1936	173 pages		$175.00	99-03
Vom Hofe, Ed	1941		EX+	$160.00	99-10
Vom Hofe, Ed.	1931	mailing envelope	mint	$300.00	99-11

BRAND	MODEL	SERIES / MFG. CODE / DESCRIPTION	GRADE	PRICE	DATE yy/mm
Vom Hofe, Ed.	1941	143 pages, 6" x 9", spine separated	EX-	$220.00	04-11
Weber	1935	80 pages	G	$36.00	99-01
Weber	1938	96 pages	VG	$46.00	99-11
Weber	1939		EX	$58.00	01-05
Weber	1957	68 pages	VG+	$11.00	05-05
William Mills	1940	#140	EX	$16.00	04-12
Winchester	Circa 1920s	31 pages, pocket size	EX-	$77.99	99-04
Winchester	1924	nice cover, NOT MET	VG+	$153.50	99-02
Winchester	1924		VG	$152.50	99-08
Wright McGill	1938	74 pages	EX-	$200.00	99-03

Checks

BRAND	MODEL	SERIES / MFG. CODE / DESCRIPTION	GRADE	PRICE	DATE yy/mm
CCBC	Garrett State Bank	unused nice company check	EX	$16.00	05-03

Creels

BRAND	MODEL	SERIES / MFG. CODE / DESCRIPTION	GRADE	PRICE	DATE yy/mm
Unknown	Split Willow	single ribs, nice leather	EX-	$167.50	00-02
Freeman/Mariner	Fancy	modern	new	$1,826.00	00-02
French	Hoiz. Supports	real nice	EX	$410.00	99-07
Lawrence	Schnell	nice patina, NOT MET	EX	$525.00	04-01
Lawrence	Split Willow	straps machined	EX	$1,550.00	99-06
Lawrence	Tillamook	pocket, from page 54 "Art of the Creel" by Chatham & McCain	EX	$1,100.00	05-04
Lawrence	15	some red paint on bottom leather	EX	$2,340.00	03-08
Lawrence Co.	#6	metal name tag & stamp	EX-	$1,560.89	99-03
Lawrence, G.	Strap #5	strap only	mint	$292.89	99-06
Macmonies	Split Willow	small repair, NOT MET	VG+	$1,825.00	99-05
Sheldon	Wide Strips	Indian Head, wood top, ugly	EX	$271.00	99-06
Simeonov	Leather	beautiful, c. 1930	EX+	$3,050.00	99-04
Simeonov	Modern	1999 made	mint	$2,700.00	99-04
Turtle	Carved Turtle Latch	turtle trademark, NOT MET	EX-	$232.50	99-11
Turtle	Tight Weave	nice turtle latch, NOT MET	EX-	$330.00	01-12
Turtle		exact one from book ($1000 – 1500)	EX-	$550.00	02-08
Turtle		beauty, nice cording	EX	$635.00	99-01
Turtle			near mint	$1,500.00	00-04

BRAND	MODEL	SERIES / MFG. CODE / DESCRIPTION	GRADE	PRICE	DATE yy/mm
Chatauqua	Ice Spearing	7⅜", GE, leather tail, NOT MET	EX	$1,215.00	01-10
Christensen	Walleye	wood box, signed "CC," 7½"	NIB	$43.00	04-12
Downey, A.J.	Trout	13¾", c. 1980, NOT MET	mint	$305.00	02-01
Heddon	4-point	bar perch	VG+	$910.00	02-10
Heddon	4-point	bar perch, nice	EX-	$2,282.00	00-09
Heddon	4-point	bar perch, top nice, awful belly, NOT MET	?	$910.00	03-01
Heddon	4-point	beater missing two fins	poor	$63.00	05-07
Heddon	4-point	crackle (re?), NOT MET	EX	$1,775.00	01-05
Heddon	4-point	green scale, belly varnish	EX-	$2,400.00	99-10
Heddon	4-point	green scale	rough	$382.00	00-09
Heddon	4-point	green scale	EX-	$2,750.00	00-05
Heddon	4-point	green scale, really ugly	avg	$600.00	99-08
Heddon	4-point	L, 4-point	VG	$616.00	99-05
Heddon	4-point	L, 4-point nice	EX	$2,351.00	99-05
Heddon	4-point	nat scale	rough	$321.00	00-09
Heddon	4-point	perch scale	VG+	$920.00	99-09
Heddon	4-point	perch scale	EX	$1,183.00	04-01
Heddon	4-point	perch scale	EX	$1,313.00	00-01
Heddon	4-point	perch scale	EX-	$1,691.66	99-09
Heddon	4-point	perch scale, belly varnish flaking, NOT MET	EX-	$560.00	05-06
Heddon	4-point	perch with box, belly rough, box EX-, RF	EXIB	$3,080.00	05-07
Heddon	4-point	perch scale	avg	$224.00	02-03
Heddon	4-point	perch scale, Down Bass box VG-, NOT MET	EXIB	$1,375.00	02-09
Heddon	4-point	perch scale, belly awful, rest ugly	poor	$305.00	01-12
Heddon	4-point	perch scale, belly varnish flaking	EX-	$1,500.00	02-01
Heddon	4-point	RB, few varnish flakes top, many belly	VG+	$1,136.00	00-08
Heddon	4-point	RB, decent, NOT MET	VG+	$1,125.00	99-12
Heddon	4-point	shiner scale, NOT MET	avg	$225.00	02-11
Heddon	4-point	white /red eye shade, NOT MET	EX-	$1,225.00	00-11
Heddon	Bat Wing	bar perch, 5 BW, NOT MET	avg	$712.00	00-11
Heddon	Bat Wing	bar perch, NOT MET	avg	$911.00	03-10
Heddon	Bat Wing	bar perch, piece of tail missing, ugly	avg-	$2,500.00	00-11
Heddon	Bat Wing	bar perch, pigtail line tie	VG	$3,250.00	02-08
Heddon	Bat Wing	carved curved tail, bar perch, pinned wings	VG+	$3,586.00	03-08
Heddon	Bat Wing	carved tail, bar perch	VG	$2,281.00	03-07
Heddon	Bat Wing	overpaint, NOT MET	poor	$306.00	00-11
Heddon	Ice Spook	perch, Up Bass 459L, Ice Spook paper!	NIB	$2,402.00	01-10
Mizera	6/1/04	red head/white/red tail, ugly	VG-	$124.72	99-04
Mizera	Pike 6¾"	solid silver, no pizzazz	EX	$130.00	99-10
Mizera	Pike 9"	r/w	EX	$385.00	99-04
Paw Paw	2906 Trout Pattern	PTCB, purty spotted decoy	NIB	$787.00	04-02
Paw Paw	7½"	replaced fin, NOT MET	avg	$77.00	00-11
Paw Paw	Ice Fishing	silver flash, revarnish	rough	$224.00	01-11
Peterson, Oscar	Pike	bear paw pattern, 6"	EX	$650.00	05-03
Stewart, Bud	Bass 8"	c. 1980, signed	new	$271.78	99-03
Thayer	6"	signed on belly	EX	$16.00	04-12

Display Boards

BRAND	MODEL	SERIES / MFG. CODE / DESCRIPTION	GRADE	PRICE	DATE yy/mm
Marathon	Tombstone	19" x 23", a few lures	EX	$102.00	05-03

Displays

BRAND	MODEL	SERIES / MFG. CODE / DESCRIPTION	GRADE	PRICE	DATE yy/mm
CCBC	Stand-up Counter	"Oh Man What Action," 14" x 10"	EX	$283.00	01-04
Heddon	Sonic	Counter stand-up display & 12 common Sonic lures	VG+	$225.00	05-07
Heddon	Tiny Punkinseed	about 9' x 12', flat with one EX CRA	EX-	$188.00	05-07
Outing	Dewey Getum	stand-up counter sign rod & reel, actual items nice	EX-	$870.00	05-07

Eyes

BRAND	MODEL	SERIES / MFG. CODE / DESCRIPTION	GRADE	PRICE	DATE yy/mm
CCBC	Glass	15/64" x 50	mint	$76.00	00-03
Unknown	Glass	on wires x 50, NOT MET	mint	$32.00	99-05

Film Splicers

BRAND	MODEL	SERIES / MFG. CODE / DESCRIPTION	GRADE	PRICE	DATE yy/mm
Heddon	Film Splicer	in large marked cardboard box	EXIB	$137.50	05-07

Fish

BRAND	MODEL	SERIES / MFG. CODE / DESCRIPTION	GRADE	PRICE	DATE yy/mm
Carved	Trout 18"	c. 1880, in shadow box, nice	EX	$1,652.00	99-01

Flies

BRAND	MODEL	SERIES / MFG. CODE / DESCRIPTION	GRADE	PRICE	DATE yy/mm
Grey, Zane	Streamer	authentication paper, framed	EX	$100.00	99-06
Shakespeare	Otsego Bass	White Miller, supernice card	NOC	$17.00	00-11

Gaffs

BRAND	MODEL	SERIES / MFG. CODE / DESCRIPTION	GRADE	PRICE	DATE yy/mm
Hardy	Telescoping	15" – 35", brass and ebony salmon gaff	EX-	$252.00	05-07
Marble	Pincer Type	spring	EX	$53.00	99-01

Grease

BRAND	MODEL	SERIES / MFG. CODE / DESCRIPTION	GRADE	PRICE	DATE yy/mm
Pflueger	Run Free	12-pack, each tube new in box	NIB	$96.00	02-01

Hangtags

BRAND	MODEL	SERIES / MFG. CODE / DESCRIPTION	GRADE	PRICE	DATE yy/mm
CCBC	New Dive Bomber/Ding Bat	small hangtag, different lure on each side	EX-	$29.00	04-03

Harpoons

BRAND	MODEL	SERIES / MFG. CODE / DESCRIPTION	GRADE	PRICE	DATE yy/mm
Vom Hofe, Ed.	10 foot	3 tips, g. silver fittings	EX	$575.00	00-08

Hooks

BRAND	MODEL	SERIES / MFG. CODE / DESCRIPTION	GRADE	PRICE	DATE yy/mm
??	Spring	patented Sept. 7th, 1897, & May 30th, 1899	EX	$177.00	01-05
Abbey & Imbrie	Snelled	A&I blade, glass beads, 2 single hooks	EX-	$24.00	03-01
Evans	Eagle Claw	5", overall brass	EX	$1,230.00	00-07
Evans	Eagle Claw Fish Trap	c. 1877, very cool but NOT MET	EX	$1,045.00	02-04
Evans & Son	Spring Hook		EX	$561.51	99-10
G.W. Evans & Son	Multispring Hook	nice shape	EX	$885.00	00-03
Greer	Patent Lever	c. 1900	EX	$28.00	02-08
Henzel	Weedless		NOC	$19.00	02-01
Lite Striking	Spring		NIB	$41.00	00-09
Parr	#2	St. Paul, MN, pat Apr. 11, 1917	EX	$124.00	03-01
Pequea	Display	3 dozen feathered hooks in 13" x 21" box	EX	$115.00	04-11
Pequea	Display	fold out, snelled hooks, 16 panels, 5" x 10", neat	EX	$220.00	04-11
West	Weedless	Council Bluffs, IA, 2-hk, little chain linking 'em	EX	$238.00	03-01
Winchester	2PCCB	box a little rough, plain Jane	VG	$200.00	99-04
Yankeedoodle	Spring Hook		EX	$300.00	99-01

Kits

BRAND	MODEL	SERIES / MFG. CODE / DESCRIPTION	GRADE	PRICE	DATE yy/mm
South Bend	Christmas Boxed	4 TE, lures NIB, flashlight, 2 spools line	NIB	$375.00	05-03

Knives

BRAND	MODEL	SERIES / MFG. CODE / DESCRIPTION	GRADE	PRICE	DATE yy/mm
Hardy	Anglers Knife #1	c. 1910 scissors & blade, missing spike	avg	$705.00	03-05
Marbles	Fish Knife?	rosewood, fish decal inlaid	very worn	$536.89	99-07

Letterhead

BRAND	MODEL	SERIES / MFG. CODE / DESCRIPTION	GRADE	PRICE	DATE yy/mm
Orvis	1933	overdue notice signed by Albert C. Orvis	EX	$27.00	04-11

Licenses

BRAND	MODEL	SERIES / MFG. CODE / DESCRIPTION	GRADE	PRICE	DATE yy/mm
AR	1938 NR	pin back, with papers	EX-	$165.05	99-05
AR	1939 NR	nonresident, badge	VG	$215.00	99-02
AR	1937	nonresident, NOT MET	EX	$167.00	04-12
AR	1938	papers	VG	$52.83	99-06
CA	1917	paper, looks like little stock certificate	EX	$63.00	05-07
CA	1934	pin back, NOT MET	EX	$66.00	99-05
CA	1934		EX	$77.00	00-11
CA	1934		EX	$78.51	00-01
CA	1934		EX	$86.15	99-09
CA	1934		EX	$87.00	00-07
CA	1941	pin	EX	$8.50	99-05
CT	1926		EX	$132.00	00-04
CT	1933	hunting & fishing	EX-	$105.00	05-07
CT	1933	pin back	EX	$63.26	99-06
CT	1943	button	EX	$61.43	99-04
DE	1932 NR	nonresident pin	VG	$212.50	99-04
DE	1932 NR		EX-	$504.00	00-07
DE	1934 NR		EX	$392.91	99-08
DE	1940	2½"	EX	$128.50	99-02
FL	1927-28	button, light corrosion on back, some stains	VG+	$735.00	02-02
HA	1948-49	Oahu County, pin back	EX	$481.00	02-06
ID	1909	paper	VG	$62.00	99-04
MA	1932	pin back, problems	avg	$47.99	99-04

BRAND	MODEL	SERIES / MFG. CODE / DESCRIPTION	GRADE	PRICE	DATE yy/mm
MI	1920 NR	paper only raggy, no pin	avg	$76.00	99-04
MI	1929 NR	#461, pin back, orange/white	EX	$1,136.00	05-06
MI	1929 Trout	ugly	VG-	$100.99	99-09
MI	1930 NR	White & Hoag Co., w/papers	EX	$261.00	00-07
MI	1930 NR	pin back	EX	$159.00	05-07
MI	1930 NR	pin back, with papers	EX	$202.00	05-07
MI	1930, 31, 32 NR	all 3 buttons with papers	EX+	$695.00	00-03
MI	1931 NR	crackling under	VG	$202.49	99-09
MI	1931 NR	nonresident badge	EX	$203.50	99-02
MI	1931 NR	NOT MET	EX	$189.38	99-05
MI	1931 NR	with paper	mint	$300.00	99-05
MI	1931 NR		EX	$214.50	99-09
MI	1932 NR	pin back	EX	$257.75	99-06
MI	1932 NR	with paper	EX	$227.00	00-05
MI	1932 NR	with paper	mint	$300.00	99-05
MI	1932 NR		EX	$227.50	99-07
MI	1932 Trout	with papers	EX	$164.01	99-09
MI	1929	nonresident, special #35373	EX	$494.00	05-02
MI	1930	nonresident, pin back	EX-	$181.00	05-07
MI	1931	nonresident, pin back, NOT MET	EX+	$181.00	04-11
MI	1932	NOT MET	EX	$137.75	99-06
MN	1927 NR	nonresident badge	EX	$148.50	99-02
MN	1927 NR	nonresident, NOT MET	EX	$100.77	99-03
MN	1927 NR	NOT MET	EX-	$100.00	99-06
MS	1937	hunting, Hinds County, NOT MET	mint	$345.00	99-07
MS	1938	hunting badge	EX-	$257.55	99-05
MS	1942	family	EX	$455.00	99-06
MY	1931	nonresident fishing, NOT MET	EX	$260.00	02-02
MY	1933 NR	nonresident	EX-	$83.00	99-02
NC	1935 – 36		EX-	$256.00	99-03
NC	1937 – 38	hunting & fishing, brass badge, nice	EX	$300.00	99-07
NC	1937	fish-shaped pin, "resident"	EX	$431.00	99-01
NC	1939	metal curved pin	EX-	$126.00	99-07
NC	1939	scratch on badge	VG	$163.50	99-03
NH	1958 NR	rectangle metal case	EX	$31.00	99-04
NY	1930 NR	pin back	EX	$229.49	99-06
NY	1931 NR	pin back	EX-	$75.00	99-06
NY	1932 NR		EX	$92.99	00-02
NY	1939 NR	pin	EX	$182.49	99-05
NY	1940 NR	button	EX	$127.50	00-03
NY	1912	minnow net, aluminum	EX	$73.35	00-01
NY	1930	hunting, fishing, trapping	EX	$18.50	99-08
NY	1932	fishing, hunting, trapping button	EX	$20.50	99-04
NY	1932	fishing, hunting	EX	$23.49	00-02
NY	1933	fishing, hunting, trapping pin	EX	$28.00	99-05
NY	1935	family fishing, hunting, trapping	EX	$208.07	99-06
NY	1938	fishing, hunting, trapping button	EX	$16.05	99-04
OH	1940	copper, pin back	EX	$11.05	99-05

BRAND	MODEL	SERIES / MFG. CODE / DESCRIPTION	GRADE	PRICE	DATE yy/mm
OH	1943	copper	?	$10.50	99-05
Ontario	1915	canvas	VG-	$36.50	99-05
PA	1923 – 59	40 diff, 1 warden badge, few modern	VG-EX	$2,300.00	99-09
PA	1927 NR		EX	$350.00	99-07
PA	1929 NR	NOT MET	EX	$61.00	99-07
PA	1931 NR	papers	EX	$307.00	00-08
PA	1937 NR	papers	EX	$283.75	99-06
PA	1938 NR	3-day, NOT MET	EX	$310.00	00-07
PA	1939 NR	3-day	EX	$200.00	00-07
PA	1939 – 47	9 different	EX-	$151.01	99-02
PA	1940	resident	EX	$43.50	99-02
PA	1941 NR	3-day	EX	$142.00	00-07
PA	1945 NR		EX	$52.00	00-08
PA	1946 NR	pin	EX	$90.00	99-05
PA	1948 NR	nonresident	EX	$48.00	99-03
PA	1922	paper license, 1st year of issue	VG	$687.00	03-05
PA	1922	sheet of paper	EX-	$610.00	02-08
PA	1923	button, NOT MET!	EX-	$280.00	99-04
PA	1923	pin	EX	$152.66	99-05
PA	1923	pin back	EX	$510.00	03-11
PA	1923	pin back	EX-	$200.00	05-07
PA	1924	pin badge	EX-	$177.50	99-05
PA	1924	pin back	EX	$295.00	03-12
PA	1925		VG	$71.00	99-07
PA	1925		EX	$178.50	99-03
PA	1925		mint	$255.00	01-03
PA	1926	pin back	VG	$18.00	03-12
PA	1926	pin back	VG	$76.00	99-06
PA	1926	pin back	EX	$305.00	99-05
PA	1927		VG+	$28.77	99-11
PA	1928		VG+	$41.13	99-07
PA	1929	button	EX	$104.50	99-04
PA	1929	button with paper	EX	$125.25	99-08
PA	1930	button	EX-	$19.50	99-05
PA	1934		EX	$64.07	00-02
PA	1935	pin back	VG+	$26.00	99-06
PA	1937		mint	$61.00	00-03
PA	1939	pin	EX	$20.00	99-04
PA	1940	unissued	EX	$30.00	99-07
PA	1950	button	mint	$29.16	99-05
PA	1950		EX	$12.00	99-03
TN	1934 – 35	hunting & fishing, NOT MET	mint	$138.50	99-06
TN	1938 – 39	with paper license in back	EX	$164.00	00-04
TN	1939 – 40	hunting & fishing	EX	$127.00	05-07
TN	1941	hunting & fishing, papers inside	EX	$142.50	99-05
VA	1930 – 31	hunting, fishing, trapping	avg	$50.00	99-06
WA	1920 NR	paper rectangle	EX	$38.00	00-02
WI	1930 NR	NOT MET	fair	$16.50	99-07

BRAND	MODEL	SERIES / MFG. CODE / DESCRIPTION	GRADE	PRICE	DATE yy/mm
WI	1930 NR	pin back	EX	$155.00	99-04
WI	1930 NR		EX	$128.49	00-01
WI	1930 NR		EX+	$145.00	99-07
WI	1932 NR	pin back	EX	$88.00	99-06
WI	1932 NR	pin back, NOT MET	EX	$121.50	99-04
WV	1939 NR	with papers	EX	$306.00	99-09
WV	1940 Hunt & Fish	papers	EX	$350.00	00-08
WV	1921	cloth	poor	$31.00	99-05
WV	1934	pin back, no paper	EX	$75.00	99-05
WV	1937	NOT MET		$27.00	99-06
WV	1938	NOT MET		$28.00	99-06

Lines

BRAND	MODEL	SERIES / MFG. CODE / DESCRIPTION	GRADE	PRICE	DATE yy/mm
Ashaway	Ship's Wheel	wood spool with linen line	EX	$39.80	00-03
Ashaway	Silk Flyline	great swastika box, nice spool	NIB	$108.00	01-03
CCBC	Lite Chub	awful, NOT MET	pig	$167.82	99-05
Cisco Kid	30 lb.	two 50 yd. spools in plastic box	NIB	$142.00	03-09
Hall	33 Different	nice display, NOT MET	NIB	$81.00	99-05
Hall	35 Different	salesman sample, NOT MET	NIB	$200.00	99-06
Hall	Salesman Sample	27 diff, NOT MET	NIB	$145.05	99-06
Heddon	Mono	Daisy/Heddon	EX	$30.00	99-01
Heddon	Pal-On	2 plastic spools of braided line, p. box	NIB	$53.00	99-12
Heddon	Pal-On 20 lb.	twin spools, leapin' bass	mint	$91.00	99-08
Heddon	Silk	Dandy-Line, waterproof pure Japanese silk	VG-	$305.00	99-03
Heddon		2 diff	EX	$26.50	99-01
Ohara	Fisherman's	24 spools, 25 yd., silk, 10 lb.	NIB	$30.75	99-06
Vom Hofe, Ed.	#27	300 yd., wood, box, nice	EXIB	$56.00	99-05
Winchester	8612 16 lb.	wood spool, holes punched	EX	$325.00	99-01
Winchester	Vacation Special	wood, Bass pic, holed, uglyish	G	$130.49	99-08

Line Dryers

BRAND	MODEL	SERIES / MFG. CODE / DESCRIPTION	GRADE	PRICE	DATE yy/mm
Hardy	Compact	fold-up, cool	EX	$455.00	00-02
Hardy	Large	windmill type, numerous "Hardy" markings odd!	EX-	$639.00	05-07
Hardy		newer looking	EX	$96.00	02-01
Vom Hofe, Ed.	Solid Brass	neat! folding 9" x 20" x 20"	EX	$338.00	02-06

Line Spools

BRAND	MODEL	SERIES / MFG. CODE / DESCRIPTION	GRADE	PRICE	DATE yy/mm
Heddon	Simpson Wood	bass, hole, one side rough	avg	$248.00	00-02

Lures

BRAND	MODEL	SERIES / MFG. CODE / DESCRIPTION	GRADE	PRICE	DATE yy/mm
Unknown	Double Spinner	barber pole paint pattern, lead head, double hooks, black/silver stripes	EX+	$1,292.50	05-04
Unknown	Florida Shiner	green/gold spot, 6"	EX-	$770.00	05-04
Unknown	Golden Shiner	w/orig box and papers, pat applied for, 6¾"	EX+	$797.50	05-04
Unknown	Lake George Floater	red/yellow/white original early bait complete with cork ball and aluminum lip, scattered pointers	VG+	$1,155.00	05-04
Unknown	Spring Hook	hollow metal minnow, 4"	EX	$550.00	00-03
4 Brothers	#5	willow leaf spinner, very nice feathered bucktail	EX+	$15.00	05-06
4 Brothers	Delite	fly reel, Bakelite, nickle plate, brass rubbed	VG	$266.00	01-11
4 Brothers	Delite	fly, hard rubber sides, nickle pltd brass	VG	$203.00	01-10
4 Brothers	Neverfail	3-hooker, crackle, maroon box	EX-IB(G)	$356.09	99-09
4 Brothers	Neverfail 5-hook	3173, maroon box EX	EXIB	$810.00	01-03
4 Brothers	Neverfail 5-hook	RB, nice maroon box 3173	EXIB	$490.00	01-04
A L&W	B. Wiggle Fish	pikie, nice	EX+	$313.88	98-12
A L&W	Pikie Triple Joint	pikie, GE	EX	$90.00	99-10
Abbey & Imbrie	3-hooker	crackle, A&I #100 (by Heddon)	VG+IB	$400.00	00-11
Abbey & Imbrie	Bass Seeker	RH, solid, no pics box nice	NIB	$42.00	01-11
Abbey & Imbrie	Basser	green perch scale, NO BIDS	EX	$10.00	01-11
Abbey & Imbrie	Big Boy	green stripe	EX	$49.00	01-08
Abbey & Imbrie	Big Boy, jntd	red/white	EX	$18.00	01-06
Abbey & Imbrie	Crab Wiggler	Heddon 1800 RET, L-rig, GE	EX-	$150.00	05-07
Abbey & Imbrie	Crawdad	frog color	EX+	$21.00	05-02
Abbey & Imbrie	Diving Mouse	RH, PE, wood checked, nice box	VG+IB	$32.00	00-02
Abbey & Imbrie	Flash-Head Wobbler	7430 CH/60, 1PCCB EX-, brass head	avgIB	$54.00	04-02
Abbey & Imbrie	Flipper	L-rig, Heddon perch scale, GE, A&I props	VG+	$250.00	01-12
Abbey & Imbrie	Floating Runt	red head/yellow, NO BIDS	EX-	$25.00	01-04
Abbey & Imbrie	Frog #8	fly rod, rubber on card	NOC	$52.00	00-01
Abbey & Imbrie	Ghost	weird metal spinner, marked	EX	$300.00	00-10
Abbey & Imbrie	Glowbody Minnow	glass tube, box (good box, one side missing end flaps)	VG+?	$1,320.00	04-11
Abbey & Imbrie	Glowbody	glass body	EX	$170.00	00-04
Abbey & Imbrie	Glowbody		EX	$70.00	00-04
Abbey & Imbrie	Go-Getter	jntd Runt, perch scale, window box	VGIB	$22.00	01-05
Abbey & Imbrie	Go-Getter	r/w in nice box, River Runt type, TE	NIB	$50.00	03-01
Abbey & Imbrie	Go-Getter	RH, fat head, Runt type, TE	EX	$15.00	01-05
Abbey & Imbrie	Go-Getter	RH, TE, great graphics, 1PCCB EX	EXIB	$50.50	99-12
Abbey & Imbrie	Go-Getter	great window box	EXIB	$63.31	00-02
Abbey & Imbrie	Go-Getter	Rush Tango type, frog, nice box	NIB	$57.00	01-03
Abbey & Imbrie	Go-Getter	y flash, PE, box VG- but decent	EXIB	$88.50	99-09
Abbey & Imbrie	Go-Getter, no code	r/w, 1PCCB window style, TE	NIB	$73.00	02-08
Abbey & Imbrie	Injured Minnow	Heddon Flipper, side hooks, L-rig, shiner scale	VG	$150.00	03-02
Abbey & Imbrie	Jennings Torpedo	metal lures, cleaned, SOLD	EX	$300.00	99-10
Abbey & Imbrie	Jointed Runt	63RBW window, TE	NIB	$71.00	01-10
Abbey & Imbrie	Jointed Vamp	blue perch, TE, belly rough, window bx, nice	VG+IB	$27.00	01-04
Abbey & Imbrie	Lawrence Gang Hook	nice box with picture card inside, c. 1890s	NIB	$311.00	01-11

BRAND	MODEL	SERIES / MFG. CODE / DESCRIPTION	GRADE	PRICE	DATE yy/mm
Abbey & Imbrie	Octopus	3-hooker, RB, SOLD	VG+	$780.00	99-10
Abbey & Imbrie	Octopus 5-hooker	rainbow, ugly back, HPGM	VG-	$405.00	03-02
Abbey & Imbrie	Octopus Minnow	staple rigged early 5-hook underwater minnow, GE, yellow glass beads, props unique only to this bait	EX	$1,787.50	05-04
Abbey & Imbrie	Pikie 4¾"	brown/y pike scale? TE	mint	$31.51	00-04
Abbey & Imbrie	Pikie, jntd	#63RH, great window box, TE	NIB	$58.00	00-09
Abbey & Imbrie	Slant Nose	black head/yellow, GE, Shur Strike	NIB	$337.00	02-10
Abbey & Imbrie	Spinner	on great bass & trout card EX	NOC	$19.00	01-04
Abbey & Imbrie	Spoon Fish	Heddon metal lure	EX	$99.00	01-09
Abbey & Imbrie	Stanley King	r/w, nice 2PCCB	EXIB	$38.25	01-04
Abbey & Imbrie	Torpedo	Jennings	EX	$382.00	00-03
Abbey & Imbrie	Torpedo	RH, A& I (Heddon) props, GE	VG	$81.00	01-05
Abbey & Imbrie	Underwater Minnow	3-hk, green perch scale	EX	$66.00	01-11
Abbey & Imbrie	Vamp	frog spot, TE	EX	$20.00	02-07
Abbey & Imbrie	Vamp	green perch scale	EX	$12.50	01-11
Abbey & Imbrie	Vamp	Heddon jointed RET, GE, L-rig	EX	$88.00	01-09
Abbey & Imbrie	Vamp	yellow perch scale	EX	$16.00	01-11
Abbey & Imbrie	Vamp, jointed	yellow perch scale	EX	$20.00	01-11
ABU	Hi-Lo	BGL	EX	$81.00	00-03
ABU	Hi-Lo	black shore	EX	$12.00	05-07
ABU	Hi-Lo	BO, brown trout	VG+	$81.00	00-03
ABU	Hi-Lo	D	EX+	$81.00	00-03
ABU	Hi-Lo	L	EX+	$81.00	00-03
ABU	Hi-Lo	LYS, luminous	EX	$81.00	00-03
ABU	Hi-Lo	M	VG	$81.00	00-03
ABU	Hi-Lo	XBG	EX+	$92.00	00-03
ABU	Hi-Lo	XBW	EX	$81.00	00-03
ABU	Hi-Lo	XBW, 2¾", Sweden	EX	$23.00	03-01
ABU	Hi-Lo	XRS	EX-	$81.00	00-03
ABU	Whirler	12-pack, 1.2 oz., odd metal spinner	NIB	$224.00	03-04
Accepted Lures	Dozy Boy	red/yellow, spring-hook type	EX	$76.00	05-03
Acme	Weedless Minnow	3-hooker, spoon, spring, worm burn!	avgIB	$39.00	00-04
Action Frog	Live Action Frog		NIB	$300.00	00-08
Adams, E.C.	Ideal Minnow	w/orig belly hooks, y GBE, some wear	G	$770.00	05-04
AL&W	Dingbat	319 pike, ½ black/rest pikie, GE	NIB	$133.00	00-05
AL&W	Pikie	17½", wood body, store display lure	EX	$627.00	05-03
Alcoe	Magic Minnow	wood/rubber fins, box VG+, golden shiner	EXIB	$455.00	03-07
Algers	Getsem Weedless	white, c. 1910	EX	$303.00	04-11
Algers	Getsum	NOT MET	VG	$100.00	00-07
Allcock	Fly	3½", open spokes, unmarked box	EX	$1,263.00	03-02
Allcock	Kastlite x 2	prototype & regular, NOT MET	VG+	$240.00	02-08
Allcock	Marvel	3", fly	EX	$197.00	02-08
Allcock	Paragon Minnow	brass, glass eyes	EX	$405.00	02-02
Allcocks	Aquatic Spider	lg size on card in great tin box	NIB	$562.00	01-06
Allcocks	Aquatic Spider	on card in cool tin (rubs)	NIB	$250.00	01-07
Allen, Forest	Ubangi	black/white ribs	EX	$23.57	99-06
Allen Tackle	Dubl Mino	rhinestone eyes	EX	$9.00	04-03

BRAND	MODEL	SERIES / MFG. CODE / DESCRIPTION	GRADE	PRICE	DATE yy/mm
American	Ball Spinner	June-bug type with luminous body, new on fish head–shaped card	EX-	$75.00	05-05
American Rod & Gun	Lucky Bunny	green	EX	$21.00	04-07
Anderson	Spring Hook Lure	perch, plastic, nice box + papers	NIB	$171.00	02-04
Anderson & Co.	Chautauqua Minnow	blue picture box EX-, 1909 papers!	NIB	$45,855.00	03-09
Arbogast	3-fin Sunfish	2", weedless, GE, hairlines, marked tail spinner, box, dirty, general wear	EXIB	$220.00	05-04
Arbogast	Flyrod Hawaiian Wiggler	yellow w/y and w hula skirt, new on card in cellophane	NOC	$15.00	05-05
Arbogast	Flyrod Hula Spinner	green w/g and w hula skirt, new on card in cellophane (torn)	NOCC	$25.00	05-05
Arbogast	Fred's Frog	white, wood body	NOC	$11.00	04-09
Arbogast	Hammerhead	2300Y, yellow back, silver	NIB	$5.00	05-03
Arbogast	Hawaiian Wiggler	scale, older pic PTCB, cat	NIB	$20.50	99-02
Arbogast	Hawaiin Wiggler	red & green, #2, new in plastic top box	NIB	$15.00	05-06
Arbogast	Hawaiin Wiggler	red & green, ¼ oz., new in box with hangtag	NIB	$10.00	05-06
Arbogast	Hawaiian Wiggler	#1, yellow w/red eyes, PE, yellow hula skirt, new in 2PSTB, w/catalog, trailer hook on card	NIB	$12.00	05-05
Arbogast	Hawaiian Wiggler	#2, solid black PE, complete package new in 2PSTB, w/catalog, trailer hook on card	NIB	$18.00	05-05
Arbogast	Hawaiian Wiggler	#2, yellow, coach dog, PE, complete unit, orig 2PSTB and cat	NIB	$22.00	05-05
Arbogast	Hula Popper	#788SRH, with correct yellow box, tail shows age	VG	$6.03	05-07
Arbogast	Hula Popper	750PTCB, rainbow trout? color, EX	NIB	$78.00	05-07
Arbogast	Hula Popper	RH, w/r&w hula skirt but it's worn, lure has very light wear	VG+	$7.00	05-05
Arbogast	Hula Popper	X780R hot pink	EX-IB	$66.00	05-05
Arbogast	Hula Popper, spinning	chipmunk	NIB	$34.00	02-09
Arbogast	Jitterbug	½ oz., smooth eye, green/blk dots	EX	$69.00	00-08
Arbogast	Jitterbug	2 WWII, frog and r/w	avg-VG	$31.56	99-01
Arbogast	Jitterbug	4 diff WWII	EX	$89.00	99-03
Arbogast	Jitterbug	⅝ oz., lum, bubble pac	NOC	$26.00	99-01
Arbogast	Jitterbug	⅝ oz., frog, clear belly, WWII lip melted	EX-?	$125.00	02-07
Arbogast	Jitterbug	⅝ oz., wood, frog, WWII lip, box VG+	EX-IB	$103.00	04-12
Arbogast	Jitterbug	b/w, ⅜ oz.	EX-	$71.95	99-03
Arbogast	Jitterbug	bare wood, special issue	NIB	$46.00	00-04
Arbogast	Jitterbug	black with black plastic lip	EX+	$30.00	05-06
Arbogast	Jitterbug	blue back herring, 2⅝"	VG+	$18.01	05-07
Arbogast	Jitterbug	blue scale	NIB	$180.00	99-03
Arbogast	Jitterbug	clear lip	NIB	$32.00	99-02
Arbogast	Jitterbug	#67, clear/gold glitter	NIB	$31.51	99-01
Arbogast	Jitterbug	flocked mouse, ⅝ oz., weedless trebles	NIB	$270.00	00-09
Arbogast	Jitterbug	fluorescent yellow	EX	$13.37	99-01
Arbogast	Jitterbug	fly rod, plastic lip, black	NOC	$32.00	00-10
Arbogast	Jitterbug	fly rod, plastic lip, silver scale	NOC	$78.00	00-10
Arbogast	Jitterbug	frog with red plastic lip, SR, 2PCCB box VG++	EX+IB	$45.00	05-06

BRAND	MODEL	SERIES / MFG. CODE / DESCRIPTION	GRADE	PRICE	DATE yy/mm
Arbogast	Jitterbug	frog, light green color, w/yellow plastic lip, in 2PCCB box VG+	EX+IB	$45.00	05-06
Arbogast	Jitterbug	frog, yellow lip	mint	$31.00	00-05
Arbogast	Jitterbug	frog, WWII, plastic lip	VG	$26.00	05-07
Arbogast	Jitterbug	frog, clear lip	EX	$17.00	99-02
Arbogast	Jitterbug	frog, wood, y plastic lip, nice box	NIB	$152.50	99-04
Arbogast	Jitterbug	frog, yellow lip	NIB	$36.00	99-06
Arbogast	Jitterbug	glow in the dark, plastic, white, topwater	GD	$13.49	05-07
Arbogast	Jitterbug	gold glitter, 3 different	NIB	$26.00	99-01
Arbogast	Jitterbug	green and yellow	GD	$5.24	05-07
Arbogast	Jitterbug	luminous, coach dog, ⅝ oz.	EX+	$56.00	04-11
Arbogast	Jitterbug	luminous, worm burn		$28.00	98-12
Arbogast	Jitterbug	metallic blue	EX+	$55.00	99-01
Arbogast	Jitterbug	musky, plastic, r/w	NIB	$28.50	99-03
Arbogast	Jitterbug	old wood, frog ugly, age lines belly	EX-?	$39.00	01-08
Arbogast	Jitterbug	orange/black dots, modern	EX	$177.50	99-06
Arbogast	Jitterbug	perch, red plastic lip, wire hdwr, in 2PCCB box VG+	EX+IB	$50.00	05-06
Arbogast	Jitterbug	perch, yellow plastic lip, wire hdwr, in 2PCCB box EX-	EX+IB	$45.00	05-06
Arbogast	Jitterbug	perch, red lip WWII	EX	$18.58	00-02
Arbogast	Jitterbug	perch, WWII lip	NIB	$158.01	00-03
Arbogast	Jitterbug	plain cedar, "Limited Edition"	NIB	$105.38	99-08
Arbogast	Jitterbug	purple CD, purple plastic lip not WWII	NIB	$455.00	00-04
Arbogast	Jitterbug	r/w, PTCB pic on bottom	EXIB	$21.50	99-02
Arbogast	Jitterbug	r/w, plastic lip, pic box	poor	$17.50	99-02
Arbogast	Jitterbug	r/w, red lip, 2PCCB, papers	EXIB	$41.00	99-03
Arbogast	Jitterbug	redwing blackbird	AVG	$31.01	05-07
Arbogast	Jitterbug	red WWII lip, wood body	EX-	$42.00	04-07
Arbogast	Jitterbug	RH, white lip, no name	EX	$31.00	00-05
Arbogast	Jitterbug	RH, 2PCCB decent	EXIB	$27.00	01-03
Arbogast	Jitterbug	RH, plastic lip, nice box	NIB	$76.00	00-10
Arbogast	Jitterbug	RH, red lip	mint	$31.00	00-05
Arbogast	Jitterbug	RH, red lip	mint	$46.00	00-05
Arbogast	Jitterbug	shiner scale, red lip	mint	$42.00	00-05
Arbogast	Jitterbug	silver/red herringbone, plastic lip	EX	$963.00	01-09
Arbogast	Jitterbug	silver scale, red lip, chips	avg	$33.00	00-08
Arbogast	Jitterbug	sparrow	NIB	$67.00	99-02
Arbogast	Jitterbug	sparrow, ⅜ oz.	NIB	$67.00	99-02
Arbogast	Jitterbug	white shore?	VG	$28.81	99-02
Arbogast	Jitterbug	wood frog, intro box, age lines, nice	NIB	$155.00	02-03
Arbogast	Jitterbug	wood, shiner scale	EX	$132.00	04-03
Arbogast	Jitterbug	wood, ⅜ oz., RH, WWII plastic lip	EX-IB	$57.00	05-01
Arbogast	Jitterbug	wood, 2¾", black shore, extra hvy rig	EX-	$665.00	00-11
Arbogast	Jitterbug	WW II, frog/black lip	VG	$39.75	99-01
Arbogast	Jitterbug	WWII lip	NIB	$51.00	01-08
Arbogast	Jitterbug	WWII lip, black with black lip	NIB	$76.00	01-08
Arbogast	Jitterbug	WWII, plastic lip, black	EX-	$14.00	05-03

BRAND	MODEL	SERIES / MFG. CODE / DESCRIPTION	GRADE	PRICE	DATE yy/mm
Arbogast	Jitterbug	WWII, plastic lip, perch/yellow lip	EX	$21.00	05-03
Arbogast	Jitterbug	WWII, y/blk lip, ugly box	VG+	$42.00	03-02
Arbogast	Jitterbug	WWII, nice box & papers	EXIB	$41.00	99-03
Arbogast	Jitterbug	WWII, r/w, red lip	EX	$39.00	99-03
Arbogast	Jitterbug	WWII, r/w, white lip	VG-	$25.00	99-01
Arbogast	Jitterbug	WWII, red lip, perch	VG	$29.00	99-02
Arbogast	Jitterbug	WWII, shiner/red, hvy rig	EX	$32.00	99-02
Arbogast	Jitterbug	XRY, red lip	EX	$29.76	99-02
Arbogast	Jitterbug 6-pack	great graphics, 1970s? 4 lures	NIB	$212.50	99-04
Arbogast	Jitterbug Flyrod x 4	4 different colors, plastic lips	avg	$44.00	01-08
Arbogast	Jitterbug Weedless	Stanley	EX	$15.50	00-04
Arbogast	Jitterbug x 2	clear lip, 4 diff	NIB	$78.50	99-09
Arbogast	Jitterbug x 2	fly rod, plastic lips, frog, RH	NOC	$72.00	00-10
Arbogast	Jitterbug, jntd	white coach dog, 2⅜", plastic	EX-	$12.00	05-06
Arbogast	Jitterbug, Musky	wood, frog spot same as previous, but just a little more wear	VG+	$34.00	05-05
Arbogast	Jitterbug, Musky	wood, RH/w, side hk, NSOB, new in EX+ orig 2PPTB w/color catalog	NIB	$55.00	05-05
Arbogast	Jitterbug, Musky	wood, yellow w/red eye shadow, side hk, NSOB, very light wear	EX	$60.00	05-05
Arbogast	Jitterbug, Musky	2-hk, back stencil, black scale, hvy teardrop	VG+	$157.00	00-04
Arbogast	Jitterbug, Musky	3-hooker, plain varnish, no paint, PTCB	NIB	$79.00	01-08
Arbogast	Jitterbug, Musky	clear cedar, wood, side hooker	NIB	$97.00	05-02
Arbogast	Jitterbug, Musky	709N, orange/blk spots, 3-hk	NIB	$197.00	04-02
Arbogast	Jitterbug, Musky	perch, plastic top box	NIB	$44.05	99-04
Arbogast	Jitterbug, Musky	plain cedar	NIB	$96.00	00-02
Arbogast	Jitterbug, Musky	plastic, flitter, 3-pack, nice	NIB	$51.00	99-02
Arbogast	Jitterbug, Musky	plastic, frog, 3-pack	NIB	$60.00	99-02
Arbogast	Jitterbug, Musky	trout, side hooks, PTCB	NIB	$71.00	99-06
Arbogast	Jitterbug, Musky	RH, 2 belly hooks, name on back	EX	$636.00	04-02
Arbogast	Jitterbug, Musky	silver scales, black back, wood	EX-	$65.00	05-06
Arbogast	Jitterbug, Musky	w/blk back & ribs, spots	NIB	$45.00	99-02
Arbogast	Jitterbug, Musky	wood side hooks, brown scale, 1 hk never attached	NIB	$217.00	04-03
Arbogast	Kicker	frog spot, glass eyes	EX-	$46.00	05-05
Arbogast	Mopar	$100, 000 contest 4-pack lures	EX	$101.00	99-03
Arbogast	Mudbug ¾ oz.	#24, 8 BIDS	NIB	$10.50	99-09
Arbogast	Pugnose	NFL team lure, Chicago Bears, NIPB	NIB	$25.00	05-05
Arbogast	Scudder	big wood lure	NIB	$39.00	01-08
Arbogast	Skinny Minny	plastic, red head/white/yellow back	NIB	$11.00	01-08
Arbogast	Skinny Minny	r/w	EX	$16.50	99-06
Arbogast	Spin Liz	golden shiner, 1/64 oz.	EX+	$17.00	05-05
Arbogast	Spin Liz	silver, ⅛ oz., new on orig card, but card is a little faded	EXOC	$17.00	05-05
Arbogast	Tin Liz	2½", musky size?	EX	$263.00	03-05
Arbogast	Tin Liz	2½", GE, RH/gold	EX	$100.00	99-07
Arbogast	Tin Liz	2¾", GE	EX	$228.00	00-10
Arbogast	Tin Liz	fly rod, PE, display card with 6 mint	NOC	$120.00	99-01
Arbogast	Tin Liz	GE	mint	$43.00	00-01

BRAND	MODEL	SERIES / MFG. CODE / DESCRIPTION	GRADE	PRICE	DATE yy/mm
Arbogast	Tin Liz	GE, in avg pic box	EX-IB	$66.00	00-10
Arbogast	Tin Liz	gold, 3½", GE, nice box	NIB	$212.50	99-03
Arbogast	Tin Liz	lg GE, silver/green	EX	$57.50	99-01
Arbogast	Tin Liz	pike	EX-	$291.00	99-03
Arbogast	Tin Liz	pike	VG+	$382.75	00-03
Arbogast	Tin Liz	pike bottom has quite a bit of rub, top is EX	VG?	$275.00	05-06
Arbogast	Tin Liz	pike shape & color	EX-	$383.00	03-01
Arbogast	Tin Liz	pike shape, one side nice, other missing 50% paint	???	$157.00	04-03
Arbogast	Tin Liz	pike, crisp un box and papers	NIB	$915.00	01-03
Arbogast	Tin Liz	pike, pointers one side, NOT MET	VG-	$177.00	00-04
Arbogast	Tin Liz	sunfish	EX	$351.00	00-07
Arbogast	Tin Liz	sunfish	EX	$222.50	98-12
Arbogast	Tin Liz	sunfish, Tin Liz, GE, r-eye has tiny nick and very light wear	VG+	$170.00	05-05
Arbogast	Tin Liz	sunfish, 4-fin, NOT MET	EX-	$152.50	99-06
Arbogast	Tin Liz	sunfish, crisp un box and papers	NIB	$415.00	01-03
Arbogast	Tin Liz	sunfish, GE	EX+	$456.00	00-01
Arbogast	Tin Liz	sunfish, GE, beauty, window box, NOT MET	NIB	$150.00	01-01
Arbogast	Tin Liz	sunfish, rough un box, NOT MET	NIB	$301.00	01-11
Arbogast	Tin Liz	sunfish, Tin Liz pic box EX, stapled pocket catalog	NIB	$455.00	04-02
Arbogast	Tin Liz	sunfish, NOT MET	EX-	$212.50	99-03
Arbogast	Tin Liz	walleye, crisp un box & papers	NIB	$1,913.00	01-03
Arbogast	Tin Liz	walleye, huge rub on one side	?	$498.00	00-10
Arbogast	Tin Liz	walleye, NOT MET	VG	$506.00	99-06
Arbogast	Tin Liz	walleye, one side all rubbed, NOT MET	avg	$498.00	00-10
Arbogast	Tin Liz #2	green shiner, WDLS, r-eye tiny crack, just a hint of wear in varnish	EX	$40.00	05-05
Arbogast	Tin Liz #2	RH/gold PE, very light wear on this	EX	$55.00	05-05
Arbogast	Tin Liz #2	RH/silver GE, WDLS, r-eye has a small chip out of glass	EX	$48.00	05-05
Arbogast	Tipsy	380 07, yellow coach dog	NOC	$14.00	04-07
Arbogast	Twin Liz	wood, red and green minnows, PPE, few light pointers on 1 minnow, orig 2PPTB	EX-IB	$30.00	05-05
Arbogast	Weedless Kicker	frog	EX	$124.07	99-09
Armax	3-hooker	Winchester, hvy age lines	NIB	$557.50	98-12
Arnold	Hop Along	fireplug, TE	EX	$86.00	00-07
Arnold	Hop Along	red/white, rubber skirt missing	mint	$41.00	03-04
Arnold	Hopalong	flourescent green frog, PTCB	NIB	$85.00	04-02
Arntz, A	Michigan Lifelike	VG box, EX paper, CHIPS	GIB	$3,635.00	99-06
Artifical Bait Co.	Superstrike Shrimp	black bead eyes, nice tail detail	EX	$632.50	05-04
Atom	Striper	1947 box with neat papers, lure so-so	VGIB	$262.00	04-12
Babbitt	Weedless	white, GE, spring-loaded wood lure, pat Oct. 26, '37	EX-	$127.00	05-07
Babbitt	Weedless		EX-	$375.00	99-10
Baby's Rattle	All Plastic		NIB	$7.00	03-01
Baby's Rattle	Baby's Rattle	orange/red chin, 2PCCB & catalog crisp	NIB	$22.00	04-12
Baby's Rattle	Mouse	yellow, wood front end only, no rattle	NIB	$32.00	03-01
Baby's Rattle	Wood/Plastic Tail	yellow/red chin, 2PCCB + papers	NIB	$34.00	03-01

BRAND	MODEL	SERIES / MFG. CODE / DESCRIPTION	GRADE	PRICE	DATE yy/mm
Baby's Rattle	Mouse	black body w/white mouth and throat, plastic w/rattle, new in blue 2PCCB w/catalog	NIB	$40.00	05-05
Baby's Rattle	Mouse	gray mouse, plastic w/rattle, blue 2PCBB w/papers and tag	NIB	$35.00	05-05
Baby's Rattle	Mouse	yellow w/red PE, scarce wood model and small size, new in orig blue 2PCBB	EX+IB	$32.00	05-05
Bacon	Spinner	double spinner, patent 1900	EX-	$18.00	04-03
Bagley	B DB1 Conetail Square Lip	chartreuse/black scale back, sm dent	VG+	$47.00	00-11
Bagley	B DB1 Square Lip	chartreuse/black scale back	EX	$70.00	00-11
Bagley	B DB1 Square Lip	coach dog, dent on top	VG	$15.00	00-11
Bagley	B DB1 Square Lip	white shad	EX	$53.00	00-11
Bagley	B DB1 Square Lip	white shad	EX	$63.00	00-11
Bagley	B DB2 Square Lip	chartreuse/black scale back	mint	$89.00	00-11
Bagley	B DB2 Square Lip	orange/black scale back	VG+	$36.00	00-11
Bagley	B DB2 Square Lip	white shad	EX-	$42.00	00-11
Bagley	B Flat8	LM9, little musky on chartreuse	NOC	$23.00	03-08
Bagley	B1	coach dog	EX-	$32.00	00-11
Bagley	B1	yellow/green scale back, square lip	EX-	$37.00	00-11
Bagley	Balsa B	square lip, common color, 15 bids	EX	$28.00	00-10
Bagley	Balsa B	white, square lip, brass line tie	EX	$35.00	00-08
Bagley	Balsa B	yellow/black scale back	NIB	$52.00	04-11
Bagley	BB2	chart/black scale back, pl box, square lip	NIB	$66.00	01-03
Bagley	BB3-4	flat lip, plastic box	NIB	$46.00	03-01
Bagley	BB3-DC	flat lip, plastic box	NIB	$50.00	03-01
Bagley	BB3-YP	yellow perch	NOC	$51.00	01-08
Bagley	BB4	green scale, pl box, square lip	NIB	$37.00	01-03
Bagley	DB04	rainbow trout	EX-	$103.00	04-11
Bagley	DB3	3", pearl/orange belly	EX	$68.00	00-11
Bagley	Diving Kill'r B2	fire-orange bar fish from Garland book	EX	$251.00	04-09
Bagley	Dredge DB3	black/chrome sides, pink chin, 4½ " long	VG	$16.50	05-07
Bagley	Dredge DB3	brown/black yellow sides, orange belly, 4½ " long	VG	$20.13	05-07
Bagley	Kill RB3	294, square lip, y back/silver stripes over white	EX	$61.00	00-05
Bagley	Killer B	KB3-04	NOC	$26.00	05-01
Bagley	Small Fry Bass	1DSF2-LB4, bass on white	mint	$31.00	00-05
Bagley	Walkin Torpedo	rapala tail prop, ES (eel skin)	NIB	$60.00	00-05
Bagley	Walkin Torpedo	rapala tail prop, GG (green on gold foil)	NIB	$50.00	00-05
Bagley	Walkin Torpedo	rapala tail prop, RS (red on silver foil)	NIB	$51.00	00-05
Bailey & Elliot	Manitou Minnow	green, papers, wrench	NIB	$2,812.00	00-01
Bailey & Elliot	Manitou Minnow	green/white belly, wrench, paper	NIB	$2,500.00	99-08
Bailey & Elliot	Manitou Minnow	green/white, wrench & papers	NIB	$1,725.00	02-04
Bailey & Elliott	Manitou Minnow	green, GE, wrench & papers, box EX	NIB	$3,000.00	05-03
Bailey & Elliott	Manitou Minnow	green, papers	NIB	$2,000.00	02-10
Ball, Horace	Floating Wiggler	white, red chin, hook drags, NOT MET	??	$191.00	01-08
Barber	Reel Shad	green/white scales, great 2PCCB, KY item	NIB	$26.00	05-03
Barr Royers	Crab	gray with black bead eyes	EX-	$80.00	05-06
Barracuda	Baby Shiner	silver shiner, plastic w/raised PE, color is a little yellowed, scarce model	EX	$30.00	05-05
Barracuda	Baby Shiner	silver shiner, YGE, POBW, wood dent on chin, light age crackling, in orig 2PPB w/card	VGIB	$35.00	05-05

BRAND	MODEL	SERIES / MFG. CODE / DESCRIPTION	GRADE	PRICE	DATE yy/mm
Barracuda	Darter	frog, GE, agelines	EX-	$500.00	00-04
Barracuda	Darter	GE	EX	$452.00	01-01
Barracuda	Gold Shiner	PE, small nick on one side and few tiny pointers	EX-	$25.00	05-05
Barracuda	May Wes	red & yellow in oval box (VG++)	VG+	$65.00	05-06
Barracuda	Shiner	green-black/red sides and silver scales, NSOP, RPE, little age cracks o/w, new in 2PPB w/card	EX-IB	$45.00	05-05
Barracuda	Silver Shiner	PE, tiny flakes at cups on belly, very light wear, last wood model	EX	$30.00	05-05
Barracuda	Tipsy Cuda	frog spot, YPE, POBW, wood crack on chin, light age crackling, in orig 2PPB w/card	VGIB	$35.00	05-05
Barracuda	Torpacuda	frog scale, little rusty	EX-	$75.00	99-08
Barracuda	Torpedo type	perch, carved tail, colorful box VG+	EXIB	$88.00	03-08
Barracuda	Twitchin Cuda	frog scale, Darter type	EX	$69.00	05-02
Bass Bird	Bass Bird	aluminum, Revolution type	EX	$61.00	04-07
Bates	Lady Bug	red/white, spring loaded	mint	$32.00	03-04
Bates	Ladybug	cream/brown stripes, spotted, 2¾"	mint	$39.00	04-02
Bates	Serpentine	pat 1865	EX-	$687.00	03-05
Bauman	Bait Cage	w/orig picture box wih papers, wire bait, c. 1920	EX	$5,500.00	05-04
Bauman	Minnow Bait Cage	box taped all around edge, ugly, NOT MET	EXIB	$2,805.00	03-07
Bauman	Minnow Cage	nice picture box	EXIB	$3,500.00	05-05
Bayou Boogie	Topwater	205, bar fish plastic box	NIB	$26.00	03-08
Bear Creek	Sucker Minnow	2½", gold scale?	EX-	$42.00	03-07
Bear Creek	Sucker Minnow	green scale, 3½"	EX	$41.00	04-07
Bear Creek	Sucker Minnow	small size, green gold scales	mint	$29.00	04-02
Bear Creek	Tweedler	frog finish	EX	$47.00	05-02
Beaver Bait Co.	Old Fighter	frog spot, weird early plastic	EX	$64.00	05-07
Benjamin-Sellar	Thumzey	BC, LW, missing end cap	EX	$750.00	02-08
Berberisch	Large	curved wood body, red/white, GE, tail hook (no metal tail)	EX	$356.00	01-12
Best O Luck	Weighted Underwater	GE, rainbow	EX-	$45.00	05-06
Bew, Charles	Chicago Spinner	spring-hook lure	VG+	$282.00	05-04
Biff	Go Devil	no paint left, metal nice	?	$67.55	00-01
Biff	Master Biff	solid red	EX-	$69.00	05-07
Biff	Master BifF Lure	black, few small pntrs, very light wear	EX	$40.00	05-05
Biff	Master Biff Plug	yellow/black dots	EX	$100.00	03-12
Biff	Master Plug	black, nice 2PCCB, sticky	NIB	$167.50	98-12
Biff	Master Plug	RH, decent box	Ex-IB	$156.00	00-10
Biff	Master Plug	y/b spotted, papers	NIB	$164.50	99-01
Biff	Master Whopee	black, crisp papers & box	NIB	$179.00	02-08
Biff	Musky Spiral	NOT MET	EX	$38.00	00-04
Biff	Musky Spiral		EX	$76.57	99-08
Biff	Musky Spiral Spinner	nice crisp box, crisp papers	NIB	$375.00	00-04
Biff	Spiral Spinner	regular size	EX-	$64.00	02-07
Biff	Spiral Spinner	small size, box VG	EXIB	$200.00	99-12
Biff	Spiral Spinner			$85.00	01-04
Biff	Spiral Spinner		NIB	$175.00	99-10
Biff	Whoopee	2⅛", r/w, ugly	VG-IB	$77.00	99-08
Biff	Spiral Spinner	pike size, NOT MET	EX	$41.09	00-02

BRAND	MODEL	SERIES / MFG. CODE / DESCRIPTION	GRADE	PRICE	DATE yy/mm
Bill's	Action Plug	RH, dent eyes, bead chain hook hangers	VG	$159.00	04-01
Bingenheimer	Nemahbin Minnow	a pig	poor	$96.00	99-04
Bingo	Rudy's Bingo Bubble	RB-2 in plastic bag	NIB	$22.00	05-01
Bishop	Beetle 14"	CCBC replica	mint	$264.00	99-01
Bite Em Bait Co.	Bait	red/white, crisp box and papers	NIB	$738.00	02-08
Bite Em Bait Co.	Bait 211	pic box, red body w/head	EX-IB	$470.00	00-02
Bite Em Bait Co.	Bate	red/white, superb pic box & pic paper (7 colors listed)	NIB	$820.00	01-09
Bite Em Bait Co.	Bite-Em-Bate	finished in white/red/copper, bright and shiney, with tight age lines, pointers, w/box EX-	EXIB	$440.00	05-04
Bite Em Bait Co.	Bite-Em-Bate	red/white, great pic box	NIB	$426.00	99-01
Bite Em Bait Co.	Bite-Em-Bate	red/silver/gold, crisp paper & box, NOT MET	NIB	$766.00	03-04
Bite Em Bait Co.	Lipped Wiggler	rare Diamond box G	EXIB	$600.00	99-10
Bite Em Bait Co.	Revolving	red/white barber pole	EX	$138.00	99-08
Bite Em Bait Co.	Revolving	red/white	EX	$142.00	01-05
Bite Em Bait Co.	Wiggler	red with white chin	EX-	$175.00	05-07
Bite Em Bait Co.	Wiggler	red/white/gold	EX	$128.00	05-07
Bite Em Bait Co.	Wiggler	RG, NE	EX-	$76.00	00-01
Bite Em Bait Co.	Wobbler	black/white/red/gold, sm lip chip, nice	VG+	$63.00	05-01
Bite Em Bait Co.	Wobbler	gold	mint	$300.00	99-03
Bite Em Bait Co.	Wobbler	wood, yellow with red on both ends	VG+	$93.90	05-07
Bleeder Bait Co.	Bleeder	perch scale in box, NOT MET	EXIB	$177.50	99-02
Bleeder Bait Co.	Bleeder	silver scale	NIB	$255.00	99-11
Bleeder Bait Co.	Bleeder	white/silver scale, 2½", papers	NIB	$177.00	00-04
Bleeder Bait Co.	Fish King	6", RH sparkle, papers	NIB	$1,000.00	00-11
Bleeder Bait Co.	Fish King	6", RH/w	EX	$375.00	99-03
Bleeder Bait Co.	Survivor	green back/white nice, GE	EX	$101.00	01-08
Blue Streak Tackle	Popper	Popper, 301, blue	NIB	$132.00	00-04
Blue Streak Tackle	Popper	Popper, 302, red	NIB	$92.00	00-04
Blue Streak Tackle	Popper	Popper, 303, white	NIB	$138.00	00-04
Blue Streak Tackle	Swimmer	bar perch blended (pikie type)	EX+	$46.00	00-04
Bobbie Bait	Junior	6" gray, 2PCCB & papers	NIB	$31.00	02-12
Bobel	Minnow	great box, NOT MET	NIB	$820.00	01-05
Bolton	ABC Minnow	GE tiny cup inserts, yellow back plate, 4"	EX	$605.00	05-04
Bolton	ABC Minnow	red/white	EX	$455.00	01-03
Bomber Bait Co.	49er	508, crisp box	NIB	$31.00	04-01
Bomber Bait Co.	Baby Spinstick	6 different babies	EX	$148.76	00-01
Bomber Bait Co.	Baby Spinstick	7243, #4 small box	EXIB	$46.75	99-06
Bomber Bait Co.	Baby Spinstick	7207 in 7240 #4 box	NIB	$95.00	00-06
Bomber Bait Co.	Baby Spinstick	7239	NIB	$42.00	00-06
Bomber Bait Co.	Baby Spinstick	black mullet, NOT MET	EX	$18.00	01-01
Bomber Bait Co.	Baby Spinstick	sm 7200 box #4	EX-IB	$37.36	99-11
Bomber Bait Co.	Baby Spinstick	7244	EX	$31.00	00-02
Bomber Bait Co.	Bomber	#400, white/silver scale, black head, date 1952	GD	$6.50	05-07
Bomber Bait Co.	Bomber	10 diff #5 boxes	NIB	$81.00	99-03
Bomber Bait Co.	Bomber	10 diff wood, PTCB	NIB	$92.00	01-04
Bomber Bait Co.	Bomber	12 diff wood	NIB	$160.00	01-04
Bomber Bait Co.	Bomber	12 diff wood, decent shape VG+ to EX	diff	$76.50	00-04
Bomber Bait Co.	Bomber	12 diff, some plastic, used	poor – EX	$15.50	99-04

BRAND	MODEL	SERIES / MFG. CODE / DESCRIPTION	GRADE	PRICE	DATE yy/mm
Bomber Bait Co.	Bomber	15 diff, common, 13 #3 & #4 boxes nice	EXIB	$204.00	99-12
Bomber Bait Co.	Bomber	1st type, black, ugly	G	$85.00	99-10
Bomber Bait Co.	Bomber	2 different	VG	$9.50	99-01
Bomber Bait Co.	Bomber	201, box #5	NIB	$15.50	99-02
Bomber Bait Co.	Bomber	201, box #4	NIB	$17.08	99-02
Bomber Bait Co.	Bomber	204, box #4	NIB	$17.00	01-03
Bomber Bait Co.	Bomber	207, #5	NIB	$13.50	00-05
Bomber Bait Co.	Bomber	207, box #4	NIB	$47.55	99-03
Bomber Bait Co.	Bomber	209, #5 box	NIB	$15.50	99-02
Bomber Bait Co.	Bomber	215, white and green back and ribs w/glitter, OPE, Tiny Dude, new in orig 2PCBB w/catalog	NIB	$20.00	05-05
Bomber Bait Co.	Bomber	216, #4 box, NOT MET	NIB	$31.20	00-02
Bomber Bait Co.	Bomber	218, #5	NIB	$21.00	00-06
Bomber Bait Co.	Bomber	219, #4 box	NIB	$16.00	99-01
Bomber Bait Co.	Bomber	220, #4 box	NIB	$19.00	99-10
Bomber Bait Co.	Bomber	221, #5 box	NIB	$27.00	99-03
Bomber Bait Co.	Bomber	236, #5	NIB	$36.00	00-07
Bomber Bait Co.	Bomber	242, #4	NIB	$146.00	00-01
Bomber Bait Co.	Bomber	245, multiflake big deal	EX	$42.00	99-10
Bomber Bait Co.	Bomber	281, wood	NIB	$24.00	05-01
Bomber Bait Co.	Bomber	300FY (like 357), 606HD, 682HD	NIB	$322.00	00-04
Bomber Bait Co.	Bomber	300TB, teal blue, wood lure	NIB	$64.00	05-03
Bomber Bait Co.	Bomber	302, #5 box	NIB	$13.00	99-02
Bomber Bait Co.	Bomber	304, #5 box	NIB	$30.00	99-04
Bomber Bait Co.	Bomber	305, wood	NIB	$17.00	05-01
Bomber Bait Co.	Bomber	305, #5 box	NIB	$19.50	99-10
Bomber Bait Co.	Bomber	305F, #3 box	NIB	$30.00	99-11
Bomber Bait Co.	Bomber	307, #5	NIB	$13.00	00-05
Bomber Bait Co.	Bomber	310, #5 box	NIB	$22.00	99-02
Bomber Bait Co.	Bomber	310, #4 box	NIB	$22.01	99-01
Bomber Bait Co.	Bomber	311, #5	NIB	$12.35	00-05
Bomber Bait Co.	Bomber	312, #5	NIB	$17.30	99-02
Bomber Bait Co.	Bomber	312, in 311 2PCCB	NIB	$30.50	99-01
Bomber Bait Co.	Bomber	312, #5 box	NIB	$10.50	99-04
Bomber Bait Co.	Bomber	313, #3 box, fat forward	NIB	$34.00	01-10
Bomber Bait Co.	Bomber	317, #4 2PCCB	NIB	$36.00	99-01
Bomber Bait Co.	Bomber	320, #5	NIB	$13.00	00-05
Bomber Bait Co.	Bomber	320, #5 box	NIB	$21.25	99-03
Bomber Bait Co.	Bomber	336, #5 box	NIB	$16.00	99-04
Bomber Bait Co.	Bomber	338, #5 box	NIB	$44.99	99-03
Bomber Bait Co.	Bomber	338, PTCB, "33?"	NIB	$133.00	01-01
Bomber Bait Co.	Bomber	340, PTCB	NIB	$15.00	00-11
Bomber Bait Co.	Bomber	355, #5 box	NIB	$17.50	99-02
Bomber Bait Co.	Bomber	355, #4 box	NIB	$32.31	00-02
Bomber Bait Co.	Bomber	356, #5 box	NIB	$16.50	99-03
Bomber Bait Co.	Bomber	358, #5 box	NIB	$14.49	99-02
Bomber Bait Co.	Bomber	359, wood	NIB	$15.00	04-07
Bomber Bait Co.	Bomber	370, #5 box	NIB	$15.50	99-02

BRAND	MODEL	SERIES / MFG. CODE / DESCRIPTION	GRADE	PRICE	DATE yy/mm
Bomber Bait Co.	Bomber	373, #5 box	NIB	$13.22	99-02
Bomber Bait Co.	Bomber	382, #5 box	NIB	$25.49	99-03
Bomber Bait Co.	Bomber	382, wood	NIB	$13.00	05-01
Bomber Bait Co.	Bomber	383, #5 box	NIB	$16.50	99-02
Bomber Bait Co.	Bomber	383, wood	NIB	$21.00	05-01
Bomber Bait Co.	Bomber	387, #5 box	NIB	$10.00	99-02
Bomber Bait Co.	Bomber	389, metascale wood	NIB	$26.00	03-06
Bomber Bait Co.	Bomber	389, wood lure, PTCB	NIB	$13.00	04-12
Bomber Bait Co.	Bomber	3MB, wood	NIB	$16.00	05-01
Bomber Bait Co.	Bomber	3YSC	NIB	$26.50	99-07
Bomber Bait Co.	Bomber	400 x 2, wood black chrome, green chrome	EX	$79.00	01-05
Bomber Bait Co.	Bomber	402, #5	NIB	$11.50	00-05
Bomber Bait Co.	Bomber	403, earliest handmade, nose chip, nice otherwise	VG+	$106.00	01-10
Bomber Bait Co.	Bomber	403, wide gap	EX-	$24.99	00-03
Bomber Bait Co.	Bomber	404, #3 box	NIB	$50.99	99-04
Bomber Bait Co.	Bomber	406, #3 box	NIB	$31.00	01-01
Bomber Bait Co.	Bomber	407, #3 box	NIB	$20.00	00-05
Bomber Bait Co.	Bomber	411, no eyes, in 411 #2, pat pend	avgIB	$22.25	99-12
Bomber Bait Co.	Bomber	412, in #4 box	NIB	$41.51	99-02
Bomber Bait Co.	Bomber	413, 49er	EX	$33.00	99-12
Bomber Bait Co.	Bomber	413, wood	NIB	$17.00	05-01
Bomber Bait Co.	Bomber	414, #5	NIB	$13.00	00-05
Bomber Bait Co.	Bomber	415, #5 box	NIB	$13.99	99-02
Bomber Bait Co.	Bomber	415, white/green back and ribs w/glitter, OPE, new in orig 2PCCB w/catalog	NIB	$18.00	05-05
Bomber Bait Co.	Bomber	416, #5 box	NIB	$12.49	99-02
Bomber Bait Co.	Bomber	416, no eyes	EX-	$26.00	00-04
Bomber Bait Co.	Bomber	417, no eyes	VG+	$30.00	01-08
Bomber Bait Co.	Bomber	418, #3 box crisp	NIB	$41.00	00-05
Bomber Bait Co.	Bomber	418, 49er in 616 #2 box (nice)	EX-IB	$46.00	99-12
Bomber Bait Co.	Bomber	418, wide gap, chip	VG	$31.00	00-02
Bomber Bait Co.	Bomber	419, #5	NIB	$13.25	00-05
Bomber Bait Co.	Bomber	419, wood	NIB	$15.00	05-01
Bomber Bait Co.	Bomber	419HD	EX	$39.00	00-06
Bomber Bait Co.	Bomber	420, #3	NIB	$12.50	99-06
Bomber Bait Co.	Bomber	420, #5 box	NIB	$15.00	99-02
Bomber Bait Co.	Bomber	443, #5 box	NIB	$19.51	99-03
Bomber Bait Co.	Bomber	444, wood	NIB	$17.00	05-01
Bomber Bait Co.	Bomber	457, #5	NIB	$12.25	00-05
Bomber Bait Co.	Bomber	458, #5	NIB	$21.00	00-07
Bomber Bait Co.	Bomber	459, #5	NIB	$13.01	00-05
Bomber Bait Co.	Bomber	470, wood	NIB	$18.00	05-01
Bomber Bait Co.	Bomber	471, #5 box	NIB	$15.49	99-02
Bomber Bait Co.	Bomber	472, #5 box	NIB	$14.25	99-02
Bomber Bait Co.	Bomber	472, wood	NIB	$18.00	05-01
Bomber Bait Co.	Bomber	480, wood	NIB	$18.00	05-01
Bomber Bait Co.	Bomber	481, wood	NIB	$19.00	05-01
Bomber Bait Co.	Bomber	482, wood	NIB	$11.00	05-01

BRAND	MODEL	SERIES / MFG. CODE / DESCRIPTION	GRADE	PRICE	DATE yy/mm
Bomber Bait Co.	Bomber	483, wood	NIB	$20.00	05-01
Bomber Bait Co.	Bomber	484, huge age lines	VG	$39.00	00-02
Bomber Bait Co.	Bomber	485, wood	NIB	$34.00	05-01
Bomber Bait Co.	Bomber	488, wood	NIB	$27.00	05-01
Bomber Bait Co.	Bomber	489, #5 box	NIB	$15.50	99-02
Bomber Bait Co.	Bomber	489, #5 box	NIB	$31.00	99-03
Bomber Bait Co.	Bomber	489, PTCB, wood lure	NIB	$16.00	04-11
Bomber Bait Co.	Bomber	489, #5 box	NIB	$21.00	99-04
Bomber Bait Co.	Bomber	620, 49er, Layne buy	EX	$431.75	99-05
Bomber Bait Co.	Bomber	605, 49er, scrapes	VG-	$20.50	99-06
Bomber Bait Co.	Bomber	49ers, 2 diff	EX	$60.99	99-04
Bomber Bait Co.	Bomber	4MK, metachrome wood	EX-IB	$53.00	03-06
Bomber Bait Co.	Bomber	4MO, wood	NIB	$31.00	01-05
Bomber Bait Co.	Bomber	5 common colors	EX	$45.50	99-02
Bomber Bait Co.	Bomber	500, "ROK," fl yellow/black ribs	NIB	$160.00	00-06
Bomber Bait Co.	Bomber	500SB, clear plastic with colored beads	NIB	$8.00	00-07
Bomber Bait Co.	Bomber	501, #3	NIB	$19.49	00-01
Bomber Bait Co.	Bomber	502, no eyes, crisp box & paper	NIB	$61.00	02-01
Bomber Bait Co.	Bomber	502, no eyes, NOT MET	NIB	$75.00	00-09
Bomber Bait Co.	Bomber	502, 2PCCB #4	NIB	$14.25	99-02
Bomber Bait Co.	Bomber	503, 49er, NOT MET	VG-	$9.50	99-12
Bomber Bait Co.	Bomber	504, #4 box	NIB	$23.50	99-03
Bomber Bait Co.	Bomber	504, mint picture box	NIB	$22.50	99-01
Bomber Bait Co.	Bomber	504, PTCB, NO BIDS	NIB	$15.00	00-11
Bomber Bait Co.	Bomber	504, wide gap, #2C, NO BIDS	VGIB	$20.00	00-05
Bomber Bait Co.	Bomber	504, yellow eye, HMLT	avg	$53.00	00-01
Bomber Bait Co.	Bomber	505, 1949 plastic, wrong 2PCCB	EX	$24.07	99-01
Bomber Bait Co.	Bomber	505, box #5	NIB	$10.00	99-03
Bomber Bait Co.	Bomber	505, 2PCCB #3	NIB	$18.00	99-02
Bomber Bait Co.	Bomber	506, 49er	EX-	$36.99	00-01
Bomber Bait Co.	Bomber	506, wide gap, #3 box	NIB	$26.75	00-04
Bomber Bait Co.	Bomber	506, #3	NIB	$15.50	99-10
Bomber Bait Co.	Bomber	506, #4 box	NIB	$19.50	99-11
Bomber Bait Co.	Bomber	506, 2PCCB #3	NIB	$33.05	99-02
Bomber Bait Co.	Bomber	507, #5 box	NIB	$16.00	99-03
Bomber Bait Co.	Bomber	508, PTCB	NIB	$18.50	02-03
Bomber Bait Co.	Bomber	508, #5 box	NIB	$15.50	99-04
Bomber Bait Co.	Bomber	509, box #4	NIB	$18.01	99-03
Bomber Bait Co.	Bomber	509, #3	NIB	$27.00	00-02
Bomber Bait Co.	Bomber	510 in 507 #3 box	NIB	$11.50	99-01
Bomber Bait Co.	Bomber	511, #3, 1781 #5 box	NIB	$27.10	00-02
Bomber Bait Co.	Bomber	511, #3 box	NIB	$31.51	99-04
Bomber Bait Co.	Bomber	511, #3	NIB	$25.00	00-01
Bomber Bait Co.	Bomber	511, 408, 2 diff #5 boxes	NIB	$27.00	99-04
Bomber Bait Co.	Bomber	511, no eyes, yellow box	VGIB	$32.99	99-10
Bomber Bait Co.	Bomber	512, 49er	EX	$27.00	00-06
Bomber Bait Co.	Bomber	512, box #5	NIB	$23.57	99-03
Bomber Bait Co.	Bomber	515 & 511, no eyes	VG	$20.00	00-07

BRAND	MODEL	SERIES / MFG. CODE / DESCRIPTION	GRADE	PRICE	DATE yy/mm
Bomber Bait Co.	Bomber	515, white green back and ribs w/glitter, OPE, new in orig 2PCBB w/catalog	NIB	$20.00	05-05
Bomber Bait Co.	Bomber	515, NE	VG-	$20.01	00-01
Bomber Bait Co.	Bomber	516, #5 box	NIB	$14.01	99-02
Bomber Bait Co.	Bomber	516, wood, 03 80 G	NIB	$7.95	05-07
Bomber Bait Co.	Bomber	516, #5 box	NIB	$29.50	99-04
Bomber Bait Co.	Bomber	516NE	EX	$56.00	99-11
Bomber Bait Co.	Bomber	516NE	EX+	$79.00	99-11
Bomber Bait Co.	Bomber	517, #3 box, lip wear	EXIB	$34.57	99-11
Bomber Bait Co.	Bomber	517NE, #2 box	EXIB	$58.77	99-11
Bomber Bait Co.	Bomber	518, #5	NIB	$15.49	00-05
Bomber Bait Co.	Bomber	519, #5 box	NIB	$30.00	99-04
Bomber Bait Co.	Bomber	520, #5	NIB	$12.25	00-05
Bomber Bait Co.	Bomber	520, #5 box	NIB	$12.55	99-03
Bomber Bait Co.	Bomber	536, #3 box	NIB	$29.50	99-07
Bomber Bait Co.	Bomber	538, #5	NIB	$38.00	00-06
Bomber Bait Co.	Bomber	543, #5 box	NIB	$15.50	99-02
Bomber Bait Co.	Bomber	553HD, 606HD	VG	$41.00	00-04
Bomber Bait Co.	Bomber	555, #4 box	NIB	$31.57	99-04
Bomber Bait Co.	Bomber	581, metascale wood	NIB	$24.00	03-06
Bomber Bait Co.	Bomber	582, metascale wood	NIB	$22.00	04-02
Bomber Bait Co.	Bomber	585, #5	NIB	$36.00	00-06
Bomber Bait Co.	Bomber	5MC, metachrome wood	NIB	$37.00	03-06
Bomber Bait Co.	Bomber	5ME, metachrome wood	NIB	$54.00	03-06
Bomber Bait Co.	Bomber	6 diff (1 Spinstick), PTCB	NIB	$96.05	99-01
Bomber Bait Co.	Bomber	600HD, flo.red/black spots	VG	$36.88	99-10
Bomber Bait Co.	Bomber	600HD, FOBD	NIB	$77.00	04-01
Bomber Bait Co.	Bomber	600HD, FYRB	NIB	$52.00	00-06
Bomber Bait Co.	Bomber	600HD x 12, flourescent, wood, early ending	NIB	$219.00	00-07
Bomber Bait Co.	Bomber	601, #3 box	NIB	$31.99	99-04
Bomber Bait Co.	Bomber	601NE	EX	$173.76	99-11
Bomber Bait Co.	Bomber	602, wood, brown/orange pic box crisp	NIB	$12.00	05-07
Bomber Bait Co.	Bomber	603, 2PCCB	NIB	$17.00	99-01
Bomber Bait Co.	Bomber	603WG, wolf gray scale	EX	$11.02	99-11
Bomber Bait Co.	Bomber	603WG, wolf gray scale	EX	$11.95	99-11
Bomber Bait Co.	Bomber	604HD, RH, smaller line tie	NIB	$23.00	01-11
Bomber Bait Co.	Bomber	605, #4	NIB	$23.00	00-03
Bomber Bait Co.	Bomber	605, #5	NIB	$17.00	99-02
Bomber Bait Co.	Bomber	605 in #2B box	EXIB	$38.00	99-04
Bomber Bait Co.	Bomber	605, wide gap	NIB	$65.00	00-05
Bomber Bait Co.	Bomber	605, 1949 plastic	EX	$18.00	99-11
Bomber Bait Co.	Bomber	605HD, green perch, smaller line tie	NIB	$35.00	01-11
Bomber Bait Co.	Bomber	606, #5 box	NIB	$17.79	99-04
Bomber Bait Co.	Bomber	607, 49er, in 518 #2 box	EXIB	$56.00	99-12
Bomber Bait Co.	Bomber	608, no eyes	VG	$10.50	99-04
Bomber Bait Co.	Bomber	608, #3 box	NIB	$18.06	99-04
Bomber Bait Co.	Bomber	608HD plus 1720	NIB	$18.00	00-09
Bomber Bait Co.	Bomber	608NE, #2 box	NIB	$72.79	99-11

BRAND	MODEL	SERIES / MFG. CODE / DESCRIPTION	GRADE	PRICE	DATE yy/mm
Bomber Bait Co.	Bomber	608NE, #2 box	EXIB	$93.00	99-11
Bomber Bait Co.	Bomber	609NE	EX	$100.10	99-11
Bomber Bait Co.	Bomber	611, #3 box	NIB	$26.56	99-12
Bomber Bait Co.	Bomber	611, 2PCCB	NIB	$31.05	99-01
Bomber Bait Co.	Bomber	611, no eyes	NIB	$141.00	00-07
Bomber Bait Co.	Bomber	611, no eyes, box #2A	NIB	$118.50	99-04
Bomber Bait Co.	Bomber	611, #5 box	NIB	$15.00	99-06
Bomber Bait Co.	Bomber	611HD, decent	VG+	$34.01	99-05
Bomber Bait Co.	Bomber	611NE	EX	$150.00	99-11
Bomber Bait Co.	Bomber	612, 49er	EX	$28.00	99-10
Bomber Bait Co.	Bomber	612, 49er	EX	$29.00	99-12
Bomber Bait Co.	Bomber	612 in 607 #3 box	EXIB	$20.50	99-01
Bomber Bait Co.	Bomber	613 x 12, #5 box, cellophane top	NIB	$305.00	00-06
Bomber Bait Co.	Bomber	613HD	EXIB	$86.00	99-08
Bomber Bait Co.	Bomber	613HD	NIB	$86.00	99-08
Bomber Bait Co.	Bomber	613HD, green shade, smaller line tie	NIB	$42.00	01-11
Bomber Bait Co.	Bomber	615, 49er	NIB	$81.00	00-06
Bomber Bait Co.	Bomber	616, wood	EXIB	$15.00	05-01
Bomber Bait Co.	Bomber	617, 49er	EX-	$46.00	02-01
Bomber Bait Co.	Bomber	617HD, lip rough, NOT MET	VG	$5.00	00-03
Bomber Bait Co.	Bomber	617HD	EX-IB	$26.00	00-04
Bomber Bait Co.	Bomber	617NE	VG+	$61.00	99-11
Bomber Bait Co.	Bomber	618, 49er in 606 #2 box	VG+IB	$41.00	99-12
Bomber Bait Co.	Bomber	618, #5 box	NIB	$39.00	99-04
Bomber Bait Co.	Bomber	618HD, red side scale, smaller line tie	NIB	$26.00	01-11
Bomber Bait Co.	Bomber	618WG	EX-	$10.50	99-11
Bomber Bait Co.	Bomber	618WG	EX+	$26.00	99-11
Bomber Bait Co.	Bomber	619, #4 box, NOT MET	NIB	$18.51	99-02
Bomber Bait Co.	Bomber	619, #4 box, NOT MET	NIB	$25.49	00-03
Bomber Bait Co.	Bomber	619, no eyes	EX-	$30.00	00-02
Bomber Bait Co.	Bomber	619, orange box crisp	NIB	$20.00	04-01
Bomber Bait Co.	Bomber	619HD	EX	$39.00	00-06
Bomber Bait Co.	Bomber	619NE	mint	$77.00	99-11
Bomber Bait Co.	Bomber	619NE, flakes on lip, otherwise nice	EX-	$10.50	99-11
Bomber Bait Co.	Bomber	638 PTCB	NIB	$51.00	04-01
Bomber Bait Co.	Bomber	639HD	G	$20.50	99-04
Bomber Bait Co.	Bomber	639HD, yellow/black dots, smaller line tie	NIB	$23.00	01-11
Bomber Bait Co.	Bomber	640, #5 box	NIB	$12.50	99-03
Bomber Bait Co.	Bomber	643, #5 box	NIB	$38.07	99-04
Bomber Bait Co.	Bomber	655, #5 box	NIB	$20.57	99-03
Bomber Bait Co.	Bomber	659HD	NIB	$70.75	99-02
Bomber Bait Co.	Bomber	671, #5	NIB	$14.50	99-06
Bomber Bait Co.	Bomber	671, wood	NIB	$26.00	05-01
Bomber Bait Co.	Bomber	671, #5 box	NIB	$19.00	99-03
Bomber Bait Co.	Bomber	671HD, purple back/flitter, smaller line tie	NIB	$26.00	01-11
Bomber Bait Co.	Bomber	682, #5 box	NIB	$35.87	99-04
Bomber Bait Co.	Bomber	688, #5	NIB	$32.88	99-10
Bomber Bait Co.	Bomber	689, box #5	NIB	$31.00	99-03

BRAND	MODEL	SERIES / MFG. CODE / DESCRIPTION	GRADE	PRICE	DATE yy/mm
Bomber Bait Co.	Bomber	6FY, wood	NIB	$57.00	02-01
Bomber Bait Co.	Bomber	6FYRB, HD	NIB	$91.00	00-05
Bomber Bait Co.	Bomber	6ME	NIB	$47.00	00-09
Bomber Bait Co.	Bomber	6ML, awful age lines	EX+??	$37.00	00-04
Bomber Bait Co.	Bomber	6SC, HD	VGIB	$67.00	99-09
Bomber Bait Co.	Bomber	6YSC, HD	VG	$26.00	99-04
Bomber Bait Co.	Bomber	7 diff, wood, used, but some decent	avg	$17.00	01-11
Bomber Bait Co.	Bomber	7 used, Bombers, 1 49er?	VG	$11.50	99-02
Bomber Bait Co.	Bomber	7 used, Bombers	VG	$52.00	99-02
Bomber Bait Co.	Bomber	7 diff, wood, 1 flourescent y	EX	$57.00	99-04
Bomber Bait Co.	Bomber	8 diff, #5 boxes, M284 plus commons	NIB	$171.50	00-02
Bomber Bait Co.	Bomber	8 diff, 2 sticks, 5 rip shad, 1 popper	NIB	$66.00	99-08
Bomber Bait Co.	Bomber	8 diff, wood, PTCB	NIB	$89.00	01-04
Bomber Bait Co.	Bomber	blue mullet, "Special" 300 box	VGIB	$29.00	99-12
Bomber Bait Co.	Bomber	clear/red bead, plastic	NIB	$17.50	99-02
Bomber Bait Co.	Bomber	no eyes, wooden in white/w black shadow, stripes, 4¾" long	VG	$10.20	05-07
Bomber Bait Co.	Bomber	plastic, 40 assorted	NIB	$187.50	99-01
Bomber Bait Co.	Bomber	r/w, 49er, NOT MET	EX	$25.01	99-04
Bomber Bait Co.	Bomber	218	NIB	$20.00	00-06
Bomber Bait Co.	Bomber	237	VG+	$38.99	00-02
Bomber Bait Co.	Bomber	256	NIB	$17.50	99-01
Bomber Bait Co.	Bomber	259	NIB	$20.22	99-02
Bomber Bait Co.	Bomber	283	NIB	$18.50	99-01
Bomber Bait Co.	Bomber	283	NIB	$23.50	00-08
Bomber Bait Co.	Bomber	389	NIB	$19.00	00-03
Bomber Bait Co.	Bomber	407	NIB	$13.00	00-06
Bomber Bait Co.	Bomber	417	NIB	$37.00	00-06
Bomber Bait Co.	Bomber	418	NIB	$21.00	01-04
Bomber Bait Co.	Bomber	421	NIB	$10.51	99-01
Bomber Bait Co.	Bomber	455	NIB	$10.51	99-01
Bomber Bait Co.	Bomber	458	NIB	$32.05	99-01
Bomber Bait Co.	Bomber	484	mint	$20.06	99-10
Bomber Bait Co.	Bomber	486	NIB	$45.00	03-06
Bomber Bait Co.	Bomber	489	EX	$9.99	99-07
Bomber Bait Co.	Bomber	506	NIB	$10.00	99-01
Bomber Bait Co.	Bomber	511	NIB	$6.00	99-01
Bomber Bait Co.	Bomber	515	NIB	$10.50	99-01
Bomber Bait Co.	Bomber	519	NIB	$11.00	99-01
Bomber Bait Co.	Bomber	543	NIB	$9.99	99-01
Bomber Bait Co.	Bomber	555	NIB	$11.00	99-01
Bomber Bait Co.	Bomber	573	NIB	$51.00	03-06
Bomber Bait Co.	Bomber	583	NIB	$26.00	00-05
Bomber Bait Co.	Bomber	585	EX	$19.00	99-05
Bomber Bait Co.	Bomber	585	NIB	$32.26	99-03
Bomber Bait Co.	Bomber	587	NIB	$26.00	00-05
Bomber Bait Co.	Bomber	587	NIB	$31.00	00-05
Bomber Bait Co.	Bomber	587	NIB	$52.00	04-01

BRAND	MODEL	SERIES / MFG. CODE / DESCRIPTION	GRADE	PRICE	DATE yy/mm
Bomber Bait Co.	Bomber	588	NIB	$20.00	00-05
Bomber Bait Co.	Bomber	603	NIB	$27.59	00-03
Bomber Bait Co.	Bomber	606	NIB	$9.99	99-01
Bomber Bait Co.	Bomber	638	NIB	$42.50	99-08
Bomber Bait Co.	Bomber	687	mint	$20.00	99-06
Bomber Bait Co.	Bomber	512, 49 plastic	VG-	$19.99	99-04
Bomber Bait Co.	Bomber	617HD, chips	VG-	$20.50	99-06
Bomber Bait Co.	Bomber 1949 plastic	4 diff, common colors, NOT MET	NIB	$22.98	99-06
Bomber Bait Co.	Bomber 1949 plastic	504, 49er	NIB	$43.00	03-06
Bomber Bait Co.	Bomber 1949 plastic	517, papers	NIB	$164.00	99-08
Bomber Bait Co.	Bomber 1949 plastic	514	EX	$39.00	99-09
Bomber Bait Co.	Bomber 1949 plastic	613	NIB	$40.00	02-01
Bomber Bait Co.	Bomber x 10	10 diff plastics	NIB	$66.00	99-12
Bomber Bait Co.	Bomber x 12	659, 12-pack, #5 boxes	NIB	$122.55	00-02
Bomber Bait Co.	Bomber x 2	no eyes, #2A boxes	VGIB	$111.50	00-03
Bomber Bait Co.	Bomber x 4	4 diff, common colors, PTCB	NIB	$47.00	00-05
Bomber Bait Co.	Bomber x 4	4 diff wood, PTCB	NIB	$56.00	01-10
Bomber Bait Co.	Bomber x 4	modern plastic, 4 diff	NIB	$18.55	99-06
Bomber Bait Co.	Bomber x 5	5 different wood, VG+ – EX	mix	$55.55	00-02
Bomber Bait Co.	Bomberette	2739, some paint off lip	EX?	$49.00	99-08
Bomber Bait Co.	Bomberette	714	NIB	$44.00	01-10
Bomber Bait Co.	Bomberette	720	EX-	$42.50	00-01
Bomber Bait Co.	Bomberette	814	EX+	$39.00	04-02
Bomber Bait Co.	Bomberette x 2	2745 box, 2 lures	NIB	$65.00	00-03
Bomber Bait Co.	Bomberettes x 2	2737 and 2747	NIB	$168.00	00-09
Bomber Bait Co.	Coca-Cola	boat scene, probably fake? NOT MET	NOC	$41.00	99-06
Bomber Bait Co.	Darter	candy, small size	EX	$350.00	01-06
Bomber Bait Co.	Earliest x 2	handmade line ties, shoe cups, 2 different, nice	EX-	$291.00	04-12
Bomber Bait Co.	Gumpy Jig	display card x 12	EX-	$10.00	99-07
Bomber Bait Co.	Jerk	4 different, VG+ – EX	EX	$72.27	99-03
Bomber Bait Co.	Jerk	4300, black/white bee, special order color	EX	$26.00	05-01
Bomber Bait Co.	Jerk	4300, Houston	VG+	$45.00	99-02
Bomber Bait Co.	Jerk	4300, Houston Special	EX	$57.00	00-05
Bomber Bait Co.	Jerk	4340, no screw variety	EX	$22.00	05-01
Bomber Bait Co.	Jerk	4351, NOT MET	NIB	$71.00	00-07
Bomber Bait Co.	Jerk	4352, y/red stripe/glitter, #3	NIB	$27.26	99-07
Bomber Bait Co.	Jerk	4400, silver scale	EX	$9.99	99-08
Bomber Bait Co.	Jerk	4400BJ, Layne buy	NIB	$120.25	99-04
Bomber Bait Co.	Jerk	4400PS	NIB	$59.00	99-04
Bomber Bait Co.	Jerk	4400SS	NIB	$33.09	99-04
Bomber Bait Co.	Jerk	4401, pearl	NIB	$62.00	99-07
Bomber Bait Co.	Jerk	4404, #3, RH/white/silver scales	NIB	$153.00	00-06
Bomber Bait Co.	Jerk	4430, NOT MET	NIB	$31.00	00-08
Bomber Bait Co.	Jerk	4515, NOT MET	EX	$20.51	99-06
Bomber Bait Co.	Jerk	4553, yellow dog	EX-	$41.00	99-02
Bomber Bait Co.	Jerk	4553, NOT MET	EX	$21.00	99-06
Bomber Bait Co.	Jerk	45MO	mint	$22.00	05-01
Bomber Bait Co.	Jerk	7239, NOT MET	EX-	$15.51	98-12

LURES

BRAND	MODEL	SERIES / MFG. CODE / DESCRIPTION	GRADE	PRICE	DATE yy/mm
Bomber Bait Co.	Jerk	black bee	EX	$51.75	99-07
Bomber Bait Co.	Jerk	4500, green/white flitter, NOT MET	EX	$37.00	99-12
Bomber Bait Co.	Jerk	4300, Houston, rare color	EX	$24.00	05-01
Bomber Bait Co.	Jerk	rainbow	VG	$21.76	99-01
Bomber Bait Co.	Jerk	yellow dog	EX	$52.00	00-05
Bomber Bait Co.	Jerk	4304	EX	$21.51	99-06
Bomber Bait Co.	Jerk	4304	EX	$37.00	00-05
Bomber Bait Co.	Jerk	4311	mint	$22.00	05-01
Bomber Bait Co.	Jerk	4322	EX	$27.50	99-02
Bomber Bait Co.	Jerk	4404	NIB	$31.23	99-04
Bomber Bait Co.	Jerk	4422	NIB	$71.00	99-07
Bomber Bait Co.	Jerk	4453	EX	$24.99	99-04
Bomber Bait Co.	Jerk	4472	NIB	$42.00	01-10
Bomber Bait Co.	Jerk	4504	EXIB	$21.00	00-07
Bomber Bait Co.	Jerk	4511	NIB	$54.00	01-10
Bomber Bait Co.	Jerk	4519	EX	$20.00	99-01
Bomber Bait Co.	Jerk	4523	NIB	$27.00	05-01
Bomber Bait Co.	Jerk	4553	EX-	$21.76	99-05
Bomber Bait Co.	Jerk	4584	VG+	$97.00	01-03
Bomber Bait Co.	Jerk, S.Stick	2 different	VG	$20.50	99-01
Bomber Bait Co.	Jerks	2 different	mint	$62.00	99-03
Bomber Bait Co.	Knothead	1204, wrong box, NOT MET	EX	$230.00	99-08
Bomber Bait Co.	Knothead	1205, crisp box & papers	NIB	$106.00	05-07
Bomber Bait Co.	Knothead	1205, green perch, small	VG+	$140.00	01-11
Bomber Bait Co.	Knothead	1214, Knothead, marked box EX, black/white ribs	NIB	$406.00	05-07
Bomber Bait Co.	Knothead	1216, NOT MET	NIB	$154.00	00-06
Bomber Bait Co.	Knothead	1218, ugly age lines, POBW	G	$83.00	99-08
Bomber Bait Co.	Knothead	1307, NOT MET	NIB	$242.50	99-12
Bomber Bait Co.	Knothead	1311, frog	avg.	$37.80	99-08
Bomber Bait Co.	Knothead	1311, lg frog	VG-	$26.00	01-11
Bomber Bait Co.	Knothead	1316, NOT MET	NIB	$134.00	00-06
Bomber Bait Co.	Knothead	1311, lg frog	VG+	$38.00	02-11
Bomber Bait Co.	Knothead	1205	EX-	$143.50	00-01
Bomber Bait Co.	Knothead	1307	EX	$178.00	00-05
Bomber Bait Co.	Knothead	1314	pig	$21.00	00-05
Bomber Bait Co.	Knothead	1315	mint	$250.00	00-09
Bomber Bait Co.	Looboyle Special	perch, NOT MET	G	$71.00	99-06
Bomber Bait Co.	Looboyle Special	white (pearl)	VG+	$515.00	01-04
Bomber Bait Co.	Midget Bomberette	2708, 2PCCB, gold scale	NIB	$38.00	05-01
Bomber Bait Co.	Mixed Plastic	100 assorted, 30 colors	NIB	$310.00	98-12
Bomber Bait Co.	No Eyes	8 diff, all nice, $88 – 122 each	NIB	$122.00	99-11
Bomber Bait Co.	Nude lure	beach scene card, NOT MET	NOC	$26.55	99-06
Bomber Bait Co.	Pinfish	2PSC	NIB	$12.00	02-08
Bomber Bait Co.	Pinfish	P00-FT, Firetiger	NIB	$12.00	00-07
Bomber Bait Co.	Popper	3X01, pearl	NIB	$7.00	99-07
Bomber Bait Co.	Popper	coach dog, PTCB	NIB	$15.00	03-04
Bomber Bait Co.	Popper	FT2T	NIB	$7.55	00-06
Bomber Bait Co.	Poppers x 2	lg & sm	NIB	$23.00	99-07

BRAND	MODEL	SERIES / MFG. CODE / DESCRIPTION	GRADE	PRICE	DATE yy/mm
Bomber Bait Co.	Poppers x 4	diff colors, $15 – 16 each	NIB	$62.00	00-05
Bomber Bait Co.	Slab Spoon	r/w, papers, PTCB	NIB	$26.00	99-03
Bomber Bait Co.	Speed Shad	frog	NIB	$15.00	01-02
Bomber Bait Co.	Speed Shad	perch?	NIB	$7.80	99-04
Bomber Bait Co.	Speed Shad x 3	all metascales, diff colors	NIB	$9.00	01-11
Bomber Bait Co.	Spin Stick	7356, black mullet, PTCB	NIB	$37.00	00-10
Bomber Bait Co.	Spin Stick	73BSBO	NIB	$10.00	05-01
Bomber Bait Co.	Spin Stick	73MO, heavy age lines	EXIB	$7.00	05-01
Bomber Bait Co.	Spin Stick	73RS	NIB	$12.30	99-01
Bomber Bait Co.	Spin Stick	73RS	NIB	$16.50	99-03
Bomber Bait Co.	Spin Stick	73RT	NIB	$67.00	99-08
Bomber Bait Co.	Spin Stick	BASS, 30 years commemorative	NIB	$10.51	99-03
Bomber Bait Co.	Spin Stick	blue scale	mint	$28.00	05-02
Bomber Bait Co.	Spin Stick	M7380	NIB	$43.00	00-08
Bomber Bait Co.	Spin Stick	7320	NIB	$6.00	99-09
Bomber Bait Co.	Spin Stick	7356	NIB	$15.50	99-04
Bomber Bait Co.	Spin Stick	7371	NIB	$26.00	99-04
Bomber Bait Co.	Spin Stick	7386	EXIB	$16.00	99-07
Bomber Bait Co.	Stick	7381, 7382	NIB	$31.00	00-08
Bomber Bait Co.	Stick	7400, chrome coach dog, hvy age lines	EX-	$50.00	00-06
Bomber Bait Co.	Stick	7406	NIB	$32.00	00-06
Bomber Bait Co.	Stick	7414	NIB	$9.75	99-01
Bomber Bait Co.	Top Bomber	4018, ugly	avg	$35.00	99-12
Bomber Bait Co.	Top Bomber	3 diff, little rough	avg	$35.00	99-03
Bomber Bait Co.	Top Bomber	4004? big black eye shadow, odd color	EX	$70.00	02-01
Bomber Bait Co.	Top Bomber	4012, 2PCCB	NIB	$41.00	05-01
Bomber Bait Co.	Top Bomber	6000, silver shad	mint	$93.00	03-04
Bomber Bait Co.	Top Bomber	6003	VG	$51.00	99-08
Bomber Bait Co.	Top Bomber	6015, in torn box	NIB	$100.00	99-01
Bomber Bait Co.	Top Bomber	4020	VG-	$26.00	00-07
Bomber Bait Co.	Top Bomber	4020	EX-	$63.00	02-06
Bomber Bait Co.	Top Bomber	4040	NIB	$77.00	00-06
Bomber Bait Co.	Top Bomber	6005	EX	$139.00	00-10
Bomber Bait Co.	Top Bomber	6014	VG	$19.99	99-06
Bomber Bait Co.	Waterdog	1501, #5	NIB	$16.00	99-02
Bomber Bait Co.	Waterdog	1504, wood	NIB	$12.00	05-01
Bomber Bait Co.	Waterdog	1506, wood	NIB	$12.00	05-01
Bomber Bait Co.	Waterdog	1508, 1511, 1615	mint	$25.00	99-01
Bomber Bait Co.	Waterdog	1508, in nice 2PCCB	NIB	$30.00	04-12
Bomber Bait Co.	Waterdog	1511, 2PCCB nice	NIB	$26.00	99-01
Bomber Bait Co.	Waterdog	1511, wood	NIB	$11.00	05-01
Bomber Bait Co.	Waterdog	1514, wood	NIB	$10.00	05-01
Bomber Bait Co.	Waterdog	1543, wood	NIB	$12.00	05-01
Bomber Bait Co.	Waterdog	1555, wood	NIB	$7.00	05-01
Bomber Bait Co.	Waterdog	1556, wood	NIB	$5.00	05-01
Bomber Bait Co.	Waterdog	1557, box #5	NIB	$15.50	99-03
Bomber Bait Co.	Waterdog	1558, wood	NIB	$7.00	05-01
Bomber Bait Co.	Waterdog	1571, wood	NIB	$6.00	05-01

BRAND	MODEL	SERIES / MFG. CODE / DESCRIPTION	GRADE	PRICE	DATE yy/mm
Bomber Bait Co.	Waterdog	1573, blue mullet, 1500SB box	EX-IB	$63.33	99-03
Bomber Bait Co.	Waterdog	15FY, plastic 12-pack	NIB	$25.00	99-03
Bomber Bait Co.	Waterdog	15MO, wood	NIB	$13.00	05-01
Bomber Bait Co.	Waterdog	1601, wood	NIB	$2.00	05-01
Bomber Bait Co.	Waterdog	1602, 1508	NIB	$20.50	99-01
Bomber Bait Co.	Waterdog	1602, in nice 2PCCB	NIB	$25.00	04-12
Bomber Bait Co.	Waterdog	1606, 2PCCB	NIB	$33.00	00-11
Bomber Bait Co.	Waterdog	1611, NO BIDS	NIB	$15.00	00-05
Bomber Bait Co.	Waterdog	1611, wood lure, PTCB	NIB	$12.00	04-12
Bomber Bait Co.	Waterdog	1620, 12-pack, #5 boxes	NIB	$180.00	00-06
Bomber Bait Co.	Waterdog	1640, wood	NIB	$7.00	05-01
Bomber Bait Co.	Waterdog	1659, #5	NIB	$9.00	99-02
Bomber Bait Co.	Waterdog	1671, 1 bid	NIB	$15.00	00-05
Bomber Bait Co.	Waterdog	16SC, wood!	NIB	$98.99	99-08
Bomber Bait Co.	Waterdog	1701, wood	NIB	$6.00	05-01
Bomber Bait Co.	Waterdog	1711, #4 box	NIB	$15.00	00-01
Bomber Bait Co.	Waterdog	1711, 2PCCB	EXIB	$12.00	05-01
Bomber Bait Co.	Waterdog	1711, wood	EXIB	$11.00	05-01
Bomber Bait Co.	Waterdog	1719, plus one common	NIB	$83.00	00-08
Bomber Bait Co.	Waterdog	1743, #5	NIB	$12.50	99-02
Bomber Bait Co.	Waterdog	1755, #4 box	NIB	$15.53	99-12
Bomber Bait Co.	Waterdog	1771, #5	NIB	$10.50	99-02
Bomber Bait Co.	Waterdog	1780, worm burn		$2.00	99-02
Bomber Bait Co.	Waterdog	17MB, age lines	NIB	$27.00	00-06
Bomber Bait Co.	Waterdog	17MC, hvy age lines	EX	$59.00	00-04
Bomber Bait Co.	Waterdog	17MO, wood	NIB	$13.00	01-05
Bomber Bait Co.	Waterdog	17YSC	NIB	$103.76	99-08
Bomber Bait Co.	Waterdog	2 plastic	NIB	$13.00	99-02
Bomber Bait Co.	Waterdog	3 in 2PCCB, 5 mixed	EXIB	$81.00	99-03
Bomber Bait Co.	Waterdog	1655	NIB	$16.50	99-01
Bomber Bait Co.	Waterdog	1720	NIB	$10.50	99-01
Bomber Bait Co.	Waterdog	1740	NIB	$16.23	99-01
Bomber Bait Co.	Waterdog	1743	NIB	$11.19	99-01
Bomber Bait Co.	Waterdog	1772	mint	$7.50	02-03
Bomber Bait Co.	Waterdog	1778	EX	$29.07	99-03
Bomber Bait Co.	Waterdog	1783	NIB	$32.99	99-01
Bomber Bait Co.	Waterdog	1784	VG	$20.00	00-06
Bomber Bait Co.	Waterdog x 10	dealer carton of 10 1711 wood lures, PTCB, all mint	NIB	$62.00	05-07
Bomber Bait Co.	Waterdog x 12	15FY, plastic, 12 pack	NIB	$82.55	00-02
Bomber Bait Co.	Waterdog x 2	two lipless, green scale, wood	NIB	$837.00	03-05
Bon Net	6-hooker	frog	VG+IB	$118.00	00-08
Bon Net	6-hooker	frog, decent box, GE, NOT MET	EX-IB	$177.00	04-11
Bon Net	6-hooker	frog, GE, NOT MET!	NIB	$164.50	99-01
Bon Net	6-hooker	glass eyes	VG+	$108.00	01-11
Bon Net	6-hooker	r/w, hardware store box	NIB	$202.50	99-08
Bon Net	6-hooker	rainbow, 6-hooker	poor	$74.00	04-12
Bon Net	6-hooker	RB, many sm pointers	GIB	$242.50	00-02

BRAND	MODEL	SERIES / MFG. CODE / DESCRIPTION	GRADE	PRICE	DATE yy/mm
Boshears Tackle Co.	Razzle Dazzle	506 black/silver scales, 2PCCB + paper EX	NIB	$62.00	05-07
Bossards	Bass Bug	large size black/yellow/red bug, near-mint box, general wear, VG with insert	EXIB	$880.00	05-04
Brady	Fish Dinner	fly rod frog, Eau Clair, WI	NIB	$510.00	99-11
Breveté	Passe Partout	France c. 1932, spring loaded, NOT MET	NIB	$405.00	00-12
British Phantom	Phantom Minnow	on card	EX	$75.00	01-04
Broen	Fisheretto	frog, PE	mint	$50.50	99-05
Brooks	#5	yellow/silver spot/red mouth, Plunker type	NIB	$36.00	02-03
Brooks	Plunker, jntd	JSP 57	NIB	$18.00	01-08
Brown	Select-A-Bait Fly Rod	neat kit with 6 interchangeable plastic bodies	NIB	$103.00	04-07
Brown Bros.	Fisheretto	frog, PE	mint	$50.50	99-04
Brown Bros.	Fisheretto	r/w, washer eyes	G	$47.87	99-01
Brunswick	Doll Top Secret		NIB	$22.00	99-10
Buckeye Bait Co.	Bug-N-Bass	brown trout, small size	EX-	$70.00	05-07
Buckeye Bait Co.	Bug-N-Bass	mullet, lg & sm sizes	EX	$295.00	04-02
Buckeye Bait Co.	Bug-N-Bass	red head & back, gold flitter, lg size	EX	$661.00	04-02
Buckeye Bait Co.	Bug-N-Bass	#10	NIB	$47.00	04-07
Buckeye Bait Co.	Bug-N-Bass	baby bass color, no code on box, color chart	NIB	$36.00	04-07
Buckeye Bait Co.	Bug-N-Bass	baby bass lg	NIB	$31.00	99-02
Buckeye Bait Co.	Bug-N-Bass	black/green circles	EX+	$230.50	98-12
Buckeye Bait Co.	Bug-N-Bass	black/silver spots, small	EX	$20.00	98-12
Buckeye Bait Co.	Bug-N-Bass	black scale, 2½"	EX	$133.21	99-06
Buckeye Bait Co.	Bug-N-Bass	black/silver markings	EX	$21.75	99-03
Buckeye Bait Co.	Bug-N-Bass	blue fish, casting size, flat yellow eye	EX	$150.00	05-06
Buckeye Bait Co.	Bug-N-Bass	BNB-7, hard plastic box	NIB	$52.00	05-03
Buckeye Bait Co.	Bug-N-Bass	brown trout, casting size, flat yellow eye	EX+	$125.00	05-06
Buckeye Bait Co.	Bug-N-Bass	brown trout, spining size, raised yellow eye	EX-	$110.00	05-06
Buckeye Bait Co.	Bug-N-Bass	frog	EX	$406.00	02-02
Buckeye Bait Co.	Bug-N-Bass	larger size, black/silver ribs	EX	$37.00	04-07
Buckeye Bait Co.	Bug-N-Bass	lg, WCD	EX	$33.52	99-03
Buckeye Bait Co.	Bug-N-Bass	lg, YCD	EX	$36.53	99-03
Buckeye Bait Co.	Bug-N-Bass	#11 crappie	NIB	$61.27	99-02
Buckeye Bait Co.	Bug-N-Bass	plastic, white with black markings, yellow eyes with black centers	MINT	$39.01	05-07
Buckeye Bait Co.	Bug-n-Bass	rainbow trout, lg?	EX	$103.48	00-02
Buckeye Bait Co.	Bug-N-Bass	rainbow trout, casting size, raised yellow eye	EX+	$125.00	05-06
Buckeye Bait Co.	Bug-N-Bass	RH/clear, black markings, no cellophane	NIB	$97.00	02-03
Buckeye Bait Co.	Bug-N-Bass	RH/clear	NIB	$81.01	99-02
Buckeye Bait Co.	Bug-N-Bass	RH/clear, 12 pack	NIB	$530.55	00-03
Buckeye Bait Co.	Bug-N-Bass	RH/clear body, sand bass #1	NIB	$90.00	99-03
Buckeye Bait Co.	Bug-N-Bass	silver, small size	EX	$67.00	99-08
Buckeye Bait Co.	Bug-N-Bass	sm, black/silver ribs	EX	$35.00	99-03
Buckeye Bait Co.	Bug-N-Bass	solid black	NIB	$129.49	00-03
Buckeye Bait Co.	Bug-N-Bass	white coach dog, 3½", unmarked crisp box	NIB	$35.00	04-09
Buckeye Bait Co.	Bug-N-Bass	y/black coach dog	EX	$27.77	99-05
Buckeye Bait Co.	Bug-N-Bass	YCD	NIB	$25.95	99-03
Buel, J.T.	#3	Arrowhead, copper back	EX-	$25.00	05-06
Buel, J.T.	#5 Arrowhead Spinner	nickle plate, red glass bead, very light wear	EX	$30.00	05-05

LURES

BRAND	MODEL	SERIES / MFG. CODE / DESCRIPTION	GRADE	PRICE	DATE yy/mm
Buel, J.T.	Arrowhead #3	Whitehall, NY, spinner	EX-	$14.00	05-03
Buel, J.T.	Arrowhead #4	2½", "Whitehall"	EX	$150.00	01-03
Buel, J.T.	Arrowhead Spinner	3 oz., big	VG-	$57.70	99-06
Buel, J.T.	Arrowhead Spinner	name only, no city	EX-	$50.00	99-05
Buel, J.T.	Empire City No. 4 Spinner	EX- 2PCCB, white paper label, "BUEL'S FLY SPOONS"	EXIB	$1,313.00	05-07
Buel, J.T.	Spinner	blade is 2⅜" long, early markings, nicely feathered	EX	$25.00	05-06
Buel, J.T.	Spinner, musky	2/0, double bladed, 4", Allure style	EX	$236.00	05-07
Bumble	Bug	red/white	EX	$34.00	01-05
Bunyan, Paul	Dinky	black & yellow	EX	$12.00	05-06
Bunyan, Paul	Dodger	white/red face	VG	$14.00	05-07
Bunyan, Paul	Dodger	window box, black ribs/yellow face	EXIB	$25.00	04-07
Bunyan, Paul	Dodger, winged	yellow head/black ribs	EX	$81.00	05-02
Bunyan, Paul	Electro Lure	RH/black ribs	VG+	$59.00	05-07
Bunyan, Paul	Electro Lure	RH/silver, w/black ribs, lots of tiny to small pointers, hardware nice	VG	$33.00	05-05
Bunyan, Paul	Electro Lure	RH/w, black ribs, can't open body, o/w, very light wear	VG+	$45.00	05-05
Bunyan, Paul	Lady Bug	flocked mouse finish	mint	$82.00	05-02
Bunyan, Paul	Lady Bug	RH, regular treble hook	EX-	$25.00	04-07
Bunyan, Paul	Lady Bug	spring loaded, yellow scale, 3½"	EX	$26.00	04-07
Bunyan, Paul	Minnie	RH/w, YPE, chip on nose and very light wear	VG+	$37.00	05-05
Bunyan, Paul	Mouse	1400, window box & papers	NIB	$98.00	03-05
Bunyan, Paul	Paul's Popper	RH, window box & papers nice	NIB	$47.00	05-02
Bunyan, Paul	Silver Shiner	1100 hardware, Rusty Tough plastic lure	VG+	$30.00	05-05
Bunyan, Paul	Tear Drop Spoon	great red box	NIB	$59.00	00-05
Bunyan, Paul	Twirl Bug Wiggler	r/w, nice 2PCCB	NIB	$100.00	99-07
Bunyan, Paul	Weaver	1900-C, NOT MET	NIB	$32.99	99-05
Bunyan, Paul	Weaver	1900-C pic box, RH	NIB	$45.00	00-05
Bunyan, Paul	Weaver	chrome	EX-	$47.00	00-09
Bunyan, Paul	Weedless Lady Bug	yellow w/silver scales, large 3¼" model in G+ 2PCCB w/catalog	EXIB	$38.00	05-05
Burke	Bass Oreno Type	blue back, silver scales, white belly, 2½"	EX-	$15.00	05-06
Burke	Big Dig	2015 X, white red around eyes	VG+	$6.05	05-07
Burke	Big Dig	perch	EX	$12.00	05-06
Burke	Chugger	black back, silver scale side, yellow belly	VG+	$12.00	05-06
Burke	Flex Plug	Big Dude model, blue scale, new in 2PSTB	NIB	$10.00	05-05
Burke	Punkinseed	perch	EX+	$15.00	05-06
Burroughs	Aqua Bat	red head/white	mint	$20.00	03-04
Burroughs	Aqua Bat	with bottle of tablets	NIB	$24.00	05-02
Burroughs	Croaker Frog	red/white, red head faded	EX-	$78.00	05-07
Burroughs	Tadpole	clear black, chartreuse spots	mint	$84.00	03-04
Burroughs	Tadpole	plastic, neat looking	mint	$80.00	03-04
Calumet Tackel	Spiral Lure	orange/black	NIB	$458.75	00-01
Calumet Tackel	Spiral Lure		NIB	$255.00	99-10
Canadian Baits	Display	pretty round display with lures	EX	$86.00	99-01
Canadian Wiggler	Fly Rod Pikie	1302 blend RH/w, tiny 1¼" PE, nose chipped, age crackling	VG-	$88.00	05-05

BRAND	MODEL	SERIES / MFG. CODE / DESCRIPTION	GRADE	PRICE	DATE yy/mm
Canadian Wiggler	Wiggler	fly rod size, chromed hollow metal that looks like flatfish	EX+	$18.00	05-05
Canadian Wiggler	Wiggler, fly rod size	plastic 9104 Ul-P, yellow w/black and red spots, new on card	NOC	$35.00	05-05
Cap N Bill	Popper	white/blue stripes, PE, 6"	EX	$222.00	04-02
Cap N Bill	Swimmer	surf lure in goldfish scale, PE	EX	$110.00	04-02
Cap N Bill	Swimmer	surf lure in green eel, PE	EX	$102.00	04-02
Captivated Lures	Lulu	electric motor operated	NIB	$21.00	04-12
Carter/Dunks	Best Ever Fly Rod	red/white, small wb	VG	$32.00	01-06
Carter/Dunks	Bestever	101 picture box VG+, black belly decal nice	EX-IB	$50.00	05-07
Carter/Dunks	Bestever	black, great pic box	NIB	$126.00	00-09
Carter/Dunks	Bestever	black, nice box and cat	NIB	$87.00	00-05
Carter/Dunks	Bestever	large RH/gold NE, flake on tail and couple nicks on lip	VG+	$22.00	05-05
Carter/Dunks	Bestever	midget RH/silver NE, early fixed hook hdwr, lip edge worn and light wear	VG-	$18.00	05-05
Carter/Dunks	Bestever	midget solid black NE, few light age lines and few teeny pntrs	EX-	$33.00	05-05
Case	Rotary Marvel	y/gold spots, NOT MET	EX	$380.00	99-05
Case Bait Co.	Rotary Marvel	Case Rotary Marvel	EX	$950.00	01-04
Case Bait Co.	Rotary Marvel	nickle plate head, Neverfail hook, hanger, alum rear	VG	$660.00	05-04
Case Bait Co.	Rotary Marvel		EX	$493.00	00-02
cast iron	Boy Fishing on Platform	post-1910, fish rises when rolled forward	mint	$3,910.00	01-10
Castaic	Baby Largemouth Bass	Series 2, number 133	NIB	$213.00	05-07
Castaic	Hardbait	baby bass	NIB	$174.00	03-11
Castaic	Hardbait	jnted rainbow trout box?	mint	$177.00	03-11
Castaic	Trout	9", wood, jntd, crisp box, modern, NOT MET	NIB	$320.00	03-06
Catch All Inc.	Catch All	smaller size, RH	VG	$14.00	04-07
Cat's Paw	Cat's Paw	red & white	EX-	$35.00	05-06
Cat's Paw	Weedless Casting	crisp box, plain	NIB	$165.00	01-04
CCBC	Wiggler	102 intro, slant-head & washer rig, NE, RH/w, DLT, age lines & few pntrs	VG	$70.00	05-05
CCBC	3-hooker	900 pikie, small chips	VG-	$162.00	01-06
CCBC	5-hooker	chub scale	VG+	$889.00	05-02
CCBC	5-hooker	silver back, rainbow, NOT MET	EX-	$1,525.00	00-11
CCBC	5-hooker	underwater minnow, chub finish	EX-	$466.00	05-07
CCBC	7000	7000, pikie, NOT MET	mint	$153.50	99-05
CCBC	7000	7001 label (torn), crawdad type	NIB	$331.00	02-02
CCBC	7000	7018, no feelers, NOT MET	mint	$128.00	99-05
CCBC	7000	Fireplug, NOT MET	VG+	$152.00	00-04
CCBC	7000	green/black ribs	EX	$103.00	00-04
CCBC	7000	Rainbow Fire	EX-	$311.00	00-05
CCBC	7000	Rainbow Fire, bead eyes	VG-	$206.50	00-03
CCBC	7000	tan/green	EX-	$88.00	00-04
CCBC	7000	white	EX	$131.00	02-03
CCBC	ALW	r/w, weedless spring hook	VG-	$650.00	99-08
CCBC	Assorted	12-pack mixed plastics	NIB	$228.51	99-03
CCBC	Beetle	black, label	EX-IB	$238.00	00-11

BRAND	MODEL	SERIES / MFG. CODE / DESCRIPTION	GRADE	PRICE	DATE yy/mm
CCBC	Beetle	2819, label, frog, GE	EXIB	$695.00	00-02
CCBC	Beetle	3800, greenish gold/y wings	EX-	$102.00	00-05
CCBC	Beetle	3818, belly sliver, otherwise nice	VG	$400.00	00-01
CCBC	Beetle	3850, label, yellow	EXIB	$438.00	00-01
CCBC	Beetle	3850W, PTCB, last of the wood beetles	NIB	$306.00	05-07
CCBC	Beetle	3851, label, back stencil	NIB	$426.00	02-01
CCBC	Beetle	3851, stencil, chain spinners	VG+IB	$202.50	00-01
CCBC	Beetle	3851, yellow-green label, missing 1 spinner	EXIB	$179.16	00-01
CCBC	Beetle	3851W, PTCB, last of the wood beetles	NIB	$358.00	05-07
CCBC	Beetle	3852, stencil, w/red wings	VG+IB	$153.00	00-04
CCBC	Beetle	3852W, PTCB, last of the wood beetles	NIB	$256.00	05-07
CCBC	Beetle	3853, orange, label	NIB	$663.00	00-10
CCBC	Beetle	3853, stencil	NIB	$530.00	02-01
CCBC	Beetle	3854, stencil bx, gold/black	NIB	$270.00	05-07
CCBC	Beetle	3853, Beetle Orange	NIB	$440.00	00-08
CCBC	Beetle	BH/red, varnish flaking	VG	$179.50	99-06
CCBC	Beetle	black and maroon	MINT	$165.00	05-07
CCBC	Beetle	black/gold	EX	$250.00	99-10
CCBC	Beetle	black/gold	EX+	$400.00	99-12
CCBC	Beetle	blk/green spots	EX	$242.50	99-02
CCBC	Beetle	blk/red wings	EX-	$228.07	00-03
CCBC	Beetle	crawdad finish	EX-	$415.00	02-01
CCBC	Beetle	g/y, no stencil, removable hook	EX	$206.00	01-08
CCBC	Beetle	gold with yellow wings, 1 spinner missing	VG+	$75.00	05-06
CCBC	Beetle	gold/black	VG+	$234.11	99-05
CCBC	Beetle	gold/blk wings, hook drag	EX-	$404.98	99-06
CCBC	Beetle	gold/orange, belly stencil, NOT MET	EX	$244.00	01-03
CCBC	Beetle	gold/y wings	EX+	$417.50	99-06
CCBC	Beetle	gold/y wings, 1 metal spinner	VG-	$331.00	99-06
CCBC	Beetle	gold/yellow, 2½", nice	EX-	$175.39	00-02
CCBC	Beetle	green/yellow, end label 3851, bx avg	EXIB	$186.00	03-01
CCBC	Beetle	green/yellow	EX	$154.00	02-02
CCBC	Beetle	green/yellow, 3851	NIB	$212.50	99-08
CCBC	Beetle	metallic green/yellow wings, gold stencil	EX-	$102.00	00-05
CCBC	Beetle	metallic green, y wings	EX-	$177.50	00-02
CCBC	Beetle	metallic green/yellow, label	NIB	$515.00	00-09
CCBC	Beetle	orange/red wings	EX-	$282.68	00-03
CCBC	Beetle	orange/red	mint	$395.00	03-04
CCBC	Beetle	red/white	VG-	$67.50	99-11
CCBC	Beetle	red/white	VG-	$118.93	99-04
CCBC	Beetle	red/white dents	VG-	$112.51	99-01
CCBC	Beetle	silver flash	VG	$171.00	02-09
CCBC	Beetle	silver flash	EX	$338.99	99-10
CCBC	Beetle	silver flash	VG+	$455.00	00-01
CCBC	Beetle	silver flash	EX-	$462.00	00-03
CCBC	Beetle	silver flash	EX	$661.00	00-11
CCBC	Beetle	white/red wings	EX-	$201.50	00-03
CCBC	Beetle	white/red wings, NOT MET	VG-	$69.33	99-06

BRAND	MODEL	SERIES / MFG. CODE / DESCRIPTION	GRADE	PRICE	DATE yy/mm
CCBC	Beetle	white/red wings, might clean up	G	$67.00	00-03
CCBC	Beetle	y/g	G	$100.00	99-03
CCBC	Beetle	y/g	EX	$202.51	00-01
CCBC	Beetle	3800, y/g	NIB	$401.51	99-05
CCBC	Beetle	y/gold, NOT MET	a pig	$48.00	00-08
CCBC	Beetle	y/green	EX	$168.00	00-10
CCBC	Beetle	y/green	EX	$230.00	99-10
CCBC	Beetle	y/green wings	EX	$158.00	03-05
CCBC	Beetle	yellow	NIB	$1,313.00	01-06
CCBC	Beetle	yellow/blk spots, age lines	VG+	$213.00	04-03
CCBC	Beetle	yellow/green wings	EX-	$114.00	03-06
CCBC	Beetle	3852	EX-IB	$325.00	99-03
CCBC	Beetle	y/g wings, #38 rough box	EXIB	$204.00	00-04
CCBC	Beetle Baby	black/maroon/red eyes	EX-	$370.00	99-12
CCBC	Beetle Baby	black/red "beetle" on belly	EX	$203.00	03-01
CCBC	Beetle Baby	blk/red wings, 6055 box	EXIB	$331.00	99-01
CCBC	Beetle Baby	gold/blk, chip on wing, shiney	VG	$130.27	99-02
CCBC	Beetle Baby	gold/y wings	EX	$247.00	00-03
CCBC	Beetle Baby	metallic green/green wings	EX	$200.00	00-04
CCBC	Beetle Baby	metallic green/y wings	EX-	$187.00	00-03
CCBC	Beetle Baby	y/g, crisp label box	NIB	$354.87	00-02
CCBC	Beetle Baby	y/green wings	EX-	$187.50	00-03
CCBC	Beetle x 2	one missing, pearl spinners	EX-	$170.00	00-07
CCBC	Beetle, Baby	6051, green	VG+	$103.00	05-07
CCBC	Beetle, Baby	golden shiner	VG	$990.00	05-07
CCBC	Beetle, Baby	yellow/green wings, un box with IM hangtag	EXIB	$116.00	05-07
CCBC	Big Bomber	6718 label	NIB	$412.61	99-06
CCBC	Big Bomber	perch	mint	$435.00	99-06
CCBC	Big Bug Wiggler	1400, red/white	EX-IB	$612.99	99-09
CCBC	Big Bug Wiggler	2½", full tail, shiny hardware, slick high-gloss original finish	EX	$330.00	05-04
CCBC	Big Bug Wiggler	black, GE	EX	$265.00	00-04
CCBC	Big Bug Wiggler	y/red wings	EX	$510.00	99-11
CCBC	Big Creek Bug Wiggler	1402, red & white, just a hint of wear	EX	$685.00	05-05
CCBC	Bomber	6000, perch, PE	mint	$52.00	00-10
CCBC	Bomber	6601, label bx, dents on belly rest nice	EX-IB	$48.00	03-02
CCBC	Bomber	6604, PE, nice label box	NIB	$198.00	99-08
CCBC	Bomber	frog!	mint	$305.00	99-03
CCBC	Bomber	red head yellow body, 3"	EX-	$95.00	05-06
CCBC	Bug Wiggler	gold bug finish, 2⅝", replaced tail	VG+	$250.00	05-06
CCBC	Bug Wiggler	gold/black ribs, sm tail burn, shiney	EX-/VG+	$350.00	00-04
CCBC	Bug Wiggler	1402, r/w, stencil rough, chip on nose	EX-IB	$315.00	02-10
CCBC	Bull Pup	green scale, unmarked box on card, fly rod lure	NIB	$125.00	05-06
CCBC	Bull Pup	metal lure, tiny 2PCCB, stamped "F-9000," VG	EXIB	$567.00	05-06
CCBC	Cast Trolla	3118, silver flash, GE	NIB	$511.00	02-02
CCBC	Castrola	green perch	EX-	$177.00	00-05
CCBC	Castrola	perch, GE	VG	$61.00	00-02

BRAND	MODEL	SERIES / MFG. CODE / DESCRIPTION	GRADE	PRICE	DATE yy/mm
CCBC	Castrola	pikie, GE	EX	$177.50	99-07
CCBC	Castrola	silver flash, GE	mint	$283.00	00-03
CCBC	Castrola		EX-IB	$152.50	99-05
CCBC	Castrolla	r/w, GE	NIB	$189.50	99-12
CCBC	Castrolla	3118	EX+	$188.50	99-10
CCBC	Champ	S30N	NIB	$95.00	99-02
CCBC	Champ S-30	pike scale, some edge wear and a few small flakes	VG+	$25.00	05-05
CCBC	Champ Spoon	3¼", pikie scale	VG+	$45.00	05-06
CCBC	Champ Spoon	3¼", white top, all silver face, white & red belly	EX-	$85.00	05-06
CCBC	Champ Spoon	white, 3½"	EX-	$5.00	05-02
CCBC	Chautaugua Special	NO BIDS	G	$1,200.00	99-10
CCBC	Cheekie	C-138, silver pearl, ½ oz., light wear	EX-	$28.00	05-05
CCBC	Clothespin	ugly at lead, rest nice, NOT MET!	?	$385.00	99-06
CCBC	Clothespin	5000, stencil	NIB	$827.00	99-10
CCBC	Clothespin Musky	5000 Special, r/w	NIB	$349.00	99-12
CCBC	Cohokie	1000G	NIB	$26.00	99-06
CCBC	Crab	Creek Crab intro box (rough)	EXIB	$260.00	01-03
CCBC	Crab Wiggler 7000?	RH, bead eyes, NOT MET	EX	$187.50	00-02
CCBC	Crab Wiggler, Baby	intro box with papers and name tag, 1909A	EXIB	$605.00	05-07
CCBC	Crawdad	2635DD box	EX-IB	$40.00	99-02
CCBC	Crawdad	300, label crisp	NIB	$102.00	00-10
CCBC	Crawdad	300, natural crab, BBE, no legs, very light wear	EX-	$22.00	05-05
CCBC	Crawdad	300, natural crab, BBE, unfished and nice legs, in EX end-label 2PCCB and with color catalog	EXIB	$80.00	05-05
CCBC	Crawdad	300, Red Devil Western Auto special, red crawdad pattern, "BBE CRAWDAD" stamp	EX-	$245.00	05-05
CCBC	Crawdad	300, stencil box crisp, missing some legs	NIB	$35.00	04-03
CCBC	Crawdad	315, tan & green, legs	NIB	$93.50	99-09
CCBC	Crawdad	b/w	EX	$588.89	99-03
CCBC	Crawdad	black bead eyes, green, no feelers, 2¼"	VG+	$25.00	05-06
CCBC	Crawdad	intro box (fair), NOT MET	EXIB	$401.50	99-01
CCBC	Crawdad	nat crawdad, NOT MET ASO	mint	$50.00	00-04
CCBC	Crawdad	peeler, blue tail	EX-	$97.00	99-03
CCBC	Crawdad	silver flash	EX	$93.00	01-12
CCBC	Crawdad	silver flash, bead eyes, NOT MET	NIB	$113.00	01-01
CCBC	Crawdad	white/purple, NOT MET	mint	$522.00	99-05
CCBC	Crawdad Baby	415, tan crab, no legs, BBE, blemishes on chin and belly, shows color well	G	$12.00	05-05
CCBC	Crawdad Baby	4208, rainbow, blue back, GE, SLT, NSOB, light age lines and few tiny pointers, tougher color to find	EX-	$62.00	05-05
CCBC	Crawdad Baby	4213, GE, black, SLT, NSOB, light age lines and few tiny pointers	VG+	$30.00	05-05
CCBC	Crawdad Baby	400, nat crab, BBE, just a hint of wear & missing 2 legs	EX	$25.00	05-05
CCBC	Crawdad, fly rod	on card F51 in box	VGIB	$40.00	04-03
CCBC	Crawdad, fly rod	red/black center, NOT MET ASO	EXIB	$91.00	00-04
CCBC	Cray-Z Fish	natural finish	EX	$11.00	05-07

BRAND	MODEL	SERIES / MFG. CODE / DESCRIPTION	GRADE	PRICE	DATE yy/mm
CCBC	Cray-Z-Fish	4 different colors	NIB	$81.00	99-02
CCBC	Cray-Z-Fish	hard plastic crab	EX	$17.50	99-02
CCBC	Creek Bug Wiggler	1400, few pointers	EX-	$250.00	99-10
CCBC	Darter	2000 S, pikie, PE, NSOB, spinner on tail, very light wear	EX-	$47.00	05-05
CCBC	Darter	2001, perch, PE, special order color	EX-	$25.00	05-05
CCBC	Darter	2005 plus 12-pack box, NOT MET	NIB	$685.03	99-12
CCBC	Darter	2014, PE, label box crisp	NIB	$29.00	04-03
CCBC	Darter	2014, y/spotted, papers, PE	NIB	$67.80	00-02
CCBC	Darter	2018, silver flash GPE, few small flakes on belly, pretty clean, in orig slightly worn 2PCCB	vg	$24.00	05-05
CCBC	Darter	2018W, PTCB rough, PE	NIB	$17.00	00-11
CCBC	Darter	2023W, chart, black/white eye, PTCB	NIB	$101.00	02-03
CCBC	Darter	8005, PTCB, redside, PE	NIB	$204.50	99-10
CCBC	Darter	8019, stencil, frog, PE	NIB	$51.00	99-06
CCBC	Darter	9000P, frog	NIB	$14.00	00-05
CCBC	Darter	9000UL	NIB	$56.00	01-05
CCBC	Darter	bumble bee, paste-on decal on back	EX	$68.00	05-03
CCBC	Darter	centennial, pike scale	NIB	$27.00	99-01
CCBC	Darter	dace, PE	EX	$68.00	00-08
CCBC	Darter	dace, 12-pack box, 1 lure with box, SOLD	NIB	$900.00	99-10
CCBC	Darter	frog in PTCB	EX-	$15.00	99-01
CCBC	Darter	frog, PE, label	NIB	$53.00	99-11
CCBC	Darter	goldfish scale, purty painted eyes	mint	$158.00	04-04
CCBC	Darter	green gar	EX-	$119.00	04-04
CCBC	Darter	2008W, rainbow, PTCB	NIB	$124.00	99-01
CCBC	Darter	1500, RH, wrong box, nice catalog	NIB	$24.00	04-03
CCBC	Darter	silver flash, plastic	NIB	$18.00	00-05
CCBC	Darter	slant dip, white nose/black DLT, red GE, age lines and tiny flks	VG	$110.00	05-05
CCBC	Darter	2000BWS, PE, PTCB, wood, special	NIB	$217.50	00-03
CCBC	Darter	y spot, PE	NIB	$31.00	99-02
CCBC	Darter	y spotted, un box	EX+IB	$30.00	00-10
CCBC	Darter	2014, yellow spotted NE, large military stencil on back, tiny spots	EX-	$27.00	05-05
CCBC	Darter Midget	8002W, r/w, PTCB	NIB	$26.50	99-01
CCBC	Darter UL	9018, plastic	EX	$26.00	00-02
CCBC	Darter, jntd	4937, PTCB, yellow flash, gold decal, PE	NIB	$165.00	05-07
CCBC	Darter, jntd	4900M, mackerel, PE, PTCB	NIB	$415.00	00-11
CCBC	Darter, jntd	4911W, PE, PTCB, NOT MET	NIB	$157.00	00-05
CCBC	Darter, jntd	4938, pearl, PTCB	NIB	$97.00	99-06
CCBC	Deepster, spinning	9633, black scale, PE	NIB	$455.00	99-04
CCBC	Ding Bat, Baby	5202, label box + cat	NIB	$119.00	05-04
CCBC	Dingbat	5100, label bx EX, box catalog	NIB	$125.00	03-07
CCBC	Dingbat	5100, PTCB, GE	NIB	$47.80	00-04
CCBC	Dingbat	5101, stencil box, sm back chip	EX-IB	$86.00	00-05
CCBC	Dingbat	5102, label	NIB	$88.00	04-03
CCBC	Dingbat	5102, label	NIB	$112.17	99-10
CCBC	Dingbat	5102, label, sm worm burn	EXIB	$125.00	99-06

BRAND	MODEL	SERIES / MFG. CODE / DESCRIPTION	GRADE	PRICE	DATE yy/mm
CCBC	Dingbat	5102, RH/w, GE, NSOB, light age lines and light wear, clean hair legs	VG+	$49.00	05-05
CCBC	Dingbat	5113, end label, black	EXIB	$103.51	99-08
CCBC	Dingbat	5118, label	NIB	$152.50	00-01
CCBC	Dingbat	5118, silver flash, GE, earliest thin body and unimp lip in orig label-end 2PCCB	NMIB	$120.00	05-05
CCBC	Dingbat	5118, stencil	EX-IB	$102.00	01-04
CCBC	Dingbat	5118, stencil bx & pocket catalog	NIB	$82.00	05-07
CCBC	Dingbat	5118 stencil, NOT MET	EXIB	$77.00	04-01
CCBC	Dingbat	5119, frog, GE	EX-	$58.00	05-05
CCBC	Dingbat	5302-P, plastic	NIB	$36.00	99-01
CCBC	Dingbat	5318, rub on nose, o/w, clean in 2PSTB with catalog	EX-IB	$28.00	05-05
CCBC	Dingbat	5401, perch, GE, lg military stencil and full legs, 1 pointer on lip, age lines and 2 thin flakes on belly	EX-	$68.00	05-05
CCBC	Dingbat	5424, redwing blackbird, tiny pointers	EX-	$325.00	05-05
CCBC	Dingbat	5499, stencil box, RH/yellow skunk, POBW	EX-IB	$823.00	04-11
CCBC	Dingbat	AL&W 3190, pikie, GE	NIB	$180.00	00-10
CCBC	Dingbat	black	VG+	$38.88	99-04
CCBC	Dingbat	black	EX-	$50.00	99-02
CCBC	Dingbat	frog	VG	$32.50	99-01
CCBC	Dingbat	frog	VG-	$37.00	99-01
CCBC	Dingbat	frog	EX-	$49.00	01-06
CCBC	Dingbat	frog, 1 eye	VG	$33.00	99-01
CCBC	Dingbat	GE, golden shiner, stamped on back, hair nice	VG+	$42.00	05-06
CCBC	Dingbat	GE, golden shiner, stamped on back, hair 85%	EX	$55.00	05-06
CCBC	Dingbat	golden shiner	EX-	$58.01	99-05
CCBC	Dingbat	golden shiner	EX	$75.00	99-08
CCBC	Dingbat	golden shiner	EXIB	$129.00	04-12
CCBC	Dingbat	golden shiner, cat, tag, nice	NIB	$98.00	99-02
CCBC	Dingbat	golden shiner, tag, cat	NIB	$138.49	99-12
CCBC	Dingbat	green scale	EX	$376.00	99-02
CCBC	Dingbat	pearl, bad varnish	VG-	$104.00	00-10
CCBC	Dingbat	perch	VG	$38.00	99-01
CCBC	Dingbat	perch	EX	$69.00	99-01
CCBC	Dingbat	perch, label	EXIB	$77.00	00-10
CCBC	Dingbat	pikie	VG	$26.00	99-01
CCBC	Dingbat	pikie	EX-	$33.52	99-05
CCBC	Dingbat	pikie	EX+IB	$56.00	99-02
CCBC	Dingbat	pikie scale	EX	$47.00	05-07
CCBC	Dingbat	pikie, worm burn, hair loss	EX?	$46.00	99-06
CCBC	Dingbat	r/w	EX	$71.00	99-01
CCBC	Dingbat	r/w	NIB	$125.00	99-06
CCBC	Dingbat	r/w, marked	VG	$48.00	99-02
CCBC	Dingbat	Rainbow Fire	EX-	$1,200.00	00-07
CCBC	Dingbat	RH	VG-	$33.00	01-08
CCBC	Dingbat	RH, GE	EX-	$52.00	05-02
CCBC	Dingbat	silver flash	VG+	$41.00	99-01
CCBC	Dingbat	WH/black	EX-	$356.57	99-12

BRAND	MODEL	SERIES / MFG. CODE / DESCRIPTION	GRADE	PRICE	DATE yy/mm
CCBC	Dingbat	white scale	EX	$655.01	98-12
CCBC	Dingbat	yellow spotted	EX	$812.00	04-02
CCBC	Dingbat	5100	EXIB	$86.00	99-02
CCBC	Dingbat x 2	black, frog (baby)	EX	$94.00	99-10
CCBC	Dingbat, Baby	5200, label, pikie	NIB	$92.00	99-10
CCBC	Dingbat, Baby	5218, label box	NIB	$67.00	04-01
CCBC	Dingbat, Baby	5218, NOT MET	EXIB	$83.00	99-01
CCBC	Dingbat, Baby	b/w, GE	VG	$526.01	99-12
CCBC	Dingbat, Baby	BW, back stencil, NOT MET	EX	$566.00	00-10
CCBC	Dingbat, Baby	golden shiner	VG-	$25.00	99-01
CCBC	Dingbat, Baby	golden shiner	EX-	$53.00	00-10
CCBC	Dingbat, Baby	golden shiner	mint	$168.50	00-01
CCBC	Dingbat, Baby	pearl	EX-	$306.33	99-04
CCBC	Dingbat, Baby	pearl, back stencil	EX	$432.00	04-11
CCBC	Dingbat, Baby	perch scale, GE	EX	$60.00	05-02
CCBC	Dingbat, Baby	perch, cat & 2 papers stencil box	NIB	$101.00	01-09
CCBC	Dingbat, Baby	pikie	EXIB	$83.00	00-10
CCBC	Dingbat, Baby	pikie, papers	NIB	$112.55	99-11
CCBC	Dingbat, Baby	silver flash	EX-	$61.00	99-01
CCBC	Dingbat, Baby	sunspot	EX	$423.00	03-09
CCBC	Dingbat, Baby	5218, silver flash, GE, brand new in orig 2PCCB	NIB	$100.00	05-05
CCBC	Dingbat, fly rod	frog, PE, huge belly sliver, top nice	VG?	$76.00	00-10
CCBC	Dingbat, fly rod	golden shiner?	EX	$200.50	99-07
CCBC	Dingbat, fly rod	pikie	NOC	$168.05	99-10
CCBC	Dingbat, fly rod	pikie, on card in box, tail flaw, NOT MET	NIB	$142.51	99-04
CCBC	Dingbat, fly rod	pikie, PE	EX	$127.00	01-02
CCBC	Dingbat, fly rod	pikie, problems	?	$154.52	99-03
CCBC	Dingbat, fly rod	rh/w, on card in box	NIB	$409.00	99-04
CCBC	Dingbat, fly rod	Shur Strike? frog	EX	$79.00	00-08
CCBC	Dingbat, Husky	frog spot, GE	EX	$144.00	05-07
CCBC	Dingbat, Husky	frog, GE	EX-	$381.00	00-07
CCBC	Dingbat, Husky	pikie, NOT MET	EX-	$106.49	99-02
CCBC	Dingbat, Husky	pikie, NOT MET	EX-	$106.49	99-02
CCBC	Dingbat, Husky	pikie, nothing special	VG+	$330.00	99-05
CCBC	Dingbat, Surface	2 diff, y skunk, golden shiner	VG/E	$460.00	99-04
CCBC	Dingbat, Surface	5113, label, cat, crisp box	NIB	$257.00	00-11
CCBC	Dingbat, Surface	5401, label box crisp, catalog, GE, wowser	NIB	$205.00	05-07
CCBC	Dingbat, Surface	5404, end label	NIB	$197.50	99-08
CCBC	Dingbat, Surface	5404, label bx, GE	NIB	$67.00	05-02
CCBC	Dingbat, Surface	5413, label, NOT MET	EXIB	$61.00	04-01
CCBC	Dingbat, Surface	5418, label	NIB	$202.50	99-09
CCBC	Dingbat, Surface	black, NOT MET	EX-	$75.00	99-05
CCBC	Dingbat, Surface	Fireplug, huge worm burn	poor	$103.49	99-12
CCBC	Dingbat, Surface	frog	EX	$61.02	99-03
CCBC	Dingbat, Surface	frog	EX+	$158.39	99-05
CCBC	Dingbat, Surface	frog	EX-	$178.49	99-07
CCBC	Dingbat, Surface	frog, 5419 stencil, catalog, crisp box	NIB	$205.00	00-11
CCBC	Dingbat, Surface	GE, golden shiner, hair nice	EX	$125.00	05-06

BRAND	MODEL	SERIES / MFG. CODE / DESCRIPTION	GRADE	PRICE	DATE yy/mm
CCBC	Dingbat, Surface	golden shiner, used but nice	EX-	$29.00	05-03
CCBC	Dingbat, Surface	golden shiner, in wrong 5402 box, GE	EX+	$226.00	05-07
CCBC	Dingbat, Surface	green back	NIB	$2,025.00	00-07
CCBC	Dingbat, Surface	perch	EX-	$90.90	98-12
CCBC	Dingbat, Surface	perch scale, GE	EX	$45.00	05-02
CCBC	Dingbat, Surface	perch, label	NIB	$225.00	99-08
CCBC	Dingbat, Surface	r/w, in box	NIB	$122.50	99-03
CCBC	Dingbat, Surface	redwing blackbird, fake stamp box	EXIB	$634.09	99-12
CCBC	Dingbat, Surface	sable	EX	$526.00	01-12
CCBC	Dingbat, Surface	sable	EX+	$610.00	99-04
CCBC	Dingbat, Surface	sable, Western Auto	VG-	$91.00	99-04
CCBC	Dingbat, Surface	sable, NOT MET	VG	$183.52	99-03
CCBC	Dingbat, Surface	sable, NOT MET	EX+	$406.00	02-01
CCBC	Dingbat, Surface	silver flash	EX	$103.50	00-02
CCBC	Dingbat, Surface	silver flash	EX+	$199.99	99-05
CCBC	Dinger	2318, label, GE	NIB	$232.50	00-03
CCBC	Dinger	5600, label	NIB	$114.00	00-09
CCBC	Dinger	5600, label, silver plate	NIB	$150.00	01-04
CCBC	Dinger	5602, r/w, label	NIB	$167.50	99-09
CCBC	Dinger	black	EX	$235.00	99-07
CCBC	Dinger	black, GE, metal plate, gold back stencil, un box	EXIB	$70.00	05-07
CCBC	Dinger	chub?	VG-	$58.00	99-07
CCBC	Dinger	dace	EX	$150.00	99-02
CCBC	Dinger	dace	EX-	$235.39	99-01
CCBC	Dinger	dace, head plate, 2 hook, hair nice	VG+	$55.00	05-06
CCBC	Dinger	dace, hook drags, but nice	VG	$145.00	00-09
CCBC	Dinger	frog	avg	$33.00	00-09
CCBC	Dinger	frog in ALW 330 18 box	EXIB	$192.49	99-04
CCBC	Dinger	frog, GE	G	$50.00	99-06
CCBC	Dinger	frog, unmarked box	NIB	$197.50	99-04
CCBC	Dinger	golden shiner	EX	$103.00	05-07
CCBC	Dinger	pikie	VG+IB	$125.00	00-05
CCBC	Dinger	pikie, couple pointers, NOT MET	EX	$67.00	02-11
CCBC	Dinger	pikie, silver plate, box un?	NIB	$143.00	00-02
CCBC	Dinger	RH/silver flash	EX	$500.00	00-07
CCBC	Dinger	RH/silver flash	EX-	$280.00	00-10
CCBC	Dinger	silver flash	EX	$128.00	99-01
CCBC	Dinger	silver flash, label box	NIB	$250.00	99-07
CCBC	Dinger, Baby	6101, nose chip	NIB	$213.00	00-08
CCBC	Dinger, Baby	frog	NIB	$150.00	00-10
CCBC	Dinger, Baby	RH	EX-	$96.00	04-12
CCBC	Dinger, Baby	RH, GE	VG	$58.00	02-06
CCBC	Dinger, Baby	special 6114, stencil, yellow spoted	NIB	$1,000.00	04-11
CCBC	Dinger, Baby	V355 stamp, W. Auto, skunk, NOT MET	NIB	$560.00	00-02
CCBC	Dinger, Husky	7500 pikie finish, GE, engraved head plate	EX-	$175.00	05-07
CCBC	Dinger, Husky	pikie	VG	$203.38	99-09
CCBC	Dinger, Husky	pikie	EX	$204.06	99-04
CCBC	Dinger, Husky	r/w, GE, thin hair	EX	$84.00	99-01

BRAND	MODEL	SERIES / MFG. CODE / DESCRIPTION	GRADE	PRICE	DATE yy/mm
CCBC	Dinger, Husky	RH, marked sm box	EX-IB	$200.00	00-10
CCBC	Dinger, Husky	silver flash	VG+	$190.37	99-10
CCBC	Dinger, Plunking	black, NOT MET	EX	$82.87	99-05
CCBC	Dinger, Plunking	golden shiner, NOT MET	EX	$117.50	99-05
CCBC	Dinger, Plunking	redwing blackbird	EX-	$157.00	04-02
CCBC	Dinger, Plunking	6200, label	NIB	$159.00	00-01
CCBC	Dinger, Plunking	6205, dace scale, GE, flake ring on BW, o/w, looks unfished, near mint	EX	$235.00	05-05
CCBC	Dinger, Plunking	6301, perch, GE, large military stencil on back, 2 chips on lip, light wear	VG-	$37.00	05-05
CCBC	Dinger, Plunking	golden shiner, nice	EX	$153.00	00-08
CCBC	Fintail Shiner	2103 stencil box	NIB	$1,327.00	04-11
CCBC	Fintail Shiner	chub finish, cloth fins intact	EX-	$157.00	05-07
CCBC	Fintail Shiner	cloth fins, chub finish, missing cloth tail, otherwise nice	EX-	$74.00	05-07
CCBC	Fintail Shiner	metal tail, perch	mint	$563.32	99-01
CCBC	Fintail Shiner	red side (chub?), all fiber fins intact, nice	EX	$1,251.00	02-03
CCBC	Fintail Shiner	red side, cloth fins	VG+	$225.00	05-07
CCBC	Fintail Shiner	shiner scale, metal dorsal fins, POBW	EX-	$300.00	02-08
CCBC	Fintail Shiner	white, metal tail	EX-	$617.00	99-03
CCBC	Flat Side Chub	1503, earliest thin body & tiny cups in nose & tail, silver shiner, very light wear	EX-	$85.00	05-05
CCBC	Flip Flap	frog, GE	EX	$250.00	00-01
CCBC	Flip Flap	frog, GE, gleamer	EX	$193.00	00-05
CCBC	Flip Flap	r/w, GE	EX-	$127.50	99-06
CCBC	Flip Flap	RH, GE	EX-	$114.00	05-07
CCBC	Flip Flap	silver flash, NOT MET	EX	$132.00	00-11
CCBC	Flip Flap	silver flash, GE	VG	$52.00	99-01
CCBC	Flip Flap	silver flash, GE	EX-	$66.00	00-11
CCBC	Flip Flop	frog spot, GE	EX-	$94.00	05-07
CCBC	Floating River Master	GE, chain perch, small nick by RE and few tiny pointers on tail	EX-	$24.00	05-05
CCBC	Fly Rod Pop-it	No. F-100, r/w and glitter on belly	EX	$82.50	05-04
CCBC	Fly Rod Injured Minnow	F90 Crippled, new on card in label bx, silver flash	NIB - NOC	$4,850.00	03-11
CCBC	Froggie	fly rod lure, PE — three-color eyes	EX	$315.00	05-07
CCBC	Froggie, fly rod	handwritten card	NIB	$184.00	04-03
CCBC	Gar	2600 GAR	NIB	$1,396.00	00-04
CCBC	Gar	2900, label a little mousy	NIB	$1,601.71	99-10
CCBC	Gar	2900, label box, stencil back	EX+IB	$1,255.00	99-04
CCBC	Gar	2900, label box, one eye cracked, SOLD	NIB	$900.00	99-10
CCBC	Gar	2920, stamped box, NOT MET	NIB	$1,025.00	01-05
CCBC	Gar	big paint slivers, ugly	avg	$72.00	04-11
CCBC	Gar	green gar, 2920 label	NIB	$1,295.00	04-02
CCBC	Gar	green gar, not awful	avg	$120.00	99-03
CCBC	Gar	green, 2BW, some POBW, NOT MET	EX	$321.00	00-11
CCBC	Gar	green, POBW, nose chip, screw, shiny	EX-?	$350.00	00-02
CCBC	Gar	green? paint off belly, 1"	?	$185.00	98-12
CCBC	Gar	grubby but might clean up	VG-	$210.00	00-07

BRAND	MODEL	SERIES / MFG. CODE / DESCRIPTION	GRADE	PRICE	DATE yy/mm
CCBC	Gar	huge belly chips, top OK	poor	$104.00	00-07
CCBC	Gar	hvy age lines, sm chip OBW, NOT MET	EX-	$511.00	00-05
CCBC	Gar	end label, pikie	NIB	$1,650.00	00-02
CCBC	Gar	natural	VG-	$248.00	01-03
CCBC	Gar	natural gar	EX	$896.00	00-04
CCBC	Gar	pikie, many pointers around tail, NOT MET	VG-	$197.00	00-04
CCBC	Gar	rings BW, chip shin, top OK, NOT MET	VG-	$306.00	99-11
CCBC	Gar	stencil box	NIB	$1,224.88	99-09
CCBC	Husky Musky	5902 (wrong) white box, GE	NIB	$242.00	00-11
CCBC	Husky Musky	600, stencil (chub), old lip	VG+IB	$151.00	00-10
CCBC	Husky Musky	601, stencil	VG+IB	$78.00	00-08
CCBC	Husky Musky	601, stencil, NOT MET	NIB	$192.00	00-09
CCBC	Husky Musky	603, box G	VG+IB	$1,525.00	99-08
CCBC	Husky Musky	607, blue nat mullet	EX	$700.00	99-10
CCBC	Husky Musky	607, mullet, 1 eye missing	EXIB	$147.61	99-11
CCBC	Husky Musky	612, white	NIB	$655.00	00-10
CCBC	Husky Musky	blue mullet (1 side faded like chub?), GE	EX-	$280.00	01-10
CCBC	Husky Musky	chub	VG	$136.89	99-04
CCBC	Husky Musky	chub finish, GE, belly very rough	avg	$21.00	05-02
CCBC	Husky Musky	chub, label	EX-IB	$285.00	99-11
CCBC	Husky Musky	chub?	VG	$86.50	99-03
CCBC	Husky Musky	DLT, RH, no eyes	EX-	$255.00	00-05
CCBC	Husky Musky	intro pic box	EXIB	$650.00	00-10
CCBC	Husky Musky	mullet finish, GE	EX	$144.00	05-07
CCBC	Husky Musky	mullet, eye replaced	VG-	$104.00	99-03
CCBC	Husky Musky	mullet?	VG-	$80.00	99-03
CCBC	Husky Musky	perch, box	VG	$82.75	99-11
CCBC	Husky Musky	RH, no eyes, flat head	VGIB	$66.00	00-04
CCBC	Husky Musky	silver flash, improved, GE	VG+	$118.00	01-08
CCBC	Husky Musky, jntd	pikie, poor box	NIB	$2,025.00	99-06
CCBC	Husky Musky, jntd	silver shiner, rear wire clipped off	VG+	$154.00	00-05
CCBC	Injured Minnow	1501, label bx, NRA, pocket catalog all crisp, GE	NIB	$326.00	05-07
CCBC	Injured Minnow	1501, GE	NIB	$104.50	99-04
CCBC	Injured Minnow	1501, perch w/correct box	NIB	$31.00	05-07
CCBC	Injured Minnow	1501, GE	EXIB	$51.00	00-06
CCBC	Injured Minnow	1501, perch, GE, cat	NIB	$76.01	99-05
CCBC	Injured Minnow	1504, GE, golden shiner	EX-	$55.00	05-06
CCBC	Injured Minnow	1504, label, box stained	NIB	$140.00	03-08
CCBC	Injured Minnow	1504, label, golden shiner, GE	NIB	$98.00	00-01
CCBC	Injured Minnow	1504, stencil, papers	EXIB	$166.50	99-08
CCBC	Injured Minnow	1505, dace, blue back, GE, just a hint of wear	EX	$65.00	05-05
CCBC	Injured Minnow	1505, label	NIB	$124.00	00-04
CCBC	Injured Minnow	1505, PTCB, GE	NIB	$76.00	99-09
CCBC	Injured Minnow	1505, GE, blue back, label	NIB	$153.49	99-09
CCBC	Injured Minnow	1505, GE, label	EXIB	$129.50	99-09
CCBC	Injured Minnow	1505, hangtag, papers, cat	NIB	$672.00	00-02
CCBC	Injured Minnow	1508, NOT MET	EXIB	$51.50	00-03
CCBC	Injured Minnow	1514 Special, stencil EX bx, y spot/red rib, GE	NIB	$474.00	02-08

BRAND	MODEL	SERIES / MFG. CODE / DESCRIPTION	GRADE	PRICE	DATE yy/mm
CCBC	Injured Minnow	1514 Special, GE, hangtag, orange spot	NIB	$810.00	05-03
CCBC	Injured Minnow	1518, box (un?)	NIB	$87.00	00-10
CCBC	Injured Minnow	1518, stencil box	NIB	$68.00	05-07
CCBC	Injured Minnow	1519, frog, GE	EXIB	$54.00	00-06
CCBC	Injured Minnow	1519, stencil, frog	NIB	$92.00	00-07
CCBC	Injured Minnow	1522, GE, crisp box	NIB	$700.00	05-07
CCBC	Injured Minnow	1524, end label, GE, catalog	NIB	$433.00	05-02
CCBC	Injured Minnow	1524, PTCB, redwing blackbird	NIB	$214.00	03-05
CCBC	Injured Minnow	1525, white scale, GE	mint	$412.00	05-03
CCBC	Injured Minnow	1531, stencil, Rainbow Fire	NIB	$214.00	00-11
CCBC	Injured Minnow	1531, stencil, Fireplug	NIB	$305.00	00-07
CCBC	Injured Minnow	1531, GE	EXIB	$301.51	99-07
CCBC	Injured Minnow	b/w, GE	EX	$1,082.00	05-02
CCBC	Injured Minnow	black back, silver flash, GE, NOT MET	mint	$361.00	00-11
CCBC	Injured Minnow	black scale, black stripe on belly, GE	EX	$135.00	05-07
CCBC	Injured Minnow	blended red head/tail, GE	G	$105.54	99-05
CCBC	Injured Minnow	broad red scale, early type	VG	$56.00	00-01
CCBC	Injured Minnow	chub in wrong box	EXIB	$51.50	99-01
CCBC	Injured Minnow	chub, GE	EX-	$51.00	99-05
CCBC	Injured Minnow	dace, GE	EX-	$30.00	02-08
CCBC	Injured Minnow	Fireplug	EX-	$73.00	00-08
CCBC	Injured Minnow	Fireplug, GE, decent	VG+	$88.00	01-10
CCBC	Injured Minnow	frog, GE, PTCB	NIB	$117.00	01-10
CCBC	Injured Minnow	frog, GE	EX-IB	$113.50	00-03
CCBC	Injured Minnow	GE, pike, looks unfished, in orig 2PCCB with catalog	NIB	$75.00	05-05
CCBC	Injured Minnow	GE, special perch with raised scales, NSOS, light wear in orig 2PCCB stamped "1501 Special"	EX-IB	$65.00	05-05
CCBC	Injured Minnow	golden shiner, rub	VG	$29.50	99-01
CCBC	Injured Minnow	goldfish scale, awesome, unmarked box	NIB	$1,250.00	04-11
CCBC	Injured Minnow	pearl, TE	NIB	$215.16	99-07
CCBC	Injured Minnow	perch, GE	EX-	$22.00	02-08
CCBC	Injured Minnow	perch, GE	mint	$41.00	99-04
CCBC	Injured Minnow	perch, GE	EX+	$60.00	99-01
CCBC	Injured Minnow	pikie color, plastic	NIB	$38.00	00-05
CCBC	Injured Minnow	pikie color, GE, sm, paint flaw	EX	$23.00	02-08
CCBC	Injured Minnow	pikie, oil-soaked box & cat, NOT MET	EXIB	$76.00	99-06
CCBC	Injured Minnow	plastic, purple scale, white eyes	EX	$88.00	00-12
CCBC	Injured Minnow	plastic, shiner scale, black back	EX	$66.00	01-03
CCBC	Injured Minnow	plastic, yellow spoted, red ribs	NIB	$111.00	05-05
CCBC	Injured Minnow	plastic, clear/purple back	EX	$364.50	00-03
CCBC	Injured Minnow	1511W, puro/BH, tack, Sioux City	NIB	$306.00	99-05
CCBC	Injured Minnow	r/w, GE	VG	$32.10	99-01
CCBC	Injured Minnow	Rainbow Fire, NOT MET	VG+	$80.00	01-06
CCBC	Injured Minnow	Rainbow Fire, stencil	NIB	$395.00	00-03
CCBC	Injured Minnow	red side (chub?)	NIB	$74.77	99-06
CCBC	Injured Minnow	red side scale (dace)	EX	$61.55	00-03
CCBC	Injured Minnow	red side, GE	EX	$160.00	99-01

LURES

BRAND	MODEL	SERIES / MFG. CODE / DESCRIPTION	GRADE	PRICE	DATE yy/mm
CCBC	Injured Minnow	redwing blackbird, sm worm burns		$65.00	99-01
CCBC	Injured Minnow	redwing blackbird	Mint	$360.00	98-12
CCBC	Injured Minnow	redwing blackbird, GE	avg/poor	$54.00	99-06
CCBC	Injured Minnow	red side label, GE	NIB	$127.50	00-01
CCBC	Injured Minnow	red side, GE, hangtag, NOT MET ASO	EX	$76.59	00-04
CCBC	Injured Minnow	red side, label, cat	G	$49.00	99-05
CCBC	Injured Minnow	redwing blackbird, GE, stencil # on box	EXIB	$169.00	03-08
CCBC	Injured Minnow	RH, GE, un? box	EXIB	$36.00	01-02
CCBC	Injured Minnow	RH, GE	EX	$35.89	00-01
CCBC	Injured Minnow	RH/w, GE, NSOS, unfished in orig EX- 2PCCB with catalog	NIB	$85.00	05-05
CCBC	Injured Minnow	RWB, GE	VG	$182.00	99-06
CCBC	Injured Minnow	silver shiner label, GE, cat + paper	NIB	$127.50	00-01
CCBC	Injured Minnow	silver flash, GE	EX	$44.61	99-05
CCBC	Injured Minnow	silver flash, GE, rough box un	EXIB	$56.55	00-02
CCBC	Injured Minnow	silver, flat side, stencil, GE	EX	$360.00	00-07
CCBC	Injured Minnow	strawberry, TE	mint	$910.00	00-04
CCBC	Injured Minnow	white scale, GE	EX	$357.00	01-05
CCBC	Injured Minnow	white, GE, stenciled name	EX-	$470.00	02-01
CCBC	Injured Minnow	white/black dots	EX	$2,603.00	01-06
CCBC	Injured Minnow	y/spots, red bloodline, GE	EX	$456.51	99-06
CCBC	Injured Minnow	yellow spotted, red lines, GE	EX	$232.00	03-01
CCBC	Injured Minnow	yellow spotted, GE	EX	$343.00	01-02
CCBC	Injured Minnow	yellow spotted with red ribs, GE	mint	$380.00	02-09
CCBC	Injured Minnow	yellow spotted, GE, PTCB	NIB	$200.01	99-04
CCBC	Injured Minnow	1501	VG-IB	$41.00	99-07
CCBC	Injured Minnow	1503P, early silver shiner, PE, plastic	EX-	$47.00	05-05
CCBC	Injured Minnow	1524, redwing blackbird, GE, few age lines, light wear and tiny pointers	VG++	$165.00	05-05
CCBC	Injured Minnow	blk/w, UL, plastic	NIB	$29.50	99-05
CCBC	Injured Minnow UL	9518UL	NIB	$66.00	99-07
CCBC	Injured Minnow UL	9518UL, plastic bowtie props	NIB	$57.00	01-05
CCBC	Injured Minnow x 7	7 diff, GE	VG-EX+	$205.00	00-05
CCBC	Injured Minnow, Baby	1505 label box, red side, GE	NIB	$75.00	05-07
CCBC	Injured Minnow, Baby	1618 GE	NIB	$97.00	00-04
CCBC	Injured Minnow, Baby	1624, worm burn	VGIB	$182.50	99-05
CCBC	Injured Minnow, Baby	baby flatside 1604 label box	NIB	$158.00	05-01
CCBC	Injured Minnow, Baby	dace, GE, NOT MET	EX	$58.00	00-09
CCBC	Injured Minnow, Baby	Fire Laquer (Rainbow Fire?), GE	EX-	$50.00	99-11
CCBC	Injured Minnow, Baby	r/w, GE	EXIB	$82.00	99-06
CCBC	Injured Minnow, Baby	Rainbow Fire, GE	EX	$92.00	00-10
CCBC	Injured Minnow, Baby	redwing blackbird, stencil	EX	$219.00	04-03
CCBC	Injured Minnow, Baby	red side, GE	EX-	$49.15	99-11
CCBC	Injured Minnow, Baby	RWB, GE	EX	$168.00	00-11
CCBC	Injured Minnow, Baby	white scale, GE	EX-	$230.00	00-05
CCBC	Injured Minnow, Baby	y/spotted/red stripe & ribs, GE	VG+	$204.01	99-09
CCBC	Injured Minnow, Baby	yellow spotted, GE	VG	$73.00	99-01
CCBC	Injured Minnow, Husky	3403 Special	EX-IB	$480.00	99-03

66

BRAND	MODEL	SERIES / MFG. CODE / DESCRIPTION	GRADE	PRICE	DATE yy/mm
CCBC	Injured Minnow, Husky	3518, GE, cat	NIB	$535.99	99-05
CCBC	Injured Minnow, Husky	black, plus black plunker	EX-	$416.52	99-11
CCBC	Injured Minnow, Husky	blue flash, GE	mint	$1,227.00	02-02
CCBC	Injured Minnow, Husky	golden shiner	VG	$93.00	99-11
CCBC	Injured Minnow, Husky	golden shiner	VG+	$250.00	02-02
CCBC	Injured Minnow, Husky	golden shiner, GE	VG	$93.00	99-11
CCBC	Injured Minnow, Husky	golden shiner, GE, decent	avg.	$62.00	99-06
CCBC	Injured Minnow, Husky	pikie, hvy age lines, chip, NOT MET	VG+	$120.00	01-05
CCBC	Injured Minnow, Husky	silver flash, GE	EX-	$355.00	99-02
CCBC	Injured Minnow, Husky	3501	EX-IB	$315.00	00-10
CCBC	Jig L Worm	red/white/blue, affidavit from CCBC	EX	$424.00	02-03
CCBC	Jigger	4202, label	NIB	$561.00	02-01
CCBC	Jigger	blk/lum head, NOT MET	EX	$415.00	00-03
CCBC	Jigger	dace	avg	$76.00	01-10
CCBC	Jigger	frog spot	VG+	$272.00	04-12
CCBC	Jigger	frog, NOT MET	G	$64.00	00-10
CCBC	Jigger	frog, ugly	VG-	$113.00	01-01
CCBC	Jigger	r/w	VG	$137.50	99-05
CCBC	Jigger	r/w, NOT MET	VG-	$87.87	99-06
CCBC	Jigger	RH	avg	$77.00	00-07
CCBC	Jigger	RH, NOT MET	VG	$130.00	01-04
CCBC	Jigger	silver flash, ugly	G	$88.00	02-02
CCBC	Jigger	silver flash, 3⅝"	VG+	$103.00	05-01
CCBC	Jigger	silver flash	EX	$330.00	05-07
CCBC	Jigger, Baby	frog	EX-	$223.00	00-03
CCBC	Jigger, Baby	frog	EX	$332.00	00-10
CCBC	Jigger, Baby	frog, NOT MET	VG	$92.00	02-01
CCBC	Jigger, Baby	frog, NOT MET	VG+	$123.00	01-10
CCBC	Jigger, Baby	frog, numerous digs	G	$130.00	99-04
CCBC	Jigger, Baby	lum head/black	EX	$403.88	99-09
CCBC	Jigger, Baby	nite glow, white head/black GE	EX	$267.00	02-10
CCBC	Jigger, Baby	silver flash, NOT MET	EX	$405.00	03-09
CCBC	Kingfish 130	strawberry, big pikie with plate	EXIB	$696.86	99-08
CCBC	Kingfish Pikie	bumblebee, GE, metal back plate	EX-	$520.00	99-09
CCBC	Kingfish Pikie	tiger stripe, GE	EX-	$405.00	00-02
CCBC	Lucky Mouse	3602 label, white	VGIB	$225.40	00-02
CCBC	Lucky Mouse	gray	EX-	$175.00	99-01
CCBC	Lucky Mouse	metal ears, gray	EX	$129.00	00-08
CCBC	Lucky Mouse	white	EX-	$180.00	99-11
CCBC	Lucky Mouse	white, red eyes, hvy age lines, ugly	avg	$26.00	05-03
CCBC	Lucky Mouse	3602	EX-	$362.99	99-10
CCBC	Mitie (Field) Mouse	639P, tiger stripe, NSOB, just a hint of wear	EX+	$40.00	05-05
CCBC	Mitie (Field) Mouse	6426, wings, RH/w w/black stripe on back, GPE, 1 pointer and very light wear in orig label-end 2PCCB	EX-IB	$90.00	05-05
CCBC	Mitie Mouse	600TM, tiger stripe, plastic box	NIB	$80.00	05-07
CCBC	Mitie Mouse	600, plastic box EX & paper, silver flash color	NIB	$76.00	05-07
CCBC	Morgan Special	perch, PE, chugger, long top lip	EX-	$80.00	99-11

BRAND	MODEL	SERIES / MFG. CODE / DESCRIPTION	GRADE	PRICE	DATE yy/mm
CCBC	Mouse	pearl, 2¾", PTCB	NIB	$80.00	01-04
CCBC	Mouse	WH/black, GE, string tail	VG	$58.00	05-05
CCBC	Musky Champ	in box, 5", metal bait, finished in pikie scale	NIB	$110.00	05-04
CCBC	Nikie	2 perch, silver flash	mint	$26.00	99-02
CCBC	Nikie	9738-P, pearl	EX	$18.00	00-05
CCBC	Nikie	r/w	NIB	$20.00	99-01
CCBC	Nikie UL	9713, black/white bars, plastic box	NIB	$31.01	99-09
CCBC	No. 6012	giant pikie, white/black eye shadow, unrigged, rear wire decal on back, paperwork w/orig box	EX	$330.00	05-04
CCBC	Open Mouth Shiner	500, purple intro box VG-	EX+IB	$2,350.00	00-01
CCBC	Open Mouth Shiner	prototype with documentation	VG+	$899.00	03-02
CCBC	Open Mouth Shiner	RH, no eyes, worm burn, rest OK	?	$49.00	01-01
CCBC	Open Mouth Weedless	intro lavender box, tear on top	EXIB	$495.00	01-05
CCBC	Peter's Special	blue mullet, GE, fluted tail	EX	$363.00	99-09
CCBC	Peter's Special	goldfish scale, GE, un box	EX-	$660.00	02-08
CCBC	Peter's Special	2606, goldfish, stencil bx Special WVS	NIB	$571.00	03-07
CCBC	Peter's Special	shad, NOT MET	NIB	$1,000.00	01-04
CCBC	Pikie	#326, AL&W, plastic, GE, triple jointed, perch scale, NOT MET	EX	$37.00	05-01
CCBC	Pikie	1706 Special Edition, modern plastic	NIB	$15.00	05-03
CCBC	Pikie	5501W, PTCB, TE	NIB	$26.50	99-01
CCBC	Pikie	6577, RH/w, plastic red hair, tail light wear	VG+	$18.00	05-05
CCBC	Pikie	6800, TE, pike, light age lines, few pointers, light wear	VG+	$33.00	05-05
CCBC	Pikie	6933W, PTCB, TE	NIB	$60.00	05-07
CCBC	Pikie	700, dirt common, GE	VG+	$10.00	00-03
CCBC	Pikie	700, DLT, label	NIB	$72.88	00-01
CCBC	Pikie	700RB, trout, plastic	NIB	$129.00	01-01
CCBC	Pikie	701, GE	NIB	$35.00	04-01
CCBC	Pikie	702, blended RH/w, DLT, GE, thin body, hk-drg on belly, light wear	VG+	$72.00	05-05
CCBC	Pikie	702 RH/w, GE, SLT, large military stencil on back, very light wear, EX- label-end 2PCCB and pikie hangtag	EX-ib	$60.00	05-05
CCBC	Pikie	702, GE	EX	$33.00	99-02
CCBC	Pikie	703, GE	NIB	$32.00	00-11
CCBC	Pikie	703, silver shiner, GE, SLT, large military stencil on back, very light wear	VG+	$22.00	05-05
CCBC	Pikie	703, silver shiner, GE, SLT, NSOB, very light wear in VG label-end 2PCCB, decent	VG+IB	$41.00	05-05
CCBC	Pikie	703, GE, box lt mold	NIB	$88.51	99-06
CCBC	Pikie	703, Special, PTCB? GE	NIB	$81.02	99-06
CCBC	Pikie	703 Special, silver chin? PTCB, GE?	NIB	$103.50	00-04
CCBC	Pikie	703SW, GE, PTCB	NIB	$137.00	01-01
CCBC	Pikie	703W, PTCB, TE EX	NIB	$77.00	05-07
CCBC	Pikie	703W, TE, PTCB missing back sticker	EXIB	$26.00	03-01
CCBC	Pikie	704, label, golden shiner, GE	NIB	$66.00	03-06
CCBC	Pikie	705, red side, DLT, GE, NOT MET	EX	$405.00	05-02

BRAND	MODEL	SERIES / MFG. CODE / DESCRIPTION	GRADE	PRICE	DATE yy/mm
CCBC	Pikie	707, blue mullet, TE, paint off both, NSOB, few minor pointers, bright aqua scales	VG-	$22.00	05-05
CCBC	Pikie	707, PTCB & catalog, GE	NIB	$91.00	04-03
CCBC	Pikie	707, stencil box EX, GE, blue mullet	NIB	$361.00	05-02
CCBC	Pikie	707, stencil, SOLD	EXIB	$255.00	99-10
CCBC	Pikie	708, label, GE, rainbow	NIB	$175.00	00-01
CCBC	Pikie	708, rainbow, DLT, thin body, blunt nose, GE (both cracked), small chip on nose and hdwr rusty	VG+	$49.00	05-05
CCBC	Pikie	710 BH, stencil, GE	NIB	$460.65	99-10
CCBC	Pikie	711, b/w, GE	NIB	$204.00	00-05
CCBC	Pikie	711 Special, b/w, GE, stencil	NIB	$290.11	99-03
CCBC	Pikie	711, WH/black, GE, hangtag, cat	NIB	$360.00	00-02
CCBC	Pikie	711, GE, cat, stencil	NIB	$237.00	01-02
CCBC	Pikie	711, GE	EX-IB	$203.00	00-04
CCBC	Pikie	711, GE, b/w, stencil box	EXIB	$185.00	99-06
CCBC	Pikie	714 Special, yellow spotted, GE	NIB	$512.00	05-02
CCBC	Pikie	714 Special, yellow/red & blk spots	NIB	$968.00	03-02
CCBC	Pikie	718, SW, TE	NIB	$63.00	00-11
CCBC	Pikie	718, GE	NIB	$51.00	99-03
CCBC	Pikie	718, GE	NIB	$56.00	99-04
CCBC	Pikie	720, stencil box, silver scale/white/purple gills	NIB	$1,424.00	01-09
CCBC	Pikie	721, Day & Nite	NIB	$191.38	99-02
CCBC	Pikie	721, Day N Nite, GE	EX-	$42.00	01-06
CCBC	Pikie	721, Nite Glow label	NIB	$108.15	00-02
CCBC	Pikie	722, GE	EXIB	$107.50	00-02
CCBC	Pikie	725, white scale, GE, NOT MET	VG	$209.50	99-05
CCBC	Pikie	731, RB Fireplug	NIB	$143.51	99-04
CCBC	Pikie	731, stencil, NOT MET	EX-IB	$100.00	02-01
CCBC	Pikie	732, Rainbow Fire, stencil box	NIB	$200.00	02-01
CCBC	Pikie	732, stencil & catalog crisp, GE	NIB	$109.00	05-07
CCBC	Pikie	732, GE, stencil box	NIB	$226.05	99-08
CCBC	Pikie	733, PTCB, GE, black scale	NIB	$200.00	02-01
CCBC	Pikie	733, black scale, GE	EX-	$169.50	99-06
CCBC	Pikie	734, blue flash, GE, SLT, small varnish blem on back, few tiny pointers, very light wear	EX-	$135.00	05-05
CCBC	Pikie	734DD, TE, blue flash, PTCB	EXIB	$48.50	99-01
CCBC	Pikie	734SW, TE, 2-hooker	NIB	$103.51	99-11
CCBC	Pikie	737DD, TE, PTCB	NIB	$270.00	00-10
CCBC	Pikie	b/w, small touch up, pointers	VG-	$82.01	99-09
CCBC	Pikie	BH, faded	G	$81.00	99-06
CCBC	Pikie	BH, no eyes, DLT	VG+	$147.50	00-03
CCBC	Pikie	black scale, GE, newer	mint	$102.51	99-04
CCBC	Pikie	black, GE	EX	$56.00	04-03
CCBC	Pikie	black, GE, back stencil	EX	$320.50	99-10
CCBC	Pikie	black/red head, GE, stencil on back	EX	$786.00	03-08
CCBC	Pikie	blk/white, GE, DLT	VG	$125.00	99-07
CCBC	Pikie	blue flash, GE	EX+	$103.00	01-04
CCBC	Pikie	blue flash, GE	EX-	$190.00	99-10

BRAND	MODEL	SERIES / MFG. CODE / DESCRIPTION	GRADE	PRICE	DATE yy/mm
CCBC	Pikie	blue/white, 710 stencil, GE, $375 NOT MET	NIB	$218.00	01-08
CCBC	Pikie	BWH, GE, back stencil only 1 picture	EX-?	$69.00	03-02
CCBC	Pikie	Day N Night Glow, GE	EX	$204.52	99-10
CCBC	Pikie	Day-N-Nite, GE	mint	$191.72	99-06
CCBC	Pikie	DD722, GE, still glows	mint	$86.00	05-02
CCBC	Pikie	DLT, GE, 720 stencil "SCHROEDER OF FINLAND," blue scale	NIB	$1,080.00	05-02
CCBC	Pikie	early RB, silver back	mint	$264.00	00-05
CCBC	Pikie	Fireplug, GE, unmarked box VG+	NIB	$137.00	05-07
CCBC	Pikie	Fireplug, GE	mint	$48.00	99-01
CCBC	Pikie	frog, TE, 6"	EX	$39.99	99-02
CCBC	Pikie	GE, silver shiner	NIB	$52.00	02-08
CCBC	Pikie	golden mullet? GE	EX-	$255.00	99-11
CCBC	Pikie	golden shiner	EX-	$35.00	99-10
CCBC	Pikie	golden shiner, GE	EX	$35.00	99-01
CCBC	Pikie	goldfish, plastic	NIB	$56.00	00-07
CCBC	Pikie	mullet, GE	EX	$111.00	00-10
CCBC	Pikie	mullet, GE	EX	$175.00	99-07
CCBC	Pikie	pearl, TE	NIB	$293.00	00-07
CCBC	Pikie	Peter's Special, pearl, GE	EX	$350.00	99-10
CCBC	Pikie	pikie finish, TE, wood	Ex	$26.00	05-07
CCBC	Pikie	pikie, GE	EX-	$14.00	99-05
CCBC	Pikie	pink pearl, TE	mint	$292.00	00-02
CCBC	Pikie	plastic, dace, new in 2PCCB, common	NIB	$21.50	00-02
CCBC	Pikie	purple eel, GE, back stencil	mint	$494.00	04-11
CCBC	Pikie	Rainbow Fire	EX	$65.00	99-04
CCBC	Pikie	Rainbow Fire, $150 NOT MET	EX+	$46.00	01-04
CCBC	Pikie	Rainbow, GE — one cracked	mint	$119.00	99-01
CCBC	Pikie	Rare Color, silver/red/white	VG	$127.00	98-12
CCBC	Pikie	RB, GE, un box	NIB	$173.00	01-08
CCBC	Pikie	redhorse, GE, DLT, 4 red fins, nice!	EX-	$2,483.00	02-09
CCBC	Pikie	RH, 7", GE, papers	NIB	$45.00	00-01
CCBC	Pikie	RH sparkles, un? box	EXIB	$167.00	00-08
CCBC	Pikie	RH/w, CA special side screws	EX-	$69.51	99-04
CCBC	Pikie	saltwater 700, 2-hk, reinforced hook hanger, GE	EX	$281.00	05-07
CCBC	Pikie	tiger stripe, GE	EX-	$100.00	99-11
CCBC	Pikie	unmarked lip, HPGM, early book-style paper box	EX	$66.00	05-04
CCBC	Pikie	w/b, DLT, GE	VG	$96.00	99-01
CCBC	Pikie	w/blk, no eyes	EX-	$229.49	99-04
CCBC	Pikie	WH/black, GE	EX-	$129.00	00-04
CCBC	Pikie	WH/black, no eyes	EX-	$100.00	00-05
CCBC	Pikie	WH/black, NE, DLT	VG	$56.00	00-01
CCBC	Pikie	WH/black, no eyes, DLT	VG+	$76.00	00-05
CCBC	Pikie	white head/black, GE, gold lettering	EX	$192.00	01-11
CCBC	Pikie	white/blended, red nose & chin, GE	EX-	$249.00	00-02
CCBC	Pikie	white/blk forward slant ribs, TE, back stenciled	mint	$999.00	03-04
CCBC	Pikie	white/red dots/green back stripe, GE	EX	$899.00	01-05
CCBC	Pikie	white scale, GE	VG+	$162.00	01-05

BRAND	MODEL	SERIES / MFG. CODE / DESCRIPTION	GRADE	PRICE	DATE yy/mm
CCBC	Pikie	wood, pikie, GE, 6" lure	VG+	$8.50	05-07
CCBC	Pikie	yellow spotted, GE, DLT	VG-	$204.01	99-11
CCBC	Pikie	yellow flash, GE	EX	$282.00	00-08
CCBC	Pikie	701	VGIB	$20.00	99-01
CCBC	Pikie	3002	EXIB	$80.99	99-04
CCBC	Pikie	2630, GE, red/o/blk spots	EX-	$204.49	99-03
CCBC	Pikie	3000MA psycho?	NIB	$134.00	04-11
CCBC	Pikie 19"	ad lure, "A L & W" on lip	EX	$1,050.00	00-04
CCBC	Pikie, 2 diff	5532, 2603, GE	NIB	$212.50	99-08
CCBC	Pikie, 3-jntd	2830P, plastic	NIB	$90.01	99-09
CCBC	Pikie, 3-jntd	AL&W, perch, GE	mint	$87.50	99-09
CCBC	Pikie, 3-jntd	golden shiner, plastic, 3 sections	EX-	$30.00	04-12
CCBC	Pikie, 3-jntd	RH/o/blk spots, plastic	EX-	$67.00	01-04
CCBC	Pikie, 5"	RH/o spotted, GE, 5", rag box	EX-	$456.00	99-04
CCBC	Pikie Display	perch scale, no extra holes, NOT MET	EX	$457.00	02-04
CCBC	Pikie, fly rod x 2	plastic long lip, pink, orange	EX	$330.25	00-03
CCBC	Pikie, jntd DD Peter's	2603DD, metal tail, GE, blk dot, stencil box	NIB	$777.00	02-01
CCBC	Pikie, jntd DD Peter's	Peter's Sp., blk scale, GE	EX	$122.00	00-08
CCBC	Pikie Kingfish	KF 135 Special, tiger, GE, plate, nice box	VG-IB	$213.62	00-02
CCBC	Pikie Kingfish	KF118, silver flash	NIB	$1,500.00	99-09
CCBC	Pikie Kingfish	white	EX	$1,100.00	99-09
CCBC	Pikie Kingfish 130	KF130, strawberry, metal flash plate	EXIB	$696.86	99-08
CCBC	Pikie Ltd. Edition	1704, modern plastic	NIB	$22.00	04-07
CCBC	Pikie Ltd. Edition	1705, modern plastic	NIB	$25.00	04-07
CCBC	Pikie Ltd. Edition	1706, modern plastic	NIB	$16.00	04-07
CCBC	Pikie Ltd. Edition	1725, modern plastic	NIB	$23.00	04-07
CCBC	Pikie Ltd. Edition	1742, modern plastic	NIB	$25.00	04-07
CCBC	Pikie Saltwater	938SW, 2-hooker, TE, PTCB	NIB	$295.00	02-09
CCBC	Pikie UL	9301, tiny, plastic	NIB	$19.00	03-08
CCBC	Pikie UL	frog, plastic, tiny UL	NOC	$46.00	00-01
CCBC	Pikie West Coast	702 Special, 2-hook, side screw, NRA	NIB	$302.50	00-01
CCBC	Pikie, wood DD	702DD, wood, 12 pack, PTCB	NIB	$305.00	99-08
CCBC	Pikie x 2	2618, 900	NIB	$150.01	99-10
CCBC	Pikie x 2	r/w, b/w, no eyes	VG+	$251.76	99-11
CCBC	Pikie x 6	all GE, decent shape	avg-VG	$31.00	99-10
CCBC	Pikie x 6	bought by newbie	avg	$91.00	00-07
CCBC	Pikie, Baby	2PCCB	NIB	$33.88	99-01
CCBC	Pikie, Baby	700DD, GE, minty box	NIB	$103.19	99-06
CCBC	Pikie, Baby	900, in white scale, GE, back stencil	EX	$1,313.00	02-04
CCBC	Pikie, Baby	900, stencil box, DLT	NIB	$80.00	02-10
CCBC	Pikie, Baby	903, label, GE	NIB	$83.00	01-04
CCBC	Pikie, Baby	903, stencil, GE	NIB	$76.01	99-10
CCBC	Pikie, Baby	908, label, GE	NIB	$156.36	99-03
CCBC	Pikie, Baby	908, RB, GE	NIB	$117.00	00-04
CCBC	Pikie, Baby	918, label, GE	NIB	$49.89	99-11
CCBC	Pikie, Baby	931, stencil, GE	NIB	$56.00	05-03
CCBC	Pikie, Baby	933, GE, PTCB	NIB	$214.00	00-10
CCBC	Pikie, Baby	934, blue flash, GE, PTCB	NIB	$189.00	05-03

BRAND	MODEL	SERIES / MFG. CODE / DESCRIPTION	GRADE	PRICE	DATE yy/mm
CCBC	Pikie, Baby	brilliant green scale, GE, DLT	VG+	$393.88	00-01
CCBC	Pikie, Baby	Fireplug, GE, wrong 900 box	EX	$164.50	99-07
CCBC	Pikie, Baby	Fireplug, GE	EX	$75.00	99-05
CCBC	Pikie, Baby	Fireplug, TE	EX	$76.00	00-10
CCBC	Pikie, Baby	pikie, GE	mint	$23.00	00-08
CCBC	Pikie, Baby	silver flash, GE	NIB	$51.00	99-02
CCBC	Pikie, Baby	white scale, GE	VG+	$366.88	99-06
CCBC	Pikie, Baby	y/red & blk spots	EX-	$154.72	99-10
CCBC	Pikie, Baby DD	RB, GE, wrong box	NIB	$189.00	01-03
CCBC	Pikie, Baby DD	RH/o and black spots, GE, NOT MET	EX-	$188.00	01-04
CCBC	Pikie, Baby jntd	#31, Rainbow Fire, GE	EX-	$61.26	99-09
CCBC	Pikie, Baby jntd	2701, perch w/underchin DLT, GE, skinny body and pointed nose, a hint of wear, in orig 2PCCB	EXIB	$150.00	05-05
CCBC	Pikie, Baby jntd	2703, GE, PTCB	NIB	$153.00	00-08
CCBC	Pikie, Baby jntd	2704, label box	EXIB	$60.99	99-05
CCBC	Pikie, Baby jntd	2708, label box	NIB	$198.00	99-04
CCBC	Pikie, Baby jntd	2718, GE, PTCB	NIB	$22.00	01-03
CCBC	Pikie, Baby jntd	2731, label, Rainbow Fire, minty box	NIB	$228.00	00-07
CCBC	Pikie, Baby jntd	4232, stamped box, Rainbow Fire	NIB	$127.52	99-05
CCBC	Pikie, Baby jntd	baby pikeral, eye crack, NOT MET	EX-	$78.50	99-04
CCBC	Pikie, Baby jntd	Rainbow Fire	EX-	$90.00	99-10
CCBC	Pikie, Baby jntd	rainbow, GE	mint	$96.00	99-11
CCBC	Pikie, Baby jntd	red Fireplug, odd label box, GE	NIB	$490.00	01-09
CCBC	Pikie, Baby jntd	RH/flitter Day & Night, "SPECIAL 2722" stencil	NIB	$770.00	04-03
CCBC	Pikie, Baby jntd	silver flash, NRA box	NIB	$162.50	99-12
CCBC	Pikie, Baby jntd	2700, GE, pike scale, 1 tiny pointer, o/w, unfished, in orig EX- label-end 2PCCB	EXIB	$38.00	05-05
CCBC	Pikie, Baby jntd	2700, GE, pike scale, light age lines, NSOB, in orig VG stamped 2PCCB	EXIB	$29.00	05-05
CCBC	Pikie, Baby jntd	2713DD Special, TE	NIB	$108.00	00-04
CCBC	Pikie, Baby jntd	silver flash, GE, box rough	EX	$59.00	05-07
CCBC	Pikie, Deep Diver jntd	TE, purple eel, label off back	VG+	$50.00	05-06
CCBC	Pikie, Deep Diving jntd	2730DD, orange with black spots and red head, w/box and papers	VG+IB	$110.00	05-07
CCBC	Pikie, fly rod	pikie color, plastic	NIB	$18.05	99-02
CCBC	Pikie, fly rod	r/w, plastic	NIB	$15.80	99-02
CCBC	Pikie, fly rod	RH, no eyes	VG+	$220.00	04-03
CCBC	Pikie, Giant	6000, goldfish scale, TE	EX	$175.00	99-04
CCBC	Pikie, Giant	6002, 2PCCB EX, TE	NIB	$81.00	05-07
CCBC	Pikie, Giant	6008 Special, RB, TE	NIB	$230.50	99-11
CCBC	Pikie, Giant	6025, black scale, PTCB	NIB	$120.02	99-10
CCBC	Pikie, Giant	6034, wood, TE, PTCB, silver flash	NIB	$99.00	01-09
CCBC	Pikie, Giant	gold scale, un 2PCCB, TE	EXIB	$102.00	00-09
CCBC	Pikie, Giant	gold scale, TE	NIB	$275.00	00-04
CCBC	Pikie, Giant	pikie	NIB	$82.50	99-09
CCBC	Pikie, Giant	rainbow, TE	NIB	$235.83	99-05
CCBC	Pikie, Giant	RB, TE, PTCB	NIB	$249.00	01-01
CCBC	Pikie, Giant	TE, silver flash	VGIB	$22.00	05-03
CCBC	Pikie, Giant	6006, TE, gold scale, green box E-	EXIB	$1,125.00	05-06

BRAND	MODEL	SERIES / MFG. CODE / DESCRIPTION	GRADE	PRICE	DATE yy/mm
CCBC	Pikie, Giant jntd	800, pikie scale, TE, few tiny pointers, light age lines	EX-	$65.00	05-05
CCBC	Pikie, Giant jntd	800, unmarked box, yellow flash, TEW	NIB	$280.00	05-07
CCBC	Pikie, Giant jntd	800, TE	NIB	$122.50	99-04
CCBC	Pikie, Giant jntd	8019, frog spot, GPE, light wear on belly in EX- hard-to-find orig 2PCCB	VG+IB	$34.00	05-05
CCBC	Pikie, Giant jntd	813, PTCB, TE	NIB	$82.00	05-07
CCBC	Pikie, Giant jntd	818, 2PCCB, TE, rub inside joint, otherwise nice	EX-IB	$52.00	05-07
CCBC	Pikie, Giant jntd	830, RH/orange spotted, TE	NIB	$146.80	00-03
CCBC	Pikie, Giant jntd	830, RH/orange spot, GE, bad joint chips	EX-?IB	$410.59	99-06
CCBC	Pikie, Giant jntd	834, 2PCCB, TE, blue flash	NIB	$57.00	99-08
CCBC	Pikie, Giant jntd	black scale, GE, nice box # 833	NIB	$177.00	05-07
CCBC	Pikie, Giant jntd	black scale, TE	NIB	$148.00	01-04
CCBC	Pikie, Giant jntd	black scale, TE, stamped box	EX-IB	$77.00	02-03
CCBC	Pikie, Giant jntd	blacks scale, TE, PTCB	EXIB	$92.01	99-11
CCBC	Pikie, Giant jntd	GE, black scale		$67.00	98-12
CCBC	Pikie, Giant jntd	RH, TE, nice 2PCCB EX	NIB	$73.00	05-07
CCBC	Pikie, Giant jntd	pearl, TE, unmarked 2PCCB	NIB	$571.00	05-07
CCBC	Pikie, Giant jntd	pikie finish, TE	EX-	$37.00	05-07
CCBC	Pikie, Giant jntd	pikie, 2PCCB, TE	EXIB	$52.00	99-06
CCBC	Pikie, Giant jntd	pikie, TE, NOT MET ASO	NIB	$61.00	00-04
CCBC	Pikie, Giant jntd	purple eel, TE	EX-	$220.00	01-05
CCBC	Pikie, Giant jntd	purple eel, TE	NIB	$321.00	01-04
CCBC	Pikie, Giant jntd	silver flash, TE	EX+IB	$95.00	99-06
CCBC	Pikie, Giant jntd	Sioux City, black	EX	$38.00	04-08
CCBC	Pikie, Giant jntd	strawberry, GE	NIB	$198.00	05-07
CCBC	Pikie, Giant jntd	823, yellow wood, PTCB, black TE	NIB	$1,009.00	03-08
CCBC	Pikie, Giant jntd	yellow spot, GE	VG+	$135.00	05-07
CCBC	Pikie, Husky	2300, unimproved lip, big screw	EX	$60.00	99-03
CCBC	Pikie, Husky	2300VCL, stamped bx VG+, 2-hk saltwater, white/red eyes, GE	NIB	$306.00	05-07
CCBC	Pikie, Husky	2302, label, cat, crisp box, GE	NIB	$128.00	00-11
CCBC	Pikie, Husky	2302 Special, w/red chin, GE	NIB	$690.00	00-02
CCBC	Pikie, Husky	2302, RH, GE, SOLD	NIB	$78.00	99-10
CCBC	Pikie, Husky	2302 Special, 2-hk, white	NIB	$1,000.00	99-03
CCBC	Pikie, Husky	2303, natural mullet, GE	EX	$200.00	99-10
CCBC	Pikie, Husky	2303, r/w, GE, pointer decent, NOT MET	VGIB	$21.00	99-01
CCBC	Pikie, Husky	2307, label, blue mullet, GE	NIB	$221.00	01-11
CCBC	Pikie, Husky	2307, nat mullet	NIB	$300.00	99-10
CCBC	Pikie, Husky	2313W, PTCB EX, TE	NIB	$77.00	05-07
CCBC	Pikie, Husky	2318, crisp box, GE	NIB	$79.00	01-05
CCBC	Pikie, Husky	2318, label, GE	NIB	$120.00	00-03
CCBC	Pikie, Husky	2321, GE, silver flash, Day N Night	VG+	$120.00	05-06
CCBC	Pikie, Husky	2333W, black scale, TE	NIB	$56.00	99-04
CCBC	Pikie, Husky	2334W, blue flash, TE	NIB	$55.00	99-04
CCBC	Pikie, Husky	2335L, GE, purple eel, 2-hk special	NIB	$698.00	99-03
CCBC	Pikie, Husky	2337, y flash, TE	EX	$115.00	00-10
CCBC	Pikie, Husky	3000 Special, mullet, GE	EX-IB	$101.00	99-06

LURES

BRAND	MODEL	SERIES / MFG. CODE / DESCRIPTION	GRADE	PRICE	DATE yy/mm
CCBC	Pikie, Husky	6902W, TE, r/w	NIB	$35.00	99-01
CCBC	Pikie, Husky	AL&W, box and lure, perch, GE	VG+IB	$28.00	00-10
CCBC	Pikie, Husky	2313, black	NIB	$750.00	99-03
CCBC	Pikie, Husky	blue flash, TE, decal, Sioux?	mint	$27.99	99-05
CCBC	Pikie, Husky	blue mullet, GE	EX-	$80.00	99-01
CCBC	Pikie, Husky	blue mullet, NOT MET	NIB	$132.50	99-02
CCBC	Pikie, Husky	blue scale (mullet?)/white belly, TE	EX-	$59.00	05-07
CCBC	Pikie, Husky	bumblebee, GE decent	VG+	$59.00	05-07
CCBC	Pikie, Husky	fireplug, GE, deep pointers, rest nice	VG+	$38.00	05-07
CCBC	Pikie, Husky	fireplug, GE, unmarked box papers	NIB	$250.00	03-07
CCBC	Pikie, Husky	pearl/bright y and red spots, TE, decal	mint	$256.00	00-08
CCBC	Pikie, Husky	perch, early hvy screw-eye hook hangers	EX-	$48.00	03-01
CCBC	Pikie, Husky	pikie	NIB	$51.00	99-02
CCBC	Pikie, Husky	pikie, GE	EXIB	$76.00	99-04
CCBC	Pikie, Husky	pikie, GE, NOT MET ASO	NIB	$36.00	00-04
CCBC	Pikie, Husky	r/w	NIB	$50.00	99-02
CCBC	Pikie, Husky	rainbow fire 2331, GE, label	NIB	$231.50	99-06
CCBC	Pikie, Husky	rainbow, GE	EX+IB	$210.00	99-02
CCBC	Pikie, Husky	RH, GE, label	NIB	$112.00	00-10
CCBC	Pikie, Husky	silver flash	EX	$65.00	99-10
CCBC	Pikie, Husky	silver flash, NOT MET	NIB	$75.00	99-02
CCBC	Pikie, Husky	2307 Special, mullet, GE	NIB	$609.00	00-09
CCBC	Pikie, Husky	2302, GE, RH/w, wire through early unimp lip, large military stencil on back, light wear	VG	$34.00	05-05
CCBC	Pikie, Husky	2308, rainbow, GE, HD wire through, NSOB, few light pointers, light age lines	VG+	$70.00	05-05
CCBC	Pikie, Husky jntd	2307, husky pikie, GE, blue or silver mullet	EX+	$150.00	05-06
CCBC	Pikie, Husky jntd	2318, crisp box	NIB	$95.00	99-11
CCBC	Pikie, Husky jntd	3000, GE, 6", pikie, in label box E-	EX-IB	$45.00	05-06
CCBC	Pikie, Husky jntd	3000, GE, pike, NSOB, HD wire thru and imp lip	NM	$40.00	05-05
CCBC	Pikie, Husky jntd	3001, light age lines, an AL&W version in orig CCBCO-AL&W 2PCCB	EX-IB	$55.00	05-05
CCBC	Pikie, Husky jntd	3001, perch, GE, wire through and imp lip, hint of wear, in orig ex 2PCCB and catalog	EXIB	$60.00	05-05
CCBC	Pikie, Husky jntd	3001, perch in nice box	NIB	$70.00	99-01
CCBC	Pikie, Husky jntd	3002, blended RH/w, TE, HD wire through, new in orig 2PPTB	NIB	$35.00	05-05
CCBC	Pikie, Husky jntd	3007, natural mullet, label	NIB	$332.00	00-07
CCBC	Pikie, Husky jntd	3007, nat mullet, label, GE	NIB	$145.02	99-11
CCBC	Pikie, Husky jntd	3031, label box, ship inside jnt, GE, Rainbow Fire	EXIB	$131.00	05-07
CCBC	Pikie, Husky jntd	3032, Fireplug, label box EX-	NIB	$143.00	04-03
CCBC	Pikie, Husky jntd	3039, tiger stripe, TE, wire through, new and unfished in EX+ orig 2PPTB, catalog	NIB	$125.00	05-05
CCBC	Pikie, Husky jntd	3044, whitefish, TE, wire through, sticker worn, 3 pointers	Ex-	$185.00	05-05
CCBC	Pikie, Husky jntd	3118, silver flash, GE, early large scale pattern, 2 nicks on lip and edge very light wear	EX-	$145.00	05-05
CCBC	Pikie, Husky jntd	3121, GE, Day N Nite, still glows, chips on lip, hk drags on belly, light wear	VG	$145.00	05-05
CCBC	Pikie, Husky jntd	3200, pike scale, GE, few light age lines, 1 pointer on lip	EX	$22.00	05-05

BRAND	MODEL	SERIES / MFG. CODE / DESCRIPTION	GRADE	PRICE	DATE yy/mm
CCBC	Pikie, Husky jntd	blue mullet	EX-	$43.00	99-01
CCBC	Pikie, Husky jntd	mullet, GE, 1 cup corroded, NOT MET	EX-	$46.00	01-04
CCBC	Pikie, Husky jntd	rainbow, GE, back stencil	EX	$42.00	03-01
CCBC	Pikie, Husky jntd	rainbow, GE, nice box, 3008 label	EXIB	$62.00	04-09
CCBC	Pikie, Husky jntd	yellow spotted, TE	EX	$76.00	99-01
CCBC	Pikie, Husky jntd	3008	EX-IB	$200.00	99-10
CCBC	Pikie, Husky jntd	3033, stenciled bx, GE	EX-IB	$67.00	05-07
CCBC	Pikie, Husky jntd	bumblebee, TE	VG+IB	$51.00	05-07
CCBC	Pikie, jointed	Fireplug	VG-	$16.04	05-07
CCBC	Pikie, jointed	2009W (IA?), TE, PTCB, NOT MET	NIB	$93.00	01-12
CCBC	Pikie, jointed	2508DDW, PTCB, TE, rainbow	NIB	$103.00	05-07
CCBC	Pikie, jointed	2600, Peter's Sp, metal tail	VG	$196.52	99-04
CCBC	Pikie, jointed	2600W, PE, wood, perch, Sioux City	NOC	$13.00	04-12
CCBC	Pikie, jointed	2600, GE, label	NIB	$71.00	99-08
CCBC	Pikie, jointed	2602, GE, RH/w, SLT, lg military stencil on back, pointers on belly	VG+	$24.00	05-05
CCBC	Pikie, jointed	2602, RH/w, SLT, GE, very light age lines, no paint loss	EX-IB	$38.00	05-05
CCBC	Pikie, jointed	2602, stencil, GE	EXIB	$46.00	00-01
CCBC	Pikie, jointed	2602, stencil, GE, crisp box	EXIB	$46.00	00-01
CCBC	Pikie, jointed	2603, GE, silver shiner	VG+	$20.00	05-06
CCBC	Pikie, jointed	2603DD, w, TE	NIB	$21.50	00-01
CCBC	Pikie, jointed	2604, golden shiner, GE, SLT, NSOB, unfinished, in orig EX 2PCCB	EXIB	$47.00	05-05
CCBC	Pikie, jointed	2604, label, golden shiner, GE	NIB	$71.00	03-06
CCBC	Pikie, jointed	2604, TE	NIB	$50.00	00-08
CCBC	Pikie, jointed	2605W, PTCB torn but VG, TE	NIB	$77.00	05-07
CCBC	Pikie, jointed	2606DD, gold scale, TE, PTCB, NOT MET	NIB	$96.00	99-08
CCBC	Pikie, jointed	2608, stencil, GE	EX-IB	$64.00	00-10
CCBC	Pikie, jointed	2608, stencil, RB, GE	NIB	$127.00	00-05
CCBC	Pikie, jointed	2608, rainbow stencil, GE	NIB	$140.49	99-11
CCBC	Pikie, jointed	2612DDW, PTCB, white with black eye shadow, TE	NIB	$205.00	05-07
CCBC	Pikie, jointed	2613, PTCB crisp, TE	NIB	$79.00	05-07
CCBC	Pikie, jointed	2614, TE, PTCB	NIB	$40.00	99-09
CCBC	Pikie, jointed	2618, GE, cat, hangtag, great set	NIB	$78.00	99-07
CCBC	Pikie, jointed	2618DD, GE, nice stencil box	NIB	$78.00	00-07
CCBC	Pikie, jointed	2619, TE	NIB	$49.00	99-01
CCBC	Pikie, jointed	2621, red/blk eye shadow, TE, PTCB	NIB	$305.00	01-08
CCBC	Pikie, jointed	2622, PTCB, GE, still glows	NIB	$256.00	05-02
CCBC	Pikie, jointed	2630, RH/orange w/black spots, GE, SLT, very light wear	EX-	$145.00	05-05
CCBC	Pikie, jointed	2630, RH/orange, blk spot, PGE!	EX-	$46.00	01-08
CCBC	Pikie, jointed	2632, Fireplug, stencil	EXIB	$96.04	99-10
CCBC	Pikie, jointed	2638, pearl, TE, Sioux City	NIB	$151.00	00-09
CCBC	Pikie, jointed	2639, tiger, TE, PTCB	NIB	$200.00	01-08
CCBC	Pikie, jointed	2643, strawberry, TE, PTCB	NIB	$300.00	01-08
CCBC	Pikie, jointed	2644, whitefish, TE, PTCB	NIB	$300.00	01-08
CCBC	Pikie, jointed	2702, label	EX-IB	$43.05	99-05

BRAND	MODEL	SERIES / MFG. CODE / DESCRIPTION	GRADE	PRICE	DATE yy/mm
CCBC	Pikie, jointed	2708, RB, GE, stencil box	NIB	$175.00	99-06
CCBC	Pikie, jointed	2725 Special, GE, white scale, tag & catalog	NIB	$686.00	05-02
CCBC	Pikie, jointed	2730, RH/orange spotted, GE	EX	$323.00	02-01
CCBC	Pikie, jointed	3000PAL, plastic, in photo alewife	EX-IB	$299.00	01-12
CCBC	Pikie, jointed	3000WS, strawberry, fake GE	EX+IB	$128.50	99-05
CCBC	Pikie, jointed	3033, black scale, GE	EX-	$175.00	99-10
CCBC	Pikie, jointed	5502, 2 RH/w, both in stamped boxes	NIB x 2	$218.51	99-04
CCBC	Pikie, jointed	730, GE, red/o/blk spots	EX	$131.39	99-03
CCBC	Pikie, jointed	black scale	EX-	$145.00	01-02
CCBC	Pikie, jointed	blue mullet, GE, 5¼"	EX	$96.00	05-07
CCBC	Pikie, jointed	#2605, dace, TE, PTCB	NIB	$77.00	05-07
CCBC	Pikie, jointed	Fireplug, GE	mint	$123.15	99-11
CCBC	Pikie, jointed	frog, TE	EX	$58.00	99-04
CCBC	Pikie, jointed	GE, golden shiner	VG+	$10.00	05-06
CCBC	Pikie, jointed	gray/red bar code stripe, TE, NOT MET	EX	$162.00	00-07
CCBC	Pikie, jointed	o spotted/RH, GE, SLT	EX	$228.00	99-05
CCBC	Pikie, jointed	TE-DD2600, pearl, tack eyes, NOT MET	EX	$21.39	05-07
CCBC	Pikie, jointed	pikeral with red tail, GE	VG+	$127.00	00-05
CCBC	Pikie, jointed	pikie, DLT, one tie under chin	mint	$81.00	99-09
CCBC	Pikie, jointed	pikie, line tie under chin	NIB	$250.00	99-08
CCBC	Pikie, jointed	plastic, RB trout, photo finish	NIB	$68.09	99-12
CCBC	Pikie, jointed	rainbow	NIB	$81.00	99-04
CCBC	Pikie, jointed	rainbow, GE, back stencil	EXIB	$66.00	03-01
CCBC	Pikie, jointed	RB, silver back	avg	$35.00	00-11
CCBC	Pikie, jointed	2608, RB, stencil, GE	NIB	$100.00	00-10
CCBC	Pikie, jointed	red head, orange spot, GE, stencil box	NIB	$248.00	04-11
CCBC	Pikie, jointed	RH/orange spotted, TE	EX-	$35.00	99-06
CCBC	Pikie, jointed	RH/sparkle, GE	EX	$237.50	99-11
CCBC	Pikie, jointed	2722 Special, GE, RH/white flitter, Day N Night	NIB	$805.00	04-03
CCBC	Pikie, jointed	shiner scale, GE, 3-hk, light age lines and very light wear	VG++	$29.00	05-05
CCBC	Pikie, jointed	shiner scale, TE, few tiny pointers	EX-	$15.00	05-05
CCBC	Pikie, jointed	TE, 3-hk, yellow perch, light wear and wear on eyes	VG	$10.00	05-05
CCBC	Pikie, jointed	tiger stripe, TE	VG	$32.55	99-03
CCBC	Pikie, jointed	tiger, TE, PTCB	NIB	$56.59	99-10
CCBC	Pikie, jointed	2600 Special, white scale, stencil bx GE	NIB	$350.00	03-11
CCBC	Pikie, jointed	yellow perch, GE, age line on nose and a hint of wear	EX	$32.00	05-05
CCBC	Pikie, jointed	yellow spotted, GE, in crisp unmarked? box	NIB	$406.00	05-01
CCBC	Pikie, jointed	2602	VGIB	$16.00	99-01
CCBC	Pikie, jointed	2632	NIB	$154.02	99-11
CCBC	Pikie, jointed DD	2600DD, strawberry spot, TE	EX-	$113.00	99-01
CCBC	Pikie, jointed DD	2607DD, GE, nice	EXIB	$100.00	02-08
CCBC	Pikie, jointed DD	2608DD, rainbow, SOLD	EXIB	$250.00	99-10
CCBC	Pikie, jointed DD	2618DD	NIB	$110.00	99-10
CCBC	Pikie, jointed DD	2618DD, crisp 2PCCB, TE painted? GE	NIB	$28.00	04-03

BRAND	MODEL	SERIES / MFG. CODE / DESCRIPTION	GRADE	PRICE	DATE yy/mm
CCBC	Pikie, jointed DD	2618DD, crisp 2PCCB, stencil, TE (painted glass?)	NIB	$28.00	04-03
CCBC	Pikie, jointed DD	2618DD, GE, crisp box	NIB	$187.00	00-09
CCBC	Pikie, jointed DD	DD703, cat	NIB	$152.50	99-08
CCBC	Pikie, jointed DD	frog, TE	EX	$76.00	00-07
CCBC	Pikie, jointed DD	golden shiner, GE	EX-	$22.55	99-01
CCBC	Pikie, jointed DD	pearl, GE	EX	$355.00	99-05
CCBC	Pikie, jointed DD	RH, GE, crisp box	NIB	$65.00	99-09
CCBC	Pikie, jointed DD	silver flash, TE, PTCB	NIB	$18.00	01-03
CCBC	Pikie, jointed DD	yellow flash, GE	VG	$50.00	99-03
CCBC	Pikie, jointed DD	yellow spotted, TE	EX	$39.25	99-02
CCBC	Pikie, Midget	2218, silver flash, GE, large military stencil on back, light wear and age lines	VG	$19.00	05-05
CCBC	Pikie, Midget	2200, pikie, GE, in label box (VG++)	VG+IB	$40.00	05-06
CCBC	Pikie, Midget	2201 intro, rare slant head, tiny body & GPE, DLT, chip at lip and tail	VG	$65.00	05-05
CCBC	Pikie, Midget	2202 intro, RH/w, GE, DLT, few age cracks and tiny flake on belly, earlier thin body	VG	$24.00	05-05
CCBC	Pikie, Midget	2204, midget pikie, GE, golden shiner	VG+	$85.00	05-06
CCBC	Pikie, Midget	2207, mullet, GE, NOT MET	EX	$169.00	05-07
CCBC	Pikie, Midget	2213 intro, black, GE, SLT, just a few tiny pointers at tail o/w	EX-	$42.00	05-05
CCBC	Pikie, Midget	2213, stamp, GE, back stencil	NIB	$76.00	00-11
CCBC	Pikie, Midget	2222, luminous, RH/white flitter, GE, glows!	mint	$321.00	05-02
CCBC	Pikie, Midget	GE, red & white, wide lip style	EX+	$30.00	05-06
CCBC	Pikie, Midget	pikie scale, GE, A-lip, just a hint of wear on this one	EX	$30.00	05-05
CCBC	Pikie, Midget	w/tough B-lip like anteater, GE, pike scale, 1 age line on belly	EX+	$35.00	05-05
CCBC	Pikie, Midget jntd	4214 Special, stencil bx, GE, y spotted	NIB	$331.00	03-04
CCBC	Pikie, Midget jntd	RB	NIB	$112.72	00-02
CCBC	Pikie, Midget jntd	RB, blue back	EX+	$202.50	00-01
CCBC	Pikie, Peter's Special	2605WSS, metal tail, jointed dace	EXIB	$247.38	99-03
CCBC	Pikie, Peter's Special	golden shiner, GE	EX	$112.50	00-04
CCBC	Pikie, Peter's Special	silver scale/red, metal tail, jointed	EX	$511.33	99-03
CCBC	Pikie, Pikeral	gold head flitter/red, GE	EX-	$146.00	00-11
CCBC	Pikie, Pikeral	silver/red tail, GE	G	$32.80	00-03
CCBC	Pikie, Pikeral jntd	silver glitter/red, GE, 2600R	NIB	$361.00	99-06
CCBC	Pikie, Snook	18, side screw, NRA box	NIB	$430.00	00-01
CCBC	Pikie, Snook	3001, papers, GE	NIB	$52.00	00-10
CCBC	Pikie, Snook	3400, GE	NIB	$40.00	01-02
CCBC	Pikie, Snook	3400, pike, early thin body and unimp lip, light pointers and light age lines, early snook	VG+	$50.00	05-05
CCBC	Pikie, Snook	3400, pike scale, rare factory prototype, heavy duty hdwr, rig looks like EXAG	VG	$260.00	05-05
CCBC	Pikie, Snook	3401, GE, perch, strap hdwr	VG+	$15.00	05-06
CCBC	Pikie, Snook	3401, label, GE	NIB	$202.00	00-10
CCBC	Pikie, Snook	3402, mint box	NIB	$213.50	99-07
CCBC	Pikie, Snook	3403, new silver shiner, TE, wire through, few light pointers	EX-	$42.00	05-05
CCBC	Pikie, Snook	3403 Special, silver shiner	EXIB	$78.11	99-02

BRAND	MODEL	SERIES / MFG. CODE / DESCRIPTION	GRADE	PRICE	DATE yy/mm
CCBC	Pikie, Snook	3404, box poor	EXIB	$125.00	99-10
CCBC	Pikie, Snook	3408, rainbow, GE, lg military stencil OB, 1 nick at tail & few tiny pointers on nose	EX-	$110.00	05-05
CCBC	Pikie, Snook	3408, rainbow, GE	NIB	$270.59	99-06
CCBC	Pikie, Snook	3421, Day N Nite, with white bucktail, special order, 2 small nicks on head	EX	$185.00	05-05
CCBC	Pikie, Snook	5¼", GE, strawberry	NIB	$722.00	02-11
CCBC	Pikie, Snook	5503 Special	NIB	$460.00	00-03
CCBC	Pikie, Snook	5508, GE, label	EX-IB	$105.00	01-02
CCBC	Pikie, Snook	5508, box for jntd, rainbow	EX-	$200.00	99-10
CCBC	Pikie, Snook	b/w, GE	VG+	$297.50	99-01
CCBC	Pikie, Snook	blue flash	NIB	$192.50	05-07
CCBC	Pikie, Snook	blue flash, GE	VG	$25.00	01-09
CCBC	Pikie, Snook	blue mullet, box #? GE	NIB	$242.50	00-01
CCBC	Pikie, Snook	mullet, GE, un box, NOT MET	EX	$102.00	02-01
CCBC	Pikie, Snook	nat mullet, GE, label	NIB	$336.00	00-03
CCBC	Pikie, Snook	purple eel	EX+	$476.44	00-02
CCBC	Pikie, Snook	r/w, GE, label box	NIB	$85.00	99-06
CCBC	Pikie, Snook	rainbow, TE, NOT MET	mint	$59.00	01-12
CCBC	Pikie, Snook	silver flash, GE	mint	$55.00	01-02
CCBC	Pikie, Snook	special hardware, NRA box	NIB	$440.00	03-01
CCBC	Pikie, Snook	3400	EXIB	$150.00	99-10
CCBC	Pikie, Snook jntd	5502, GE	NIB	$51.69	99-05
CCBC	Pikie, Snook jntd	5507, GE	NIB	$198.00	99-08
CCBC	Pikie, Snook jntd	5507 Special, metal tail	NIB	$539.00	99-05
CCBC	Pikie, Snook jntd	5518, GE, silver flash in label box (VG++)	EX+IB	$65.00	05-06
CCBC	Pikie, Snook jntd	5518, GE, label box VG	EX-IB	$22.00	05-03
CCBC	Pikie, Snook jntd	5531, RB Fire, cat, GE	EXIB	$125.00	99-06
CCBC	Pikie, Snook jntd	6818, SOLD	EX	$1,225.00	99-10
CCBC	Pikie, Snook jntd	pearl, TE, back stencil in gold, lt hk drag	EX-	$204.00	01-10
CCBC	Pikie, Snook jntd	RH/gold (repaint?), NOT MET	VG+	$73.00	00-04
CCBC	Pikie, Snook jntd	3400	EXIB	$46.10	99-04
CCBC	Pikie, Snook jntd	5501, perch, GE, NSOB, few light age lines, in EX+ label-end 2PCCB	EXIB	$85.00	05-05
CCBC	Pikie, Snook jntd	5502 RH/w, TE, NSOB, age lines and small flake on belly, RE, unfished in orig 2PPTB	VGIB	$28.00	05-05
CCBC	Pikie, Snook jntd	5503, silver shiner, GE, chip on nose and large flake under tail, few tiny pointers	VG	$44.00	05-05
CCBC	Pikie, Snook jntd	5513, black, TE, gold lable on back	EX	$50.00	05-05
CCBC	Pikie, spinning jntd	frog color, plastic bait	EX	$18.00	05-06
CCBC	Pikie, spinning jntd	PE, pikie, wood bait, 2½"	EX-	$12.00	05-06
CCBC	Pikie, Striper	6802, TE	NIB	$32.00	99-06
CCBC	Pikie, Striper	6900, lg white box crisp, GE, cat	NIB	$238.00	00-11
CCBC	Pikie, Striper	6900 Special, TE, PTCB, pearly blue/blk tiger stripes	NIB	$647.00	05-07
CCBC	Pikie, Striper	6907, mullet, label box	VG+IB	$113.50	99-04
CCBC	Pikie, Striper	6918, TE, PTCB	NIB	$51.00	00-10
CCBC	Pikie, Striper	6919, silver flash, SOLD	EX-	$125.00	99-10
CCBC	Pikie, Striper	6919W, frog, TE	NIB	$178.00	03-01

BRAND	MODEL	SERIES / MFG. CODE / DESCRIPTION	GRADE	PRICE	DATE yy/mm
CCBC	Pikie, Striper	6931, Fireplug, tag	NIB	$188.49	99-10
CCBC	Pikie, Striper	mullet, GE, hooks rusty but paint nice	EX-	$62.00	04-02
CCBC	Pikie, Striper	Rainbow Fire	NIB	$600.00	00-05
CCBC	Pikie, Striper	Rainbow Fire, tack eyes, fuzzy pictures	mint	$320.00	04-02
CCBC	Pikie, Striper	Rainbow Fire, GE, un box, NOT MET!	mint	$886.00	00-03
CCBC	Pikie, Striper	silver flash, GE	NIB	$243.00	01-09
CCBC	Pikie, Striper	TE, PTCB, no top	NIB	$43.00	98-12
CCBC	Pikie, Striper jntd	3033, black scale, TE, PTCB	NIB	$132.00	00-10
CCBC	Pikie, Striper jntd	5502, GE	NIB	$137.50	00-03
CCBC	Pikie, Striper jntd	6800, GE, NOT MET	mint	$280.00	01-01
CCBC	Pikie, Striper jntd	6807, GE, blue mullet, label box VG+	EX-IN	$165.00	05-06
CCBC	Pikie, Striper jntd	6807, label, GE	NIB	$415.00	01-12
CCBC	Pikie, Striper jntd	6818, stencil box, GE	NIB	$156.00	05-07
CCBC	Pikie, Striper jntd	6818, silver flash, GE	EXIB	$52.07	99-04
CCBC	Pikie, Striper jntd	6824W, shrimp color, TE, PTCB	NIB	$455.00	05-07
CCBC	Pikie, Striper jntd	6831, GE, Rainbow Fire, stamped on back, in box E-	EX-IB	$225.00	05-06
CCBC	Pikie, Striper jntd	6833, TE	NIB	$76.00	00-10
CCBC	Pikie, Striper jntd	6839, GE, blue flash, 2PCCB, papers	NIB	$125.00	98-12
CCBC	Pikie, Striper jntd	blue flash	EX	$210.00	99-10
CCBC	Pikie, Striper jntd	Fireplug, GE	VG	$125.55	99-08
CCBC	Pikie, Striper jntd	6819, frog, PTCB, TE, joint chip	EX-IB	$100.00	02-09
CCBC	Pikie, Striper jntd	frog, TE	VG	$76.00	99-06
CCBC	Pikie, Striper jntd	6819W, frog, TE, PTCB	EXIB	$103.50	99-02
CCBC	Pikie, Striper jntd	6835, purple eel, stencil box, GE	EX-IB	$178.00	05-07
CCBC	Pikie, Striper jntd	RB, blue back, GE	NIB	$433.00	00-05
CCBC	Pikie, Striper jntd	RB, GE	EX+	$100.00	99-06
CCBC	Pikie, Tarpon	4002, single hooks, label box	EX-IB	$730.00	05-02
CCBC	Pikie, Tarpon	4002, single hooks, GE, box VG+, SOLD	EX-IB	$600.00	99-10
CCBC	Pikie, Tarpon	4002, trebles, hooks rusty	NIB	$305.00	99-05
CCBC	Pikie, Tarpon	4018, treble hooks, label box	NIB	$1,700.00	99-05
CCBC	Pikie, Tarpon	7002, 2 single hooks	EXIB	$797.43	99-04
CCBC	Pikie, Tarpon	mullet, treble hooks	EX-	$1,136.00	05-02
CCBC	Pikie, Tarpon	RH, GE, 2 treble hooks	VG+	$410.00	05-07
CCBC	Pikie, Tarpon	RH, GE, 2 trebles, reenforcing screws	EX-	$937.00	05-07
CCBC	Pikie, Tarpon	single hooks, GE, r/w	EX-	$421.00	99-08
CCBC	Pikie, Tarpon	single hooks, mullet	EX-	$579.00	99-09
CCBC	Plunker	3131, stencil, couple pointers	EXIB	$151.00	02-03
CCBC	Plunker	3200, pike scale, early humpback style, GE, few nicks and pointers	VG	$38.00	05-05
CCBC	Plunker	3201, label	NIB	$77.50	00-01
CCBC	Plunker	3202, early humpback, RH/w, GE, light age lines and few tiny pointers	EX-	$40.00	05-05
CCBC	Plunker	3202, label, GE	EXIB	$45.00	04-03
CCBC	Plunker	3204, label	NIB	$100.00	02-02
CCBC	Plunker	3204, label, lip chip	EX-IB	$41.00	02-03
CCBC	Plunker	3204, PTCB, TE	NIB	$36.55	99-01
CCBC	Plunker	3204, stencil, golden shiner, GE	NIB	$117.00	01-08

BRAND	MODEL	SERIES / MFG. CODE / DESCRIPTION	GRADE	PRICE	DATE yy/mm
CCBC	Plunker	3206, end label, goldfish	EXIB	$800.00	03-05
CCBC	Plunker	3208, stencil bx EX, blue back, rainbow, GE, p cat	NIB	$129.00	05-07
CCBC	Plunker	3213, stencil box, GE	NIB	$62.00	02-03
CCBC	Plunker	3213, stencil, GE	NIB	$77.00	99-11
CCBC	Plunker	3213, GE, stencil	EXIB	$66.52	99-10
CCBC	Plunker	3213, GE, stencil	NIB	$112.50	99-10
CCBC	Plunker	3214, stencil, y/r & blk spots, GE	EXIB	$266.99	99-10
CCBC	Plunker	3218, label, GE	NIB	$45.00	00-09
CCBC	Plunker	3219, frog, GE, a few light age lines, 1 pointer on lip and 1 pointer on RS	EX-	$24.00	05-05
CCBC	Plunker	3224, red wing, label box EX-, NOT MET	EXIB	$126.00	04-11
CCBC	Plunker	3238, pearl, GE, brass cups, few tiny pointers on chin, WWII, hazy eyes	EX	$225.00	05-05
CCBC	Plunker	black, 3213 box	VGIB	$34.00	99-01
CCBC	Plunker	black, GE, nice box	NIB	$131.99	99-12
CCBC	Plunker	black scale, TE, PTCB, NOT MET	NIB	$86.00	00-10
CCBC	Plunker	Fire? GE	EX	$134.09	99-05
CCBC	Plunker	frog, GE	mint	$135.00	99-09
CCBC	Plunker	GE, black	EX-	$48.00	98-12
CCBC	Plunker	golden shiner, GE	EX-	$50.00	02-08
CCBC	Plunker	Henry Dills, letter fron Heizerling, NOT MET	VG	$810.00	99-04
CCBC	Plunker	no-scale perch, GE, special order	EX	$205.38	99-04
CCBC	Plunker	pearl, GE	VG+	$104.00	01-05
CCBC	Plunker	perch, GE	EX	$21.00	02-08
CCBC	Plunker	pikie, GE	EX-	$21.00	02-08
CCBC	Plunker	pikie, GE, label	NIB	$55.00	00-08
CCBC	Plunker	plastic, black shore	EX	$66.00	05-03
CCBC	Plunker	plastic, coach dog	EX	$51.00	05-03
CCBC	Plunker	plastic, shad, 9209 Special box	NIB	$51.00	05-03
CCBC	Plunker	r/w	EX+	$49.99	98-12
CCBC	Plunker	Rainbow Fire, GE, decent	VG+	$154.00	01-10
CCBC	Plunker	rainbow, TE	EX	$51.35	99-01
CCBC	Plunker	RB, GE	EX	$175.00	00-07
CCBC	Plunker	redwing blackbird	VG+	$66.00	04-11
CCBC	Plunker	redwing blackbird, GE	avg+	$154.48	99-07
CCBC	Plunker	redwing blackbird, 2 cracked eyes	VG+	$61.00	02-08
CCBC	Plunker	RH, GE, crisp box and cat	NIB	$115.00	01-03
CCBC	Plunker	WH/black, GE	EX-	$229.00	00-04
CCBC	Plunker	white scale	VG-	$39.00	99-01
CCBC	Plunker	white scale, stencil	NIB	$331.66	99-12
CCBC	Plunker	y spotted, decal	mint	$41.00	00-11
CCBC	Plunker	y/blk spots, TE	EX	$25.00	00-02
CCBC	Plunker	yellow spoted, GE	EX	$168.30	99-02
CCBC	Plunker	yellow/short black ribs, TE	EX-	$154.00	05-01
CCBC	Plunker	1500, GE, PTCB, sm chip	EXIB	$71.00	99-05
CCBC	Plunker Bass Bug	1000, on card in box	NIB	$184.00	04-03
CCBC	Plunker, Baby	redwing blackbird	EX	$161.00	04-03

BRAND	MODEL	SERIES / MFG. CODE / DESCRIPTION	GRADE	PRICE	DATE yy/mm
CCBC	Plunker, Baby	redwing blackbird	VG	$87.00	04-11
CCBC	Plunker, Husky	5800, lip chip, rest nice	?	$129.00	99-06
CCBC	Plunker, Husky	5801, label, GE	NIB	$332.00	01-03
CCBC	Plunker, Husky	5807, mullet scale, GE, wire through, deep blue scales, few pointers	VG	$95.00	05-05
CCBC	Plunker, Husky	5831, stencil box	EXIB	$1,022.00	04-03
CCBC	Plunker, Husky	golden shiner, NOT MET	EX-	$154.00	01-10
CCBC	Plunker, Husky	perch, GE, NOT MET	EXIB	$158.00	99-06
CCBC	Plunker, Husky	pikie, GE	EX	$129.00	99-06
CCBC	Plunker, Husky	RB, GE, NOT MET	EX	$405.00	00-03
CCBC	Plunker, Husky	RH, GE	VG+	$78.00	00-04
CCBC	Plunker, Husky	silver mullet, GE	EX+	$338.33	99-05
CCBC	Plunker, Midget	5900, pike, GE, few age lines, 1 blem on tail and 1 nick on chin	VG+	$15.00	05-05
CCBC	Plunker, Midget	5913, black, GE, large stenciled "PLUNKER" on back, chips in mouth and tail	VG-	$18.00	05-05
CCBC	Plunker, Snook	7102, GE	NIB	$380.00	00-09
CCBC	Plunker, Snook	7107, PE, PTCB	NIB	$169.16	99-09
CCBC	Plunker, Snook	7134, BT, GE	NIB	$182.00	00-09
CCBC	Plunker, Snook	7134B blue flash/bucktail, GE, NOT MET	NIB	$262.00	01-04
CCBC	Plunker, Snook	b/w, GE	avg	$67.00	00-04
CCBC	Plunker, Spinning	plastic, golden shiner?	EX	$25.75	99-06
CCBC	Polly Wiggle	1700, BBE, meadow frog, light wear, original weed guard	VG++	$295.00	05-05
CCBC	Polly Wiggle	brown pollywog	VG	$102.00	00-09
CCBC	Polly Wiggle	pollywog	VG+	$71.00	99-09
CCBC	Polly Wiggle	red head/white/flitter, weed guard intact, NOT MET	EX	$75.00	05-07
CCBC	Poly Wiggle	r/w	EX	$311.58	99-11
CCBC	Pop N Dunk	6301, perch, GE, 1 tiny pointer and paint bubble in mouth, w/orig 2PCCB and hangtag	EX+IB	$125.00	05-05
CCBC	Pop N Dunk	BH/red body, NOT MET	EX-	$202.00	00-04
CCBC	Pop N Dunk	black head/red, GE	EX-	$400.00	99-03
CCBC	Pop N Dunk	dace	avg	$26.50	00-01
CCBC	Pop N Dunk	GE, frog	EX+	$95.00	05-06
CCBC	Pop N Dunk	GE, perch	EX+	$85.00	05-06
CCBC	Pop N Dunk	GE, red & white in 2PCCB box (VG++), marked	EXIB	$100.00	05-06
CCBC	Pop N Dunk	GE, red side	VG+	$85.00	05-06
CCBC	Pop N Dunk	golden shiner, mouth rough, rest OK	avg	$86.00	03-07
CCBC	Pop N Dunk	perch	VG	$42.41	99-01
CCBC	Pop N Dunk	perch scale, GE	mint	$53.00	05-07
CCBC	Pop N Dunk	perch, TE, NOT MET	EX	$41.00	99-06
CCBC	Pop N Dunk	pikie finish, GE	EX+	$53.00	05-07
CCBC	Pop N Dunk	r/w, GE, label	NIB	$175.00	99-09
CCBC	Pop N Dunk	redwing blackbird	VG+	$40.00	04-11
CCBC	Pop N Dunk	redwing blackbird, GE	VG+	$104.00	00-09
CCBC	Pop N Dunk	redwing blackbird, GE, lg rub on belly, rest nice	?	$61.00	05-07
CCBC	Pop N Dunk	redwing blackbird, unmarked box	EXIB	$159.00	04-04
CCBC	Pop N Dunk	red/black	EX-	$623.00	99-04

BRAND	MODEL	SERIES / MFG. CODE / DESCRIPTION	GRADE	PRICE	DATE yy/mm
CCBC	Pop N Dunk	redwing blackbird	EX	$110.00	05-07
CCBC	Pop N Dunk	redwing blackbird	EX-	$112.50	99-09
CCBC	Pop N Dunk	RWB, GE	EX+	$306.00	01-08
CCBC	Pop N Dunk	RWB, small chips inside, rest nice	EX-	$69.00	00-04
CCBC	Pop N Dunk	silver flash, pikie, GE	EX-	$76.00	00-06
CCBC	Pop N Dunk	white scale	EX-	$302.00	00-04
CCBC	Pop N Dunk	white scale	EX	$202.00	00-11
CCBC	Pop N Dunk	white scale, big tail chip	VG	$62.00	00-12
CCBC	Pop-It	101, yellow, on ugly card	NOC	$287.00	99-06
CCBC	Pop-It	RH, on card in box unmarked	NIB	$88.00	04-03
CCBC	Pop-It		VG-	$38.50	99-01
CCBC	Popper	r/w, PE, name on back	EX-	$159.50	99-06
CCBC	Popper	yellow, PE, long saltwater lure	VG-	$36.50	99-07
CCBC	River Rustler	3702, stencil, GE	EXIB	$316.00	00-09
CCBC	River Rustler	3700 intro, tag, cat, nice box	NIB	$178.00	00-11
CCBC	River Rustler	no lip surface type, dark shiner? scale	VG+	$136.00	04-12
CCBC	River Rustler	perch, GE	EX	$162.50	99-09
CCBC	River Rustler	RH, GE, big nose chip	avg	$27.50	00-01
CCBC	River Rustler	silver flash, GE, belly chips	VG	$45.00	05-03
CCBC	River Scamp	4301, perch, GE, few light age lines on belly	EX	$65.00	05-05
CCBC	River Scamp	4304, golden shiner, GE, SLT, varn flakes on belly and some light general wear	VG-	$32.00	05-05
CCBC	River Scamp	4305, label, TE?	NIB	$227.50	99-08
CCBC	River Scamp	4318, label box, GE	NIB	$192.00	01-11
CCBC	River Scamp	chub finish, GE	mint	$52.00	05-03
CCBC	River Scamp	chub, GE	mint	$52.00	05-02
CCBC	River Scamp	dace, GE	EX	$135.00	00-09
CCBC	River Scamp	dace, GE	EX	$57.99	99-05
CCBC	River Scamp	golden shiner, uncataloged, GE	EX	$293.88	00-03
CCBC	River Scamp	red side	EX+	$123.61	99-10
CCBC	River Scamp	red sides	VG+	$47.00	01-04
CCBC	Sail Shark	RH, Lazy Ike type but on Creek Chub card	NOC	$31.00	03-07
CCBC	Sail Shark x 2	2 different, on bubble pack cards	NOC	$26.00	01-05
CCBC	Salt Spin Darter	7702, r/w, PE, stencil box, name on back	EX-IB	$238.51	99-06
CCBC	Sarasota	pikie	avg	$67.00	99-04
CCBC	Sarasota	pikie	VG-	$120.50	99-10
CCBC	Sarasota	pikie	VG-	$150.00	00-05
CCBC	Sarasota	pikie scale, 3300 stencil box VG	EX-IB	$255.00	05-02
CCBC	Sarasota	side hooker, silver flash, GE	EX	$730.00	99-11
CCBC	Sarasota	side hooks, silver flash, GE, nice except belly	VG+	$328.00	02-10
CCBC	Sarasota	silver flash, GE, unmarked box	NIB	$400.00	99-02
CCBC	Sarasota	silver flash	EX	$462.00	05-02
CCBC	Sarasota	silver flash, 3-hk, side hooker, GE	EX-	$424.00	05-07
CCBC	Sarasota	white/red chin	avg	$41.00	00-02
CCBC	Sarasota Special	2 side hooks, NOT MET, silver flash GE	VG-	$191.39	99-06
CCBC	Silver Shiner	103, GE, SLT, hint of wear, factory blem on nose & tiny chip under lip	EX	$280.00	05-05
CCBC	Silversides	1703, PTCG, mint & papers	NIB	$130.00	05-07

BRAND	MODEL	SERIES / MFG. CODE / DESCRIPTION	GRADE	PRICE	DATE yy/mm
CCBC	Silversides	perch, PE, like Devil Horse	EX	$125.00	99-11
CCBC	Silversides	silver flash, PE, like Devil Horse	EX	$125.00	99-11
CCBC	Skipper	4600, pikie scale, GE, light age lines, wear on lip and edge indent in back	VG+	$62.00	05-05
CCBC	Skipper	BWH, GE	EX	$155.00	03-07
CCBC	Skipper	strawberry, big hook, drag belly	VG+	$334.00	00-10
CCBC	Slant Dip	111 intro, white head/black, slant head & NE, DLT, rubs in black	G+	$78.00	05-05
CCBC	Snark	frog	mint	$24.00	03-04
CCBC	Snark Eel	frog	mint	$34.00	03-04
CCBC	Snark Eel	red head/white	mint	$27.00	03-04
CCBC	Snook Plunker	GE, buck tail, treble, purple eel pattern	EX	$192.50	05-04
CCBC	Spin Darter	blue flash, 5¾", PE, stencil on back	EX	$229.00	01-10
CCBC	Spinning Darter	9019 P, frog, plastic, NSOS	EX	$12.00	05-05
CCBC	Spinning Darter	902, blended RH/w, DLT, GE, age lines and light wear, in orig EX 2PCCB	VG+IB	$95.00	05-05
CCBC	Spinning Darter	914, yellow spotted, light general wear with few chips and age lines	G+	$68.00	05-05
CCBC	Spinning Inj Minnow	9501, perch, GPE, wood, earlier larger body, hk drag on nose	VG+IB	$18.00	05-05
CCBC	Spinning Jntd Pikie	9401, perch, GPE, earliest version from the jntd midget pikie (4200 series) body	VG+	$19.00	05-05
CCBC	Spinning Jntd Pikie	9418, silver flash, plastic, NSOB, new in orig 2PSTB w/catalog	NIB	$15.00	05-05
CCBC	Spinning Pikie	9318, wood, silver flash, GPE, just a hint of wear	EX	$15.00	05-05
CCBC	Spinning Pikie	9330, RH/orange w/black spots, wood, GPE, brand new in orig 2PPTB, but # faded	NIB	$100.00	05-05
CCBC	Spoon Tail	500, RH, PE, ugly lure	EX	$202.00	00-08
CCBC	Spoon Tail	g/w, silver flakes	NIB	$67.00	99-06
CCBC	Spoontail	silver flash	EX	$87.00	00-10
CCBC	Spoontail	silver flash	EX	$27.00	04-09
CCBC	Striper Strike	1916 P, 5", banana, white, in orig 2PCCB (# faint)	EX-IB	$80.00	05-05
CCBC	Striper Strike	1934 P, 5", blue flash, white, stained	EX	$25.00	05-05
CCBC	Striper Strike	1940 P, 5", chrome, white, some paint flkd off red mouth	EX	$28.00	05-05
CCBC	Striper Strike	2138 P, 4", pearl, big pink and yellow spots, full white bucktail	EX+	$33.00	05-05
CCBC	Striper Strike	2220 P, 4", mackeral, white BT, very light wear and hks rusty	EX-	$30.00	05-05
CCBC	Striper Strike	2403 P, 2½", new silver shiner, white BT, tie loss, very light wear	EX-	$27.00	05-05
CCBC	Striper Strike	2420 P, 2½", mackeral, white BT, very light wear and hks rusty	VG+	$24.00	05-05
CCBC	Striper Strike	2501 P, 3", perch, full white bucktail, special order color	NM	$40.00	05-05
CCBC	Striper Strike	2516 P, 3", banana, full white bucktail, small nick on lip edge	EX	$25.00	05-05
CCBC	Striper Strike	2100AM, amber	NIB	$16.00	04-02
CCBC	Sucker	3900B, black	EXIB	$750.00	99-04
CCBC	Sucker	black	poor	$46.00	01-09

BRAND	MODEL	SERIES / MFG. CODE / DESCRIPTION	GRADE	PRICE	DATE yy/mm
CCBC	Sucker	nice	EX	$775.00	02-09
CCBC	Sucker	NOT MET	EX-	$520.00	00-02
CCBC	Sucker	yellow	VG	$460.00	04-03
CCBC	Sucker	yellow	EX-	$510.00	00-07
CCBC	Sucker	yellow sucker, GE	EX	$1,525.00	00-01
CCBC	Sucker	yellow sucker, label	NIB	$1,607.00	00-02
CCBC	Super 6 Assortment	lures VG, box lid reattached VG-	VG-	$1,700.00	01-03
CCBC	Surf Darter	silver flash, in wrong 7635 box	EX-IB	$188.00	05-07
CCBC	Surf Popper	silver flash, PE	EX	$180.27	99-08
CCBC	Surf Popper	yellow flash, with 2PCCB VG	EXIB	$154.00	05-07
CCBC	Surfster	2322 Special, RH, nite & day glitter, stencil bx	NIB	$1,200.00	04-03
CCBC	Surfster	6", RH/w, GE	EX	$163.50	99-04
CCBC	Surfster	7200, blue flash, GE	EX+	$131.00	01-05
CCBC	Surfster	7200, PTCB	NIB	$219.50	99-09
CCBC	Surfster	7207 Special, mullet, GE	NIB	$405.00	99-06
CCBC	Surfster	7218, red eye shadow, GE, NOT MET	EX	$102.00	01-11
CCBC	Surfster	7218 W P, TE	NIB	$67.66	00-02
CCBC	Surfster	7218R	NIB	$160.50	99-01
CCBC	Surfster	7218R, special red around GE	NIB	$200.00	99-07
CCBC	Surfster	7234R, PTCB, GE	NIB	$177.00	01-01
CCBC	Surfster	7318, PTCB	NIB	$449.00	02-02
CCBC	Surfster	7400, purple eel, GE	VG	$127.50	99-04
CCBC	Surfster	7434, GE, blue flash, in stamped box VG++	EXIB	$135.00	05-06
CCBC	Surfster	7434, 2PCCB, hook rust	EXIB	$153.61	99-01
CCBC	Surfster	7434, blue flash, GE, rust	EXIB	$155.50	99-04
CCBC	Surfster	blue flash	EX	$59.21	99-01
CCBC	Surfster	blue flash	EX	$200.00	99-10
CCBC	Surfster	lg size, purple eel, GE	VG	$90.00	99-05
CCBC	Surfster	pearl, TE	VG+	$57.00	02-08
CCBC	Surfster	purple eel	G	$18.00	99-01
CCBC	Surfster	RH, 4¼", TE	EX	$180.00	00-03
CCBC	Surfster	silver flash, red chin & eye shadow, GE, 7¼", un box	EXIB	$64.00	05-07
CCBC	Surfster 7¼"	perch, GE, oversize box	VGIB	$202.50	99-11
CCBC	Surfster 7200	blue flash, TE	EX	$51.57	99-04
CCBC	Tiny Tim	6102W, PTCB, very modern	NIB	$108.00	00-04
CCBC	Tiny Tim	6401, label box	NIB	$102.50	99-08
CCBC	Tiny Tim	6401, perch scale, PE, label box	EXIB	$96.00	99-09
CCBC	Tiny Tim	6402, perch scale, PE, label box	NIB	$158.05	99-09
CCBC	Tiny Tim	6425, label, white scale	NIB	$255.00	00-03
CCBC	Tiny Tim	6425, stencil, white scale PE, color p cat	NIB	$472.00	01-08
CCBC	Tiny Tim	6426, white/redwings	EX-	$87.00	05-01
CCBC	Tiny Tim	7425, label, NOT MET	NIB	$218.00	00-10
CCBC	Tiny Tim	flourescent red, NOT MET	NIB	$112.00	00-07
CCBC	Tiny Tim	frog, 6419 stencil box, BW a mite rough	EXIB	$538.00	05-07
CCBC	Tiny Tim	label 6427, spotted	NIB	$354.02	99-04
CCBC	Tiny Tim	perch, one chip	EX	$41.00	99-09
CCBC	Tiny Tim	pikie	EX	$54.99	00-01

BRAND	MODEL	SERIES / MFG. CODE / DESCRIPTION	GRADE	PRICE	DATE yy/mm
CCBC	Tiny Tim	r/w, early	EX-	$90.99	99-02
CCBC	Tiny Tim	red head	NIB	$202.50	99-09
CCBC	Tiny Tim	redwing blackbird	VG-	$42.00	01-03
CCBC	Tiny Tim	redwing blackbird, 2 sm rough spots	VG-	$58.00	02-08
CCBC	Tiny Tim	RWB, PE, back stencil	avg	$88.75	00-01
CCBC	Tiny Tim	spotted, NOT MET	EX	$229.00	00-08
CCBC	Tiny Tim	white scale	EX-	$90.00	04-02
CCBC	Tiny Tim	white scale	EX-	$158.50	00-01
CCBC	Tiny Tim	white scale, un box, NOT MET	mint	$181.50	99-08
CCBC	Tiny Tim	white scale	VG+	$63.50	99-01
CCBC	Tiny Tim	white scale, gold stencil	VG+	$143.00	00-05
CCBC	Tiny Tim	yellow/2 blk dots	EX-	$71.00	99-02
CCBC	Tiny Tim	6400	NIB	$118.00	00-10
CCBC	Tiny Tim x 2	pikie, perch, 1 in correct label box	NIB/EX+	$210.00	99-06
CCBC	Tiny Tim x 5	6400 x 2, 6401, 6402, 6425	NIB	$712.00	00-08
CCBC	Top N Pop	silver flash, plastic	EX	$53.00	01-10
CCBC	Top Wiggle	yellow plastic, 2PCCB	NIB	$35.00	99-05
CCBC	Torpedo	139 PYB, Up Bass, mint	NIB	$700.00	99-02
CCBC	Trout Minnow Fly Rod	T01, NRA stamped, fly rod box VG	EXIB	$722.00	05-02
CCBC	Underwater Minnow	3-hk, TE, RH/w, blk eye shadow, age lines and flaking on eye edges	VG	$110.00	05-05
CCBC	Unfinished x 22	all different paint sticks, some Shur Strike	mint	$212.50	00-02
CCBC	Wag Tail	802, stencil, GE	EX-IB	$93.00	00-10
CCBC	Wag Tail	flat tail, pikie, GE	VG-	$41.50	99-01
CCBC	Wag Tail	frog, GE, belly wear	VG-	$282.00	99-02
CCBC	Wag Tail	goldfish, GE	EX+	$611.00	01-08
CCBC	Wag Tail	perch early, fluted	VG	$68.00	00-05
CCBC	Wag Tail Chub	nat chub, plain tail	EX-IB	$222.22	00-03
CCBC	Wag Tail Chub	805, early red side, GE, DLT, fluted tail, 2 small flakes and age lines	VG	$77.00	05-05
CCBC	Wag Tail Chub	901, GE, perch, SLT, 1 tiny pointer and 2 faint age lines, few pointers on nose	EX+IB	$15.00	05-05
CCBC	Wag Tail Chub	901, GE, perch, SLT, 1 tiny pointer and 2 faint age lines, o/w, new in orig 2PPTB with color catalog	EX+IB	$39.00	05-05
CCBC	Wag Tail Chub	gold flash	EX-	$266.00	99-05
CCBC	Wag Tail Chub	golden shiner	EX	$122.50	99-01
CCBC	Wag Tail Chub	804, golden shiner, plain tail	EXIB	$115.00	04-03
CCBC	Wag Tail Deluxe	RH	EX+	$135.00	99-10
CCBC	Wag Tail Deluxe	806, ugly golden shiner		$52.00	99-02
CCBC	Wag Tail Deluxe	goldfish scale, GE	mint	$549.00	99-05
CCBC	Wee Dee	4800, bug finish, NOT MET	NIB	$1,115.00	99-10
CCBC	Wee Dee	bug finish	EX-	$610.00	00-08
CCBC	Wee Dee	bug finish	EX	$615.00	99-11
CCBC	Wee Dee	bug finish	EX	$637.33	99-03
CCBC	Wee Dee	bug finish, ship under 1 eye nice	EX-?	$455.00	02-09
CCBC	Wee Dee	frog	G??	$300.00	99-08
CCBC	Wee Dee	frog	EX	$405.00	99-06
CCBC	Wee Dee	frog	EX-	$415.02	99-09
CCBC	Wee Dee	frog spot	VG+	$394.00	99-11

BRAND	MODEL	SERIES / MFG. CODE / DESCRIPTION	GRADE	PRICE	DATE yy/mm
CCBC	Wee Dee	frog, GE	EX+	$746.00	01-08
CCBC	Wee Dee	frog, GE, NOT MET	VG+	$306.00	01-06
CCBC	Wee Dee	frog, un box	EXIB	$500.00	00-10
CCBC	Wee Dee	frog, GE, nice	EX	$536.99	99-04
CCBC	Wee Dee	r/w, SOLD	EX-	$975.00	99-10
CCBC	Wee Dee	small plastic new model, frog	NIB	$67.00	05-02
CCBC	Wee Dee	black scale, plastic	mint	$34.90	99-09
CCBC	Wee Dee	Fire Laquer, plastic	mint	$34.90	99-09
CCBC	Wee Dee No 4800	GE, wire leader and weed guards, frog-finished bait, several tiny edge chips	EX	$330.00	05-04
CCBC	Wee Dee, plastic	frog, plastic box & papers	NIB	$49.00	02-05
CCBC	Weed Bug	2800, weed bug finish, label box VG	EX+IB	$1,290.00	99-10
CCBC	Weed Bug	2819, frog, label, GE, 2 papers	EXIB	$692.32	00-03
CCBC	Weed Bug	2819, label, frog, short wires	EX	$800.00	99-10
CCBC	Weed Bug	bug color, 1st type	VG+IB	$501.00	03-08
CCBC	Weed Bug	bug color, new weed guard	VG+	$515.52	99-01
CCBC	Weed Bug	bug color, red BE, weed guard missing	EX-	$296.00	99-12
CCBC	Weed Bug	frog	EX	$430.33	99-03
CCBC	Weed Bug	frog, GE, big worm burn	avg	$103.00	04-11
CCBC	Weed Bug	frog, GE	avg	$157.51	00-02
CCBC	Weed Bug	frog, GE	EX-?	$426.51	99-05
CCBC	Weed Bug	frog, GE	EX-	$462.00	00-02
CCBC	Weed Bug	frog, GE	EX-	$493.88	00-01
CCBC	Weed Bug	frog, GE, worm burn small	VG	$191.00	01-05
CCBC	Weed Bug	frog, GE, stamped box, NOT MET	NIB	$503.00	99-03
CCBC	Weed Bug	frog, belly chip, NOT MET	VG+/EX-	$305.00	99-03
CCBC	Weed Bug	frog, NRA unmarked box	avg	$215.02	99-05
CCBC	Weed Bug	frog, rusty hardware	EX	$450.00	99-11
CCBC	Weed Bug	Weed Bug finish, SOLD	EX-	$870.00	99-10
CCBC	Weed Bug	white, GE	EX-	$309.00	00-11
CCBC	Weed Bug	white/red eyes	VG+	$317.11	99-12
CCBC	Weed Bug	y/g, 1 bead eye	VG	$250.85	99-05
CCBC	Weed Bug	2819, Meadow Brown frog, GE, type 3, unfished, in 2PCCB stmpd "SPECIAL 2819"	EXIB	$850.00	05-05
CCBC	Weed Bug	bug finish, red bead eyes	EX	$180.00	05-07
CCBC	Weed Bug	bug finish, red bead eyes	EX	$593.00	04-02
CCBC	Weed Bug No. 2800	GE, wire leader and weed guards, frog-finished bait, minor chipping around eye	VG	$220.00	05-04
CCBC	Weed Bug Type II	2802, white, red eyes, GE, some fine age lines and very light wear	EX-	$400.00	05-05
CCBC	Weed Chunk	Weed Chunk 2802 label, white & red GE, papers	NIB	$905.00	03-10
CCBC	Weed Frog	frog, GE	EX+	$539.00	00-08
CCBC	Wiggle Diver	5041, red/yellow, plastic?	NIB	$66.00	99-09
CCBC	Wiggle Diver	red & white plastic bait	EX	$18.00	05-06
CCBC	Wiggle Diver	silver flash	EX	$32.00	05-03
CCBC	Wiggle Diver	wood, tiger stripe	EX-	$70.00	99-03
CCBC	Wiggle Fish	#2405, TE	VG	$58.50	99-01
CCBC	Wiggle Fish	2400 stencil box VG+, fluted tail, GE	EXIB	$170.00	05-07

BRAND	MODEL	SERIES / MFG. CODE / DESCRIPTION	GRADE	PRICE	DATE yy/mm
CCBC	Wiggle Fish	2400 stencil, GE	EXIB	$357.00	02-06
CCBC	Wiggle Fish	2400-W-PE, PTCB	NIB	$64.00	00-10
CCBC	Wiggle Fish	2402 RH, GE, fluted	EX	$128.00	00-04
CCBC	Wiggle Fish	2402W, PTCB & paper, R, TE	NIB	$130.00	05-07
CCBC	Wiggle Fish	2403, label	EX-IB	$190.00	00-10
CCBC	Wiggle Fish	2404, golden shiner, TE, SLT, few tiny pointers & age lines on forehead	EX-	$64.00	05-05
CCBC	Wiggle Fish	2404, GE	NIB	$280.00	00-09
CCBC	Wiggle Fish	2405, label, red sides	NIB	$481.00	99-11
CCBC	Wiggle Fish	2405W, PTCB, dace, TE	NIB	$81.00	05-07
CCBC	Wiggle Fish	2418 Special, frog stencil, tiny chip	EX-IB	$1,310.00	00-10
CCBC	Wiggle Fish	2418, stencil bx, glass eyes	NIB	$175.00	03-10
CCBC	Wiggle Fish	2418, stencil, gold tail	NIB	$178.50	99-08
CCBC	Wiggle Fish	blended RH, TE	mint	$69.00	00-02
CCBC	Wiggle Fish	centennial	NIB	$46.00	99-08
CCBC	Wiggle Fish	chub, GE	EX	$102.50	99-05
CCBC	Wiggle Fish	collector's edition, perch	NIB	$42.00	99-06
CCBC	Wiggle Fish	commemorative	NIB	$57.00	00-11
CCBC	Wiggle Fish	dace, GE	VG+	$72.00	00-05
CCBC	Wiggle Fish	DLT #2401, stencil box	EXIB	$145.00	99-01
CCBC	Wiggle Fish	DLT #2402, GE, great	EX+	$407.50	99-01
CCBC	Wiggle Fish	frog; Sioux City, Iowa, version	EX+	$78.00	03-02
CCBC	Wiggle Fish	golden shiner, GE, fluted tail	VG	$51.00	00-05
CCBC	Wiggle Fish	golden shiner	VG-	$56.00	01-03
CCBC	Wiggle Fish	golden shiner	EX	$123.50	99-07
CCBC	Wiggle Fish	golden shiner	EX-	$140.50	00-02
CCBC	Wiggle Fish	golden shiner, fluted tail	EX-	$159.00	00-05
CCBC	Wiggle Fish	golden shiner, GE	EX-	$76.02	99-08
CCBC	Wiggle Fish	perch scale, TE	EX	$64.00	05-07
CCBC	Wiggle Fish	perch, DLT, GE	EX-	$70.00	00-04
CCBC	Wiggle Fish	perch, GE	VG+	$71.00	00-05
CCBC	Wiggle Fish	perch, GE, DLT	EX-	$91.25	99-04
CCBC	Wiggle Fish	perch, NOT MET	avg	$34.55	99-01
CCBC	Wiggle Fish	perch, TE	EX	$72.55	00-02
CCBC	Wiggle Fish	r/w, GE, DLT	VG+	$79.00	99-01
CCBC	Wiggle Fish	Rainbow Fire, rub to primer on top	EX-	$1,385.00	01-04
CCBC	Wiggle Fish	red with gold scales/silver nose, GE	EX-	$1,594.50	99-12
CCBC	Wiggle Fish	red side, box	VG+IB	$139.00	99-05
CCBC	Wiggle Fish	red sides, GE	EX-	$202.50	99-10
CCBC	Wiggle Fish	RH, label, GE, NOT MET	EXIB	$132.00	00-10
CCBC	Wiggle Fish	RH, un lip, fluted tail, age lines	EX	$75.00	00-10
CCBC	Wiggle Fish	shiner scale, TE, back tag	EX	$49.01	99-11
CCBC	Wiggle Fish	silver flash	EX	$140.00	99-10
CCBC	Wiggle Fish	silver flash, TE	mint	$65.00	99-05
CCBC	Wiggle Fish	TE, frog, PTCB 2418	NIB	$202.50	98-12
CCBC	Wiggle Fish	TE, perch	VG-	$26.87	99-01
CCBC	Wiggle Fish	2402	EX+	$125.00	99-10

BRAND	MODEL	SERIES / MFG. CODE / DESCRIPTION	GRADE	PRICE	DATE yy/mm
CCBC	Wiggle Fish, Baby	2501, perch, GE, very early small body, some light age lines	EX-	$125.00	05-05
CCBC	Wiggle Fish, Baby	gold shiner, DLT, fluted tail	EX	$260.00	99-08
CCBC	Wiggle Fish, Baby	golden shiner	EX-	$255.00	99-06
CCBC	Wiggle Fish, Baby	golden shiner, GE, DLT	mint	$271.00	99-07
CCBC	Wiggle Fish, Baby	golden shiner, GE, NOT MET	EX	$227.61	00-03
CCBC	Wiggle Fish, Baby	perch, DLT, HPGM, GE, fluted tail	EX	$762.00	00-04
CCBC	Wiggle Fish, Husky	chub scale, 2 hook drags but rest nice	VG	$388.00	99-12
CCBC	Wiggle Fish, Husky	pikie, big hook drag	G-	$327.22	99-10
CCBC	Wiggle Fish, Husky		EX	$1,275.00	01-06
CCBC	Wiggle Wizard	4500, red sides	VG	$160.00	00-10
CCBC	Wiggler 100	100 nat scale, intro box EX, HPGN	NIB	$1,051.00	03-04
CCBC	Wiggler 100	101 intro, slant head, washer hdwr, early perch, HPGMs & fins, DTL, light pointers	VG+	$50.00	05-05
CCBC	Wiggler 100	101, DLT	EXIB	$128.50	99-06
CCBC	Wiggler 100	101, intro box, pamphlet	EXIB	$1,150.00	99-04
CCBC	Wiggler 100	107, intro box, cat, NOT MET	EX-IB	$1,251.00	01-03
CCBC	Wiggler 100	109, green back, label box EX-, GE, DLT, wowser!	NIB	$817.00	05-07
CCBC	Wiggler 100	205, with papers, intro box, SOLD	NIB	$1,920.00	99-10
CCBC	Wiggler 100	2401, Sioux City? metal tail	NIB	$99.99	99-05
CCBC	Wiggler 100	b/w	VG	$86.00	99-01
CCBC	Wiggler 100	chub	EX	$93.00	99-01
CCBC	Wiggler 100	chub scale, GE	EX	$81.00	04-07
CCBC	Wiggler 100	chub, DLT, GE	VG	$16.00	05-07
CCBC	Wiggler 100	chub, GE, stencil	VG+IB	$84.00	00-10
CCBC	Wiggler 100	chub, HPGM	EX-	$129.00	02-02
CCBC	Wiggler 100	chub, label, DLT	EXIB	$140.00	01-03
CCBC	Wiggler 100	chub, NOT MET	EX+	$77.00	01-08
CCBC	Wiggler 100	chub, GE, DLT	EX+	$150.00	99-11
CCBC	Wiggler 100	chub, HPGM, DLT	EX-	$104.01	99-05
CCBC	Wiggler 100	chub, NRA box	NIB	$100.00	99-06
CCBC	Wiggler 100	chub, sm chin chip	EX-IB	$78.00	00-04
CCBC	Wiggler 100	GE, chub, DBLT, blush gill marks	VG+	$45.00	05-06
CCBC	Wiggler 100	GE, early perch scale, 2 HPGM, unmarked lip, DBLT	VG+	$55.00	05-06
CCBC	Wiggler 100	golden shiner, GE	VG+	$80.00	99-10
CCBC	Wiggler 100	goldfish	EX-	$232.00	01-07
CCBC	Wiggler 100	goldfish scale, HPGM, unmarked prop	mint	$475.00	03-07
CCBC	Wiggler 100	green back	VG+	$112.00	00-07
CCBC	Wiggler 100	intro #2 pic box, washer rig	EXIB	$600.00	00-10
CCBC	Wiggler 100	intro box VG-, nat chub, NOT MET	EXIB	$685.00	99-06
CCBC	Wiggler 100	intro box	EXIB	$700.00	00-03
CCBC	Wiggler 100	intro box 100, nat chub scale, NOT MET	EXIB	$676.00	03-11
CCBC	Wiggler 100	intro box, beater	VG+IB	$131.00	00-08
CCBC	Wiggler 100	intro box Natural No. P EX & 1917 pocket catalog EX-, perch	EXIB	$588.00	05-07
CCBC	Wiggler 100	intro box nice, papers	NIB	$700.00	00-03
CCBC	Wiggler 100	intro box Natural No. C.C. VG+, NOT MET	EXIB	$675.00	04-02
CCBC	Wiggler 100	intro box	NIB	$2,001.00	99-09

BRAND	MODEL	SERIES / MFG. CODE / DESCRIPTION	GRADE	PRICE	DATE yy/mm
CCBC	Wiggler 100	intro pic box VG-	VGIB	$565.55	00-01
CCBC	Wiggler 100	old chub, GE	NIB	$150.00	99-06
CCBC	Wiggler 100	pearl, GE	EX	$470.00	02-09
CCBC	Wiggler 100	perch early, HPGF, washer rig	EX-	$200.00	99-03
CCBC	Wiggler 100	perch, HPGM, a beauty	EX	$188.00	02-08
CCBC	Wiggler 100	perch, GE	EX	$87.99	99-10
CCBC	Wiggler 100	r/w, GE, DLT, older	EX-	$37.00	99-01
CCBC	Wiggler 100	102, RH, no eyes	VG+IB	$40.00	04-03
CCBC	Wiggler 100	stencil box VG	EXIB	$135.09	00-02
CCBC	Wiggler 100	WH/black, GE	EX	$480.00	00-02
CCBC	Wiggler 200	205, green back, intro box avg	VG+IB	$660.00	00-12
CCBC	Wiggler 200	206, goldfish scale	NIB	$685.00	99-05
CCBC	Wiggler 200	212, all red end label	NIB	$2,125.00	02-02
CCBC	Wiggler 200	black/white, GE, nice	EX	$355.00	99-08
CCBC	Wiggler 200	chub, DLT, GE, NOT MET ASO	EX-	$63.00	00-04
CCBC	Wiggler 200	golden shiner, GE, DLT	EX	$125.00	99-11
CCBC	Wiggler 200	goldfish, DLT	EX	$152.22	99-10
CCBC	Wiggler 200	green back, 209 label box EX	NIB	$406.00	05-07
CCBC	Wiggler 200	perch	NIB	$162.50	99-08
CCBC	Wiggler 200	perch, un box, cat	EX-IB	$50.00	00-10
CCBC	Wiggler 200	perch, GE, DLT	VG	$53.99	99-05
CCBC	Wiggler 200	red side label, NRA box	NIB	$157.00	01-03
CCBC	Wiggler 200	shiner, special Toad Hounton lip (chipped)	EX	$62.00	03-02
CCBC	Wiggler 200	special, silver scale/red, stencil	VGIB	$91.00	01-03
CCBC	Wiggler 200	VanHouten, red side label box	NIB	$1,275.00	99-11
CCBC	Wiggler 200	yellow spotted	EX	$437.00	04-11
CCBC	Wiggly Rind	metal	EX	$61.00	01-01
Chain O Lakes	Musky Duck	papers, NOT MET	NIB	$142.50	99-05
Chapman	#1 Kidney	red/brass, NOT MET	VG-	$51.00	99-05
Chapman	#2 Teardrop	"Chapman & Son Thereasa, NY"	EX-	$150.00	00-10
Chapman	2 Diff	#6 Willow, buzz notched, pat 3-84	EX-	$567.50	00-04
Chapman	Allure	odd swivel, dents	VG-	$155.50	99-06
Chapman	Double Fish Spinner	"I.XL Theresa, NY," 2½"	EX-	$128.00	05-07
Chapman	Electric Bait	#2	VG+	$273.00	05-07
Chapman	Kidney Spinner	2/0, red on one side	VG+	$98.00	05-07
Chapman	Kidney Spinner		VG	$76.00	99-10
Chapman	Metal Fish	buzzer spinner in front, scale textured	EX	$1,525.00	01-02
Chapman	Minnow Propeller #5	pat 1870, "THERESA, NY," brass dble arrowhead? polished	EX-	$450.00	05-07
Chapman	Muskee Allure		EX	$500.00	01-04
Chapman	Perfect #2	"Chapman & Son, Theresa NY," blue bead	EX	$641.00	03-05
Chapman	Spinner	double blades like fluted spoon handles	EX	$3,500.00	05-02
Chapman	Water Nymph	3½", no hooks, scale finish, NOT MET	EX	$430.00	02-11
Chapman	Water Nymph	middle size	EX	$1,550.00	02-08
Chapman & Son	Minnow Propeller	fish shape spoon sith twist tails fins	EX-	$300.00	02-01
Chapman & Son	Spinner		EX-	$96.00	02-01
Charmer	3 hooks	orange/green stripes, GE, uglyish	VG+?	$432.50	00-03

LURES

BRAND	MODEL	SERIES / MFG. CODE / DESCRIPTION	GRADE	PRICE	DATE yy/mm
Charmer	Charmer	GE, brown crackleback head, red stripes on brown tail, slight split in wood on bottom head section	EX-	$650.00	05-06
Charmer	Charmer	gold/red stripe	EX-	$450.00	02-01
Charmer	Charmer	gold/red stripe, 3⅜", NOT MET	EX-	$700.00	04-01
Charmer	Charmer	green head, white/green stripes	EX-	$585.00	05-07
Charmer	Charmer	orange/green stripe, white label box VG+	EX-IB	$3,000.00	03-07
Charmer	Charmer	orange/red stripe, yellow label box avg	EXIB	$3,000.00	03-07
Charmer	Midget	dark "puter" head/yellow tail, NO BIDS	EX	$2,000.00	02-08
Charmer	Midget	no eyes	EX	$1,820.00	99-10
Charmer	Minnow	brown/red, nice	VG+	$610.00	01-04
Charmer	Minnow	gold/red stripe, $600 minimum, NO BIDS	VG		02-08
Charmer	Minnow	missing 1½ props, checked, ugly	avg	$230.00	00-04
Charmer	Minnow	o/red stripe, orange box rough, $1200 minimum, NO BIDS	avgIB		02-08
Charmer	Minnow	orange/red tail, orange head, many age lines but paint present, very scarred, orange/red border box avg	VG+IB	$935.00	05-04
Charmer	Minnow	orange/green stripe, lots age lines but OK	EX-?	$522.00	03-04
Charmer	Minnow	orange/orange stripes	EX-	$881.00	02-02
Charmer	Minnow	orange/red stripes	EX-	$1,300.00	01-04
Charmer	Minnow	orange/green stripe, GE	EX	$811.00	02-09
Charmer	Minnow	r/w, ugly line burns, 3-hooker	G	$450.00	99-08
Charmer	Minnow	white/red stripe	EX	$1,600.00	01-06
Charmer	Minnow	white/red stripe, SOLD	EX-	$1,250.00	00-05
Charmer	Surface	orange/green	EX-	$600.00	99-03
Charmer	Surface	white head, green spots, yellow tail, 1 BID	EX-	$1,800.00	02-08
Charmer	Minnow	white head, green stripes	EX-	$1,020.00	99-10
Chicago	Spinner	pat 1900, hooks rusty	EX-	$56.00	02-12
Chicago	Wobbler	weird metal, pat 1900	EX	$265.00	00-05
Chicago Tackle Co.	King Chub	RH, 2", 202 PTCB	NIB	$28.00	04-09
Childre, Lew	BB-1N	made in Japan	EX	$62.00	05-05
Chix	Salmon	3-pack, white bluegill	NIB	$151.00	99-06
Christiansen	Viking Frog	small size	EX-/EX	$715.00	05-07
Chub Products	King Chub	sm size scale pattern	EX	$17.00	04-02
Chucky Duck Ltd	Chucky Duck	wood duck, varniched bare wood #00030	NIB	$41.00	04-08
Cisco Kid	10-pack	nice shipping box	NIB	$129.00	99-01
Cisco Kid	12-pack	y/green 1PCCB with 12 common? lures NIB	mint	$345.00	03-05
Cisco Kid	Cisco Kid	black, rhinestone-studded pointed lip	EX	$21.00	05-01
Cisco Kid	Cisco Kid	green, rhinestone-studded rounded lip	EX	$21.00	05-01
Cisco Kid	Injured Cisco	806, injured minnow type	EX	$22.00	03-03
Cisco Kid	Injured Cisco	807, (new) orange coach dog	EX	$13.00	03-03
Cisco Kid	Injured Cisco	810, pikie color	EX	$16.00	03-03
Cisco Kid	Injured Minnow	green scale over yellow/green back	mint	$138.00	03-05
Cisco Kid	Skin-N-Cisco	1513, red head/white scale	EX	$22.00	03-03
Cisco Kid	Skin-N-Cisco	1521, black back/silver scale	EX-	$22.00	03-03
Cisco Kid	Skip-N-Cisco	white, blue sparkles, g/y PTCB	NIB	$63.00	03-02
Cisco Kid	Topper	703, RH/white flitter	EX-	$23.00	03-03

BRAND	MODEL	SERIES / MFG. CODE / DESCRIPTION	GRADE	PRICE	DATE yy/mm
Cisco Kid	Topper	705, black/flitter	EX	$23.00	03-03
Cisco Kid	Topper	705, black/flitter/red chin	EX	$22.00	03-03
Cisco Kid	Topper	712, green back, coach dog	EX	$22.00	03-03
Cisco Kid	Topper	719, green back/gold scale	EX-	$23.00	03-03
Cisco Kid	Topper	721, dark back/silver scale	EX	$22.00	03-03
Cisco Kid	Zara Type?	blue scale, white 2PCCB	EXIB	$259.00	03-12
Cisco Kid	110	FL PTCB	NIB	$13.00	03-02
Cisco Kid	1353	yellow/brown squiggle, PTCB	NIB	$50.00	02-03
Cisco Kid	1417	Lazy Ike type, plastic, rare	VG	$19.00	03-03
Clark	Darter Scout	gold scale, PTE, chip on r-eye and light wear under tail	VG	$77.00	05-05
Clark	Duckbill #600	yellow shore	NIB	$46.00	01-05
Clark	Duckbill Waterscout	white shore	VG+	$68.75	00-02
Clark	Duckbill, jointed	green shore/red scale stripe, plastic	mint	$201.00	05-03
Clark	Duckling	scale pattern	VG-	$58.00	02-07
Clark	Expert 5-hooker	Expert, GE, hole props	VG+	$1,302.00	00-12
Clark	Expert 5-hooker	green/w, hole props, many back digs	?	$360.00	01-08
Clark	Make 'Em bite	Flawless bait, red crackleback, w/orig box, paper mint	EX+	$3,795.00	05-04
Clark	Popper Scout	frog spot, card	NIB	$36.00	02-12
Clark	Popper Scout	PE, steel back, shiner	VG+	$15.00	05-06
Clark	Popper Scout	silver scale, nice card and box	NIB	$54.00	01-08
Clark	Popper Scout	y/red ribs	EX	$21.49	99-08
Clark	Water Scout	317, black shore, TE, great box & papers	NIB	$59.00	01-08
Clark	Water Scout	3241, dent eye, new in tube	NIT	$207.00	02-03
Clark	Water Scout	32CS	NIB	$42.00	98-12
Clark	Water Scout	400 Series, pearl w/blue eyes, PTE, light age crackling and few pointers	VG+	$35.00	05-05
Clark	Water Scout	400 Series, yellow shore, PTE, very light wear	EX	$28.00	05-05
Clark	Water Scout	300, black shore, TE	EX-	$18.00	99-01
Clark	Water Scout	blk/y, red dot, PE?	NIB	$127.50	99-04
Clark	Water Scout	dent eyes altered by addition of white bead eyes	VG+	$20.00	05-06
Clark	Water Scout	dent eye, brown with gold stripes & green eyes	VG+	$61.00	05-07
Clark	Water Scout	dent eye, perch scale	EX-	$30.00	99-03
Clark	Water Scout	duckbill, perch, TE	mint	$88.00	00-11
Clark	Water Scout	early 2PCCB, dent eye, dace?	NIB	$310.00	04-11
Clark	Water Scout	frog finish, bump eye, 403 bx & papers nice	NIB	$58.00	05-02
Clark	Water Scout	frog, nice box, TE	NIB	$68.00	01-03
Clark	Water Scout	green perch, TE	NIB	$59.00	00-10
Clark	Water Scout	nice box, papers	EXIB	$50.00	99-03
Clark	Water Scout	perch	NIB	$26.00	01-04
Clark	Water Scout	perch scale, nice box	NIB	$41.00	99-09
Clark	Water Scout	perch scale, tack eye	mint	$23.50	99-07
Clark	Water Scout	perch, indent red eye, tube	NIT	$172.50	99-01
Clark	Water Scout	rainbow, box & papers	NIB	$66.99	98-12
Clark	Water Scout	RH/white	NIB	$27.00	01-05
Clark	Water Scout	scale pattern, oval indent eye	EX	$28.95	98-12

BRAND	MODEL	SERIES / MFG. CODE / DESCRIPTION	GRADE	PRICE	DATE yy/mm
Clark	Water Scout	white shore/red spine	EXIB	$49.99	99-04
Clark	Water Scout	yellow shore, "Springfield Casket Mfg. Co, Crane, MO"	EX	$106.00	05-07
Clark	Water Scout Jr.	214, dent eye, new in tube	NIT	$217.00	02-03
Clark	Water Scout, jntd	frog spot, 1524 PTCB & papers EX	NIB	$135.00	05-07
Clark	Waterscout, duckbill	white shore	mint	$126.00	05-03
Cleopatra	Musky Size	articulated metal minnow, lamp shade	NOT MET	$720.00	99-11
Clewell	Snake Bait	ugly	avg	$149.50	99-01
Clewell	Snake Bait	black finish, 1 rusty treble hook, rarest color	EX	$770.00	05-04
Clewell	Snake Bait	green finish, w/box EX-	EX+IB	$1,540.00	05-04
Clewell	Snake Bait	#4 crisp bx, reddish hard plastic worm	NIB	$924.00	03-05
Clewell	Snake Bait	green, NOT MET	NIB	$1,825.00	04-03
Clewell	Snake Bait	r/w, blemish free	EX+	$247.50	05-04
Clewell	Snake Bait	SOLD	NIB	$1,350.00	99-10
Clink	Salmon	red head/white, tail perfect, crisp box	NIB	$123.00	02-02
Clinton	Champion	barber pole, NOT MET	EX	$1,535.00	04-03
Clinton	Wilt Champion Minnow	SOLD	EX-	$2,500.00	99-10
Clinton	Wilt Little Wonder	SOLD	EX-	$2,200.00	99-10
Clinton Wilt Co.	Champion Minnow	orange/green stripe	EX	$1,425.00	03-02
Clipper	Metal	dual fish spinner, GE, 3", embossed, inside painted red	EX	$366.00	05-07
Coldwater	Ghost	lum, avg picture box	avgIB	$449.00	00-10
Coldwater	Helldiver	big chip on back	avg	$65.50	99-09
Coldwater	Wiggler	strawberry, pic box nice, GE cracked	EX-IB	$640.00	02-08
Coleman	New Thing	white pasteboard box EX-, Tiverton, lure just a jig	RI	$181.00	05-01
Colorama	Lure 100	multilure with 100 inserts on card	NOC	$8.00	04-12
Comstock	Flying Hellgrimite	FAKE, NOT MET!	fake EX	$1,475.00	00-12
Conroy	Wood Body Spinner	Conroy textured blade with Brush patent #	VG+	$326.00	04-12
Cook	Colorado Moth	1⅛", brown/red	VG	$202.50	99-06
Cook	Colorado Moth	1¾", nice color	EX	$290.05	99-04
Cook	Colorado Moth	dull brown mottled	EX	$136.50	99-04
Cook	Colorado Moth		EX-	$255.00	00-10
Cook	Moth	large Buck? type	mint	$405.00	99-08
Cooper, Gene	Cooper	white/blk dots	EX	$31.00	04-02
Cooper Lures	Ubangi	yellow/brown back	EX	$58.00	05-07
Cordell	Big O x 2	plastic, 2 diff, plastic box	NIB	$19.99	99-06
Cordell	Big O x 6	neat egg carton 6-pack	NIB	$127.50	00-03
Cordell	GTO	4676 plastic box, RH, black dots	NIB	$7.00	05-03
Coxe	1315L	papers included, lt saltwater reel	NIB	$86.00	03-12
Coxe	95C	black	EX	$22.00	03-12
Cra-Bug	Cra-Bug	RH/w, NE, dbl hk on belly	EX-	$60.00	05-05
Crazylegs	Mixed	5 diff	NIB	$120.00	99-03
Crazylegs	500	green	NIB	$31.50	99-05
Cree-Duk	Cree-Duk	4", y/brown	NOC	$60.00	99-06
Cree-Duk	Cree-Duk	black and white, bufflehead, small size and light wear	VG+	$28.00	05-05
Cree-Duk	Cree-Duk	small size, black & white, new on card	NOC	$65.00	05-06

BRAND	MODEL	SERIES / MFG. CODE / DESCRIPTION	GRADE	PRICE	DATE yy/mm
Cree-Duk	Cree-Duk	small size, brown & white	VG+	$35.00	05-06
Cree-Duk	Cree-Duk	yellow and brown, mallard, small size, very light use wear	VG+	$25.00	05-05
Crowder	Wobbing Willie	hot pink	mint	$23.00	04-02
Cummings	Marvelous Bass Getter	RH, like a Decker, plain label 2PCCB VG+	EXIB	$622.00	01-11
Cummings, Ed	1937	32 pages	EX	$106.00	01-05
Cunningham & Son	Millie Mouse	1", wood body, BBE, single hook, c. 1960, Mass.	NM	$25.00	05-05
D.A.M.	Baby Wooden Woobler	#1618, poor box, "Spinner"	EXIB	$50.00	99-07
D.A.M.	Pikie	jointed perch, NOT MET	EX	$255.00	02-04
D.A.M.	"Eveready" on Lip	3-jntd minnow, 4¾", GE, carved tail	mint	$779.00	03-08
D.A.M.		5085, box VG, 5", double-jointed pike, GE	EXIB	$960.00	03-07
D.A.M.		made for Goble, GE, pike on yellow box	EX-IB	$1,281.00	03-11
D.A.M.	Fish Getter	5085, Heddon-made L-rig, dbl jntd	NIB	$650.00	04-04
D.A.M.	Fliegen	salmon fly, new on card	NOC	$25.00	05-05
D.A.M.	Fly Rod Jntd Pikie	red and gold scale w/black spots, 1⅞", wood, 3-hk	EX+	$55.00	05-05
D.A.M.	Gerat Qualitat	jointed, carved tail, painted eye, perch	mint	$114.00	04-11
D.A.M.	Gerat Qualitat	rapala type, red plastic flippers	EX	$46.00	05-01
D.A.M.	Midge-Oreno type	tiny, GE, RH/yellow, SR, belly hk hanger and rig-type tail hanger	EX+	$110.00	05-05
D.A.M.	Mouse Bait	leather ears + tail, black bead eye, black back, olive green sides	VG	$115.50	04-11
D.A.M.	Sea Devil Wobbler	nice 2PCCB, shiner scale, PE	NIB	$142.50	00-02
D.A.M.	Spinner	nice pike graphic box, embossed spoon	NIB	$40.00	04-11
D.A.M.	Vamp Style	Heddon? pike shape, perch scale color, GE	mint	$710.00	03-11
D.A.M.	Vampire	like Heddon Gamefisher, neat scale pattern	EX	$430.00	03-02
Dalton	Barracuda	Dalton Special, wood, St. Pete FL fishing lure, white/black back stripe, glitter	EX	$5.51	05-07
Dalton	Special	"Clearwater Fl" on belly	EX	$21.03	99-01
Damyl	Spinner	neat pic box, perch, crank bait, PE	NIB	$258.30	00-01
Damyl	Wobbler	neat pic box, pikie, PE	NIB	$257.80	00-01
Dandy	Reyhu	yellow spots, Florida wood lure	EX	$7.00	05-02
Darby	Spin Head	crisp box & paper, green, red & white head	NIB	$495.00	05-04
Darby	Spring Bait	globe with bunch of wires & hooks	avg	$105.00	00-01
Darby Bait	Rotary Head w/Spring-Loaded Hooks	unique wood lure, superclean, green	EX	$650.00	05-05
Davis Tackle	Trigger Fish	great 2PCCB, red/black lure	NIB	$56.00	05-07
Dean, Pop	Musky Bait	GE, showing obvious wear	G-	$137.50	05-04
Decker	Bass Bait	brown box, papers	NIB	$1,027.99	99-04
Decker	Bass Bait	yellow picture box	NIB	$455.00	99-04
Decker	Surface	r/w, printing inside box (EX-)	EXIB	$434.00	02-07
Decker	Surface	slender body, red/white, front prop marked "Decker"	EX+	$250.00	03-07
Decker	Surface (globe)	brown box, c. 1908, SOLD	EXIB	$650.00	99-10
Decker	Surface Water Bass Bait	white bait, Jersey rigged hooks, box VG+	NIB	$990.00	04-11
Decker	Surface Water Casting Bass Bait	mouse (shiny), papers, pic box VG+	NIB	$620.00	01-11
Decker	Top Water Bait	yellow with orange spots	GD	$27.50	04-11
Decker	Top Water	r/w	EX	$980.00	99-10
Decker	Underwater	Manhattan	EXIB	$2,870.00	99-10
Dekalb	Corn Cob	novelty lure, perfect wings	mint	$130.00	04-02

BRAND	MODEL	SERIES / MFG. CODE / DESCRIPTION	GRADE	PRICE	DATE yy/mm
Delavan	North Channel Minnow	5-hooker	EX-	$1,310.00	99-10
Demon	Sail Shark	#35 PEP (pink eye pearl), plastic bx & paper	NIB	$26.00	02-11
Demon	Sail Shark	"#YD-60" on belly	NIB	$32.00	04-12
Demon	Sail Shark	12-pack picture box x 12 lures NIB	NIB	$207.00	04-11
Demon	Sail Shark	blk head/clear, hard plastic box	NIB	$10.00	00-08
Demon	Sail Shark	Demon's Sail Shark, gold CD	NIB	$28.99	00-01
Demon	Sail Shark	PB, name on belly	NIB	$15.00	01-01
Demon	Sail Shark	"PB-20" on belly	NIB	$23.00	03-02
Demon	Sail Shark	yellow, paper and box	EXIB	$21.51	00-03
Detroit Bait Co.	Bass Caller	3½", GE, green back/white belly/red chin	VG+	$159.50	04-11
Detroit Bait Co.	Bass Caller	bar perch	NIB	$294.00	00-03
Detroit Bait Co.	Bass Caller	cream, crisp box & papers	VG+IB	$227.00	02-03
Detroit Bait Co.	Glass Minnow Tube	4¼", couple rusty hooks	EX-	$560.00	02-02
Detroit Bait Co.	Glass Minnow Tube	aluminum-capped, picture box top slight edge wear, box bottom corners are split	EXIB	$1,760.00	05-04
Detroit Bait Co.	Glass Minnow Tube	box VG+, papers EX	EX-IB	$2,500.00	02-07
Detroit Bait Co.	Glass Minnow Tube	marked end cap	EX	$547.00	05-03
Detroit Bait Co.	Glass Minnow Tube	nice pic. box & paper, NOT MET	EXIB	$1,136.00	03-11
Detroit Bait Co.	Glass Minnow Tube	NOT MET	EX-	$560.00	99-03
Detroit Bait Co.	Glass Minnow Tube	pic box EX-, paper EX, sliding cap	NIB	$4,650.00	01-06
Detroit Bait Co.	Glass Minnow Tube	VG+ box, crisp papers	EX-IB	$1,426.00	02-08
Detroit Bait Co.	Glass Minnow Tube		EX	$660.00	99-10
Detroit Bait Co.	Minnow Bait Cage	great box & paper, no rust	NIB	$7,000.00	04-02
Detroit Bait Co.	Minnow Cage	3½", light rust but nice	EX-	$613.00	05-06
Detroit Bait Co.	Minnow Tube	3¼", one tiny chip	EX-	$451.00	05-07
Detroit Bait Co.	Minnow Tube	picture box VG+, crisp papers, $2500 NOT MET	NIB	$2,225.00	05-07
Detroit Bait Co.	North Channel	green/silver belly, two hks missing, not bad	VG	$255.00	02-02
Detroit Bait Co.	North Channel Minnow	3 hooks	VG	$255.00	02-02
Detroit Bait Co.	North Channel Minnow	5-hk, GE, black back/white, no markings, many paint slivers	avg	$330.00	05-07
Detroit Bait Co.	North Channel Minnow	white pastebord box VG+, lure belly rough	EX-IB	$3,039.00	05-01
Detroit Bait Co.	Weedless Wizard	frog, 2 papers, EX box	NIB	$2,313.00	00-10
Detroit Bait Co.	Weedless Wizard	mechanical chunk bait, 1930s, fully functional, stamped on hook release mechanism	EX+	$1,182.50	05-04
Dewey	Du-Getum	picture box VG+, white coach dog	NIB	$735.00	04-11
Diamond Mfg.	Ultra Casting	crackle (Pflueger Surprise), superb box, MO	NIB	$1,295.00	01-09
Dickens	Duplex Darter	in nice box, r/w	NIB	$450.00	99-02
Dillonbeck	Runt Type	frog spot, window box, NJ item	EX-IB	$83.00	05-02
Dineen	Spinning Minnow	hollow metal ugly thing, IL item	EX	$381.00	02-02
Doll	Top Secret	black/1 white shad spot	VG+	$29.00	00-04
Doll	Top Secret	green/white blended, lg size	EX-	$15.00	04-09
Doll	Top Secret	perch, nice box and tag	NIB	$28.50	99-03
Doll	Top Secret	shad	NIB	$20.53	00-01
Doll	Top Secret	yellow/red	EX	$9.99	99-06
Donaly	Catchumbig	ugly Woodpecker type with spinners	avg	$1,400.00	02-01
Donaly	Jersey Wow	black/yellow design, 3 single hooks	EX	$565.00	99-04
Donaly	Jersey Wow	hand-painted bait, white/red/black, black ribs, roughness at tail end	VG	$148.50	05-04

BRAND	MODEL	SERIES / MFG. CODE / DESCRIPTION	GRADE	PRICE	DATE yy/mm
Donaly	Jersey Wow	y/red/blk, 1 treble	mint	$710.00	99-04
Donaly	Redfin	3 metal flippers, g/w GE, NOT MET	VG	$295.00	02-04
Donaly	Redfin Floater	yellow/black ribs	VG+	$230.00	99-04
Donaly	Redfin Minnow	green/white, w/red accents, few pointers, c. 1911	EX	$1,650.00	05-04
Donaly	Redfin	NOT MET	VG+	$710.00	99-05
Donaly	Redfin Floater	3-hooker (like Fishcake), very faded box	EXIB	$950.00	02-03
Donaly	Redfin Floater	black skeletal rib design, marked prop	G	$183.00	05-07
Donaly	Redfin Floater		VG-	$355.00	99-09
Donaly	Redfin Minnow	white/red stripe, nice pic box, NOT MET	EXIB	$2,827.00	05-05
Donaly	Redfin Minnow		G+	$450.00	02-02
Drake	Sea Bat	crisp box & papers	EXIB	$432.00	05-01
Drake	Sea Bat	r/w	NIB	$168.00	01-04
Drake	Sea Bat	red/white age lines and both paperwork and box	EXIB	$440.00	05-04
Drake	Sea Bat	RH	NIB	$209.50	00-03
Dunks	Baby Duck	yellow w/brown back and wings, just a hint of wear on this rare duck lure	EX	$150.00	05-05
Dunks	Swim O Lure, musky	chipmunk finish, PE, jointed, adjustable diving lip	EX	$150.00	05-07
Dunks	Worry Wart	metal	mint	$66.00	03-04
Dura-Flote	Nipple Dipper	in tube & paper	NIT	$38.00	03-02
Eau Claire Fly Co.	Chippewa	globe type, same lure as in Slade's book	VG-	$550.00	04-03
Eau Claire Fly Co.	Courderay	same lure as in Slade's book	EX	$852.00	04-03
Edgren	Spinning Minnow	metal, nice pic box	NIB	$228.60	99-09
Edward, Jacob	Horsefly	few blemishes, ¼" nick on one wing, some small spots to primer under wings, all original, wings and lip work well	EX	$742.50	05-04
Eger	Bull Nose	OPE, 3", frog skin–covered bait	EX+	$35.00	05-06
Eger	Bull Nose	silver flash, PE	EX	$156.00	00-07
Eger	Darter	1512, 2PCCB VG+, frog skin–covered lure, 3⅞"	VG+IB	$177.00	05-07
Eger	Darter	frog spot, YPE, red mouth, 3-hk, 3⅞", few scattered pointers and light age cracks	VG	$16.00	05-05
Eger	Dillinger	w/red stripe, short fat type	NIB	$40.00	99-01
Eger	Dillinger	308	NIB	$36.00	98-12
Eger	Frog Pappy	covered in frog skin, YPE, red mouth, 3-hk, 3⅞"	EX	$37.00	05-05
Eger	Junior Dillinger	yellow w/black ribs, YPE, light pointers and light age cracks, 3⅜"	VG	$13.00	05-05
Eger	Master Dillinger	3⅞", green with black side stripe, yellow belly	EX-	$20.00	05-06
Eger	Sergeant Sea Diver	RH/flitter, PE	EX	$112.00	01-05
Eger	Shrimp	Victory, box EX	EXIB	$464.00	99-02
Eger	Spinner	Foss-type blade, cone-shaped body	EX	$256.00	01-11
Eger	Sub-Pedo	York production period, yellow and red shore minnow, YPE, NSOB, 2 small flakes on BW	EX	$30.00	05-05
Eger	Torpedo	201, w/blk stripes, PE	NIB	$34.52	99-09
Eger	Torpedo	bar perch? carved fish tail, PTCB #301, PE	NIB	$40.00	01-10
Eger	Weedless Dillinger	white/red ribs, r/w skirt, flakes on BW, very light wear	EX-	$28.00	05-05
Eger	Weedless Dillinger	yellow/red ribs, white hula skirt replaced, flk at BW, tail bright colors	EX-	$23.00	05-05
Electro	Lure	Paul Bunyan type	EXIB	$131.00	00-08

BRAND	MODEL	SERIES / MFG. CODE / DESCRIPTION	GRADE	PRICE	DATE yy/mm
Electrolure	Electrolure	RH, Illinois	EX	$25.00	00-10
Electronic Units Inc.	Jumping Jo	hot orange, papers included	NIB	$57.00	03-02
Electronics Units Co.	Jumpin Joe	scale	NIB	$31.00	99-04
Elkay Bait Co.	Puddle Jumper	b&w bead eyes	EX	$51.00	04-02
Ellis	Salmon Plug	white/silver scale	mint	$51.00	99-01
Emmell	Chippewa	4", sienna crackle	avg	$175.00	02-02
Emmell Bait	Chpipewa	RB, 4" pike size, Blair box VG	NIB	$4,506.00	01-03
Emmells	Chippewa Mausky	white, ugly, NOT MET	VG-	$380.00	02-01
English?	Paragon Minnow	GE, embossed, scale finish, rear hook hanger broken, c. 1890	VG+/EX-	$2,090.00	05-04
Enterprise Mfg. Co.	Flying Helgramite	type 1	EX-	$2,310.00	04-03
Enterprise Mfg. Co.	Maybug	Pflueger, nice lure, NOT MET	EX	$1,064.00	05-06
Eppinger	Husly Devle Jr.	wood slide box, nice, NOT MET	EX-	$46.09	99-12
Eppinger	Winged Devil	b/w scaled, wrong box	VG	$39.00	01-03
Etchen Tackle	Helga Devil	novelty lure, red head/white	EX	$20.00	04-07
Evans-Walton	Weed Queen	aluminum	G	$56.00	99-12
Ewelure	Ewelure	small early jntd plastic from Texas, perch scale?	EX	$23.00	05-07
Excel	Silver Streak	rubber minnow	NIB	$152.00	00-08
Fair Play Ind.	Bubble Minnie	square 2PCCB VG, orange	EXIB	$69.00	04-09
Fenner	Fenner's Wab	Weedless Automatic bait, c. 1924, r/w, pyralin, spring-hook activated lure	EX	$37.00	05-05
Fenner	W.A.B.	red/white	EX	$48.00	00-05
Fin Wing	Glow Wing		NIB	$141.49	00-03
Fishathon	Dizzy Diver	RH	EX	$16.00	04-02
Fishathon	Dizzy Floater	black scale over green back	EX	$16.00	04-07
Fish-Rite	Auto Hook Setter	nice box	NIB	$21.60	99-08
Fishtrap	#700 Junior	r&w, spring hook, weedless, nice box	NIB	$27.00	01-08
Flood	Florida Shiner	5", brown/gold, box avg, paper tears	EX	$330.00	04-11
Flood	Florida Shiner	5", brown/gold, brown accents, large gold dots, box VG, paper tears	EX	$330.00	04-11
Flood	Florida Shiner	5", brown/gold, green stripe, black accents, box avg (large stain), paper tears	EX	$220.00	04-11
Flood	Florida Shiner	6", brown/gold, green stripe, black accents, box G, paper tears	VG	$247.50	04-11
Flood	Florida Shiner	box & papers, gold scales, black fins	EX-IB	$612.00	05-06
Flood	Florida Shiner	dark brown back, cream belly, silver spots, 6½", minnow, w/papers and box	EXIB	$990.00	05-04
Flood	Florida Shiner	lg size box EX-, papers EX	EXIB	$500.00	04-07
Flood	Florida Shiner	minnow, 5", finished in brown with gold spots pattern, with painted tack eyes, side hook hangers, belly weight protruding	EXIB	$550.00	05-04
Flood	Florida Shiner	minnow, 6" long, small belly crack, w/papers	EX+IB	$550.00	05-04
Flood	Florida Shiner	NOT MET	NIB	$387.99	99-09
Flood	Florida Shiner	papers	NIB	$317.00	99-12
Flood	Florida Shiner	POBW, light stain on box	NIB	$285.00	01-10
Flood	Florida Shiner	small, 4¾", box VG	NIB	$400.00	01-06
Flood	Florida Shiner	SOLD	NIB	$590.00	99-10

BRAND	MODEL	SERIES / MFG. CODE / DESCRIPTION	GRADE	PRICE	DATE yy/mm
Flood	Florida Shiner	w/orig box and papers, brown/gold spots, age lines, eye chip free	EX-	$412.50	05-04
Florida Artifical Bait Co.	Superstrike	articulated shrimp, pic box VG-, 2 papers	NIB	$1,394.00	02-01
Florida Artifical Bait Co.	Celluloid Superstrike Shrimp Bait	4", black bead eyes, 7 segments	EX	$93.50	04-11
Florida Artifical Bait Co.	Celluloid Superstrike Shrimp Bait	5", black bead eyes, 8 segments	VG	$132.00	04-11
Florida Artifical Bait Co.	Super Strike Shrimp	picture 2PCCB with patent # VG+, articulated celluloid	NIB	$5,520.00	05-07
Florida Artificial Bait Co.	Super Strike Shrimp	6 segment celluloid, green	EX	$355.00	01-03
Florida Fishing Tackle	Injured Minnow	barracuda, silvery, GE, 3-hk, 3¾"	VG-	$456.00	05-01
Folk Art	Mud Puppy Type	GE, 7", mud puppy bait, 2 belly cup rig hooks	EX	$104.50	05-04
Foss, Al	#3	black/white, nice tin box correctly marked	NIB	$166.00	02-03
Foss, Al	#4	GE, tin box	GD	$28.50	05-07
Foss, Al	#4 Weedless	GE, red and white, very light wear	EX+	$13.00	05-05
Foss, Al	#5 R-W Bucktail	in VG+ orig red tin	EX-IB	$28.00	05-05
Foss, Al	#5 Yellow Bucktail		EX	$12.00	05-05
Foss, Al	Egypt Spinner	early red glass eyes, very light wear	EX-	$25.00	05-05
Foss, Al	Fan Dancer #18	crisp box & papers	NIB	$48.00	02-03
Foss, Al	Frog #11	brown hair, patent blade	EX-	$35.00	05-06
Foss, Al	Frog #12	nice blue tin box	EXIB	$61.00	00-09
Foss, Al	Frog Wiggler	#12	EX	$45.99	99-05
Foss, Al	Frog Wiggler #12	tin box avg, lure mint	NIB	$80.00	99-02
Foss, Al	Jazz Wiggler	#10 lead body painted red, few small flakes	EX-	$12.00	05-05
Foss, Al	Little Egypt Wiggler	light blue glass eyes perfect	EX	$118.00	01-10
Foss, Al	Minnow	white, GE, hinged tin, papers	NIB	$50.00	99-01
Foss, Al	Musky Oriental Wiggler	r/w, GE, very light wear	EX	$58.00	05-05
Foss, Al	Oriental Wiggler	white, GE, blue hinged box EX-, papers	EXIB	$152.00	02-09
Foss, Al	Oriental Wiggler #4	white, nice hinged green box, pig papers	EXIB	$100.00	04-02
Foss, Al	Shimmy	Jr. #7 Parma Bell Fly tail	EX	$40.00	05-05
Foss, Al	Shimmy Spinner #7	red bucktail	EX	$15.00	05-05
Foss, Al	Shimmy Wiggler	red #5 musky, red tin VG, papers	EXIB	$66.51	00-02
Foss, Al	Shimmy Wiggler #6	black & white hair weedless in plastic box (E)	EXIB	$40.00	05-06
Foss, Al	Shimmy Wiggler #6	red tin box E-, box is unmarked, American Fork & Hoe	EXIB	$50.00	05-06
Foss, Al	Skidder	Figure 4 blade, very light wear	EX-	$30.00	05-05
Foss, Al	Skidder	pic 2PCCB VG+	EXIB	$455.00	02-01
Foss, Al	Skidder	red tin box EX-	NIB	$102.00	02-01
Foss, Al	Tin Liz	GE, gold	EX	$53.00	99-01
Foss, Al	True Temper	#27, red and black bucktail, clean lure, bucktail gone	VG+	$25.00	05-05
Four Tees	Darter	wood, frog spot, fatter darter style, PE	EX	$139.00	05-07
Francis Fly Co.	#10 Brann's Ranger	silver head; brn, yel, red feathers; tad bit dirty, 2 tiny pointers	EX-	$49.00	05-05
Francis Fly Co.	#5 Irvin Cobb	YPE, 2 tiny pointers, tail tad bit dirty	EX-	$38.00	05-05
Francis Fly Co.	Bass Bug	#55 Bucking Hams Glory, very light wear	EX	$66.00	05-05
Francis Fly Co.	Black Cricket	cork body, YPE, black wings, very light wear	EX	$12.00	05-05

BRAND	MODEL	SERIES / MFG. CODE / DESCRIPTION	GRADE	PRICE	DATE yy/mm
Francis Fly Co	Fly Rod Flap Tail	trout size, gray flock mouse, very light wear	EX	$75.00	05-05
Francois	The Frog	ragged box	NIB	$133.50	99-04
Freeport	Fluted Spinner	1904 pat, 2 blue glass beads	EX-	$62.00	02-12
Freeport	Hook	blue beads, blade & weed guard, $250 NOT MET	EX	$156.00	04-02
Freeport	Hook	wood box EX + papers, trailer hook	NIB	$660.00	99-06
Froelich	Twin Treble Diver x 2	2¾", c. 1935, black/white spots, red accents	EX	$121.00	04-11
Frost, Cary	Chippewa	bass size, eyes & spinner OK, paint bad	poor	$90.00	05-02
Frost, Cary	Chippewa	bass, sienna/yellow, sow	poor	$177.50	99-04
Fury	Crab Pup #40	3 diff removable hook harnesses	NIB	$23.00	03-01
Fury Mfg. Co.	Fury	4-pack, #60 PTCB, 4 wood bodies, 1 harness	NIB	$20.00	04-09
Gabbard	R2	Lucky 13 type wood lure, PE	NIB	$9.00	04-02
Gaide, C.J.W.	Baite	ugly nothing bucktail thing, NOT MET	EX-	$383.00	02-02
Game Guide	Phantom Flattie	salmon lure, rainbow scale?	EX	$14.00	04-07
Gardner	Twin Dancer	perch scale, name on back	mint	$50.00	03-04
Gardner	Twin Dancer	window bx, black	NIB	$7.00	04-09
Garland	Cork Head Minnow	never been rigged, w/box EX	EX+IB	$1,567.50	05-04
Gateway	River Master	RB, nice, HR5 Gateway box, GE	NIB	$103.00	01-09
Gateway	River Master, jntd	rainbow, GE, unmarked in Gateway box	NIB	$97.00	03-12
Gee Wiz	Action Frog	#23, nice box	NIB	$183.00	00-10
Gee Wiz	Action Frog	4½", nice box and paper	NIB	$175.00	99-05
Gee Wiz	Action Frog	counter display w/red/white frog	EX	$460.00	04-03
Gee Wiz	Action Frog	musky size, 2 single hooks	EX-	$316.00	03-04
Gee Wiz	Action Frog	box EX-, tiny cracks in rubber feet	NIB	$127.00	05-07
Gee Wiz	Action Frog	no wheel	EX	$175.00	99-03
Gee Wiz	Action Frog	on large yellow thick card	EX	$99.00	05-07
Gee Wiz	Action Frog	small size	NIB	$202.50	99-04
Gee Wiz	Action Frog	with box	EXIB	$132.00	05-07
Gee Wiz	Action Frog		EX	$75.00	00-02
Genalure	Electric	built-in generator, no batteries needed, not working	EX-	$31.00	04-07
General Tool	Spoon Fin	green, GE	EX	$177.00	01-03
Gen-Shaw	Genshaw	180 perch? nice mtn. scene box & paper	NIB	$34.00	04-12
Gen-Shaw	Wiggle Lure	rough box, nice paper, sow, NOT MET	poorIB	$42.00	99-06
Gibbs, Stan	Cast-A-Lure	blue/white, 4½", 2PCCB crisp	NIB	$63.00	05-07
Gibbs, Stan	Cast-A-Lure	silver eel, 2½ oz., decent 2PCCB	EXIB	$73.00	03-05
Glenwillow's	Safety Lure	RH, TE, mint lure and box!	NIB	$92.00	00-09
Globe Lure	3-section Bait	c. 1920, three-section bait, age lines, minor wear, w/box edge wear, box faded on end	VG+	$632.50	05-04
Glo-Boy	Minnow	plastic GE? single weedless hook	EX-	$14.00	03-08
Glow-Bug	Spinner	June bug type with luminous body, new on fish head–shaped card	NOC	$12.00	05-05
Goble	Tulsa Wiggler	poor papers	NIB	$1,400.00	00-11
Gobles	Wiggler	with correct box, smaller size	NIB	$1,500.00	01-04
Goite	Arrowhead Spinner	silver full tail, very light wear	EX-	$28.00	05-05
Goite	Indiana	aluminum, agate guide	EX	$66.00	02-02
Gopher	Gopher		NIB	$56.59	00-03
Gowan	Bumble Bug		NIB	$36.02	99-05
Graves	Minnow Tube	wood box, paper label VG+, lure 3¾", NOT MET	EXIB	$1,975.00	04-07

BRAND	MODEL	SERIES / MFG. CODE / DESCRIPTION	GRADE	PRICE	DATE yy/mm
Graves	Spinner	2PCCB with pic label, 3⁹⁄₁₆" VG, "Caught at Last"	NIB	$1,913.00	04-07
Green-Wylie	Klipon	scale patter, GE, nice	EX	$238.00	03-04
Gregory	Cleopatra Minnow	4-section metal	EX	$820.00	02-09
Gregory	Metal	double fish spoon, GE, c. 1870s, marked "GREGORY NEAT!"	EX	$433.00	05-07
Gresh	Bender	r/w, B-Flat shiner type, GE, 5¼"	VG	$371.00	99-11
Gresh	Darter	RH, PE, nice box, "Gresh" on belly	NIB	$208.00	00-07
Gruber	Glow Worm	r/w, wood box nice	NIB	$185.05	00-01
Gruber	Glow Worm	r/w, with papers	EX	$152.50	99-05
Gruber	Glow Worm	w/red stripes, top box missing	EXIB	$275.00	99-04
Gruber	Glow Worm	white/red stripes, crisp papers	mint	$51.00	05-07
Gruber	Glow Worm	white/red stripes, crisp paper	EX+	$51.00	05-07
Gruber	Glow Worm	y/green stripes	EX+	$150.00	00-04
Gudebrod	Blabber Mouth		NIB	$13.00	99-02
Gudebrod	Nimble Nose	2200 S10, yellow/foil insert	NIB	$18.00	04-07
H & I Pflueger	3-hooker	sienna crackle, GE, Neverfail old box	EXIB	$688.00	01-08
H H Lure Co.	Scorpion	metal spinner bait in great 2PCCB, papers	NIB	$11.00	01-08
H&H	Scorpion	2PCCB, metal spinner bait Arizona item	NIB	$14.00	04-11
H&I	Shurkatch Surface Mouse	gray w/silver belly, PTE, "A Squeaky" clean mouse	NM	$42.00	05-05
H&I	Shurkatch Surface Mouse	musky jntd pikie, RH/w, PTE, in orig huge 2PCBB	EX+IB	$75.00	05-05
H&I	Wood Jitterbug	frog spot, yellow plastic lip, ⅝ oz., very light wear on back, EX in 2PCCB	EX-ib	$75.00	05-05
Haas	4-segment Minnow	some paint off lip	EX-	$185.00	99-05
Haas	Beetle		VG	$250.00	00-10
Haas	Haas Lure	3-jointed, corroded lip	EX_	$91.51	99-12
Haas	Liv Minnow	fly rod	mint	$247.00	03-08
Haas	Minnow	red & white single joint, 3½"	VG+	$375.00	05-06
Hagen	Impeller	red/yellow, Wis., c. 1930, Globe type	VG+	$104.00	03-01
Hagen	Spinner	PTCB	NIB	$14.00	03-01
Hagen	Spinner	PTCB, metal lure	NIB	$13.00	02-03
Hagrett	Cat's Paw	orange/red spots, wood, spring-hook lure	EX	$60.00	04-07
Halco	Giant Trembler	photo finish, green back; blue, pink, and yellow color desending to belly; 7" rattles	VG	$8.51	05-07
Halik	Frog	lg size	EX-	$40.00	05-06
Halik	Frog	medium size, 3½"	EX+	$45.00	05-06
Halik	Frog	medium size, 3½"	EX+	$45.00	05-06
Halik	Frog	medium size, 3½", in box VG+	EX+IB	$55.00	05-06
Halik	Frog Jr		EXIB	$51.01	99-06
Halik	Frog Jr.		EX-	$29.00	99-01
Halik	Frog Jr.		NIB	$64.00	99-01
Halik	Halik Frog	large size, green frog, very light use wear, in graphic orig 2PCBB	EXIB	$45.00	05-05
Hampton	Kentucky Leader	shrink-wrap box	NIB	$61.00	02-06
Handkamer	Jasper	wood, made in Canada, no eyes	VG	$34.00	02-02
Hansen	Michigan Lifelike	3 hooks	avg	$600.00	01-03

BRAND	MODEL	SERIES / MFG. CODE / DESCRIPTION	GRADE	PRICE	DATE yy/mm
Hansen	Michigan Lifelike	5-hook, decent, 1-1-1997 photo?	avg	$360.00	02-08
Hansen	Michigan Lifelike	5-hooker	EX	$1,662.01	99-11
Hansen	Michigan Lifelike	5-hooker, chips and slivers	avg	$910.00	00-01
Hansen	Michigan Lifelike	a sow, NOT MET	poor	$431.00	99-04
Hansen	Michigan Lifelike	an oinker	poor	$350.00	03-02
Hansen	Michigan Lifelike	black splatter back/white, triple rear prop, GE	VG+	$455.00	05-07
Hansen	Michigan Lifelike	c. 1910, circular hardware	EX+	$1,680.00	99-10
Hansen	Michigan Lifelike	GE, unmarked props, cup and screw belly rig	VG	$1,155.00	05-04
Hansen	Michigan Lifelike	pat Feb. 25, 1908, articulated minnow arntz, triple rear prop, GE, second style hook hangers, silver/blue back, yellow belly, minnow	EX	$6,270.00	05-04
Hansen	Michigan Lifelike	Pic box EX, paper EX	NIB	$8,000.00	01-12
Hansen	Michigan Lifelike	ugly	avg	$565.00	99-10
Hansen	Michigan Lifelike	yellow/black splatter back	VG+	$835.00	05-06
Hansen	Michigan Lifelike	yellow/dark green back, GE, 3-blade rear prop	VG+	$519.00	05-07
Hansen	Michigan Lifelike	yellow/green back splatter, egg yolk, GE, NOT MET	EX	$1,325.00	05-07
Hansen	Spoonjack Minnow	g/y splatter finish	VG+	$463.89	99-07
Hansen	Sub Master	plastic lure, 2PCCB from Kansas	NIB	$152.00	03-02
Hansen, Jacob	Spoon Jack	minnow, 4¼", 3-hook, cup rigged, GE, trademark Hansen prop	EX	$880.00	05-04
Hardy	Jock Scott Wiggler	blue/ivory, marked box EX, wood lure, PE, external BW, cool!	NIB	$148.00	05-07
Hardy	Phantom	maroon box rough, rainbow? lure	NIB	$139.00	04-03
Hardy	St.George	fly, 3⅜", Mark II check	EX-	$225.00	99-08
Hargreet	Cat's Paw	wood, RH, painted eyes, 1946 Michigan item	AVG	$25.02	05-07
Harkauf	Trout Minnow	wood, fly rod lure on superb card, 1 BW, a wowser	NOC	$1,703.00	05-06
Harkauf	Wooden Minnow	2½", with 3-blade prop, painted eye, HPGM, chip around belly weight	G+	$852.50	05-04
Harlow	Spoon	pat 1888, nice	EX	$77.61	99-11
Harris	Manistee Minnow	Globe type, name on one side, NOT MET	VG	$905.00	05-07
Harrison Inds	Vibra Bat	cool bat card!	NOC	$32.00	05-03
Harron & Son	Spinner	marked blade on wrong shaft	VG+	$39.00	04-02
Haskell	Minnow	10" saltwater size in wood box	EXIB	$101,200.00	03-11
Hass	Live Minnow	scale	EX	$168.00	01-01
Hastings	Frog	weedless external belly weight	EX	$175.00	05-06
Hastings	Rubber Frog	hand-painted frog	EX	$137.50	04-11
Hastings	Rubber Frog	hand-painted frog	VG	$247.50	04-11
Hastings	Weedless Frog	early rubber frog w/ext BW, light age cracks and right foot reattached, G 2PCBB	EX-IB	$115.00	05-05
Hastings	Weedless Frog	pic box nice, legs missing	?IB	$900.00	01-08
Hastings-Jamison	Frog		VG+	$75.00	00-04
Hawk	Walleye	black shore	minty	$36.00	05-02
Hayes	Feather Minnow	fly, in nice box	NIB	$342.76	99-03
Hayes	Flapper	ugly spinner with lead keel, weedless hook	VG+	$43.00	03-01
Heddon	0	a real pig, NOT MET! ASO seller	poor	$54.67	00-02
Heddon	0	red & blk spots, cup, un, varnish flk	EX-	$1,100.00	99-10
Heddon	0	red/black spots, L-rig	EX-	$385.00	03-07

BRAND	MODEL	SERIES / MFG. CODE / DESCRIPTION	GRADE	PRICE	DATE yy/mm
Heddon	0	red/black spots, L-rig	EX-	$385.00	03-07
Heddon	0	red and black	EX	$1,100.00	01-04
Heddon	0	red spotted, Down Bass box VG+	EXIB	$611.00	03-12
Heddon	0	red, blk spots, HPGM, sm body, c. 1911	EX	$850.00	99-08
Heddon	0	red/black spots, cup rig, Down Bass bx	VG+IB	$265.00	05-07
Heddon	0	spotted	VG	$333.33	00-03
Heddon	0	spotted, Up Bass nice, NOT MET	EXIB	$910.00	01-01
Heddon	0	spotted, varnished over	ugly	$60.00	99-06
Heddon	0	strawberry	EX-	$520.01	99-12
Heddon	0	strawberry	EX-	$550.00	00-05
Heddon	0	strawberry, cup rig	VG+/EX-	$387.00	00-11
Heddon	0	strawberry, Down Bass bx	EXIB	$797.00	03-11
Heddon	0	white spotted	VG+	$175.00	02-11
Heddon	0	yellow spotted	VG-	$150.00	99-04
Heddon	0	yellow spotted, marked tall Down Bass	EX-IB	$685.00	00-02
Heddon	0	yellow with red with black spots, GE, L-rig	VG+	$135.00	05-06
Heddon	0		VG+	$248.00	00-04
Heddon	0	001, yellow spotted, GE, L-rig, chip on back, light general wear	G+	$130.00	05-05
Heddon	0	001, Brush box VG+, toilet	EXIB	$736.00	02-12
Heddon	0	02, Down Bass box nice, lure nice	EXIB	$890.00	02-11
Heddon	0	4", GE, white/red with green decoration, 3 HPGM	GD	$220.00	04-11
Heddon	0	a real pig, NOT MET!!	poor	$97.00	00-02
Heddon	0	awful	poor	$100.00	00-04
Heddon	0	cup rig, spotted	avg	$86.00	03-07
Heddon	0	cup rig, spotted	VG	$139.00	03-07
Heddon	0	five-sided bait, marked props, gill marks, GE	EX	$467.50	05-04
Heddon	0	great Down Bass box	EXIB	$2,075.00	00-02
Heddon	0	most paint there	avg	$150.00	00-03
Heddon	0	Pine tree rough, NOT MET	EX-IB	$675.00	00-03
Heddon	0	r&b dots, varnish	EX-	$1,600.00	99-10
Heddon	0	red and black	EX-	$900.00	01-04
Heddon	0	red spotted, L-rig, decent	VG	$513.00	01-01
Heddon	0	red/black dots, L-rig, full paint, but many varnish flakes	VG+	$207.00	05-07
Heddon	0	red/black spots, L-rig	VG+	$380.00	04-12
Heddon	0	red/black spots	EX	$710.00	01-05
Heddon	0	red/black spots, missing 2 hooks	VG	$266.00	03-01
Heddon	0	red/black spots, varnish, chips	avg+	$280.55	99-03
Heddon	0	red/blk spt, 002 Down Bass VG, NOT MET	VG+IN	$256.00	03-02
Heddon	0	spotted, a sow	ugly	$124.05	99-04
Heddon	0	spotted, Down Bass VG, papers	EXIB	$2,500.00	99-11
Heddon	0	strawberry, SOLD	EX-	$650.00	00-05
Heddon	0	strawberry, cup	VG-	$240.00	00-08
Heddon	0	strawberry, Down Bass VG+	EXIB	$3,054.00	00-08
Heddon	0	strawberry, L-rig	VG+	$440.00	00-05
Heddon	0	strawberry, L-rig	EX	$611.00	05-03
Heddon	0	strawberry, POBW, problems	VG-	$200.00	99-12

BRAND	MODEL	SERIES / MFG. CODE / DESCRIPTION	GRADE	PRICE	DATE yy/mm
Heddon	0	strawberry, L-rig, yellowed	VG+	$250.98	99-11
Heddon	0	tall 002 Down bass	EX-IB	$860.00	99-05
Heddon	0	tall Down Bass box VG, strawberry	EX-IB	$970.00	00-05
Heddon	0	white spotted, nice	EX-	$677.00	02-09
Heddon	0	y spotted, un Down Bass	VG+IB	$410.00	99-09
Heddon	0	y spotted, in unmarked Up Bass bx VG	avgIBS	$129.00	04-07
Heddon	0	yellow spotted	avg	$198.00	00-10
Heddon	0	yellow spotted	VG+	$477.00	02-03
Heddon	0	yellow/r&b spots, cup rig	VG	$373.00	99-01
Heddon	0	yellow strawberry, NOT MET	EX-	$384.00	02-12
Heddon	0		VG	$266.00	00-04
Heddon	0		EX-	$409.00	00-04
Heddon	10	strawberry, like a small "00"	avg	$414.00	99-11
Heddon	10	w/spotted pointers	G	$255.00	98-12
Heddon	10	y/r & blk spots	VG-	$248.27	99-06
Heddon	10 Big Mary	white/sparkle	EX	$480.00	01-05
Heddon	10 FL Special	white/red eye, L-rig, NOT MET	VG	$143.00	00-10
Heddon	10 Light Casting Minnow	strawberry	VG+	$625.00	00-05
Heddon	20	#20-GCB, newer type	NIB	$92.00	05-07
Heddon	20	#20-8'-0-F-HD H or E, 2/2	EX-	$661.00	01-12
Heddon	20	20RHF, Banner box, papers	VG+IB	$103.50	99-03
Heddon	20	21 Down Bass	VG+IB	$300.00	01-01
Heddon	20	Artistic Minnow bx #22, papers, white lure	EX-IB	$616.00	03-01
Heddon	20	Banner box 20L, plastic eye/nail	NIB	$150.00	03-10
Heddon	20	crackle, GE, cup	VG+	$177.00	01-03
Heddon	20	crackleback	avg	$36.00	98-12
Heddon	20	crackleback, white box, "Artisitic Minnow 20"	box EX-	$1,225.00	99-04
Heddon	20	crackleback, intro box VG	EXIB	$1,525.00	99-03
Heddon	20	frog scale, $1,500 minimum, NO BIDS	EX	no bids	05-01
Heddon	20	frog scale, GE	EX-	$599.00	05-06
Heddon	20	goldfish scale, GE, Stanley prop	EX-	$500.00	01-12
Heddon	20	No. 20, GE, cup rig hardware, unmarked prop, rainbow finish, 2 HPGM	G	$110.00	05-04
Heddon	20	P, TE, Banner box	NIB	$150.00	99-01
Heddon	20	perch, PTE, 20L Banner box	EX-IB	$100.00	00-10
Heddon	20	rainbow, cup rig, BW bulge	EX-	$334.00	04-01
Heddon	20	RB, fat body, cup	EX-	$316.00	00-05
Heddon	20	RB, cup, POBW	EX-	$285.00	00-05
Heddon	20	RB, GE, 2 HPGM, L-rig	EX-	$335.00	99-07
Heddon	20	RB, GE, belly chip but nice	EX-	$390.50	00-03
Heddon	20	red, GE, cup, lg touch-up	??	$89.00	02-07
Heddon	20	red, GE, cup, not awful	G	$182.00	01-04
Heddon	20	RH/silver scale, TE	EX	$82.00	00-01
Heddon	20	shiner scale, GE, cup un box	EXIB	$270.00	03-12
Heddon	20	tack glass eye, RH/SS	NIB	$154.00	98-12
Heddon	20	w/red tip of tail, eye pointer	decent	$62.55	99-01
Heddon	20	w/sil & gold sparkle, cup, POBW	EX	$616.00	00-07
Heddon	20	white, GE, POBW	VG	$193.50	98-12

BRAND	MODEL	SERIES / MFG. CODE / DESCRIPTION	GRADE	PRICE	DATE yy/mm
Heddon	20	white/red eye, GE, cup	VG	$208.50	00-01
Heddon	100	100, rainbow, wood box & papers EX	EX-IB	$1,336.00	02-04
Heddon	100	101, RB wood box VG	VG+IB	$535.00	01-12
Heddon	100	101, wood box EX-, "Why of it" paper, rainbow, cup, HPGM	VGIB	$635.00	05-07
Heddon	100	102, Down Bass EX-, white/red eye shadow, NOT MET	EXIB	$400.00	05-07
Heddon	100	102RET, Brush bx, 2pc, odd color paint	NIB	$425.00	03-01
Heddon	100	103, alum/green back, cup	VG-	$207.00	00-08
Heddon	100	103, aluminum, wood box	VGIB	$1,025.00	99-05
Heddon	100	103, wood box, alum,"Why of it" papers	EXIB	$1,685.00	00-01
Heddon	100	104, Down Bass, red, L, NOT MET	EX-IB	$430.00	00-10
Heddon	100	104, wood box, crisp paper	NIB	$4,596.00	00-04
Heddon	100	107, white box (seams repaired), sienna, POBW	EX-IB	$1,375.00	03-02
Heddon	100	107, wood box, lid replaced, NOT MET	VG+IB	$696.00	02-02
Heddon	100	109A, white Down Bass VG+, cup	EX-IB	$1,284.00	00-01
Heddon	100	109L, Brush bx crisp, NOT MET	NIB	$312.00	04-12
Heddon	100	109L, Down Bass	VG+IB	$212.50	99-08
Heddon	100	109L, Down Bass	VG+IB	$305.00	99-10
Heddon	100	109P, L, NOP	EX	$400.00	99-08
Heddon	100	151, wood box, RB, cup, nice box	EXIB	$1,878.73	00-01
Heddon	100	153, wood box, alum, cup, nice box	EX-IB	$1,580.45	00-01
Heddon	100	2BW, cup, HPGM, green/yellow	VG+	$280.00	03-04
Heddon	100	3 belly weights, crackle, NOT MET	VG+	$1,100.00	99-03
Heddon	100	bar perch, Down box 109A rough, L-rig	EXIB	$456.00	04-01
Heddon	100	bar perch, L-rig, marked props	EX	$342.00	05-07
Heddon	100	bar perch, L-rig, un box Down Bass	EXIB	$384.00	02-10
Heddon	100	bar perch, cup rig decent	VG-	$255.00	99-01
Heddon	100	bar perch, cup, HPGM	EX-	$300.00	99-07
Heddon	100	bar perch, cup, HPGM, front prop marked	EX	$350.00	99-08
Heddon	100	bar perch, cup, HPGM, un, wood box avg	VG+IWB	$686.05	99-10
Heddon	100	bar perch, fat, cup, unmarked props	EX-	$405.00	00-11
Heddon	100	bar perch, L, Down Bass	NIB	$1,775.00	00-09
Heddon	100	bar perch, L-rig, ugly belly, rest nice	VG	$300.00	99-02
Heddon	100	bar perch, cup, 2 HPGM, Down, papers	VGIB	$540.00	99-08
Heddon	100	black head/yellow, with correct box	VG+IB	$550.00	05-07
Heddon	100	black head/yellow? (white?), L-rig	VG+	$519.00	03-10
Heddon	100	blend red, 104 wood box EX-, ROBW	EX-IB	$1,600.00	01-10
Heddon	100	blended red, cup, HPGM, GE	VG+	$100.00	05-07
Heddon	100	blended red, L-rig	EX-	$150.00	05-07
Heddon	100	blended red/blk, cup, HPGM, unmarked	EX-	$430.00	99-08
Heddon	100	blended w/slate back, cup, HPGM	EX	$800.00	99-08
Heddon	100	blue back, purty	EX-	$872.00	00-01
Heddon	100	blue bordered bx 101 avg	EX-IB	$850.00	02-04
Heddon	100	blue/silver, 2 HPGM, 2 BW, cup	G	$232.50	99-05
Heddon	100	blue scale, L-rig, NOT MET	VG	$265.00	02-02
Heddon	100	box G	VGIB	$512.00	01-03
Heddon	100	copper, cup, thin	EX-	$855.00	99-12

BRAND	MODEL	SERIES / MFG. CODE / DESCRIPTION	GRADE	PRICE	DATE yy/mm
Heddon	100	crackle, "2nd"	EX	$375.00	00-09
Heddon	100	crackle, 3? (2 maybe) BW, nickle cups	avg	$258.00	02-01
Heddon	100	crackle, cup, tail chip	EX-IB	$1,025.00	00-10
Heddon	100	crackle, L, fat body	EX-	$192.00	01-05
Heddon	100	crackle, 3 BW, brass cups & ties	G	$370.00	00-12
Heddon	100	crackle, Brush, 2pc	NIB	$406.00	99-12
Heddon	100	crackle, cup, Down Bass	EXIB	$408.78	00-03
Heddon	100	crackle, cup, HPGM, fat body	EX	$655.00	99-08
Heddon	100	crackle, cup, unmarked, sweeping gills	EX	$305.00	99-10
Heddon	100	crackle, cup, HPGM, un, tapered	EX+	$765.00	99-08
Heddon	100	crackle, GE, L-rig, fat, NOT MET	EX-	$202.52	99-06
Heddon	100	crackle, high forehead, 2 BW, NOT MET	VG	$255.00	02-02
Heddon	100	crackle, high, 2 BW, brass cups tie	EX	$800.00	99-10
Heddon	100	crackle, high, brass	ugly chips	$280.70	99-11
Heddon	100	crackle, L, blush	EX-	$375.00	99-10
Heddon	100	crackle, L, fat body, blush, Down Bass	NIB	$740.00	00-09
Heddon	100	crackle, L-rig	EX-	$242.50	00-01
Heddon	100	crackle, L-rig, cracked eyes, OK	EX-	$153.00	00-05
Heddon	100	crackle, L-rig, Down Bass EX, NOT MET	NIB	$472.00	00-07
Heddon	100	crackle, L-rig, HPGM, fat body	EX-	$202.00	01-05
Heddon	100	crackle, taper, un, HPGM, cup, crack?	EX-	$231.50	99-12
Heddon	100	crackleback, brass cups, 3 BW	avg	$450.00	04-11
Heddon	100	crackleback, Brush box, 2pc	NIB	$356.00	02-10
Heddon	100	crackleback, cup, HPGM	VG+	$114.00	05-07
Heddon	100	crackleback, wood bx faded, top/sides nice	EX-IB	$650.00	02-12
Heddon	100	crisp wood box	NIB	$2,125.00	02-01
Heddon	100	crackleback, cup, fat body, MO, HPGM	EX+	$451.25	99-04
Heddon	100	crackleback, L-rig, marked front prop	VG	$132.50	99-05
Heddon	100	crackleback, broad, L-rig, nice	EX	$355.55	99-12
Heddon	100	DBB, high forehead, brass cup, 2 BW, ugly belly, NOT MET	VG-IB	$364.00	04-07
Heddon	100	Down Bass 101 EX, L-rig, NO BIDS	NIB	$500.00	04-11
Heddon	100	fancy light green crackle, cup, HPGM, fat	EX	$601.00	99-12
Heddon	100	fancy back wood box, slim body	NIB	$2,751.00	00-09
Heddon	100	fat, cup, 2HPGM, crkleback, chip belly weight	EX-	$375.00	99-03
Heddon	100	FG, NNOP, cup, pre-1910	VG	$305.00	99-01
Heddon	100	frog scale, fat body, belly varnish	EX-	$510.00	01-03
Heddon	100	frog scale, L-rig	EX-	$450.00	03-07
Heddon	100	frog scale, L-rig	EX	$595.00	00-07
Heddon	100	frog scale, belly varnish, SOLD	VG+	$375.00	00-05
Heddon	100	frog scale, fat body, L-rig	EX-	$676.00	98-12
Heddon	100	GE, old rainbow, 2 HPGM, box EX and all writing legible	EX	$104.50	04-11
Heddon	100	gold scale, L-rig, varnish loss	EX-	$405.00	99-07
Heddon	100	goldfish, L-rig	EX-	$950.00	00-05
Heddon	100	goldfish, L-rig, NOT MET	EX-	$425.00	01-03
Heddon	100	green crackleback, 2pc-rig, GE, hint of wear, in orig G- Brush 2PCCB	EXIB	$290.00	05-05
Heddon	100	green crackleback, fat body, L-rig, some varnish loss	VG	$95.00	05-05

BRAND	MODEL	SERIES / MFG. CODE / DESCRIPTION	GRADE	PRICE	DATE yy/mm
Heddon	100	green scale, L-rig, marked props	VG+	$76.00	05-07
Heddon	100	green scale, L, broad scale	VG	$255.00	99-06
Heddon	100	green scale, L-rig, ugly varnish	avg	$97.00	99-09
Heddon	100	high forehead, brass, 2 BW, NOT MET	VG+	$700.00	04-01
Heddon	100	high forehead, red back/y, 3 sweeping HPGM	VG-	$510.00	01-08
Heddon	100	L, in 109 Up Bass, L-rig, marked	EX-	$330.00	99-05
Heddon	100	nice wood box, crackleback lure	EXIB	$1,407.00	00-06
Heddon	100	perch scale, L-rig	VG	$82.00	05-07
Heddon	100	perch scale, L-rig, decent	VG+	$188.87	00-03
Heddon	100	perch scale, L-rig, nice	VG+	$256.00	99-06
Heddon	100	Pine Tree bx rough, 109A bar perch, cup HPGM	EX-IB	$660.00	04-03
Heddon	100	rainbow, cup, HPGM	VG+	$107.00	05-07
Heddon	100	rainbow, cup, HPGM, 1 BW	VG+	$107.00	05-07
Heddon	100	rainbow, cup, HPGM, no name on props	VG-	$59.00	05-07
Heddon	100	rainbow, toilet seat, POBW, Down Bass unmarked	EXIB	$228.00	04-11
Heddon	100	rainbow, cup	VG	$310.99	99-02
Heddon	100	RB, cup, white pasteboard box avg	EX-IB	$360.00	02-10
Heddon	100	RB, fat, L-rig, un box avg	EX	$302.00	00-11
Heddon	100	RB, L, some sm chips	VG++	$191.00	00-08
Heddon	100	RB, L-rig, fat body nice	EX	$243.00	00-08
Heddon	100	RB, L-rig, varnish belly but nice	VG+	$130.00	00-04
Heddon	100	RB, cup, HPGM, BW missing, plugged	VG+	$92.00	00-04
Heddon	100	RB, cup, HPGM, "Gem" WYSIWYG	EX?	$126.00	99-08
Heddon	100	RB, cup, nice	EX/EX-	$287.86	00-01
Heddon	100	RB, high head, brass, poor wood, NOT MET	VG-IB	$751.00	01-01
Heddon	100	RB, L-rig, big chips but not awful	avg	$52.00	00-04
Heddon	100	RB, L-rig, fat body, gleamer	EX+	$458.53	00-01
Heddon	100	RB, L-rig, GE, nice	EX	$355.00	99-11
Heddon	100	RB, L-rig, marked	EX-	$280.00	99-08
Heddon	100	red head/white/red tail, L-rig	EX	$522.00	01-03
Heddon	100	red stripe, RB? copper in eyes, L-rig	EX-	$202.49	99-10
Heddon	100	red, black HPGM, cup	VG	$139.00	00-05
Heddon	100	red, cup rig	EX	$405.00	01-03
Heddon	100	red, ugly	poor	$76.00	98-12
Heddon	100	red, cup, ugly	avg	$231.50	00-01
Heddon	100	salt flitter, cup, fat, SOLD	EX+	$950.00	00-05
Heddon	100	sienna crackle, c. 1908, cup, blunt nose	EX	$595.00	05-02
Heddon	100	shiner scale, L	VG+	$338.00	00-08
Heddon	100	sienna crackle, c. 1907, cup rig, no name on prop	VG	$144.00	05-07
Heddon	100	sienna crackle, 2 BW, cup, HPGM	EX-	$1,000.00	00-07
Heddon	100	sienna crackle, cup, un, HPGM	G	$168.50	00-01
Heddon	100	sienna, cup, HPGM	EX-	$735.00	99-06
Heddon	100	sienna, drags, chips, ugly	avg	$167.50	99-02
Heddon	100	silver, HPGM, cup, some sm chips but not awful	avg	$49.00	04-11
Heddon	100	slate back, fat, cup, HPGM	EX-	$259.44	99-12
Heddon	100	slate back, red eye shadow, cup, HPGM	EX	$810.00	00-04
Heddon	100	slate, cup, wood box not marked	VG-IB	$1,225.00	99-06
Heddon	100	slate/red eye	EX-	$575.00	00-05

BRAND	MODEL	SERIES / MFG. CODE / DESCRIPTION	GRADE	PRICE	DATE yy/mm
Heddon	100	Stanley props, cup, RH	EX	$749.00	00-05
Heddon	100	white, red eye shadow, L-rig, varnish flaking, NOT MET	VG	$102.00	05-07
Heddon	100	white, red eye, cup, Down Bass bx 102	NIB	$767.00	04-11
Heddon	100	white, cup, HPGM, tiny varnish, real	EX-	$388.00	00-04
Heddon	100	white, wood box, NOT MET	VG-IB	$810.00	99-09
Heddon	100	white/red eyes, cup, fat body	VG+	$300.00	99-03
Heddon	100	wood box	EXIB	$1,200.00	00-07
Heddon	100	wood box & paper nice, crackle	EXIB	$1,575.00	00-05
Heddon	100	wood box nice, RB	VG+IB	$1,500.00	01-03
Heddon	100	wood box VG+, $1,000 NOT MET	VG+IB	$790.00	01-03
Heddon	100	wood box, crackle, cup, HPGM, nice box	EXIB	$2,000.00	00-02
Heddon	100	wood box & papers 101 EX, cup, HPGM	EXIB	$1,691.00	03-05
Heddon	100	y, high forehead, 2 BW, brass cups	VG	$1,300.00	99-08
Heddon	100	yellow, high, brass, wood, NOT MET	VG-IB	$1,505.02	99-11
Heddon	101 RB	blunt nose, marked wood box EX	EXIB	$2,000.00	99-10
Heddon	101 RB	blunt nose, marked wood box VG+	EXIB	$1,650.00	99-10
Heddon	101	L-rig, Down Bass VG-	VG+IB	$511.00	01-01
Heddon	101	RB, fat, cup, name on props	VG+/EX-	$425.00	99-10
Heddon	103 ALUM	wood box nice, POBW, black HPGM	VG+IB	$2,550.00	00-12
Heddon	104	blended red, cup, un	EX	$700.00	99-10
Heddon	104	solid red, L, chip OBW	EX-	$625.00	99-10
Heddon	107	sienna crackle, cup, no name, slim	EX	$1,000.00	99-10
Heddon	107	sienna, fat, cup, un, HPGM	EX-	$1,000.00	99-10
Heddon	109 D UW Minnow	green scale, L-rig, age lines and flakes on belly	VG+	$85.00	05-05
Heddon	109	blue border, Down Bass VG+, cup	EX-IB	$2,000.00	99-10
Heddon	109D	cup, marked props	EX-	$500.00	99-10
Heddon	109D	Down Bass	EX-IB	$500.00	99-10
Heddon	119N	dace, 2pc, Up Bass	EXIB	$171.00	00-11
Heddon	150	150RET, underwater minnow, GPE, SR, red eye & tail	VG+	$75.00	05-06
Heddon	150	150, Up Bass, L-rig, crackle	EXIB	$301.00	01-07
Heddon	150	150P, S-rig, Banner	EXIB	$154.01	99-09
Heddon	150	150RB, S-rig, Banner	NIB	$125.00	99-12
Heddon	150	150RHF, Banner box, S-rig, PE	NIB	$187.00	01-01
Heddon	150	151, Down Bass bx EX, L-rig, NOT MET	EXIB	$305.00	05-07
Heddon	150	151, in nice wood box, papers	EX-	$1,810.00	99-02
Heddon	150	151, Up Bass, L-rig	EX-IB	$305.00	01-07
Heddon	150	151, wood box VG	VGIB	$788.00	01-11
Heddon	150	151, wood box, no writing lid top	EXIB	$1,450.00	99-05
Heddon	150	152, tall Down Bass VG+, L-rig fat body	EX-IB	$455.00	02-06
Heddon	150	152, Down, L, w/red eyes and tail	NIB	$1,884.00	00-01
Heddon	150	152, Down Bass, L-rig, nice box	EXIB	$960.00	99-03
Heddon	150	154, Down Bass bx "154" looks bogus, NOT MET	NIB	$940.00	02-02
Heddon	150	154, Down Bass EX-, L-rig NOT MET	EXIB	$691.00	05-07
Heddon	150	159, Down(VG), L-rig, HPGM NOT MET	EXIB	$610.00	00-10
Heddon	150	159, pasteboard box, saltwater, cup, HPGM, NOT MET	NIB	$898.00	02-10

BRAND	MODEL	SERIES / MFG. CODE / DESCRIPTION	GRADE	PRICE	DATE yy/mm
Heddon	150	159A, Down Bass crisp, bar perch, L-rig	NIB	$898.00	03-09
Heddon	150	159A, Up Bass EX, bar perch, L	VGIB	$510.00	00-12
Heddon	150	159A, Up Bass rough, L-rig	VGIB	$257.00	04-05
Heddon	150	159D, Down VG, L-rig, screamer lure	NIB	$2,000.00	00-04
Heddon	150	159D, Up Bass EX, L-rig NOT MET	EXIB	$585.00	05-07
Heddon	150	159J, Down, L-rig, frog scale, nice box	EXIB	$1,400.00	99-08
Heddon	150	159L, Up Bass box, NOT met	EX-IB	$600.00	99-03
Heddon	150	159L, Up Bass bx, toilet seat, GE, NOT MET	NIB	$611.00	05-07
Heddon	150	159L, Up Bass VG, toilet seat NOT MET	EXIB	$611.00	05-07
Heddon	150	159PL, L-rig, Up Bass EX	NIB	$2,932.00	02-07
Heddon	150	159RH, Up, flitter, cup, age lines	VG+IB	$460.00	00-02
Heddon	150	all red finish, GE, marked props, toilet seat hardware, few tiny hook dings, Brush bx VG+	EXIB	$660.00	05-04
Heddon	150	alum (bluish back), HPGM	EX-	$799.00	02-08
Heddon	150	aluminum, c. 1908, blunt nose, cup rig, no name on prop	EX-	$860.00	05-07
Heddon	150	aluminum, cup, HPGM	VG+	$256.00	02-07
Heddon	150	aluminum, L-rig	EX-	$214.00	04-02
Heddon	150	aluminum, L-rig, iffy paint job	EX	$455.00	00-04
Heddon	150	Banner bx 150GCB, crackleback, PE	EXIB	$132.00	05-07
Heddon	150	bar perch, cup rig, name on props, GE	avg	$76.00	05-07
Heddon	150	bar perch, Down box 159A rough, L-rig	VG+IB	$274.00	04-01
Heddon	150	bar perch, cup, fat	VG	$290.00	00-01
Heddon	150	bar perch, cup, NOT MET ASO	poor	$66.00	00-02
Heddon	150	bar perch, L-rig	G	$120.00	99-12
Heddon	150	bar perch, L-rig	VG	$282.77	00-02
Heddon	150	bar perch, L-rig, decent	G+	$170.00	99-03
Heddon	150	bar perch, L-rig, fat body	EX-	$1,100.00	99-05
Heddon	150	bar perch, toilet, POBW	EX-	$550.00	00-05
Heddon	150	bar perch, L-rig	EX	$556.00	01-01
Heddon	150	black crackleback, L-rig	EX	$380.00	00-04
Heddon	150	blended alum, NOP, L, thin body, varnish	EX-	$650.00	99-08
Heddon	150	blended red, L-rig, fat body	G	$161.00	99-12
Heddon	150	blk, sucker, brass, high forehead	EX-	$2,550.00	99-04
Heddon	150	blue crackle, Brush, 2pc	EXIB	$950.00	99-10
Heddon	150	blue Down Bass 159A VG+, cup	VG+IB	$2,700.00	01-11
Heddon	150	CB, Up Bass	EX-IB	$417.00	00-08
Heddon	150	CBK, cup, 3 HPGM	VG+	$285.00	99-07
Heddon	150	CBK, cup, much varnish flaking	G	$164.50	99-05
Heddon	150	copper, 3 BW, POBW, brass cups, c. 1904	EX-	$31,857.00	03-02
Heddon	150	crackle, cup, HPGM, Down Bass bx	EXIB	$305.00	03-11
Heddon	150	crackle, high forehead, 3 BW, brass cups	VG-	$2,005.00	01-12
Heddon	150	crackle, L-rig	EX-	$242.00	01-05
Heddon	150	crackle, L-rig, Up Bass	VGIB	$260.00	00-10
Heddon	150	crackle, PE	EXIB	$158.00	02-01
Heddon	150	crackle, cup, HPGM, 1 BW	mint	$1,075.00	99-08
Heddon	150	crackle, cup, HPGM, POBW	VG	$151.00	99-12
Heddon	150	crackle, cup, HPGM, unmarked	VG+	$284.88	99-09

BRAND	MODEL	SERIES / MFG. CODE / DESCRIPTION	GRADE	PRICE	DATE yy/mm
Heddon	150	crackle, cup, HPGM, un props, nice	EX+	$616.00	99-11
Heddon	150	crackle, faded wood box	VG+IB	$1,450.00	00-05
Heddon	150	crackle, L-rig, blush, thin w/pointed nose	EX	$555.00	99-06
Heddon	150	crackle, L-rig, blush, ugly belly varnish	VG	$200.00	99-08
Heddon	150	crackle, L-rig, Down Bass	EX-IB	$501.57	00-02
Heddon	150	crackle, L-rig, POBW, Down, NOT MET	EX-IB	$301.55	99-08
Heddon	150	crackle, PE, PTCB	NIB	$112.50	00-03
Heddon	150	crackle, toilet, crisp Brush box, catalog, POBW	NIB	$432.00	02-02
Heddon	150	crackle, wood box & paper EX	EXIB	$2,285.00	01-05
Heddon	150	crackleback, poor picture	EX-?	$200.00	99-01
Heddon	150	crackleback, 3 BW, brass cups, NOT MET	EX	$4,611.00	03-02
Heddon	150	crackleback, blush chin, marked props	mint	$609.00	02-11
Heddon	150	crackleback, Brush bx EX, 2pc, POBW	EXIB	$165.00	05-07
Heddon	150	crackleback, c. 1920s, cup rig, name on prop, name on belly, blush chin	mint	$472.00	05-07
Heddon	150	crackleback, fat, HPGH, L-rig nice, c. 1915	EX	$352.00	02-09
Heddon	150	crackleback, fat body, Up Bass	EXIB	$535.00	99-04
Heddon	150	crackleback, L-rig	G	$166.50	99-03
Heddon	150	crackleback, L-rig, 3 HPGM	EX-	$300.00	99-01
Heddon	150	crackleback, PE	VG	$104.00	99-05
Heddon	150	crackleback, round body, cup, unmarked props	VG+	$375.00	99-03
Heddon	150	crackleback, wood bx (hung!) & papers EX-	NIB	$2,559.00	03-05
Heddon	150	crackle, L, Down Bass, decent	G+IB	$173.50	99-06
Heddon	150	cup rig, ugly	poor	$153.00	99-01
Heddon	150	cup, marked props, most paint gone	beater	$69.00	01-03
Heddon	150	cup, slate, not awful	avg	$100.00	99-02
Heddon	150	D. Double papers, blended RH, cup	EX? (G)	$811.00	99-05
Heddon	150	Down Bass box 150 VG, cup, D. Double papers	EX-IB	$561.00	03-10
Heddon	150	Down Bass EX, L-rig, blush chin, NOT MET	EX+IB	$405.00	05-07
Heddon	150	fat, sienna crackle, cup, HPGM, tail chip	VG+	$456.00	00-01
Heddon	150	frog scale, L-rig, huge chips	poor	$88.00	00-03
Heddon	150	frog scale?	avg	$91.00	98-12
Heddon	150	frog spot, L-rig, name on belly, marked props	EX	$467.00	04-03
Heddon	150	frog, L-rig, NOT MET	EX	$560.00	02-10
Heddon	150	frog, L-rig	EX	$910.00	99-09
Heddon	150	frog, L-rig, varnish flake	VG	$485.00	98-12
Heddon	150	frog, L-rig, champagne eyes, fat	VG	$422.00	00-02
Heddon	150	frog scale, L, fat body, belly varnish	VG+	$494.00	00-11
Heddon	150	frog scale, L-rig	EX-	$810.00	02-06
Heddon	150	frog scale, L-rig, sm tail chip	EX-	$711.00	03-01
Heddon	150	frog scale, 2pc, flawless, SOLD	mint	$2,850.00	00-05
Heddon	150	frog scale, L	VG-	$407.00	01-03
Heddon	150	frog scale, L, looks OK	VG-	$296.00	01-04
Heddon	150	GE		$148.50	04-11
Heddon	150	GE, brown back/red, 3 black HPGM, box good	VG	$27.50	04-11
Heddon	150	GE, green crackleback, 3 HPGM, box 150 good	VG	$137.50	04-11
Heddon	150	GE, green crackleback, red chin blush	EX?	$165.00	04-11
Heddon	150	GE, green scale	EX	$77.00	04-11

BRAND	MODEL	SERIES / MFG. CODE / DESCRIPTION	GRADE	PRICE	DATE yy/mm
Heddon	150	GE, red, 3 HPGM	VG	$121.00	04-11
Heddon	150	GE, rainbow	avg	$75.00	99-01
Heddon	150	glitter, L-rig, marked props, HPGM	EX-	$400.00	00-10
Heddon	150	gold, cup, HPGM, fat, 2 ugly sm chips	VG-	$251.00	00-02
Heddon	150	goldfish, L-rig	EX-	$1,850.00	00-05
Heddon	150	goldfish scale, L-rig, decent	VG+	$361.00	01-10
Heddon	150	goldfish scale, L-rig, POBW, nice	EX-	$898.00	04-12
Heddon	150	goldfish scale, un box rough	EXIB	$450.00	04-12
Heddon	150	goldfish, toilet seat	EX	$1,525.00	04-03
Heddon	150	goldfish, fat body, L-rig	VG	$565.00	00-04
Heddon	150	goldfish scale, L-rig, ugly belly	VG	$300.00	00-10
Heddon	150	green back/yellow, L-rig, fat, NO BIDS	avg	$355.00	99-12
Heddon	150	green scale with glass eyes, two-piece toilet seat hardware	EX	$330.00	05-07
Heddon	150	green scale, L, NOP, fat body	VG+	$375.00	99-08
Heddon	150	green/white, 3 BW, slim body	avg	$660.00	02-10
Heddon	150	green scale, L-rig, NOP	EX+	$875.00	00-05
Heddon	150	green scale, L-rig, fat, purty	EX-/EX	$810.00	01-03
Heddon	150	green scale, L	EX-	$393.00	00-03
Heddon	150	green scale, L-rig	VG	$255.00	00-02
Heddon	150	high forehead, brass, 2 BW, rainbow	VG-	$2,025.00	99-04
Heddon	150	high forehead, POBW, 2 BW, crackleback, wood box	EX-IB	$5,100.00	03-11
Heddon	150	HPGM, NOP, L-rig, missing hardware	poor	$128.00	00-08
Heddon	150	L-rig, bar perch, Up Bass box	both mint	$2,700.00	99-01
Heddon	150	L-rig, high forehead, varnish	VG	$300.00	99-01
Heddon	150	L-rig, w/flitter	rough	$61.00	99-02
Heddon	150	nice wood box, "Fancyback"	EXIB	$1,426.00	00-05
Heddon	150	o/blk spot, L-rig, marked props	VG-	$1,047.22	99-05
Heddon	150	orange	EX-	$78.00	04-11
Heddon	150	orange/blk spots, L-rig	VG+	$1,025.00	01-06
Heddon	150	P, PE, papers, NOT MET	NIB	$153.00	01-03
Heddon	150	painted eye, S-rig, perch scale	mint	$100.00	04-11
Heddon	150	PE, crackleback	EX	$126.00	99-01
Heddon	150	pearly gold/red eye shadow, L-rig	VG	$565.00	00-10
Heddon	150	perch scale, L-rig	EX	$330.00	99-04
Heddon	150	perch scale, L, ugly varnish	VG	$280.55	00-03
Heddon	150	perch scale, L, wrong Down Bass	VG	$251.05	99-08
Heddon	150	perch scale, L-rig, 159A Down Bass	EX+IB	$1,875.00	99-04
Heddon	150	Pine Tree box poor	EX-	$885.00	00-05
Heddon	150	Pine tree box VG+, lure belly varnish	VG+IB	$1,226.00	01-01
Heddon	150	r/w, PE, age lines	EX	$97.00	99-01
Heddon	150	rainbow, cup, HPGM, NOP, thin body	EX-	$425.00	03-01
Heddon	150	rainbow, L-rig, GE, big chips	poor	$41.00	04-12
Heddon	150	rainbow, L-rig, HPGM	VG+	$270.00	03-07
Heddon	150	rainbow, L-rig, looks nice! junk box	EX	$204.00	02-10
Heddon	150	rainbow, PE	avg	$77.90	99-01
Heddon	150	RB, 2pc, Brush bx, belly stencil, GE	NIB	$367.00	03-11

BRAND	MODEL	SERIES / MFG. CODE / DESCRIPTION	GRADE	PRICE	DATE yy/mm
Heddon	150	RB, cup	poor	$66.00	00-10
Heddon	150	RB, L-rig	EX	$310.00	01-04
Heddon	150	RB, L-rig, un box VG, NOT MET	EXIB	$305.00	01-05
Heddon	150	RB, L-rig, light touch-up	VG	$86.00	00-05
Heddon	150	RB, NOP, cup, fat body, varnish	avg	$131.00	00-10
Heddon	150	RB, PE, Banner box VG	NIB	$213.00	00-05
Heddon	150	RB, Pine Tree box & papers, NOT MET	?	$1,512.00	01-10
Heddon	150	RB, thin body, cup, Up Bass bx nice, NOT MET	NIB	$522.00	02-03
Heddon	150	RB, 2pc, marked, belly stencil	EX-	$244.56	99-09
Heddon	150	RB, 2pc, POBW	EX	$455.00	99-11
Heddon	150	RB, cup, 3 HPGM, ugly varnish	VG	$179.00	99-08
Heddon	150	RB, cup, HPGM, lt hook drag	EX-	$450.00	00-03
Heddon	150	RB, cup, HPGM, round, poor wood bx	EXIB	$850.00	00-02
Heddon	150	RB, cup, HPGM, unmarked, POBW	VG+	$188.37	99-09
Heddon	150	RB, cup, un Down Bass box	EX-	$300.00	99-07
Heddon	150	RB, GE, L-rig, belly varnish, NOT MET	EX-	$202.50	99-07
Heddon	150	RB, lg scrape on back, Down, NOT MET	avgIB	$177.00	01-03
Heddon	150	RB, L-rig, Down Bass VG-, decent	VGIB	$255.00	99-12
Heddon	150	RB, L-rig, fat body, varnish flakes	VG-	$203.50	99-11
Heddon	150	RB, L-rig, NOT MET	VG	$180.50	99-10
Heddon	150	RB, PE, PTCB, cat	NIB	$325.00	00-04
Heddon	150	RB, zinc eyes, 2pc	EX	$565.00	00-06
Heddon	150	red, 2pc, POBW	G	$148.00	00-05
Heddon	150	red scale, L-rig	G	$326.00	99-01
Heddon	150	red scale, L-rig	VG+	$483.00	99-12
Heddon	150	red scale, L-rig, ROBW, purty	EX	$1,975.00	99-09
Heddon	150	red, cup	EX-	$750.00	00-05
Heddon	150	red, cup, HPGM, NOP	EX	$900.00	99-08
Heddon	150	red, huge belly chips, top OK	fair	$75.00	99-01
Heddon	150	red, L-rig, fat, NO BIDS	VG-	$355.00	99-12
Heddon	150	red/dark back, cup, HPGM, POBW	VG	$191.50	99-05
Heddon	150	red/orange, cup, HPGM, varnish problems	VG+	$898.00	03-04
Heddon	150	red scale	EX	$1,200.00	01-04
Heddon	150	red scale, L-rig	VG	$213.00	01-10
Heddon	150	red scale, GE, L-rig, Down Bass unmarked	avg	$305.00	99-02
Heddon	150	red scale, L-rig	VG	$371.00	00-05
Heddon	150	red scale, un Down Bass	VG	$685.00	99-10
Heddon	150	repaint, 2pc	awful	$46.00	99-02
Heddon	150	RET, 2pc	EX-	$301.00	00-03
Heddon	150	RH & tail, L-rig, marked "2nd"	EX-	$480.00	05-02
Heddon	150	RH, saltwater, cup rig, a few hvy agelines	EX-	$350.00	04-02
Heddon	150	RH, PE, S-rig, NOT MET	NIB	$102.00	01-04
Heddon	150	RH, PE, cat, NOT MET	EXIB	$102.51	99-06
Heddon	150	RSF (South Bend color), NOT MET	rough	$280.00	01-06
Heddon	150	saltwater, cup, unmarked Down Bass bx	NIB	$675.00	03-01
Heddon	150	saltwater, L, NOT MET	EX	$356.00	01-01
Heddon	150	saltwater, w/flakes, L, NOT MET	EX	$720.00	01-01

BRAND	MODEL	SERIES / MFG. CODE / DESCRIPTION	GRADE	PRICE	DATE yy/mm
Heddon	150	seinna crackle, cup, fat body, HPGM, marked props	EX	$890.00	04-12
Heddon	150	shiner scale, L-rig	EX+	$522.00	99-12
Heddon	150	shiner scale, PE	VGIB	$96.00	99-04
Heddon	150	shinerscale, L-rig	VG	$127.00	03-07
Heddon	150	sienna CB, cup, marked props, belly stencil	EX	$555.00	02-03
Heddon	150	sienna crackle, c. 1907, blunt nose, cup rig, no name on prop	EX-	$385.00	05-07
Heddon	150	sienna crackle, cup, HPGM, poor wood box	EX-	$1,198.00	02-02
Heddon	150	sienna crackle, L-rig, sm tail chip, nice	EX-	$637.00	02-05
Heddon	150	sienna crackle, cup, POBW	EX-	$750.00	00-05
Heddon	150	sienna crackle, L-rig, HPGM, purty	EX-	$910.00	01-10
Heddon	150	sienna, cup, HPGM, fat body	VG+	$730.00	03-11
Heddon	150	silver, HPGM, ugly varnish, "looks gold"	??	$1,000.00	01-09
Heddon	150	slate, cup, HPGM, blunt nose, POBW	EX-	$330.00	01-12
Heddon	150	slate, cup, HPGM, NOT MET	VG	$128.00	02-02
Heddon	150	slate, cup, MP, HPGM	VG-	$225.00	99-06
Heddon	150	strawberry, L-rig, bad varnish ugly	G	$351.00	00-11
Heddon	150	w/red eyes, L-rig	EX-	$349.00	00-07
Heddon	150	w/RH and tail, L-rig	EX-	$750.00	00-05
Heddon	150	w/sparkles, cup, HPGM	EX-	$301.99	00-03
Heddon	150	white paste bx rough, NOT MET	GIB	$302.00	02-11
Heddon	150	white sparkles, L-rig, Down Bass	EXIB	$560.00	00-02
Heddon	150	white, cup, HPGM, NOP, fat body	EX-	$625.00	03-01
Heddon	150	white, red eye blush, L, marked props	EX-	$355.00	99-10
Heddon	150	white, red eye, L-rig, POBW	EX-	$240.00	02-01
Heddon	150	white/red eyes, cup	EX	$255.00	05-07
Heddon	150	white/flitter, GE, L-rig	EX+	$685.00	99-11
Heddon	150	white/glitter, fat, L-rig	EX	$661.00	99-04
Heddon	150	white/red blush eyes, L-rig	EX-	$198.00	02-12
Heddon	150	white/silver flakes, L-rig	EX-	$605.00	99-03
Heddon	150	Wilbourn Special No. 250 finish, in original box, unmarked high Down Leaping Bass box, GE, marked props, L-rig hardware, 3 HPGM, some varnish flaking	EXIB	$3,960.00	05-04
Heddon	150	wood box 151RB VG+, cup	VG+IB	$935.00	00-12
Heddon	150	y/blk head, L-rig, varnish throat	VG	$453.00	00-08
Heddon	150	yellow spotted, pointers, NOT MET	VG+	$91.00	99-01
Heddon	150 x 2	crackle cup rig, frog L-rig	avg	$187.00	00-10
Heddon	150 x 2	RHF and OS, PE, S-rig	EX	$330.50	99-08
Heddon	151 Special UW Minnow	07-08 model, rainbow w/white back, GE, CR, light general wear	VG-	$140.00	05-05
Heddon	151 Wood Box	RB, nice box, lure decent	VG+IB	$1,077.00	00-11
Heddon	151	great wood box, NOT MET	VG+IB	$908.00	00-08
Heddon	151	RB, L, Down Bass (cut)	NIB	$1,350.00	99-10
Heddon	151	wood box, RB, cup, HPGM, unmarked	EXIB	$1,750.00	99-08
Heddon	152 Slate	cup, blunt nose, wood box VG	EXIB	$2,500.00	99-10
Heddon	152	r/w/r, L, chip OBW	EX-	$1,000.00	99-10

BRAND	MODEL	SERIES / MFG. CODE / DESCRIPTION	GRADE	PRICE	DATE yy/mm
Heddon	154	blended red, Down Bass, cup, high	VGIB	$400.03	00-01
Heddon	155	early YRB, wood box type	VG+/EX-	$1,500.00	99-10
Heddon	159 D UW Minnow	deluxe green scale, silver strip on back, scales wrap around belly	EXIB	$1,750.00	05-05
Heddon	159A	bar perch, L-rig, nice Up Bass box	EX-IB	$636.00	00-11
Heddon	159A	bar perch, L-rig, sm flakes by eyes	EX-	$800.00	99-10
Heddon	159B	Down Bass EX, cup, tail chip, dent	VGIB	$669.00	00-12
Heddon	159D	2pc, chip OBW	EX-	$675.00	99-10
Heddon	159D	deluxe green scale, L, marked props	EX	$1,000.00	99-10
Heddon	159H	red scale, L, no blush, no name on belly	EX	$2,000.00	99-10
Heddon	159L	2pc, Brush VG	EX+IB	$900.00	99-10
Heddon	159P	2pc, Brush 159L	EXIB	$950.00	99-10
Heddon	159P	ROBW	EX	$700.00	99-10
Heddon	1600 Deep Diving Wiggler	1600, white, L-rig nice	EX	$229.48	00-03
Heddon	1600 Deep Diving Wiggler	1600S, Down Bass	NIB	$500.00	04-12
Heddon	1600 Deep Diving Wiggler	1600S, Down Bass VG+	EXIB	$456.00	04-12
Heddon	1600 Deep Diving Wiggler	1600S, NOT MET	EX-IB	$408.03	00-01
Heddon	1600 Deep Diving Wiggler	1609S, tall Down Bass, side hooks	EX-IB	$305.00	00-11
Heddon	1600 Deep Diving Wiggler	bar perch, L-rig	EX-	$350.00	03-01
Heddon	1600 Deep Diving Wiggler	bar perch, side hooker, pigtail line tie	VG	$168.00	03-05
Heddon	1600 Deep Diving Wiggler	crackle, Down Bass VG, L-rig	NIB	$520.00	99-12
Heddon	1600 Deep Diving Wiggler	crackleback belly, 3-hk, inchworm tie	EX	$266.00	03-11
Heddon	1600 Deep Diving Wiggler	crackleback, inchworm	EX-	$179.50	98-12
Heddon	1600 Deep Diving Wiggler	crackleback, pigtail	VG	$163.00	99-01
Heddon	1600 Deep Diving Wiggler	crisp tall Down Bass bx, hangtag, crab paper	NIB	$1,225.00	02-01
Heddon	1600 Deep Diving Wiggler	Down Bass bx VG+, inchworm line tie, L-rig hardware, white/red/green finish, tight age lines, 2 small varnish flakes on left side	EX+IB	$852.50	05-04
Heddon	1600 Deep Diving Wiggler	Down, "Wiggler" on side r/w	EXIB	$293.88	99-08
Heddon	1600 Deep Diving Wiggler	frog finish	VG	$137.50	04-11
Heddon	1600 Deep Diving Wiggler	frog spot	avg	$77.00	04-11
Heddon	1600 Deep Diving Wiggler	frog spot, inchworm tie, GE, L-rig	VG+	$110.00	05-02
Heddon	1600 Deep Diving Wiggler	frog, pigtail	EX	$331.00	00-08
Heddon	1600 Deep Diving Wiggler	frog, tough side hook type, 3-hk	VG-	$98.00	03-07
Heddon	1600 Deep Diving Wiggler	mint box, hangtag, papers	NIB	$1,225.00	02-01
Heddon	1600 Deep Diving Wiggler	r/w, inchworm, NOT MET	avg	$46.00	99-01
Heddon	1600 Deep Diving Wiggler	RB, inchworm, tall Down un box, NOT MET	EX-IB	$315.00	01-10
Heddon	1600 Deep Diving Wiggler	RH, inch, hangtag, papers, tall Down Bass	NIB	$779.00	01-09
Heddon	1600 Deep Diving Wiggler	S, 1600S deep Down Bass, avg	VG+IB	$365.00	00-10
Heddon	1600 Deep Diving Wiggler	SB, un Down Bass, varnish	VG-IB	$102.00	00-11
Heddon	1600 Deep Diving Wiggler	strawberry, side hooks	VG+	$375.00	00-05
Heddon	1600 Deep Diving Wiggler	strawberry, inchworm	EX-	$153.00	05-07
Heddon	1600 Deep Diving Wiggler	strawberry, inchworm	VG	$63.00	04-12
Heddon	1600 Deep Diving Wiggler	strawberry, pigtail	EX	$474.00	04-01
Heddon	1600 Deep Diving Wiggler	strawberry, bottom cup, pigtail	EX	$400.00	99-03
Heddon	1600 Deep Diving Wiggler	white/red flakes, varnish, inchworm	VG	$150.00	00-03
Heddon	1600 Deep Diving Wiggler	y/strawberry, L-rig, 3-hooker side	VG+	$104.00	00-05
Heddon	1600 Deep Diving Wiggler	y/blk & red spots, inchworm	VG+	$79.00	99-08

BRAND	MODEL	SERIES / MFG. CODE / DESCRIPTION	GRADE	PRICE	DATE yy/mm
Heddon	1600 Deep Diving Wiggler	yellow spotted, nice eye appeal	EX-	$121.00	03-06
Heddon	1600 Deep Diving Wiggler	yellow spotted, tall Down Bass box EX-	EXIB	$1,400.00	01-12
Heddon	1700 Near Surface Wiggler	1609B, tall Down Bass Wiggler box	EXIB	$1,330.00	99-10
Heddon	1700 Near Surface Wiggler	1700S Down Bass bx, some varnish flaking	EXIB	$450.00	03-11
Heddon	1700 Near Surface Wiggler	1705 Down, pigtail, strawberry, paper	NIB	$1,027.00	01-01
Heddon	1700 Near Surface Wiggler	5-hooker plus Vamp	poor	$155.00	99-01
Heddon	1700 Near Surface Wiggler	blue scale, several pointers, ugly	VG-	$431.00	00-11
Heddon	1700 Near Surface Wiggler	crackleback, L-rig, 3 belly hooks	EX	$256.00	03-12
Heddon	1700 Near Surface Wiggler	Down Bass unmarked, Crab Wiggler paper, strawberry inchworm	VG+IB	$225.00	05-07
Heddon	1700 Near Surface Wiggler	frog scale	avg	$328.00	05-07
Heddon	1700 Near Surface Wiggler	frog spot, pigtail line tie, GE	VG	$160.00	04-11
Heddon	1700 Near Surface Wiggler	frog, GE, inchworm, varnish	VG	$118.00	00-05
Heddon	1700 Near Surface Wiggler	GE, frog finish	VG	$82.50	04-11
Heddon	1700 Near Surface Wiggler	goldfish, inchworm tie	EX-	$1,200.00	01-10
Heddon	1700 Near Surface Wiggler	L-rig, strawberry, belly varnish flakes, inchworm	EX-	$173.00	05-07
Heddon	1700 Near Surface Wiggler	RH, inchworm, GE, L-rig, no belly varnish, otherwise nice	VG+	$78.00	05-07
Heddon	1700 Near Surface Wiggler	strawberry, inchworm, hvy age lines	VG+	$146.00	05-07
Heddon	1700 Near Surface Wiggler	strawberry, GE, cup	VG	$158.00	99-01
Heddon	1700 Near Surface Wiggler	strawberry, pigtail, L-rig	VG	$176.00	99-03
Heddon	1700 Near Surface Wiggler	thin bodied, Depression era	RET	$121.00	05-07
Heddon	1700 Near Surface Wiggler	y spotted, inchworm, eye crack, SOLD	EX-	$550.00	00-05
Heddon	1700 Near Surface Wiggler	y/blk & red spots, pigtail	EX-	$230.50	99-08
Heddon	1700 Near Surface Wiggler	frog spot, inchworm, GE	avg	$75.00	04-11
Heddon	175	crackle	avg	$205.00	00-10
Heddon	175	crackle, SOLD	EX	$1,550.00	00-05
Heddon	175	crackle, NOT MET	VG+	$345.00	00-07
Heddon	175	crackle, L-rig, NOT MET	VG-	$565.00	99-03
Heddon	175	crackleback, c. 1912 – 15, minimum bid $500, NO BIDS	EX-	no bids	05-07
Heddon	175	crackleback, cup rig	EX-	$500.00	05-07
Heddon	175	gray slate, 2 BW, varnish	VG	$350.00	99-08
Heddon	175	rainbow, cup	EX-	$1,325.00	01-05
Heddon	175	rainbow, cup rig	VG+	$760.00	99-03
Heddon	175	RB, cup rig, decent	VG+	$333.00	01-06
Heddon	175	slate, HPGM, un props	EX-	$1,587.00	01-03
Heddon	175	slate, NOT MET	VG	$463.00	00-09
Heddon	175	yellowed white?	VG-	$393.50	00-03
Heddon	200	no eyes, red/lum? bubbly	avg	$117.00	98-12
Heddon	200	200BH, Up Bass, 2pc hardware, no eyes	NIB	$480.00	00-05
Heddon	200	200LUM, Down Bass box VG	EX-IB	$500.00	05-03
Heddon	200	200LUM, Down Bass, 3 hooks	EX-IB	$1,000.00	00-11
Heddon	200	200S Down Bass, 3 pins, varnish	VG+IB	$736.00	00-09
Heddon	200	4-hooker, 200SW Down Bass, blue head	EX-IB	$910.00	02-02
Heddon	200	4-hooker, BH, 2 pins, un Pine Tree VG+	EX-IB	$3,500.00	00-11
Heddon	200	b/w, L-rig, 3-screw collar	VG	$137.00	99-01
Heddon	200	b/w, 3 pins, varnish flk	VG?	$246.50	99-05
Heddon	200	BH, 4-hooker	poor	$111.00	03-02

LURES

BRAND	MODEL	SERIES / MFG. CODE / DESCRIPTION	GRADE	PRICE	DATE yy/mm
Heddon	200	BH, slope nose, repainted collar, NOT MET	EX	$1,006.00	00-08
Heddon	200	BH, 2 pins, c. 1912, Down Bass bx	EXIB	$1,500.00	02-02
Heddon	200	BH, 4 hooker! tail cap	VG	$710.00	01-03
Heddon	200	BH, 4-hooker! age lines	EX-	$800.00	04-01
Heddon	200	BH, L-rig, Up Bass, NOT MET	EXIB	$350.00	00-08
Heddon	200	BH, 4 hooks, 2 sides	VG+	$885.00	00-02
Heddon	200	BH, L, Up Bass nice box, cat	NIB	$599.00	00-03
Heddon	200	BH, L-rig, no eyes, ugly varnish	VG	$127.00	00-05
Heddon	200	BH, type C, 3 pins, double name collar	VG+	$153.00	00-08
Heddon	200	blue head, L-rig	VG+	$105.00	05-07
Heddon	200	Down Bass 200BH nice	EXIB	$513.00	01-09
Heddon	200	Down Bass box 200SW avg, blue head	VG+IB	$220.00	04-11
Heddon	200	Down Bass bx 200SL EX, RH lum	EXIB	$685.00	04-03
Heddon	200	frog finish	VG	$82.50	04-11
Heddon	200	frog spot, no eyes, 2pc, belly stencil	EX	$310.00	03-04
Heddon	200	frog, no eyes, L-rig	VG-	$98.00	05-07
Heddon	200	frog, L-rig, no eyes	EX-	$191.00	00-10
Heddon	200	frog, NE, L-rig, Down Bass	EXIB	$307.00	00-01
Heddon	200	frog, no eyes, L-rig, tail cap	EX-?	$128.00	00-10
Heddon	200	frog, tail cap, 3 pins, cup, no eyes	G	$112.00	99-04
Heddon	200	frog, Up Bass nice, 3 pins, small chips	VG+IB	$205.00	00-04
Heddon	200	green scale, no eyes, L-rig, belly varnish	VG+	$261.00	02-12
Heddon	200	green scale, no eyes, L-rig	EX	$1,428.00	00-04
Heddon	200	mouse, 2pc	EX-	$962.00	03-02
Heddon	200	nickle-plated hardware, 2-pin collar retaining most of its red, general wear	VG+	$247.50	05-04
Heddon	200	r/w, GE	EX	$237.50	99-02
Heddon	200	red scale, L-rig, no eyes, decent	G	$866.00	00-05
Heddon	200	RH, GE, 2pc, small wrinkle in paint	EX-	$306.00	02-02
Heddon	200	RH/LUM 200SL Down box	EX-IB	$500.00	01-09
Heddon	200	RH/LUM unmarked, 3-pin collar	VG	$114.00	03-11
Heddon	200	SB, L, Down, tail cap, ugly varn, NOT MET	VG+IB	$305.00	00-11
Heddon	200	solid red repaint? 2 pins	EX	$898.00	00-05
Heddon	200	Up Bass bx LUM EX, lure ugly varnish, NOT MET	avgIB	$68.00	04-07
Heddon	200	w/red & green spots, L-rig, tail cap	EX-	$800.00	99-12
Heddon	210	210 BH, blue head/white, GE, 2pc rig, just a hint of wear	EX	$125.00	05-05
Heddon	210	210 BH, GH/w, powder blue head, NE, LR, some light varnish flaking and very light wear	EX-	$95.00	05-05
Heddon	210	210BF Banner, PE	NIB	$104.00	02-08
Heddon	210	210BLH Banner box, wood lure, PE	NIB	$224.00	04-12
Heddon	210	210BLH Banner box, PE	NIB	$101.99	99-02
Heddon	210	210BLH Banner bx EX, wood lure, PE	NIB	$96.00	05-07
Heddon	210	210BM, 2pc, Brush	NIB	$249.50	99-11
Heddon	210	219 B, frog spot, NE, TS-rig, NSOB, few tiny varn pointers and hint of wear, rare in toilet seat	EX-	$90.00	05-05
Heddon	210	219 D, green scale, GE, 2pc, very minor flks and light wear, orig VG- Brush Surf Orena box	VG+IB	$125.00	05-05
Heddon	210	219B, minty Down Bass box, L-rig	NIB	$405.00	99-03

114

BRAND	MODEL	SERIES / MFG. CODE / DESCRIPTION	GRADE	PRICE	DATE yy/mm
Heddon	210	219B, frog, 2pc, GE, Brush, cat	NIB	$698.00	99-05
Heddon	210	219B, frog, L-rig, NE, Up Bass, cat	NIB	$568.00	99-05
Heddon	210	BF, GE, NOT MET	EX-	$81.00	01-03
Heddon	210	BF, white eye	NIB	$88.02	99-09
Heddon	210	BH, GE	VG	$61.00	99-03
Heddon	210	BH, GE, Brush	VGIB	$100.00	99-06
Heddon	210	BH/w, GE, Up Bass box	NIB	$521.99	99-02
Heddon	210	blue head/white wood, PE	EX-	$46.00	04-10
Heddon	210	Brush box 210RH, GE, 2pc	VG+IB	$76.00	01-10
Heddon	210	cream/blue head, GE	VG-	$50.00	05-07
Heddon	210	frog spot, GE, 2pc	VG+	$76.00	05-07
Heddon	210	frog, 2pc, GE	EX+	$188.00	04-01
Heddon	210	frog, GE	EX	$154.00	00-07
Heddon	210	frog, PE	EX	$62.00	99-01
Heddon	210	frog scale, L-rig	VG+	$830.00	02-01
Heddon	210	GM		$29.50	99-02
Heddon	210	GM, looks poor	VG	$49.99	99-03
Heddon	210	GM, 2pc	EX	$82.00	01-02
Heddon	210	GM, S-rig	EX	$81.00	00-03
Heddon	210	GM, worn box, 2pc, NOT MET	EX+IB	$104.00	00-03
Heddon	210	green scale, L-rig	VG+	$50.00	03-07
Heddon	210	green scale, GE, 2pc	VG+	$212.00	02-01
Heddon	210	LUM, nice box, awful chips, NOT MET	poorIB	$112.00	01-05
Heddon	210	LUM, 2pc, red eye & tail	EX+	$350.00	99-03
Heddon	210	luminous, GE	EX-	$375.00	99-01
Heddon	210	mouse	EX-	$103.50	99-01
Heddon	210	mouse, ears & tail	VG	$61.99	99-04
Heddon	210	mouse, S-rig	EX	$56.00	99-02
Heddon	210	r/w, Banner box	NIB	$152.00	99-01
Heddon	210	r/w, GE	VG	$45.00	99-01
Heddon	210	r/w, GE, 2pc, NOT MET	EX	$62.00	99-01
Heddon	210	red head/white, GE	EX-	$66.00	99-01
Heddon	210	red scale, L-rig, NE	VG	$340.00	01-03
Heddon	210	RH, no eyes, L-rig	EX-	$41.00	04-11
Heddon	210	RH, PE	EX	$66.00	05-07
Heddon	210	RH, S-rig, PE	EX-	$37.00	00-11
Heddon	210	RH, GE, 2pc, NOT MET	EX+	$100.00	99-05
Heddon	210	RH/white, GE, 2pc, stencil	mint	$179.50	00-01
Heddon	210 Spook	210B	NIB	$133.50	99-12
Heddon	210 Spook	210BF	NIB	$78.00	99-10
Heddon	210 Spook	210BF	NIB	$82.00	99-06
Heddon	210 Spook	210BH	NIB	$207.51	99-06
Heddon	210 Spook	210BH, window box	NIB	$140.00	05-07
Heddon	210 Spook	210BO	NIB	$197.51	99-06
Heddon	210 Spook	210CDF, NOT MET	NIB	$73.00	03-01
Heddon	210 Spook	210SD	NIB	$61.00	04-02
Heddon	210 Spook	210SS	NIB	$203.00	00-07
Heddon	210 Spook	210SSD	NIB	$81.00	99-06

BRAND	MODEL	SERIES / MFG. CODE / DESCRIPTION	GRADE	PRICE	DATE yy/mm
Heddon	210 Spook	210Y	NIB	$127.50	99-06
Heddon	210 Spook	BF, white eye	NIB	$103.50	99-03
Heddon	210 Spook	BH	NIB	$163.50	99-06
Heddon	210 Spook	BH	mint	$194.00	02-08
Heddon	210 Spook	BH	NIB	$212.50	99-02
Heddon	210 Spook	BH	EX	$217.00	00-05
Heddon	210 Spook	BH	NIB	$223.00	02-10
Heddon	210 Spook	BH	NIB	$229.00	99-04
Heddon	210 Spook	BH	NIB	$265.00	00-03
Heddon	210 Spook	black	EX+	$102.50	99-08
Heddon	210 Spook	black	NIB	$137.00	00-04
Heddon	210 Spook	black, white eyes	EX	$106.50	99-01
Heddon	210 Spook	blk, J.Yates! NOT MET	EX	$84.00	99-02
Heddon	210 Spook	blue head	EX	$134.00	03-07
Heddon	210 Spook	blue head	NIB	$255.00	04-01
Heddon	210 Spook	blue head/white	EX-	$160.00	01-11
Heddon	210 Spook	blue shore	EX	$179.00	03-07
Heddon	210 Spook	BO	NIB	$258.00	99-04
Heddon	210 Spook	bone, NOT MET	NIB	$107.00	01-01
Heddon	210 Spook	BSO on card	NOC	$151.00	03-07
Heddon	210 Spook	BSO, orange dace, NOT MET	mint	$325.00	99-04
Heddon	210 Spook	bullfrog	EX	$61.00	01-07
Heddon	210 Spook	chart coach dog	EX	$86.89	99-02
Heddon	210 Spook	CDF	NIB	$80.00	04-02
Heddon	210 Spook	coach dog	EX	$68.00	01-07
Heddon	210 Spook	frog	VG	$56.55	99-01
Heddon	210 Spook	frog	mint	$91.00	99-01
Heddon	210 Spook	frog scale, no hardware, salesman sample	EX	$530.00	03-07
Heddon	210 Spook	frog spot, gold eye	EX	$91.00	03-07
Heddon	210 Spook	RH blended	EX	$127.00	03-07
Heddon	210 Spook	SD	NIB	$141.00	99-03
Heddon	210 Spook	shad	EX	$71.00	01-07
Heddon	210 Spook	shad	EX	$43.00	05-07
Heddon	210 Spook	silver scale	mint	$167.50	00-03
Heddon	210 Spook	silver scale	AVG	$83.00	05-07
Heddon	210 Spook	silver scale, belly rough	VG-	$83.00	05-07
Heddon	210 Spook	SS	EX+	$122.50	99-04
Heddon	210 Spook	white/flitter, no code on box	NIB	$132.50	99-01
Heddon	210 Spook	white/red eye shadow	EX	$105.00	00-10
Heddon	210 Spook	y	NIB	$127.50	99-06
Heddon	210 Spook	y coach dog	NIB	$125.00	00-08
Heddon	210 Spook	YCD	EX	$102.00	02-10
Heddon	210 Spook	YCD	NIB	$106.00	02-10
Heddon	210 Spook	YCD	NIB	$107.50	99-06
Heddon	210 Spook	YCD, no code on box	NIB	$125.50	99-01
Heddon	210 Spook	yellow	NIB	$127.50	99-04
Heddon	210 Spook	yellow	EX	$152.50	99-05
Heddon	210 Spook	yellow	EX	$160.00	99-01

BRAND	MODEL	SERIES / MFG. CODE / DESCRIPTION	GRADE	PRICE	DATE yy/mm
Heddon	210 Spook	yellow/red chin	EX	$117.00	04-12
Heddon	210 Spook x 3	3 different	NIB	$385.00	99-11
Heddon	250	rainbow, ugly varnish, L-rig	rough	$175.00	03-11
Heddon	250	green scale	VG	$450.00	00-10
Heddon	250	red scale, L-rig, not awful	G	$360.00	00-05
Heddon	260 Surface Minny	green scale, GE, toilet, NOBP	VG+	$364.00	00-09
Heddon	260 Surface Minny	perch scale, 2pc, NOT MET	EX	$407.00	01-05
Heddon	260 Surface Minny	strawberry, GE	EX	$1,035.00	99-02
Heddon	269L	Up Bass 261 VG	EXIB	$650.00	99-10
Heddon	300	3⅛", white/red eyes and tail	VG?	$55.00	04-11
Heddon	300	3¾", GE, rainbow	VG	$66.00	04-11
Heddon	300	300S Down Bass VG, 2-hk, L-rig	EXIB	$550.00	05-07
Heddon	300	301 white box poor	VG-IB	$518.00	00-04
Heddon	300	302 3H Brush crisp	NIB	$1,200.00	01-09
Heddon	300	4-hooker in slate	EX-	$495.00	05-07
Heddon	300	6-hook, marked, repaint	new	$232.00	02-03
Heddon	300	6-hooker, 2pc, strawberry decent	EX-	$600.00	02-05
Heddon	300	6-hooker, crackleback	fair	$1,052.50	99-01
Heddon	300	XRY, 6-hooker	VG+	$1,501.00	99-01
Heddon	300	7-hooker, perch scale, 2pc	EX-	$600.00	02-06
Heddon	300	all varnish missing, was RB, now white	fair	$156.00	00-07
Heddon	300	crackle, ugly belly varnish, L-rig, blush	VG	$137.50	99-08
Heddon	300	crackleback, brass cup, long HPGM, early one	VG+	$350.00	03-04
Heddon	300	crackleback, L-rig, fat body	VG+	$281.00	02-11
Heddon	300	crackle, 2-hk, blush	EX	$395.00	02-03
Heddon	300	crackle, 2-hk, HPGM, brass? cup, early white-eye model	VG+	$1,250.00	05-07
Heddon	300	crackle, brass cup, 3-hooks, HPGM	VG+	$242.00	04-01
Heddon	300	crackle, cup, 2-hk	EX-	$685.00	00-09
Heddon	300	crackle, cup, long gill marks, reserve	EX+	$2,400.00	00-11
Heddon	300	crackle, cup, $2400 NOT MET	EX	$356.00	00-12
Heddon	300	crackle, cup, thin, NOT MET	EX-	$898.00	00-10
Heddon	300	crackle, L, HPGM	EX-	$515.00	01-04
Heddon	300	crackle, 2pc, chip OBW	EX-	$400.00	99-10
Heddon	300	crackle, 3-hk, cup, round body, SOLD	EX	$775.00	00-05
Heddon	300	crackle, 5-hook, DL box	NIB	$5,600.00	00-01
Heddon	300	crackle, cup, HPGM, a pig	ugly	$81.00	99-08
Heddon	300	crackle, cup, HPGM, un, NOT MET	EX-	$300.00	99-09
Heddon	300	crackle, flat L-rig, 3 HPGM	EX-	$300.00	99-08
Heddon	300	crackle, L, blush chin	VG+	$255.00	99-08
Heddon	300	crackle, L, HPGM, NOT MET	VG+	$178.00	00-12
Heddon	300	crackle, L, HPGM, NOT MET	EX-	$260.00	99-11
Heddon	300	crackle, L-rig, blush	VG+	$229.00	00-08
Heddon	300	crackle, L-rig, red chin	VG+	$227.50	00-03
Heddon	300	crackleback, 2pc, Up Bass bx 300 2H, VG	VG+IB	$212.00	04-02
Heddon	300	crackleback, 3-hk, 2pc, name on belly, blush chin	EX+	$539.00	05-07
Heddon	300	crackleback, cup, belly chip, decent	EX-	$204.00	02-07

BRAND	MODEL	SERIES / MFG. CODE / DESCRIPTION	GRADE	PRICE	DATE yy/mm
Heddon	300	crackleback, cup, HPGM ugly, age lines, NOT MET	VG+	$393.00	03-04
Heddon	300	crackleback, HPGM, L-rig	EX	$344.00	02-12
Heddon	300	crackleback, L-rig, air gills, x-holes!	holes	$157.50	99-08
Heddon	300	cup, high forehead, unmarked	EX	$4,650.00	99-02
Heddon	300	frog scale, one side awful, L-rig	poor	$227.00	03-01
Heddon	300	frog spot, L-rig	EX-	$1,500.00	02-09
Heddon	300	frog spot, L-rig, small tail sliver	EX	$1,500.00	02-09
Heddon	300	green back, RB, 3-hk	VG+	$775.00	00-05
Heddon	300	high forehead, HPGM, crackleback, brass cup	EX+	$6,101.00	03-09
Heddon	300	L, 2pc, bad bleed through, NOT MET	VG	$188.50	99-05
Heddon	300	L-rig, 302 Up Bass crisp, tissue, NOT MET	NIB	$877.00	02-05
Heddon	300	L-rig, fat body, HPGM, dull, rust	VG+	$300.00	99-12
Heddon	300	made on a wire, through rigged, South Bend Surf Oreno box	EX-	$650.00	05-05
Heddon	300	nat scale, 6-hooker	EX-	$935.00	99-09
Heddon	300	perch scale, 2pc, 6-hooker	EX-	$490.00	01-06
Heddon	300	perch scale, 6-hooker, 2pc, NOT MET	EX-	$433.00	02-01
Heddon	300	pike scale, 2pc, 3-hooker, big burn, POBW	VG	$410.00	01-09
Heddon	300	pike scale, 6-hooker	EX-	$787.77	00-03
Heddon	300	rainbow, 2-hk, L-rig	EX-	$288.00	04-03
Heddon	300	rainbow, 2pc	EX-	$230.00	03-07
Heddon	300	rainbow, L-rig, decent, NOT MET	VG+	$260.00	01-11
Heddon	300	RB, 4-hooker, L-rig	EX-	$1,100.00	01-11
Heddon	300	RB, 6-hooker, L-rig	VG+	$1,205.00	00-03
Heddon	300	RB, 7-hooker, 2pc	VG+	$910.00	01-03
Heddon	300	RB, cup, fat, NOT MET	VG	$183.00	00-10
Heddon	300	RB, L-rig, I bid $1065	EX	$1,090.00	00-11
Heddon	300	RB, L-rig, missing rear hook & prop, NOT MET	VG	$109.00	02-11
Heddon	300	RB, cup, HPGM, un, ugly varnish	VG-?	$178.50	99-09
Heddon	300	RB, cup, POBW	EX	$1,025.00	99-11
Heddon	300	RB, cup, ugly varnish, otherwise nice	VG	$255.00	99-11
Heddon	300	RB, L-rig, marked, NOT MET	EX-	$240.50	99-09
Heddon	300	RB, L-rig, NOT MET	EX	$510.00	99-07
Heddon	300	red, L-rig, repaint?	EX-	$645.00	99-05
Heddon	300	red scale, L-rig	avg	$81.00	02-10
Heddon	300	RET, L-rig	EX-	$798.00	00-02
Heddon	300	RH, cup rig, varnish loss, NOT MET	EX-?	$205.00	99-03
Heddon	300	saltwater finish, 2-hk, L-rig, HPGM	EX-	$345.00	04-03
Heddon	300	saltwater flitter, 3-hook, L-rig, chip on tail	VG+	$262.00	05-07
Heddon	300	SB, 2pc, unmarked props	EX-	$800.00	01-08
Heddon	300	slate back, cup, thin, NOT MET	EX-	$765.00	00-10
Heddon	300	slate, cup, HPGM	EX	$425.00	03-07
Heddon	300	slate, cup, HPGM, lg crunch, age lines	avg	$124.00	00-09
Heddon	300	slate, cup, HPGM, name on props	VG-	$150.00	04-11
Heddon	300	strawberry	VG-	$158.50	99-05
Heddon	300	strawberry, 2pc	avg	$228.00	03-07
Heddon	300	strawberry, 2pc	EX	$355.00	03-07

BRAND	MODEL	SERIES / MFG. CODE / DESCRIPTION	GRADE	PRICE	DATE yy/mm
Heddon	300	strawberry, 3-hk, cup	avg	$112.00	03-04
Heddon	300	strawberry, L-rig, many pointers & sm chips	avg	$182.00	04-01
Heddon	300	strawberry, L-rig, 3-hk, SOLD	VG+	$325.00	00-05
Heddon	300	strawberry, L-rig, HPGM, Down Bass	VG+IB	$760.00	99-06
Heddon	300	strawberry, 300S X3 Brush box	NIB	$2,125.00	00-06
Heddon	300	red eye, L-rig	EX-	$283.88	99-04
Heddon	300	white/red eye shadow, L-rig	EX-	$220.00	04-07
Heddon	300	white spotted, 6-hk, toilet	VG+	$566.00	01-04
Heddon	300	white, cup, HPGM, ugly varnish	G	$166.00	01-01
Heddon	300	white, red eye shadow, L-rig	EX-	$197.00	02-07
Heddon	300	white, red eye, L-rig, age lines, decent	VG+	$206.00	02-01
Heddon	300	white, L-rig, spotty varnish, NOT MET	G	$296.00	99-02
Heddon	300	white, red eye, 6-hooker	VG	$585.00	00-03
Heddon	300	white, red eye, 2pc, 3 hooks	EX-	$334.00	00-09
Heddon	300	white/glitter, L-rig, 2-hk, hook drags	VG+	$589.00	01-06
Heddon	300	white/red eye shadow, L-rig, fat body	VG+	$181.00	05-07
Heddon	300	white/red eye, L-rig	VG+	$264.00	00-04
Heddon	300	white/red eye, L-rig	EX-	$390.00	00-11
Heddon	300	XRY, 2pc	EX	$1,000.00	99-10
Heddon	300	y spotted, 2pc	avg	$188.00	00-10
Heddon	300	yellow, cup, unmarked props	G	$129.00	02-07
Heddon	302	slate back, cup, POBW	EX	$1,350.00	99-10
Heddon	350	350S Fish Flesh bx	EXIB	$778.00	03-11
Heddon	350	green scale, 1 side nice, 1 ugly	VG	$620.00	00-08
Heddon	350	green scale, hook drag, chip	VG	$400.00	00-09
Heddon	350	nat scale, hook drag, ugly belly	VG-	$178.50	99-11
Heddon	350	nat scale, small tail chip	EX-	$562.51	99-12
Heddon	350	natural scale (green)	VG+	$433.00	00-10
Heddon	350	natural scale, 359CP	VGIB	$361.00	99-08
Heddon	350	RH, GE, NOT MET	EX-	$383.00	99-05
Heddon	350	SB, nice	EX-	$735.00	99-11
Heddon	350	strawberry, Fish Flesh bx avg	NIB	$725.00	04-12
Heddon	350	yellow spotted	EX-	$898.00	99-09
Heddon	352	Fish Flesh box, toilet	NIB	$1,026.00	01-02
Heddon	400	alum, all brass, 3 BW, POBW, hook drag	VG	$800.00	99-08
Heddon	402	blue crackleback head	EX	$575.00	02-03
Heddon	402	sienna crackle	VG+	$400.00	01-01
Heddon	402	white, crackle forehead, NOT MET	EX	$768.00	01-06
Heddon	402	y/crackleback skullcap, GE	EX	$611.00	00-04
Heddon	402 Bucktail	yellow/sienna, crackleback forehead	EX	$465.00	04-04
Heddon	402 Killer Surface Minny	rainbow, varnish flaking	VG-	$175.00	02-08
Heddon	402 Surface	white/crackle, NOT MET	EX	$797.00	01-03
Heddon	450 Killer	lavender, 3 BW, repaint?	VG+	$1,480.00	00-09
Heddon	450 Killer	red/white/red, $500 NOT MET	EX	$240.00	00-05
Heddon	450 Killer	red/white/red, 1 BW, repaint?	EX	$1,200.00	99-08
Heddon	508	y/flitter, crack ABW, rust hooks	EX-	$400.00	99-10
Heddon	508RH	sm tail chip	EX-	$200.00	99-10
Heddon	600 Saltwater Special	RH, GE, 3⅝"	EX	$120.50	00-03

BRAND	MODEL	SERIES / MFG. CODE / DESCRIPTION	GRADE	PRICE	DATE yy/mm
Heddon	700	3-hk, sienna, a pig, big chips, overspray	poor	$560.00	99-08
Heddon	700	fancy sienna	EX-	$4,850.00	01-04
Heddon	700	3-hk, pikie, L-rig	VG-	$1,302.00	99-02
Heddon	700	3-hk, sway belly, crackleback, NOT MET	VG+	$1,225.00	02-12
Heddon	700	3-hk, sway belly, crackleback, GE, cup rig	EX-	$798.00	05-07
Heddon	700	3-hk, sway belly, 3 BW	VG	$457.00	01-10
Heddon	700	3-hk, sienna crackle, NOT MET	VG+	$2,850.00	00-02
Heddon	700	3-hk, sway back, 4 BW, crackle, SOLD	mint	$5,500.00	00-05
Heddon	700	3-hook, sway belly, sienna, ugly, NOT MET	poor	$505.00	03-02
Heddon	700	5-hk, round body, 701 intro box EX, POBW	NIB	$23,600.00	02-04
Heddon	700	701 Musky Vamp box G, sway, 3-hk, NOT MET	VG+IB	$1,229.00	01-11
Heddon	700	bar perch, 3-hk, sway belly, varnish flaking	VG-	$511.00	04-02
Heddon	700	bar perch, 3-hook, sway belly, decent	VG	$2,348.00	02-08
Heddon	700	bar perch, 3-hooker	avg	$458.00	04-12
Heddon	700	bar perch, sway belly, 3-hk, 4 BW, decent	VG	$1,116.00	01-10
Heddon	700	bar perch, 3-hk, sway belly	VG+	$3,451.00	00-02
Heddon	700	bar perch, POBW2, sway belly, cup	VG	$2,735.00	99-10
Heddon	700	crackle, 3-hk, sway belly, blush, ugly varnish	VG	$1,300.00	01-08
Heddon	700	crackle, 3-hook, sway, ugly belly, NOT MET	VG-	$685.00	02-03
Heddon	700	crackle, sway belly, HPGM nice	VG+	$3,050.00	02-01
Heddon	700	crackle, 3-hk, bad varnish on belly	avg	$885.55	00-02
Heddon	700	crackle, cup, HPGM, big chip, NOT MET	?	$2,247.00	00-12
Heddon	700	green scale, 709D box, 3-hook, min $20K, NO BIDS	VG+IB	$20,000.00	03-11
Heddon	700	large round body style, GE, gill marks, 4 belly weights and unmarked props, small areas restored	VG	$1,320.00	05-04
Heddon	700	old perch, 4 BW, hvy L, chips on BW	VG+	$6,327.50	99-11
Heddon	700	rainbow, sway belly	VG-	$1,401.00	02-07
Heddon	700	RB, sway belly, 3-hk, could be worse	avg	$1,550.00	02-05
Heddon	700	RB, 3-hook, decent	VG+	$1,683.00	00-02
Heddon	700	round body! sienna rainbow, 5-hk, lg hooks	EX-	$13,100.00	02-08
Heddon	700	sienna crackle, 3-hk, sway belly	VG-	$2,500.00	01-06
Heddon	700	sienna crackle, 3-hk, 5 touch-ups, NOT MET	repaired	$1,326.00	01-12
Heddon	700	sienna crackle, ugly, NOT MET	avg	$375.00	02-03
Heddon	700	sienna, perch, big chips ugly, 5-hk, sway belly	avg.	$5,200.00	02-02
Heddon	700	sienna, 3-hk, touched-up, still ugly	??	$512.00	03-04
Heddon	700	sienna, 3-hook, huge slice out of belly	?	$630.00	00-10
Heddon	800 Swimming Minnow	802 Up Bass nice	VG+IB	$182.00	01-10
Heddon	800 Swimming Minnow	c. 1911, 3⅛", GE, yellow/green, red spots, 2 HPGM	EX-	$198.00	04-11
Heddon	800 Swimming Minnow	spotted	VG	$275.00	00-02
Heddon	800 Swimming Minnow	strawberry, SOLD	EX	$1,750.00	00-05
Heddon	800 Swimming Minnow	3¼", finished in yellow/red/green decoration, large GE, 2 HPGM, trailing treble, chipping on edges, w/correct box VG-, minor moisture stains and paper tears	EXIB	$5,500.00	05-04
Heddon	800 Swimming Minnow	white pasteboard box VG+, 3-lure paper	EXIB	$5,300.00	04-12
Heddon	850 Swimming Minnow	3¾", GE, white/green, red spots, 3 HPGM	VG+	$137.50	04-11

BRAND	MODEL	SERIES / MFG. CODE / DESCRIPTION	GRADE	PRICE	DATE yy/mm
Heddon	850 Swimming Minnow	HPGM, fat body, L-rig, spotted, nice	VG+	$1,450.00	03-07
Heddon	900 Swimming Minnow	901 white DLB crisp bx, orange? spot	NIB	$8,800.00	04-11
Heddon	900 Swimming Minnow	awful chips, ugly	poor	$123.00	04-11
Heddon	900 Swimming Minnow	bad varnish, no chips, NOT MET	avg	$158.00	00-09
Heddon	900 Swimming Minnow	orange spotted	VG+	$520.00	05-02
Heddon	900 Swimming Minnow	SB, chips	VG-	$500.00	01-07
Heddon	900 Swimming Minnow	spotted, ugly edge rubs bad	fair	$256.00	00-03
Heddon	900 Swimming Minnow	spotted, nice	VG+	$600.00	03-07
Heddon	900 Swimming Minnow	spotted, normal rubs on sharp edges	VG	$203.00	05-07
Heddon	900 Swimming Minnow	spotted	VG-	$422.00	98-12
Heddon	900 Swimming Minnow	4½", surface bait, GE, trailing treble, belly double with locking pin, yellow/red/green decorations, 3 HPGM, 1 tiny chip near tail, minor varnish flaking	EX	$550.00	05-04
Heddon	900 Swimming Minnow	w/red spots, big belly chips, NOT MET	G	$760.55	99-03
Heddon	900 Swimming Minnow	white/red spots, HPGM, screw eye hook hanger	VG-	$242.00	02-12
Heddon	900 Swimming Minnow	y spotted, decent, NOT MET	VG+?	$447.00	00-04
Heddon	900 Swimming Minnow	y spotted, HPGM, box rough, SOLD	EX-IB	$1,900.00	00-05
Heddon	900 Swimming Minnow	yellow spotted, $500 NOT MET	VG+	$405.00	01-04
Heddon	900 Swimming Minnow	yellow spotted, HPGM, GE	EX	$588.00	05-07
Heddon	900 Swimming Minnow		EX	$2,750.00	00-04
Heddon	900 Swimming Minnow	4⅜", GE, yellow/red/green spots, 3 HPGM	VG	$192.50	04-11
Heddon	ABU Hi-Lo	9440XBW, Heddon ABU PTCB crisp, Heddon ABU on belly	NIB	$225.00	05-07
Heddon	Artistic Minnow	#51 blended gold, white 2PCCB	EXIB	$960.00	99-05
Heddon	Artistic Minnow	#51 blended gold, white box	EXIB	$960.00	99-04
Heddon	Artistic Minnow	#51 white pasteboard bx, blended gold, bouy, paper (torn)	EXIB	$1,100.00	04-02
Heddon	Artistic Minnow	#51, paper EX, bouy EX, NOT MET	EX-IB	$1,175.00	99-08
Heddon	Artistic Minnow	gold	EX-	$151.00	00-10
Heddon	Artistic Minnow	green back/gold digs, NOT MET	G	$76.00	99-01
Heddon	Artistic Minnow	green/gold label rough, papers, weight	EXIB	$1,600.00	00-05
Heddon	Artistic Minnow	seinna, crackleback	EX	$300.00	99-01
Heddon	Artistic Minnow	sienna	VG+	$126.00	00-07
Heddon	Artistic Minnow	sienna	EX	$178.19	99-02
Heddon	Artistic Minnow	sienna, crackle, beater box	EX-	$775.00	00-05
Heddon	Artistic Minnow	sienna, tail chip, otherwise OK	VG-	$112.50	99-01
Heddon	Artistic Minnow	sienna, weight & papers, box VG	NIB	$1,375.00	01-09
Heddon	Artistic Minnow	sienna, with bouy weight	EX	$402.61	99-02
Heddon	Artistic Minnow	white box VG-, papers taped, sienna	NIB	$972.00	01-04
Heddon	Artistic Minnow	white box, weight, nice	NIB	$1,755.00	00-02
Heddon	Artistic Minnow	blended gold, pointers	VG	$175.00	01-07
Heddon	Artistic Minnow No. 50	GE, 2 HPGM, gold wash	EX	$181.50	04-11
Heddon	Artistic Minnow with Weight	sienna, crackleback, GE, 2 HPGM, box VG	EX	$187.00	04-11
Heddon	Babe Oreno	red Pagin scale, long sliver of missing paint	??	$52.00	04-03
Heddon	Baby Cobra	9910B, black Fish Flash (silver glitter sides), NI2PSTB	NIB	$9.00	05-04

LURES

BRAND	MODEL	SERIES / MFG. CODE / DESCRIPTION	GRADE	PRICE	DATE yy/mm
Heddon	Baby Cobra	9910SD, green shad, WPE, new in orig 2PSTB	NIB	$9.00	05-04
Heddon	Baby Cobra	9910Y, Yellow Fish Flash (silver glitter sides)	NM	$9.00	05-04
Heddon	Baby Zara	black w/white ribs	EX	$5.25	05-07
Heddon	Bass Bug	#56 Chadwick's Sunbeam Up Bass bx crisp	NIB	$522.00	04-02
Heddon	Bass Bug	#58, wood, NOT MET	mint	$42.55	99-05
Heddon	Bass Bug	#60, tiny Down Bass	NIB	$1,428.00	00-08
Heddon	Bass Bug #53	Up Bass bx EX, Chadwick's Sunbeam	NIB	$753.00	04-03
Heddon	Bass Bug #58	Up Bass	EXIB	$280.00	99-11
Heddon	Bass Bug #50	window bx, NOT MET	NIB	$202.00	03-02
Heddon	Bass Bug Spook	974BW, window box, card, NOT MET	NIB	$66.00	01-08
Heddon	Bass Bug Spook	974WR, card, Banner box 2PCCB	NIB	$80.00	00-05
Heddon	Bass Bug Spook	975BR, on card, window box	NIB	$29.00	04-11
Heddon	Bass Bug Spook	975WR, on card, NOT MET	NIB	$75.50	00-05
Heddon	Bass Bug Spook	975BR, window box crisp & card	NIB	$200.00	02-08
Heddon	Bass Bug Spook	975DG, mint card and window box	NIB	$261.00	00-05
Heddon	Bass Bug Spook	975WR, window box, NOT MET	NOCIB	$79.00	99-06
Heddon	Bass Bug Spook	975Y, window box	NIB	$55.00	03-01
Heddon	Bass Bug Spook	975Y, mint card and window box	NIB	$261.00	00-05
Heddon	Bass Bug Spook	brown	EX-	$27.55	99-07
Heddon	Bass Bug Spook	brown, NOT MET	EX	$36.00	99-06
Heddon	Bass Bug Spook	green shore, Muma's #353 on page 97	EX-	$70.00	05-06
Heddon	Bass Bug Spook	white shore, red letter–stamped belly	EX+	$20.00	05-06
Heddon	Bass Bug Spook	yellow shore, feathers & hackle a little faded	VG	$15.00	05-06
Heddon	Bass Bug Wood	S875BW, on nice card, window box, wood	NIB	$426.00	01-12
Heddon	Basser	8409L, perch scale, GE, TS-hdwr	EX++	$185.00	05-04
Heddon	Basser	8500FRH, RH/w and silver glitter, new in orig EX- Brush 2PCBB, color catalog	NIB	$225.00	05-04
Heddon	Basser	8500FRH, red head/flitter, 2pc, Brush bx EX	NIB	$227.00	02-12
Heddon	Basser	8500RH, Banner bx crisp & papers, PE	NIB	$29.00	05-02
Heddon	Basser	8501, L-rig, papers, Down crisp, NOT MET	NIB	$361.00	01-11
Heddon	Basser	8502, Basser Down Bass box	EXIB	$157.00	02-03
Heddon	Basser	8502, Brush bx, hvy L-rig, GE	EXIB	$65.00	05-07
Heddon	Basser	8502, Brush EX, HD hardware nice!	NIB	$100.00	03-02
Heddon	Basser	8502, Down Bass	NIB	$255.00	01-03
Heddon	Basser	8502LUM, Brush VG	avgIB	$41.00	00-10
Heddon	Basser	8509H, red scale, GE, L-rig, odd blem on back, light age lines and very light wear	EX-	$125.00	05-04
Heddon	Basser	8509H, red scale, GE, L-rig, some scuffs and pointers, hdwr has heavy corrosion	G	$47.00	05-04
Heddon	Basser	8509L, perch scale, TS-rig, flks on edge of lip and eyes, light age lines on belly, toilet seat hdwr	EX-	$72.00	05-04
Heddon	Basser	8509D, L-rig	NIB	$212.00	03-01
Heddon	Basser	8509J, frog scale, Down Bass	NIB	$836.00	99-03
Heddon	Basser	8509K, Down Bass EX, goldfish scale	NIB	$635.00	02-07
Heddon	Basser	8509L, Brush crisp, L-rig? perch scale	NIB	$303.00	01-08
Heddon	Basser	8509L, Brush, 2pc	NIB	$263.00	99-09
Heddon	Basser	8509M, hvy duty L-rig, Brush box	NIB	$415.00	99-04
Heddon	Basser	8509M, Up Bass box mint	NIB	$716.00	99-03
Heddon	Basser	8509M, Brush, 2pc	NIB	$247.50	00-01

BRAND	MODEL	SERIES / MFG. CODE / DESCRIPTION	GRADE	PRICE	DATE yy/mm
Heddon	Basser	8509P, Down crisp	NIB	$286.00	01-06
Heddon	Basser	8529PAS Deluxe, GE, Allen Stripey in Brush box with paper	NIB	$320.00	05-06
Heddon	Basser	Allen Stripey with bar rig	EX	$110.00	05-07
Heddon	Basser	blue scale (pale)	EX	$385.00	05-07
Heddon	Basser	brown natural scale, GE, L-rig, red eye shadow	EX	$101.00	05-07
Heddon	Basser	deep green scale, GE, L-rig	EX+	$140.00	01-03
Heddon	Basser	Down Bass bx 8502, L-rig	EXIB	$148.00	03-11
Heddon	Basser	frog scale	EX-	$275.00	05-07
Heddon	Basser	frog scale, L-rig, NOT MET	EX	$143.00	02-06
Heddon	Basser	frog scale, L-rig	EX-	$550.00	00-05
Heddon	Basser	frog scale, GE, L-rig nice	EX-	$155.00	05-07
Heddon	Basser	frog scale, heavy L-rig, GE	EX+	$456.00	01-03
Heddon	Basser	frog scale, Down un?	EX-	$410.99	99-08
Heddon	Basser	frog scale, Head-On, not awful	avg	$155.00	00-04
Heddon	Basser	frog scale, L-rig, GE	EX-	$299.76	99-10
Heddon	Basser	goldfish scale, L-rig	EX+	$347.00	05-03
Heddon	Basser	goldfish scale, L-rig, NOT MET	EX	$256.00	02-10
Heddon	Basser	green scale, Head-On	EX-	$152.00	00-07
Heddon	Basser	green scale, Up Bass EX-	BIB	$274.00	01-10
Heddon	Basser	green scale, Up Bass, NOT MET	EXIB	$168.00	00-07
Heddon	Basser	Head-On, green scale	VG+	$51.00	99-02
Heddon	Basser	Head-On, natural scale	EX-	$168.00	02-02
Heddon	Basser	Head-On, goldfish scale	EX	$505.00	02-01
Heddon	Basser	Head-On, P, GE, L-rig, fat	EX-	$228.50	99-05
Heddon	Basser	M, Head-On	EX	$160.00	01-01
Heddon	Basser	M, Head-On, un Down Bass, NOT MET	EXIB	$114.00	00-04
Heddon	Basser	natural scale, Head-On, GE, L-rig	VG	$112.00	05-07
Heddon	Basser	orange/black spots, GE, NOT MET	EX-	$481.00	02-09
Heddon	Basser	orange/blk spots, Head-On	VG+	$600.00	01-11
Heddon	Basser	original wood, GE, S-rig, strawberry	mint	$192.00	02-10
Heddon	Basser	perch scale, GE, hvy L-rig	VG+	$38.00	04-11
Heddon	Basser	perch scale, Head-On	EX-	$154.49	99-08
Heddon	Basser	pike scale, Head-On	EX	$155.00	00-10
Heddon	Basser	pike scale, L-rig, unmarked Up Bass bx EX-	EXIB	$127.00	05-07
Heddon	Basser	r/w, PE, S-rig	EX	$57.00	99-01
Heddon	Basser	red scale	EX-	$165.00	05-07
Heddon	Basser	red scale	EX+	$760.00	99-06
Heddon	Basser	red scale, Head-On, L-rig, un box	EX-	$380.00	00-05
Heddon	Basser	RH, PE, Navy #s	NIB	$150.00	99-04
Heddon	Basser	RH, XL-rig, Brush EX-	NIB	$116.00	01-10
Heddon	Basser	RH, 2pc, GE	EX-	$31.00	04-07
Heddon	Basser	RH, GE, L-rig	EX	$76.00	01-08
Heddon	Basser	RH, GE, 2pc, nice	VG?	$26.00	00-04
Heddon	Basser	RH, L-rig	EX	$43.00	00-05
Heddon	Basser	SB, L-rig	EX-	$129.00	02-01
Heddon	Basser	shiner scale, GE	fair	$19.00	99-01
Heddon	Basser	shiner scale, 2pc	EX-	$62.80	00-03

BRAND	MODEL	SERIES / MFG. CODE / DESCRIPTION	GRADE	PRICE	DATE yy/mm
Heddon	Basser	strawberry, PE, original	mint	$89.88	99-06
Heddon	Basser	white/gold flitter, 2pc, GE	EX	$256.29	99-05
Heddon	Basser Deluxe	8529P, Brush bx EX, NOT MET	NIB	$208.00	03-02
Heddon	Basser Deluxe	Allen Stripey, GE	mint	$291.00	00-08
Heddon	Basser Deluxe	LUM, salmon lure in wrong 8519P bx	EX	$300.00	02-07
Heddon	Basser Head-On	pike scale in 8509P Up Bass	VG-	$81.00	99-01
Heddon	Basser Jr.	shiner scale, "Plunking," GE	EX	$381.56	00-02
Heddon	Basser Spook	9849P, 2pc, 3-hooker, in Up Bass Box E-	VG-	$75.00	05-06
Heddon	Basser Spook	9855, GE, green scale, 2pc, Up Bass Box E-	VG-	$75.00	05-06
Heddon	Basser x 2	8509P, 9L, Brush, 2pc	VG+IB	$315.00	99-06
Heddon	Big Bud	clear with dice inside	NOC	$58.00	02-03
Heddon	Big Chug	GDS (mackerel)	EX	$175.00	99-03
Heddon	Big Chug	SS, NOT MET	VG	$24.99	99-04
Heddon	Big Chug	white/red ribs	EX+	$40.51	99-09
Heddon	Big Chug	XRY	EX	$150.00	99-03
Heddon	Big Chug	XRY	EX	$150.00	99-03
Heddon	Big Chug		EX	$90.00	00-07
Heddon	Big Hedd	9330BGL, bluegill new in intro Big Hedd 2PSTB, includes earlier 6-pack dealer carton	NIB	$40.00	05-04
Heddon	Big Hedd	9330BJY, 12-pack, NOT MET	NIB	$80.00	99-03
Heddon	Big Hedd	9330GSD, green shad, NI2PSTB	NIB	$18.00	05-04
Heddon	Big Hedd	9330SSD, silver shad, OPE	EX+	$20.00	05-04
Heddon	Big Hedd	9330BJO, PTCB EX	NIB	$52.00	05-07
Heddon	Big Hedd	9330BRR	EXIB	$34.00	04-11
Heddon	Big Hedd	9330BWR	EXIB	$32.00	04-11
Heddon	Big Hedd	9330-CD, ⅝ oz.	NIB	$23.00	00-07
Heddon	Big Hedd	9330GSD	EXIB	$34.00	04-11
Heddon	Big Hedd	9330XBW	NIB	$39.99	99-02
Heddon	Big Hedd	9410, silver shad, OPE, light wear	EX-	$20.00	05-04
Heddon	Big Hedd	BGL, NOT MET!	NIB	$32.00	99-04
Heddon	Big Hedd	black coach dog	NIB	$96.00	98-12
Heddon	Big Hedd	black shore, PTCB, unbelievable! 11 BIDS	NIB	$1,225.00	05-07
Heddon	Big Hedd	BSO, big hook drag, NOT MET!	VG	$410.00	03-11
Heddon	Big Hedd	chrome/flourescent orange shore	EX	$360.00	02-02
Heddon	Big Hedd	rainbow? yellow/black dots	VG+	$305.00	02-05
Heddon	Big Joe	608RH, RH/w w/gold flitter, GE, TS-rig, NSOB, PO3BWs, very light age crackling	VG	$110.00	05-05
Heddon	Big Joe	spotted	EX-IB	$300.88	99-03
Heddon	Big Mary	802, RH/w, GE, TS-rig, some bold age lines, small nick at nose and few varnish flks on red	VG-	$57.00	05-05
Heddon	Big Mary	808RH, RH/w w/gold flitter, GE, TS-rig, few light pointers on shin and wear at tail edge	EX-	$100.00	05-05
Heddon	Big Mary	808RH, flitter, avg lure, Up Bass	avgIB	$87.00	99-08
Heddon	Big Mary	RH/flitter, Down Bass 802 VG+, NOT MET	NIB	$357.00	01-10
Heddon	Big Mary	RH/y flitter, GE	EX-	$88.00	00-10
Heddon	Big May	prop? r/w flitter, GE	EX-	$177.50	99-02
Heddon	Black Sucker	3-hook, huge chips	poor	$800.00	03-11
Heddon	Black Sucker	4 BW, 3-hk, huge chips to wood	poor	$566.00	04-02

BRAND	MODEL	SERIES / MFG. CODE / DESCRIPTION	GRADE	PRICE	DATE yy/mm
Heddon	Black Sucker	5-hk, many hook drags	avg.	$3,050.00	00-02
Heddon	Black Sucker	a beauty	EX	$5,400.00	02-09
Heddon	Black Sucker	attractive	EX-	$2,850.00	02-08
Heddon	Black Sucker	bottom of tail missing, varnish flakes	??	$460.00	05-03
Heddon	Black Sucker	hooks, cups missing on side	avg.	$651.00	99-03
Heddon	Black Sucker	huge chip between eyes, NOT MET	fair	$339.00	99-11
Heddon	Black Sucker	L-rig, bottom tail missing, decent otherwise	VG-	$1,028.00	02-02
Heddon	Black Sucker	more white than normal, nice	VG+	$2,807.00	02-04
Heddon	Black Sucker	odd color, much varnish	avg	$2,638.00	00-09
Heddon	Black Sucker	only primer left except on back	poor	$400.00	02-01
Heddon	Black Sucker	POBW, real nice	EX-	$4,351.00	02-01
Heddon	Black Sucker	rainbow, 5-hook, ugly varnish	VG	$2,500.00	03-11
Heddon	Black Sucker	ugly age lines, minimum bid $6125	EX-	no bids	02-08
Heddon	Black Sucker	ugly varnish, NOT MET	avg	$710.00	02-02
Heddon	Bottlenose Tadpolly	yellow spotted	VG+	$328.00	01-04
Heddon	Brush Popper	4 diff	NIB	$81.00	99-04
Heddon	Brush Popper	5440RFY, large size	NIB	$36.51	00-02
Heddon	Brush Popper	lg size	NIB	$19.10	99-03
Heddon	Bubbling Bug	90YB	EX	$99.00	02-05
Heddon	Bubbling Bug	blk/y stripes, big chips	avg	$170.00	00-02
Heddon	Bubbling Bug	copper/green, bad belly chip, rest nice	?	$153.00	01-12
Heddon	Bubbling Bug	r/w	EX	$310.00	01-04
Heddon	Bubbling Bug	RH	VG	$103.00	01-07
Heddon	Bubbling Bug	y/black, NOT MET	EX	$272.00	01-01
Heddon	Bucktail Surface Minnow	w pasteboard box 401 RB VG (tape)	VG+IB	$2,725.00	02-02
Heddon	Bug A Bee	silver/black ribs	EX	$103.00	04-12
Heddon	Bug A Bee	yellow/green stripes	EX	$95.00	03-07
Heddon	Catalina	crackle, wrapped line ties	EX-?	$830.00	01-10
Heddon	Chugger	14KCD	EX	$129.00	01-02
Heddon	Chugger	14KCD?	EX	$138.00	00-09
Heddon	Chugger	2 diff gold eye, XBW, RH	EX	$42.00	99-05
Heddon	Chugger	9450L box (wrong) BRS	NIB	$81.00	00-05
Heddon	Chugger	9540BRSO, brown scale/y eyes	NIB	$218.00	00-05
Heddon	Chugger	9540BRY	NIB	$307.00	03-01
Heddon	Chugger	9540GFBS, white eye, window box	NIB	$73.00	00-10
Heddon	Chugger	9540GRA	NIB	$107.00	00-09
Heddon	Chugger	9540OYG	NIB	$56.00	99-05
Heddon	Chugger	9540SWBS	NIB	$122.50	99-02
Heddon	Chugger	9540VCD	NIB	$87.00	01-10
Heddon	Chugger	9540VCD	NIB	$127.00	00-09
Heddon	Chugger	9540WTG YB	NIB	$81.00	99-02
Heddon	Chugger	9540YBS	NIB	$226.00	03-01
Heddon	Chugger	9540YFSL	NIB	$359.00	02-10
Heddon	Chugger	9540CDYS	NIB	$172.00	00-09
Heddon	Chugger	9540CDYS, white eye, 1PCWB	NIB	$130.00	00-07
Heddon	Chugger	beige/gold shore ribs, y eyes	EX	$153.00	00-05
Heddon	Chugger	black, gold eye	EX-	$41.00	99-03
Heddon	Chugger	black/gold foil, gold eye	EX-	$34.50	00-02

BRAND	MODEL	SERIES / MFG. CODE / DESCRIPTION	GRADE	PRICE	DATE yy/mm
Heddon	Chugger	black/orange spots, GE	EX	$117.50	00-04
Heddon	Chugger	black/orange spots & eyes	EX	$91.00	99-06
Heddon	Chugger	BLGF, gold eye, NOT MET	EX	$51.00	00-09
Heddon	Chugger	blk head & tail; clear/red, w, y spots; w eye	EX	$79.00	00-04
Heddon	Chugger	blk/gold foil, gold eyes	EX	$95.50	99-04
Heddon	Chugger	blk/silver reflecter, gold eyes	EX-	$20.55	99-03
Heddon	Chugger	blue shore, gold eyes	mint	$127.00	02-07
Heddon	Chugger	bone, y eye, blk eye shadow	EX	$151.00	00-04
Heddon	Chugger	brown/caramel to silver scales, white eyes	EX	$215.00	02-03
Heddon	Chugger	BRS	EX	$100.00	00-09
Heddon	Chugger	BRS, NOT MET	EX-	$54.00	00-09
Heddon	Chugger	CDF	EX-	$100.00	00-09
Heddon	Chugger	CDF, red eye	NIB	$47.00	00-10
Heddon	Chugger	chart, spotted, gold eye	VG	$61.01	99-05
Heddon	Chugger	chrome/blue scale	EX	$82.59	00-03
Heddon	Chugger	clear/blue scale, red gill	EX	$100.00	01-02
Heddon	Chugger	clear white/blk spot/gold foil	EX	$100.00	99-06
Heddon	Chugger	clear, white eye	mint	$56.50	99-06
Heddon	Chugger	clear/green back/lime & red spots	EX	$103.59	99-10
Heddon	Chugger	clear y/blk dots, white eye	EX	$64.00	00-04
Heddon	Chugger	CPS	NIB	$159.00	00-09
Heddon	Chugger	CRA	EX	$122.00	00-09
Heddon	Chugger	crackle	EX	$182.50	99-06
Heddon	Chugger	crawdad? brown, white eye	EX	$305.00	99-08
Heddon	Chugger	CRWS	EX	$172.00	00-09
Heddon	Chugger	foil inset	EX	$71.00	99-06
Heddon	Chugger	foil inset	EX-	$96.00	99-06
Heddon	Chugger	frog, white eye	EX	$72.00	00-04
Heddon	Chugger	GDS	EX	$208.00	00-09
Heddon	Chugger	GFB, gold eye	NIB	$88.00	00-10
Heddon	Chugger	GFBS, white eye	NIB	$88.00	00-10
Heddon	Chugger	GLDS	NIB	$160.00	00-08
Heddon	Chugger	gold/blk spots, gold foil, gold eyes	EX-	$60.00	99-04
Heddon	Chugger	gold/dark bronze scale, white eye	EX	$89.88	00-03
Heddon	Chugger	green scale/white, gold eyes	EX	$200.00	99-10
Heddon	Chugger	GYH/silver scale	EX	$198.00	00-08
Heddon	Chugger	KCD, NOT MET	NIB	$122.50	00-02
Heddon	Chugger	LBL	EX	$169.00	00-09
Heddon	Chugger	natural bluegill	mint	$400.00	04-12
Heddon	Chugger	natural striper	EX	$125.00	99-11
Heddon	Chugger	NBL	EX	$49.00	00-09
Heddon	Chugger	NPY	NIB	$78.00	00-08
Heddon	Chugger	orange/blk ribs	EX	$255.00	99-11
Heddon	Chugger	PC	NIB	$207.00	00-08
Heddon	Chugger	perch, 2pc	EX+	$40.00	99-02
Heddon	Chugger	pike scale, white eye	EX	$177.00	00-10
Heddon	Chugger	RB, white eye	EX	$162.50	00-01
Heddon	Chugger	red/clear/gold foil	EX	$51.00	00-04

BRAND	MODEL	SERIES / MFG. CODE / DESCRIPTION	GRADE	PRICE	DATE yy/mm
Heddon	Chugger	red/gold foil	EX	$60.00	99-01
Heddon	Chugger	red/gold foil	EX	$62.00	99-04
Heddon	Chugger	red/silver foil, 9540-SP Banner	EXIB	$48.52	00-03
Heddon	Chugger	red/silver foil, gold eye	EX	$52.00	99-12
Heddon	Chugger	red/textured silver insert	EX	$68.01	99-05
Heddon	Chugger	RH/frog scale, gold eye	EX	$170.50	99-10
Heddon	Chugger	SD, NOT MET	EX-	$47.00	00-09
Heddon	Chugger	SD, clear belly	EX	$118.00	00-09
Heddon	Chugger	SFB, 12-pack counter display box neat	NIB	$600.00	04-04
Heddon	Chugger	SFBS, white eye	NIB	$47.00	00-10
Heddon	Chugger	SFSXS	NIB	$104.00	00-08
Heddon	Chugger	SFSXS, white eye	NIB	$77.00	00-10
Heddon	Chugger	SFSXS, silver head/tail, silver foil inset	EX	$156.00	99-11
Heddon	Chugger	SFYS, white eye	NIB	$93.00	00-10
Heddon	Chugger	shad, red gill, y eyes	EX	$42.00	01-09
Heddon	Chugger	silver shad, orange eye	mint	$95.00	00-06
Heddon	Chugger	silver, silver scale/w dots/y eye, NOT MET	EX	$115.00	00-10
Heddon	Chugger	SSRHYB, gold eyes	EX	$114.00	00-04
Heddon	Chugger	strawberry, horribly oxidized	?	$156.00	00-10
Heddon	Chugger	tiger stripe, white eye	EX	$72.00	99-11
Heddon	Chugger	WCD, NOT MET	EX	$51.00	00-09
Heddon	Chugger	white tiger stripe, white eye	EX	$77.00	05-07
Heddon	Chugger	white/black zebra, white eye	EX	$103.00	01-03
Heddon	Chugger	white/blk spots	EX	$89.00	99-03
Heddon	Chugger	XBW	mint	$12.50	99-02
Heddon	Chugger	XRS, NOT MET	EX	$31.00	00-09
Heddon	Chugger	XRYBB	EX-	$59.80	00-02
Heddon	Chugger	XRYBB, white eye	NIB	$121.00	00-10
Heddon	Chugger	y shad	EX	$73.00	99-04
Heddon	Chugger	y/black spots, red eyes	VG+	$128.00	00-07
Heddon	Chugger	y/blk dots, silver foil insert	EX-	$53.00	01-08
Heddon	Chugger	YCD, gold eye	EX	$56.00	00-11
Heddon	Chugger	YCD, NOT MET	EX-	$51.00	00-09
Heddon	Chugger	yellow bird	EX	$467.00	02-01
Heddon	Chugger	yellow bird/black wings	EX	$455.00	01-10
Heddon	Chugger	yellow, black wings, red eye shadow	mint	$590.00	04-11
Heddon	Chugger	zebra	EX-	$80.00	00-02
Heddon	Chugger	14KCD, white eye	EX	$305.00	00-11
Heddon	Chugger	159 different Spooks, NOT MET	EX-NIB	$11,800.00	00-12
Heddon	Chugger	y/blk tiger stripe	EX	$150.00	99-05
Heddon	Chugger Jr.	9520SJ	NIB	$41.00	01-05
Heddon	Chugger Jr.	9520BB, blk triangle box, NOT MET	NIB	$18.49	99-03
Heddon	Chugger Jr.	9520BRS, gold eye	NIB	$52.00	99-06
Heddon	Chugger Jr.	black wing, yellow bird	EX	$417.00	01-10
Heddon	Chugger Jr.	CPS (clear purple seagull), white eye	EX	$67.00	05-01
Heddon	Chugger Jr.	green/y spots, gold eye	EX	$66.59	00-03
Heddon	Chugger Jr.	nat bluegill	EX	$51.00	99-03
Heddon	Chugger Jr.	red, white, yellow spots	EX	$33.50	99-01

BRAND	MODEL	SERIES / MFG. CODE / DESCRIPTION	GRADE	PRICE	DATE yy/mm
Heddon	Chugger Jr.	white/black dots, red gills, black/red eyes	EX	$67.00	05-07
Heddon	Chugger Jr.	y wing, black bird	EX	$367.00	01-10
Heddon	Chugger Jr.	yellow/silver foil	VG	$32.00	99-01
Heddon	Chugger Jr. x 3	w/blk spot, o/blk spot, red foil	EX-	$104.00	99-07
Heddon	Chugger Jr.	bar fish	EX	$81.00	04-07
Heddon	Chugger Spook	9540SD, white eyes, box rough	NIB	$27.00	06-05
Heddon	Chugger Spook	Banner box 9540L & catalog, gold eyes	NIB	$34.00	05-02
Heddon	Chugger Spook	blended red head/white, white eyes	EX	$38.00	06-05
Heddon	Chugger Spook	Fish Flash, silver & black, gold eyes	EX	$17.00	06-05
Heddon	Chugger Spook	natural photo finish (stamped "Chugger," size of Chugger Jr.)	EX	$18.50	05-07
Heddon	Chugger Spook	one-eyed Willie, clear w/1 eye on belly, NOT MET	EX	$611.00	04-01
Heddon	Chugger Spook	RH/frog scale, gold eyes	EX	$132.00	04-11
Heddon	Chugger Spook	yellow-backed bird, hooks bent, few pointers	EX-	$790.00	04-01
Heddon	Chugger x 2	XRY, gold eye, 2 the same, PTCB	NIB	$46.53	99-08
Heddon	Chugger, Baby	chrome, chart, 9520UY	NIB	$26.00	99-02
Heddon	Chugger, Baby	9520XRW	NIB	$12.99	05-07
Heddon	Clatter Tad	9900LBL, MO, listed 1977, only in Daisy Box (E)	EX+IB	$40.00	05-06
Heddon	Clatter Tad	MO, green crawdad	EX+	$18.00	05-06
Heddon	Clatter Tad	MO, nickel plate chrome	EX+	$12.00	05-06
Heddon	Clatter Tad	MO, rainbow trout	EX+	$40.00	05-06
Heddon	Clatter Tad	MO, yellow-green florescent	EX+	$18.00	05-06
Heddon	Coast Minnow	6½", spotted, HPGM, varnish, decent	VG-	$921.00	00-04
Heddon	Coast Minnow	crackle, 4½", HPGM, NOT MET	EX+	$1,250.00	03-02
Heddon	Coast Minnow	green scale back, o belly, beauty	EX-	$2,283.00	00-10
Heddon	Coast Minnow	rainbow, NOT MET	VG+	$273.00	04-12
Heddon	Coast Minnow		EX-	$2,600.00	01-04
Heddon	Coast Minnow, Musky	7", strawberry, lt varnish	EX	$2,550.00	99-04
Heddon	Cobra	9930 SF, PTCB	NIB	$20.50	99-01
Heddon	Cousin	shad	mint	$26.00	99-02
Heddon	Cousin 1	7725GSD	NIB	$25.00	04-07
Heddon	Cousin II	7735 RS, silver scale	NIB	$26.65	99-06
Heddon	Cousin II	bass	EX	$22.50	99-02
Heddon	Cousin II	red/blk spots	EX	$26.50	99-01
Heddon	Crab Spook	LUM, nice Brush box 9909LC and cat	NIB	$293.88	99-11
Heddon	Crab Spook, Baby	eyes missing	EX-	$31.00	01-08
Heddon	Crab Wiggler	1800P, L-rig	EX	$423.00	99-05
Heddon	Crab Wiggler	1800S, Down Bass nice	VG+IB	$229.00	02-05
Heddon	Crab Wiggler	1809B, frog, intro Down Bass	EXIB	$400.00	00-08
Heddon	Crab Wiggler	1809D, crisp "CRAB" Down Bass	EXIB	$337.00	00-05
Heddon	Crab Wiggler	1809J, frog scale	VG-	$158.00	00-05
Heddon	Crab Wiggler	1900, green scale, L-rig	EX	$320.00	99-06
Heddon	Crab Wiggler	1900, Brush	VG+IB	$70.00	00-03
Heddon	Crab Wiggler	1900, crackleback, Down Bass	EXIB	$330.00	99-03
Heddon	Crab Wiggler	1900, crackleback, L-rig, Up Bass	EXIB	$202.50	00-02
Heddon	Crab Wiggler	1900, Down Bass box VG+, RET lure, GE, L-rig	VG+IB	$118.00	05-07
Heddon	Crab Wiggler	1900, pike scale, GE, vivid colors nice	EX	$96.00	05-07

BRAND	MODEL	SERIES / MFG. CODE / DESCRIPTION	GRADE	PRICE	DATE yy/mm
Heddon	Crab Wiggler	1900, red scale deluxe, un box	EX-IB	$260.00	00-05
Heddon	Crab Wiggler	1909C, nat crab, 2pc, NSOB, GE, tiny flake on nose and pointer at l-eye, few light age lines	EX-	$62.00	05-05
Heddon	Crab Wiggler	1909P, shiner scale, L-rig, GE, light carn wear and few light points in unmrkd DLB 2PCCB	VG+IB	$90.00	05-05
Heddon	Crab Wiggler	5009D, Down, special card & paper	NIB	$1,077.99	00-03
Heddon	Crab Wiggler	crab, unmarked intro box, U collar	EX-IB	$300.00	99-08
Heddon	Crab Wiggler	crackle, GE	VG+	$153.00	01-01
Heddon	Crab Wiggler	crackle, NOT MET	EX	$148.00	00-10
Heddon	Crab Wiggler	crackle, Down Bass intro, NOT MET	VG+IB	$140.00	00-07
Heddon	Crab Wiggler	crackleback, GE, L-rig	VG	$91.99	99-05
Heddon	Crab Wiggler	frog, "Crab" Down Bass VG, papers	VGIB	$168.00	00-11
Heddon	Crab Wiggler	frog, GE, L-rig, inchworm	VG+	$177.00	00-07
Heddon	Crab Wiggler	g scale, Down Bass poor, NOT MET	EX-IB	$105.00	00-09
Heddon	Crab Wiggler	GE, white with red/blk/green spots, U-collar L-rig	VG+	$65.00	05-06
Heddon	Crab Wiggler	green scale, no eyes (1600 body)	VG+	$400.00	02-02
Heddon	Crab Wiggler	no eyes! rainbow, Depression era, cup (drilled for L-rig & eyes)	EX-	$699.00	05-07
Heddon	Crab Wiggler	r/w, L-rig, un Up Bass	VG+IB	$125.00	99-07
Heddon	Crab Wiggler	rainbow scale, age lines	EX-	$598.00	02-08
Heddon	Crab Wiggler	lum? red head & tail, not marked	EX-	$400.00	02-08
Heddon	Crab Wiggler	RH blended, white with flitter	VG	$272.75	99-03
Heddon	Crab Wiggler	strawberry, larger size	avg	$19.00	04-07
Heddon	Crab Wiggler	Up Bass EX, 1909C	EXIB	$203.00	05-07
Heddon	Crab Wiggler	white, GE, with leather tail	EX+	$227.51	99-06
Heddon	Crab Wiggler	1950	EX-	$156.00	00-06
Heddon	Crab Wiggler	strawberry, 3½"	VG	$141.19	99-01
Heddon	Crab Wiggler	y spotted, intro Down Bass, cat	EX-IB	$300.00	00-10
Heddon	Crab Wiggler, Baby	1902, Brush box crisp	NIB	$330.00	99-04
Heddon	Crab Wiggler, Baby	1909B, Down Bass bx, EX-, NOT MET	VG+IB	$122.00	02-10
Heddon	Crab Wiggler, Baby	1909J, Down Bass nice	EX-IB	$408.00	02-04
Heddon	Crab Wiggler, Baby	1959C, Brush bx VG-, natural crab, GE, pocket catalog	EX-IB	$55.00	05-07
Heddon	Crab Wiggler, Baby	1959P, Brush box, 2pc, tiny nose chip	EXIB	$282.00	00-10
Heddon	Crab Wiggler, Baby	bar perch, GE, U-collar	VG+	$51.00	05-07
Heddon	Crab Wiggler, Baby	Brush bx 1959C EX, 2pc	EXIB	$221.00	04-07
Heddon	Crab Wiggler, Baby	crab, later	EX+	$370.00	00-05
Heddon	Crab Wiggler, Baby	crackle	EX-	$350.00	00-05
Heddon	Crab Wiggler, Baby	crackleback & matching papers EX	EX-	$79.00	05-07
Heddon	Crab Wiggler, Baby	frog	EX-	$48.00	01-03
Heddon	Crab Wiggler, Baby	frog scale with intro box	EXIB	$247.50	05-07
Heddon	Crab Wiggler, Baby	frog, 2pc	EX	$250.00	99-10
Heddon	Crab Wiggler, Baby	frog, L-rig, varnish	VG	$53.00	00-10
Heddon	Crab Wiggler, Baby	frog, Down Bass, intro paper, tag	EXIB	$330.00	99-01
Heddon	Crab Wiggler, Baby	GE RET, red eye & tail, L-rig	VG+	$40.00	05-06
Heddon	Crab Wiggler, Baby	GE, green scale, box marked "1909D GD"	VG	$137.50	04-11
Heddon	Crab Wiggler, Baby	goldfish scale, L-rig, chip on back, otherwise decent	VG+	$128.00	05-07

BRAND	MODEL	SERIES / MFG. CODE / DESCRIPTION	GRADE	PRICE	DATE yy/mm
Heddon	Crab Wiggler, Baby	goldfish, bad varnish ugly	VG-	$58.00	00-04
Heddon	Crab Wiggler, Baby	L-rig, unmarked, Down Bass box	EX-IB	$234.00	02-05
Heddon	Crab Wiggler, Baby	natural scale, age lines but nice	EX-	$1,000.00	01-07
Heddon	Crab Wiggler, Baby	perch scale	VG-	$80.00	99-01
Heddon	Crab Wiggler, Baby	red scale fancy, pork rind pin on back	EX+	$538.00	00-09
Heddon	Crab Wiggler, Baby	saltwater, Down Bass 1900 bx & paper avg	EX+IB	$425.00	03-01
Heddon	Crab Wiggler, Baby	y/black, L-rig	EX	$284.00	00-11
Heddon	Crackleback	5 different	NIB	$111.26	99-04
Heddon	Crackleback	8000BAR, bar fish, WPE, 3⅞", smaller size, few nicks on lip and light wear	VG+	$15.00	05-04
Heddon	Crackleback	8050GBC	NIB	$35.26	99-05
Heddon	Crackleback	8050GCB, green crackleback on white	MINT	$35.00	05-04
Heddon	Crackleback	8050GSD, green shad	MINT	$25.00	05-04
Heddon	Crackleback	blue/green, NOT MET	EX	$12.50	99-05
Heddon	Crackleback	small size, yellow	EX+	$65.00	05-06
Heddon	Crar Wiggler	1909B, Down Bass, frog spot	EX-IB	$191.00	05-02
Heddon	Craw Shrimp	3 diff, NOT MET	EX	$61.08	99-04
Heddon	Craw Shrimp	375AMR, window box	NIB	$52.00	00-01
Heddon	Craw Shrimp	375BAM	NIB	$41.00	05-07
Heddon	Craw Shrimp	375PRL, purple shrimp, plastic, NSOB, very light wear	EX	$40.00	05-04
Heddon	Craw Shrimp	375BAM	NIB	$26.00	03-11
Heddon	Craw Shrimp	amber/blk	EX	$21.50	99-05
Heddon	Craw Shrimp	amber/red spots	mint	$25.49	99-06
Heddon	Craw Shrimp	black/red	EX	$62.50	98-12
Heddon	Craw Shrimp	blue	EX	$87.15	00-03
Heddon	Craw Shrimp	dark	EX	$42.00	99-02
Heddon	Craw Shrimp	g/blk	VG	$27.50	99-02
Heddon	Craw Shrimp	natural brown (clear)	EX	$28.00	01-08
Heddon	Craw Shrimp	root beer color	EX	$55.00	98-12
Heddon	Crazy Crawler	2100BWH, zinc eyes	EXIB	$307.00	05-07
Heddon	Crazy Crawler	2100GM, gray flock mouse, 2pc, Donaly rig, BBE set on top of head, light pointers on belly	EX-	$170.00	05-05
Heddon	Crazy Crawler	2100GW, Crawler intro paper + catalog	NIB	$343.00	02-10
Heddon	Crazy Crawler	2100XRS, 3-color eye, intro papers	EXIB	$127.50	99-01
Heddon	Crazy Crawler	2100XRW, RH, white shore, SR, chip on butt and a hint of wear	EX-	$40.00	05-05
Heddon	Crazy Crawler	2100XRW, Banner box, cat	NIB, nice	$103.50	99-02
Heddon	Crazy Crawler	2100YRH, RH, yel S-rig	MINT	$55.00	05-05
Heddon	Crazy Crawler	2100YRH, Brush box EX- & intro paper, 2pc, black eyes	NIB	$179.00	05-07
Heddon	Crazy Crawler	2100BF, Banner, papers	NIB	$66.60	01-06
Heddon	Crazy Crawler	2100BF, S-rig	EX+	$25.00	00-10
Heddon	Crazy Crawler	2100BF, 2pc, blk eye, cat	NIB	$111.00	99-04
Heddon	Crazy Crawler	2100BF, Brush, 2pc	NIB	$150.50	99-08
Heddon	Crazy Crawler	2100BF, Donaly	NIB	$256.51	99-05
Heddon	Crazy Crawler	2100BF, Donaly clip	mint	$200.00	99-06
Heddon	Crazy Crawler	2100BF, S-rig, Brush, papers	NIB	$104.09	00-02
Heddon	Crazy Crawler	2100BF, Banner, paper, cat	NIB	$131.38	99-06

BRAND	MODEL	SERIES / MFG. CODE / DESCRIPTION	GRADE	PRICE	DATE yy/mm
Heddon	Crazy Crawler	2100BWH, Donaly clips	EX-	$215.00	04-12
Heddon	Crazy Crawler	2100BWH, zinc (tack) eye, 2pc, NOT MET	EX	$201.00	04-02
Heddon	Crazy Crawler	2100BWH, 2pc	EX	$88.57	99-09
Heddon	Crazy Crawler	2100BWH, Banner	NIB	$92.00	99-11
Heddon	Crazy Crawler	2100BWH, black eyes, un Brush	EXIB	$89.99	99-09
Heddon	Crazy Crawler	2100BWH, Donaly, crisp Brush box	NIB	$260.59	99-04
Heddon	Crazy Crawler	2100BWH, intro paper, blk eye	NIB	$128.49	99-04
Heddon	Crazy Crawler	2100BWH, S-rig	EX-	$38.99	99-02
Heddon	Crazy Crawler	2100CM, colors faded, NOT MET	VG	$275.00	02-02
Heddon	Crazy Crawler	2100CM, sm tail chip, nice	VG+	$536.00	01-05
Heddon	Crazy Crawler	2100CM, decent	VG+	$375.00	03-12
Heddon	Crazy Crawler	2100GM	VG	$30.50	99-01
Heddon	Crazy Crawler	2100GM	NIB	$144.49	99-10
Heddon	Crazy Crawler	2100GM, Banner crisp	NIB	$188.00	00-08
Heddon	Crazy Crawler	2100GM, Donaly clips	EX	$87.00	00-08
Heddon	Crazy Crawler	2100GM, S-rig	EX	$61.00	99-04
Heddon	Crazy Crawler	2100GM, Brush	NIB	$142.50	99-07
Heddon	Crazy Crawler	2100GM, Brush, 2pc	EX-IB	$52.00	99-12
Heddon	Crazy Crawler	2100GM, green intro, Brush	EXIB	$204.50	00-02
Heddon	Crazy Crawler	2100GW	VG	$103.50	99-01
Heddon	Crazy Crawler	2100GW	EX	$169.00	00-01
Heddon	Crazy Crawler	2100GW	NIB	$315.00	00-05
Heddon	Crazy Crawler	2100GW	NIB	$332.00	00-12
Heddon	Crazy Crawler	2100GW, Donaly clips	EX	$256.00	00-04
Heddon	Crazy Crawler	2100GW, Donaly clips	EX-	$213.51	99-03
Heddon	Crazy Crawler	2100GW, mint bx & paper, NOT MET	NIB	$207.00	03-07
Heddon	Crazy Crawler	2100GW, Donaly	EX	$180.00	00-10
Heddon	Crazy Crawler	2100GW, crisp intro box & glow papers	NIB	$255.00	04-12
Heddon	Crazy Crawler	2100GW, 2100YRH, red eye	EX	$305.00	99-04
Heddon	Crazy Crawler	2100LUM, usual heavy flaking	VG-	$154.00	04-01
Heddon	Crazy Crawler	2100XBW, black eye, 2pc	mint	$449.00	04-02
Heddon	Crazy Crawler	2100XBW, black eye	VG+	$333.00	00-07
Heddon	Crazy Crawler	2100XBW, box avg	VG+IB	$202.56	99-11
Heddon	Crazy Crawler	2100XBW, red eye	EX	$370.59	99-03
Heddon	Crazy Crawler	2100XBW, red eye	EX	$665.00	99-08
Heddon	Crazy Crawler	2100XRS	NIB	$130.00	99-08
Heddon	Crazy Crawler	2100XRS, black eyes	EX	$60.00	04-11
Heddon	Crazy Crawler	2100XRS, Banner, paper, cat	NIB	$142.29	99-06
Heddon	Crazy Crawler	2100XRS, red eye, Brush, papers	NIB	$260.01	99-05
Heddon	Crazy Crawler	2100XRW, bad age lines	decent	$23.50	99-01
Heddon	Crazy Crawler	2100XRW, Banner	NIB	$163.77	00-01
Heddon	Crazy Crawler	2100XRW, Banner crisp	NIB	$104.00	00-08
Heddon	Crazy Crawler	2100XRW in XRS Brush, 2pc, intro paper	NIB	$154.00	00-04
Heddon	Crazy Crawler	2100XRW, Donaly clips superb	EX	$89.00	04-11
Heddon	Crazy Crawler	2100XRY	rough	$56.00	00-11
Heddon	Crazy Crawler	2100XRY	mint	$394.00	00-01
Heddon	Crazy Crawler	2100XRY, red eye	EX-	$226.00	00-10
Heddon	Crazy Crawler	2100YRH	NIB	$86.00	99-02

BRAND	MODEL	SERIES / MFG. CODE / DESCRIPTION	GRADE	PRICE	DATE yy/mm
Heddon	Crazy Crawler	2100YRH	NIB	$152.50	99-05
Heddon	Crazy Crawler	2100YRH, zinc (raised) eye, 2pc	EX+	$405.00	05-01
Heddon	Crazy Crawler	2100YRH, zinc eyes, lg chip at throat, rest nice	VG-	$151.00	05-07
Heddon	Crazy Crawler	2100YRH, Banner	NIB	$78.01	99-08
Heddon	Crazy Crawler	2100YRH, Banner box	NIB	$61.01	99-06
Heddon	Crazy Crawler	2100YRH, S-rig	NIB	$100.99	99-04
Heddon	Crazy Crawler	2100YRH, tape on Banner box	NIB	$86.00	99-09
Heddon	Crazy Crawler	2102XS, Donaly, intro papers	EXIB	$255.99	99-04
Heddon	Crazy Crawler	2120, 2pc, red dot in black eye, nice tail & ears	VG+	$40.00	05-06
Heddon	Crazy Crawler	2120, black shore, red eye	EX-	$162.50	99-10
Heddon	Crazy Crawler	2120BWH, cone tail	EX	$150.00	04-11
Heddon	Crazy Crawler	2120BWH, Banner box, cat	NIB nice	$112.50	99-02
Heddon	Crazy Crawler	2120, glowworm	EX-	$143.00	99-01
Heddon	Crazy Crawler	2120GM	EX	$33.77	05-07
Heddon	Crazy Crawler	2120XRS, silver shore, 2pc, GPE, hks dirty, orig Brush 2PCCB w/intro papers	EX+IB	$90.00	05-05
Heddon	Crazy Crawler	2120, yellow shore, red eye	EX-	$157.00	99-10
Heddon	Crazy Crawler	2120BF, Banner bx + paper EX	NIB	$36.00	05-07
Heddon	Crazy Crawler	2120BF, chip, age lines	avg	$21.00	99-01
Heddon	Crazy Crawler	2120BF, cone tail	VG+	$155.00	02-04
Heddon	Crazy Crawler	2120BF, cone tail	EX-	$229.00	04-01
Heddon	Crazy Crawler	2120BF, Banner, CC paper, cat, crisp, NO BIDS		$50.00	01-01
Heddon	Crazy Crawler	2120BF, black eye, Brush, cat	NIB	$46.00	00-10
Heddon	Crazy Crawler	2120BF, 2pc, red eye, Banner	NIB	$146.50	99-05
Heddon	Crazy Crawler	2120BF, NOT MET	EX-IB	$42.00	99-01
Heddon	Crazy Crawler	2120BF, S-rig, decent	VG	$16.00	99-04
Heddon	Crazy Crawler	2120BWH, Banner	NIB	$53.00	00-05
Heddon	Crazy Crawler	2120BWH, Banner — sm peel on top of box	NIB	$51.00	01-10
Heddon	Crazy Crawler	2120BWH, S-rig	avg	$41.00	99-01
Heddon	Crazy Crawler	2120BWH, surface rig	EX	$41.50	99-01
Heddon	Crazy Crawler	2120BWH, red eye, S-rig?	EX+	$41.00	00-03
Heddon	Crazy Crawler	2120BWH, Banner, paper	VGIB	$53.00	99-05
Heddon	Crazy Crawler	2120CHP	EX-	$203.00	03-07
Heddon	Crazy Crawler	2120CM, colors faded, NOT MET	VG-	$138.00	02-02
Heddon	Crazy Crawler	2120GM	VG+	$36.00	99-01
Heddon	Crazy Crawler	2120GM	NIB	$65.00	99-02
Heddon	Crazy Crawler	2120GM	EXIB	$135.50	99-07
Heddon	Crazy Crawler	2120GM, Banner, papers, nice!	NIB	$66.00	02-01
Heddon	Crazy Crawler	2120GM, Banner, NOT MET	EXIB	$49.00	01-06
Heddon	Crazy Crawler	2120GW	EX-	$152.00	00-09
Heddon	Crazy Crawler	2120GW, cone tail	EX	$515.00	99-12
Heddon	Crazy Crawler	2120GW, intro papers	EXIB	$271.01	99-07
Heddon	Crazy Crawler	2120RHW	EX	$61.00	99-02
Heddon	Crazy Crawler	2120RHY	EX	$66.00	99-02
Heddon	Crazy Crawler	2120WRH, cone tail	EX	$203.00	02-02
Heddon	Crazy Crawler	2120WRH, in Banner 2120YRH box	EXIB	$41.00	01-01
Heddon	Crazy Crawler	2120XBW	EX-	$189.00	02-02
Heddon	Crazy Crawler	2120XBW	EX-	$313.77	00-01

BRAND	MODEL	SERIES / MFG. CODE / DESCRIPTION	GRADE	PRICE	DATE yy/mm
Heddon	Crazy Crawler	2120XBW, nice	EX	$306.00	99-03
Heddon	Crazy Crawler	2120XBW, red eye	EX-	$453.00	99-01
Heddon	Crazy Crawler	2120XBW, NOT MET	VG+	$203.00	99-03
Heddon	Crazy Crawler	2120XBW, red eye, intro, cat	EXIB	$450.00	99-05
Heddon	Crazy Crawler	2120XBW, red eye	EX	$238.50	00-02
Heddon	Crazy Crawler	2120XBW, red eye	EX	$271.06	00-01
Heddon	Crazy Crawler	2120XRS	EX	$31.00	03-01
Heddon	Crazy Crawler	2120XRS, Banner crisp, catalog & CC paper, great combo	NIB	$76.00	05-07
Heddon	Crazy Crawler	2120XRS, Banner, papers	NIB	$60.00	02-01
Heddon	Crazy Crawler	2120XRS, Brush, 2pc, 3-color eyes	EXIB	$67.00	05-07
Heddon	Crazy Crawler	2120XRS, cone tail	EX-	$130.00	03-07
Heddon	Crazy Crawler	2120XRS, cone tail	EX	$205.00	02-02
Heddon	Crazy Crawler	2120XRS, cone tail, intro papers, NOT MET	NIB	$265.00	02-04
Heddon	Crazy Crawler	2120XRS, red eye, y intro papers	EXIB	$91.00	00-02
Heddon	Crazy Crawler	2120XRS, 2pc, black iris	EX-	$87.00	05-05
Heddon	Crazy Crawler	2120XRS, Banner	NIB	$69.00	99-11
Heddon	Crazy Crawler	2120XRS, Banner, cat	NIB	$85.00	99-08
Heddon	Crazy Crawler	2120XRS, cone tail	VG	$133.50	99-12
Heddon	Crazy Crawler	2120XRS, S-rig, Banner	NIB	$84.00	99-10
Heddon	Crazy Crawler	2120XRY	avg	$46.51	99-04
Heddon	Crazy Crawler	2120XRY	avg	$314.18	99-03
Heddon	Crazy Crawler	2120XRY, Brush decent, decent lure	EX-IB	$217.00	02-03
Heddon	Crazy Crawler	2120XRY, 3-color eyes	EX	$246.00	03-10
Heddon	Crazy Crawler	2120XRY, red eye	VG	$154.00	05-07
Heddon	Crazy Crawler	2120XRY, black eyes	EX+	$324.99	99-04
Heddon	Crazy Crawler	2120XRY, red eye	VG-	$164.50	99-12
Heddon	Crazy Crawler	2120XRY, red eye	EX-	$192.50	99-06
Heddon	Crazy Crawler	2120XRY, red eye	EX+	$362.00	00-03
Heddon	Crazy Crawler	2120XRY, red eye, Brush	NIB	$432.00	00-02
Heddon	Crazy Crawler	2120XRY, red eye, not awful	avg	$42.00	99-09
Heddon	Crazy Crawler	2120YRH, Brush box, cat	NIB	$125.00	99-01
Heddon	Crazy Crawler	2120YRH, cone tail	EX	$306.00	03-07
Heddon	Crazy Crawler	2120YRH, fat body, NOT MET	EXIB	$78.50	99-01
Heddon	Crazy Crawler	2120YRH, S-rig	mint	$35.00	01-05
Heddon	Crazy Crawler	2120YRH, 2pc, blk eye	EX	$53.00	99-01
Heddon	Crazy Crawler	2120YRH, 2pc, red eye	EX	$50.00	99-08
Heddon	Crazy Crawler	2120YRH, blk eye, 2pc	EX	$54.50	99-05
Heddon	Crazy Crawler	2120YRH, cat, papers	NIB	$102.50	99-04
Heddon	Crazy Crawler	2122LUM, papers, crisp box, mint	NIB	$1,326.00	03-04
Heddon	Crazy Crawler	2122LUM, papers	NIB	$1,200.00	03-11
Heddon	Crazy Crawler	2122LUM, crisp papers, never wet, 1 flake	EX?IB	$305.00	01-11
Heddon	Crazy Crawler	2150BF	EX	$260.00	99-12
Heddon	Crazy Crawler	2150BF	EX-	$300.00	99-10
Heddon	Crazy Crawler	2150BF, Banner box	NIB	$406.00	00-11
Heddon	Crazy Crawler	2150BF, NO BIDS!	NIB	$525.00	99-07
Heddon	Crazy Crawler	2150BF, Banner, NOT MET	NIB	$405.03	99-06
Heddon	Crazy Crawler	2150BF, Banner, NOT MET again!	NIB	$307.00	99-08

BRAND	MODEL	SERIES / MFG. CODE / DESCRIPTION	GRADE	PRICE	DATE yy/mm
Heddon	Crazy Crawler	2150GM	VG+	$182.49	99-04
Heddon	Crazy Crawler	2150RH, red eye	EX-	$300.00	00-09
Heddon	Crazy Crawler	2150RHW, decent, NOT MET	VG+	$168.09	99-03
Heddon	Crazy Crawler	2150WRH, black eye	EXIB	$370.00	00-10
Heddon	Crazy Crawler	2150XRW, black eye	EX	$650.00	99-01
Heddon	Crazy Crawler	2150YRH, black eye	EX-	$183.00	00-11
Heddon	Crazy Crawler	2150YRH, black eye	mint	$285.00	00-02
Heddon	Crazy Crawler	2150YRH, Brush, red eye, NOT MET	NIB	$330.00	99-09
Heddon	Crazy Crawler	2 diff 2120BWH, fat & reg, 1 box	EXIB	$152.00	99-04
Heddon	Crazy Crawler	320BF, 3-color eye, way too high!	EX	$41.00	99-07
Heddon	Crazy Crawler	4 diff, nice S-rig	VG+-EX-	$134.00	99-01
Heddon	Crazy Crawler	9120CYG, modern Smith color	EX	$38.01	99-04
Heddon	Crazy Crawler	9120, flocked mouse	VG	$22.00	99-06
Heddon	Crazy Crawler	9120GR, plastic	NIB	$950.00	05-02
Heddon	Crazy Crawler	9120GR, plastic!	NIB	$2,850.00	00-09
Heddon	Crazy Crawler	9120BF, early 3-color eyes, plastic	EX	$17.00	03-01
Heddon	Crazy Crawler	9120BRS, plastic	EX-	$113.00	02-10
Heddon	Crazy Crawler	9120GR	NIB	$1,600.00	00-10
Heddon	Crazy Crawler	9120YRH, green triangle bubble pack	NOC	$33.00	00-11
Heddon	Crazy Crawler	black shore, white eye	EX	$650.00	01-08
Heddon	Crazy Crawler	black with white head, intro papers	NIB	$99.00	05-07
Heddon	Crazy Crawler	BWH	VG+	$66.00	99-01
Heddon	Crazy Crawler	BWH, zinc eye	EX	$250.00	01-08
Heddon	Crazy Crawler	cone tail, 2120GW Brush bx VG+, intro paper, cat	EX-IB	$191.00	05-07
Heddon	Crazy Crawler	green scale	VG+	$28.51	05-07
Heddon	Crazy Crawler	musky	G	$89.00	99-04
Heddon	Crazy Crawler	red head/silver shore	VG	$406.00	02-05
Heddon	Crazy Crawler	RHW, Donaly	EX	$214.49	99-05
Heddon	Crazy Crawler	short bodied, heavy duty toilet seat hardware, red/white finish, Donaly-type hardware, 3½" bait	VG	$192.50	05-04
Heddon	Crazy Crawler	tiny, frog, 3-color eye	EX	$20.52	99-01
Heddon	Crazy Crawler	WBH2100	VG	$25.00	99-01
Heddon	Crazy Crawler	XRS, fat body	G	$17.50	99-01
Heddon	Crazy Crawler	XRW2120	EX-	$21.00	99-01
Heddon	Crazy Crawler	XRY, red eye, sm paint flaw	EX-	$177.00	00-09
Heddon	Crazy Crawler	YRH, zinc eye	EX	$300.00	01-08
Heddon	Crazy Crawler	2100, chipmunk, NOT MET	VG+	$249.00	03-01
Heddon	Crazy Crawler	2100BF, Banner, cat	NIB	$75.00	99-08
Heddon	Crazy Crawler	2120, chipmunk, purty nice	EX-	$443.00	01-08
Heddon	Crazy Crawler	2120XRS, red eye	EX	$43.00	02-12
Heddon	Crazy Crawler	2120XRY, box avg	VGIB	$204.00	02-11
Heddon	Crazy Crawler Spook	9120GR, blk/green triangle box mint, NOT MET	NIB	$999.00	04-02
Heddon	Crazy Crawler Spook	9120YRH, marked "2nd"	EX	$20.50	99-08
Heddon	Crazy Crawler, Musky	2150BF, Banner bx, red eye, toilet	NIB	$256.00	02-12
Heddon	Crazy Crawler, Musky	2150BF, Banner nice, NOT MET	EXIB	$256.00	01-08
Heddon	Crazy Crawler, Musky	2150CM, "N" backwards in "HEDDON"?	EX	$1,500.00	02-03
Heddon	Crazy Crawler, Musky	2150GM, Banner box	EXIB	$180.00	03-02

BRAND	MODEL	SERIES / MFG. CODE / DESCRIPTION	GRADE	PRICE	DATE yy/mm
Heddon	Crazy Crawler, Musky	2150GM, Banner, NOT MET	EX-IB	$231.00	01-03
Heddon	Crazy Crawler, Musky	2150WRH, Banner	EXIB	$148.00	01-09
Heddon	Crazy Crawler, Musky	2150WRH, Banner box rough	EXIB	$113.00	02-05
Heddon	Crazy Crawler, Musky	2150YRH, Banner	EX+IB	$307.00	01-08
Heddon	Crazy Crawler, Musky	2150YRH, Banner bx crisp	NIB	$295.00	03-01
Heddon	Crazy Crawler, Musky	2150YRH, 3-color eye	EX-	$177.00	02-01
Heddon	Crazy Crawler, Musky	2150YRH, red eye, NOT MET	EX	$228.00	00-05
Heddon	Crazy Crawler, Musky	BF, red eye	VG+	$137.00	02-06
Heddon	Crazy Crawler, Musky	frog, 3-color eyes	VG+	$138.00	04-04
Heddon	Crazy Crawler, Musky	RHY, black eyes	mint	$314.00	02-07
Heddon	Crazy Crawler, Musky	WRH, red eye	mint	$153.00	03-11
Heddon	Crazy Crawler, Musky	WRH, red eyes	VG	$113.00	02-05
Heddon	Crazy Crawler, Musky	WRH, toilet, Donaly clips	EX	$626.00	01-04
Heddon	Crazy Crawler, Musky	XRS, huge worm burn	poor	$130.00	03-07
Heddon	Crazy Crawler, Musky	XRW, black eye, NOT MET	EX	$311.00	02-11
Heddon	Crazy Crawler, Musky	YRH, black eyes, toilet seat	VG-	$103.00	04-11
Heddon	Crazy Crawler, Musky	YRH, Donaly hardware, bleed through	VG+	$269.00	01-08
Heddon	Crazy Crawler, Musky	YRH, red eyes, NOT MET	EX	$180.00	01-10
Heddon	Crazy Crawler, Tiny	3 diff, 3-color eyes, common colors	EX	$71.00	99-08
Heddon	Crazy Crawler, Tiny	320XRS, 3-color eye, PTCB	NIB	$38.00	01-12
Heddon	Crazy Crawler, Tiny	frog spot, painted eye yellow and black with red center	EX	$7.63	05-07
Heddon	Crazy Crawler, Tiny	redwing blackbird	EX	$18.00	05-05
Heddon	Crazy Crawler, Tiny	XRS, 3-color eyes	EX	$15.00	02-08
Heddon	Crazy Crawlers	3 diff — YRH, XRS, BF	EX	$152.00	99-01
Heddon	Daddy Basser	perch scale, lip edge rough, NOT MET	VG+	$658.00	02-08
Heddon	Darting Zara	6500, green scale, 2pc, GE	EX	$412.00	05-01
Heddon	Darting Zara	9210XRW, white shore, GPE, just a hint of wear	EX	$22.00	05-04
Heddon	Darting Zara	BF, nail in mouth	EX	$550.00	00-05
Heddon	Darting Zara	frog, GE	EX	$493.00	00-04
Heddon	Darting Zara	frog, GE, 2pc, wood	VG+	$130.00	99-05
Heddon	Darting Zara	frog, gold eye, no prop	EX-	$43.43	99-11
Heddon	Darting Zara	GE, bullfrog finish, box (correct condition of box unknown)	EX	$489.50	04-11
Heddon	Darting Zara	GE, frog, Lurebob, NO BIDS	EX	$399.00	00-02
Heddon	Darting Zara	RB? dent, 2pc, GE, wood	VG	$112.00	99-04
Heddon	Darting Zara	silver scale	EX-	$250.00	01-07
Heddon	Darting Zara	SS, GE, wood	EX	$132.49	99-02
Heddon	Darting Zara	SS, PE, prop	EX	$41.01	99-05
Heddon	Darting Zara	XRW, with prop gold eye	EX	$40.00	99-02
Heddon	Darting Zara	XRW, gold eye, NOT MET	NIB	$61.06	00-01
Heddon	Deep 6	green shad scale	EX	$5.00	05-03
Heddon	Deep O Diver	black head/yellow, ugly varnish	VG	$68.00	05-07
Heddon	Deep O Diver	deluxe green scale	VG+	$85.00	00-04
Heddon	Deep O Diver	goldfish scale	VG+	$147.50	00-03
Heddon	Deep O Diver	intro box EX, varnish a mite ugly	VG+IB	$450.00	02-05
Heddon	Deep O Diver	intro box avg, white/blk spots, NOT MET	EX-IB	$356.00	00-11
Heddon	Deep O Diver	y/blk spots	VG+	$96.00	00-08

BRAND	MODEL	SERIES / MFG. CODE / DESCRIPTION	GRADE	PRICE	DATE yy/mm
Heddon	DLX Salmon Plug	RH/golden shiner, Up Bass box	EX-	$143.50	99-02
Heddon	Dowagiac Spook	9100 XRY, PE	NIB	$48.85	99-04
Heddon	Dowagiac Spook	9109XRG, Super Spook crisp box & paper, GE, wowser	NIB	$350.00	05-07
Heddon	Dowagiac Spook	amber center/white/red spots ends	EX	$227.00	00-08
Heddon	Dowagiac Spook	amber spotted, 9100S Up, papers	NIB	$809.99	00-02
Heddon	Dowagiac Spook	clear GE	EX	$657.58	99-10
Heddon	Dowagiac Spook	GE, green perch scale, 2pc	EX+	$95.00	05-06
Heddon	Dowagiac Spook	GE, common color	EX	$93.00	02-01
Heddon	Dowagiac Spook	perch, GE	EX	$100.00	99-03
Heddon	Dowagiac Spook	perch scale, GE	EX-	$108.50	99-09
Heddon	Dowagiac Spook	pike scale, GE, pocket catalog, no box	EX-	$406.00	05-07
Heddon	Dowagiac Spook	pikie scale, GE, 2pc	EX+	$399.00	03-07
Heddon	Dowagiac Spook	shiner scale, GE	EX-	$82.50	99-09
Heddon	Dowagiac Spook	silver shore, GE, 2pc	EX	$227.00	05-07
Heddon	Dowagiac Spook	strawberry, GE	EX	$499.00	04-03
Heddon	Dowagiac Spook	strawberry, painted eye	EX	$71.00	02-08
Heddon	Dowagiac Spook	strawberry, PE	EX	$112.00	02-02
Heddon	Dowagiac Spook	strawberry, PE	EX-	$20.51	99-05
Heddon	Dowagiac Spook	strawberry, PE	mint	$37.00	99-12
Heddon	Dowagiac Spook	strawberry/amber belly, GE	poor	$139.00	03-06
Heddon	Dowagiac Spook	XBW, GE	EX-	$366.00	01-11
Heddon	Dowagiac Spook	XBW, glass eyes, rare, black shore	EX-	$309.00	03-01
Heddon	Dowagiac Spook	XBW, GE	EX-	$305.00	99-08
Heddon	Dowagiac Spook	XRG, glass eye, crisp Up Bass box unmarked?	NIB	$333.00	04-11
Heddon	Dowagiac Spook	XRS, painted eyes	mint	$34.00	05-02
Heddon	Dowagiac Spook	XRW, Flesh box, GE	EXIB	$96.00	00-01
Heddon	Dowagiac Spook	XRY, gold eyes	EX	$30.00	05-07
Heddon	Dowagiac Spook	XRY, PE	mint	$28.00	04-03
Heddon	Dowagiac Spook	XRY, PE	VG	$12.50	99-01
Heddon	Dowagiac Super Spook	9109XRG, Brush crisp, GE, P?	NIB	$193.00	01-06
Heddon	Dowagiac Super Spook	clear amber/spots, GE, curved	VG+	$42.23	99-04
Heddon	Drop Zara	silver scale	NOC	$52.50	99-01
Heddon	Dummy Double	1500S, Down Bass bx EX-, papers VG, L-rig	EX-IB	$887.00	04-07
Heddon	Dummy Double	1509B, frog, L-rig, NOT MET	EX-	$1,725.00	01-08
Heddon	Dummy Double	1509S, Down avg, crisp paper	VG+IB	$1,703.78	00-01
Heddon	Dummy Double	bar perch	avg	$390.00	99-01
Heddon	Dummy Double	crackle, L-rig, 23 bids	EX-	$3,250.00	00-04
Heddon	Dummy Double	crackleback, Down Bass 1500 EX, L-rig, NOT MET	EX-IB	$776.00	05-06
Heddon	Dummy Double	crackleback, L-rig	EX-	$1,400.00	02-08
Heddon	Dummy Double	Dummy Double, fancy spot finish, football hardware, marked props	VG+	$330.00	05-04
Heddon	Dummy Double	football rig, white, red, and green spots; GE, 3¼" body, earliest model with no tail hook	VG++	$600.00	05-05
Heddon	Dummy Double	football rig, ugly	avg	$512.00	00-04
Heddon	Dummy Double	football rig, red/blk spots	EX-	$3,100.00	99-04
Heddon	Dummy Double	football rig, spotted	VG+	$1,277.00	00-03

BRAND	MODEL	SERIES / MFG. CODE / DESCRIPTION	GRADE	PRICE	DATE yy/mm
Heddon	Dummy Double	football, wrong rear hook, big chip, NOT MET	VG+	$457.00	01-01
Heddon	Dummy Double	frog spot, L-rig	VG-	$180.00	04-12
Heddon	Dummy Double	frog spot, L-rig	VG+	$430.00	04-11
Heddon	Dummy Double	frog, L-rig, ugly varnish	VG	$406.00	03-02
Heddon	Dummy Double	frog, L-rig, heavy age lines	VG-	$1,025.00	00-10
Heddon	Dummy Double	L-rig, decent, NOT MET	VG	$431.00	01-11
Heddon	Dummy Double	lure crap, 3 good hooks	poor	$510.00	00-07
Heddon	Dummy Double	orange spotted, decent	VG+	$725.00	99-11
Heddon	Dummy Double	RB	avg?	$500.00	99-05
Heddon	Dummy Double	SB, football, DD papers, unmarked box	VG+IB	$1,400.00	02-03
Heddon	Dummy Double	slate/red eye, NOT MET	VG	$775.00	99-02
Heddon	Dummy Double	spotted, fairly ugly, NOT NET	VG-	$500.00	99-07
Heddon	Dummy Double	spotted, football rig	VG	$1,200.00	02-08
Heddon	Dummy Double	spotted, football rig, huge chip	?	$575.00	02-06
Heddon	Dummy Double	spotted, ugly, NOT MET	VG-	$365.00	99-08
Heddon	Dummy Double	spotted, L-rig	VG+	$1,225.00	99-04
Heddon	Dummy Double	strawberry	EX-	$2,200.00	00-05
Heddon	Dummy Double	white spotted, L-rig	VG-	$436.00	02-02
Heddon	Dummy Double	y spotted, L-rig	VG+	$737.00	00-10
Heddon	Dummy Double	y spotted, football, huge belly chip, rest OK	?	$1,000.00	00-12
Heddon	Dummy Double	y/red/green spots, L-rig	VG	$598.00	99-03
Heddon	Dying Flutter	2 diff, frog, blk/silver, w eye	EX	$22.00	99-01
Heddon	Dying Flutter	3 different	NIB	$35.01	99-01
Heddon	Dying Flutter	9205Y	NIB	$12.99	05-07
Heddon	Dying Flutter	black over yellow with orange belly	NIB	$10.50	05-07
Heddon	Dying Flutter	gold color, yellow stripes, black eyes, 4" long	VG	$15.50	05-07
Heddon	Expert	alum, ugly	avg	$510.00	00-01
Heddon	Expert	BH, slope nose, brass cup, tail cap	VG	$786.00	00-09
Heddon	Expert	BH/w, red collar	VG+	$1,654.00	00-01
Heddon	Expert	short, fat, long sweeping gill marks, tiny	avg	$2,550.00	00-10
Heddon	Fidget	401, BW, red and white, window box	NIB	$14.99	05-07
Heddon	Fidgit 3-Pack kit	plastic flip-top divided box, 1 lure has paint flakes, 2 clean lures	EX-	$33.00	05-05
Heddon	Flap Tail	7000RH, Banner bx crisp & papers, PE	NIB	$47.00	05-02
Heddon	Flap Tail	gold PE, perch scale SR	EX+	$35.00	05-06
Heddon	Flap Tail Jr.	9700SS, silver scale (flash), GPE, shorter 3" body style, very light wear	EX-	$32.00	05-04
Heddon	Flaptail	7000GM, Banner	NIB	$78.50	99-09
Heddon	Flaptail	7000L, PE	NIB	$55.55	99-05
Heddon	Flaptail	7002, Brush, GE, small chip	VGIB	$50.00	99-04
Heddon	Flaptail	7002, GE, 2-pc, Brush	NIB	$174.49	99-05
Heddon	Flaptail	7009SS, Brush nice, 2pc	EX-IB	$75.00	01-10
Heddon	Flaptail	frog, 2pc, flaw on back burn?	VG+	$129.00	01-01
Heddon	Flaptail	L, S-rig, big eyes	EX-	$39.00	00-10
Heddon	Flaptail	mouse, lt belly drag	EX+	$100.00	00-10
Heddon	Flaptail	P, GE, 2pc, looks nice	EX	$122.50	99-06
Heddon	Flaptail	perch, GE, 2pc	EX	$147.50	99-05
Heddon	Flaptail	perch scale, GE, S-rig	EX	$77.00	00-11

BRAND	MODEL	SERIES / MFG. CODE / DESCRIPTION	GRADE	PRICE	DATE yy/mm
Heddon	Flaptail	r/w, GE	EX+	$100.00	99-01
Heddon	Flaptail	RH, GE, 2pc	EX	$72.00	05-07
Heddon	Flaptail	RH, GE, 2pc	EX	$102.00	01-03
Heddon	Flaptail	RH, GE	EX	$52.50	00-03
Heddon	Flaptail	shiner scale, GE, 2pc	EX	$98.00	00-05
Heddon	Flaptail	silver scale, GE nice!	EX-	$41.00	04-11
Heddon	Flaptail	SS, painted eye	EX	$35.00	02-12
Heddon	Flaptail	SS, GE, 2pc	mint	$107.50	99-09
Heddon	Flaptail Fly Rod	710, r/w, Up Bass bx avg	EXIB	$181.00	04-12
Heddon	Flaptail Fly Rod	710, y, Up Bass	NIB	$180.00	00-10
Heddon	Flaptail Fly Rod	710BR, Up Bass, VG	NIB	$291.00	00-04
Heddon	Flaptail Fly Rod	720WR, rough box	NIB	$102.50	99-06
Heddon	Flaptail Fly Rod	740GM, Up Bass	EXIB	$154.50	99-08
Heddon	Flaptail Fly Rod	b/w	EX	$138.02	99-04
Heddon	Flaptail Fly Rod	black/white wings	EX	$309.00	99-09
Heddon	Flaptail Fly Rod	gold?	EX	$103.00	00-05
Heddon	Flaptail Fly Rod	r/w	EX	$90.00	01-04
Heddon	Flaptail Fly Rod	r/w pointers, cracks	avg	$35.00	99-01
Heddon	Flaptail Fly Rod	RH	VG+	$42.00	00-03
Heddon	Flaptail Fly Rod	RH	EX	$45.00	00-11
Heddon	Flaptail Fly Rod	RH	EX	$68.00	00-08
Heddon	Flaptail Fly Rod	yellow, NOT MET	EX	$52.99	99-06
Heddon	Flaptail Fly Rod	yellow, NOT MET	EX-	$66.99	99-05
Heddon	Flaptail Fly Rod	yellow, on card (no box)	NOC	$71.50	99-12
Heddon	Flaptail Fly Rod	mouse	EX	$40.00	04-11
Heddon	Flaptail Giant	natural scale, teddy bear eyes	EX	$461.00	04-02
Heddon	Flaptail Giant	strawberry, teddy bear eyes	EX	$330.00	04-02
Heddon	Flaptail Jr.	7110GM, Brush bx & papers	NIB	$153.00	03-10
Heddon	Flaptail Jr.	chipmunk, NOT MET	EX-	$430.00	00-01
Heddon	Flaptail Jr.	green scale? 2pc, GE	EX+	$132.50	99-01
Heddon	Flaptail Jr.	gray mouse, 2pc	EX	$81.00	02-02
Heddon	Flaptail Jr.	nat scale, GE	EX	$123.51	99-06
Heddon	Flaptail Jr.	perch scale, GE, 2pc	EX	$131.38	00-02
Heddon	Flaptail Jr.	pike scale, GE	mint	$127.50	99-06
Heddon	Flaptail Jr.	shiner scale, GE	EX	$89.01	99-05
Heddon	Flaptail Jr.	shiner scale, GE	mint	$250.00	00-02
Heddon	Flaptail Jr.	silver scale	EX	$39.00	01-04
Heddon	Flaptail Jr.	SS, GE, 2pc, a beauty	EX+	$64.00	03-01
Heddon	Flaptail Vamp	r/w, golfish scale flapper	EX	$300.00	99-01
Heddon	Flaptail Vamp Musky	SS, toilet, GE	EX	$228.00	01-02
Heddon	Flaptail Vamp Musky?	shiner scale, fat body, L-rig	EX	$325.00	99-08
Heddon	Flaptail, Musky	7040GM, Banner	NIB	$207.55	99-04
Heddon	Flaptail, Musky	7040PAS, PE, Banner avg	EXIB	$75.00	00-10
Heddon	Flaptail, Musky	7050GM, gray flock mouse, BBE, toilet hdwr, some light consistent wear to flock, few flks	VG-	$75.00	05-05
Heddon	Flaptail, Musky	7050SS, strawberry spotted, lg GEs, HDTS hdwr	EX-	$130.00	05-05
Heddon	Flaptail, Musky	7050PAS, red Brush box, PE	NIB	$81.00	00-03

BRAND	MODEL	SERIES / MFG. CODE / DESCRIPTION	GRADE	PRICE	DATE yy/mm
Heddon	Flaptail, Musky	7050PAS, PE, Banner	NIB	$56.00	99-10
Heddon	Flaptail, Musky	7050RH, PE, Banner papers	NIB	$56.00	99-11
Heddon	Flaptail, Musky	7059CP, GE, Flesh box, wowser	NIB	$986.00	01-03
Heddon	Flaptail, Musky	chipmunk	VG+	$400.00	05-01
Heddon	Flaptail, Musky	copper sheen! reg GE, beauty! toilet seat	EX	$420.00	04-02
Heddon	Flaptail, Musky	gray mouse, light hook drags, toilet seat	VG	$137.00	05-03
Heddon	Flaptail, Musky	mouse	G	$31.77	99-02
Heddon	Flaptail, Musky	natural scale	EX-	$128.55	99-04
Heddon	Flaptail, Musky	natural scale, GE	EX-	$132.00	05-01
Heddon	Flaptail, Musky	P, in 7052 Brush box, GE, toilet	NIB	$382.00	00-10
Heddon	Flaptail, Musky	pike scale, toilet	VG+	$133.00	05-07
Heddon	Flaptail, Musky	r/w, GE, unmarked Brush box	EXIB	$157.50	99-01
Heddon	Flaptail, Musky	RH, glass eyes	EX	$66.00	04-03
Heddon	Flaptail, Musky	RH, GE	EX-	$77.00	02-06
Heddon	Flaptail, Musky	RH, GE, toilet	EX-	$70.00	05-07
Heddon	Flaptail, Musky	SB, teddy eyes, sm chip	EX-	$250.00	01-01
Heddon	Flaptail, Musky	SD, PE? in crisp Brush box	NIB	$187.00	00-09
Heddon	Flaptail, Musky	shiner scale, regular GE	EX	$198.00	04-03
Heddon	Flaptail, Musky	shiner scale, teddy eyes, toilet seat	EX-	$130.00	03-02
Heddon	Flaptail, Musky	shiner scale, GE, toilet seat	EX	$221.00	03-07
Heddon	Flaptail, Musky	SS, GE, light hook drag, chew mark, decent	VG+	$87.00	03-02
Heddon	Flaptail, Musky	strawberry, teddy bear GE	EX	$361.00	00-02
Heddon	Flipper	140, GE, RH/white	GD	$132.00	04-11
Heddon	Flipper	149M, great box	NIB	$2,820.00	00-11
Heddon	Flipper	bar perch, chip on back, otherwise nice	VG	$204.00	04-11
Heddon	Flipper	frog scale, repaint? min $895, NO BIDS	EX	$895.00	03-11
Heddon	Flipper	frog spot, awful worm burn, $650 NOT MET	??	$153.00	02-08
Heddon	Flipper	No. 140, GE, white/red/green decoration, fat body	EX	$71.50	04-11
Heddon	Flipper	green scale, $595, NOT MET	EX-	$345.00	03-12
Heddon	Flipper	green scale, Down Bass bx EX-	EX-IB	$450.00	05-07
Heddon	Flipper	green scale, NOT MET	poor	$56.00	00-04
Heddon	Flipper	nat scale	EX-	$1,200.00	00-05
Heddon	Flipper	perch scale, L-rig	EX	$372.00	02-02
Heddon	Flipper	RET	EX-	$350.00	01-07
Heddon	Flipper	shiner scale, L-rig, NOT MET	EX-	$315.00	00-08
Heddon	Flipper	Stanley props, nicks, NOT MET	?	$261.00	01-05
Heddon	Flipper	strawberry, Down Bass unmarked bx	avgIB	$178.00	02-10
Heddon	Flipper	strawberry, fat body, Stanley props	EX	$800.00	04-12
Heddon	Flipper	strawberry, age lines, no missing paint	VG	$475.00	99-11
Heddon	Flipper	white, bull's-eye, otherwise nice	EX-	$114.00	01-05
Heddon	Flipper	white, red nose	avg	$69.00	02-02
Heddon	Flipper	white/red eye shadow, Heddon prop, NOT MET	VG	$135.00	01-10
Heddon	Flipper	JRH, frog scale, tail chip	VG	$800.00	00-08
Heddon	Flipper Musky?	RET, fat body, Stanley props, 3 dbl hooks	VG+	$521.00	01-04
Heddon	Florida Lure 19S	y flitter, L-rig, HPGM	EX-	$500.00	99-10
Heddon	Florida Special	12S, RH/w, GE, NSOP, TS-rig, little flaking on BW and tail, stamped "2nd"	EX-	$110.00	05-05
Heddon	Florida Special	green scale	EX-	$300.00	00-10

139

BRAND	MODEL	SERIES / MFG. CODE / DESCRIPTION	GRADE	PRICE	DATE yy/mm
Heddon	Florida Special	green scale	VG+	$525.00	00-05
Heddon	Florida Special	red scale, 2¾", decent	VG	$307.00	00-05
Heddon	Florida Special	strawberry, unmarked Down Bass bx	EX	$767.00	03-11
Heddon	Florida Special 10B	marked props, gold flitter, saltwater finish, decent	VG	$152.00	05-07
Heddon	Florida Special Baby	green scale, SOLD	VG+/EX-	$575.00	00-05
Heddon	Fuzzi Bug	black, bass size	mint	$175.00	02-12
Heddon	Fuzzi Bug	white, large bass size	EX	$250.00	02-11
Heddon	Gamefisher	5400S	EX-	$1,138.00	00-12
Heddon	Gamefisher	5401, rainbow, L-rig, few minor nicks and varnish pointers	EX-	$75.00	05-05
Heddon	Gamefisher	5409P, shiner scale, L-rig, 3 tiny varnish pointers	EX	$55.00	05-05
Heddon	Gamefisher	5409P, shiner scale, TS-rig, 1 tiny pointer and hint of wear in orig Up Bass 2PCCB	EXIB	$250.00	05-05
Heddon	Gamefisher	5501, Down Bass & papers	EXIB	$238.00	04-01
Heddon	Gamefisher	5501, Down Bass bx, nice papers	EX+IB	$238.00	04-02
Heddon	Gamefisher	5501, RB, L-rig, Down Bass, nice	NIB	$238.00	99-08
Heddon	Gamefisher	5502, Down Bass bx & paper	NIB	$138.00	05-07
Heddon	Gamefisher	5502, Down Bass bx, crisp catalog	NIB	$288.00	03-05
Heddon	Gamefisher	5502, Down Bass, nice	NIB	$255.00	99-05
Heddon	Gamefisher	5502, crisp Up Bass, wowser	NIB	$315.00	00-04
Heddon	Gamefisher	5502, L-rig, Down Bass	EX-IB	$195.00	00-01
Heddon	Gamefisher	5509D, Down Bass VG	EX-IB	$112.00	00-10
Heddon	Gamefisher	5509D, Up Bass	EXIB	$242.50	99-07
Heddon	Gamefisher	5509M, DLB VG	EXIB	$125.00	04-03
Heddon	Gamefisher	5509M, unmarked Down Bass	EX-IB	$200.00	99-10
Heddon	Gamefisher	blue scale	EX-	$258.00	04-03
Heddon	Gamefisher	green scale	VG-	$21.50	05-07
Heddon	Gamefisher	green scale	EX?	$34.00	00-06
Heddon	Gamefisher	green scale	G	$37.00	99-01
Heddon	Gamefisher	green scale, GE, expert thinks fake	VG-	$578.00	02-02
Heddon	Gamefisher	pike scale, L-rig	mint	$177.00	00-01
Heddon	Gamefisher	pike scale, un Down Bass VG	EX-	$151.00	99-08
Heddon	Gamefisher	r/w	EX	$73.00	99-01
Heddon	Gamefisher	rainbow	VG	$22.00	04-07
Heddon	Gamefisher	rainbow	VG-	$35.00	99-01
Heddon	Gamefisher	rainbow	VG-	$50.00	99-01
Heddon	Gamefisher	rainbow	EX	$106.00	01-10
Heddon	Gamefisher	RB	EX-	$51.00	00-05
Heddon	Gamefisher	red head & tail	EX	$133.50	00-01
Heddon	Gamefisher	RET	VG	$27.00	00-03
Heddon	Gamefisher	shiner scale	VG	$48.00	99-01
Heddon	Gamefisher	shiner scale	VG+	$44.00	05-07
Heddon	Gamefisher	shiner scale, Down Bass	NIB	$228.37	99-02
Heddon	Gamefisher	shiner scale, L-rig, nice	EX	$125.00	99-03
Heddon	Gamefisher	shiner scale, unmarked Down Bass bx, crisp catalog	NIB	$342.00	03-05
Heddon	Gamefisher	shiner scale	VG+	$38.00	00-04
Heddon	Gamefisher	white/red	EX	$57.00	00-05

BRAND	MODEL	SERIES / MFG. CODE / DESCRIPTION	GRADE	PRICE	DATE yy/mm
Heddon	Gamefisher x 2	green scale, RET	EX-	$113.00	00-06
Heddon	Gamefisher x 2	shiner scale, red & white, both nice	EX	$188.01	99-09
Heddon	Gamefisher x 2	sm and large in RB, nice	EX	$203.55	00-02
Heddon	Gamefisher, Baby	5402, Up Bass & papers	NIB	$227.00	00-12
Heddon	Gamefisher, Baby	blue scale	VG+	$175.00	00-10
Heddon	Gamefisher, Baby	blue scale, looks repainted in pictures	EX	$450.00	03-04
Heddon	Gamefisher, Baby	blue scale, sm worm burn top tail	VG	$371.00	01-03
Heddon	Gamefisher, Baby	RET	EX	$76.00	01-02
Heddon	Gamefisher, Baby	shiner scale, 5402 Down Bass bx, crisp catalog	NIB	$169.00	03-05
Heddon	Gamefisher, Baby	5501, rainbow, L-rig, long thin varn flake on head and couple of nicks	VG	$40.00	05-05
Heddon	Giant Runt	RH, papers, 2PCCB	NIB	$812.00	98-12
Heddon	Go Deeper Crab	9909L, perch scale, BBE, 2pc, nice feelers, light varnish wear	EX-	$45.00	05-05
Heddon	Go Deeper Crab	crackleback	EX	$36.00	05-07
Heddon	Go Deeper Crab	D1900NC, natural crab, GPE, 1 pointer and a hint of age lines, EX+ Banner 2PCCB	EX+IB	$55.00	05-05
Heddon	Go Deeper Crab	D1900NC, PE, S-rig, cat	EXIB	$40.00	99-05
Heddon	Go Deeper Crab	D1900GCB, green crackleback, GPE, SR, few light age lines and hint of wear	EX	$35.00	05-05
Heddon	Go Deeper Crab	gold PE, SR, orange with black & red spots	VG+	$20.00	05-06
Heddon	Go Deeper Crab	r/w, PE, Banner	NIB	$56.00	99-09
Heddon	Go Deeper Crab	spotted orange, PE	NIB	$80.00	99-01
Heddon	Great Vamp	LUM	VG+	$300.00	99-12
Heddon	Great Vamp	blue herring (SS?), $125 NOT MET	VG	$68.00	00-05
Heddon	Great Vamp	Shiner scale, GE, toilet, NOT MET	VG	$212.50	99-04
Heddon	Hardins Whiz	belly stencil, POBW, floppy, NOT MET	VG	$355.00	01-01
Heddon	Hardins Whiz	shiner scale	EX	$1,245.00	00-07
Heddon	Hedd Hunter	9300BB baby bass, shallow lip, WPE	EX	$7.00	05-04
Heddon	Hedd Hunter	9310CBO, crackleback, orange paint great, very light wear on lip and hdwr	EX-	$10.00	05-04
Heddon	Hedd Hunter	9310YFO, flor yellow w/flor orange ribs and blk back, light wear and few scratches	VG	$5.00	05-04
Heddon	Hedd Hunter	9320CD	NOC	$37.00	00-02
Heddon	Hedd Hunter	9320NPB	NOC	$37.00	00-02
Heddon	Hedd Hunter	9325LC, natural perch finish, very light wear	EX-	$8.00	05-04
Heddon	Hedd Hunter	9325SUC, natural sucker finish	NM	$11.00	05-04
Heddon	Hedd Hunter	9350NSN (Rapala shape)	NOC	$34.63	00-02
Heddon	Hedd Hunter	Day-glo neon green scale/cream	EX	$66.00	05-07
Heddon	Hedd Plug	3 diff	EX	$132.50	99-04
Heddon	Hedd Plug	big size, chrome	EX-	$28.00	01-06
Heddon	Hedd Plug	chart/silver scale	EX	$42.00	99-01
Heddon	Hedd Plug	chart green/RB scale	mint	$49.99	99-03
Heddon	Hedd Plug	nat striper, photo finish	EX	$103.50	00-01
Heddon	Hedd Plug	pearl	EX	$61.00	99-06
Heddon	Hedd Plug Magnum	FL, orange/blk spots, 4½"		$100.00	99-03
Heddon	Hedd Plug Magnum	musky color, 4½"	EX+	$100.00	99-03
Heddon	Hedd Plug Magnum	pike scale lime green?	EX	$150.00	02-05

BRAND	MODEL	SERIES / MFG. CODE / DESCRIPTION	GRADE	PRICE	DATE yy/mm
Heddon	Hep Spinners	easel display board, 3 lures	EX	$32.00	99-01
Heddon	Hi Tail	105B, gold eye, "Topkick" covered	NIB	$106.00	00-04
Heddon	Hi Tail	305SS, gold eyes	NIB	$70.00	04-02
Heddon	Hi Tail	6 diff, NOT MET	EX	$203.00	99-01
Heddon	Hi Tail	black	VG	$37.00	99-01
Heddon	Hi Tail	black	EX+	$46.90	98-12
Heddon	Hi Tail	black, gold eyes, "Topkick" painted over	EX	$105.00	05-02
Heddon	Hi Tail	black, white eye	EX	$48.00	01-08
Heddon	Hi Tail	black/gold eye	EX	$62.00	99-05
Heddon	Hi Tail	Budweiser, NOT MET	avg	$307.00	99-03
Heddon	Hi Tail	Budweiser, decal scrape	VG-	$150.00	01-05
Heddon	Hi Tail	BWC, black & white checkerboard	EX-	$257.00	03-07
Heddon	Hi Tail	checkerboard	EX	$370.00	01-03
Heddon	Hi Tail	checkerboard	EX+	$416.00	02-04
Heddon	Hi Tail	checkerboard, black scales on white belly	EX	$230.00	05-07
Heddon	Hi Tail	frog	mint	$66.50	99-02
Heddon	Hi Tail	frog	NIB	$69.00	99-02
Heddon	Hi Tail	frog, white eye, NOT MET	EX	$36.06	00-01
Heddon	Hi Tail	Indy 500	EX+	$380.00	01-12
Heddon	Hi Tail	P, white eye	EX	$39.00	99-05
Heddon	Hi Tail	perch	EX	$46.00	99-02
Heddon	Hi Tail	perch	EX-	$51.00	99-01
Heddon	Hi Tail	perch	EX	$66.08	99-02
Heddon	Hi Tail	perch, white eyes	mint	$63.89	99-03
Heddon	Hi Tail	perch, white eye	EX	$46.10	99-04
Heddon	Hi Tail	perch, white eye	mint	$49.99	99-05
Heddon	Hi Tail	perch, white eyes	EX-	$51.00	99-05
Heddon	Hi Tail	perch scale	NIB	$69.00	02-01
Heddon	Hi Tail	r/w	VG	$25.00	99-01
Heddon	Hi Tail	r/w, gold eye, "Heddon" only	VG+	$44.50	99-04
Heddon	Hi Tail	r/w, white eye	mint	$61.00	99-04
Heddon	Hi Tail	r/w, white eye	EX	$50.00	99-06
Heddon	Hi Tail	RH, PTCB	NIB	$96.00	05-07
Heddon	Hi Tail	RH, white eye	EX	$51.00	99-05
Heddon	Hi Tail	silver scale	mint	$40.00	00-04
Heddon	Hi Tail	silver scale	EX	$40.00	98-12
Heddon	Hi Tail	silver scale	EX	$41.00	99-01
Heddon	Hi Tail	silver scale, UNLISTED	EX-	$585.00	99-06
Heddon	Hi Tail	silver scale, white eye, NOT MET	EX	$35.02	99-07
Heddon	Hi Tail	SS	EX	$28.25	99-01
Heddon	Hi Tail	SS	EX-	$41.00	99-03
Heddon	Hi Tail	SS	VG	$41.00	99-03
Heddon	Hi Tail	SS	EX-	$46.00	99-03
Heddon	Hi Tail	store display with 4 colors, 12 lures	NOC	$600.00	00-05
Heddon	Hi Tail	XRY, NOT MET	EX	$338.00	02-03
Heddon	Hi Tail	XRY, white eye, NOT MET	EX	$356.00	02-04
Heddon	Hi Tail	yellow, white eye	VG+IB	$48.78	99-05
Heddon	Hi Tail	yellow, white eye	EX	$41.00	99-06

BRAND	MODEL	SERIES / MFG. CODE / DESCRIPTION	GRADE	PRICE	DATE yy/mm
Heddon	Hi Tail	yellow/yellow eyes	EX	$78.25	99-03
Heddon	Hi Tail		EX-	$40.99	99-01
Heddon	Hi Tail x 5	5 different, all white eye	EX	$168.51	99-08
Heddon	Hi Tail x 12	stand-up display, 6 colors x 2	NOC	$691.00	00-03
Heddon	Hi Tail x 4	305RH, 305F, 305L, 305SS	NIB	$205.00	03-01
Heddon	Hi-Jacker	9355BAR	NIB	$39.00	05-01
Heddon	Improved Hedd Plug	3 diff flourescent, NOT MET	NIB	$122.50	99-08
Heddon	Killer	450, r/w/r	EX	$850.00	99-10
Heddon	Killer	intro pic box avg, alum, 3 BW	EX-IB	$5,000.00	99-10
Heddon	Killer	picture box avg, r/w/r, no eyes	EX-IB	$721.00	05-03
Heddon	Killer	r/w/r, NOT MET	avg	$233.50	99-01
Heddon	Killer	solid red, with three belly weights and box (avg)	VG+IB	$1,210.00	05-07
Heddon	Killer 400	blue/white pic box VG+	EX-IB	$6,750.00	01-06
Heddon	Killer 450	pic box VG-, red/white, NOT MET	EX-IB	$5,001.00	00-12
Heddon	King Basser	8540PAS, Allen Stripey, r-chipped, l-cracked, few pointers, o/w, new in EX- Brush box and cat	EXIB	$115.00	05-04
Heddon	King Basser	PAS, teddy bear, string	EX-	$50.00	99-03
Heddon	King Basser	pearl? (white) shore, rope	EX-	$44.51	00-01
Heddon	King Basser	XRY, TBGE, Brush box, breakaway	NIB	$162.00	00-07
Heddon	King Cobra	9940BL, blue back and silver glitter sides, WPE	EX-	$37.00	05-04
Heddon	King Stanley	pike scale, 299M up bx	NIB	$87.00	02-09
Heddon	King Zig Wag	8352M crisp Brush box, varnish? on eyes	NIB	$152.00	04-03
Heddon	King Zig Wag	8369 Brush, A. Stripey, 1 crack eye	EXIB	$127.50	00-04
Heddon	King Zig Wag	8369PAS, Brush	NIB	$318.00	01-05
Heddon	King Zig Wag	8369PBH, GE, POBW	NIB	$140.00	00-10
Heddon	King Zig Wag	blue scale	EX	$171.00	00-08
Heddon	King Zig Wag	white shore, box has no codes but EX	NIB	$46.00	05-03
Heddon	King Zig Wag	white, GE, POBW	EX-	$152.50	00-01
Heddon	King Zig Wag	XRW, pearl? string hook	EX-	$237.50	00-01
Heddon	King Zig Wag	XRW, PE, Banner	NIB	$75.00	00-03
Heddon	King Zig Wag Salmon	8350P, string, crisp Brush & cat	NIB	$134.00	00-11
Heddon	Kinney Bird	GE, cup rigged, bird shows age lines, chipping and flaking to primer	EX-	$3,080.00	05-04
Heddon	Lagauna Runt	L10XBP, Brush, PE	NIB	$102.50	00-01
Heddon	Laguana Runt 10S	SB, GE, Up Bass VG+, POBW	EX-IB	$189.00	01-08
Heddon	Laguna Rung	119SS, silver scale, GE, TS-rig, PO1BW, few small varn flaks on nose and light age lines	VG+	$78.00	05-05
Heddon	Laguna Runt	L10XPB, crisp Brush box, PE	NIB	$114.50	99-02
Heddon	Laguna Runt	pearl, painted eyes	mint	$41.00	02-07
Heddon	Little Joe	502, RH/w, GE, L-rig, part POBW, flakes on tail, light wear	VG-	$62.00	05-05
Heddon	Little Joe	508RH, RH/w w/gold flitter, GE, TS-rig, light ring on BW	NM	$150.00	05-05
Heddon	Little Joe	RH glitter, GE, NOT MET	EX	$212.49	99-10
Heddon	Little Mary	802 Down Bass EX-	EX-IB	$400.00	99-10
Heddon	Little Mary	858 RH RH/w w/gold fleck, rare zinc eyes, TS-hdwr, part POBW	EX-	$225.00	05-05
Heddon	Lucky 13	2500BL, Spook? blue scale	NIB	$870.00	03-06
Heddon	Lucky 13	2500BRS	NIB	$128.00	01-08

BRAND	MODEL	SERIES / MFG. CODE / DESCRIPTION	GRADE	PRICE	DATE yy/mm
Heddon	Lucky 13	2500PG, golden shiner, YPE, plastic, few scuffs and light wear	VG+	$14.00	05-05
Heddon	Lucky 13	2500PRH, RH/shiner, plastic, WPE, SR, unfished condition	EX+	$18.00	05-05
Heddon	Lucky 13	2500RH, RH/w, GE, ST, NSOB, very light wear	EX	$45.00	05-05
Heddon	Lucky 13	2500GRA	NIB	$107.00	00-09
Heddon	Lucky 13	2500XRY, PTCB	NIB	$275.00	05-07
Heddon	Lucky 13	2502, RH/w, NE, deep cup rig, light age lines, hole in chin, chip at tail	VG++	$85.00	05-05
Heddon	Lucky 13	2502, Up Bass, L-rig, long lip	NIB	$300.00	01-09
Heddon	Lucky 13	2509PLRH, no eyes, Brush	EX-IB	$167.50	99-08
Heddon	Lucky 13	b/w, tack glass eyes, tough color	EX-	$61.00	99-08
Heddon	Lucky 13	Charlie Campbell frog	EX	$113.00	00-05
Heddon	Lucky 13	frog spot, eye	EX	$220.00	05-07
Heddon	Lucky 13	goldfish scale, NE, cup, varnish	avg	$78.00	00-10
Heddon	Lucky 13	golfish scale	VG+	$177.00	04-12
Heddon	Lucky 13	green scale, no eyes, 2pc	NIB	$141.00	02-07
Heddon	Lucky 13	BEE, in black/yellow	EX	$550.00	05-07
Heddon	Lucky 13	JRH, Brush bx, GE, S-rigged	NIB	$127.00	02-08
Heddon	Lucky 13	long lip, L-rig, in 2501 Brush box	EXIB	$300.00	99-01
Heddon	Lucky 13	natural scale, no eyes, L-rig, couple bull's-eye dents	EX-	$174.00	05-07
Heddon	Lucky 13	no eyes, RH/shiner scale, toilet seat	EX-	$62.00	05-07
Heddon	Lucky 13	no eyes, yellow/black head, cup rig, rough on black paint	VG-	$115.00	05-07
Heddon	Lucky 13	orange with black spots, no eyes	EX	$413.00	05-07
Heddon	Lucky 13	r/w, no eyes, L-rig, long lip	EX-	$102.50	99-05
Heddon	Lucky 13	red/white with box	NIB	$176.00	05-07
Heddon	Lucky 13	red head/shiner, toilet seat hardware	EX-	$137.00	05-07
Heddon	Lucky 13	red scale, no eyes	VG+	$325.00	00-05
Heddon	Lucky 13	red scale, no eyes	VG	$163.51	99-06
Heddon	Lucky 13	RH, NE, long lip	EX-	$165.00	00-12
Heddon	Lucky 13	RH/frog scale, tack glass eye	NIB	$102.50	99-02
Heddon	Lucky 13	RH/frog scale, no eyes	EX	$344.00	01-11
Heddon	Lucky 13	RH/frog scale, no eyes, L-rig	EX-	$243.01	00-02
Heddon	Lucky 13	RH/frog scale, GE, S-rig	EX	$30.00	00-10
Heddon	Lucky 13	SS, wood, painted eyes, S-rig	mint	$61.00	02-07
Heddon	Lucky 13	W2500PRH, "Original," S-rig	NIB	$32.00	00-11
Heddon	Lucky 13	X2500W-BF, collector's edition	NIB	$23.93	05-07
Heddon	Lucky 13	XBW, PE	EX	$202.00	00-05
Heddon	Lucky 13	XRYBB, PE, thin lip chip	EX-	$265.00	00-11
Heddon	Lucky 13	yellow/silver/black	GD	$13.50	05-07
Heddon	Lucky 13 Jr.	3409H, Wiggle King intro box fair	avgIB	$267.00	00-05
Heddon	Lucky 13 Spook	GRA, Florescent Green Crawfish	NIB	$75.00	02-03
Heddon	Lucky 13 Spook	natural bass?	mint	$89.00	02-03
Heddon	Lucky 13 Spook	NF, natural frog	NIB	$152.00	02-03
Heddon	Lucky 13 Spook	photo finish pikie	EX	$204.00	00-08
Heddon	Lucky 13 Spook	shad, yellow eyes, light lip wear, gold belly stencil	EX-	$330.00	05-07
Heddon	Lucky 13 Spook	SS, white eyes	EX	$6.00	06-05
Heddon	Lucky 13 Spook	TORA, tiger stripe	EX	$1,009.00	03-07

BRAND	MODEL	SERIES / MFG. CODE / DESCRIPTION	GRADE	PRICE	DATE yy/mm
Heddon	Lucky 13 Spook	XRY	NIB	$275.00	03-07
Heddon	Lucky 13 Spook	XRY, S-rig, tail bell rig, white eye	mint	$290.00	02-06
Heddon	Lucky 13 Spook	XRY, white eyes	EX	$230.00	04-11
Heddon	Lucky 13 Spook	YCD	EX	$265.00	03-07
Heddon	Lucky 13 Spook	yellow coach dog?	EX	$35.00	99-01
Heddon	Lucky 13 Spook	yellow coach dog?	mint	$76.00	99-01
Heddon	Lucky 13 Spook	yellow tiger	mint	$518.00	01-12
Heddon	Lucky 13, Baby	GE, frog	avg	$12.50	99-01
Heddon	Lucky 13, Baby	perch, NE	EX-	$425.00	99-01
Heddon	Lucky 13, Baby	photo, nat bass?	EX	$54.00	00-04
Heddon	Lucky 13, Baby	SB color, silver head/black-silver spots	EX-	$355.00	00-11
Heddon	Lucky 13, Baby	2400B, bullfrog, plastic, SR, GPE, slight rub on lip edge	EX-	$12.00	05-05
Heddon	Lucky 13, Baby	2400JRH, RH/frog scale, plastic, SR, YPE, looks unfished, in orig VG+ 2PPTB	EXIB	$22.00	05-05
Heddon	Lucky 13, Baby	2409K, goldfish, NE, long lip, belly and lip have chips and varnish loss	G++	$32.00	05-05
Heddon	Lucky 13, Baby	2409SS, silver scale, NE, long lip, TS-hdwr, few small nicks on lip edge	EX	$85.00	05-05
Heddon	Lucky 13?	silver scale/blue eye & back, no stencil?	EX-	$401.00	02-04
Heddon	Luny Frog	3502WRH, Up Bass box, red head, white, a beauty	NIB	$510.00	05-06
Heddon	Luny Frog	3509B, closed legs	mint	$150.00	99-10
Heddon	Luny Frog	3509BB, Up Bass	NIB	$355.00	99-07
Heddon	Luny Frog	3509RH, Up Bass box EX	EX-IB	$1,326.99	00-02
Heddon	Luny Frog	closed leg	EX	$350.00	99-05
Heddon	Luny Frog	closed leg, lip missing much paint	VG-	$58.00	04-12
Heddon	Luny Frog	hangtag, Down Bass bx VG+, open leg	NIB	$385.00	03-02
Heddon	Luny Frog	lip chips, NOT MET	?	$61.66	99-02
Heddon	Luny Frog	meadow frog	EX+	$134.00	00-10
Heddon	Luny Frog	nice box	EXIB	$305.00	00-04
Heddon	Luny Frog	NOT MET	mint	$103.50	00-02
Heddon	Luny Frog	open legs	?	$85.00	99-02
Heddon	Luny Frog	open legs	EX-	$102.00	00-04
Heddon	Luny Frog	open legs	VG+	$66.00	05-07
Heddon	Luny Frog	r/w	EX	$1,075.00	99-12
Heddon	Luny Frog	red head/white, poor pictures	??	$901.00	03-04
Heddon	Luny Frog	red/white	VG	$425.00	05-01
Heddon	Luny Frog	RH	VG+	$408.00	01-05
Heddon	Luny Frog	RH, 1 foot broken off (toes)	VG	$260.00	01-03
Heddon	Luny Frog	RH, hairline crk in web, NOT MET	EX-	$455.00	03-02
Heddon	Luny Frog	RH, NOT MET	VG	$349.00	00-09
Heddon	Luny Frog	Up Bass nice	NIB	$243.00	01-04
Heddon	Luny Frog	Up Bass nice	NIB	$430.00	00-01
Heddon	Luny Frog	Up Bass VG-, nice hangtag	NIB	$270.00	04-02
Heddon	Luny Frog		avg	$42.00	00-02
Heddon	Luny Frog		EX-	$57.00	00-05
Heddon	Luny Frog		VG	$62.55	99-01
Heddon	Luny Frog		VG-	$66.00	99-02

BRAND	MODEL	SERIES / MFG. CODE / DESCRIPTION	GRADE	PRICE	DATE yy/mm
Heddon	Luny Frog		EX	$86.50	99-06
Heddon	Luny Frog		EX	$96.00	99-01
Heddon	Luny Frog		EX	$110.00	00-06
Heddon	Luny Frog, Little	in wrong box 3327, neat papers	NIB	$280.00	99-03
Heddon	Luny Frog, Little	perfect D. Bass 3209B, hangtag, receipt	NIB	$481.00	99-07
Heddon	Luny Frog, Little	Up Bass 3409B EX, mint hangtag	NIB	$561.00	99-10
Heddon	Luny Frog, Little	Up Bass bx EX	NIB	$308.00	02-11
Heddon	Luny Frog, Little		EX-	$71.00	00-04
Heddon	Luny Frog, Little		EX	$78.77	99-09
Heddon	Luny Frog, Little		VG+	$79.55	00-02
Heddon	Luny Frog, Little		EX	$99.00	00-01
Heddon	Luny Frog, Little		EX	$123.50	99-02
Heddon	Luny Frog, Little		EX	$129.00	00-08
Heddon	Luny Frog, Little		EX+	$152.50	99-05
Heddon	Luny Frog, Little		EX	$225.99	99-04
Heddon	Magnum Hedd Plug	8850MG, golden black, muskie	NOC	$255.00	03-01
Heddon	Magnum Hedd Plug	natural striper	EX	$437.00	03-01
Heddon	Magnum Hedd Plug	NG, "Northern Green," special order color	mint	$565.00	03-11
Heddon	Magnum Hedd Plug	solid chrome, no eyes, NOT MET!	mint	$305.00	05-03
Heddon	Magnum Hedd Plug	white, pink sides, gold eyes	EX	$1,469.00	04-11
Heddon	Magnum Tadpolly	clear	EX	$31.99	99-02
Heddon	Magnum Torpedo	362LC	NOC	$83.00	99-02
Heddon	Magnum Torpedo	362RH, window box, solid white belly	NIB	$400.00	03-08
Heddon	Magnum Torpedo	BF	EX-	$84.00	99-02
Heddon	Magnum Torpedo	BF, white eye	EX	$61.51	99-06
Heddon	Magnum Torpedo	BF, white eyes	EX	$84.00	99-01
Heddon	Magnum Torpedo	black shore	mint	$66.00	04-12
Heddon	Magnum Torpedo	blue shore	EX	$580.00	01-06
Heddon	Magnum Torpedo	color SS, white eyes	mint	$415.00	05-02
Heddon	Magnum Torpedo	frog	EX	$77.00	99-01
Heddon	Magnum Torpedo	frog scale	EX	$119.99	05-07
Heddon	Magnum Torpedo	frog scale/black eye shadow, missing hook	EX	$122.00	05-07
Heddon	Magnum Torpedo	frog spot	EX	$60.00	04-12
Heddon	Magnum Torpedo	frog, white eyes	NOC	$77.00	98-12
Heddon	Magnum Torpedo	hot bar perch	EX	$541.00	98-12
Heddon	Magnum Torpedo	KHC	EX	$228.00	03-07
Heddon	Magnum Torpedo	MG	EX	$300.00	03-08
Heddon	Magnum Torpedo	modern Smith color	EX	$56.01	99-03
Heddon	Magnum Torpedo	modern Smith color, red CD	EX	$80.99	99-03
Heddon	Magnum Torpedo	nat striper	EX	$137.00	00-10
Heddon	Magnum Torpedo	nat perch? photo finish	mint	$110.00	00-01
Heddon	Magnum Torpedo	nat striper	NIB	$77.00	99-04
Heddon	Magnum Torpedo	o/blk spots, modern	EX	$46.00	99-04
Heddon	Magnum Torpedo	pale yellow, coach dog	mint	$31.00	99-05
Heddon	Magnum Torpedo	perch scale, gold eyes	EX+	$355.00	04-07
Heddon	Magnum Torpedo	perch, white eye, 2 others	EX	$102.50	99-03
Heddon	Magnum Torpedo	perch?	EX	$200.50	99-02
Heddon	Magnum Torpedo	purple shore, red eye shadow	EX	$3,500.00	01-09

BRAND	MODEL	SERIES / MFG. CODE / DESCRIPTION	GRADE	PRICE	DATE yy/mm
Heddon	Magnum Torpedo	r/w	EX+	$405.00	99-01
Heddon	Magnum Torpedo	RH, clear belly with white scales	EX	$154.00	05-07
Heddon	Magnum Torpedo	RH, white eye, window box	NIB	$278.00	01-10
Heddon	Magnum Torpedo	RH/SS	EX	$910.00	05-07
Heddon	Magnum Torpedo	SS, white eye	mint	$335.00	01-12
Heddon	Magnum Torpedo	SS, white eyes, PTCB	NIB	$182.50	99-06
Heddon	Magnum Torpedo	strawberry	EX+	$203.50	99-12
Heddon	Magnum Torpedo	white, blue eyes	NIB	$285.35	98-12
Heddon	Magnum Torpedo	white, blue eyes	NIB	$355.00	99-02
Heddon	Magnum Torpedo	white, blue eyes	EX-	$406.00	99-03
Heddon	Magnum Torpedo	white shore, white eye, NOT MET	EX	$83.00	00-10
Heddon	Magnum Torpedo	XBS, white eye	EX	$410.00	99-09
Heddon	Magnum Torpedo	XBW, white eyes	EX	$68.00	05-07
Heddon	Magnum Torpedo	XRS, white eye	EX	$69.00	05-07
Heddon	Magnum Torpedo	XRS, white eye	EX	$83.01	99-09
Heddon	Magnum Torpedo	XRW	VG	$82.00	99-04
Heddon	Magnum Torpedo	XRY	EX	$305.00	00-03
Heddon	Magnum Torpedo	XRY, red around white eyes	EX-	$311.00	03-02
Heddon	Magnum Torpedo	XRY, white eye	NIB	$525.00	01-04
Heddon	Magnum Torpedo x 2	frog, striper	EX	$112.50	99-09
Heddon	Meadow Mouse	4000BM, Brush crisp	NIB	$500.00	01-05
Heddon	Meadow Mouse	4000GM, Up Bass	NIB	$270.50	99-11
Heddon	Meadow Mouse	4000GM, Up Bass, L-rig	EXIB	$202.50	99-08
Heddon	Meadow Mouse	4000WM, Up Bass, red stripe on back	NIB	$510.00	00-02
Heddon	Meadow Mouse	4000WM, Up Bass box EX, L-rig	NIB	$351.00	03-07
Heddon	Meadow Mouse	4000WM, L-rig	EX-	$155.00	02-03
Heddon	Meadow Mouse	9800GM, NOT MET	NIB	$30.00	99-12
Heddon	Meadow Mouse	9800W	NIB	$57.00	99-03
Heddon	Meadow Mouse	b/w, earliest version, beauty	EX	$611.00	99-02
Heddon	Meadow Mouse	b/w, L-rig, purty	EX	$535.11	99-05
Heddon	Meadow Mouse	9800BLM, black	NIB	$36.00	99-01
Heddon	Meadow Mouse	black/white head, L-rig	VG+	$405.00	01-10
Heddon	Meadow Mouse	brown, L-rig, bead nose?	EX	$152.50	99-05
Heddon	Meadow Mouse	chipmunk, wrong box 9800DL	EX	$91.04	99-06
Heddon	Meadow Mouse	F4000GM, Banner wrong, L-rig	EXIB	$189.02	99-07
Heddon	Meadow Mouse	F4000BM, brown flock, TS-hdwr, BBE, light consistent wear to flock	VG	$75.00	05-05
Heddon	Meadow Mouse	F4000GM, gray mouse, 2pc, looks new in EX- Brush box w/catalog	NMIB	$125.00	05-05
Heddon	Meadow Mouse	molded ears, plastic	VG+	$27.00	99-01
Heddon	Meadow Mouse	Up Bass 4000BM, L-rig	NIB	$280.00	03-11
Heddon	Meadow Mouse	white/black head, L-rig	EX	$510.00	05-02
Heddon	Meadow Mouse	white, cup rig, narrow lip, red blush eyes	EX	$127.00	05-07
Heddon	Meadow Mouse	white, later plastic version	mint	$50.00	02-07
Heddon	Meadow Mouse	white, L-rig	EX+	$263.00	02-12
Heddon	Meadow Mouse	white, L-rig, "2nd," nice!	mint	$222.00	02-12
Heddon	Meadow Mouse	white/black back stripe, red glass nose, L-rig	EX	$179.00	05-07
Heddon	Meadow Mouse	wood, greenish brown, black leather ears and tail	VG	$38.99	05-07

BRAND	MODEL	SERIES / MFG. CODE / DESCRIPTION	GRADE	PRICE	DATE yy/mm
Heddon	Meadow Mouse	wooden, w/leather ears and tail, one eye paint off, 4¾" long, light gray	VG	$16.12	05-07
Heddon	Meadow Mouse	4000	EXIB	$36.01	99-04
Heddon	Meadow Mouse	4000GM, Up Bass bx, L-rig, a beauty	NIB	$171.00	03-04
Heddon	Meadow Mouse 4000	b/w, L-rig	VG+	$406.22	99-08
Heddon	Meadow Mouse 4000	green? leather ears, tail, nice	EX	$103.50	99-06
Heddon	Meadow Mouse 4000	white, red blush, green stripe, nice ears	EX	$192.00	01-08
Heddon	Midget Crab Wiggler	1902RET, red eyes and tail, GE, TS-rig, light age lines and 1 pntr at r-eye	EX-	$75.00	05-05
Heddon	Midget Crab Wiggler	1959L, perch scale, GE, TS-rig, age lines and very light wear	EX-	$62.00	05-05
Heddon	Midgit Digit	110XRS, wood, PE, nice box	EXIB	$104.50	99-09
Heddon	Midgit Digit	9020M, gold eyes, Runt box	NIB	$32.00	05-01
Heddon	Midgit Digit	9020XRW, window	NIB	$18.00	99-02
Heddon	Midgit Digit	B119XRW, POBW, w/shopworn orig tiny Brush 2PCCB	VG+IB	$65.00	05-05
Heddon	Midgit Digit	B119XRW, white shore, GPE, NSOB, very light wear and some light bleed through	EX-	$60.00	05-05
Heddon	Midgit Digit	B110, wood, gold PE, red & white, 2pc, in box VG, paper	EX+	$95.00	05-06
Heddon	Midgit Digit	black shore, with box	NIB	$88.00	05-07
Heddon	Midgit Digit	green shore, plastic	NIB	$35.00	99-02
Heddon	Midgit Digit	red head/saltwater, with box and papers	NIB	$143.00	05-07
Heddon	Midgit Digit	shiner, with box and papers	NIB	$88.00	05-07
Heddon	Midgit Digit	silver shore, with box and papers	NIB	$88.00	05-07
Heddon	Midgit Digit	wood, dace	EX	$261.00	03-02
Heddon	Midgit Digit	wood, rainbow	EX	$278.00	03-02
Heddon	Midgit Digit	wood, B119LUM Brush EX, varnish flakes, NOT MET	EX-IB	$80.00	01-10
Heddon	Midgit Digit	wood, green scale, PE, ROBW, tail hook, 2pc	EX	$660.00	05-07
Heddon	Midgit Digit	XBW, wood, POBW	EX-	$23.00	04-11
Heddon	Midgit Digit	XRW, white eye, PTCB	NIB	$21.00	04-02
Heddon	Midgit Digit	y/black dots, red eyes	VG+	$181.00	00-07
Heddon	Mulitple Metal Minnow		EX	$250.00	03-01
Heddon	Multiple Metal Minnow	replaced hooks, $500 NOT MET	EX*	$355.00	00-05
Heddon	Multiple Metal Minnow	hooks rough	VG+	$458.00	02-08
Heddon	Multiple Metal Minnow	nickle, NOT MET!	EX	$711.00	99-02
Heddon	Multiple Metal Minnow	nickle plated	EX	$327.00	05-07
Heddon	Multiple Metal Minnow	silver	EX	$358.00	02-01
Heddon	Multiple Metal Minnow	silver, c. 1908	EX	$365.00	05-07
Heddon	Multiple Metal Minnow		EX	$425.00	99-12
Heddon	Multiple Metal Minnow		EX	$900.00	01-04
Heddon	Munk Mouse	chipmuck color, 2pc	VG+	$294.00	02-12
Heddon	Munk Mouse	chipmunk, 2pc	EX-	$160.00	03-07
Heddon	Munk Mouse	chipmunk, lt drag	VG+	$152.50	99-01
Heddon	Munk Mouse	F4200CM, Brush crisp, rev lip, 2pc	NIB	$433.88	99-11
Heddon	Musky Surfusser	359R, Fish Flesh box	NIB	$1,000.00	04-04
Heddon	Musky Surfusser	natural scale	VG	$228.00	03-05

BRAND	MODEL	SERIES / MFG. CODE / DESCRIPTION	GRADE	PRICE	DATE yy/mm
Heddon	Musky Surfusser	natural scale	EX-	$339.00	02-06
Heddon	Musky Surfusser	red/green, heavy duty toilet seat hardware, tight age lines and pointers	VG	$302.50	05-04
Heddon	Musky Surfusser	RH	EX-	$345.00	04-03
Heddon	Musky Surfusser	shiner scale	EX	$1,850.00	00-05
Heddon	Musky Surfusser	strawberry, only 1 prop, NOT MET	EX-	$333.00	02-08
Heddon	Natural Minnow	neat box, 5", plastic lure, dace?	NIB	$56.00	03-01
Heddon	Pikie?	L-rig, pikie, supposedly Heddon, NOT MET	VG+	$255.00	02-04
Heddon	Polly Runt	3½", green scale, 2pc, GE, belly marked "Heddon"	EX-	$458.00	05-07
Heddon	Polly Runt	shiner scale, GE, 2pc	EX-	$323.58	99-04
Heddon	Pop Eye Frog	85GF, window box, on card	NIB	$133.50	99-03
Heddon	Pop Eye Frog	chrome, plastic lure	NIB	$15.50	99-05
Heddon	Pop Eye Frog	in box	NIB	$99.99	99-01
Heddon	Pop Eye Frog	Luly pad factory card VG+	EXOC	$178.00	04-12
Heddon	Pop Eye Frog	unmarked window box	mint	$76.00	99-02
Heddon	Popper Spook	4 diff	VG	$16.06	99-03
Heddon	Popper Spook	930XRW, on card in window box	NIB	$76.00	99-05
Heddon	Popper Spook	fly rod, 5 diff	VG-EX	$76.51	99-06
Heddon	Popper Spook	green, rough box	NIB	$29.00	99-01
Heddon	Popper Spook	white	EX	$15.00	05-06
Heddon	Popper Spook	XRS	EX-	$31.00	02-03
Heddon	Popper Spook	yellow shore	EX	$15.00	05-06
Heddon	Pork Rind Minnow	red, GE, Down Bass nice	NIB	$229.10	00-01
Heddon	Preyfish	natural bass? photo finish	EX	$44.00	04-02
Heddon	Prowler	3½", brown crackle	EX	$129.00	00-09
Heddon	Prowler	7025SSD	NIB	$18.99	05-07
Heddon	Prowler	7025SSD, ⅜ oz.	NIB	$22.50	99-06
Heddon	Prowler	7025BWX	NIB	$16.50	99-01
Heddon	Prowler	7050BWB, ⅝ oz., musky, L	NIB	$51.00	99-05
Heddon	Prowler	7050SSD, silver shad, OPE, very light wear	EX	$25.00	05-04
Heddon	Prowler	7205BWB	NIB	$18.21	99-01
Heddon	Prowler	BGL, 4½"	EX	$11.50	99-01
Heddon	Prowler	green scale?	EX	$31.00	99-04
Heddon	Prowler	perch, 3½"	EX	$66.77	99-04
Heddon	Prowler, Musky	7075B, NOT MET	NIB	$41.50	99-05
Heddon	Prowler, Musky	7075SU	NIB	$57.00	00-04
Heddon	Prowler, Musky	mackeral, 6¼", NOT MET	VG	$41.99	99-06
Heddon	Prowler, Musky	y/silver stripe	NIB	$46.00	00-02
Heddon	Punkinseed	2 diff — 730CRA, 380BGL	EX	$159.06	99-04
Heddon	Punkinseed	320BGL, big scales, w eye	EX+	$86.00	99-06
Heddon	Punkinseed	320SUN, gold eye	EX	$76.00	99-06
Heddon	Punkinseed	380, blue chrome, NOT MET	EX	$393.55	99-10
Heddon	Punkinseed	380, strawberry, NOT MET	EX	$687.99	99-10
Heddon	Punkinseed	380BGL	VG	$40.00	99-01
Heddon	Punkinseed	380BGL, gold eye	EX	$67.01	99-05
Heddon	Punkinseed	380BGL, gold eye	NIB	$113.51	99-12

BRAND	MODEL	SERIES / MFG. CODE / DESCRIPTION	GRADE	PRICE	DATE yy/mm
Heddon	Punkinseed	380BGL, gold eyes	EX	$48.00	99-01
Heddon	Punkinseed	380CRA	NIB	$137.50	99-04
Heddon	Punkinseed	380CRA, gold eyes	avg.	$38.50	99-03
Heddon	Punkinseed	380, perch?	EX	$80.00	98-12
Heddon	Punkinseed	380SD, orange eyes	EX	$153.50	99-12
Heddon	Punkinseed	380, strawberry	EX	$610.00	99-03
Heddon	Punkinseed	380SUN	VG	$40.00	99-01
Heddon	Punkinseed	380SUN	EX	$56.56	99-01
Heddon	Punkinseed	380SUN, gold eye	EX-	$51.50	99-02
Heddon	Punkinseed	380SUN, gold eyes	EX	$80.99	99-03
Heddon	Punkinseed	380SUN x 2, gold eyes	mint	$104.00	99-12
Heddon	Punkinseed	380XBW, gold eye	EX+	$111.00	00-11
Heddon	Punkinseed	380XBW, gold eye	EX	$64.53	99-02
Heddon	Punkinseed	380XBW, white eye, bell rig	EX	$113.00	99-02
Heddon	Punkinseed	380XRW, gold eyes	EX	$132.00	99-01
Heddon	Punkinseed	380XRY	VG	$41.53	99-05
Heddon	Punkinseed	380XRY	EX	$91.00	99-02
Heddon	Punkinseed	380XRY	EX+	$103.51	99-05
Heddon	Punkinseed	380XRY, gold eye	mint	$108.00	99-01
Heddon	Punkinseed	380XRY, gold eye	mint	$128.05	99-10
Heddon	Punkinseed	380XRY, red eye shadow	EX	$136.00	00-04
Heddon	Punkinseed	380XRY, white eye	mint	$113.61	99-06
Heddon	Punkinseed	730BGL, bluegill, GPE, 2PCCB, couple teeny pointers and ring on BW	EX+	$120.00	05-04
Heddon	Punkinseed	730XBW, black shore, 2pc, GPE	MINT	$250.00	05-04
Heddon	Punkinseed	730XRW, S-rig, S-rig/2pc	VG+	$109.00	05-07
Heddon	Punkinseed	730BGL	EX	$91.00	03-07
Heddon	Punkinseed	730BGL	EX	$102.00	03-09
Heddon	Punkinseed	730BGL, Banner, S-rig, 2pc	NIB	$200.50	00-03
Heddon	Punkinseed	730BGL, Brush bx EX-	EXIB	$142.00	05-07
Heddon	Punkinseed	730BGL, Banner, S-rig, 2pc	NIB	$224.51	99-05
Heddon	Punkinseed	730BGL, S-rig, 2pc, mouth	EX	$163.52	00-01
Heddon	Punkinseed	730CRA	EX-IB	$82.00	03-09
Heddon	Punkinseed	730CRA	EX	$152.50	99-07
Heddon	Punkinseed	730CRA, orange PE, box VG+	EX-IB	$165.00	05-06
Heddon	Punkinseed	730CRA, 2pc, chin	EX	$188.35	00-01
Heddon	Punkinseed	730CRA, 2pc	EX	$150.00	99-10
Heddon	Punkinseed	730CRA, 2pc	EX+	$208.50	99-06
Heddon	Punkinseed	730CRA, Brush, mouth, 2pc	NIB	$333.88	99-08
Heddon	Punkinseed	730CRA, Brush, S-rig	EXIB	$142.50	00-02
Heddon	Punkinseed	730CRA, chin, 2pc	mint	$212.50	99-05
Heddon	Punkinseed	730CRA, orange eye, S-rig!	EX	$112.50	99-12
Heddon	Punkinseed	730L, POBW, tough color in a 730	EX	$540.00	02-01
Heddon	Punkinseed	730ROB, 2pc, chin	EX-	$405.02	00-01
Heddon	Punkinseed	730SD	G	$50.00	99-01
Heddon	Punkinseed	730SD	EX	$81.00	03-09
Heddon	Punkinseed	730SD	EX-IB	$85.00	03-09
Heddon	Punkinseed	730SUN	EX	$96.00	03-02

BRAND	MODEL	SERIES / MFG. CODE / DESCRIPTION	GRADE	PRICE	DATE yy/mm
Heddon	Punkinseed	730SUN	NIB	$281.00	00-04
Heddon	Punkinseed	730SUN, awful glue spot	poor	$23.36	99-02
Heddon	Punkinseed	730SUN, dents	VG-	$54.00	04-07
Heddon	Punkinseed	730SUN, POBW	EX	$75.00	03-09
Heddon	Punkinseed	730SUN, Brush bx EX & catbelly a mite rough	EX-IB	$125.00	05-07
Heddon	Punkinseed	730SUN, cat	EX-IB	$415.01	99-03
Heddon	Punkinseed	730SUN, mouth	EX-	$157.50	99-04
Heddon	Punkinseed	730XBW	EX	$126.00	03-09
Heddon	Punkinseed	730XBW	EX	$203.50	99-04
Heddon	Punkinseed	730XBW, in Brush box	NIB	$384.00	99-01
Heddon	Punkinseed	730XBW, NOT MET	EXIB	$204.00	00-07
Heddon	Punkinseed	730XBW, cat	NIB	$382.00	99-04
Heddon	Punkinseed	730XBW, mouth tie, S-rig, NOT MET	EX	$137.00	05-07
Heddon	Punkinseed	730XBW, surface belly, 2-piece tail hardware	EX	$192.50	05-04
Heddon	Punkinseed	730XBW, POBW	G	$61.00	99-08
Heddon	Punkinseed	730XBW, S-rig, 2pc, mouth	EX	$270.02	00-01
Heddon	Punkinseed	730XBW, uglyish	VG-	$112.50	99-01
Heddon	Punkinseed	730XRS	EX-	$560.00	99-04
Heddon	Punkinseed	730XRS, 2pc, chin	VG+	$610.00	99-06
Heddon	Punkinseed	730XRW, "Sinker," odd stencil	EX	$406.00	00-10
Heddon	Punkinseed	730XRW, Banner! S-rig, NOT MET	NIB	$725.00	00-07
Heddon	Punkinseed	730XRW, Banner, S-rig, cat, insp tag	NIB	$1,080.00	99-08
Heddon	Punkinseed	730XRY, Banner, 2pc, S-rig, cat	NIB	$394.00	01-04
Heddon	Punkinseed	730XRY, S-rig, 2pc, bleed	EX	$150.00	00-04
Heddon	Punkinseed	730XRY, S-rig, 2pc, NOT MET	VG+	$104.50	99-05
Heddon	Punkinseed	740, goldscale? blue eye, BOZ	VG-	$154.05	99-06
Heddon	Punkinseed	740, green perch? chin	EX+	$535.00	99-08
Heddon	Punkinseed	740ROC, chip on belly, otherwise nice	VG+IB	$149.00	04-02
Heddon	Punkinseed	740SD, early shad, w/glitter flakes on lip edge and tiny nick on back	VG+	$100.00	05-04
Heddon	Punkinseed	740, silver herring, POBW, NOT MET	EX-	$511.00	05-07
Heddon	Punkinseed	740XBW, POBW	EX	$442.00	05-01
Heddon	Punkinseed	740BGL	G	$70.00	99-01
Heddon	Punkinseed	740BGL	EX-IB	$143.00	00-08
Heddon	Punkinseed	740BGL	VG+	$152.51	99-02
Heddon	Punkinseed	740BGL	EX+IB	$280.00	99-02
Heddon	Punkinseed	740BGL in CRA box, POBW, chin	EX chip	$118.00	99-01
Heddon	Punkinseed	740BGL, touch-up	??	$81.00	03-09
Heddon	Punkinseed	740BGL, "FLOATER" POBW	EX	$160.00	00-08
Heddon	Punkinseed	740BGL, 740ROC, 2 diff	VG+	$304.00	99-04
Heddon	Punkinseed	740BGL, avg box, NOT MET!	GIB	$228.00	98-12
Heddon	Punkinseed	740BGL, Brush box avg, chin	VG+IB	$250.00	99-04
Heddon	Punkinseed	740CRA	EX-IB	$92.00	03-09
Heddon	Punkinseed	740CRA	EX-	$158.50	99-07
Heddon	Punkinseed	740CRA	EXIB	$380.00	99-01
Heddon	Punkinseed	740CRA, "FLOATER"	EX	$160.00	00-08
Heddon	Punkinseed	740CRA, soft spot, chin tie, POBW	EX-	$647.00	05-02
Heddon	Punkinseed	740CRA, Brush	EXIB	$425.00	99-07

BRAND	MODEL	SERIES / MFG. CODE / DESCRIPTION	GRADE	PRICE	DATE yy/mm
Heddon	Punkinseed	740CRA, chin tie, 2pc	EX	$107.00	05-07
Heddon	Punkinseed	740CRA, 2pc, POBW	EX	$180.50	99-09
Heddon	Punkinseed	740CRA, blue eye, ROBW, NOT MET	EX	$127.00	99-12
Heddon	Punkinseed	740CRA, chin, POBW, NOT MET	EX-	$83.00	99-08
Heddon	Punkinseed	740CRA, POBW	EX	$102.00	99-08
Heddon	Punkinseed	740CRA, POBW	EX	$175.00	99-07
Heddon	Punkinseed	740CRA, stain one side, nice Brush	VGIB	$191.16	99-08
Heddon	Punkinseed	740K, red shore, NOT MET	EX-	$960.00	00-02
Heddon	Punkinseed	740K, goldfish scale	VG+	$455.00	04-05
Heddon	Punkinseed	740K, goldfish scale	VG+	$640.00	04-04
Heddon	Punkinseed	740L, ROBW	EX-	$272.99	99-11
Heddon	Punkinseed	740PCH, Brush bx avg, paper	EX-IB	$152.00	05-07
Heddon	Punkinseed	740, red shore, goldfish, ugly burn	fair	$442.00	00-04
Heddon	Punkinseed	740ROB	NIB	$411.50	99-02
Heddon	Punkinseed	740ROB	NIB	$620.00	99-04
Heddon	Punkinseed	740ROB, nose chip, shiny	EX-IB	$230.00	00-08
Heddon	Punkinseed	740ROB	EX-IB	$273.00	99-10
Heddon	Punkinseed	740ROC	EX	$201.00	03-09
Heddon	Punkinseed	740ROC, nice used example	VG+	$46.00	04-02
Heddon	Punkinseed	740ROC or 740L	EX	$310.00	00-02
Heddon	Punkinseed	740ROC, chin tie, NOT MET	EX	$167.00	02-06
Heddon	Punkinseed	740ROC, NOT MET	NIB	$270.00	00-02
Heddon	Punkinseed	740ROC, 2pc, chin	EX-	$255.01	99-08
Heddon	Punkinseed	740ROC, red eye, nice, NOT MET	VG+	$61.00	99-12
Heddon	Punkinseed	740SD	EX-	$96.00	00-03
Heddon	Punkinseed	740SD, old shad color with flitter	EX	$117.00	03-09
Heddon	Punkinseed	740SD, old shad color, nice	EX-	$175.00	99-03
Heddon	Punkinseed	740SD, 2pc, NOT MET	EX	$128.50	99-08
Heddon	Punkinseed	740SH, Brush, chin, 2pc	NIB	$380.00	00-10
Heddon	Punkinseed	740SHA, couple chips, cat	VGIB	$235.00	99-06
Heddon	Punkinseed	740SUN	EX-IB	$114.00	03-09
Heddon	Punkinseed	740SUN	NIB	$325.00	00-08
Heddon	Punkinseed	740SUN, box, early shad, 2pc	EX-IB	$149.00	01-03
Heddon	Punkinseed	740SUN, Brush bx EX, floater, POBW	EXIB	$101.00	05-07
Heddon	Punkinseed	740SUN, Brush bx VG, chin tie	EXIB	$137.00	05-07
Heddon	Punkinseed	740SUN, POBW	EX-	$144.00	01-03
Heddon	Punkinseed	740SUN, chin tie, POBW	EX-	$69.00	05-07
Heddon	Punkinseed	740SUN, NOT MET	EX-	$142.60	00-03
Heddon	Punkinseed	740SUN, POBW nice	EX-	$154.00	01-06
Heddon	Punkinseed	740SUN, worm burn tail, NOT MET	decent	$71.00	99-08
Heddon	Punkinseed	740SUN, POBW	EX	$255.00	99-05
Heddon	Punkinseed	740SUN, shiny	EX	$258.88	00-02
Heddon	Punkinseed	740, sunfish?	G	$147.50	99-09
Heddon	Punkinseed	740XBW, chin tie	EX-	$586.00	05-02
Heddon	Punkinseed	740XBW, chin, POBW, 2pc	VG+	$237.50	99-08
Heddon	Punkinseed	740XBW, ring around BW	EX	$675.11	99-06
Heddon	Punkinseed	740XRS, Skelton, chin tie	EX	$565.00	05-02
Heddon	Punkinseed	740XRW	EX	$338.00	99-10

BRAND	MODEL	SERIES / MFG. CODE / DESCRIPTION	GRADE	PRICE	DATE yy/mm
Heddon	Punkinseed	740XRW, 2pc, varnish ugly	G	$102.51	99-02
Heddon	Punkinseed	740XRW, POBW	EX-	$80.00	03-09
Heddon	Punkinseed	740XRW, POBW, otherwise nice	EX-	$76.00	04-02
Heddon	Punkinseed	740XRW	EX	$260.55	99-06
Heddon	Punkinseed	740XRW, chin, red line	EX+	$200.00	00-10
Heddon	Punkinseed	740XRW, 2pc	VG+	$114.57	00-01
Heddon	Punkinseed	740XRW, 2pc, NOT MET	EX-	$210.00	99-05
Heddon	Punkinseed	740XRW, 2pc, POBW	VG	$168.50	99-06
Heddon	Punkinseed	740XRW, chin	VG-	$168.50	99-06
Heddon	Punkinseed	740XRW, POBW	EX-	$180.27	99-08
Heddon	Punkinseed	740XRY in 740ROB box	NIB	$1,180.00	99-04
Heddon	Punkinseed	740XSK, goldfish shore, chin tie, Brush	NIB	$3,719.00	00-12
Heddon	Punkinseed	742XS, white shore, 2pc, GPE, light age crackling and light bleed through	VG+	$115.00	05-04
Heddon	Punkinseed	742XS, white shore, red scale on sides, 2pc, GPE, part POBW and ¼" blem on tail	VG	$125.00	05-04
Heddon	Punkinseed	742XS, Brush, 2pc	NIB	$550.00	01-10
Heddon	Punkinseed	742XS, Brush box	EXIB	$1,775.00	99-04
Heddon	Punkinseed	742XS, crisp box & papers, 2pc, chin tie	NIB	$317.00	05-07
Heddon	Punkinseed	742XS, white shore	NIB	$338.00	02-04
Heddon	Punkinseed	742XS, white shore, red side stripe	NIB	$333.00	03-01
Heddon	Punkinseed	8630SUN, gold eye, 740XRW	EX/VG+	$161.38	99-12
Heddon	Punkinseed	9630BGL, gold eye, Banner	NIB	$112.00	00-10
Heddon	Punkinseed	9630BGL, white eye, S-rig/bell	mint	$76.00	05-07
Heddon	Punkinseed	9630BGL, window box, bell/bell, white eye	NIB	$76.00	05-07
Heddon	Punkinseed	9630, bluegill, rear bell, gold eye	VG-	$42.23	99-02
Heddon	Punkinseed	9630, brown shore, unique (silver ribs)	EX	$2,184.99	99-10
Heddon	Punkinseed	9630, chrome, red ribs, no Heddon markings (fake?), NOT MET	VG+	$406.00	05-07
Heddon	Punkinseed	9630, coach dog	EX+	$350.00	99-11
Heddon	Punkinseed	9630CRA, orange eye, Banner	NIB	$102.00	00-10
Heddon	Punkinseed	9630, crappie, white eye	mint	$78.77	99-11
Heddon	Punkinseed	9630GRA	mint	$359.00	05-07
Heddon	Punkinseed	9630, green scale, g/b triangle box	NIB	$598.88	99-06
Heddon	Punkinseed	9630, green scale?	mint	$1,135.00	02-01
Heddon	Punkinseed	9630, green scale, bell, blk shadow	NIB	$511.00	99-04
Heddon	Punkinseed	9630RH, flitter, gold eyes	EX	$511.00	05-07
Heddon	Punkinseed	9630, SD, PTCB, white eye	NIB	$77.00	00-10
Heddon	Punkinseed	9630SUN, Banner box	NIB	$136.00	02-02
Heddon	Punkinseed	9630SUN, gold eye, Banner	NIB	$102.00	00-10
Heddon	Punkinseed	9630SUN, Banner, tail 2pc	NIB	$123.71	99-02
Heddon	Punkinseed	9630, white coach dog	EX	$228.00	04-12
Heddon	Punkinseed	9630, shad? gray scale/white, o eye	EX-	$810.00	99-04
Heddon	Punkinseed	9630, bar perch?	mint	$578.00	99-03
Heddon	Punkinseed	9630BG, gold PE	VG+	$35.00	05-06
Heddon	Punkinseed	9630BGL	VG	$46.00	99-01
Heddon	Punkinseed	9630BGL	EX	$65.00	99-01
Heddon	Punkinseed	9630BGL, Banner box	NIB	$137.00	99-01

BRAND	MODEL	SERIES / MFG. CODE / DESCRIPTION	GRADE	PRICE	DATE yy/mm
Heddon	Punkinseed	9630BGL, bell rig	EXIB	$66.00	03-09
Heddon	Punkinseed	9630BGL, gold eye	EX	$53.00	03-09
Heddon	Punkinseed	9630BGL, gold eyes	EX	$46.00	03-09
Heddon	Punkinseed	9630BGL, tail bell rig	EX	$43.00	03-09
Heddon	Punkinseed	9630BGL, 9630CRA	VG-	$63.00	99-01
Heddon	Punkinseed	9630BGL, gold eye, PTCB	NIB	$97.00	05-07
Heddon	Punkinseed	9630-BGL, gold eye, S-rig, PTCB	NIB	$105.00	00-11
Heddon	Punkinseed	9630BGL, Banner	NIB	$123.51	00-02
Heddon	Punkinseed	9630BGL, bell tail, S-rig	NIB	$129.49	99-05
Heddon	Punkinseed	9630BGL, gold eye, Banner box	EXIB	$117.50	99-03
Heddon	Punkinseed	9630BGL, S-rig, PTCB	NIB	$149.00	99-05
Heddon	Punkinseed	9630CD	EX	$275.00	99-03
Heddon	Punkinseed	9630CD	mint	$331.00	00-09
Heddon	Punkinseed	9630CD	NIB	$430.00	00-02
Heddon	Punkinseed	9630CD, Whopper Stopper card	NOC	$385.00	99-03
Heddon	Punkinseed	9630CD, coach dog, S-rig, gold eye	EX+	$177.00	03-07
Heddon	Punkinseed	9630CD, gold eye, red gills	VG+	$96.00	99-06
Heddon	Punkinseed	9630CRA	EX	$48.09	99-01
Heddon	Punkinseed	9630CRA	EX-	$53.00	99-01
Heddon	Punkinseed	9630CRA	VG	$62.67	99-03
Heddon	Punkinseed	9630CRA, Banner box	NIB	$127.00	99-01
Heddon	Punkinseed	9630CRA, Banner box, o eye	NIB	$202.50	99-04
Heddon	Punkinseed	9630CRA, gold eyes	EXIB	$70.00	03-09
Heddon	Punkinseed	9630CRA, NOT MET	EX	$66.00	99-01
Heddon	Punkinseed	9630CRA, S-rig, gold eye	EX-	$62.99	99-02
Heddon	Punkinseed	9630CRA, tail 2pc rig, orange eyes	EX	$42.00	03-09
Heddon	Punkinseed	9630CRA, tail 2pc rig, orange eyes	EX	$45.00	03-09
Heddon	Punkinseed	9630CRA, tail bell rig, white eyes	EXIB	$58.00	03-09
Heddon	Punkinseed	9630CRA, orange eyes	NIB	$81.00	00-04
Heddon	Punkinseed	9630CRA, bell	EX	$49.99	99-09
Heddon	Punkinseed	9630CRA, S-rig/bell	VG	$62.00	99-05
Heddon	Punkinseed	9630GRA, bell rig	EX+	$308.00	03-07
Heddon	Punkinseed	9630GRA, on Whopper Stopper card	NOC	$705.00	00-11
Heddon	Punkinseed	9630GSD, green shad triangle box crisp	NIB	$620.00	04-02
Heddon	Punkinseed	9630RH, flitter	EX	$836.00	00-05
Heddon	Punkinseed	9630RH, flitter, gold eye, $1,200 NOT MET	EX	$735.00	02-02
Heddon	Punkinseed	9630RH, ugly, NOT MET	VG-	$225.05	99-08
Heddon	Punkinseed	9630SD	EX	$56.78	99-01
Heddon	Punkinseed	9630SD	EXIB	$74.00	03-09
Heddon	Punkinseed	9630SD	EXIB	$106.49	99-03
Heddon	Punkinseed	9630SD, old plastic slide box	NIB	$153.00	00-07
Heddon	Punkinseed	9630SD, tail bell rig	EXIB	$62.00	03-09
Heddon	Punkinseed	9630SD, yellow eye, older	VG+	$75.00	99-03
Heddon	Punkinseed	9630SD, NOT MET	NIB	$67.00	00-09
Heddon	Punkinseed	9630SD, gold eyes	EX-	$71.50	99-12
Heddon	Punkinseed	9630SD, S-rig/bell, rub	VG	$51.00	99-02
Heddon	Punkinseed	9630SD, y eyes	EX-	$53.68	99-01
Heddon	Punkinseed	9630SSD	NOC	$75.00	99-05

BRAND	MODEL	SERIES / MFG. CODE / DESCRIPTION	GRADE	PRICE	DATE yy/mm
Heddon	Punkinseed	9630SSD, gold eye, S-rig/bell	EX-	$71.00	99-06
Heddon	Punkinseed	9630SUN	EX-	$43.00	01-03
Heddon	Punkinseed	9630SUN	VG	$45.50	99-02
Heddon	Punkinseed	9630SUN	NIB	$83.00	99-01
Heddon	Punkinseed	9630SUN	NIB	$177.50	99-07
Heddon	Punkinseed	9630SUN, Banner	VG+IB	$76.00	99-09
Heddon	Punkinseed	9630SUN, Banner box	NIB	$147.00	99-01
Heddon	Punkinseed	9630SUN, Banner bx, gold eyes, NOT MET	NIB	$152.00	04-12
Heddon	Punkinseed	9630SUN, bell rig	EX	$53.00	03-09
Heddon	Punkinseed	9630SUN, gold eyes	EX	$49.00	03-09
Heddon	Punkinseed	9630SUN, gold eyes	EXIB	$78.00	03-09
Heddon	Punkinseed	9630SUN, gold PE	VG+	$45.00	05-06
Heddon	Punkinseed	9630SUN, tail bell rig	EX-	$44.00	03-09
Heddon	Punkinseed	9630SUN, gold eye, Banner box + papers	EXIB	$85.00	01-12
Heddon	Punkinseed	9630SUN, gold, window? box	NIB	$127.00	00-08
Heddon	Punkinseed	9630SUN, NOT MET	NIB	$117.00	99-06
Heddon	Punkinseed	9630SUN, PTCB, bell	NIB	$79.00	00-07
Heddon	Punkinseed	9630SUN, Banner	EXIB	$127.29	99-12
Heddon	Punkinseed	9630SUN, Banner, S-rig	VGIB	$81.00	99-06
Heddon	Punkinseed	9630SUN, gold eye, Banner, cat	NIB	$160.50	99-09
Heddon	Punkinseed	9630SUN, gold eye, PTCB	NIB	$104.52	99-04
Heddon	Punkinseed	9630SUN, gold eyes	EX+	$43.55	99-12
Heddon	Punkinseed	9630SUN, S-rig, Banner box	NIB	$192.50	99-05
Heddon	Punkinseed	9630SUN, white eye, bell rig	EX	$52.00	00-03
Heddon	Punkinseed	9630XBW, Banner, papers, gold, S-rig/2pc	NIB	$293.01	99-12
Heddon	Punkinseed	9630XBW, gold eye	EX-	$63.00	03-09
Heddon	Punkinseed	9630XBW, gold, PE, plastic top box	NIB	$135.00	05-06
Heddon	Punkinseed	9630XBW, gold eye	EX-	$78.00	05-07
Heddon	Punkinseed	9630XBW, gold eye, x holes	??	$53.00	99-04
Heddon	Punkinseed	9630XBW, gold eye, S-rig/2pc	EX-	$67.00	00-04
Heddon	Punkinseed	9630XBW, S-rig	EX	$147.50	99-06
Heddon	Punkinseed	9630XBW, S-rig/2pc, gold, Brush	NIB	$333.88	99-08
Heddon	Punkinseed	9630XRW	EX-	$86.85	99-01
Heddon	Punkinseed	9630XRW	NIB	$203.51	99-05
Heddon	Punkinseed	9630XRW, gold eye, avg box	NIB	$318.50	00-03
Heddon	Punkinseed	9630XRW, gold eyes	EXIB	$136.00	03-09
Heddon	Punkinseed	9630XRW, Banner box crisp	EXIB	$183.00	03-07
Heddon	Punkinseed	9630XRW, gold eye, Banner box & papers	NIB	$192.00	02-01
Heddon	Punkinseed	9630XRW, S-rig/bell, gold eye	EX	$255.00	00-04
Heddon	Punkinseed	9630XRW, Banner, gold, s-rig/2pc, cat	NIB	$360.01	99-05
Heddon	Punkinseed	9630XRW, gold eye, S-rig/2pc	EX	$330.00	00-04
Heddon	Punkinseed	9630XRW, gold eye, S-rig, cat	NIB	$360.01	99-05
Heddon	Punkinseed	9630XRY	EX	$128.00	99-02
Heddon	Punkinseed	9630XRY, bell rig	mint	$90.00	99-02
Heddon	Punkinseed	9630XRY, gold eyes	EX	$86.00	03-09
Heddon	Punkinseed	9630XRY, S-rig/bell, white eye	NIB	$200.00	00-06
Heddon	Punkinseed	9630XRY	NIB	$167.50	00-01
Heddon	Punkinseed	9630XRY, 2-bell, PSTCB	NIB	$82.50	99-12

BRAND	MODEL	SERIES / MFG. CODE / DESCRIPTION	GRADE	PRICE	DATE yy/mm
Heddon	Punkinseed	9630XRY, bell, no seam, cream eye	NIB	$125.56	99-03
Heddon	Punkinseed	9630XRY, bell, w eye	NIB	$103.50	99-04
Heddon	Punkinseed	9630XRY, gold eye	EX-IB	$77.00	99-06
Heddon	Punkinseed	9630XRY, gold eye, S-rig	EX	$90.99	99-03
Heddon	Punkinseed	980SUN, on card, fly	NOC	$255.00	99-01
Heddon	Punkinseed	BGL, fly rod	EX	$76.00	04-07
Heddon	Punkinseed	SD, fly rod	EX	$71.00	04-07
Heddon	Punkinseed	fly rod, Spook, crappie color, single hook	EX	$70.00	05-07
Heddon	Punkinseed	fly rod, sunfish, treble, NOT MET	mint	$159.00	01-01
Heddon	Punkinseed	RH/flitter, NOT MET	VG+	$355.00	00-10
Heddon	Punkinseed	shad	EX	$65.00	05-07
Heddon	Punkinseed	730SUN, wood	EX	$117.50	05-07
Heddon	Punkinseed	X9630CD	NIB	$475.00	99-09
Heddon	Punkinseed	XRY, Brush box + catalog, S-rig, mouth tie	NIB	$341.00	02-06
Heddon	Punkinseed	380CRA, white eye	NIB	$88.56	99-02
Heddon	Punkinseed	730, silver shore	VG++	$935.00	05-07
Heddon	Punkinseed	730, white shore/black ribs, 2pc	EX-	$838.00	02-01
Heddon	Punkinseed	740, goldfish shore, NOT MET (asking $2100)	EX	$1,225.00	05-05
Heddon	Punkinseed	740, perch scale	EX	$127.00	02-08
Heddon	Punkinseed	740, perch scale, NOT MET	EX+	$253.00	01-12
Heddon	Punkinseed	740, perch scale, POBW, NOT MET	EX	$330.00	01-09
Heddon	Punkinseed	740, sunfish, with line tie on chin	EX	$137.50	05-07
Heddon	Punkinseed	740BGL, paint off BW	EXIB	$256.00	99-02
Heddon	Punkinseed	740XRW	EX-	$291.00	00-03
Heddon	Punkinseed	742XS, Brush box, chin line tie	NIB	$515.00	05-05
Heddon	Punkinseed	9630SD, shad, YPE, SR, few tiny nicks and very light wear	VG+	$49.00	05-04
Heddon	Punkinseed	9630SUN, sunfish, GPE, SR, in orig early EX 2PPTB	EX+IB	$80.00	05-04
Heddon	Punkinseed	9630CD	EX-	$147.00	01-03
Heddon	Punkinseed	9630CD, gold eye, bell rig	mint	$209.00	04-04
Heddon	Punkinseed	9630GSD, green shad, NOT MET	NIB	$695.00	04-11
Heddon	Punkinseed	9630XBW, gold eye, Banner	NIB	$152.00	02-01
Heddon	Punkinseed	9630XBW, gold eyes	EX-	$54.00	02-08
Heddon	Punkinseed	Brush bx 740ROC EX-	NIB	$417.00	04-12
Heddon	Punkinseed, 20 diff	740 x 8, 730 x 5, plastic, NOT MET	VG-mint	$1,935.00	99-05
Heddon	Punkinseed x 2	both BGL, white eyes	EX+	$103.51	99-10
Heddon	Punkinseed x 5	730 x 2, 740 x 3, all nice, NOT MET	EX-EX	$570.00	01-10
Heddon	Punkinseed x 7	380 set, 7 diff, gold eyes, NOT MET	EX	$565.00	00-11
Heddon	Punkinseed, fly rod	320SUN	EX	$315.00	99-06
Heddon	Punkinseed, fly rod	980CRA, PTCB	NIB	$305.00	01-09
Heddon	Punkinseed, fly rod	980SD, box rough, NOT MET	NIB	$140.00	01-03
Heddon	Punkinseed, fly rod	980SUN, window bx EX, on card	NIB	$255.00	04-03
Heddon	Punkinseed, fly rod	BG, single hook	EX	$261.00	00-07
Heddon	Punkinseed, fly rod	BGL	mint	$190.00	00-02
Heddon	Punkinseed, fly rod	BGL	EX	$108.00	03-02
Heddon	Punkinseed, fly rod	BGL	EX+	$168.00	00-10
Heddon	Punkinseed, fly rod	BGL	mint	$367.00	99-06

BRAND	MODEL	SERIES / MFG. CODE / DESCRIPTION	GRADE	PRICE	DATE yy/mm
Heddon	Punkinseed, fly rod	BGL, "shiner scale," a joke	EX	$244.00	02-02
Heddon	Punkinseed, fly rod	BGL, treble hook	EX	$260.00	00-03
Heddon	Punkinseed, fly rod	BGL, treble hook	EX-	$260.55	00-02
Heddon	Punkinseed, fly rod	BGL, 1 hook	EX	$214.00	00-10
Heddon	Punkinseed, fly rod	BGL, 2 big pointers	VG?	$114.00	00-04
Heddon	Punkinseed, fly rod	BGL, treble hook	MINT	$356.99	99-05
Heddon	Punkinseed, fly rod	BGL, treble hook	EX	$270.00	99-03
Heddon	Punkinseed, fly rod	bluegill, ugly	avg/poor	$123.52	99-05
Heddon	Punkinseed, fly rod	CRA	EX-	$131.00	00-10
Heddon	Punkinseed, fly rod	CRA	EX	$231.38	00-01
Heddon	Punkinseed, fly rod	CRA	EX	$256.00	99-05
Heddon	Punkinseed, fly rod	CRA, treble hook	EX	$201.00	05-02
Heddon	Punkinseed, fly rod	CRA, single hook	EX	$104.00	05-07
Heddon	Punkinseed, fly rod	CRA, treble	EX-	$162.00	00-10
Heddon	Punkinseed, fly rod	CRA, treble	EX+	$256.00	99-06
Heddon	Punkinseed, fly rod	CRA, treble, NOT MET	EX	$187.50	99-05
Heddon	Punkinseed, fly rod	crappie	EX+	$108.00	04-11
Heddon	Punkinseed, fly rod	crappie, 3-hk	EX	$330.01	99-03
Heddon	Punkinseed, fly rod	crappie, treble hook	EX	$195.00	00-11
Heddon	Punkinseed, fly rod	rock bass	EX+	$257.00	02-02
Heddon	Punkinseed, fly rod	rock bass?	EX	$260.99	99-06
Heddon	Punkinseed, fly rod	SD	EX	$157.50	00-01
Heddon	Punkinseed, fly rod	SD, treble hook	EX	$142.00	03-01
Heddon	Punkinseed, fly rod	shad	EX	$152.00	02-03
Heddon	Punkinseed, fly rod	shad	EX	$159.00	00-04
Heddon	Punkinseed, fly rod	shad	EX	$242.00	02-03
Heddon	Punkinseed, fly rod	shad	EX	$265.00	99-08
Heddon	Punkinseed, fly rod	shad	EX	$267.00	99-05
Heddon	Punkinseed, fly rod	shad, NOT MET	EX-	$124.00	00-03
Heddon	Punkinseed, fly rod	shad, window box, NOT MET	NIB	$243.00	00-12
Heddon	Punkinseed, fly rod	shad, worn box	NIB	$179.00	01-01
Heddon	Punkinseed, fly rod	shad, single hook	EX	$310.00	99-03
Heddon	Punkinseed, fly rod	SUN	EX	$137.50	99-03
Heddon	Punkinseed, fly rod	SUN	EX	$189.00	99-03
Heddon	Punkinseed, fly rod	SUN, treble, lip puckered	EX-	$201.50	99-06
Heddon	Punkinseed, fly rod	SUN, 3-hook, unmarked Brush	NIB	$400.99	99-04
Heddon	Punkinseed, fly rod	SUN, treble, no iris	EX	$167.50	00-02
Heddon	Punkinseed, fly rod	sunfish	EX	$186.00	01-05
Heddon	Punkinseed, fly rod	sunfish	EX	$225.00	00-08
Heddon	Punkinseed, fly rod	sunfish	NIB	$355.00	99-11
Heddon	Punkinseed, fly rod	white shore, GE, single hook	EX	$1,000.00	00-10
Heddon	Punkinseed, fly rod	x 5, easy colors, NOT MET	EX	$1,400.99	99-07
Heddon	Punkinseed, fly rod	XRW	EX	$305.00	03-05
Heddon	Punkinseed, fly rod	XRW, a beauty, NOT MET	EX+	$810.00	01-12
Heddon	Punkinseed, fly rod	XRW, single hook nice	EX	$721.00	00-11
Heddon	Punkinseed, Tiny	380FLS	NIB	$256.00	04-12
Heddon	Punkinseed, Tiny	380XRY, gold PE, bell hdwr	NIB	$125.00	05-06
Heddon	Punkinseed, Tiny	380BGL	NIB	$67.01	99-09

BRAND	MODEL	SERIES / MFG. CODE / DESCRIPTION	GRADE	PRICE	DATE yy/mm
Heddon	Punkinseed, Tiny	380CRA, gold eyes	NIB	$123.51	99-11
Heddon	Punkinseed, Tiny	380SUN, white eyes	mint	$68.00	03-04
Heddon	Punkinseed, Tiny	380SUN, gold eyes	NIB	$96.99	99-09
Heddon	Punkinseed, Tiny	380XBW	NIB	$209.50	00-03
Heddon	Punkinseed, Tiny	380XBW, gold eye, PTCB	NIB	$180.00	01-12
Heddon	Punkinseed, Tiny	380XRW, gold eye	EX+	$257.00	99-09
Heddon	Punkinseed, Tiny	380XRY	NIB	$99.99	99-03
Heddon	Punkinseed, Tiny	380XRY	NIB	$117.50	99-08
Heddon	Punkinseed, Tiny	BGL	EX	$42.00	03-09
Heddon	Punkinseed, Tiny	BGL	EX	$48.00	03-09
Heddon	Punkinseed, Tiny	BGL, gold eyes	EX	$48.00	03-09
Heddon	Punkinseed, Tiny	BGL, gold eyes	EX	$54.00	03-09
Heddon	Punkinseed, Tiny	BGL, pale	EX	$38.00	03-09
Heddon	Punkinseed, Tiny	BGL, gold eye	EX	$66.00	00-09
Heddon	Punkinseed, Tiny	blue scale/red dots	mint	$385.00	02-08
Heddon	Punkinseed, Tiny	CRA	EX	$45.00	03-09
Heddon	Punkinseed, Tiny	CRA, gold eyes	EXIB	$62.00	03-09
Heddon	Punkinseed, Tiny	CRA, gold eyes	mint	$71.00	00-04
Heddon	Punkinseed, Tiny	CRA, white eye, rusty hooks	mint	$38.00	02-08
Heddon	Punkinseed, Tiny	crappie, gold eye	EX	$81.00	99-08
Heddon	Punkinseed, Tiny	flourescent chartreuse	mint	$671.00	02-08
Heddon	Punkinseed, Tiny	FLS, green triangle box, no pupil	NIB	$559.00	03-08
Heddon	Punkinseed, Tiny	FLS, silver eye, gray scale/blk dots	NOC	$650.00	00-11
Heddon	Punkinseed, Tiny	gold eye, 6 diff, no hardware	EX	$232.00	02-06
Heddon	Punkinseed, Tiny	golden shiner, no belly stencil, NOT MET	mint	$2,385.00	00-03
Heddon	Punkinseed, Tiny	GRA, NOT MET	EX-	$777.00	00-12
Heddon	Punkinseed, Tiny	hot chartreuse shore	mint	$636.00	02-07
Heddon	Punkinseed, Tiny	NPB, chrome	EX	$499.00	00-02
Heddon	Punkinseed, Tiny	OGG, 1980s, Smith color for Japan	NOC	$660.00	02-02
Heddon	Punkinseed, Tiny	OOG (chart/gold ribs), NOT MET	EX	$305.00	01-03
Heddon	Punkinseed, Tiny	SD	EX	$46.00	03-09
Heddon	Punkinseed, Tiny	SD, gold eyes	EX	$41.00	03-09
Heddon	Punkinseed, Tiny	SD, orange eyes	EX	$49.00	03-09
Heddon	Punkinseed, Tiny	SD, gold eye	EX	$103.50	99-03
Heddon	Punkinseed, Tiny	strawberry spot, gold eye (sm chips)	EX-	$359.00	02-02
Heddon	Punkinseed, Tiny	strawberry, gold eyes	EX	$417.00	05-07
Heddon	Punkinseed, Tiny	strawberry, gold eyes	EX+	$226.00	05-07
Heddon	Punkinseed, Tiny	SUN	EX	$45.00	03-09
Heddon	Punkinseed, Tiny	SUN	EXIB	$64.00	03-09
Heddon	Punkinseed, Tiny	SUN, gold eyes	EX	$42.00	03-09
Heddon	Punkinseed, Tiny	SUN, gold eyes	mint	$50.00	00-03
Heddon	Punkinseed, Tiny	SUN, white eye, 3 BIDS OVER $70	mint	$86.00	00-04
Heddon	Punkinseed, Tiny	SUN, white eye, 12 BIDS!	EX	$117.50	99-11
Heddon	Punkinseed, Tiny	sunfish pattern, raised eyes, bell hardware	EX+	$38.00	05-07
Heddon	Punkinseed, Tiny	tiny crappie shore	EX+	$40.00	05-07
Heddon	Punkinseed, Tiny	white shore, gold eye	mint	$104.00	05-07
Heddon	Punkinseed, Tiny	XBW	EX	$74.00	03-09
Heddon	Punkinseed, Tiny	XBW, gold eyes	EX	$76.00	03-09

BRAND	MODEL	SERIES / MFG. CODE / DESCRIPTION	GRADE	PRICE	DATE yy/mm
Heddon	Punkinseed, Tiny	XBW, gold eye	EX	$148.00	00-09
Heddon	Punkinseed, Tiny	XRW, gold eyes	EXIB	$134.00	03-09
Heddon	Punkinseed, Tiny	XRY	EX	$74.00	03-09
Heddon	Punkinseed, Tiny	XRY, gold eye	EX	$81.00	03-09
Heddon	Punkinseed, Tiny	XRY, gold eyes	mint	$63.00	05-02
Heddon	Punkinseed, Tiny	yellow coach dog, gold eye	EX	$517.00	00-10
Heddon	Punkinseed, Tiny	380XBW, black shore, GPE, bell rig, looks new but spot of varnish loss	EX-	$60.00	05-04
Heddon	Punkinseed, Tiny	black shore, gold eye	MINT	$81.52	05-07
Heddon	Punkinseed, Tiny	OGG, hot chartreuse/gold ribs	NOC	$735.00	01-10
Heddon	Punkinseed, Tiny x 2	BGL SUN, white eyes	mint	$132.51	99-09
Heddon	Punkinspin	382PRL, pearls pink PE and gills, NSOB, bell rig, new in intro 2PSTB, paperwork	NIB	$190.00	05-04
Heddon	Punkinspin	382PRL, yellow w/pearl belly, NSOB, very light wear	EX	$120.00	05-04
Heddon	Punkinspin	382PRL, NOT MET	NIB	$127.00	00-10
Heddon	Punkinspin	382YPR, yellow w/pearl belly, new in orig intro 2PSTB	NIB	$170.00	05-04
Heddon	Punkinspin	382NP	NIB	$155.00	02-01
Heddon	Punkinspin	382NP, chrome	NIB	$282.50	99-07
Heddon	Punkinspin	382NP, chrome	NIB	$191.00	00-03
Heddon	Punkinspin	chrome	EX	$142.49	99-08
Heddon	Punkinspin	chrome	EX	$255.99	99-03
Heddon	Punkinspin	chrome, NO BIDS	EX+	$150.00	99-10
Heddon	Punkinspin	chrome, blue scale	EX-	$131.38	00-02
Heddon	Punkinspin	ivory	EX	$162.00	00-06
Heddon	Punkinspin	NPB	NIB	$213.00	04-12
Heddon	Punkinspin	pearl, 1 bid	EX+	$150.00	99-10
Heddon	Punkinspin	PRL	EXIB	$83.00	03-09
Heddon	Punkinspin	SD	EX	$78.00	03-09
Heddon	Punkinspin	Smokey Joe	EX	$90.00	03-09
Heddon	Punkinspin	Smokey Joe	mint	$91.00	02-07
Heddon	Punkinspin	white pearl	mint	$300.00	99-11
Heddon	Punkinspin	white, ugly	poor	$32.99	99-03
Heddon	Punkinspin	yellow pearl	NIB	$162.50	00-03
Heddon	Punkinspin	yellow pearl	EX	$139.00	00-09
Heddon	Punkinspin	yellow pearl	EX	$68.00	04-11
Heddon	Punkinspin	yellow pearl	mint	$170.00	99-06
Heddon	Punkinspin	yellow pearl, 1 BID	EX+	$130.00	99-10
Heddon	Punkinspin	YPL	EX	$84.00	03-09
Heddon	Punkinspin, Tiny	crackleback, salesman sample, no hooks, "#2" on side	EX	$345.00	05-07
Heddon	Punkinspin, Tiny	salesman sample #12, no hooks, black/glitter, NOT MET	EX	$227.00	05-07
Heddon	Punkinspin, Tiny	salesman sample #1, crackleback/ red eye shadow, NOT MET	EX	$174.00	05-07
Heddon	Punkinspin, Tiny	salesman sample #6, pearl/blue gills & eye shadow	EX	$145.00	05-07
Heddon	Punkinspin, Tiny	salesman sample #7, blue/ yellow pearl, NOT MET	EX	$152.00	05-07

BRAND	MODEL	SERIES / MFG. CODE / DESCRIPTION	GRADE	PRICE	DATE yy/mm
Heddon	Punkinspin, Tiny	salesman sample #8, blue shad, NOT MET	EX	$130.00	05-07
Heddon	Queen Stanley	280NP, nickel plate w/red feather tail, new in tiny Up Bass Banner 2PCCB	NIB	$45.00	05-05
Heddon	River Runt	9400W-L, centennial, wood	NIB	$19.00	04-12
Heddon	River Runt 110	110, dace, GE, 2pc	VG(EX?)	$134.09	99-05
Heddon	River Runt 110	110, shiner scale	mint	$137.50	00-02
Heddon	River Runt 110	110, silver herring, GE	mint	$700.00	00-02
Heddon	River Runt 110	110BWH, Up Bass small, 2pc	NIB	$360.00	00-03
Heddon	River Runt 110	110GWH, Brush, 2pc	EXIB	$182.00	02-02
Heddon	River Runt 110	110RB, GE	VG+	$381.00	99-04
Heddon	River Runt 110	110RH, GE, 2pc, poor box	EXIB	$104.00	99-05
Heddon	River Runt 110	111, rainbow, GE, 2pc, Up Bass	EXIB	$300.00	99-10
Heddon	River Runt 110	112, Brush	EX-IB	$91.00	00-03
Heddon	River Runt 110	112, Brush bx EX, 2pc, superb	NIB	$205.00	05-07
Heddon	River Runt 110	112, small Down Bass box	NIB	$203.25	00-02
Heddon	River Runt 110	112, RH/w, 2pc-rig, GE, few tiny pointers and some light age crackling in white	VG+	$50.00	05-05
Heddon	River Runt 110	112, RH/w, L-rig, narrow, marked, lip varn flaked off RH and small chip at tail	VG-	$38.00	05-05
Heddon	River Runt 110	114, all red, GE, L-rig, thin lip, small body, age crackling and flaking on nose and eyes	G+	$58.00	05-05
Heddon	River Runt 110	119GWH, black w/white head, GE, TS-rig, NSOB, varn flakes and very light wear	VG	$80.00	05-05
Heddon	River Runt 110	119G, black	EX-IB	$202.00	00-10
Heddon	River Runt 110	119L, Up Bass, L-rig	VGIB	$301.00	01-07
Heddon	River Runt 110	119L, name OB	EX	$160.00	99-10
Heddon	River Runt 110	119M, 2pc	EX	$87.00	00-11
Heddon	River Runt 110	119N, 2pc, Brush, NOT MET	NIB	$228.00	00-09
Heddon	River Runt 110	119R, Brush box, 2pc	EX-IB	$150.00	00-11
Heddon	River Runt 110	119R, Brush bx, 2pc, NOT MET	NIB	$164.00	02-10
Heddon	River Runt 110	119R, Up Bass bx EX-	EXIB	$168.00	03-02
Heddon	River Runt 110	119R, Up Bass, GE	NIB	$390.00	00-05
Heddon	River Runt 110	119XRY, GE, 2pc, tiny chip	EXIB	$384.00	05-07
Heddon	River Runt 110	BW, 2pc, NOT MET	EX+	$275.00	00-11
Heddon	River Runt 110	dace, GE, 2pc	VG+	$52.00	00-01
Heddon	River Runt 110	dace, L-rig, heavy crazing, NOT MET	VG+	$66.00	00-03
Heddon	River Runt 110	GE, perch	mint	$182.49	99-02
Heddon	River Runt 110	green scale, GE	EX	$158.56	99-10
Heddon	River Runt 110	L, 2pc, GE, NOT MET	VG	$59.00	00-05
Heddon	River Runt 110	L, GE, 2pc, sm eye crack	EX+	$147.50	99-05
Heddon	River Runt 110	L, GE, decent	VG+	$62.00	99-06
Heddon	River Runt 110	nat scale, 2pc, NOT MET	EX-	$75.99	00-03
Heddon	River Runt 110	natural scale, 2pc	mint	$261.00	00-04
Heddon	River Runt 110	natural scale, GE, 1 crk	VG	$63.00	99-08
Heddon	River Runt 110	P, GE, L-rig, ugly age lines	VG+	$125.00	00-05
Heddon	River Runt 110	perch scale, GE, 2pc	EX-	$38.00	04-07
Heddon	River Runt 110	RB, #111, Up Bass small, 2pc	NIB	$227.50	00-03
Heddon	River Runt 110	red, GE	EX+	$430.33	00-02
Heddon	River Runt 110	RH, silver flitter, GE	mint	$139.88	99-06

BRAND	MODEL	SERIES / MFG. CODE / DESCRIPTION	GRADE	PRICE	DATE yy/mm
Heddon	River Runt 110	shiner scale, GE	VG+	$56.00	00-10
Heddon	River Runt 110	shiner scale, L-rig	EX	$78.00	05-07
Heddon	River Runt 110	silver shore, 110XRS crisp box, GE, 2pc	NIB	$500.00	05-07
Heddon	River Runt 110	strawberry, 2pc, EX	EX	$260.00	05-07
Heddon	River Runt 110	strawberry, 2pc, GE, NOT MET	EX+	$128.00	05-07
Heddon	River Runt 110	Up Bass bx, 119G	EX-IB	$138.00	04-03
Heddon	River Runt 110	WH/blk, GE, 2pc, NOT MET	VG-	$76.00	99-05
Heddon	River Runt 110	wood, red & white, GE, 2pc, Up Bass box VG++	EX-	$125.00	05-06
Heddon	River Runt 110	wood, GE, shiner scale	EX	$77.65	05-07
Heddon	River Runt 110	wood, rainbow, GE, TS	EX-	$110.00	05-06
Heddon	River Runt 110	wood, white, GE, missing 1 eye	AVG	$48.80	05-07
Heddon	River Runt 110	XRS, GE, 2pc	VG+	$66.00	05-07
Heddon	River Runt 110	GE, RH/w, silver flakes	EX	$110.00	98-12
Heddon	River Runt 110	perch scale	EX+	$165.00	00-05
Heddon	River Runt Flash Kit	hard plastic box, 4 different FF lures	NIB	$511.00	03-02
Heddon	River Runt Floater	9400-GR-CO, ½ oz.	NIB	$50.00	02-01
Heddon	River Runt Floater	9400P, shiner scale, GPE, SR, a hint of wear in orig EX RR-2PCCB and BandW catalog	EX+IB	$40.00	05-04
Heddon	River Runt Floater	9400RH, RH/w, with clear and silver-scaled belly, WPE, SR	NM	$10.00	05-04
Heddon	River Runt Floater	9400SD, green shad, 2pc, YPE, just a hint of wear	EX+	$37.00	05-04
Heddon	River Runt Floater	9400SR-XRW, Spook Ray, red and white, pink shore, SR, varn flk at tail and light wear on r-side	VG	$24.00	05-04
Heddon	River Runt Floater	9400XRY, floating River Runt, w/box and papers	NIB	$9.51	05-07
Heddon	River Runt Floater	9400XRY, yellow shore, GPE, 2pc, no box, couple tiny pointers	EX	$14.00	05-04
Heddon	River Runt Floater	9400XRY, yellow shore, WPE, SR, unfished	MINT	$10.00	05-04
Heddon	River Runt Floater	9400RB	VGIB	$40.00	99-10
Heddon	River Runt Floater	9400RB, crisp box & papers	NIB	$97.00	04-01
Heddon	River Runt Floater	9400RB, Banner	NIB	$31.50	99-09
Heddon	River Runt Floater	9400RH, Runt box	NIB	$37.55	99-09
Heddon	River Runt Floater	9400-SR-XRW, pink shore	NIB	$51.00	99-05
Heddon	River Runt Floater	9400XRG, Runt bx EX	NIB	$81.00	05-07
Heddon	River Runt Floater	9400XRW, S-rig, gold eye	NIB	$35.00	01-04
Heddon	River Runt Floater	9400XRY, 2pc, catalog	NIB	$42.00	02-07
Heddon	River Runt Floater	9401, Brush bx EX & catalog, rainbow, 2pc	EX-IB	$70.00	05-07
Heddon	River Runt Floater	9409L, perch, 2pc, GPE, very light wear	EX	$18.00	05-04
Heddon	River Runt Floater	9409M, pike scale, 2pc, GPE, very minor hk mark on RS, in orig Brush box with faint #	EXIB	$39.00	05-04
Heddon	River Runt Floater	9409XRG, green shore, 2pc, GPE, in orig EX- Brush 2PCCB	NMIB	$45.00	05-04
Heddon	River Runt Floater	9409XRS, silver shore, 2pc, GPE, in orig EX- Brush 2PCCB	EX+IB	$42.00	05-04
Heddon	River Runt Floater	9409XRY, yellow shore, GPE, 2pc, in orig EX Brush box w/color RR insert	EX+IB	$45.00	05-04
Heddon	River Runt Floater	9409XRS, Brush box	EXIB	$32.00	99-02
Heddon	River Runt Floater	9409XRY, Brush, 2pc	EXIB	$17.30	00-02
Heddon	River Runt Floater	9409XRY, 2pc	NIB	$41.00	01-05
Heddon	River Runt Floater	BF, white eyes	EX	$53.01	99-03

BRAND	MODEL	SERIES / MFG. CODE / DESCRIPTION	GRADE	PRICE	DATE yy/mm
Heddon	River Runt Floater	BF, white eye	EX	$46.00	01-03
Heddon	River Runt Floater	black, 2pc, NOT MET	mint	$56.00	99-06
Heddon	River Runt Floater	BRS, white eye	EX	$33.50	99-06
Heddon	River Runt Floater	Brush bx 9409XRS, 2pc, narrow lip	EXIB	$138.00	04-03
Heddon	River Runt Floater	bx 9409XWB poor, blistered, NOT MET	VG?IB	$148.00	02-08
Heddon	River Runt Floater	chart/silver CD, NOT MET	EX	$178.00	00-09
Heddon	River Runt Floater	dace, 2pc	EX	$35.00	01-02
Heddon	River Runt Floater	dace, 2pc	EX	$179.00	04-11
Heddon	River Runt Floater	dace, 2pc, rusty	EX-	$86.52	99-08
Heddon	River Runt Floater	E9400RW, Everlasting, red/white, Waterwave	EX	$199.00	02-02
Heddon	River Runt Floater	E9400RW, Waterwave, catalog	NIB	$325.00	02-10
Heddon	River Runt Floater	FFGB	mint	$54.00	02-07
Heddon	River Runt Floater	FFGR	mint	$77.00	02-07
Heddon	River Runt Floater	FF-RGF	EX	$31.00	03-02
Heddon	River Runt Floater	FF-RSF, no lip, marked "2nd"	EX	$225.00	03-03
Heddon	River Runt Floater	FF-RSP, red/silver sparkle filled	EX	$52.00	03-02
Heddon	River Runt Floater	FFSB	mint	$43.00	02-07
Heddon	River Runt Floater	FFSR	mint	$54.00	02-07
Heddon	River Runt Floater	frog, white eye	EX	$54.00	03-05
Heddon	River Runt Floater	frog/y belly, white eyes, Pradco?	EX	$86.00	00-04
Heddon	River Runt Floater	GFS, 2pc, stripe	EX+	$57.00	00-10
Heddon	River Runt Floater	golden shiner, Banner box	NIB	$104.25	99-02
Heddon	River Runt Floater	Gray Ghost	mint	$41.00	03-02
Heddon	River Runt Floater	GW, puckered	poor	$46.00	99-11
Heddon	River Runt Floater	LUM, unmarked belly, bubbling	VG-	$160.00	05-07
Heddon	River Runt Floater	no lip, FF-RG	EX	$104.50	99-04
Heddon	River Runt Floater	pearl shore, jointed, box, cat	NIB	$46.50	99-01
Heddon	River Runt Floater	RB, 2pc, Brush	NIB	$60.00	99-08
Heddon	River Runt Floater	red nose/tail, silver stripes/sparkles, NOT MET		$55.00	00-07
Heddon	River Runt Floater	red Waterwave, Everlasting color	EX	$315.00	99-06
Heddon	River Runt Floater	red/s scale with silver flitter inside	EX	$102.50	99-08
Heddon	River Runt Floater	red/white Everlasting, 2pc	VG	$177.00	01-06
Heddon	River Runt Floater	red/white marble, 2pc, sunk eye	EX+	$212.50	99-08
Heddon	River Runt Floater	red/white Waterwave, NOT MET	mint	$280.00	04-04
Heddon	River Runt Floater	LUM? RET, 2pc, blister	VG+	$76.00	02-07
Heddon	River Runt Floater	silver glitter liner/red head & tail	EX	$76.00	99-03
Heddon	River Runt Floater	silver herring, 2pc	EX	$338.00	03-05
Heddon	River Runt Floater	Smokey Joe, white eye	EX	$51.00	05-01
Heddon	River Runt Floater	SP, red/gold, no lip, NOT MET	EX	$163.16	99-03
Heddon	River Runt Floater	Spook floater, RH, 3½"	EX	$7.97	05-07
Heddon	River Runt Floater	SR, red & white in VG box	VG+	$12.00	05-06
Heddon	River Runt Floater	Waterwave, red/white	EX	$157.00	04-04
Heddon	River Runt Floater	XRY, red belly stencil, 2pc	VG+	$44.00	02-07
Heddon	River Runt Floater	XRY, g&b triangle box	NIB	$11.01	99-06
Heddon	River Runt Floater	XRY, white eye, b&g box	NIB	$11.01	99-07
Heddon	River Runt Floater, jntd	Brush box & catalog VG+	EXIB	$128.00	05-07
Heddon	River Runt Floater, jntd	9430M, pike scale, GPE, SR, hint of wear and hdwr little dirty	EX	$27.00	05-04

BRAND	MODEL	SERIES / MFG. CODE / DESCRIPTION	GRADE	PRICE	DATE yy/mm
Heddon	River Runt Floater, jntd	9430RH, RH/w, GPE, SR	NM	$22.00	05-04
Heddon	River Runt Floater, jntd	9430SD, Shad, YPE, SR, hint of wear	EX	$40.00	05-04
Heddon	River Runt Floater, jntd	9430XRG, green shore, GPE, SR	NM	$38.00	05-04
Heddon	River Runt Floater, jntd	9430XRS	NIB	$61.00	01-03
Heddon	River Runt Floater, jntd	9430XRS, Runt box + catalog, 2pc	NIB	$31.00	05-03
Heddon	River Runt Floater, jntd	9430XRW, white shore, GPE, SR-hdwr, just a hint of wear	NM	$35.00	05-04
Heddon	River Runt Floater, jntd	9430XRY, yellow shore, GPE, SR, red eye shadow, little shy	EX-	$22.00	05-04
Heddon	River Runt Floater, jntd	9430L	NIB	$36.00	99-04
Heddon	River Runt Floater, jntd	9430SD, 2 papers	EXIB	$40.00	04-02
Heddon	River Runt Floater, jntd	9430XRS, gold eyes, crisp box & catalog	NIB	$45.00	05-02
Heddon	River Runt Floater, jntd	9430XRY	NIB	$32.00	02-03
Heddon	River Runt Floater, jntd	9439XRS, silver shore, GPE, SR, in orig EX- RR2PCCB	EX+IB	$45.00	05-04
Heddon	River Runt Floater, jntd	9439N, Runt bx, dace, 2pc, 2 papers	EXIB	$95.00	05-07
Heddon	River Runt Floater, jntd	9439XRG, Brush EX, S-rig, newer lure	NIB	$47.00	02-07
Heddon	River Runt Floater, jntd	dace, 2pc	EX-	$65.00	02-07
Heddon	River Runt Floater, jntd	PXBW, box	EXIB	$51.01	99-03
Heddon	River Runt Floater, jntd	r/w, gold eye	EX	$29.00	99-05
Heddon	River Runt Floater, jntd	RH, gold eyes, Banner, NOT MET	NIB	$29.09	99-09
Heddon	River Runt Floater, jntd	silver scale	EX-	$133.81	00-03
Heddon	River Runt Floater, jntd	silver scale, gold eye, 2pc?	EX-	$133.81	00-03
Heddon	River Runt Floater, jntd	XRW	VG+	$24.50	99-02
Heddon	River Runt Floater, jntd	XRY, gold eye	EX-	$26.65	99-05
Heddon	River Runt Floater, jntd	XRY, gold eyes, Banner	NIB	$39.99	99-09
Heddon	River Runt Fly Rod	950XRS, on card in box	NIB	$141.00	02-01
Heddon	River Runt Fly Rod	dace	EX	$71.01	99-06
Heddon	River Runt Fly Rod	fly rod	EX+	$69.00	99-01
Heddon	River Runt Fly Rod	950XBW, fly rod, River Runt, gold stencil	EX	$404.00	02-01
Heddon	River Runt Fly Rod	fly rod, wood, NOT MET	EX	$266.00	00-06
Heddon	River Runt Fly Rod	fly rod, red head	EX	$96.00	02-03
Heddon	River Runt Fly Rod	goldfish shore, fly rod lure	EX	$360.00	03-01
Heddon	River Runt Fly Rod	rainbow, wood lure	EX-	$187.00	04-04
Heddon	River Runt Fly Rod	RH, NOT MET	EX	$76.50	99-07
Heddon	River Runt Fly Rod	RH/w	EX	$56.00	99-04
Heddon	River Runt Fly Rod	shiner scale	EX	$51.99	99-09
Heddon	River Runt Fly Rod	shiner scale, a little wrinkly	EX-	$76.00	02-03
Heddon	River Runt Fly Rod	wood, shiner scale	VG	$222.50	99-07
Heddon	River Runt Fly Rod	wood, rainbow	VG-	$175.00	03-01
Heddon	River Runt Fly Rod	XBW	EX	$432.00	05-02
Heddon	River Runt Fly Rod	XRG	mint	$107.49	99-07
Heddon	River Runt Fly Rod	XRG, NOT MET	mint	$109.50	99-06
Heddon	River Runt Fly Rod	XRG, fly rod	EX	$122.51	00-01
Heddon	River Runt Fly Rod	XRS	EX	$66.00	00-01
Heddon	River Runt Fly Rod	yellow	EX	$162.00	00-05
Heddon	River Runt Fly Rod x 2	XRW, fly rod, shiner scale	EX	$115.00	02-01
Heddon	River Runt Go-Deeper	9119XRY, Brush, scoop lip	NIB	$66.50	99-09

BRAND	MODEL	SERIES / MFG. CODE / DESCRIPTION	GRADE	PRICE	DATE yy/mm
Heddon	River Runt Go-Deeper	9XYB, scoop lip	EX-	$463.00	02-07
Heddon	River Runt Go-Deeper	b/w ribs, sq lip	mint	$30.00	99-01
Heddon	River Runt Go-Deeper	blue shore, gold eyes, S-rig	EX-	$74.00	05-07
Heddon	River Runt Go-Deeper	crackleback, gold eyes	mint	$90.00	05-07
Heddon	River Runt Go-Deeper	D9010XRY, yellow shore, early deep diver, scoop lip, 2pc	EX	$40.00	05-04
Heddon	River Runt Go-Deeper	D9010-SR XCW	NIB	$207.00	02-02
Heddon	River Runt Go-Deeper	D9110M, pike scale, GPE, SR, DD-lip, new in orig RR2PCCB, catalog	NIB	$45.00	05-04
Heddon	River Runt Go-Deeper	D9110P, shiner scale, GPE, SR, DD, scoop Lip, 1 nick at tail and 2 tiny pntrs	EX-	$27.00	05-04
Heddon	River Runt Go-Deeper	D9110RH, RH/w, GPE, SR, DD, scoop lip, 1 pointer on nose and very light wear	EX	$21.00	05-04
Heddon	River Runt Go-Deeper	D9110RH, gold eye, square lip	NIB	$35.00	99-02
Heddon	River Runt Go-Deeper	D9010SR-XBY	EXIB	$42.00	00-10
Heddon	River Runt Go-Deeper	D9110SR-XRW, crisp	NIB	$63.00	01-10
Heddon	River Runt Go-Deeper	D9110SP, red/silver/silver sparkles	NIB	$113.00	00-07
Heddon	River Runt Go-Deeper	D9110XBW	EXIB	$25.06	99-07
Heddon	River Runt Go-Deeper	D9110XBW, papers	NIB	$103.51	00-02
Heddon	River Runt Go-Deeper	D9110XBW, Banner box	NIB	$45.00	99-01
Heddon	River Runt Go-Deeper	D9119GWH, b/w, puckered, nice box	avgIB	$113.61	99-12
Heddon	River Runt Go-Deeper	D9119XRY, scoop lip, catalog	EXIB	$47.00	02-07
Heddon	River Runt Go-Deeper	DD9400BRS, brown crawdad, red angle lip	NIB	$50.00	99-02
Heddon	River Runt Go-Deeper	DD9400CBO	NIB	$56.75	99-03
Heddon	River Runt Go-Deeper	FFD9110SB, gold, PE, silver flash, black scale, SR	NIB	$70.00	05-06
Heddon	River Runt Go-Deeper	FFD9110SR	NIB	$52.00	04-11
Heddon	River Runt Go-Deeper	FF-SB, Midget	EX	$49.99	99-04
Heddon	River Runt Go-Deeper	GFR-D9010, NOT MET	NIB	$74.00	01-07
Heddon	River Runt Go-Deeper	gold PE, green perch scale	EX-	$12.00	05-06
Heddon	River Runt Go-Deeper	gold PE, white shore, SR	EX-	$20.00	05-06
Heddon	River Runt Go-Deeper	gold PE, black shore	EX+	$35.00	05-06
Heddon	River Runt Go-Deeper	gold PE, black shore in box (E+)	NIB	$75.00	05-06
Heddon	River Runt Go-Deeper	gold PE, V-lip, silver scale	EX+	$55.00	05-06
Heddon	River Runt Go-Deeper	gold PE, shiner scale in box (E), nice pink stripe	EX+IB	$70.00	05-06
Heddon	River Runt Go-Deeper	natural scale, 2pc	EX	$33.30	05-07
Heddon	River Runt Go-Deeper	OCB, flourescent lip	EX	$58.00	03-02
Heddon	River Runt Go-Deeper	orange crackle, modern lip	EX	$37.00	00-05
Heddon	River Runt Go-Deeper	red/silver foil	EX	$41.15	99-05
Heddon	River Runt Go-Deeper	RH, gold eyes, Banner, step lip	NIB	$39.99	99-09
Heddon	River Runt Go-Deeper	RH/w flitter, square lip	EX	$51.00	99-01
Heddon	River Runt Go-Deeper	SGOY, stair	EX	$46.00	99-06
Heddon	River Runt Go-Deeper	strawberry spot, square lip	VG+	$29.50	99-01
Heddon	River Runt Go-Deeper	strawberry, scoop, 2pc, sunk eyes	EX+	$203.50	99-08
Heddon	River Runt Go-Deeper	white, PE, perch scale, bell hdwr, gold lip	E	$12.00	05-06
Heddon	River Runt Go-Deeper	XRG, scoop, Midget	mint	$42.99	99-01
Heddon	River Runt Go-Deeper	XRS, scoop, wrong 9010P box	EXIB	$20.50	99-02
Heddon	River Runt Go-Deeper	XRY, scoop lip	mint	$21.00	99-08
Heddon	River Runt Go-Deeper	coach dog, angle lip, NOT MET	EX	$22.50	99-01
Heddon	River Runt Go-Deeper	yellow PE, shad, SR	EX	$25.00	05-06

BRAND	MODEL	SERIES / MFG. CODE / DESCRIPTION	GRADE	PRICE	DATE yy/mm
Heddon	River Runt Go-Deeper, jntd	D9430M, jntd	NIB	$37.00	99-05
Heddon	River Runt Go-Deeper, jntd	gold PE, sinker, red & white, flat lip	EX-	$15.00	05-06
Heddon	River Runt Go-Deeper Midget	XGF, in 9119GW Brush box	NIB	$134.00	02-02
Heddon	River Runt Go-Deeper Midget	D9010, red/silver glitter, stair lip	EX	$104.50	99-09
Heddon	River Runt Go-Deeper Midget	D9010, SFB, stair lip	EX	$58.00	99-09
Heddon	River Runt Go-Deeper Midget	D9010SS, SR, in box with paper	NIB	$75.00	05-06
Heddon	River Runt Go-Deeper Midget	D9010XBW, SR in box with paper	NIB	$75.00	05-06
Heddon	River Runt Midget	9010GCB, gold eye, Banner box	NIB	$237.00	00-09
Heddon	River Runt Midget	9010SFB	NIB	$44.00	04-01
Heddon	River Runt Midget	9010BR, brown scale	NIB	$179.00	04-12
Heddon	River Runt Midget	9010D, green scale, gold eyes, Runt box	NIB	$175.00	04-11
Heddon	River Runt Midget	9010GFB	NIB	$46.00	04-11
Heddon	River Runt Midget	9010SFR	EXIB	$53.00	04-11
Heddon	River Runt Midget	9019XBW, 2pc, catalog	NIB	$47.00	02-07
Heddon	River Runt Midget	9020RH, Midgit-Digit w/box	VG	$15.25	05-07
Heddon	River Runt Midget	Allen Stripey, 2pc, lousy picture, not sure of grade	EX?	$255.00	05-07
Heddon	River Runt Midget	Allen Stripey, gold eyes, S-rig	EX	$278.00	03-10
Heddon	River Runt Midget	Banner box 9010P	NIB	$37.00	99-01
Heddon	River Runt Midget	black crappie, white eye	VG+	$179.00	05-07
Heddon	River Runt Midget	black with yellow ribs/eye shadow	EX	$187.00	04-03
Heddon	River Runt Midget	black, 2pc? NOT MET		$28.27	99-05
Heddon	River Runt Midget	black/gold eyes, S-rig	EX	$24.99	99-02
Heddon	River Runt Midget	black/gold foil, NOT MET	EX	$43.09	99-06
Heddon	River Runt Midget	black/silver foil, NOT MET	EX	$27.17	99-07
Heddon	River Runt Midget	blue shore, gold eyes, S-rig	EX	$76.00	03-10
Heddon	River Runt Midget	crackleback, gold eyes, S-rig	EX	$91.00	03-10
Heddon	River Runt Midget	dace	mint	$33.00	03-02
Heddon	River Runt Midget	early silver herring	EX	$155.00	01-01
Heddon	River Runt Midget	FF9010GB, Mahinske, NOT MET	NIB	$46.00	99-08
Heddon	River Runt Midget	FF9010GFYBS	VG+	$73.00	04-11
Heddon	River Runt Midget	FF9010GR	VG+IB	$38.00	04-11
Heddon	River Runt Midget	FF9010GR	NIB	$53.00	04-11
Heddon	River Runt Midget	FF9010SR, Mahinske, NOT MET	NIB	$61.00	99-08
Heddon	River Runt Midget	Fish Flash, silver & black	EX	$16.00	06-05
Heddon	River Runt Midget	golden shiner, un box	EX-IB	$46.00	00-04
Heddon	River Runt Midget	goldfish scale, tan stripe, gold eye, NOT MET	mint	$181.00	01-12
Heddon	River Runt Midget	goldfish, pearl, 2 diff	EX	$105.01	99-08
Heddon	River Runt Midget	goldfish? S-rig, newer, Jacomet seller	EX	$68.00	99-10
Heddon	River Runt Midget	GR, green crawdad, S-rig/bell	EX	$321.00	04-02
Heddon	River Runt Midget	green scale, gold eye	mint	$90.00	04-02
Heddon	River Runt Midget	black/gold reflector	VG	$30.00	99-09
Heddon	River Runt Midget	new silver herring, gold eye, "2nd"	EX	$53.00	03-04
Heddon	River Runt Midget	orange crackleback, w eye, NOT MET	EX	$36.66	99-08
Heddon	River Runt Midget	pearl, gold eyes	EX	$41.00	99-06
Heddon	River Runt Midget	RB, gold eye	EX	$31.01	99-06
Heddon	River Runt Midget	red/silver foil, NOT MET	EX	$66.00	99-06
Heddon	River Runt Midget	silver herring	EX-	$99.00	99-03
Heddon	River Runt Midget	silver herring, early, 2pc, wowser!	mint	$112.00	02-08

BRAND	MODEL	SERIES / MFG. CODE / DESCRIPTION	GRADE	PRICE	DATE yy/mm
Heddon	River Runt Midget	silver shore, 2pc	VG+	$15.00	05-06
Heddon	River Runt Midget	SR-BW, yellow ribs, NOT MET	NIB	$35.00	99-02
Heddon	River Runt Midget	strawberry, gold eyes, chips	avg	$24.50	99-01
Heddon	River Runt Midget	white, gold eye, 18 bids, poor box	EX	$229.00	00-07
Heddon	River Runt Midget	white/black spots, part transparent, gold PE	EX	$129.00	05-07
Heddon	River Runt No-Snag	9119XGF	NIB	$182.00	00-10
Heddon	River Runt No-Snag	9XGF, 2pc	EX	$57.00	02-07
Heddon	River Runt No-Snag	black	EX	$330.00	04-03
Heddon	River Runt No-Snag	black/white head, gold eyes	EX	$437.00	05-07
Heddon	River Runt No-Snag	blue shore	EX	$685.00	04-11
Heddon	River Runt No-Snag	D9119L, Brush avg	NIB	$52.00	02-07
Heddon	River Runt No-Snag	D9119RH flitter, Brush EX	NIB	$152.00	02-07
Heddon	River Runt No-Snag	D9119XRY, Brush EX-, paper!	NIB	$64.00	02-07
Heddon	River Runt No-Snag	dace	EX	$56.55	00-02
Heddon	River Runt No-Snag	dace	EX	$80.00	03-08
Heddon	River Runt No-Snag	dace	mint	$104.01	99-10
Heddon	River Runt No-Snag	dace	NIB	$177.50	00-03
Heddon	River Runt No-Snag	GFS, NOT MET	EX	$66.00	01-02
Heddon	River Runt No-Snag	goldfish shore	EX	$135.00	00-08
Heddon	River Runt No-Snag	green scale	EX-	$293.00	02-07
Heddon	River Runt No-Snag	M, wrong box	EX	$52.00	00-04
Heddon	River Runt No-Snag	N9109XRX	EXIB	$861.00	04-11
Heddon	River Runt No-Snag	N9110, dace	NIB	$202.50	99-10
Heddon	River Runt No-Snag	N9110S, no hook guards!	NIB	$384.00	01-06
Heddon	River Runt No-Snag	N9110XRG	EXIB	$37.00	00-05
Heddon	River Runt No-Snag	N9112, Brush bx VG+, paper	NIB	$72.00	05-07
Heddon	River Runt No-Snag	N9112, EX box, papers, cat	NIB	$95.00	00-05
Heddon	River Runt No-Snag	N9119P	EXIB	$74.00	00-05
Heddon	River Runt No-Snag	N9119R	NIB	$123.00	00-07
Heddon	River Runt No-Snag	N9119XGF, No-Snag papers crisp	NIB	$178.00	01-08
Heddon	River Runt No-Snag	N9119XGF, papers	EXIB	$112.50	99-05
Heddon	River Runt No-Snag	N9119XRS	NIB	$57.00	99-06
Heddon	River Runt No-Snag	nat scale, lt rust	EX-	$83.00	00-10
Heddon	River Runt No-Snag	natural or pike?	EX	$93.92	99-02
Heddon	River Runt No-Snag	PAS	EX-	$585.00	02-03
Heddon	River Runt No-Snag	perch scale	EX	$31.00	00-03
Heddon	River Runt No-Snag	perch, in N9119P box	VGIB	$49.99	99-05
Heddon	River Runt No-Snag	rainbow	EX-	$113.00	04-02
Heddon	River Runt No-Snag	RH, flitter	EX	$71.00	01-03
Heddon	River Runt No-Snag	RH, flitter	EX	$118.60	00-02
Heddon	RIver Runt No-Snag	RH/w glitter	EX	$93.00	00-04
Heddon	River Runt No-Snag	shad, yellow eyes	VG+	$330.00	05-07
Heddon	River Runt No-Snag	shiner scale	rough	$20.00	02-08
Heddon	River Runt No-Snag	shiner scale	EX	$37.50	99-01
Heddon	River Runt No-Snag	shiner scale	EX	$77.99	00-02
Heddon	River Runt No-Snag	white	EX	$261.51	00-03
Heddon	River Runt No-Snag	XBW	EX	$45.00	00-05
Heddon	River Runt No-Snag	XBW	EXIB	$40.00	99-04

BRAND	MODEL	SERIES / MFG. CODE / DESCRIPTION	GRADE	PRICE	DATE yy/mm
Heddon	River Runt No-Snag	XBW, nice Brush box	NIB	$95.50	99-08
Heddon	River Runt No-Snag	XBX, nice box, catalog & No-Snag paper	EXIB	$51.00	02-05
Heddon	River Runt No-Snag	XGF	EX-	$66.00	99-01
Heddon	River Runt No-Snag	XGF	VG	$76.00	98-12
Heddon	River Runt No-Snag	XGF, closed guard	EX	$65.01	99-06
Heddon	River Runt No-Snag	XGF, closed guard	EX	$73.75	99-06
Heddon	River Runt No-Snag	XRG	mint	$43.75	99-03
Heddon	River Runt No-Snag	XRS	mint	$49.99	99-06
Heddon	River Runt No-Snag	XRS, $75 NOT MET	NIB	$41.00	01-06
Heddon	River Runt No-Snag	XRS, small closed guard	EX	$41.00	00-03
Heddon	River Runt No-Snag	XRS, Brush	EXIB	$76.33	00-03
Heddon	River Runt No-Snag	XRY	rough	$21.00	02-08
Heddon	River Runt No-Snag	XRY	EX-	$31.50	99-08
Heddon	River Runt No-Snag	XRY	VG	$36.00	99-01
Heddon	River Runt No-Snag	XRY	EX	$50.00	99-03
Heddon	River Runt No-Snag	XRY, Brush	EXIB	$56.33	00-03
Heddon	River Runt No-Snag	XWB, luminous, blisters	VG	$663.00	05-02
Heddon	River Runt Salmon	8859SPRH, Brush, 2pc, RH spotted	NIB	$1,393.00	00-09
Heddon	River Runt Salmon	XRY, deep diver, teddy bear eyes, string	EX	$228.50	00-01
Heddon	River Runt Salmon	shiner scale, TBE, NOT MET	NIB	$331.00	01-03
Heddon	River Runt Salmon	XRW, teddy GE	VG+	$150.00	99-09
Heddon	River Runt Sinker x 4	P, RH, jntd	NIB	$62.00	99-02
Heddon	River Runt Sinker x 3	R, fltr, snkr, Midget, all 2pc	EX	$48.00	99-02
Heddon	River Runt Sinker	2 r/w flitter, SS	EX-	$21.00	99-01
Heddon	River Runt Sinker x 4	9400 — P, SD, RH, M	EXIB	$103.55	99-01
Heddon	River Runt Sinker	9010BHY, Daisy box	NIB	$49.99	99-03
Heddon	River Runt Sinker	9010PG, golden shinner, SR, GPE, few light pointers	EX-	$39.00	05-04
Heddon	River Runt Sinker	9010SFR	NIB	$51.01	99-07
Heddon	River Runt Sinker	9010GFR	VG-	$22.01	99-09
Heddon	River Runt Sinker	9010GFR	EX	$31.00	99-09
Heddon	River Runt Sinker	9010M, 2pc, catalog	NIB	$40.00	02-07
Heddon	River Runt Sinker	9010S, cat, hangtag, crisp, S-rig	NIB	$78.00	00-04
Heddon	River Runt Sinker	9010SE-XBY, b/w, yellow ribs	BIB	$56.20	98-12
Heddon	River Runt Sinker	9010XBL, w eye, Daisy box	NIB	$98.50	99-05
Heddon	River Runt Sinker	9010XGF, w eye, Daisy box	NIB	$48.02	99-05
Heddon	River Runt Sinker	9019XBY, 2pc, paper	NIB	$43.00	02-07
Heddon	River Runt Sinker	9110BB, baby bass, WPE, SR, few tiny pointers	EX-	$38.00	05-04
Heddon	River Runt Sinker	9110CBO	NIB	$61.00	03-01
Heddon	River Runt Sinker	9110L, perch, WPE; SR, in red, white, and blue striped 2PSTB	NIB	$18.00	05-04
Heddon	River Runt Sinker	9110M, pike scale, GPE, SR, few light pointers	VG+IB	$19.00	05-04
Heddon	River Runt Sinker	9110PG, golden shiner, GPE, SR	EX+	$40.00	05-04
Heddon	River Runt Sinker	9110, red and white, Waterwave, 2pc, GPE, hks dirty, hint of wear	EX	$295.00	05-04
Heddon	River Runt Sinker	9110RH, RH/w, GPE, 2pc, scratches on nose	VG+	$18.00	05-04

167

BRAND	MODEL	SERIES / MFG. CODE / DESCRIPTION	GRADE	PRICE	DATE yy/mm
Heddon	River Runt Sinker	9110RH, RH/w, GPE, SR, bright and shiny in orig VG RR2PCCB	EX+IB	$18.00	05-04
Heddon	River Runt Sinker	9110SD, green shad, YPE, SR, new on VG+ earliest blister card	NOC	$18.00	05-04
Heddon	River Runt Sinker	9110SG-XGY	EX	$100.00	99-08
Heddon	River Runt Sinker	9110SG-XYS, Spook Glow, yellow and silver ribs	NM	$65.00	05-04
Heddon	River Runt Sinker	9110SR-XBY, papers	NIB	$129.49	99-12
Heddon	River Runt Sinker	9110SR-XLB, nice box	EXIB	$76.00	01-08
Heddon	River Runt Sinker	9110XBP, pearl shore, GPE, SR, very light wear	EX-	$24.00	05-04
Heddon	River Runt Sinker	9110XBW, black shore, GPE, 2pc, very light wear	EX	$25.00	05-04
Heddon	River Runt Sinker	9110XRG, green shore, 2pc, GPE, very light wear, in orig VG RR2PCCB	EXIB	$40.00	05-04
Heddon	River Runt Sinker	9110XRW, white shore, WPE, SR, hint of wear	EX	$14.00	05-04
Heddon	River Runt Sinker	9110XRY, yellow shore, GPE, 2pc, very light wear in orig Brush 2PCCB	EXIB	$38.00	05-04
Heddon	River Runt Sinker	9110L, gold eye	NIB	$35.99	99-07
Heddon	River Runt Sinker	9110M, PTCB	NIB	$15.00	04-12
Heddon	River Runt Sinker	9110RB	NIB	$39.00	99-03
Heddon	River Runt Sinker	9110RH, S-rig	NIB	$38.00	01-03
Heddon	River Runt Sinker	9110RH, 2pc	EXIB	$35.00	99-02
Heddon	River Runt Sinker	9110Runt SG-XYS	EX-IB	$74.00	02-01
Heddon	River Runt Sinker	9110SP, red/silver flitter inside	NIB	$168.00	98-12
Heddon	River Runt Sinker	9110XRG, gold eyes, papers	NIB	$25.57	99-08
Heddon	River Runt Sinker	9110XRW	EXIB	$15.50	98-12
Heddon	River Runt Sinker	9110XRY, gold eyes	NIB	$25.00	99-07
Heddon	River Runt Sinker	9112, Brush	NIB	$29.51	00-02
Heddon	River Runt Sinker	9119GW, Runt box, 2pc, glow papers	EXIB	$129.00	03-11
Heddon	River Runt Sinker	9119L, perch, GPE, SR, very light wear	EX	$15.00	05-04
Heddon	River Runt Sinker	9119M, pike scale, GPE, 2pc, small scuff on its belly and no box	EX-	$24.00	05-04
Heddon	River Runt Sinker	9119GW	EX-IB	$112.00	03-06
Heddon	River Runt Sinker	9119GWH, b/w, nice box	VG-IB	$115.91	99-12
Heddon	River Runt Sinker	9119L, GE, Up Bass box, perch scale, GE	EXIB	$152.50	99-04
Heddon	River Runt Sinker	9119XRG, Brush box	EXIB	$45.01	99-02
Heddon	River Runt Sinker	9119XRS, Brush box	EX-	$43.52	99-05
Heddon	River Runt Sinker	9119XSK, Brush bx EX-	NIB	$300.00	03-05
Heddon	River Runt Sinker	9400WL, centennial	NIB	$36.00	99-03
Heddon	River Runt Sinker	9XBW, 2pc	NIB	$47.00	02-07
Heddon	River Runt Sinker	9XRG	mint	$41.00	02-07
Heddon	River Runt Sinker	9XRS, 2pc	NIB	$47.00	02-07
Heddon	River Runt Sinker	9XRS-XL, early type, narrow lip	VG	$30.00	02-07
Heddon	River Runt Sinker	b/w ribs, Runt box	EX	$31.50	99-01
Heddon	River Runt Sinker	baby bass, white eye	EX	$30.00	01-10
Heddon	River Runt Sinker	black, gold eye, 2pc	EX	$129.00	00-04
Heddon	River Runt Sinker	black, 2pc, NOT MET		$76.00	99-05
Heddon	River Runt Sinker	black/silver foil	EX-	$46.26	00-02
Heddon	River Runt Sinker	black/silver reflector box	NIB	$40.00	99-01
Heddon	River Runt Sinker	blue shore, white eye, window box	NIB	$90.99	99-12

BRAND	MODEL	SERIES / MFG. CODE / DESCRIPTION	GRADE	PRICE	DATE yy/mm
Heddon	River Runt Sinker	BRS, yellow eyes	EX	$58.00	00-07
Heddon	River Runt Sinker	CBO, white eye, NOT MET	EX-	$31.99	99-03
Heddon	River Runt Sinker	clear orange spotted	EX	$225.00	99-06
Heddon	River Runt Sinker	clear orange/red & black spots, gold eyes	EX	$76.00	05-07
Heddon	River Runt Sinker	clear plum/blk ribs	EX	$59.00	00-07
Heddon	River Runt Sinker	cobalt blue shore, white eyes	EX	$302.00	02-11
Heddon	River Runt Sinker	crackle, Spook, gold eyes	EX	$102.00	01-10
Heddon	River Runt Sinker	deep M, deep XBW, jntd	NIB	$98.00	99-02
Heddon	River Runt Sinker	FF9010GB	NIB	$68.00	00-10
Heddon	River Runt Sinker	FF9010GFYBS	EX-	$145.00	02-03
Heddon	River Runt Sinker	FFGB	mint	$67.00	02-07
Heddon	River Runt Sinker	FFGR	mint	$78.00	02-07
Heddon	River Runt Sinker	FFRGF, red/gold foil	EX-	$24.00	02-08
Heddon	River Runt Sinker	FFSB	mint	$67.00	02-07
Heddon	River Runt Sinker	FFSR	mint	$63.00	02-07
Heddon	River Runt Sinker	XRY, floater	EX	$14.49	99-01
Heddon	River Runt Sinker	floater, pink shore, w eye	EX	$7.50	99-01
Heddon	River Runt Sinker	glowworm, 2pc	EX	$150.00	99-06
Heddon	River Runt Sinker	Go-Deeper, gold eye, stair	NIB	$42.00	98-12
Heddon	River Runt Sinker	gold PE, pearl black shore	VG+	$45.00	05-06
Heddon	River Runt Sinker	green scale, 2pc	EX	$160.00	04-11
Heddon	River Runt Sinker	green scale, gold eyes, S-rig	mint	$106.00	03-05
Heddon	River Runt Sinker	green scale, gold eye	EX	$202.00	00-10
Heddon	River Runt Sinker	GW, no picture	mint	$127.50	00-02
Heddon	River Runt Sinker	LUM, bad bubbling	poor	$152.00	00-07
Heddon	River Runt Sinker	LUM, fat black ribs, 9119XBW box	blistered	$290.00	02-01
Heddon	River Runt Sinker	M, 2pc	NIB	$40.00	02-07
Heddon	River Runt Sinker	nat photo gold/green/orange, gold eyes	EX	$75.00	01-04
Heddon	River Runt Sinker	neon green shore	EX-	$41.00	99-01
Heddon	River Runt Sinker	OCB, $20 postage	EX+	$32.00	00-04
Heddon	River Runt Sinker	orange crackleback, white eyes	EX	$35.13	00-03
Heddon	River Runt Sinker	orange crackleback, white eye, NOT MET	EX	$46.51	99-08
Heddon	River Runt Sinker	orange crackleback, white eye	EX	$46.01	99-06
Heddon	River Runt Sinker	pearl, gold eye	EX	$53.52	99-05
Heddon	River Runt Sinker	perch, GE	EX	$149.00	99-01
Heddon	River Runt Sinker	pink shore, 9400SP box	EX	$67.00	00-07
Heddon	River Runt Sinker	r/blk, Spook Glow, white eye	EX	$50.00	99-02
Heddon	River Runt Sinker	r/w, Waterwave	EX-	$256.75	99-08
Heddon	River Runt Sinker	RB flitter, M flitter, Deeper XRS	NIB	$105.00	99-02
Heddon	River Runt Sinker	RB, 2pc	EX-	$52.51	99-06
Heddon	River Runt Sinker	red gold foil	mint	$41.00	00-11
Heddon	River Runt Sinker	red Waterwave	EX	$174.00	04-11
Heddon	River Runt Sinker	red/clear/silver flitter, insert, NOT MET	EX	$65.50	99-05
Heddon	River Runt Sinker	red/gold foil	VG	$32.00	00-04
Heddon	River Runt SInker	red/white, Waterwave	EX-	$177.00	05-05
Heddon	River Runt Sinker	RH	NIB	$24.50	99-03
Heddon	River Runt Sinker	SG-RB	EX	$79.00	99-02
Heddon	River Runt Sinker	SG, red/blk ribs	EX	$51.00	00-03

BRAND	MODEL	SERIES / MFG. CODE / DESCRIPTION	GRADE	PRICE	DATE yy/mm
Heddon	River Runt Sinker	SG-XOY	EX	$30.00	04-02
Heddon	River Runt Sinker	SG-XOY	EX	$60.00	99-03
Heddon	River Runt Sinker	SG-XRO, NOT MET	EX	$41.00	99-03
Heddon	River Runt Sinker	SG-XRO, NOT MET!	EX	$42.00	99-02
Heddon	River Runt Sinker	SG-XYS	NIB	$74.00	02-07
Heddon	River Runt Sinker	shiner scale, 2pc	mint	$128.50	00-03
Heddon	River Runt Sinker	silver herring (new), S-rig	VG+	$50.00	03-02
Heddon	River Runt Sinker	SP, silver	EX	$81.00	99-04
Heddon	River Runt Sinker	Spook Glow, green/yellow ribs	EX	$56.00	01-10
Heddon	River Runt Sinker	Spook Glow, orange/yellow ribs	mint	$72.00	00-08
Heddon	River Runt Sinker	Spook Ray, red/black ribs, gold eye	EX	$72.00	00-06
Heddon	River Runt Sinker	Spook Ray, red/orange/blk ribs	EX	$65.00	98-12
Heddon	River Runt Sinker	spotted pearl, 9110RB box	EX	$179.51	99-04
Heddon	River Runt Sinker	strawberry, 2pc	EX	$109.00	04-11
Heddon	River Runt Sinker	strawberry, gold eyes, cat	NIB	$117.50	99-07
Heddon	River Runt Sinker	strawberry, gold eyes, S-rig	EX	$51.06	99-05
Heddon	River Runt Sinker	trans w/blk dots, silver foil	EX-	$80.00	00-07
Heddon	River Runt Sinker	Waterwave, r&w Everlasting	EX+	$300.00	01-12
Heddon	River Runt Sinker	wood, PE, dace, POBW	VG+	$86.00	99-05
Heddon	River Runt Sinker	XBW	NIB	$31.00	02-07
Heddon	River Runt Sinker	XBW, black shore, 2pc, GPE, hooks darkened	EX	$27.00	05-04
Heddon	River Runt Sinker	XRG, green shore, GPE, SR	EX	$15.00	05-04
Heddon	River Runt Sinker	XRG, XRW Brush box	EX	$16.00	99-01
Heddon	River Runt Sinker	XRS	NIB	$26.00	02-07
Heddon	River Runt Sinker	XRS, jointed sinker, Banner bx	NIB	$26.50	99-01
Heddon	River Runt Sinker	XRY, Midget, gold eyes	EX-	$12.00	99-01
Heddon	River Runt Sinker	XRY, sinker, gold eyes	EX-	$10.00	99-01
Heddon	River Runt Sinker	yellow PE, black head, white body, orange ribs	VG+	$45.00	05-06
Heddon	River Runt Sinker	E9110YB, yellow/black, NOT MET	NIB	$636.00	04-04
Heddon	River Runt Sinker, jntd	9330RH, red front half and white back half, new in EX+ orig RR-2PCCB, b&w catalog	NIB	$50.00	05-04
Heddon	River Runt Sinker, jntd	9330RH, RH/w and clear belly, GPE, SR, just a hint of wear	EX+	$30.00	05-04
Heddon	River Runt Sinker, jntd	9330XBW, black shore, GPE, SR, very light wear, in orig VG- RR2PCCB	EXIB	$44.00	05-04
Heddon	River Runt Sinker, jntd	9330XPB, pearl shore, GPE, SR, very light wear, in orig EX RR2PCCB, color catalog	Ex-IB	$75.00	05-04
Heddon	River Runt Sinker, jntd	9330XRG, green shore, GPE, 3", body has light wear	VG	$21.00	05-04
Heddon	River Runt Sinker, jntd	9330XRG, green shore, SR, GPE, 3", body new in VG+ orig RR2PCCB	EXIB	$62.00	05-04
Heddon	River Runt Sinker, jntd	9330XRS, silver shore, GPE, SR	MINT	$40.00	05-04
Heddon	River Runt Sinker, jntd	9330XRW, white shore, GPE, SR, light wear, in VG orig RR2PCCB, BandW catalog	EX-IB	$42.00	05-04
Heddon	River Runt Sinker, jntd	9330XRW, white shore, GPE, SR, very light wear	EX	$38.00	05-04
Heddon	River Runt Sinker, jntd	9330L, with color catalog, nice Runt box	NIB	$25.00	04-03
Heddon	River Runt Sinker, jntd	9330L, Banner, NOT MET	NIB	$29.00	00-10
Heddon	River Runt Sinker, jntd	9330RH	NIB	$46.00	99-07

BRAND	MODEL	SERIES / MFG. CODE / DESCRIPTION	GRADE	PRICE	DATE yy/mm
Heddon	River Runt Sinker, jntd	9330RHF, silver scale	NIB	$151.00	00-10
Heddon	River Runt Sinker, jntd	9330XRY	NIB	$29.00	02-03
Heddon	River Runt Sinker, jntd	strawberry, gold eye, S-rig	EX	$190.00	00-03
Heddon	River Runt Sinker, jntd	XRS, gold eyes, Banner, NOT MET	NIB	$26.00	99-09
Heddon	River Runt Tiny	353SDN, natural shad	NIB	$27.00	98-12
Heddon	River Runt Tiny	353SUC, natural sucker	NIB	$67.00	99-01
Heddon	River Runt Tiny	blk/silver foil, GE	EX	$77.51	00-02
Heddon	River Runt Tiny	blk/silver foil, GE	EX	$77.99	00-02
Heddon	River Runt Tiny	BRS	mint	$51.00	03-02
Heddon	River Runt Tiny	FF350GB	NIB	$55.00	04-11
Heddon	River Runt Tiny	FF350GR	EX+	$42.00	04-11
Heddon	River Runt Tiny	FFD350SB	EX-IB	$29.00	04-11
Heddon	River Runt Tiny	MG	EX	$56.00	03-02
Heddon	River Runt Tiny	natural shad	NIB	$27.55	99-02
Heddon	River Runt Tiny	OBS	EX	$58.00	03-02
Heddon	River Runt Tiny	PTCB	NIB	$16.50	99-01
Heddon	River Runt Tiny Floating	FF340GB	EX+	$35.00	04-11
Heddon	River Runt Tiny Floating	FF340GR	NIB	$46.00	04-11
Heddon	River Runt Tiny Go-Deeper	blk/silver foil, GE	EX	$80.99	00-02
Heddon	River Runt Tiny Go-Deeper	white/black dots, black/red eyes	EX	$63.00	05-07
Heddon	River Runt Tiny Go-Deeper	D350, in uncataloged shiner scale	EX	$87.00	05-07
Heddon	River Runt Tiny Go-Deeper	FFD350GB	NIB	$67.00	04-11
Heddon	River Runt x 12	12-pack of all 4 Spook Glow colors	NIB	$2,778.00	00-01
Heddon	River Runt x 4	4 diff SGs, XGY, XLB, XOY, XYS	EX-	$151.00	01-09
Heddon	River Runt x 4	4 diff Spook Glows, NOT MET	EX	$163.00	00-07
Heddon	River Runt x 9	9 diff common, all with cats, nice	NIB	$362.00	99-08
Heddon	River Runt XBW	Spook Sinker in correct box	EX	$26.00	99-01
Heddon	River Runt	6 red/sil, blk/sil, OS	EX	$164.50	99-02
Heddon	River Runt	9110SGXGY, crackle, blk/red	NIB (1/3)	$130.16	99-06
Heddon	Salmon River Runt	8859XRX, Brush, white shore? teddy bear eyes	NIB	$615.00	02-02
Heddon	Salmon River Runt	8859PLXR, big Go-Deeper lip, teddy eyes	NIB	$427.00	02-12
Heddon	Salmon River Runt	scoop lip, herring scale	EX-	$345.00	04-03
Heddon	Salmon River Runt	white/red gills, teddy bear eyes	EX	$138.00	04-03
Heddon	Saltwater Special	RH flitter	EX	$325.00	00-05
Heddon	Scissortail Go-Deeper	3 diff	EX	$89.88	99-04
Heddon	Scissortail	9830P, Banner box	NIB	$57.00	99-03
Heddon	Scissortail	9830XBW	NIB	$39.80	99-02
Heddon	Scissortail	OS, catalog	NIB	$71.00	01-10
Heddon	Scissortail	pike scale	EX	$27.00	01-08
Heddon	Scissortail	9830M, pike scale	NIB	$49.51	05-07
Heddon	Scissortail	r/w	EX	$23.35	99-05
Heddon	Scissortail	shiner scale, missing hook	EX	$21.01	99-02
Heddon	Scissortail	XRY	EX	$61.00	99-10
Heddon	Scissortail		VG	$28.00	99-02
Heddon	Scissortail	9830XRS, silver shore	EX+	$40.00	05-04
Heddon	Scissortail x 3	M, XRS, RH, all EX	EX	$64.66	00-04
Heddon	Sea Runt	210S, strawberry spot, GE, TS-rig, NSOB, PO1BW, chin flake and nick on l-side	VG+	$95.00	05-05

171

BRAND	MODEL	SERIES / MFG. CODE / DESCRIPTION	GRADE	PRICE	DATE yy/mm
Heddon	Sea Runt	YRH, painted eyes	mint	$43.00	02-07
Heddon	Shark Mouth Minnow	RH/flitter, "cast aluminum"?	EX	$513.00	01-10
Heddon	Shark Mouth Minnow	red/yellow	EX-	$110.00	05-07
Heddon	Shrimpy Spook	½ whiskers	EX	$290.00	99-08
Heddon	Shrimpy Spook	9009NS, Up Bass	EXIB	$250.00	00-10
Heddon	Shrimpy Spook	nat shrimp	EX+	$350.00	01-07
Heddon	Shrimpy Spook	nice	EX	$300.00	99-04
Heddon	Shrimpy Spook	NOT MET	EX-	$149.00	00-09
Heddon	Shrimpy Spook	r/w flitter, st tail	EX	$305.00	99-03
Heddon	Shrimpy Spook	whiskers, eyes OK	VG+	$227.50	99-03
Heddon	Sienna 100	2 belly weights, marked wood box VG	EXIB	$990.00	05-07
Heddon	Skipper	RET	VG-	$348.00	00-09
Heddon	Slopenose	2-pin collar, blue head, NOT MET	EX-	$307.00	03-11
Heddon	Slopenose	L-rig? 3-pin	?	$356.00	00-09
Heddon	Slopenose	b/w, red collar, rare papers	EX-	$2,060.00	99-12
Heddon	Slopenose	BH, 4 hooks, tail cap, NOT MET	avg	$169.00	01-03
Heddon	Slopenose	BH, NOT MET	EX-	$550.00	00-11
Heddon	Slopenose	BH, pinned collar, brass tail	avg	$201.00	02-06
Heddon	Slopenose	BH, single pin, c. 1903, chips, NOT MET	VG?	$587.00	00-09
Heddon	Slopenose	brass tail & cups, NOT MET	VG	$510.00	02-06
Heddon	Slopenose	c. 1912, 4½", blue head/white body, w/rare box VG+ and papers		$11,110.00	05-04
Heddon	Slopenose	gold-washed cup and cap and box, ½ label missing	VG+	$1,320.00	05-07
Heddon	Slopenose	pic box avg, lure decent but collar repainted	VG+IB	$610.00	02-07
Heddon	Slopenose	poor pic box, BH	EX-IB	$1,274.00	00-10
Heddon	Slopenose 4-hooker	BH, 2 pin, red collar, tail cap	VG+	$1,000.00	00-04
Heddon	Sonar	2-433-GF & 431-SF	NIB	$16.00	99-01
Heddon	Sonar	26 diff salesman, marked, odd colors	mint	$56.01	99-02
Heddon	Sonic	14KCD	VG	$61.25	99-04
Heddon	Sonic	385, black scale, gold eye, thunderbolt	EX	$284.00	03-06
Heddon	Sonic	385CBO, crackleback, orange WPE, little wear on tip of nose	EX-	$33.00	05-04
Heddon	Sonic	385CD, white coach dog, very light wear	EX-	$8.00	05-04
Heddon	Sonic	385DD, dark dace, black scale on white body, WPE, POBW	EX-	$12.00	05-04
Heddon	Sonic	385GF, green fish (light green scale over pearly body), YPE	EX+	$20.00	05-04
Heddon	Sonic	385SF, silverfish, YPE, light wear on nose	VG+	$12.00	05-04
Heddon	Sonic	385SJ, Smokey Joe, gray scales on clear body, YPE	EX-	$35.00	05-04
Heddon	Sonic	385L, PTCB	NIB	$15.50	99-02
Heddon	Sonic	385L, 12-pack w/9 lures	NIB	$90.00	99-05
Heddon	Sonic	385SF	NIB	$17.00	99-01
Heddon	Sonic	388PUM, nat Pumkinseed	NIB	$27.00	00-04
Heddon	Sonic	9385 SD, plus yellow scale	NIB	$23.02	99-01
Heddon	Sonic	baby bass	mint	$34.00	99-01
Heddon	Sonic	blue scale, rubbed on one side	GD	$36.99	05-07
Heddon	Sonic	BRS	EX	$57.00	04-01

LURES

BRAND	MODEL	SERIES / MFG. CODE / DESCRIPTION	GRADE	PRICE	DATE yy/mm
Heddon	Sonic	checkerboard, NOT MET	EX	$228.00	00-11
Heddon	Sonic	chrome/black scale	mint	$21.50	99-02
Heddon	Sonic	chrome/black scale, no T-bolt, paint off by belly	VG	$31.00	05-07
Heddon	Sonic	chrome/blue scale	VG	$20.50	99-01
Heddon	Sonic	clear y, blk dots	EX	$61.00	00-03
Heddon	Sonic	coach dog, gold bolt	mint	$26.00	99-02
Heddon	Sonic	frog, gold eye, 325BAR box	EX	$43.00	99-06
Heddon	Sonic	GBP	NOC	$30.00	99-04
Heddon	Sonic	Johnson Outboard logo, NOT MET	EX	$112.00	00-07
Heddon	Sonic	Johnson Seahorse logo	EX	$355.00	99-04
Heddon	Sonic	natural shad	NIB	$28.50	99-02
Heddon	Sonic	NSN, photo perch?	EX	$46.00	01-10
Heddon	Sonic	o crackle	EX	$30.00	00-03
Heddon	Sonic	perch	VG	$9.75	99-01
Heddon	Sonic	perch, molded hangers	mint	$36.00	99-01
Heddon	Sonic	shad	mint	$14.00	99-02
Heddon	Sonic	shad, paint raised on BW	EX	$10.50	99-01
Heddon	Sonic	white w/black, gold eyes	VG	$15.50	05-07
Heddon	Sonic	white/blk bolt, newer	NOC	$45.99	99-06
Heddon	Sonic	y, coach dog?	EX	$36.80	99-02
Heddon	Sonic	y/b, coach dog, gold eye	mint	$33.00	99-01
Heddon	Sonic	y/blk, coach dog	mint	$22.50	99-02
Heddon	Sonic x 15	stand-up display, common colors	EX	$500.00	00-10
Heddon	Sonic, Firetail	2 black, coach dog	EX	$31.00	99-02
Heddon	Sonic, Firetail	395B, black w/white lightning, bold GPE, very light wear	EX-	$13.00	05-05
Heddon	Sonic, Firetail	395CD, white coach dog, GPE, very light wear	EX+	$17.00	05-05
Heddon	Sonic, Firetail	395RH, RH/white and silver scales on belly, YPE	EX+	$15.00	05-05
Heddon	Sonic, Firetail	395SD, shad, GPE, few minor scuffs on forehead	VG+	$10.00	05-05
Heddon	Sonic, Firetail	395RH, PTCB EX, paper	NIB	$77.00	05-07
Heddon	Sonic, Firetail	SD, blk/green triangles card	NOC	$13.00	01-08
Heddon	Sonic, Super	9385BB, baby bass, gold-plated hdwr and hooks	EX	$15.00	05-04
Heddon	Sonic, Super	9385CD, white coach dog, Heddon's Classic series, gold-plated hdwr and hooks	NM	$5.00	05-04
Heddon	Sonic, Super	9385CR, Crystal Rainbow, WPE, very light wear on this early Sonic	EX	$12.00	05-04
Heddon	Sonic, Super	9385CS, crystal shad	NIB	$22.00	01-08
Heddon	Sonic, Super	9385GFB, gold foil black?	NIB	$53.00	01-08
Heddon	Sonic, Super	9385NP, nickle plate	NIB	$52.00	01-08
Heddon	Sonic, Super	9385NRT, natural trout	NIB	$98.00	01-10
Heddon	Sonic, Super	9385NSD, nickle shad, black scale back	NIB	$53.00	01-08
Heddon	Sonic, Super	9385, shad, WPE	Mint	$10.00	05-04
Heddon	Sonic, Super	9385VRB, chrome rainbow scale, tiny pointers on belly and very light wear	VG+	$24.00	05-04
Heddon	Sonic, Super	9385Y, yellow scale, WPE	EX+	$10.00	05-04
Heddon	Sonic, Super	9385Y, yellow scale, WPE, in orig EX- 2PSTB	NIB	$15.00	05-04
Heddon	Sonic, Super	9385BC, black crappie, PTCB	NIB	$20.50	99-01
Heddon	Sonic, Super	9385CD	NIB	$19.00	99-01

173

BRAND	MODEL	SERIES / MFG. CODE / DESCRIPTION	GRADE	PRICE	DATE yy/mm
Heddon	Sonic, Super	9385CR, PTCB	NIB	$46.00	99-01
Heddon	Sonic, Super	9385GRA	NIB	$71.25	00-03
Heddon	Sonic, Super	9385L, ABU Record	NIB	$31.00	99-03
Heddon	Sonic, Super	9385L, PTCB	NIB	$18.00	99-04
Heddon	Sonic, Super	9385LC, nat perch	NIB	$56.00	00-03
Heddon	Sonic, Super	9385NRT, nat rainbow trout, NOT MET	NIB	$87.00	03-01
Heddon	Sonic, Super	9385NSN, nat sunfish	NOC	$71.00	03-01
Heddon	Sonic, Super	9385PUM	NIB	$76.51	00-03
Heddon	Sonic, Super	9385RFL	NIB	$50.00	02-08
Heddon	Sonic, Super	9385SUC, nat sucker	NIB	$134.02	00-03
Heddon	Sonic, Super	9386RH, RH/w w/white scales and spots on sides, WPE, clean	EX	$15.00	05-04
Heddon	Sonic, Super	9386SD, nat shad	NIB	$30.00	00-04
Heddon	Sonic, Super	985CS, old plastic lid box	NIB	$19.00	00-07
Heddon	Sonic, Super	albino	EX+	$76.00	00-03
Heddon	Sonic, Super	bronze chrome/blk scale	EX	$41.00	99-02
Heddon	Sonic, Super	CS, gold eye	EX	$25.21	99-02
Heddon	Sonic, Super	GLDS	EX-	$36.46	99-04
Heddon	Sonic, Super	gold spot	EX	$51.00	02-08
Heddon	Sonic, Super	gold spot	EX+	$60.00	99-01
Heddon	Sonic, Super	GPB, gold/blk back	EX+	$33.00	99-02
Heddon	Sonic, Super	green scale, blk coach dog	EX	$56.50	99-02
Heddon	Sonic, Super	nat redfish	mint	$325.00	02-04
Heddon	Sonic, Super	natural perch? name on side	EX	$77.00	05-07
Heddon	Sonic, Super	orange crackle	mint	$52.00	99-08
Heddon	Sonic, Super	pearl scale	EX	$27.00	99-05
Heddon	Sonic, Super	purple bar scale	EX	$67.00	00-04
Heddon	Sonic, Super	red head/blue tail/silver scale	EX	$16.00	99-02
Heddon	Sonic, Super	salesman sample, NRE, no hdwr, NOT MET	EX	$127.00	04-01
Heddon	Sonic, Super	Smith 1999 color!	mint	$257.51	99-07
Heddon	Sonic, Super	V9385GF, gold flitter	NIB	$70.00	99-02
Heddon	Sonic, Super	X9385BYY, Smith color, black w/yellow shadow wave	NOC	$20.00	05-04
Heddon	Sonic, Super	X9385WPS, undereye Smith color, white/purple spots	NOC	$20.00	05-04
Heddon	Sonic, Super	X9385WSL, undereye Smith color, white/black wave and spots	NOC	$20.00	05-04
Heddon	Sonic, Super	plastic with blue and yellow pattern	VG	$9.00	05-07
Heddon	Sonic, Top	300NGL, nat BGL	NIB	$89.88	99-04
Heddon	Sonic, Top	bar fish	EX	$36.00	99-01
Heddon	Sonic, Top	black scale	EX+	$47.00	99-05
Heddon	Sonic, Top	blue scale (purple?)	EX	$31.67	99-06
Heddon	Sonic, Top	MG?	EX	$129.00	02-11
Heddon	Sonic, Top	MG?	mint	$250.00	02-11
Heddon	Sonic, Top	perch (yellow scale?)	EX	$22.00	99-01
Heddon	Sonic, Top	purple scale	NIB	$61.00	99-03
Heddon	Sonic, Top	purple scale	NIB	$61.00	99-03
Heddon	Sonic, Top	Y	NIB	$35.00	99-06
Heddon	Sonic, Ultra	325B	NIB	$6.00	05-02

BRAND	MODEL	SERIES / MFG. CODE / DESCRIPTION	GRADE	PRICE	DATE yy/mm
Heddon	Sonic, Ultra	325BAR, nice PTCB	NIB	$52.71	99-01
Heddon	Sonic, Ultra	325SD, nice PTCB	NIB	$42.00	99-01
Heddon	SOS 140	140RHF, RH/w w/flitter, GPE, SR, varnish lightly tan	EX	$50.00	05-05
Heddon	SOS 140	140L, PE, Banner	NIB	$75.00	00-10
Heddon	SOS 140	140P, PE, Banner	NIB	$86.00	00-10
Heddon	SOS 140	frog spot, 2pc, GE	EX	$374.00	02-09
Heddon	SOS 140	green scale, 2pc	EX	$163.00	01-04
Heddon	SOS 140	L, GE, chip between eyes, OK	VG	$51.01	99-02
Heddon	SOS 140	perch, PE	EX	$42.00	99-02
Heddon	SOS 140	r/w, GE, 2pc	mint	$106.50	99-10
Heddon	SOS 140	RH, L-rig	EX-	$63.00	02-01
Heddon	SOS 140	RH, GE, 2pc, NOT MET	mint	$105.02	99-05
Heddon	SOS 140	shiner scale	EX	$132.50	99-01
Heddon	SOS 140	shiner scale, GE, 2pc	mint	$114.00	00-11
Heddon	SOS 140	SS, GE, 2pc, dent belly	EX-	$51.00	00-09
Heddon	SOS 160	160, GE	VG+	$39.00	05-07
Heddon	SOS 160	169N, dace, GE, TS-hdwr and wire through, couple very minor marks	EX-	$105.00	05-05
Heddon	SOS 160	169L, Brush box EX, 2pc, GE, chip on nose, otherwise minty	EX-IB	$75.00	05-07
Heddon	SOS 160	169L, Brush bx VG+, small chip, otherwise nice	EX-IB	$75.00	05-07
Heddon	SOS 160	169N, Up Bass nice, NOT MET	NIB	$305.00	01-12
Heddon	SOS 160	crackleback, POBW, 2pc	avg	$190.00	04-11
Heddon	SOS 160	dace, Up Bass bx 169N, L-rig	VGIB	$132.00	04-03
Heddon	SOS 160	dace, L-rig	EX	$176.00	02-08
Heddon	SOS 160	frog scale, L-rig	EX	$899.00	02-11
Heddon	SOS 160	frog scale, L-rig decent	EX-	$766.00	04-11
Heddon	SOS 160	green scale, L-rig	VG+	$65.00	04-12
Heddon	SOS 160	green scale, L-rig	EX	$133.50	99-08
Heddon	SOS 160	multi 170, Up Bass bx, shiner scale, L-rig	EXIB	$129.00	04-11
Heddon	SOS 160	P, L-rig, decent	VG+	$51.01	99-06
Heddon	SOS 160	RH, L-rig, yellowed varnish, nice	VG+	$63.00	04-11
Heddon	SOS 160	shiner scale, L-rig, GE, 1 pointer	EX-	$101.00	00-10
Heddon	SOS 160	silver scale	EX-	$127.00	00-10
Heddon	SOS 160	SS, 2pc	EX	$92.50	99-03
Heddon	SOS 160	SS, 2pc	EX	$104.00	01-01
Heddon	SOS 160	SS, GE, L-rig	EX-	$122.00	99-03
Heddon	SOS 170	172, Brush bx, 2pc, red head/white	NIB	$381.00	02-11
Heddon	SOS 170	179SS, silver scale, GE, TS-hdwr, few varn flks on nose and eyes, o/w, EX in VG Brush 2PCCB	EX-IB	$145.00	05-05
Heddon	SOS 170	179N, Up Bass, L-rig, NOT MET	EX-IB	$178.00	02-03
Heddon	SOS 170	179P, Brush, 2pc	NIB	$302.00	00-11
Heddon	SOS 170	Brush 179L, 2pc, pike scale, lure not L	EXIB	$165.00	04-03
Heddon	SOS 170	crackleback, L-rigs, huge hook drags	poor	$382.00	04-12
Heddon	SOS 170	dace, 2pc, NOT MET	mint	$214.00	02-12
Heddon	SOS 170	frog spot, L-rig, lot of pointers	G	$262.00	01-10
Heddon	SOS 170	green scale, L-rig	VG+	$121.00	01-11
Heddon	SOS 170	green scale, 2pc	EX-	$168.50	99-01

BRAND	MODEL	SERIES / MFG. CODE / DESCRIPTION	GRADE	PRICE	DATE yy/mm
Heddon	SOS 170	P tan back, L-rig, $3000 NOT MET	EX+	$1,331.00	00-03
Heddon	SOS 170	perch scale, L-rig	EX	$172.00	03-07
Heddon	SOS 170	perch scale, L-rig, nice	VG+	$82.00	04-12
Heddon	SOS 170	perch scale, 2pc, NOT MET	EX-	$122.50	99-12
Heddon	SOS 170	pike scale, 2pc, GE	VG+?	$127.50	99-06
Heddon	SOS 170	r/w, 2pc, looks super	EX	$126.50	99-03
Heddon	SOS 170	RET, L-rig, nice	VG+	$66.00	03-05
Heddon	SOS 170	RH, 2pc	EX-	$91.00	04-12
Heddon	SOS 170	RH, 2pc, big varnish flake, ugly bleed	VG+	$107.00	00-12
Heddon	SOS 170	RH, toilet seat	EX	$293.00	03-09
Heddon	SOS 170	RH, toilet seat hdwr	EX	$293.00	03-09
Heddon	SOS 170	RH, 2pc, sm dent nice	EX	$157.51	00-02
Heddon	SOS 170	RH, L-rig	EX-	$160.00	99-03
Heddon	SOS 170	RH/w, L-rig	VG	$97.00	99-04
Heddon	SOS 170	shiner scale, 2pc, belly stencil	mint	$203.00	03-03
Heddon	SOS 170	shiner scale, 2pc, NOT MET	EX-	$70.00	00-07
Heddon	SOS 170	shiner, L-rig, GE	EX-	$225.00	99-05
Heddon	SOS 170	shiner scale, 2pc	mint	$305.00	02-02
Heddon	SOS 170	silver scale, 2pc, GE, nice one	EX-	$72.00	04-12
Heddon	SOS 170	SS, silver scale, L-rig nice!	EX	$165.00	04-02
Heddon	SOS 170	SS, 2-pc, name on belly	EX-	$90.00	03-03
Heddon	SOS 170	SS, L-rig	VG	$88.00	99-04
Heddon	SOS 370	black sucker, Heddon props, L-rig	beater	$160.00	01-08
Heddon	SOS 370	pike scale, Stanley props, cup rig	EX-	$765.00	02-06
Heddon	SOS 370	pike scale, Stanley props, minty	EX+	$939.00	02-02
Heddon	SOS 370	RH, L-rig, Heddon props	EX	$1,009.00	01-09
Heddon	SOS 370	RH, Stanley props, cup rigged	EX-	$617.00	02-08
Heddon	SOS 370	RH, Stanley props	VG-	$670.00	00-02
Heddon	SOS 370	RH, Stanley props	VG-	$355.00	99-11
Heddon	SOS 370	SS, L-rig, Heddon props, several chips	VG-	$462.00	02-11
Heddon	Spindiver	bar perch	VG	$310.00	04-01
Heddon	Spindiver	bar perch	VG-	$760.00	99-07
Heddon	Spindiver	bar perch, ugly	avg	$265.00	01-04
Heddon	Spindiver	bar perch, $700 BUY NOW NOT MET	VG	$390.00	02-01
Heddon	Spindiver	bar perch, wood chip on tail, NOT MET	VG-	$485.00	01-08
Heddon	Spindiver	bar perch, NOT MET	avg	$362.85	99-01
Heddon	Spindiver	correct 3002 Down box!	EX-IB	$1,649.00	01-03
Heddon	Spindiver	crackleback	EX-	$405.00	02-01
Heddon	Spindiver	crackle	VG+	$649.00	01-04
Heddon	Spindiver	crackle, belly varnish problems	VG+	$1,136.00	00-07
Heddon	Spindiver	crackleback	VG	$590.00	04-02
Heddon	Spindiver	frog	EX-	$1,825.00	01-03
Heddon	Spindiver	frog	EX-	$2,427.00	01-05
Heddon	Spindiver	frog scale, rear hook missing	VG+	$596.00	05-06
Heddon	Spindiver	frog scale, missing center hook, belly varnish flaking	EX-	$660.00	05-07
Heddon	Spindiver	frog, not awful	avg	$285.00	00-06

BRAND	MODEL	SERIES / MFG. CODE / DESCRIPTION	GRADE	PRICE	DATE yy/mm
Heddon	Spindiver	frog, sm nose chip, lt tail rub	EX-	$1,075.00	01-10
Heddon	Spindiver	frog, ugly, NOT MET	avg	$180.00	99-05
Heddon	Spindiver	frog, varnish tail & belly	VG-	$1,055.00	99-05
Heddon	Spindiver	frog scale	avg	$468.00	03-10
Heddon	Spindiver	frog scale, sm touch-up on tail	VG+	$921.00	02-07
Heddon	Spindiver	frog scale, varnish flaking but decent	VG+	$653.00	04-02
Heddon	Spindiver	frog spot	EX	$1,750.00	01-04
Heddon	Spindiver	frog spot, ugly belly varnish	avg	$272.00	04-02
Heddon	Spindiver	GE, white/red/green decoration	GD+	$154.00	04-11
Heddon	Spindiver	goldfish scale, NOT MET	VG+	$1,044.00	00-03
Heddon	Spindiver	goldfish, NOT MET	beater	$228.00	00-05
Heddon	Spindiver	green scale	avg	$348.00	02-03
Heddon	Spindiver	green scale	VG	$1,126.01	99-04
Heddon	Spindiver	green scale, ugly!	poor	$305.00	01-07
Heddon	Spindiver	green scale, nice	EX-	$580.00	02-09
Heddon	Spindiver	green scale, belly varnish	VG	$334.00	05-07
Heddon	Spindiver	green scale, decent	VG+	$898.88	00-01
Heddon	Spindiver	green scale, side rough, 1 nice	½ VG+	$263.00	00-05
Heddon	Spindiver	rainbow, lt vanish flakes	EX	$880.00	04-03
Heddon	Spindiver	rainbow	fair	$142.00	99-01
Heddon	Spindiver	RB, varnish, $700 NOT MET	EX-	$660.00	01-06
Heddon	Spindiver	RB, sm nose chip, lt varnish, NOT MET	EX-/VG+	$660.00	01-06
Heddon	Spindiver	RB, missing spinner, hook	poor	$109.16	99-09
Heddon	Spindiver	red and white Spindiver w/correct 3002 box	EX-	$1,700.00	01-04
Heddon	Spindiver	red scale, decent	VG	$462.00	01-04
Heddon	Spindiver	red scale deluxe, sm chip on back, touch-up	VG	$1,125.00	01-09
Heddon	Spindiver	red scale	VG	$383.00	04-02
Heddon	Spindiver	red scale, decent, NOT MET	VG	$234.00	02-05
Heddon	Spindiver	RET, junk box	EXIB	$889.00	02-10
Heddon	Spindiver	RET, L-rig	VG	$510.00	03-05
Heddon	Spindiver	RET, hvy varnish flaking, otherwise OK	VG-	$404.00	00-03
Heddon	Spindiver	strawberry	rough	$289.00	99-08
Heddon	Spindiver	strawberry	G	$269.00	04-11
Heddon	Spindiver	strawberry, ugly	avg	$350.00	01-04
Heddon	Spindiver	white, RET, SOLD	VG+	$900.00	00-05
Heddon	Spindiver	white, RET, varnish loss but nice	VG+	$685.00	02-04
Heddon	Spindiver	white w/red nose	AVG	$250.00	05-07
Heddon	Spindiver	white, red eyes & tail	VG+	$394.00	03-11
Heddon	Spindiver	white, red eye & tail	EX-	$1,554.00	00-01
Heddon	Spoon Kit	3 sm Ace-type spoons in broken plastic box	NIB	$26.00	04-12
Heddon	Spoony Frog	8209B, Up Bass, frog finish	EXIB	$462.00	02-05
Heddon	Spoony Frog	frog but awful paint		$27.00	99-01
Heddon	Spoony Frog	frog color, sm chip	EX-	$125.00	05-06
Heddon	Spoony Frog	frog color, minor feet chips	EX-	$198.50	99-07
Heddon	Spoony Frog	frog, 50% paint loss on legs	VG-?	$134.06	99-08
Heddon	Spoony Frog	gold, NOT MET	VG	$26.00	99-01
Heddon	Spoony Frog	silver	EX	$20.52	99-11
Heddon	Spoony Frog	silver, NOT MET	EX	$36.25	00-02

BRAND	MODEL	SERIES / MFG. CODE / DESCRIPTION	GRADE	PRICE	DATE yy/mm
Heddon	Spoonyfish	5¾"	EX	$238.50	99-02
Heddon	Spoonyfish	large size, NOT MET	EX	$157.00	99-01
Heddon	Stanley #70	pike scale, GE, Skitter attached bx rough	NIB	$350.00	02-02
Heddon	Stanley Perfection Weedless	12-pack, hooks on cards, cool	NIB	$300.00	99-11
Heddon	Stanley Pork Rind	odd heart-shaped metal lip, M	EX	$361.00	00-08
Heddon	Stanley Pork Rind Minnow	72, red and white, Pyrolin, very light wear	EX	$35.00	05-04
Heddon	Stanley Pork Rind Minnow	shiner scale, GE	EX	$60.00	00-10
Heddon	Stingaree	9930, RH/w, GPE, SR	EX-	$25.00	05-04
Heddon	Stingaree	9930RH	NIB	$34.00	02-08
Heddon	Stingaree	9930RH, PTCB	NIB	$26.99	99-02
Heddon	Stingaree	frog, large size	EX-	$36.00	99-05
Heddon	Stingaree	large size, gold PE, white shore	EX+	$20.00	05-06
Heddon	Stingaree	perch	EX-	$26.00	99-02
Heddon	Stingaree	perch scale	EX	$66.00	05-07
Heddon	Stingaree	r/w	NIB	$52.01	99-03
Heddon	Stingaree	sm size, gold PE, red/white	EX+	$20.00	05-06
Heddon	Stingaree	tiny frog	VG	$15.57	99-01
Heddon	Stingaree	wood, unmarked	avg	$132.50	99-02
Heddon	Stingaree	XBW	EX+	$19.60	99-02
Heddon	Stingaree	XBW	NIB	$65.00	05-07
Heddon	Stingaree	XRY	EX	$27.00	99-02
Heddon	Stingaree Tiny x 2	XRY, perch scale	EX	$34.00	02-08
Heddon	Stingaree x 12	set of all 12, only one box — 330 XRY	EX	$610.00	02-02
Heddon	Stingaree, Tiny	perch	EX	$25.57	99-02
Heddon	Stingaree, Tiny	XRW, gold eyes	EX+	$52.00	05-07
Heddon	Stingaree, Tiny	XRY	EX	$64.00	05-07
Heddon	Super Dowagiac Spook	9108RH, amber body, RH/gold flitter, FE, TS-rig, very light wear	EX	$55.00	05-04
Heddon	Super Dowagiac Spook	L, in crisp Fish Flesh box, GE	NIB	$125.00	00-10
Heddon	Super Dowagiac Spook	perch, GE	EX	$80.52	99-04
Heddon	Super Dowagiac Spook	perch, GE, toilet	EX	$46.51	99-05
Heddon	Super Dowagiac Spook	shiner scale, GE, 1 broken	EX-	$56.00	99-01
Heddon	Super Spook	strawberry, PE	EX	$31.00	99-01
Heddon	Surface Bucktail	green back, rainbow	EX-	$950.00	00-05
Heddon	Surface Bucktail	white/blue crackle forehead	EX-	$950.00	00-05
Heddon	Surface Cobra	330XRW, white shore, GPE, SR	EX+	$32.00	05-04
Heddon	Surface Cobra	330XRY, yellow shore, GPE	EX+	$35.00	05-04
Heddon	Surface Cobra	9960Y, yellow, Fish Flash (silver glitter sides), NSOP	NM	$5.00	05-04
Heddon	Surface Minnie	RET	EX-	$875.00	00-05
Heddon	Surface Vamp Spook	silver flitter filling, red head	EX	$177.50	99-04
Heddon	Surfusser	350S, Fish Flesh bx VG	EXIB	$677.00	04-11
Heddon	Surfusser	yellow spot	avg	$255.00	04-11
Heddon	Tad Polly 5000	3⅞", GE, green scale finish	EX	$137.50	04-11
Heddon	Tad Polly 5000	GE, frog scale finish	EX-	$49.50	04-11
Heddon	Tadpolly	5000, frog, GE	EX	$205.00	05-07
Heddon	Tadpolly	5000, green scale, toilet set, wowser	EX+	$227.00	05-07
Heddon	Tadpolly	5000, RET, GE, in intro box VG, heart plate	VG	$95.00	05-06

BRAND	MODEL	SERIES / MFG. CODE / DESCRIPTION	GRADE	PRICE	DATE yy/mm
Heddon	Tadpolly	5000S, strawberry spot, GE, turned-up, TS-hdwr, very light wear	EX	$195.00	05-05
Heddon	Tadpolly	5000D, L-rig, intro box	VG+IB	$380.00	99-06
Heddon	Tadpolly	5002, Down Bass nice, NOT MET	NIB	$140.00	02-11
Heddon	Tadpolly	5002, Brush, 2pc	NIB	$222.50	99-10
Heddon	Tadpolly	5002, Down Bass, L-rig	NIB	$390.01	99-10
Heddon	Tadpolly	5009J, frog scale, GE, L-rig, few light varn nicks and age lines, in orig VG+ Down Bass 2PCCB	VG+IB	$345.00	05-05
Heddon	Tadpolly	5009L, early perch scale, GE, L-rig, varn flaking is on back	VG	$36.00	05-05
Heddon	Tadpolly	5009A, Down crisp, sm chip back	EX-IB	$430.00	01-08
Heddon	Tadpolly	5009D, Down bx, bar perch	EXIB	$505.00	02-09
Heddon	Tadpolly	5009D, intro box EX-	EXIB	$750.00	99-10
Heddon	Tadpolly	5009D, Up Bass	VG-IB	$73.10	00-03
Heddon	Tadpolly	5009D, Brush crisp	EXIB	$280.00	99-11
Heddon	Tadpolly	5009K, intro box EX-, nice goldfish scale lure	EX-IB	$1,201.00	02-02
Heddon	Tadpolly	5009L, intro box VG+, perch scale, GE	EXIB	$319.00	05-07
Heddon	Tadpolly	5009M, flawless Down Bass box	NIB	$562.00	99-09
Heddon	Tadpolly	5900, crackleback, glass eyes, big belly sliver	VG-	$59.00	05-07
Heddon	Tadpolly	6000, frog scale, belly varnish flaking	EX-	$400.00	05-01
Heddon	Tadpolly	6000, goldfish scale, GE	EX-	$179.00	05-07
Heddon	Tadpolly	6000, intro box, RET	EXIB	$513.00	00-05
Heddon	Tadpolly	6000, perch scale, GE, heart, Down Bass	NIB	$612.00	00-08
Heddon	Tadpolly	6000 size, rainbow, L-rig	VG	$58.00	05-07
Heddon	Tadpolly	6009D, intro box VG+	EXIB	$613.03	00-01
Heddon	Tadpolly	bar perch, Down Bass	VG+IB	$525.00	00-05
Heddon	Tadpolly	crackle	EX-	$300.00	01-10
Heddon	Tadpolly	5009P(WRG), crackle, Up Bass EX	EX	$500.00	99-10
Heddon	Tadpolly	fancy green scale, L-rig, Down Bass 6000	EXIB	$169.00	03-04
Heddon	Tadpolly	frog spot, L-rig, GE	VG	$48.00	04-12
Heddon	Tadpolly	frog, intro box avg, varnish flakes belly	EX-IB	$300.00	02-10
Heddon	Tadpolly	frog, GE, L-rig	VG+	$203.51	99-08
Heddon	Tadpolly	frog scale, cracked eyes	avg	$68.00	99-01
Heddon	Tadpolly	green scale, L-rig	VG?	$99.99	99-02
Heddon	Tadpolly	intro box	VGIB	$565.87	99-04
Heddon	Tadpolly	intro box EX	EXIB	$400.00	04-11
Heddon	Tadpolly	intro box VG+, shiner scale	EXIB	$467.00	04-03
Heddon	Tadpolly	intro box EX-, shiner scale	NIB	$488.00	04-03
Heddon	Tadpolly	RB, intro box, pointers	VG+	$650.00	99-03
Heddon	Tadpolly	RB, small belly chip at hook, nice	VG+	$81.25	00-04
Heddon	Tadpolly	red scale, intro box	EXIB	$600.00	99-04
Heddon	Tadpolly	RET, intro box avg	EX-IB	$251.00	03-02
Heddon	Tadpolly	saltwater (white/flitter), 5000 size	EX	$238.00	03-11
Heddon	Tadpolly	shiner scale, GE	EX+	$462.50	00-02
Heddon	Tadpolly	shiner scale, GE, age lines	EX+	$182.00	02-09
Heddon	Tadpolly	spotted	avg	$42.76	99-07
Heddon	Tadpolly	strawberry, 5000, toilet, GE	EX+	$466.00	05-07
Heddon	Tadpolly	strawberry, GE, decent used	G+	$57.00	03-02

BRAND	MODEL	SERIES / MFG. CODE / DESCRIPTION	GRADE	PRICE	DATE yy/mm
Heddon	Tadpolly	white, GE	VG-	$53.00	99-03
Heddon	Tadpolly	white, GE	VG-	$74.00	99-01
Heddon	Tadpolly	white/flitter, GE	VG+	$82.00	01-10
Heddon	Tadpolly	white/red eye, L-rig	VG	$75.00	99-01
Heddon	Tadpolly 5000	5009D	EXIB	$290.00	00-02
Heddon	Tadpolly 5000	blk head/yellow, bad varnish, rest OK	VG	$390.00	00-03
Heddon	Tadpolly 5000	blk head/yellow, crackleback, 2 diff	EX-	$579.00	99-04
Heddon	Tadpolly 5000	crab, L-rig	EX-	$158.49	00-01
Heddon	Tadpolly 5000	crackle, varnish, L-rig	EX-	$150.00	99-08
Heddon	Tadpolly 5000	green scale, L-rig, beauty	EX+	$500.00	99-01
Heddon	Tadpolly 5000	nice, Down Bass	EXIB	$510.50	00-02
Heddon	Tadpolly 5000	rainbow	EX-	$320.75	99-03
Heddon	Tadpolly 5000	red head blended	EX+	$312.00	02-03
Heddon	Tadpolly 5000	strawberry, L, bell plate, lt age lines, SOLD	EX+	$450.00	99-12
Heddon	Tadpolly 5000	strawberry, 2pc	EX-	$256.00	00-07
Heddon	Tadpolly 5000	y/black back stripe, NOT MET	VG+	$291.95	99-12
Heddon	Tadpolly 6000	crackle, L-rig	VG+	$150.00	99-08
Heddon	Tadpolly 6000	frog, decent	VG	$93.00	01-01
Heddon	Tadpolly 6000	goldfish scale, L-rig	EX-	$448.99	00-02
Heddon	Tadpolly 6000	green scale, huge chips	fair	$28.76	99-01
Heddon	Tadpolly 6000	green scale, L-rig	EX-	$250.00	99-08
Heddon	Tadpolly 6000	red scale	VG	$208.00	00-06
Heddon	Tadpolly 6000	white/flitter, SOLD	EX	$700.00	99-12
Heddon	Tadpolly Baby	green scale, ugly belly varnish, NOT MET	EX-	$91.00	02-03
Heddon	Tadpolly Baby	red scale, intro box	EX-IB	$560.00	99-05
Heddon	Tadpolly Runt	5109D, green scale, TS-hdwr, GE, dark bleed through on most of the bait	FAIR	$95.00	05-05
Heddon	Tadpolly Runt	SB, GE, NOT MET	VG+	$536.00	00-01
Heddon	Tadpolly Spook	½ oz., PEPSI	EX	$86.00	99-08
Heddon	Tadpolly Spook	9000FYR-BB	NIB	$12.20	05-07
Heddon	Tadpolly Spook	9000XBW, black shore, GPE, NSOB, early narrow lip, very light wear	EX-	$15.00	05-04
Heddon	Tadpolly Spook	9000XRS, silver shore, GPE, SR, in orig Up Bass Banner 2PCCB	EXIB	$40.00	05-04
Heddon	Tadpolly Spook	9000XRY, yellow shore, GPE, NSOF, hint of wear	EX+	$15.00	05-04
Heddon	Tadpolly Spook	9000FYR, Tadpolly, MO, Fire Herring	EX+	$323.00	05-06
Heddon	Tadpolly Spook	9000RH, MO, white with red head, in diamond box E	EXIB	$20.00	05-06
Heddon	Tadpolly Spook	9000RH, SR, white with red head, gold eye	EX+	$20.00	05-06
Heddon	Tadpolly Spook	clear, no Heddon markings	EX	$10.00	05-06
Heddon	Tadpolly Spook	9000YB, Coho	NIB	$18.00	05-03
Heddon	Tadpolly Spook	MO, Golden Bay Shiner, new in 1980	EX	$35.00	05-06
Heddon	Tadpolly Spook	MO, yellow florescent, red ribs	EX+	$25.00	05-06
Heddon	Tadpolly Spook	MO, flourescent black spot	EX	$20.00	05-06
Heddon	Tadpolly Spook	MO, Glo-Tadpolly Pink Alewife	EX+	$25.00	05-06
Heddon	Tadpolly Spook	MO, Sea Pearl	EX+	$40.00	05-06
Heddon	Tadpolly Spook	orange spot	EX	$6.30	05-07
Heddon	Tadpolly Spook	Pepsi ad logo, green/black triangle, PTCB dented	NIB	$54.00	05-07

BRAND	MODEL	SERIES / MFG. CODE / DESCRIPTION	GRADE	PRICE	DATE yy/mm
Heddon	Tadpolly Spook	r/w, Banner 2PCCB	NIB	$27.88	99-02
Heddon	Tadpolly Spook	red bullfrog	NIB	$21.50	99-02
Heddon	Tadpolly Spook	SR, green scale, gold eye, marked "2nd"	EX+	$18.00	05-06
Heddon	Tadpolly Spook	SR, silver flitter, red head, gold eye	EX+	$18.00	05-06
Heddon	Tadpolly Spook	SR, yellow shore, minnow, gold eye	EX+	$12.00	05-06
Heddon	Tadpolly Spook	SR, black with white eyes	EX+	$25.00	05-06
Heddon	Tadpolly Spook	SR/Bell, perch, yellow belly, gold eye	EX+	$18.00	05-06
Heddon	Tadpolly Spook	XBW, gold eyes, Banner bx EX	NIB	$29.00	05-02
Heddon	Tadpolly Spook Magnum	9000GRS, green scale, GPE, SR, few light pointers	EX-	$15.00	05-04
Heddon	Tadpolly Spook Magnum	9006HR, Herring, molded hdwr, little wear	VG+	$17.00	05-04
Heddon	Tadpolly Spook Magnum	9006NP, nickle plated in orig unopened 2PSTB with papers	NIB	$28.00	05-04
Heddon	Tiger	1010TG	NIB	$35.00	00-05
Heddon	Tiger	1020TG	NIB	$26.85	99-04
Heddon	Tiger	1020TG, 3¼"	EX	$12.45	99-04
Heddon	Tiger	1020XBW, green/blk, triangle card crisp	NOC	$79.00	05-07
Heddon	Tiger	1040GSCD, 5"	NIB	$191.00	00-02
Heddon	Tiger	1040PM	mint	$53.00	00-04
Heddon	Tiger	1040TG	NIB	$54.01	00-02
Heddon	Tiger	1040TG, opaque tiger color	NIB	$45.00	05-05
Heddon	Tiger	3 sizes	EX-	$81.00	99-03
Heddon	Tiger	3½", silver/black back	EX	$6.00	06-05
Heddon	Tiger	4", blk/gold	EX	$10.60	99-02
Heddon	Tiger	4", tiger	EX	$34.00	00-05
Heddon	Tiger	4½", clear/blk/gold insert	EX	$51.00	99-05
Heddon	Tiger	4¼", blk/silver	EX	$13.01	99-02
Heddon	Tiger	5", blue flash with flitter	EX	$41.01	99-02
Heddon	Tiger	5¼", clear/sparkles on back	EX	$338.00	00-04
Heddon	Tiger	CDF, but stripes	EX	$75.00	00-10
Heddon	Tiger	4¼", gold/stripes	VG	$11.00	99-02
Heddon	Tiger	large size, yellow/orange eye shadow, flitter	EX	$114.00	05-07
Heddon	Tiger	purple/silver reflector	NIB	$32.01	99-04
Heddon	Tiger x 2	1030Y, 1030GF	NIB	$56.01	99-05
Heddon	Tiny Clatter Tad	990LBL, blue Spook, blue scale, shad, new in orig 2PSTB	NIB	$30.00	05-04
Heddon	Tiny Crazy Crawler	320XRW, RH, white shore, plastic, gold PE	EX	$15.00	05-05
Heddon	Tiny Lucky 13	black/white	Mint	$28.50	05-07
Heddon	Tiny Runt	XBW	mint	$98.00	02-08
Heddon	Tiny Spook	310BGL	NIB	$143.00	01-05
Heddon	Tiny Spook	RH	EX	$66.00	00-02
Heddon	Tiny Spook	XBW	EX	$48.00	03-07
Heddon	Tiny Spook	XBW, gold eyes	EX	$71.00	05-07
Heddon	Tiny Spook	XRY	EX+	$81.00	99-09
Heddon	Tiny Tease	dace	EX	$395.00	03-01
Heddon	Tiny Tease	nat scale	VG+	$192.45	99-04
Heddon	Tiny Tease	perch	EX	$407.00	99-03
Heddon	Tiny Tease	RH, fly rod lure	VG	$35.00	05-06

BRAND	MODEL	SERIES / MFG. CODE / DESCRIPTION	GRADE	PRICE	DATE yy/mm
Heddon	Tiny Tease	RH/white, cup	EX-	$66.00	00-01
Heddon	Tiny Torpedo	0360VY, 8 BIDS	NIB	$46.59	00-03
Heddon	Tiny Torpedo	360X, PTCB, clear lure, gold eye, belly stencil nice!	NIB	$58.00	05-07
Heddon	Tiny Torpedo	black/gold foil, gold eye	mint	$41.50	99-04
Heddon	Tiny Torpedo	CD, black belly stencil, gold eyes	EX	$47.00	01-04
Heddon	Tiny Torpedo	weird blue/black color	EX	$11.00	99-01
Heddon	Top Kick	black, like Hi-Tail gold eyes	EX	$317.00	03-01
Heddon	Top Kick	yellow, white eyes, fake?	EX	$281.00	03-02
Heddon	Torpedo	120RET, Abbey & Imbrie props	VG+	$109.00	05-07
Heddon	Torpedo	122, Down nice	EXIB	$250.00	01-09
Heddon	Torpedo	129D, L	EX-	$275.00	99-10
Heddon	Torpedo	130L, Banner bx crisp & paper, PE, perch scale	NIB	$69.00	05-07
Heddon	Torpedo	130L, shiner scale, PE, cat	NIB	$66.00	99-05
Heddon	Torpedo	130P, Banner, PE, cat	NIB	$124.00	01-10
Heddon	Torpedo	130XWB, Banner box	EX-IB	$41.00	04-11
Heddon	Torpedo	139Z, rainbow scale, GE, TS-rig, light age lines and 2 tiny pointers	EX	$410.00	05-05
Heddon	Torpedo	30RHF, Banner bx, PE	NIB	$85.00	02-12
Heddon	Torpedo	4", RET, GE, 2pc	EX	$192.00	04-12
Heddon	Torpedo	blue scale, Up Bass VG, tail chip	NIB	$1,400.00	00-05
Heddon	Torpedo	dace, Brush 139M(WRG) EX-	EXIB	$375.00	99-10
Heddon	Torpedo	green scale, L-rig	EX	$301.00	02-02
Heddon	Torpedo	rainbow scale, GE, 2pc, mint but POBW	EX	$343.00	02-12
Heddon	Torpedo	rainbow, painted eye	mint	$51.00	02-07
Heddon	Torpedo	Stanley, cup rig, pikie scale, GE	mint	$650.00	00-03
Heddon	Torpedo	w/blk ribs, GE, no props	EX	$250.00	99-09
Heddon	Torpedo	XWB, GE, POBW	EX-	$150.00	99-08
Heddon	Torpedo	yellow/silver flakes	EX-	$480.00	98-12
Heddon	Torpedo	122	EX	$250.00	99-10
Heddon	Torpedo	blue scale, GE, marked props	EX	$535.00	01-03
Heddon	Torpedo 120	green scale	mint	$650.00	00-05
Heddon	Torpedo 120	M, Stanley props	mint	$480.00	01-03
Heddon	Torpedo 120	M, Stanley props, NOT MET	EX-	$178.50	99-05
Heddon	Torpedo 120	RET, GE, age lines	VG+	$53.00	05-07
Heddon	Torpedo 120	shiner scale, L-rig, GE	EX	$129.00	05-07
Heddon	Torpedo 130	crackle, L-rig	EX	$1,200.00	01-07
Heddon	Torpedo 130	green scale nice	EX-	$126.51	00-01
Heddon	Torpedo 130	green scale, GE, nice	EX-	$238.15	99-02
Heddon	Torpedo 130	perch scale, 2pc	EX	$52.00	05-07
Heddon	Torpedo 130	pike scale, GE, toilet rig	EX	$223.00	01-05
Heddon	Torpedo 130	shiner scale, GE, L-rig	VG+	$45.00	04-12
Heddon	Torpedo 130?	green scale, GE, L-rig	EX	$202.50	99-05
Heddon	Torpedo Spook	green scale, 2pc, best I have ever seen	EX	$450.00	03-08
Heddon	Torpedo Spook	pike scale, tenite, no puckering, c. 1933	EX	$1,236.00	04-12
Heddon	Torpedo Tiny	22 different	EX+	$134.50	99-02
Heddon	Torpedo, Baby	RH flitter, 2pc, GE	EX	$405.00	03-08

BRAND	MODEL	SERIES / MFG. CODE / DESCRIPTION	GRADE	PRICE	DATE yy/mm
Heddon	Torpedo, Baby	orange, black ribs	mint	$152.00	04-11
Heddon	Triple Teazer	1000, yellow BT, yellow hair, gold-plated hdwr, 3 fish blades, full tail	EX	$65.00	05-05
Heddon	Trout Size Wilder Dilg	fancy pattern bait in new condition, correct Down Bass box, wowser	NIB	$330.00	05-04
Heddon	Ultra Sonic	325B, black, GPE, very light wear	EX-	$12.00	05-05
Heddon	Ultra Sonic	325RH, RH/w, WPE, new in early 2PPTB on insert card	NIB	$21.00	05-05
Heddon	Ultra Sonic	325, yellow, WPE	EX	$15.00	05-05
Heddon	Underwater Expert	#3, white, 2 BW, sm belly chips	VG++	$3,738.00	02-01
Heddon	Underwater Expert	white, 2 BW, huge/tiny props	VG	$1,725.00	00-10
Heddon	Underwater Expert	white, big front prop, big chip by one cup, c. 1904	avg	$750.00	05-02
Heddon	Underwater Expert	white, gold wash still on hardware	EX-	$3,001.00	02-02
Heddon	Unknown Saltwater	RH, NOT MET	EX	$677.00	04-02
Heddon	Vamp	7500M, Spook, PE, NOT MET	NIB	$77.50	99-05
Heddon	Vamp	7500PG, tack-on eyes, Banner	EX-IB	$223.00	01-03
Heddon	Vamp	7500RHF, plastic tack eye, PTCB	EXIB	$103.00	05-07
Heddon	Vamp	7500S, L-rig, Up Bass	EX-IB	$372.00	00-10
Heddon	Vamp	7502RET, GE, L-rig, Up Bass EX	NIB	$151.50	99-12
Heddon	Vamp	7502, red eyes and tail, GE, L-rig, few light age lines, looks almost new in G+ orig Up-Bass 2PCCB	EX+IB	$130.00	05-04
Heddon	Vamp	7502, GE, 2pc, Brush	NIB	$300.00	99-10
Heddon	Vamp	7509BB, Luny frog (dark green), GE, 2pc rig, few pointers and light wear	VG	$95.00	05-04
Heddon	Vamp	7509BB, Luny frog, GE, L-rig, few varn flakes and light wear	VG	$120.00	05-04
Heddon	Vamp	7509D, green scale, GE, turned-up, TS-hdwr, very light wear, comes with orig VG+ Up 2PCCB	EX-IB	$140.00	05-04
Heddon	Vamp	7509M, pikie scale, GE, L-rig, 1 pointer and light age lines, orig EX 1st Up Bass 2PCCB	EX+IB	$200.00	05-04
Heddon	Vamp	7509M, pikie scale, GE, L-rig, few small pntrs on back and light age lines, orig VG Up Bass 2PCCB	EX-IB	$110.00	05-04
Heddon	Vamp	7509R, brown nat scale, GE, L-rig, few tiny pntrs, 2 small flks on BW, orig 1st Up Bass 2PCCB	EX-IB	$170.00	05-04
Heddon	Vamp	7509D, Up nice, green scale	NIB	$197.00	01-05
Heddon	Vamp	7509M, Down Bass box EX, L-rig, & catalog	NIB	$560.00	05-06
Heddon	Vamp	7509M, Down Bass	NIB	$350.00	00-03
Heddon	Vamp	7509M, Down Bass, L-rig	EXIB	$325.00	99-04
Heddon	Vamp	7509M, GE, 2pc, Brush	EXIB	$200.00	99-10
Heddon	Vamp	7509M, Up Bass, L-rig	EXIB	$131.50	00-01
Heddon	Vamp	7509P, age lines	EX-	$100.00	99-10
Heddon	Vamp	7509P, L-rig, Up Bass	VG-IB	$79.01	99-06
Heddon	Vamp	7509PL, pearl, 2pc	VGIB	$191.38	99-05
Heddon	Vamp	7509R, Down Bass EX, L	NIB	$1,025.00	00-12
Heddon	Vamp	7509RET, Brush, 2pc	EX-IB	$170.27	00-01
Heddon	Vamp	8500M, Down, L-rig	NIB	$312.55	00-01
Heddon	Vamp	9502, Down Bass box	EX+IB	$205.00	99-01
Heddon	Vamp	blue scale	fair	$56.01	00-02
Heddon	Vamp	blue scale, Down Bass 7509X	EX-IB	$1,275.00	99-03

BRAND	MODEL	SERIES / MFG. CODE / DESCRIPTION	GRADE	PRICE	DATE yy/mm
Heddon	Vamp	blue scale, L-rig	VG+	$375.00	99-06
Heddon	Vamp	chartreuse CD, L-rig, GE	VG+	$305.00	03-01
Heddon	Vamp	crackle, L, red eye shadow, belly crack, nice	EX-/VG+	$405.00	01-11
Heddon	Vamp	crackle, plastic tack eye, "Original"	EX+	$150.00	01-07
Heddon	Vamp	crackleback, L-rig, red eye shadow	EX	$455.00	05-03
Heddon	Vamp	dace, 2pc, GE	VG+	$176.00	01-03
Heddon	Vamp	frog scale, L-rig	VG-	$128.50	00-02
Heddon	Vamp	frog spot, full paint but ugly age lines, L-rig, GE	VG-	$116.00	05-07
Heddon	Vamp	frog, L-rig	VG+	$353.00	01-05
Heddon	Vamp	frog scale	EX+	$875.00	00-05
Heddon	Vamp	frog scale, GE	EX-	$525.00	99-01
Heddon	Vamp	frog scale, L-rig, beauty	EX	$1,425.00	00-07
Heddon	Vamp	frog spot, L-rig	EX-	$284.00	02-08
Heddon	Vamp	GE, green scale, sm nose chip	VG	$35.00	99-01
Heddon	Vamp	GE, rainbow	EX-	$74.79	98-12
Heddon	Vamp	green head/y (BH/w yellowed?), GE, L-rig	EX-	$1,275.00	00-04
Heddon	Vamp	green pike scale, 2pc	EX+	$175.00	99-08
Heddon	Vamp	green scale with red head, L-rigged	EX	$220.00	05-07
Heddon	Vamp	green scale, GE	VG-	$60.00	99-01
Heddon	Vamp	green scale, GE, 2pc	EX	$117.00	01-02
Heddon	Vamp	green scale, L-rig, purty	EX	$63.00	02-03
Heddon	Vamp	green scale, L-rig	EX	$122.49	99-05
Heddon	Vamp	Luny frog, GE, L-rig	mint	$1,313.00	99-04
Heddon	Vamp	Luny frog, L-rig, NOT MET	VG-	$88.75	99-08
Heddon	Vamp	Luny frog, L	VG-	$201.00	01-03
Heddon	Vamp	M in Down Bass, p catalog!	EX-IB	$255.00	99-05
Heddon	Vamp	M, L-rig	EX	$93.00	00-05
Heddon	Vamp	nat scale, L-rig	EX-	$139.00	00-05
Heddon	Vamp	natural scale, L-rig	EX	$187.00	00-08
Heddon	Vamp	orange/black spots, GE, L-rig	EX	$1,975.00	01-04
Heddon	Vamp	orange/blk dots	EX-	$306.00	02-10
Heddon	Vamp	orange/blk spots, hdwr corroded, un Down box	EX-	$907.50	99-07
Heddon	Vamp	P, L-rig, Up Bass nice	NIB	$325.00	01-10
Heddon	Vamp	P, GE, S-rig odd, Banner box	NIB	$193.05	00-02
Heddon	Vamp	PAS, GE, 2pc, decent	VG	$31.00	00-10
Heddon	Vamp	perch, PE, jointed, Banner box	EX-	$32.00	99-01
Heddon	Vamp	pike scale, GE, 2pc	EX-	$60.00	05-07
Heddon	Vamp	pike scale, L	EX-	$78.77	00-03
Heddon	Vamp	pike scale, L	EX	$142.50	00-03
Heddon	Vamp	pike scale, PE	EX+	$21.50	99-01
Heddon	Vamp	pike, GE, Down Bass end miss	VGIB	$72.00	99-02
Heddon	Vamp	pike scale, L-rig	EX	$104.00	00-11
Heddon	Vamp	PRH, L-rig	VG+	$170.27	00-01
Heddon	Vamp	rainbow scale, L-rigged	EX	$440.00	05-07
Heddon	Vamp	rainbow, L-rig, GE	VG+	$61.00	05-07
Heddon	Vamp	RB, round nose, age lines	VG	$450.00	00-09
Heddon	Vamp	RB, tack-on eyes, S-rig	EX	$53.00	01-03
Heddon	Vamp	RB, GE, jointed, nose chip	G	$28.00	99-01

BRAND	MODEL	SERIES / MFG. CODE / DESCRIPTION	GRADE	PRICE	DATE yy/mm
Heddon	Vamp	RB, L-rig, Up Bass EX	EX-IB	$182.50	99-12
Heddon	Vamp	RB, TE	EX	$41.00	99-08
Heddon	Vamp	red/frog spot, GE, 2pc, NOT MET	VG-	$201.00	99-05
Heddon	Vamp	RH/flitter	EX+	$305.00	99-03
Heddon	Vamp	RH/flitter, L-rig, GE	VG+	$60.00	05-07
Heddon	Vamp	RH/flitter, L-rig	EX	$229.00	00-05
Heddon	Vamp	RH/Luny frog, toilet, NOT MET	EX	$699.00	00-10
Heddon	Vamp	RHF, GE, 2pc	EX-	$112.50	99-09
Heddon	Vamp	round nose, RB, L-rig	EX-	$888.00	00-10
Heddon	Vamp	round nose, Zara body, RB, GE, L-rig	VG+	$1,000.00	00-02
Heddon	Vamp	SB, PE	NOC	$56.00	00-09
Heddon	Vamp	strawberry, GE, surface rig!	EX	$76.00	03-01
Heddon	Vamp	strawberry, L-rig nice	EX	$99.00	00-11
Heddon	Vamp	strawberry, L-rig, GE	EX	$72.00	05-07
Heddon	Vamp	strawberry, 2pc, GE, hvy checking	VG	$50.00	00-02
Heddon	Vamp	strawberry, GE	EX	$79.99	99-08
Heddon	Vamp	strawberry, GE	EX-	$142.50	00-03
Heddon	Vamp	strawberry, PE	EX	$33.50	99-06
Heddon	Vamp	Vampire, L-rig, green scale, GE	EX	$154.00	02-03
Heddon	Vamp + Flaptail	both RH with PE	EX+	$76.00	99-10
Heddon	Vamp Kingfisher Spook	KF9759YBS, Brush (+$500)	NIB	$1,500.00	01-01
Heddon	Vamp Kingfisher Spook	KF9752 box, strawberry, metal banded	EXIB	$711.00	04-02
Heddon	Vamp Spook	7000M, Banner box	NIB	$53.50	99-01
Heddon	Vamp Spook	9509P, GE, hangtag, Up Bass EX+	NIB	$430.00	99-07
Heddon	Vamp Spook	9750F, frog color, gold eyes, PTCB EX	NIB	$55.00	05-07
Heddon	Vamp Spook	9750L, perch w/box, box with no identifying numbers	VG+	$35.29	05-07
Heddon	Vamp Spook	9750M, pikie w/box	VG+	$36.65	05-07
Heddon	Vamp Spook	9750M, pikie w/box	EX	$31.31	05-07
Heddon	Vamp Spook	9750M, window box EX, clear plastic lip	NIB	$68.00	05-07
Heddon	Vamp Spook	9750M, window box, clear plastic lip	NIB	$63.00	05-07
Heddon	Vamp Spook	9750L, Banner box, Navy stock numbers	NIB	$84.00	99-04
Heddon	Vamp Spook	9750R, Banner box EX, gold eye, S-rig	NIB	$67.00	05-07
Heddon	Vamp Spook	9750RHF, Banner box	NIB	$109.50	99-01
Heddon	Vamp Spook	9750XRY, molded plastic lip, new	NIB	$101.00	99-03
Heddon	Vamp Spook	9759GW, Flesh box poor, NOT MET	EXIB	$264.00	02-03
Heddon	Vamp Spook	9759L, GE, perch, TS-hdwr box E-, with paper	VGIB	$55.00	05-06
Heddon	Vamp Spook	Brush bx 9759M, glass eyes, bar rig badly puckered	poorIB	$105.00	05-07
Heddon	Vamp Spook	FFBSF, no lip surface, Vamp, gold eyes	EX+	$172.00	03-07
Heddon	Vamp Spook	frog, vertical center mold, fake?	EX	$250.00	00-07
Heddon	Vamp Spook	GE, RH	VG	$72.50	98-12
Heddon	Vamp Spook	GE, shiner scale	EX	$128.00	00-08
Heddon	Vamp Spook	GE, shiner scale, NOT MET	EXIB	$230.00	00-12
Heddon	Vamp Spook	glass eyes, RET, Fish Flesh box	EXIB	$222.59	99-08
Heddon	Vamp Spook	glowworm, decent	VG+	$115.00	02-08
Heddon	Vamp Spook	gold PE, black shore, SR	EX+	$75.00	05-06
Heddon	Vamp Spook	M, navy numbers on box	NIB	$150.00	99-06

BRAND	MODEL	SERIES / MFG. CODE / DESCRIPTION	GRADE	PRICE	DATE yy/mm
Heddon	Vamp Spook	pearl? with silver scale, white eyes	EX	$241.00	02-03
Heddon	Vamp Spook	pike scale, gold eye	EX-	$17.50	99-02
Heddon	Vamp Spook	RB, gold eye, wrong box	EX	$88.59	99-06
Heddon	Vamp Spook	red/silver flitter inside	EX	$102.50	99-09
Heddon	Vamp Spook	RET, GE, hook drag but nice	VG+	$51.00	00-04
Heddon	Vamp Spook	RH, in VG Banner box	NIB	$52.01	99-02
Heddon	Vamp Spook	RH/brown middle/white tail/gold eyes	EX	$285.00	03-05
Heddon	Vamp Spook	RHF, GE, Up Bass, NOT MET	EXIB	$136.00	01-03
Heddon	Vamp Spook	strawberry, gold eye	EX	$66.00	00-04
Heddon	Vamp Spook	strawberry, plastic lip	EX	$67.00	04-01
Heddon	Vamp Spook	strawberry, plastic lip, PE, surface, NOT MET	EX	$71.00	00-07
Heddon	Vamp Spook	XBW, clear plastic lip, NOT MET	mint	$86.00	03-12
Heddon	Vamp Spook	XBW, clear plastic lip, painted eye	EX	$152.00	04-08
Heddon	Vamp Spook	XBW, gold eyes	EX	$69.00	99-02
Heddon	Vamp Spook	XRB, gold eyes	VG+	$96.55	99-10
Heddon	Vamp Spook	XRW, gold eye, 2pc	mint	$46.00	00-04
Heddon	Vamp Spook	XRY Banner, gold eye	NIB	$33.00	00-09
Heddon	Vamp Spook, jntd	7309M, pike scale, GE, TS-hdwr, 2 tiny age lines on nose, gold scales turning green	EX	$95.00	05-05
Heddon	Vamp Spook, jntd	9XRK	EX	$343.00	02-07
Heddon	Vamp Spook, jntd	9XRW, 2pc, a beauty	EX	$137.00	02-08
Heddon	Vamp Spook, jntd	green scale, GE, metal lip, wrong box	EX	$305.00	00-11
Heddon	Vamp Spook, jntd	natural scale	EX-	$60.00	99-11
Heddon	Vamp Spook, jntd	XRG, 2pc	EX-	$128.05	99-09
Heddon	Vamp, Baby	7400S, Down Bass bx EX, no hooks	NIB	$395.00	03-05
Heddon	Vamp, Baby	7400S, GE, white with small black & red spots, 2pc, POBW	EX-	$135.00	05-06
Heddon	Vamp, Baby	7409D, Down Bass crisp, L-rig	NIB	$365.00	02-02
Heddon	Vamp, Baby	7409M, Down Bass, L-rig	EX-IB	$196.00	00-09
Heddon	Vamp, Baby	7409M, GE, pike scale in correct marked box (VG+), L-rig	EXIB	$135.00	05-06
Heddon	Vamp, Baby	7409M, sharp Down Bass, L-rig	EXIB	$238.04	99-09
Heddon	Vamp, Baby	Allen Stripey, chips, NOT MET	G	$68.00	00-06
Heddon	Vamp, Baby	crackle, 2pc, POBW	EX-	$931.00	01-03
Heddon	Vamp, Baby	frog scale, GE, L-rig	EX-	$265.00	01-01
Heddon	Vamp, Baby	frog spot, L-rig, ring on BW	EX	$277.00	02-11
Heddon	Vamp, Baby	frog, GE, L-rig, Down Bass, paper	NIB	$1,525.00	99-05
Heddon	Vamp, Baby	frog scale	EX	$500.00	03-04
Heddon	Vamp, Baby	goldfish scale, L-rig	EX-	$405.00	01-03
Heddon	Vamp, Baby	P, GE, L-rig, Down Bass + cat	NIB	$284.00	00-09
Heddon	Vamp, Baby	RET, GE, 2-pc, no lip	VG+	$305.00	05-01
Heddon	Vamp, Baby	RET, L-rig	EX	$160.00	00-04
Heddon	Vamp, Baby	RET, L-rig	mint	$180.50	99-05
Heddon	Vamp, Baby	RH/white, silver flakes	VG	$95.00	98-12
Heddon	Vamp, Baby	w/r eyes and tail, repaint?	mint	$156.03	99-03
Heddon	Vamp, Baby	7409R, small nick at tail, few tiny pointers, L-rig, bx rough	EXIB	$104.50	05-04
Heddon	Vamp, Baby, surface	SS, GE, 2pc, NOT MET	EX-	$76.00	00-08
Heddon	Vamp, Giant	7550PAS	EX-IB	$200.00	99-10

BRAND	MODEL	SERIES / MFG. CODE / DESCRIPTION	GRADE	PRICE	DATE yy/mm
Heddon	Vamp, Giant	green scale, 8", L-rig, ugly varnish by eyes	VG+??	$584.00	03-01
Heddon	Vamp, Giant	shiner scale, Brush box, GE	NIB	$227.00	04-12
Heddon	Vamp, Giant jntd	7350RHT, PE, Banner	NIB	$100.00	99-08
Heddon	Vamp, Giant jntd	7352, GE, Brush	NIB	$179.25	99-06
Heddon	Vamp, Giant jntd	7359 PAS	EXIB	$141.00	00-05
Heddon	Vamp, Giant jntd	7359PAS, Brush box	EXIB	$227.50	99-07
Heddon	Vamp, Giant jntd	Brush box, #7352, GE	NIB	$227.00	00-10
Heddon	Vamp, Giant jntd	PAS, GE, toilet seat	EX	$133.00	04-03
Heddon	Vamp, Giant jntd	pike scale, GE, L-rig, Up Bass 7359M rough	avgIB	$114.00	04-11
Heddon	Vamp, Giant jntd	RET, GE, Brush lg, box, cat	NIB	$292.00	00-10
Heddon	Vamp, Giant jntd	shiner scale, PE, Banner	NIB	$122.50	99-05
Heddon	Vamp, Giant jntd	7350PAS, hook drag, surface rig	VGIB	$41.00	04-08
Heddon	Vamp, Giant jntd	7352, white/RH and tail, TS, GE huge	EX+IB	$250.00	05-04
Heddon	Vamp, Giant jntd	r/w, GE, Brush box rough	NIB	$163.11	99-04
Heddon	Vamp, Great	natural scale, 6", toilet seat hdwr	EX-	$242.00	04-01
Heddon	Vamp, Great	PAS, GE, toilet	EX+	$578.88	99-05
Heddon	Vamp, Great	strawberry, GE, toilet	EX-	$423.88	99-05
Heddon	Vamp, Jointed	7300RET, L-rig	EX	$152.00	00-04
Heddon	Vamp, Jointed	7309L, L rig, nice Up Bass box	NIB	$255.00	99-12
Heddon	Vamp, Jointed	7309P, Brush, L-rig	EXIB	$162.50	00-03
Heddon	Vamp, Jointed	7309PRH, 2pc, GE	NIB	$566.00	03-01
Heddon	Vamp, Jointed	7309S Brush bx, 2pc, strawberry	NIB	$239.00	02-11
Heddon	Vamp, Jointed	7359M, lg red border Up Bass	NIB	$265.01	99-11
Heddon	Vamp, Jointed	7509D, NOT MET	EXIB	$118.49	00-03
Heddon	Vamp, Jointed	Brush bx (EX) 7350PAS, 2pc, GE	NIB	$150.00	04-03
Heddon	Vamp, Jointed	Brush, cat	NIB	$445.00	01-02
Heddon	Vamp, Jointed	crackleback, L-rig, GE	avg	$90.00	99-05
Heddon	Vamp, Jointed	green scale, Brush	EXIB	$247.50	00-01
Heddon	Vamp, Jointed	green scale, GE, Brush	NIB	$325.00	99-11
Heddon	Vamp, Jointed	nat pike?	?	$19.73	99-05
Heddon	Vamp, Jointed	nat scale, GE, L-rig nice	EX	$179.00	00-11
Heddon	Vamp, Jointed	pike scale, GE, L-rig	VG	$38.00	04-07
Heddon	Vamp, Jointed	rainbow? or rainbow scale, 2pc	EX	$251.00	03-07
Heddon	Vamp, Jointed	red tail, GE	rough	$21.00	99-02
Heddon	Vamp, Jointed	XRY, PE, wood	EX	$26.56	00-03
Heddon	Vamp, Musky	6", 7550S Brush VG+, toilet seat	EXIB	$457.00	00-07
Heddon	Vamp, Musky	6", GE, natural scale finish, box No. 7559R VG	EX	$71.50	04-11
Heddon	Vamp, Musky	6", shad, GE, red gills	VG+	$207.00	02-06
Heddon	Vamp, Musky	6", white spotted, bad hook drags, GE, toilet seat	avg	$76.00	04-02
Heddon	Vamp, Musky	6", 9550RH, toilet seat, GE	NIB	$382.00	05-05
Heddon	Vamp, Musky	6", frog, GE	VG+	$2,550.00	00-02
Heddon	Vamp, Musky	6", pike scale, $595 NOT MET	EX	$370.00	02-05
Heddon	Vamp, Musky	6", L-rig, pike scale	EX	$357.50	05-07
Heddon	Vamp, Musky	7550S, Up Bass VG-, L-rig nice	EXIB	$600.00	02-08
Heddon	Vamp, Musky	7559M, Up Bass rough, hvy L-rig	NIB	$718.00	00-11
Heddon	Vamp, Musky	7559R, Brush, "Great Vamp," toilet seat NOT MET	NIB	$382.00	02-02
Heddon	Vamp, Musky	7600- 8" M, L-rig, all paint gone forehead	?	$56.00	00-09
Heddon	Vamp, Musky	7600P, Down avg, hook drag, L, NOT MET!	EX-IB	$2,235.00	00-12

BRAND	MODEL	SERIES / MFG. CODE / DESCRIPTION	GRADE	PRICE	DATE yy/mm
Heddon	Vamp, Musky	8", shiner scale, 2 big chips	G	$261.00	99-08
Heddon	Vamp, Musky	8", green scale, varnish flakes	VG	$925.00	00-05
Heddon	Vamp, Musky	8", nice Down Bass box, asking price	EX-IB	$2,400.00	02-08
Heddon	Vamp, Musky	8", pike scale, L-rig, beauty	EX	$887.00	04-02
Heddon	Vamp, Musky	8", pike scale nice	EX-	$710.00	02-03
Heddon	Vamp, Musky	8", GE, nice Down Bass box 7609M, L-rigs	EX-IB	$2,285.00	02-09
Heddon	Vamp, Musky	Down Bass 7609M, L-rig, new seller	NIB	$2,902.00	03-08
Heddon	Vamp, Musky	frog spot, 8", L-rig, great tight age lines, GE	EX	$4,805.00	05-07
Heddon	Vamp, Musky	goldfish scale, 6", rough but not awful, min $190, NO BIDS	VG-	$190.00	05-07
Heddon	Vamp, Musky	green scale, hvy L-rig, 6", used but not awful	VG-	$51.00	05-07
Heddon	Vamp, Musky	nat scale, 6", NOT MET	VG+	$202.00	01-04
Heddon	Vamp, Musky	pike scale, 6", NOT MET	EX+	$430.00	01-04
Heddon	Vamp, Musky	shiner scale, 8", GE, L-rig, NOT MET	VG+	$503.00	02-08
Heddon	Vamp, Musky	8", pike scale	EX-	$605.00	05-07
Heddon	Vamp, Musky jntd	7", nat scale, GE, L-rig	EX-	$164.50	99-07
Heddon	Vamp, Musky jntd	7258M, Fish Flesh bx, zinc eyes! L-rig	NIB	$1,136.00	02-12
Heddon	Vamp, Musky jntd	7352, GE, Brush	NIB	$227.00	00-10
Heddon	Vamp, Musky jntd	7352RH, GE, 2pc, Brush	NIB	$247.27	99-10
Heddon	Vamp, Musky jntd	7359PAS, Brush bx, toilet seat	NIB	$391.00	02-11
Heddon	Vamp, Musky jntd	jointed Musky Vamp in Allen Stripey, with box 7550 Banner, GE ?	EXIB	$132.00	05-07
Heddon	Vamp, Round Nose	rainbow	EX	$1,900.00	01-04
Heddon	Vamp, jntd	9732, red eyes and tail, 2pc rig, GPE, very light wear in orig long Brush 2PCCB	EXIB	$85.00	05-04
Heddon	Vampire	7502, red eyes and tail, L-rig in lip, GE, few tiny varn pntrs, light age crack on BW	EX-	$65.00	05-05
Heddon	Vampire	7509M, Down Bass	EXIB	$182.50	99-05
Heddon	Vampire	crackleback, L-rigged	EX	$440.00	05-07
Heddon	Vampire	GE, orange with black spots, L-rig	EX	$445.00	05-06
Heddon	Vampire	goldfish scale, NOT MET	VG+	$168.00	03-01
Heddon	Vampire	M, real nice	EX	$87.00	00-10
Heddon	Vampire	perch scale, L-rig	EX-	$102.50	00-01
Heddon	Vampire	pike scale, L-rig	EX	$92.00	02-08
Heddon	Vampire	pike scale, nice	EX-	$83.00	00-02
Heddon	Vampire	strawberry	EX-	$99.00	00-04
Heddon	Vampire, Musky	7600, nat scale, GE, L-rig, 8"	avg	$360.00	99-12
Heddon	Vampire, Musky	pike scale, 8", GE, corr metal, nice	EX-	$769.99	99-11
Heddon	Vampire, Musky	spotted, bite marks	VG-	$105.38	98-12
Heddon	Walton Feather Tail	42, blush eye, ROBW	EX-	$250.00	99-10
Heddon	Walton Feather Tail	49G, black	EX+	$275.00	99-10
Heddon	Walton Feather Tail	black, NOT MET	EX	$217.00	00-08
Heddon	Walton Feather Tail	GE, red/white	EX	$154.00	04-11
Heddon	Walton Feather Tail	M, GE, nice	EX	$150.00	00-05
Heddon	Walton Feather Tail	pike scale, NOT MET	EX	$59.00	00-05
Heddon	Walton Feather Tail	r/w	VG	$86.00	99-01
Heddon	Walton Feather Tail	r/w, tail dirty but full, tiny flk at nose and light age lines, orig EX- Down Bass box	EX-IB	$250.00	05-05
Heddon	Walton Feather Tail	RB, GE, gleamer	EX-	$364.00	00-01

BRAND	MODEL	SERIES / MFG. CODE / DESCRIPTION	GRADE	PRICE	DATE yy/mm
Heddon	Wee Tad	590BRS	NIB	$260.00	01-09
Heddon	Wee Willie	strawberry, GE	VG+	$305.00	99-11
Heddon	Wee Willie	white/flitter, cup rigged, un Up Bass box VG-	NIB	$425.00	01-11
Heddon	Wee Willie	YH/white, flitter, Brush, GE	NIB	$500.00	01-03
Heddon	Weedless Widow	220XRY, yellow shore, 2pc, POBW, varnish flkd and yellowed	G+	$77.00	05-05
Heddon	Weedless Widow	222, RH/w, NE, TS-hdwr, NSOB, new in orig 2PCCB	NIB	$175.00	05-05
Heddon	Weedless Widow	222, POBW, Brush, NO BIDS	NIB	$49.99	99-06
Heddon	Weedless Widow	229BB, Meadow Frog, PE, single hk, NSOB, very minor varn wear but hair tail is short	EX-	$66.00	05-05
Heddon	Weedless Widow	BWH, white wings, Crazy Crawler color!	EX-	$306.00	03-05
Heddon	Weedless Widow	green scale, no eyes	EX-	$52.00	99-06
Heddon	Weedless Widow	y/sparkles	EX	$54.00	00-09
Heddon	Westchester Bug	green	EX	$686.00	02-08
Heddon	Widget	300BF, window box, on card	NIB	$177.00	00-02
Heddon	Widget	BF	EX+	$50.00	01-03
Heddon	Widget	black/spotted, NOT MET	EX	$71.01	99-08
Heddon	Widget	mouse	VG+	$64.55	99-11
Heddon	Widget	mouse	EX	$124.72	99-05
Heddon	Widget	perch scale, red window box	NIB	$143.00	00-07
Heddon	Widget	perch scale, NOT MET	EX-	$52.00	00-04
Heddon	Widget	RH SS	EX	$66.00	01-10
Heddon	Widget	silver/red & black spots	mint	$75.00	99-08
Heddon	Widgets x 9	9 different, nice	EX-, EX	$310.00	99-11
Heddon	Wiggle King	frog spot, belly decal	AVG	$88.99	05-07
Heddon	Wiggle King	M, un Down Bass, no eyes, belly stencil	VG-	$285.00	00-11
Heddon	Wiggle King	red scale, PE? cup	EX-	$406.00	00-05
Heddon	Wiggle King	RH	VG+	$63.00	06-05
Heddon	Wiggle King	RH, belly decal, ugly varnish	avg	$75.00	99-11
Heddon	Wiggle King	shiner scale	NIB	$2,000.00	00-04
Heddon	Wiggle King	strawberry, intro slant head, SOLD	VG+	$750.00	00-05
Heddon	Wiggle King 2000	r/w blended	VG	$127.50	99-11
Heddon	Wilder Dilg	#10, Down Bass bx, on card, Brann's Glory, NOT MET	NIB	$222.00	03-12
Heddon	Wilder Dilg	#10, on card, window box	NIB	$141.00	03-04
Heddon	Wilder Dilg	#12, Up Bass, Bob Davis card	NIB	$433.00	02-01
Heddon	Wilder Dilg	#12, yellow, Down Bass box	EXIB	$113.02	99-03
Heddon	Wilder Dilg	#30, Down Bass, red	NIB	$431.00	00-03
Heddon	Wilder Dilg	#4, Kemper's Charge, box EX	EXIB	$812.00	00-08
Heddon	Wilder Dilg	#56, Chadwick's Sunbeam, fly rod, NOT MET	mint	$43.00	01-01
Heddon	Wilder Dilg	#6, bass size, Down Bass, card	NIB	$861.00	00-08
Heddon	Wilder Dilg	#6, in pic box rough	EXIB	$87.05	00-02
Heddon	Wilder Dilg	#6, Wilder's fancy, great box	NIB	$1,002.00	00-08
Heddon	Wilder Dilg	#7, Up Bass crisp	NIB	$225.00	00-02
Heddon	Wilder Dilg	#8, Zane Gray, picture box, card	EXIB	$271.05	99-03
Heddon	Wilder Dilg	bass size, Pete's Choice, No. 7 Down Bass EX	NIB	$325.00	04-12

BRAND	MODEL	SERIES / MFG. CODE / DESCRIPTION	GRADE	PRICE	DATE yy/mm
Heddon	Wilder Dilg	Bob Davis #12, yellow w/yellow hackle and feathers, in Down Bass box VG+, on a marked card that is stamped	EX-IB	$125.00	05-06
Heddon	Wilder Dilg	Bob Davis pic box VG, NOT MET	EXIB	$177.50	00-01
Heddon	Wilder Dilg	Bob Davis pic box VG+	NIB	$277.99	00-01
Heddon	Wilder Dilg	Brann's Glory No. 10, in picture box VG++, some bleeding	EXIB	$290.00	05-06
Heddon	Wilder Dilg	Brann's Glory, pic box rough, papers	NIB	$138.55	00-02
Heddon	Wilder Dilg	Down Bass "bass size" EX, red lure	EX-IB	$52.00	04-11
Heddon	Wilder Dilg	Down Bass box crisp	NIB	$255.00	99-09
Heddon	Wilder Dilg	Down Bass unmarked VG+, NOT MET	NIB	$85.00	02-06
Heddon	Wilder Dilg	Down Bass, trout #33, card, NOT MET	NOB	$237.00	01-10
Heddon	Wilder Dilg	fancy black head, orange & black hackle	VG+	$35.00	05-06
Heddon	Wilder Dilg	intro box	NIB	$356.50	99-04
Heddon	Wilder Dilg	Irving Cobb pic box EX-	NIB	$627.00	02-06
Heddon	Wilder Dilg	lure is awful, odd box VG		$305.00	99-01
Heddon	Wilder Dilg	Mannfeld's Coaxer pic box	NIB	$560.00	03-03
Heddon	Wilder Dilg	red head, red hackle & red feathers with black streaks	EX-	$30.00	05-06
Heddon	Wilder Dilg	red, Down Bass	NIB	$326.00	99-07
Heddon	Wilder Dilg	red, picture box avg	EXIB	$204.55	99-11
Heddon	Wilder Dilg	red/yellow	mint	$34.00	00-01
Heddon	Wilder Dilg	Up Bass bx	NIB	$153.00	03-11
Heddon	Wilder Dilg	Venable's Charmer	EXIB	$148.00	99-01
Heddon	Wilder Dilg	Venable's Charmer, nice pic box	NIB	$450.00	02-06
Heddon	Wilder Dilg	Venable's Charmer, pic box	#3	$200.00	99-09
Heddon	Wilder Dilg	white, Up Bass VG+	VGIB	$145.00	00-07
Heddon	Wilder Dilg	Zane Gray, nice box	EXIB	$610.00	00-08
Heddon	Wilder Dilg	#2, Mannfeld Coaxer, un Heddon box VG	NIB	$462.00	01-05
Heddon	Wilder Dilg	#32, Wilder's Fancy, white/red intro box & papers, trout size	NIB	$566.00	04-01
Heddon	Wilder Dilg Spook	XRS, NOT MET	mint	$22.27	99-08
Heddon	Wilder Dilg Spook	yellow shore, nice hackle & feathers	EX	$25.00	05-06
Heddon	Wood Zara	frog	mint	$37.00	99-05
Heddon	Wood Zara	frog scale, PE, no hardware	EX	$16.00	02-07
Heddon	Wood Zara	SS	NOC	$18.00	99-02
Heddon	Woodpecker	1001, RH, blue brdr Down, paper & LUM pap EX-	NIB	$3,550.00	02-04
Heddon	Woodpecker	hand marked bx 1001RH, Heddon tissue, NOT MET	??	$1,025.00	02-02
Heddon	Wounded Spook	perch scale, white eye	mint	$44.00	01-05
Heddon	Wounded Spook	1940SD, 1940 lure, with box	EX	$18.50	05-07
Heddon	Wounded Spook	XRY, 2 diff, perch, gold eyes	EX	$90.00	99-03
Heddon	Wounded Spook	2 XRY, PRH, gold eyes	EX	$75.00	99-03
Heddon	Wounded Spook	9140XRS, gold eye	NIB	$81.00	99-04
Heddon	Wounded Spook	9140XRW, 2PCCB, 2pc rig!	NIB	$151.50	99-01
Heddon	Wounded Spook	9140XRY	EXIB	$71.00	99-04
Heddon	Wounded Spook	9140L, Banner, gold eye	NIB	$56.00	00-04
Heddon	Wounded Spook	9140RHF, Banner bx EX, catalog	NIB	$81.00	05-07
Heddon	Wounded Spook	9140SD, white eye, PTCB	NIB	$80.00	00-10

BRAND	MODEL	SERIES / MFG. CODE / DESCRIPTION	GRADE	PRICE	DATE yy/mm
Heddon	Wounded Spook	9140XRW, Banner, gold eye	EXIB	$63.00	00-04
Heddon	Wounded Spook	9140XRY, Banner, gold eye	NIB	$37.00	00-06
Heddon	Wounded Spook	BF, gold eye	VG+	$69.99	99-04
Heddon	Wounded Spook	crackle	EX	$345.00	99-06
Heddon	Wounded Spook	frog	EX-	$61.00	99-01
Heddon	Wounded Spook	frog, white eye, PSTB	NIB	$46.00	00-01
Heddon	Wounded Spook	frog, white eye	EX	$28.08	99-08
Heddon	Wounded Spook	frog, white eye	EX	$52.00	00-04
Heddon	Wounded Spook	frog, white eyes	EX	$25.02	99-12
Heddon	Wounded Spook	frog, white eye	VG	$56.00	99-03
Heddon	Wounded Spook	frog, white eyes	EX-	$26.01	99-08
Heddon	Wounded Spook	gold PE, white shore, SR	VG+	$15.00	05-06
Heddon	Wounded Spook	gold PE, white shore, SR	EX	$25.00	05-06
Heddon	Wounded Spook	GRA	EX	$335.00	02-01
Heddon	Wounded Spook	green/pink/white	EX	$26.50	98-12
Heddon	Wounded Spook	L, gold eye	mint	$66.00	00-09
Heddon	Wounded Spook	L, gold eyes, crisp box & cat	NIB	$89.00	01-01
Heddon	Wounded Spook	L, gold eye, other $5 lure	EX	$27.51	99-07
Heddon	Wounded Spook	L, gold eyes, NOT MET	mint	$46.53	99-06
Heddon	Wounded Spook	L, white eye, PTCB	VGIB	$47.00	99-05
Heddon	Wounded Spook	perch, gold eyes	EX-	$29.00	99-09
Heddon	Wounded Spook	perch, box papers	NIB	$40.00	99-02
Heddon	Wounded Spook	perch, white eye	EX	$18.51	99-05
Heddon	Wounded Spook	perch, white eye	mint	$20.00	99-04
Heddon	Wounded Spook	perch, white eye	EX	$34.00	99-08
Heddon	Wounded Spook	pike scale, white eyes, PTCB	NIB	$63.00	05-07
Heddon	Wounded Spook	r/w, gold eyes	EX	$71.01	99-02
Heddon	Wounded Spook	RH/flitter, gold eye	mint	$61.00	99-08
Heddon	Wounded Spook	RH, yellow eyes	EX	$89.50	99-06
Heddon	Wounded Spook	RHF, gold eye, 2PCCB	NIB	$112.50	99-05
Heddon	Wounded Spook	RHF, gold eyes	EX	$92.00	99-08
Heddon	Wounded Spook	shad	NIB	$40.00	00-08
Heddon	Wounded Spook	shad, white eye	EX	$100.00	01-08
Heddon	Wounded Spook	shad, white eye	VG	$22.50	99-12
Heddon	Wounded Spook	shad, white eye	EX-	$32.07	99-02
Heddon	Wounded Spook	shad, white eye	EX	$55.00	99-06
Heddon	Wounded Spook	shad, white eye, PTCB	NIB	$89.00	99-11
Heddon	Wounded Spook	XBW	VG	$37.99	98-12
Heddon	Wounded Spook	XBW, recessed gold eye	EX	$67.00	00-04
Heddon	Wounded Spook	XBW, white eye	EX	$47.00	00-04
Heddon	Wounded Spook	XBW, white eyes	EX	$89.00	00-02
Heddon	Wounded Spook	XBW, white eyes	EX	$122.00	05-03
Heddon	Wounded Spook	XBW, window box, white eye	NIB	$65.00	00-03
Heddon	Wounded Spook	XRS, gold eye	EX	$39.00	99-04
Heddon	Wounded Spook	XRS, gold eyes with box	VGIB	$53.00	99-04
Heddon	Wounded Spook	XRS, white eye	VG	$30.00	00-01
Heddon	Wounded Spook	XRW recessed eyes, S-rig	EX	$77.00	99-01
Heddon	Wounded Spook	XRW, gold eyes	EX+	$46.50	99-03

BRAND	MODEL	SERIES / MFG. CODE / DESCRIPTION	GRADE	PRICE	DATE yy/mm
Heddon	Wounded Spook	XRW, gold eyes	EX	$87.00	99-01
Heddon	Wounded Spook	XRW, gold sunken eyes	EX	$22.25	99-11
Heddon	Wounded Spook	XRY, gold eyes	VG	$69.99	99-04
Heddon	Wounded Spook	XRY, white eyes	EX-	$31.51	99-04
Heddon	Wounded Spook	XRY, gold eye	EX	$26.51	99-04
Heddon	Wounded Spook	XRY, gold eye	EX-	$33.50	00-01
Heddon	Wounded Spook	XRY, gold eye	EX	$50.99	99-03
Heddon	Wounded Spook	XRY, gold eye	EX	$52.02	99-06
Heddon	Wounded Spook	XRY, gold eyes	VG	$17.54	00-02
Heddon	Wounded Spook	XRY, white eye, NOT MET	VG-	$9.99	99-05
Heddon	Wounded Spook	XRY, white eye, ugly	VG-	$28.89	99-03
Heddon	Wounded Spook		mint	$44.51	99-01
Heddon	Zara Baby	crackleback, gold eye	EX	$123.06	99-06
Heddon	Zara II	9240ORH, looks red to me	NIB	$79.00	01-08
Heddon	Zara II	9240ORH, looks red	NIB	$134.00	00-12
Heddon	Zara II	9240XBL	NIB	$42.00	01-08
Heddon	Zara II	chrome, white eye	NIB	$233.00	01-09
Heddon	Zara II	frog, gold eyes	NIB	$37.00	01-10
Heddon	Zara II	GRA	EX	$61.00	99-04
Heddon	Zara II	red	EX+	$36.00	99-01
Heddon	Zara II	scale/red ribs	EX	$75.00	99-02
Heddon	Zara II	y/2 black dots, red gills	EX	$91.50	99-06
Heddon	Zara Spook	3 XRY, XBL, SS nose	EX-	$65.00	99-02
Heddon	Zara Spook	17 Pradcos	EX	$156.00	99-03
Heddon	Zara Spook	2 diff, XRB, clear, chin, no hole	EX	$133.50	99-04
Heddon	Zara Spook	3 RH, XRY, SS	VG	$82.00	98-12
Heddon	Zara Spook	3 RH, XRY, BF	VG	$162.00	98-12
Heddon	Zara Spook	9250XRW	NIB	$50.00	99-03
Heddon	Zara Spook	9250GSCD, nose line tie	EXIB	$505.00	04-07
Heddon	Zara Spook	9250RH, PTCB, lg black eye shadow, white belly scales, nose tie	NIB	$110.00	05-07
Heddon	Zara Spook	9250SS, white eye	NIB	$32.00	99-06
Heddon	Zara Spook	9255NSE	NIB	$203.00	04-12
Heddon	Zara Spook	9255XBL, triangle card	NOC	$84.00	01-05
Heddon	Zara Spook	9256NF, Charlie Campbell, chin swayback	NIB	$88.00	00-07
Heddon	Zara Spook	baby bass, chin, no hole, swayback	EX	$94.00	00-05
Heddon	Zara Spook	baby bass, chin, no hole, original	EX	$60.01	99-06
Heddon	Zara Spook	bar perch? chin, no hole, swayback	EX	$260.00	00-04
Heddon	Zara Spook	BB, swayback	NIB	$92.00	00-08
Heddon	Zara Spook	BF, white eye nose	EX	$46.99	99-01
Heddon	Zara Spook	BF, white eye, nose, window	NIB	$50.00	99-02
Heddon	Zara Spook	9255C, blue shore, orig chin	NIB	$63.00	99-08
Heddon	Zara Spook	brown crawdad, chin tie, swayback	mint	$68.00	03-02
Heddon	Zara Spook	brown crawdad, swayback, "Original" on belly	EX	$71.00	05-07
Heddon	Zara Spook	BRS	EX	$110.00	02-11
Heddon	Zara Spook	BRS	EX	$137.00	02-10
Heddon	Zara Spook	BRS, swayback, NOT MET	EX	$79.00	02-03
Heddon	Zara Spook	BRS, chin tie, swayback	EX	$114.00	01-10

BRAND	MODEL	SERIES / MFG. CODE / DESCRIPTION	GRADE	PRICE	DATE yy/mm
Heddon	Zara Spook	C. Campbell, swayback, nat bass	EX	$53.00	01-08
Heddon	Zara Spook	Campbell, nat striper, chin	EX	$41.00	99-03
Heddon	Zara Spook	Campbell, nat mullet? chin, no hole	VG+	$68.00	99-05
Heddon	Zara Spook	Campbell, nat y mullet? chin, no hole	VG+	$71.00	99-05
Heddon	Zara Spook	Charlie Campbell, photo finish perch, swayback	EX	$51.00	05-07
Heddon	Zara Spook	GD, chin, no hole, color	EX	$41.00	99-06
Heddon	Zara Spook	GR, chin, no hole, lum belly	EX	$70.00	00-04
Heddon	Zara Spook	chin, Charlie Campbell, shad, NOT MET	EX	$104.00	00-04
Heddon	Zara Spook	chin, no hole, baby bass, CC	EX	$142.00	98-12
Heddon	Zara Spook	chin, no hole, brown, crawdad?	EX	$120.50	99-06
Heddon	Zara Spook	chin, no hole, frog, Charlie Campbell	EX	$69.00	00-02
Heddon	Zara Spook	chin, no hole, green scale/CD/lum belly	EX	$70.00	00-04
Heddon	Zara Spook	chin, no hole, nat green perch	EX	$153.28	00-02
Heddon	Zara Spook	chin, no hole, nat striper	EC	$38.00	00-05
Heddon	Zara Spook	chin, no hole, swayback, baby bass	EX	$128.50	00-02
Heddon	Zara Spook	chrome, chin, no hole, original	VG	$73.00	99-04
Heddon	Zara Spook	chrome/blk scale, nose tie	NIB	$69.00	99-04
Heddon	Zara Spook	clear HD, white eye and nose	EX-	$107.50	99-01
Heddon	Zara Spook	clear, chin, no hole	EX	$137.50	98-12
Heddon	Zara Spook	clear, chin, swayback	EX	$55.00	02-06
Heddon	Zara Spook	clear, heavy duty hardware	EX+	$80.50	00-04
Heddon	Zara Spook	clear, chin, swayback	EX	$178.50	00-03
Heddon	Zara Spook	clear, nose	NIB	$132.50	99-01
Heddon	Zara Spook	clear, nose, molded hardware	EX	$86.00	99-05
Heddon	Zara Spook	clear, nose, molded	EX	$56.00	99-05
Heddon	Zara Spook	clear, white eye, chin, no hardware	mint	$62.00	99-02
Heddon	Zara Spook	Cohiba Cuban Cigar sp order	NOC	$11.00	99-02
Heddon	Zara Spook	Color-C-lector, bl/red/sil, EBSCO	NOC	$12.49	99-02
Heddon	Zara Spook	Color-C-lector 6-pack	NIB	$217.50	98-12
Heddon	Zara Spook	crawdad, original	EX	$102.50	99-08
Heddon	Zara Spook	Dowluck sp order	NOC	$11.01	99-02
Heddon	Zara Spook	FF9250GR, NOT MET	NIB	$137.50	99-10
Heddon	Zara Spook	FF-GB	EX	$86.00	98-12
Heddon	Zara Spook	FF-GB		$86.00	98-12
Heddon	Zara Spook	FF-GR, NOT MET	EX	$112.51	99-03
Heddon	Zara Spook	FL, brown crawdad, "Original"	VG	$126.00	99-01
Heddon	Zara Spook	frog, C. Campbell, no hole	EX	$39.87	99-09
Heddon	Zara Spook	frog scale, looks Pradco	EX	$232.00	00-06
Heddon	Zara Spook	frog, chin, no hole	EX	$107.50	99-04
Heddon	Zara Spook	frog, chin, no hole, NOT MET	EX	$73.00	00-02
Heddon	Zara Spook	frog, gold eye, chin, no hole	EX	$79.00	99-05
Heddon	Zara Spook	frog, gold eye, chin, swayback	EX	$72.00	01-05
Heddon	Zara Spook	frog, gold eye, chin, no hole	mint	$100.00	99-05
Heddon	Zara Spook	frog, Charlie Campbell	EX	$67.00	99-01
Heddon	Zara Spook	GRA, chin tie, swayback, no hole	NIB	$79.00	02-02
Heddon	Zara Spook	green/red/black spots, chin	NIB	$185.00	99-03
Heddon	Zara Spook	green scale, coach dog, chin, no hole	EX-	$191.38	00-02
Heddon	Zara Spook	kamikaze quality tackle, sp order	NOC	$24.50	99-02

BRAND	MODEL	SERIES / MFG. CODE / DESCRIPTION	GRADE	PRICE	DATE yy/mm
Heddon	Zara Spook	KCH, 6 stripes, swayback, chin	EX	$242.00	01-04
Heddon	Zara Spook	lum, baby bass, swayback, chin	EX	$48.00	01-04
Heddon	Zara Spook	MG, chin tie, swayback, no hole	NIB	$236.00	02-02
Heddon	Zara Spook	MG, musky gold scale	NOC	$133.50	99-02
Heddon	Zara Spook	MG, musky gold, chin, no hole	NOC	$167.50	99-01
Heddon	Zara Spook	nat chrome shad, chin, no hole, clear silver foil, NOT MET	EX	$76.01	00-02
Heddon	Zara Spook	nat bluegill? C. Campbell, chin, no hole	EX	$167.50	99-12
Heddon	Zara Spook	nat frog, chin, no hole, "Original"	EX	$143.50	99-04
Heddon	Zara Spook	nat shad? C. Campbell, chin, no hole	EX	$157.10	99-12
Heddon	Zara Spook	natural striper, NOT MET!	EX	$110.00	01-04
Heddon	Zara Spook	nose, black/silver foil	EX	$200.00	00-02
Heddon	Zara Spook	NSP (nat spotted bass), C. Campbell	EX	$138.00	99-12
Heddon	Zara Spook	NVRB, nat rainbow chrome	NIB	$67.00	00-03
Heddon	Zara Spook	9255XBW, original, swayback	NIB	$100.00	00-09
Heddon	Zara Spook	original, green/blk, bass?	EX	$182.50	99-01
Heddon	Zara Spook	perch? chin tie swayback	VG	$114.00	02-07
Heddon	Zara Spook	photo frog, chin, no hole, NOT MET	EX	$51.00	99-06
Heddon	Zara Spook	purple, chin, no hole	EX	$50.00	99-01
Heddon	Zara Spook	r/w, molded hardware	NIB	$26.51	99-04
Heddon	Zara Spook	r/w, white eye, nose	EX-	$43.99	99-01
Heddon	Zara Spook	r/w, chin, no hole	EX-	$71.00	99-05
Heddon	Zara Spook	r/w, nose, white eye	EX	$36.00	99-02
Heddon	Zara Spook	red/gold foil, nose tie	EX-	$102.00	04-02
Heddon	Zara Spook	red/gold foil, nose tie	EX-	$87.00	02-02
Heddon	Zara Spook	red/silver foil, nose tie	EX	$121.00	04-11
Heddon	Zara Spook	red/gold flitter inside	EX	$247.50	99-07
Heddon	Zara Spook	red/gold foil, gold eyes	EX	$102.70	99-11
Heddon	Zara Spook	red/sparkle filled, Banner bx	NIB	$177.00	03-02
Heddon	Zara Spook	RH	NIB	$69.00	98-12
Heddon	Zara Spook	RH/flitter, nose, white eye	EXIB	$18.50	99-10
Heddon	Zara Spook	S9250SFB	NIB	$200.00	02-02
Heddon	Zara Spook	shad, nose	EX	$77.02	99-01
Heddon	Zara Spook	silver glitter filled	EX	$261.00	98-12
Heddon	Zara Spook	silver scale, gold eye, nose	VG	$31.00	99-01
Heddon	Zara Spook	silver scale, nose, white eye	EX-	$14.01	99-08
Heddon	Zara Spook	SS	NIB	$46.05	98-12
Heddon	Zara Spook	SS, Banner, gold eyes	NIB	$40.00	00-01
Heddon	Zara Spook	SS, nose	EX-	$41.99	99-01
Heddon	Zara Spook	SS, nose tie	EXIB	$19.00	99-01
Heddon	Zara Spook	SS, chin tie, swayback, 4-seam, no hole nose	mint	$41.00	02-08
Heddon	Zara Spook	SS, chin, swayback	EX	$37.00	02-02
Heddon	Zara Spook	SS, nose, white eye	EX-	$10.49	01-08
Heddon	Zara Spook	SS, "original" shin, no hole	EX	$85.00	99-04
Heddon	Zara Spook	SS, Banner, gold eye, "Spoon"	NIB	$22.00	99-11
Heddon	Zara Spook	SS, gold eye, nose tie	EX-	$22.05	99-04
Heddon	Zara Spook	SS, nose, molded	EX+	$22.16	99-05
Heddon	Zara Spook	SS, nose, molded hook hangers	NIB	$22.51	99-08

194

BRAND	MODEL	SERIES / MFG. CODE / DESCRIPTION	GRADE	PRICE	DATE yy/mm
Heddon	Zara Spook	SS, w eye, hvy salt rig	NIB	$41.00	99-03
Heddon	Zara Spook	XRY, SS, chin, no hole	VG, VG	$24.94	98-12
Heddon	Zara Spook	swayback, chin, baby bass, green scale	EX	$44.00	01-04
Heddon	Zara Spook	swayback, chrome	EX	$16.00	05-07
Heddon	Zara Spook	swayback, clear w/black dot	EX	$33.00	05-07
Heddon	Zara Spook	white, black down back and around eyes, glitter, 4½" long	avg	$11.11	05-07
Heddon	Zara Spook	white, gold eye, nose	VG	$16.51	99-08
Heddon	Zara Spook	wood, frog	EX	$16.00	99-01
Heddon	Zara Spook	XBW, chin tie, swayback	EX	$17.00	05-07
Heddon	Zara Spook	XBW, nose, white eye, NOT MET	EX	$32.00	99-03
Heddon	Zara Spook	XBW, chin, no hole	VG	$59.50	99-03
Heddon	Zara Spook	XBW, chin, no hole	VG+	$68.00	99-05
Heddon	Zara Spook	XBW, gold eye	EX	$57.50	99-08
Heddon	Zara Spook	XRB	EX	$54.10	99-01
Heddon	Zara Spook	XRB	NIB	$80.00	98-12
Heddon	Zara Spook	XRB, white eyes	NIB	$81.01	98-12
Heddon	Zara Spook	XRB, chin, no hole	EX-	$51.00	99-06
Heddon	Zara Spook	XRB, gold eye, nose	EX	$33.00	99-06
Heddon	Zara Spook	XRB, white eye	EX	$22.00	99-10
Heddon	Zara Spook	XRS clear, swayback, chin	EX	$65.00	01-05
Heddon	Zara Spook	XRS, white eye, chin, swayback	mint	$79.00	99-11
Heddon	Zara Spook	XRW	EX	$52.01	98-12
Heddon	Zara Spook	XRW	NIB	$82.00	98-12
Heddon	Zara Spook	XRW, nose, molded hook hangers	NIB	$24.01	99-08
Heddon	Zara Spook	XRW, nose, molded	EX	$26.01	99-05
Heddon	Zara Spook	XRY	NIB	$44.00	02-05
Heddon	Zara Spook	XRY	NIB	$66.00	98-12
Heddon	Zara Spook	XRY, gold eye, nose	EX-	$46.99	99-01
Heddon	Zara Spook	XRY, gold eye, nose tie	VG	$40.00	99-01
Heddon	Zara Spook	XRY, gold eyes, Banner box	NIB	$52.00	99-01
Heddon	Zara Spook	XRY, nose tie	VG+	$4.00	05-07
Heddon	Zara Spook	XRY, white eye, nose	VG	$33.99	99-01
Heddon	Zara Spook	XRY, white eye, PSTB	NIB	$51.01	00-01
Heddon	Zara Spook	XRY, chin, swayback	EX	$59.00	02-06
Heddon	Zara Spook	XRY, chin, swayback	EX	$44.00	02-02
Heddon	Zara Spook	XRY, 2PCCB, gold eye	NIB	$152.50	98-12
Heddon	Zara Spook	XRY, nose	EX-IB	$36.00	99-01
Heddon	Zara Spook	XRY, nose tie	EX	$41.00	99-01
Heddon	Zara Spook	XRY, nose, molded hook hangers	NIB	$23.01	99-08
Heddon	Zara Spook	XRY, nose, white eye	EX	$18.50	99-04
Heddon	Zara Spook	XRY, nose, white eye	mint	$30.70	99-02
Heddon	Zara Spook	XRY, white eye, nose	VG	$10.51	99-04
Heddon	Zara Spook x 13	13 diff swaybacks	EX – mint	$800.00	02-07
Heddon	Zara Spook x 2	blue shore, nose, 1 molded, 1 S-rig	EX	$20.50	00-03
Heddon	Zara Spook x 2	red Fish Flash, blk Fish Flash Banner	VGIB/VG	$124.72	99-06
Heddon	Zara Spook x 2	XRW, GE, RH, WE, nose	VG	$76.95	99-02
Heddon	Zara Spook x 2	XRY, SS, GE, nose	EX	$71.00	99-02

BRAND	MODEL	SERIES / MFG. CODE / DESCRIPTION	GRADE	PRICE	DATE yy/mm
Heddon	Zara Spook x 3	2 nose, 1 chin, no hole, nat bluegill, GD?	EX-	$65.99	99-06
Heddon	Zaragossa	4⅝", green scale, Zara equipped, heavy duty hardware, obvious signs of use	VG	$495.00	05-04
Heddon	Zaragossa	6500SO, PE, Banner box	NIB	$125.00	99-06
Heddon	Zaragossa	6502, white with red eyes and chin, TS-hdwr, GE, shows light age	VG++	$195.00	05-05
Heddon	Zaragossa	6509DYB, 2pc, Brush, yellow belly	EXIB	$504.99	99-11
Heddon	Zaragossa	6509K, Down Bass, L-rig, NOT MET	NIB	$2,550.00	99-12
Heddon	Zaragossa	6509P	VG+	$375.00	99-10
Heddon	Zaragossa	6509PRH	EX-	$700.00	99-10
Heddon	Zaragossa	6509PRH, 2H, 2pc, Brush, NOT MET	NIB	$525.00	00-01
Heddon	Zaragossa	6509RH, 2H, Brush bx, RH/flitter, 2pc	EXIB	$699.00	02-05
Heddon	Zaragossa	6609SS, silver scale, 2pc, GE, tiny bit front lip edge wear	EX	$140.00	05-05
Heddon	Zaragossa	Banner box, PE	VGIB	$62.00	99-01
Heddon	Zaragossa	BF, Banner box, PE	NIB	$75.75	99-03
Heddon	Zaragossa	blue scale, L-rig	EX	$2,250.00	02-08
Heddon	Zaragossa	blue scale, GE, L-rig	VG+	$536.00	99-12
Heddon	Zaragossa	centennial BB	NIB	$81.00	02-01
Heddon	Zaragossa	centennial F (not BF), GE	NIB	$101.00	02-01
Heddon	Zaragossa	centennial, crackleback	NIB	$29.00	99-01
Heddon	Zaragossa	centennial, frog	NIB	$32.00	99-01
Heddon	Zaragossa	centennial reissue, CBO, crackleback orange	NIB	$59.00	05-07
Heddon	Zaragossa	centennial, white shore	NIB	$42.50	99-01
Heddon	Zaragossa	centennial X6500W-GNS	NIB	$49.05	99-07
Heddon	Zaragossa	centennial, green scale, GE	NIB	$30.00	99-08
Heddon	Zaragossa	crackle, L	EX-	$650.00	99-10
Heddon	Zaragossa	Down Bass nice, L-rig	NIB	$725.00	01-09
Heddon	Zaragossa	centennial, frog	NIB	$42.00	99-01
Heddon	Zaragossa	frog scale	VG+	$302.50	05-07
Heddon	Zaragossa	frog, GE, centennial	NIB	$36.00	00-07
Heddon	Zaragossa	frog, PE, wood, 2 hooks, Banner box	NIB	$52.00	03-07
Heddon	Zaragossa	centennial, frog	NIB	$26.00	99-01
Heddon	Zaragossa	centennial, frog	NIB	$29.67	99-01
Heddon	Zaragossa	GE, red head, shiner scale, SR, stamped on belly	VG+	$75.00	05-06
Heddon	Zaragossa	GE, shiner scale finish	EX	$60.50	04-11
Heddon	Zaragossa	goldfish scale, blunt nose	VG+	$2,200.00	00-05
Heddon	Zaragossa	green scale, 6509D Down Bass bx VG	EXIB	$400.00	04-12
Heddon	Zaragossa	green scale, GE, L-rig	VG+	$91.55	99-09
Heddon	Zaragossa	green scale, GE, L-rig	EX-	$280.00	00-01
Heddon	Zaragossa	late dace, toilet seat	EX-	$405.00	02-10
Heddon	Zaragossa	orange/black dots, GE, L-rig, Down Bass 6600W EX	NIB	$1,825.00	05-07
Heddon	Zaragossa	perch scale, 2pc	VG+	$201.00	99-08
Heddon	Zaragossa	red scale, L-rig	EX-	$676.00	04-12
Heddon	Zaragossa	red scale, no chin, L-rig	VG-	$1,300.00	00-11
Heddon	Zaragossa	shiner scale, L-rig, GE	EX	$376.00	05-07
Heddon	Zaragossa	sienna, serial #0001 Centennial	NIB	$77.00	99-01

BRAND	MODEL	SERIES / MFG. CODE / DESCRIPTION	GRADE	PRICE	DATE yy/mm
Heddon	Zaragossa	silver scale, PE, "Original"	mint	$20.50	00-03
Heddon	Zaragossa	DLX, snub nose, green scale, L-rig	EX-	$425.00	99-03
Heddon	Zaragossa	strawberry, GE, L	VG-	$187.00	00-08
Heddon	Zaragossa	strawberry, L-rig	EX-	$560.00	02-12
Heddon	Zaragossa	w/red eye, extra hook screwed in	EX+	$140.50	99-11
Heddon	Zaragossa	white/red eye, L-rig	VG+	$216.00	01-03
Heddon	Zaragossa	y/spotted, centennial	NIB	$96.00	01-03
Heddon	Zaragossa Jr.	RB, GE, for Japan	EX	$96.00	00-08
Heddon	Zaragossa, Baby	SO, Banner box, NOT MET	NIB	$316.88	99-03
Heddon	Zaragossa, Centennial	6 different	NIB	$261.50	99-05
Heddon	Zig Wag	8302, RH/w, intro, Gold Zig Wag decal on belly, GE, l rig, 3-hk, light age lines	EX-IB	$270.00	05-04
Heddon	Zig Wag	8302, Up Bass	VG+IB	$60.00	99-04
Heddon	Zig Wag	8308RH, RH/w w/gold flitter, 2-hk, 2pc, small chip in jnt, varn wear on lip edge	EX-	$95.00	05-04
Heddon	Zig Wag	8309M, Down Bass ad box!	EXIB	$255.00	99-04
Heddon	Zig Wag	black head/white body	EX	$522.50	05-07
Heddon	Zig Wag	crackle	EX-	$525.00	99-08
Heddon	Zig Wag	frog spot, 8309 BF Up Bass bx EX	VG+IB	$168.00	05-07
Heddon	Zig Wag	frog, GE	poor	$27.00	99-02
Heddon	Zig Wag	herring with heavy L-rig	EX-	$522.50	05-07
Heddon	Zig Wag	herring, PE, 5"	mint	$96.00	02-09
Heddon	Zig Wag	Luny frog, RH/nat, 2 diff	G	$220.37	99-04
Heddon	Zig Wag	Luny frog, GE, one med chip	EX	$306.00	99-01
Heddon	Zig Wag	orange with black spots	EX-	$302.50	05-07
Heddon	Zig Wag	perch scale, older L-rig	mint	$314.99	99-08
Heddon	Zig Wag	pike scale, Down Bass	NIB	$310.00	00-03
Heddon	Zig Wag	r/w, GE, L-rig, purty, too cheap	EX+	$81.07	99-08
Heddon	Zig Wag	r/w, Up Bass box has "8302"	EXIB	$80.50	99-01
Heddon	Zig Wag	RH, L-rig, Up Bass	EXIB	$127.50	00-02
Heddon	Zig Wag	RH, Up Bass, L-rig, GE	NIB	$90.00	99-06
Heddon	Zig Wag	RH/green scale, 2pc, Brush box	NIB	$256.51	00-02
Heddon	Zig Wag	RH/green scale, belly stencil, wowser	EX+	$240.60	99-12
Heddon	Zig Wag	RH/nat scale, GE	EX-	$86.00	00-11
Heddon	Zig Wag	RH/nat scale, L-rig	VG+	$30.00	00-10
Heddon	Zig Wag	RH/natural scale, GE	mint	$200.00	99-09
Heddon	Zig Wag	RH/pike scale, hangtag EX	mint	$293.00	01-04
Heddon	Zig Wag	shiner scale, 2pc, POBW, lip chip	VG	$47.00	04-07
Heddon	Zig Wag	solid pearl with heavy L-rig	EX	$467.50	05-07
Heddon	Zig Wag	solid red	EX-	$302.50	05-07
Heddon	Zig Wag	Up Bass avg	EX-IB	$64.99	99-10
Heddon	Zig Wag 8300	8300, RH/natural scale, old stencil	EX	$263.00	99-08
Heddon	Zig Wag 8300	8300, shiner scale, old stencil, L-rig	EX+	$100.55	99-08
Heddon	Zig Wag Jr.	8349R-RH, RH/natural scale, GE, TS-hdwr, 1 pntr and tiny nick on lip	EX	$70.00	05-04
Heddon	Zig Wag Jr.	PRH, painted eye	mint	$34.00	02-07
Heddon	Zig Wag, King	8359SPRH, Brush bx VG+, RH spotted, GE	NIB	$305.00	05-07
Heddon	Zig Wag, King	8359YS, Banner box, string, teddy bear eyes	NIB	$82.00	05-07

197

BRAND	MODEL	SERIES / MFG. CODE / DESCRIPTION	GRADE	PRICE	DATE yy/mm
Heddon	Zig Wag, King	8369PLXR, RH, Brush box	EXIB	$203.50	99-07
Heddon	Zig Wag, King	white, Brush box 8362M, NOT MET	EX-IB	$42.00	04-02
Helin	Fishcake	#11	NIB	$39.00	99-04
Helin	Fishcake	#11, black/glitter	mint	$11.50	99-05
Helin	Fishcake	#11, flor orange	EX	$10.99	99-12
Helin	Fishcake	#11, orange/blk spots	NIB	$29.95	99-02
Helin	Fishcake	#11, silver	NIB	$30.99	99-02
Helin	Fishcake	#11F	NIB	$38.00	99-05
Helin	Fishcake	#7, black spots, blk prop	NIB	$20.50	99-06
Helin	Fishcake	#7, hot orange spotted, no marking on box	NIB	$26.00	04-02
Helin	Fishcake	#7, red/white	NIB	$22.05	99-12
Helin	Fishcake	#7, scale finish	EX	$7.00	05-03
Helin	Fishcake	#7, y/red dots	NIB	$20.00	99-06
Helin	Fishcake	#9, b/gold scale	NIB	$32.00	99-06
Helin	Fishcake	#9, FL, o/blk spots, pointers, dirt	VG	$24.50	99-03
Helin	Fishcake	#9FR	NIB	$33.00	99-04
Helin	Fishcake	#9, orange/red spots	mint	$30.56	99-02
Helin	Fishcake	#9B	NIB	$27.60	99-06
Helin	Fishcake	4 #9s, 1 #11, 6-pack, 5 lures	NIB	$164.50	99-06
Helin	Fishcake	black scale	mint	$16.01	99-03
Helin	Fishcake x 2	frog, y/r spot	VG	$25.00	99-01
Helin	Fishcake x 6	6-pack, assorted, 2 flourescent	NIB	$114.00	00-04
Helin	Fishcake x 2	2 diff, frog, blk/o spots	mint	$47.00	99-03
Helin	Fishcake x 4	4 assorted	EX	$51.00	99-11
Helin	Flatfish	#U20, yellow with red & black spots, in 2PCCB box	EX+	$20.00	05-06
Helin	Flatfish	12-pack, dealer display window boxes	NIB	$161.50	99-03
Helin	Flatfish	6", wood, o/blk stripe/red dots	EX	$36.01	99-03
Helin	Flatfish	F-7, orange with red spots, in 2PCCB box VG++	EX-	$20.00	05-06
Helin	Flatfish	frog, "U20" marked on lure and box, original pamphlet	NIB	$18.50	05-07
Helin	Flatfish	LU, orange back w/red spot and full glitter belly, wood, VG picture 2PCCB	EXIB	$22.00	05-05
Helin	Flatfish	S3, frog, tag burn, 2 papers 1937 – 38 crisp	NIB	$51.00	02-03
Helin	Flatfish	S3, frog spot, wood, light crazing all over, no paint loss	VG+	$7.00	05-05
Helin	Flatfish	S3, gold glitr back and silver glitr belly, SG, wood, very light edge wear on lip, nice in early 2PST	EX-IB	$15.00	05-05
Helin	Flatfish	S3, orange w/black back and red spots, wood, few light age cracks	EX	$8.00	05-05
Helin	Flatfish	T4, white w/black back and red spots, wood shows light age, VG picture 2PCCB	EX-IB	$20.00	05-05
Helin	Flatfish	U20, orange w/black and red spots, wood, very light wear	EX	$7.00	05-05
Helin	Flatfish	U20, silver scales on black, 4-hk, wood, light age crackling, no paint loss	VG+	$6.00	05-05
Helin	Flatfish	U20, silver w/black spots, 4-hk, wood	ex+	$9.00	05-05
Helin	Flatfish	U20, yellow, RH, black and red spots, 3¼" long, w/original box.	AVG	$6.50	05-07
Helin	Flatfish	X4, orange back w/red spot, gold glitter belly, wood, 3-hk, hint orig wear	EX+	$12.00	05-05

BRAND	MODEL	SERIES / MFG. CODE / DESCRIPTION	GRADE	PRICE	DATE yy/mm
Helin	Flatfish	X4, white w/black back and red spots, wood, very light wear	EX	$7.00	05-05
Helin	Flatfish	X5, gold (all gold glitter), wood, 3-hk, varn flk on tail and few tiny varn pointers	EX-	$9.00	05-05
Helin	Flatfish x 12	12-pack, plastic, nice display box	NIB	$81.00	02-11
Helin	Flatfish x 56	plastic, special display board, no hooks	new	$455.00	00-03
Helin	Flatfish x 8	2PCCB pic bx, all with 1948 papers crisp, 8 diff lures & boxes	NIB	$103.00	05-07
Helin	Flatfish, F7	white, fly rod, 2PCCB 1945	NIB	$15.50	99-05
Helin	Swimmerspoon	w/red & blk spots	NIB	$18.26	99-05
Helin	Swimmerspoon x 4	4 different	NIB	$33.00	99-12
Hendryx	#2	fluted spinner, lg single Bing hook	EX	$26.00	04-03
Hendryx	American Spinner	ball type, 5"	VG+	$32.00	99-06
Hendryx	American Spinner	gold & silver plated, textured, pat 1905, 5"	EX-	$112.00	05-07
Hendryx	Serpentine	correct Bing's bucktail	EX-	$500.00	99-10
Hendryx	Serpentine Minnow	ugly spiral thing, green	VG	$400.00	00-01
Hendryx	Snake Bait	c. 1886, EX- Doc Herr, NOT MET	EX-	$256.00	04-11
Henning	Glass Minnow	un wood box, NOT MET	EX	$1,075.00	99-07
Henning	Glass Minnow Tube	Wiltom Mfg. Co.	EX+	$1,482.00	03-08
Herters	Pikie, jntd Giant	RH, TE	NIB	$76.00	05-07
Herters	spoon	2 bead eyes, Japan	EX	$5.00	03-01
Hex	Bunty	r&w with paper, Canada	EX+	$25.00	05-06
Higgins, J.C.	Injured Minnow	Paw Paw, plastic box #3377, perch	NIB	$29.00	03-01
Higgins, J.C.	Pikie	Paw Paw, TE, plastic box #3376, perch	NIB	$20.00	03-01
Higgins, J.C.	Pikie, jntd	Paw Paw, plastic box #3369, perch	NIB	$29.00	03-01
Hildreth	Wonder Bug	black w/white head/spots/belly hair/wings, new in orig 2PPB w/paperwork	NIB	$32.00	05-05
Hill, L.S.	Spinner	tandem minnows, pat dates May 23, 1876, and Feb. 4, 1879	EX-	$357.00	05-07
Hinckley	#4 Phantom	unmarked plain box & nice paper	EXIB	$442.00	05-07
Hinckley	Aluminum Fish Phantom #4	paper with line drawing listing 4 sizes, unmarked box	EXIB	$442.00	05-07
Hinckley	Fish Phantom	2⅜", hollow aluminum w/rotating head, few noticable dents	VG	$49.00	05-05
Hinckley	Phantom Float	alum (polished), Jan. 12, 1905	EX cleaned	$286.00	00-10
Hinckley	Phantom Minnow		EX	$75.00	01-04
Hinckley	Yellow Bird	1897 pat	VG	$76.50	99-08
Hinckley	Yellow Bird Fish Phantom	#3, white pasteboard box VG+	avgIB	$334.00	01-08
Hinkle	Lizard	green scale	EX+	$97.00	00-05
Hinkle	Lizard	green/black	EX	$86.00	00-05
Hi-Sport	Hi-Sport Lure	green/blk ribs, silver scale, 2½", plastic, few pointers and small scratch on chin	EX-	$13.00	05-05
Hi-Sport	Hi-Sport Lure	orange/black stripe on sides, 2½", plastic, NSOS	NM	$20.00	05-05
Hi-Sport	Hi-Sport Lure	white/red stripes down sides (left stripe slight fade), 2½", plastic, neat r&w variation	EX	$15.00	05-05
Hi-Yo	Activated Lure	gold scale, hollow metal, runs with dry ice, in EX- 1PCCB w/papers, 3 tails	EX+IB	$45.00	05-05
Hoage	Magnetic Weedless	brown/green	EX	$24.99	99-05
Hoage	Magnetic Weedless	r/w	EX	$29.00	99-06
Hoage	Magnetic Weedless	RH/black	EX	$39.88	99-08

BRAND	MODEL	SERIES / MFG. CODE / DESCRIPTION	GRADE	PRICE	DATE yy/mm
Hoage	Spoon Fin	green, yellow GE	EX	$100.00	00-10
Hoage	Spoon Fin		EX	$400.00	99-10
Hoage, Clyde	Spoon Fin Minnow	4½", wood, glass eyed bait, metal side fins, blended red back, general wear and pointer, yellow GE	VG	$440.00	05-04
Hobbs Supply	Bon Net	RB, GE, 6-hooker, nice box	VGIB	$242.50	00-02
Hofschneider	Red Eye Wiggler	2PCCB nice, gold, old box	EXIB	$42.00	03-02
Hofschneider	Wiggle Plug	plastic in window box	NIB	$8.00	04-12
Hollowhead	Hollowhead	black & yellow box EX-	EX+IB	$20.00	05-06
Hom-Art	Dipper	frog spot	mint	$126.00	03-04
Hom-Art	Dipper	silver/black ribs	mint	$40.00	04-02
Hom-Art	Skipper	black	mint	$49.00	03-04
Hom-Art	Skipper	blue/white, nice papers & box	NIB	$108.00	04-12
Hom-Art	Skipper	frog	mint	$46.00	03-04
Hom-Art	Skipper	frog spot, plastic, very light wear on lure, hdwr looks great	EX	$30.00	05-05
Hom-Art	Skipper	perch scale (Arbo-like color)	mint	$30.00	03-04
Hom-Art	Skipper	RB	NIB	$46.00	00-04
Homemade	Huge Bomber	red/white, 12"	EX	$28.00	99-01
Hook Bros.	Salmon Plug	herring scale	NIB	$99.00	04-11
Hootenanna		red head/white sparkles, plastic box & paper	NIB	$41.00	02-12
Horrock - Ibbotson	3-hook	yellow/green crackleback, GE, great 2PCCB	NIB	$685.00	03-11
Horrock - Ibbotson	Babe Oreno	scramble finish, TE	EX	$25.00	01-05
Horrock - Ibbotson	Rangley Minnow	RH/w, plastic spin size, new in orig 2PPB w/card, bonus RH/w, fly size	NIB	$10.00	05-05
Horrock - Ibbotson	Success Spinner	3-hooker, nice box, c. 1910	VGIB	$260.00	01-03
Horvath	Twiggler	novelty jointed lure	EX	$43.00	04-07
Hoseney	Kicking Frog Bait Don Hoseney	2¼", HP, frog, signed on belly	EX	$88.00	04-11
Hosmer, J.D.	Mechanical Frog	green frog spot, pattern, white belly, 6-part hinged wood	EX	$5,170.00	05-04
Howes	Vacuum	dragonfly	VG	$406.00	99-01
Howes	Vacuum	white, tin box VG-	EXIB	$780.00	99-10
Howes	Vacuum Bait	NE, white/blk? dragonfly	EX+	$473.98	99-04
Howes	Vacuum Bait	r&w, swivel hdwr, light flaking, w/some age cracks and light wear	G	$95.00	05-05
Howes	Vacuum Bait	white/red gills, nice tin box, NOT MET	VG-IB	$224.50	99-06
Howe's	Vacuum	white, tin box, nice paper, NOT MET	EX-IB	$536.00	01-02
Howe's	Vacuum	white/red gills	VG-	$130.00	05-07
Howe's	Vacuum bait	white/red, box avg, flyer VG	VG	$770.00	04-11
Hub	Muck Ko Chuck	y/black spots, NOT MET	EX	$102.00	00-05
Hubbs	Bon Net	frog, great Hobb's box	NIB	$310.01	99-09
Hump Lure Co.	Mighty Minnow	clear/y dots, plastic box EX	NIB	$31.00	03-04
Humpy	Humpy	black & white L, 3-color, 20 in plastic top box (E)	EX	$15.00	05-06
Illingsworth	No-5 MK-2	spin, ½ bail, Bakelite sides	VG+	$187.00	01-10
Immell	Chippewa	3", red? no middle hook	VG	$228.00	00-08
Immell	Chippewa	3½", crackleback	VG	$204.00	02-08
Immell	Chippewa	3½", rainbow	EX	$965.00	02-09
Immell	Chippewa	4", crackle/spotted sides, box VG-, NOT MET	VGIB	$690.00	02-10

BRAND	MODEL	SERIES / MFG. CODE / DESCRIPTION	GRADE	PRICE	DATE yy/mm
Immell	Chippewa	4", rainbow, NOT MET	EX-	$372.00	05-07
Immell	Chippewa	4", rainbow, Blair box P-55 EX-, $2,000 NOT MET	EXIB	$1,628.00	05-07
Immell	Chippewa	bass, sienna crackle	G	$270.00	99-03
Immell	Chippewa	bass size, rainbow	VG	$330.00	04-03
Immell	Chippewa	bass, white	EX-	$890.00	99-10
Immell	Chippewa	bass, chips, NOT MET	G?	$229.50	00-01
Immell	Chippewa	bass, rainbow	EX-	$700.00	99-12
Immell	Chippewa	brown/sienna, bass size	EX+	$1,650.00	01-04
Immell	Chippewa	crackle, bass size, nice box	NIB	$3,250.00	01-12
Immell	Chippewa	musky Chippewa. Ever seen one EX? Now you have.	EX	$3,000.00	01-04
Immell	Chippewa	musky crackleback, chips, NOT MET	G	$775.00	99-03
Immell	Chippewa	musky red/yellow, big chips, NOT MET	avg	$305.00	99-05
Immell	Chippewa	musky, crackleback	G	$1,550.00	02-05
Immell	Chippewa	pike size, RB, box avg, chips but nice	VGIB	$1,025.00	02-05
Immell	Chippewa	pike size, sienna crackleback, full paint on bar	EX-	$636.00	04-12
Immell	Chippewa	pike size, crackleback, ugly	fair	$275.00	99-03
Immell	Chippewa	pike size, crackleback	EX-	$970.00	99-10
Immell	Chippewa	pike, a pig, missing belly hook	poor	$250.00	99-05
Immell	Chippewa	RB, "Pike" box avg, NOT MET (wanted $2100!)	EXIB	$870.00	02-03
Immell	Chippewa	red and aluminum, pike size, correctly marked box	NIB	$3,600.00	01-04
Immell	Chippewa	red, pike size, big chips, NOT MET	avg	$167.50	99-11
Immell	Chippewa	red/orange, NOT MET	avg	$237.50	99-08
Immell	Chippewa	sienna, belly awful, NOT MET	avg+	$257.00	00-10
Immell	Chippewa	silver/red back, GE, nice	EX-	$430.34	00-02
Immell	Chippewa	yellow/sienna, 3½"	EX-	$500.00	05-02
Immell	Chippewa #99	crackle, intro box EX-	VG+IB	$3,450.00	01-06
Immell	Chippewa, Musky	perfect glass eyes, full red paint on marked spinner, nearly flawless green fancy back paint finish, minor paint chips on metal belly	EX	$2,310.00	05-04
Immell	Chippewa, Musky	white with spots, chips, metal strip, NO BIDS	EX-?	$2,000.00	02-08
Immell	Chippewa, Pike	brown/sienna	EX	$999.00	99-11
Immell	Skipper	strawberry, light rust on lip, nice!	EX	$811.00	04-12
Interchangable Bait Co.	Bubble Sally	with pills & papers, NOT MET	NIB	$48.00	01-08
International	Pelican	black head/white, Indiana Co.	NIB	$55.00	04-01
Isle Royale	Featherwood	RW, w/r and w feather tail	NM	$18.00	05-05
Isle Royale	Pike Chub	wood, pikie scale, nice yellow/black 2PCCB	NIB	$58.00	04-12
Isle Royale	Woblit	3333-H, RH, Bass Oreno type, PE	NIB	$36.00	00-05
Jack's Tackle	Pogo Spinner	lt green shad/flitter, SPS4 box EX-	EXIB	$37.00	04-09
Jack's Tackle	Rip-L-Lure	green scale	mint	$49.00	03-04
Jacobs	Polly Frog	neat wood with hair legs, 4¼"	EX	$159.00	01-08
James, W.H.	Metal Fish Spin	pat date Jan. 27th, 1874	avg	$88.00	99-01
Jamison	#2 Winged Mascot	nice pasteboard box EX-	EXIB	$380.00	02-02
Jamison	Beetle Plop	red head/white	mint	$27.00	03-04

BRAND	MODEL	SERIES / MFG. CODE / DESCRIPTION	GRADE	PRICE	DATE yy/mm
Jamison	Blatz Beer	wooden beer bottle lure, label VG++	VG+	$20.00	05-06
Jamison	Coaxer	#1, c. 1916, 2PCCB	VG+	$177.50	99-05
Jamison	Coaxer #1	frog finish, box EX- (text only on box top)	NIB	$485.00	02-08
Jamison	Coaxer #2	nice box & papers	NIB	$150.00	04-03
Jamison	Fly Rod Bass Coaxer	r/w, 1" body, 2" w/tail	NM	$70.00	05-05
Jamison	Fly Rod Wiggler	yellow perch, crisp box	NIB	$455.00	03-09
Jamison	Luminous Coaxer	#1, crisp box & 2 papers, wowser	NIB	$475.00	05-07
Jamison	Mascot	r/w	EX+	$200.00	99-08
Jamison	Mascot	RH	EX	$154.00	04-11
Jamison	Nemo	w/orig box, small dent in box, light wear	EX	$715.00	05-04
Jamison	Nemo	white, external belly weight	EX-	$427.00	05-07
Jamison	Nemo		EX-IB	$417.00	03-09
Jamison	Nemo Bass Bait	nice box VG+, RH	EXIB	$817.00	04-11
Jamison	Single Spin Shannon	pre-1920, looks like Coaxer Underwater with spinner	EX-	$24.00	05-05
Jamison	Struggling Mouse	bar perch	VG+	$280.00	03-04
Jamison	Struggling Mouse	frog finish, 2 chips but still decent	??	$50.00	04-11
Jamison	Struggling Mouse	frog spot, light tiny pointers and small chip under tail	EX-	$110.00	05-05
Jamison	Struggling Mouse	PE, NOT MET	EX-	$102.50	00-02
Jamison	Struggling Mouse		EX	$112.50	00-01
Jamison	Underwater Coaxer	decent pasteboard box, NOT MET	EXIB	$230.00	02-02
Jamison	Wig Wag	RH, GE, lip chips, rest nice	VG-	$66.00	05-07
Jamison	Wig Wag	RH/white, GE	EX	$57.00	05-02
Jamison	Wiggle Twin	brown head & wings, silver scale	mint	$122.50	00-03
Jamison	Wiggle Twin	brown scale	EX-	$34.33	00-01
Jamison	Wiggle Twin	perch	EX	$36.51	99-05
Jamison	Wiggle Twin	RH	EX	$38.00	01-03
Jamison	Wiggle Twin	white/blk head	EX	$103.00	00-04
Jamison	Wiggler Fly Rod	bar perch	VG	$46.00	99-05
Jamison	Wiggler Fly Rod	bar perch, nice box marked, y perch	NIB	$295.00	00-02
Jamison	Wig-L-Twin	red/white	EX	$26.01	99-02
Jamison	Wig-L-Twin	black/gold scales	EX	$37.00	99-01
Jamison	Wig-L-Twin	green scale, nice box	NIB	$134.00	04-11
Jamison	Wig-L-Twin	red/black, orange wings	EX	$54.00	04-11
Jamison	Winged Mascot	large 4" and 3-hk model, RH/w, NE, age lines and some pointers	VG	$88.00	05-05
Jamison	Winged Mascot	RH	EX	$103.00	01-03
Jamison	1500	strawberry, nice	EX	$27.08	99-02
Jamison	Nemo Bass Bait	RH	VG	$247.50	04-11
Japan	Bone Jig	large saltwater jig, made of bone	EX-	$10.00	04-12
Jennings	Torpedo	metal barber pole–type spinner	VG	$407.00	99-04
Jennings	Torpedo	metal spiral body, glass bead	VG	$497.00	99-03
Jennings	Torpedo	silver spiral shape	VG+	$227.00	05-07
Jennings Decoy Co.	Shad Quack	duck novelty lure on card	NOC	$30.00	04-09
Jensen	Frogleg Kicker	extendable legs	VG	$12.27	05-07
Jensen	Froglegs	#608, red head/white, small sixe	EXIB	$127.00	05-07
Jensen	Froglegs	bass size	EX	$29.00	99-07

BRAND	MODEL	SERIES / MFG. CODE / DESCRIPTION	GRADE	PRICE	DATE yy/mm
Jensen	Froglegs		NIB	$41.00	00-01
Jensen	Froglegs Frog	green frog, blem on left cheek and tiny flk on nose, no cupped mouth, very light wear	EX-	$42.00	05-05
Jensen	Kicker Frog		NIB	$58.25	99-02
Jensen	Wood Froglegs Kicker	green frog, blem on l cheek and tiny flk on nose	EX-	$75.00	05-05
Jensen	Zipper	perch scale	mint	$7.00	05-02
Jersey	Expert	weird chin spinner, 3 single hooks	EX	$3,170.00	99-10
Jersey	Wow	black shore, one treble	EX-	$388.88	00-01
Jim Dandy	Fish Bait	picture box VG-	EX-IB	$52.00	05-02
Johansson	Spring Hook	fish trap, large 6", steel, unmrkd, very light wear	EX+	$30.00	05-05
Johnson	Auto Striker	2"	EX	$500.00	99-10
Johnson	Auto Striker	2"	NIB	$2,100.00	99-10
Johnson	Auto Striker	3", papers, box VG+	EXIB	$1,600.00	00-11
Johnson	Auto Striker	6½"	EXIB	$1,580.00	99-10
Johnson	Auto Striker	bx EX-, belly chip	EX-IB	$712.00	03-03
Johnson	Auto Striker	huge chip on tail, rest EX	?	$438.00	99-05
Johnson	Auto Striker	large, some tail, paint missing	VG-	$300.00	99-05
Johnson	Auto Striker	medium size	EX	$585.00	00-03
Johnson	Auto Striker	small size	VG-	$200.00	99-05
Johnson	Auto Striker	small size	EX	$497.00	99-07
Johnson	Auto Striker	small size	EX	$535.25	99-11
Johnson	Auto Striker	small size, PE, hair gone	VG+	$270.00	00-10
Johnson	Auto Striker	white/blk stripes	VG-	$257.00	99-02
Johnson	Auto Striker Jr.	b/w, no eyes	VG+	$354.00	00-03
Johnson	Auto Striker Jr.	beige/brown stripe	EX	$431.00	99-11
Johnson	Auto Striker Jr.	on card	NIB	$1,031.88	99-05
Johnson	Automatic Striker	small size, 3¼"	EX	$391.00	04-02
Johnson	Automatic Striker, jntd	lg size, front EX, back poor, NOT MET!	poor	$202.50	99-06
Johnson	Weedo	RH/w, YPE, wood body, w/spring action to reveal hooks	EX	$58.00	05-05
Johnson, Bill	Darto	r/w	NIB	$76.00	02-11
Judas	Frog	black	mint	$109.00	03-04
K & K	Animated Minnow	4¼", professional repaint by Bud Stewart, initaled	EX	$93.50	05-04
K & K	Animated Minnow	4", GE, metal tail, dark green back, silver belly	VG	$220.00	04-11
K & K	Animated Minnow	4", green/gold pattern, obvious wear and chipping bow, 6½" size, wear, missing end, taped corners, paper loss	VG	$1,980.00	05-04
K & K	Animated Minnow	green/silver, later style, 4¼", minnow, few age lines	EX	$880.00	05-04
K & K	Animated Minnow	jointed, green ugly chips	avg	$150.00	02-01
K & K	Animated Minnow	missing one hook, 30% paint loss	avg	$305.00	04-02
K & K	Animated Minnow	rare maroon pic box G	EX-IB	$6,500.00	01-12
K & K	Animated Minnow	scale pattern on back, much paint loss	rough	$214.00	05-07
K & K	Antimated Minnow	green back/white, GE, 3-hk, 2 side hooks	poor	$380.00	05-07
K & K	Antimated Minnow	probably never wet but huge chips, NOT MET	poor?	$202.00	01-12
K & K	Minnowette	3½", bait black/gold, crosshatch finish, some chipping to wood	G	$522.50	05-04
K & K	Minnowette	4¼", finished Heddon, rainbow, normal chipping	VG	$165.00	05-04
K & K	Minnowette	green/silver belly, jntd, GE, sm chips but nice	EX-	$655.00	04-12
K & K	Minnowette	pinkish back, white belly, slight chipping, glued chin	G	$495.00	05-04

BRAND	MODEL	SERIES / MFG. CODE / DESCRIPTION	GRADE	PRICE	DATE yy/mm
K & K	Minnowette	ugly	avg	$125.00	99-08
Kalamazoo	#1 3-hooker	lime green back/silver belly	EX-	$835.00	00-10
Kalamazoo	#2 5-hooker	lime green back/silver belly	EX-	$1,714.00	00-10
Kalamazoo	Minnow #1 3-hooker	nice shape	EX	$4,307.00	99-09
Kalamazoo	Minnow #2	4 doubles, 1 treble (missing)	EX	$5,357.00	00-09
Kalamazoo Fishing Tackle Co.	Rhodes Mechanical Frog	picture 2PCCB VG+, upper left pic of frog	VG+IB	$5,600.00	03-05
Kaufman	Harkauf	green/white, PE	EX	$612.00	00-08
Kauth	Streamline Jointed Minnow	green perch scale, GE, like an L&S	EX	$53.00	05-07
Kautzky	Lazy Ike	frog, bass plug	NIB	$2.25	05-07
Kautzky	Lazy Ike	KL-37 SC, gold scale over orange, blk back	NIB	$74.00	03-11
Kautzky	Musky Ike	r/w	EX	$15.00	99-03
Kautzky	Sail Ike x 6	6-pack	NIB	$63.50	99-06
Kautzky	Sail Shark	#166, RH/gold scale	NIB	$9.99	99-04
Kautzky	Sail Shark	orange/blk spots, PTCB	NIB	$15.51	99-11
Kautzky	Sail Shark	r/w, intro card	NIB	$26.00	99-05
Kautzky	Sail Shark	RH, on card	NIB	$12.51	00-03
Kautzky	Sail Shark	silver	NIB	$13.00	99-07
Kautzky	Sail Shark, jntd	light shad with scales	EX	$101.00	04-07
Kautzky	Sail Shark x 4	4 diff	NIB	$38.77	00-01
Kautzky	Shark Ike	3 diff, old plastic box	NIB	$33.00	99-04
Kautzky	Shark Ike	blk/y ribs	NIB	$9.99	99-04
Kautzky	Top Ike	r/w, NOT MET!	NIB	$21.00	99-03
Kautzky	Top Ike	y/r dots, NOT MET	EX	$10.50	99-07
K-B	K-B Spoon	#4 K-B, spoon w/mint box	NIB	$14.99	05-07
Keeling	5-hooker	silver-green, GE	avg	$361.00	00-02
Keeling	Baby Expert		VG+	$375.00	99-10
Keeling	Baby Tom	1⅜", red/yellow/green stripe pattern	EX-	$77.00	04-11
Keeling	Baby Zara	GE, pikie	EX+	$300.00	99-08
Keeling	Crab	black/white	EX+	$150.00	99-08
Keeling	Expert	5-hook, yellow GE, 2BW, 3 HPGM, nice	EX-	$396.00	05-07
Keeling	Expert	5-hook, red, HPGM, hole props	VG+	$638.00	99-10
Keeling	Expert	5-hooker, round body, hole props, looks odd	EX+	$511.00	01-10
Keeling	Expert	no eyes, screw hangers, HPGM	EX-	$430.00	99-07
Keeling	Expert	y, no eyes, 2 HPGM	VG-	$392.00	99-06
Keeling	Flapper	450, rainbow, no eyes	EX	$125.00	99-03
Keeling	Flapper	4½", green scale, no eyes	EX-	$82.55	99-12
Keeling	General Tom	bar fish, GE, spinner?	VG-	$159.00	00-01
Keeling	Musky Expert	5", 3-hk, 4BW, props missing & broken	VG	$785.00	02-09
Keeling	Surface Tom	strawberry, GE, rough box	EXIB	$255.77	99-03
Keeling	Tom Thumb	3 diff	rough	$20.50	99-03
Keeling	Tom Thumb	dark green scale, great box & paper	NIB	$500.00	99-08
Keeling	Tom Thumb	pig lure with box, Hobbs buy	poor	$67.00	99-03
Keeling	Tom THumb	RB, big chips, Hobbs buy	poor	$47.00	99-03
Keeling	Tom Thumb	red/white, fair box, newby bought it	EXIB	$200.00	00-07
Keeling	Tom Thumb	yellow scale, papers, hvy age lines	NIB	$163.00	01-01
Keeling?	Expert	5-hk, silver, "EXPERT" on side	VG+	$850.00	00-05
Keeling?	Expert	lg bowtie props, GE	VG	$1,082.50	99-03

BRAND	MODEL	SERIES / MFG. CODE / DESCRIPTION	GRADE	PRICE	DATE yy/mm
Keeling?	Zaragossa Type	pikie, GE	EX	$152.50	99-10
Keen	Kicker Frog		EX	$1,025.00	01-11
Keen	Knight	black scale/yellow, wood, Tadpolly shaped	EX-	$24.00	03-08
Keetchum	Frog Casting Frame Gang	hooks replaced, decent box	NIB	$80.00	99-01
Kellman	Charles C. Kellman Lure	2½", HP frog pattern	EX	$88.00	04-11
Kent	5-hooker	green/white	avg	$1,275.00	02-10
Kent	Floater	frog, GE, sm tail chip, NOT MET	EX-	$400.00	01-08
Kent	Floater	GE, twisted wire, side hook hangers, I&R stamped props	G	$440.00	04-11
Kent	Floater (frog)	copper/black spots, original model	VG	$4,406.00	02-02
Kent	Frog	GE, 6 spots, one sm chip	EX-	$472.00	02-08
Kent	Frog	repaint on back		$153.50	99-01
Kentucky Bait Co.	Flying Fish	frog/yellow wings	mint	$81.00	03-04
Ketchall	Wobbler	red/white, age lines but nice	EX	$71.00	02-08
Ketchum	Frog Gang	rough box	EXIB	$102.00	00-04
Kiffe	200	lots of wear & light corr, but works OK	avg	$57.00	03-04
Kimmich	Mouse	bead eyes, in pic box	EXIB	$575.00	99-01
Kimmich	Mouse	brown, picture box VG+	NIB	$287.00	04-03
Kimmich	Mouse	great box & papers, snipers	NIB	$526.10	99-11
Kimmich	Mouse	head tiger stripe pattern on top, diamond shaped lip w/box and papers	EX	$440.00	05-04
Kimmich	Mouse	nice box, hair little rough	EXIB	$472.00	01-04
King	Spiral	white/red stripes	EX-	$52.00	02-12
King Chub	3½"		NIB	$34.00	01-03"
Kingfisher	3-hooker	chub scale, NOT MET	EXIB	$256.00	99-11
Kingfisher	3-hooker	white, GE, HPGM, unmarked props	EX-IB	$405.00	99-03
Kingfisher	Bass Oreno type	r/w, TE, decent newer box	EX-IB	$22.50	99-11
Kingfisher	Moonlight Floater	woodpecker, red & blue label box VG	EXIB	$898.00	05-02
Knight Mfg.	Bad Shad	green, 3" long, made in Tyler TX	NIB	$22.50	05-07
Kono Mfg.	Myopic Minnow	yellow flitter, novelty lure with eye glasses	EX	$431.00	05-07
Kwiki	Kwiki	2 interchangable wood bodies, metal frame	NIB	$89.00	04-02
L & S	Baby Cat	gold/blk window box	NIB	$25.39	99-01
L & S	Bass Master	plastic w/box & pamphlet, 3" white belly, green scales, green back, yellow eyes	VG+	$21.50	05-07
L & S	Bass Master 2519	green/yellow, sparkles, clear eye, window box	NIB	$44.00	01-06
L & S	MirrroLure	sinker	NIB	$19.49	05-07
L & S	Mixed	5 common colors	EX-	$52.50	99-01
L & S	Mudcat	brown	EX	$20.00	05-06
L & S	Musky Master	gold/black box, common color, o eyes	NIB	$137.00	01-05
L & S	Musky Master	J-435	EX	$24.75	99-01
L & S	Musky Master	perch, opaque red eye	EX	$55.00	00-12
L & S	Musky Master	scale, opaque eyes	EX-	$55.00	01-05
L & S	Musky Master	y/green scale, clear eye, NOT MET	EX	$29.00	01-01
L & S	Panfish Master	#00-32	NIB	$8.74	99-01
L & S	Panfish Master	nice box with papers	NIB	$16.50	98-12
L & S	Pike Master	common color, o eyes	EX	$10.00	01-05
L & S	Pike Master	silver/blk back, ribs	NIB	$27.80	99-02

BRAND	MODEL	SERIES / MFG. CODE / DESCRIPTION	GRADE	PRICE	DATE yy/mm
L & S	PikeMaster	3021, blue scale	NIB	$22.17	99-01
L & S	Troutmaster	opaque eyes	EX	$18.00	01-04
Lake George	Floater	alum nose, spoon bent, maroon/cream	EX-	$455.00	04-01
Lake George	Floater	red/white, ball has chips, lure nice	EX	$580.00	03-04
Lamay	Creeper	frog, modern 2PCCB, NOT MET	NIB	$25.00	00-10
Land-Em	Lure	red mechanical lure, White's P 85 D 6 in box with paper	NIB	$90.00	05-06
Land-em	Spring Lure	papers, plain box	EXIB	$449.00	00-01
Lane	Spinner, spoon	3 diff	NOC	$7.99	99-05
Lane	Wagtail	silver/green	mint	$655.00	00-08
Lane	Wagtail Shinner	CCBC lip?	EX-	$183.50	99-05
Lane	Wagtail Wobbler	2¾", HP, black/green/silver, 1 HPGM	EX	$49.50	04-11
Lane	Wagtail Wobbler	2¾", HP, black/green/silver, 1 HPGM	VG	$77.00	04-11
Lane	Wagtail Wobbler	2¾", HP, green back/gold scale, 1 HPGM	VG-	$49.50	04-11
Lane	Wagtail Wobbler	2¾", HP, green back/gold scale, 1 HPGM	VG	$137.50	04-11
Lane	Wagtail Wobbler		EX-	$318.00	00-01
Lane	Wagtail Wobbler		EX	$376.00	99-11
Lanes	Automatic Minnow	paint flaking	VG	$2,100.00	02-08
Larson	Fishtrap	spring action spoon, r&w paint like a daredevil, neat graphics on 2PCCB, catalog	NIB	$20.00	05-05
Larson	Weed Splitter	black head, scale pattern, odd weedless hooks	EX	$21.00	02-08
Lauby	4¼ inch	w/black back/spots, nice	EX	$127.50	99-08
Lauby	Fly Rod	strawberry, thick body	EX-	$132.50	00-01
Lauby	Fly Rod	strawberry, thin body	EX-	$153.50	00-01
Lauby	Lauby	strawberry	EX-	$182.00	04-11
Lauby	Musky Size	w/age lines, couple of pointers, w/orig box marked "wonder spoon"	EX-	$1,980.00	05-04
Lauby	Pike Size	spotted	EX-	$157.00	00-01
Lauby	Spoon	4", RH, with flippers	EX-	$74.00	00-04
Lauby	Spoon	bigger one, yellow & black top, spotted belly	EX	$345.00	04-03
Lauby	Spoon	medium in box B37-R, tiger spot, back/white spot belly	NIB	$517.00	04-03
Lauby	Weedless	strawberry	VG+	$68.00	00-10
Lauby	Weedless	w spotted, nicks around hook guard	VG	$87.00	00-03
Lauby	WonderSpoon	3½", yellow/black dots, nice box & papers	NIB	$709.00	01-05
Lauffer	Scientific Lures	Bakelite, interchangeable 4 heads & 4 bodies, great box EX	NIB	$990.00	05-04
Layfield	Sunnybrook	103, Skunk Black, made in Tyler, TX, about 2" long	AVG	$13.00	05-07
Lazy Dazy	Lazy Dazy	red & white, in plastic top box VG++	VG+	$10.00	05-06
Lazy Ike	12-pack	2PCCB EX, includes 6 lures new in PTCB	NIB	$96.00	03-07
Lazy Ike	Fly Ike	silver scale/ black ribbed	VG+	$10.00	05-06
Lazy Ike	Husky Ike	KL-42 BLSC, PTCB with card crisp, blue scale	NIB	$68.00	05-07
Lazy Ike	Natural Ike	rainbow trout finish, 20 RT	NIB	$46.00	05-04
Lazy Ike	Sail Shark	145, sm size, red head/white	NIB	$40.00	03-10
Lazy Ike	Sail Shark	200MO, silver/orange head	NIB	$21.00	02-11
Lazy Ike	Sail Shark	200S, green head/silver	NIB	$22.00	02-11
Lazy Ike	Sail Shark	235, PTCB	NIB	$17.00	05-02
Lazy Ike	Sail Shark	260, yellow, coach dog	NIB	$11.00	02-11

BRAND	MODEL	SERIES / MFG. CODE / DESCRIPTION	GRADE	PRICE	DATE yy/mm
Lazy Ike	Sail Shark	6-pack, PTCB, clear red/flitter	NIB	$113.00	03-07
Lazy Ike	Sail Shark	jointed, clear red/flitter	EX	$47.00	03-03
Lazy Ike	Sail Shark	purple/chrome	NIB	$27.50	01-07
Lazy Ike	Sail Shark	yellow body, black head, yellow eye w/black center, gold glitter	EX	$27.00	05-07
Lazy Ike	Sail Shark	105	NIB	$32.03	99-07
Lazy Ike	Sail Shark	205	NIB	$14.01	99-07
Lazy Ike	Sail Shark	235	NIB	$26.01	99-07
Lazy Ike	Sail Shark	240	NIB	$15.01	99-07
Lazy Ike	Sail Shark	245	NIB	$31.01	99-07
Lazy Ike	Sail Shark	265	NIB	$15.01	99-07
Lazy Ike	Sail Shark	frog spot, missing belly hook	EX-	$142.00	03-11
Lazy Ike	Sail Shark, jointed	fire tiger	EX	$46.00	03-04
Lazy Ike	Sail Shark, jointed	red head/yellow, black ribs	NIB	$32.00	05-07
Lazy Ike	Sail Shark, jointed	PEP, white	EX	$27.00	02-10
Lazy Ike	Stinger	yellow/ silver flakes	NIB	$23.00	04-01
Lazy Ike	Tail Shark	jointed Sail Shark, golden shiner, rounded tail	VG+	$33.00	03-11
Le Boeuf	Creeper	frog color, smaller size	EX	$34.00	05-01
Le Boeuf	Creeper	green	VG	$34.00	99-01
Le Boeuf	Creeper	frog	EXIB	$72.00	00-08
Le Boeuf	Creeper	light frog	NIB	$75.00	99-12
Le Boeuf	Creeper	light frog, 2PCCB	NIB	$56.00	01-06
Le Boeuf	Creeper Frog	green/black squiggles	EX	$76.00	05-03
Le Lure	Creeper	black, signed newer model, NOT MET	EX	$78.00	03-11
Le Lure	Creeper	green, wedding veil, unmarked Frenchy	EX	$82.00	04-01
Le Lure	Creeper	pointed nose & tail	EX	$128.00	04-03
Le Lure	Fetch-In-Catch	red scale, modern box, NOT MET	NIB	$456.00	03-07
Le Lure	Flat Globe	crackleback, unsigned, 8¾", NOT MET	avg	$275.00	03-11
Le Lure	Globe	perch scale, Frenchy LeMay	mint	$131.00	04-01
Le Lure	Musky Water Thumper	modern box & lure autographed "Frenchy"	NIB	$195.00	03-05
Leon Tackle	Chase A Bug	gray Waterwave	EX	$84.00	99-03
Lews	BB1	Speed Spool	VG	$51.00	99-02
Lews	BB-1L	Speed Spool	mint	$69.00	00-09
Lex Baits	Kentucky Leader	green/yellow/red chin	EX	$18.00	05-02
Lido Lures	Swimmer	dark mullet scale, GE, 8", wood box stained	EXIB	$227.00	05-07
Little Jul	Little Jul	yellow/spots, plastic box, lg size, 3"	NIB	$16.00	04-07
Live Action	Frog	box VG+	NIB	$202.00	05-07
Live Action	Frog	nice box	NIB	$189.00	05-01
Live Action	Frog	nice box	NIB	$237.50	00-02
Livesey	Metal Minnow (Livesev?)	neat curved tail, 3 hooks, NOT MET	EX-	$960.00	03-02
Livingstone, J.	8	kidney spinner, Ganaoque, Ontario	EX-	$130.00	05-07
Lloyd & Co.	Hunger Jack	few pointers	EX	$550.00	05-04
Lloyd & Co.	Hungry Jack	NOT MET	VG+	$356.99	99-05
Lloyd & Co.	Hungry Jack	NOT MET	EX-	$279.00	99-08
Lloyd & Co.	Hungry Jack	scale finish, ugly	poor	$278.00	05-03
Lloyd & Co.	Hungry Jack		EX-	$501.00	02-03
Lloyd & Co.	Hungry Jack		EX-	$356.01	99-03
Lloyd's	Mermaid Queen	gold hair/green tail, papers	NIT	$71.00	05-01

BRAND	MODEL	SERIES / MFG. CODE / DESCRIPTION	GRADE	PRICE	DATE yy/mm
Lockhart	Wagtail Witch	red, L-rig	EX-	$83.00	05-07
Long Island	Flasher	box & paper	EXIB	$225.00	05-07
Lucky Day	Go Getter	black shore	EX	$18.00	04-02
Lucky Strike	Jntd Submarine Plug	5", jntd pikie, silver flash, rubber fused on belly, very light wear	EX-	$32.00	05-05
Luhr Jenson	Dogwalker		EX	$27.00	99-01
Lur-All	Beetle Bug	#164, on card in box	NIB	$51.00	99-06
Lur-All	Beetle Bug	lg 2PCCB, fish with lure in mouth	EXIB	$67.00	05-02
Lurette	Glass Tube	#2	?	$925.00	01-07
Lurk Live Lures Inc.	Lurk Live Lure	minnow tube, crisp box and paper	NIB	$27.00	04-09
Macatawa Bait Co.	Hopper	3½", Bead Eye Bug	NM	$165.00	05-04
Macatawa Bait Co.	Musky Bird	bumblebee color, 6" body, metal tail & wings	mint	$175.00	03-01
Macatawa Bait Co.	Musky Frog	cool	NIB	$165.00	99-01
Macatawa Bait Co.	Musky Minnow	5-hk, bar perch, modern lure	NIB	$92.00	05-07
Mack	The Mack Hook	#7, fancy fluted spinner and pat hook, ornate glass beads pat 1891	EX	$125.00	05-05
Mackenzie	Bait Life	bobber/minnow tube thing	NIB	$15.00	04-09
Mack's	Winner Bait x 2	frog spot, blue flash	EX	$63.00	04-11
Magic Bait Co.	Magic Minnow	hollow metal, nice box, NOT MET	NIB	$48.00	03-02
Makinen	6-pack	graphics inside lid, 6 diff common lures	EXIB	$480.00	02-03
Makinen	Holi Comet	tenite yellow/black/red spots, papers	NIB	$27.00	04-02
Makinen	Holi Comet, jntd	frog, cat, NOT MET	NIB	$17.50	99-06
Makinen	Holi Comet, Musky	pike, has no eyes, wood	EX+	$35.00	05-06
Makinen	Holy Comet	pikie	EXIB	$60.00	99-01
Makinen	Makilure	wood, frog spot, L10C box & catalog	NIB	$19.00	05-03
Makinen	Merry Widow	frog spot	EX	$13.00	05-02
Makinen	Merry Widow	red hed/white scales, papers	NIB	$39.00	03-10
Makinen	Musky Holi Comet	pike scale, 6" long, jntd, plastic, light pointers and few light scratches	VG	$20.00	05-05
Makinen	Musky Holi Comet	plastic model, gray back and ribs with gold scales, light wear, in lg 2PCCB	VGIB	$38.00	05-05
Makinen	Waddle Bug	frog spot, NE, few tiny pointers and light age lines, in orig EX- 2PCCB w/paperwork	ex-IB	$38.00	05-05
Makinen	Waddle Bug	NOT MET	NIB	$37.00	99-04
Makinen	Wonderlure		NIB	$42.30	99-10
Makinen	Wonderlure Jr.	fly rod? pike scale, brass flippers	EX-	$66.00	03-07
Manatou	Minnow	red, hook drag	VG+	$1,082.00	02-03
Manistee	Surface Bait	sm Globe type, carved? eyes, "MANISTEE" on side	VG-	$2,358.00	04-01
Manistee	Minnow	retains most paint, "the manistee" stenciled on side, minor paint flaking on base of spinner and tip of tail	EX-	$3,080.00	05-04
Manitou	Minnow	green back, small nick on tail, nice box & papers	EXIB	$1,325.00	05-06
Manitou	Minnow	green/y belly, wrench & paper	NIB	$2,000.00	00-08
Manitou	Minnow	wrench & papers, NOT MET	NIB	$2,107.00	99-09
Manitou	Minnow	wrench, papers, dark green	NIB	$3,190.00	99-10
Mann	Dancer	frog, Zara type	NOC	$26.97	99-02
Mann	Dancer	Zara with fin, frog	EX	$63.00	98-12

BRAND	MODEL	SERIES / MFG. CODE / DESCRIPTION	GRADE	PRICE	DATE yy/mm
Mann	Frog	black	NIB	$51.00	99-02
Mann	Frog?	hourglass shape, rear spinner	NIB	$57.00	99-01
Mann	Hackleback	wounded Spook with fin	EX	$48.00	98-12
Mann	Hard Worm x 4	4 diff	EX	$42.00	00-11
Mann	Mann Dancer	finned Zara type, shad	NOC	$10.51	99-02
Mann	Mann Frog	green pearl/blk spot	EX	$42.00	99-02
Mann	Mann Frog	y/blk spots	EX	$42.00	99-02
Mann J.H.	Spinner	Syracuse, NY, bent	avg	$83.00	00-10
Mann, J. H.	#1 Tandem Spinner	4¼", blades look sterling silver, sm dents	VG	$102.00	03-05
Manning	Tasty Shrimp		EX	$34.00	99-03
Manucraft	Tubulure	silver, 2PCCB & papers	NIB	$35.00	04-07
Marathon	1947 Book	9 lures	NIB	$42.00	99-01
Marathon	Joes Deep Runner x 3	Froelich plastic lure, 3 diff colors	mint	$66.00	02-03
Marathon	Musk-E-Hound	red/yellow, PE, 2PCCB VG+	EXIB	$100.00	05-07
Marathon	Musk-E-Munk	red/yellow, painted eye	NIB	$67.00	04-11
Marathon	Musk-E-Munk	yellow/red head, GE, hooks very rusty, rest nice	VG+	$20.00	04-12
Marathon	Muskie Huskie	No. 10522 scale, black scale	NIB	$107.00	05-07
Marathon	Musky Munk	GE, brown/white, belly pntrs on l-side and light wear, full hair tail	VG+	$64.00	05-05
marathon	Musky Muskrat Bait	5", covered in muskrat fur, bead eyes	EX	$121.00	04-11
Marathon	Waterfrog	GE, hair frog	NIB	$56.00	00-08
Maratrhon	Musk-E-Monk	rainbow, TE, 2PCCB	VGIB	$65.00	98-12
Marsh	Darter	plastic Florida lure	NIB	$151.00	05-07
Marsh	Marvel	y shore, plastic, box VG+, FL	NIB	$60.00	01-03
Marsh	Marvel #2 Darter	leaping bass 2PCCB VG, green back/white sides	EXIB	$146.00	05-07
Martin	7"	green scale back/white, NOT MET	NIB	$27.00	01-05
Martin	Fetchi Lizard	RH, PE	NIB	$23.49	00-04
Martin	Injured Minnow	white/light silver scale, GE, belly stencil	EX-	$67.00	03-02
Martin	Lizzard	#51SW, w/blk spots & line	NIB	$46.00	99-05
Martin	Lizzard	25G, corners rough on box	NIB	$52.00	00-01
Martin	Lizzard	green perch	NIB	$76.00	99-04
Martin	Salmon lure	7KS/c-3, yellow/red gill, crisp box	NIB	$43.00	05-03
Martin	Salmon lure	pearl pink, no hooks, old fish pic box #5	EXIB	$28.00	05-03
Martin	Shrimp	r&w swirled, window bx 1102 EX	NIB	$21.00	04-09
Martin	Tad	green scale, "TAD" on belly	EX	$66.00	01-01
Martin Fly Rod	Crawfish	plastic like Martin shrimp, but tiny brown and w/red feelers	mint	$45.00	05-05
Martin Fly Rod	Minnow-Darter	gray plastic body like Martin shrimp, but tiny and brown with yellow hair tail, very light wear	EX+	$45.00	05-05
Marvelus	3-hooker	Neverfail, white, box VG	VG+IB	$406.00	01-09
Mason	4"	silver herring, NOT MET	NIB	$102.00	01-05
Mason	4"	white herring, NOT MET	NIB	$102.00	01-05
Mason	4"	yellow/red gill	NIB	$250.00	01-05
Mason	Delux Salmon lure	silver herring, great box and papers, PE	NIB	$225.00	01-08
Mason	Mason	white, crisp box & paper, Salmon plug	NIB	$189.00	01-01
Mason	Mason	white, crisp box & paper, Salmon plug	NIB	$197.00	01-01
Mason	Salmon Delux	white herring, Seattle, WA	NIB	$333.00	00-09
Mason	Salmon Delux	yellow herring, Seattle, WA	NIB	$355.00	00-09

BRAND	MODEL	SERIES / MFG. CODE / DESCRIPTION	GRADE	PRICE	DATE yy/mm
Master	Lure	Pikie type, GE?	EX	$22.50	00-01
Masterlure	Pikie Type	RH, jointed, 8", GE, 2PCCB, Brooklyn, NY	NIB	$293.00	03-08
Masterlure	Snook Jr.	yellow spray, ugly GE, DD, pikie type	NIB	$421.00	01-02
MB Mfg. Co.	Kitchen Sink	novelty lure on EX- card	NOC	$25.00	04-09
McCagg	Barney	2½" brown scale, paper in original cellophane bag	new	$59.00	05-07
McCagg	Barney	large size black, with scale back stripe	NIB	$53.00	05-01
McCagg	Barney	red/white, lg size	mint	$76.00	03-04
McCagg	Barney	side hook, lg, blk/grn scale stripe, nice	NIB	$165.00	00-10
Medley	Wiggly Crawfish	green/silver/red	VG+	$137.00	01-03
Medley	Wiggly Crawfish	green/y stripes	VG	$155.00	00-10
Medley	Wiggly Crawfish	red/yellow	EX-	$160.00	01-03
Medley	Wiggly Crawfish	white pasteboard B-1 box EX, white/red lure	EXIB	$810.00	05-06
Medley	Wiggly Crawfish	yellow/brown	EX-	$148.00	01-03
Medley	Wiggly Crawfish	yellow/red/brown	EX-	$150.00	01-03
Mepps	Harley Davidson	13 BIDS! Mepps with decal	NIB	$41.00	99-09
Mercury	Mercury Worm	yellow w/mercury in clear middle section new in plastic tube w/catalog	NIB	$35.00	05-05
Mercury Worm	Mercury Worm	purple, hollow, large drop of mercury in it for ballast, hand painted, w/clear box	EX	$15.51	05-07
Mercury Worm Lure Co.	Mercury Worm	yellow/black skirt, in tube	NIT	$30.00	04-08
Mermaid Bait Co.	4 different	NOT MET	EX-	$71.00	99-04
Mermaid Bait Co.	MerMinnow	spoon, NOT MET	mint	$9.99	99-01
Mermaid Bait Co.	Scatback	2PCCB	NIB	$137.50	99-03
Mermaid Bait Co.	Scatback	black scale, plastic, bass size, in orig 2PPTB	EX+IB	$70.00	05-05
Mermaid Bait Co.	Scatback	frog spot, ⅝ oz. bass size, unused, in EX- orig 2PPTB	EX+IB	$70.00	05-05
Mermaid Bait Co.	Scatback	papers	NIB	$20.00	99-05
Mermaid Bait Co.	Virgin	red hair & green fins	EX+	$55.00	05-06
Messinger Fly Rod	Frog	brown and green frog, small body, GPE, hint of wear	EX+	$40.00	05-05
Messinger Fly Rod	Frog	brown-yellow and green frog, large size, very light wear	EX-	$30.00	05-05
Messinger Fly Rod	Frog	tan and white frog, GPE, 1 eye gone, hair is a little stained	VG	$18.00	05-05
Michigan Lake	Fin-Win	wood, GE, green scale, cream belly, darker around eyes, red chin, 3¾"	VG	$18.25	05-07
Miller	#5	Springwater, NY, Colorado Blade, nice red beads	VG+	$12.00	05-06
Miller	Reversible	RH	EX	$3,300.00	03-11
Miller	Reversible	RH/white (lum?) + gold spots	EX	$2,976.00	04-11
Miller	Reversible	RH/w, NOT MET	G	$860.00	99-05
Miller	Reversible	strawberry, Neverfail hardware	EX	$4,500.00	05-07
Miller	Reversible	y/gold spots, Neverfail hardware	mint	$6,000.00	01-12
Miller	Reversible	yellow with gold spot, minnow, w/picture box with broken corner and some label damage, 2 box flyers	EXIB	$6,875.00	05-04
Miller	Reversible Spinner	full red, yellow, and white tail accents, marked "pat applied for," wire leader	EX	$440.00	05-04
Miller	Reversible Spinner	in picture 2PCCB	VGIB	$1,100.00	98-12
Miller	Reversible Spinner	pic box with cut on top but OK, papers	NIB	$986.00	04-03

BRAND	MODEL	SERIES / MFG. CODE / DESCRIPTION	GRADE	PRICE	DATE yy/mm
Miller	Reversible Spinner	yellow, white feathers, full leader	EX	$440.00	05-04
Millsite	28 Diff Commons	salesman display, NOT MET	EX	$362.00	00-03
Millsite	6 Commons	mixed grades		$27.00	99-07
Millsite	Bassor	y/black spots	NIB	$24.00	00-05
Millsite	Dail Double x 4	one lg, 3 small	VG+	$46.52	00-03
Millsite	Daily Double	3 different	EX	$57.00	99-03
Millsite	Daily Double	4 different	EX	$36.25	99-03
Millsite	Daily Double	834, orange/black spots	NIB	$36.00	04-03
Millsite	Daily Double	8401, perch	NIB	$27.80	99-03
Millsite	Daily Double	frog, NOT MET	NIB	$11.51	99-06
Millsite	Daily Double	gray	VG+	$10.00	05-06
Millsite	Daily Double	perch?	EX	$28.00	99-01
Millsite	Daily Double	pikie/blk heads	EXIB	$20.50	99-05
Millsite	Daily Double	r/w	EX	$11.49	99-01
Millsite	Daily Double	sil/blk spots, NOT MET	EX-	$9.99	99-05
Millsite	Fly Rod Daily Double	y/black dots	EX	$150.00	00-07
Millsite	Paddle Plug	Rattle Bug, 2 diff	EX	$47.00	99-03
Millsite	Paddle Plug	brown scale	EX-	$20.49	99-06
Millsite	Paddle Plug	perch scale	VG	$31.50	98-12
Millsite	Paddle Plug	pikie	VG	$15.58	99-02
Millsite	Paddle Plug	r/w, with tag	mint	$20.50	99-02
Millsite	Paddle Plug	r/w, with hangtag	EX	$28.50	99-02
Millsite	Paddle Plug	red, NOT MET	EXIB	$26.00	00-02
Millsite	Paddle Plug	silver flash	avg	$27.01	99-02
Millsite	Paddle Plug	yellow	EX+	$31.05	99-05
Millsite	Paddle Plug	671, r/w	NIB	$29.99	99-06
Millsite	Paddle Plug	red and black scale	EX	$62.99	00-02
Millsite	Rattel Bug	green scale	EX	$21.07	99-05
Millsite	Rattle Bug	blk/red	EX	$39.00	99-08
Millsite	Rattle Bug	r/w, PTCB	EXIB	$27.25	00-03
Millsite	Rattle Bug	yellow/black, wrong box	EXIB	$47.00	98-12
Millsite	Rattle Bug	brown	EX-	$24.00	99-03
Millsite	Rattle Bug	brown/yellow	EX	$36.00	99-01
Millsite	Rattle Bug	frog	NIB	$21.00	05-02
Millsite	Rattle Bug	frog finish	EX-	$6.00	04-12
Millsite	Rattle Bug	gold, NOT MET	EX-IB	$21.00	99-05
Millsite	Rattle Bug	orange	EX-	$12.50	99-02
Millsite	Rattle Bug	r/w		$11.10	99-01
Millsite	Rattle Bug	r/w, early indent eyes, nice 2PCCB	NIB	$41.00	01-03
Millsite	Rattle Bug	red (black lines)	EX	$48.00	01-08
Millsite	Rattle Bug	y/blk spots, sm chip	EX-	$42.00	01-01
Millsite	Rattle Bug	y/r, nice papers, 2PCCB	EX-IB	$104.00	01-08
Millsite	Rattle Bug	yellow/blk	EX	$36.52	99-02
Millsite	Rattle Bug			$18.76	99-01
Millsite	Runt Types	2 diff, 530, 530T?	NIB	$38.09	99-04
Millsite	Runt Types	4 different	EX	$16.00	01-03
Millsite	Runt Types x 3	common colors, PTCB	NIB	$27.03	99-09
Millsite	Spin E Bee	frog spot, ¼ oz.	EX	$53.00	05-07

BRAND	MODEL	SERIES / MFG. CODE / DESCRIPTION	GRADE	PRICE	DATE yy/mm
Millsite	Wig Wag	blue scale	VG+	$25.00	99-08
Millsite	Wig Wag	red/blk dots	EX	$10.00	00-01
Milwards	Trout Archer	England, nice 2PCCB, on crisp card	NIB	$13.00	05-03
Minnow tube	Unknown	3-hooker, nice harness	VG	$760.00	99-03
Minser	Lucky Louie	5¼", salmon plug, blue back/white, crisp box	NIB	$204.00	05-07
Minser	Wee Louie	pearl pink, nice graphic 2PCCB	NIB	$25.00	04-07
Miracle Lure	Miracle Lure	LS1, small size	NIB	$21.00	04-09
Mitey Atom	Mitey Atom	b/w, wood?	EX	$30.30	99-06
Mitey Atom	Mitey Atom	RH, VG+ box	EXIB	$49.00	04-09
Modern Sporting Goods	Froglegs	flattened tail, lily pad box VG	NIB	$90.00	03-08
Modern Sporting Goods	Froglegs	molded front legs, great box knife & fork	NIB	$152.00	01-05
Mohawk River	Bubble Dancer	RH	NIB	$38.00	04-11
Mohawk River Tackle	Bubble Dancer	dark scale, auto bubble forming lure	NIB	$43.00	03-06
Montgomery Ward	Bass Oreno Type	RH, 7480 PTCB, TE	NIB	$20.00	04-12
Moonlight	#2 Weedless	great box, woodpecker type	EXIB	$532.22	99-09
Moonlight	3000 2-hooker	frog, GE, surface?	EX	$405.00	99-11
Moonlight	5-hook Wobbler	white, ugly, cup, 3¾"	EX-	$262.63	99-12
Moonlight	5-hooker	green/w, tiny cups, ugly age lines, chips	avg	$424.00	99-10
Moonlight	5-hooker	red, nice	VG+	$585.77	99-05
Moonlight	Aristocrat Torpedo	w/red ribs, GE	EX-	$136.00	00-04
Moonlight	Babe-Eat-Us	Mossback, black back/green top/white belly, NE, ST, lg blem on belly and light wear	VG-	$34.00	05-05
Moonlight	Baby Surface Pikaroon	uncataloged, little size, 3", near-pikaroon shape, surface lure, RH/w	EX	$150.00	05-05
Moonlight	Bass Seeker	bar perch, GE	EX	$148.00	00-06
Moonlight	Bass Seeker	perch, GE	EX	$129.00	03-04
Moonlight	Bass Seeker	perch/sparkles, GE	EX	$113.00	00-10
Moonlight	Crawfish	weight & legs	EX	$520.00	99-04
Moonlight	Cup-Faced Wobbler	brown back, RB, GE, hook drag on back	VG-	$71.00	00-10
Moonlight	Dreadnaught	b/w	EX-	$3,738.00	00-03
Moonlight	Dreadnaught	red & white, white overpainted	EX-	$612.00	04-11
Moonlight	Floating Bait	3-pack, self-glowing Nite bait	NIB	$1,620.00	99-03
Moonlight	Floating Bait	very early box & papers, lum	EXIB	$500.00	01-05
Moonlight	Floating Bait	white woodpecker type, early 2PCCB EX- white, papers	NIB	$588.00	05-07
Moonlight	Floating Bait #1	LUM, woodpecker, great box	EXIB	$815.00	00-05
Moonlight	Jointed Pikaroon	in correct box	NIB	$750.00	01-04
Moonlight	Ladybug Wiggler	bright and shiny, with slight paint chip on head, w/box general wear	EX-IB	$1,430.00	05-04
Moonlight	Ladybug Wiggler		EX	$900.00	01-04
Moonlight	Ladybug Wiggler	y/blk spots w/gold centers, PE	VG	$300.00	99-06
Moonlight	Midget Woodpecker	luminous	VG+	$69.50	00-01
Moonlight	Mossback 1103	(Surf Oreno type), box VG, POBW	EXIB	$610.00	02-08
Moonlight	Paw Paw #5 Fishspear	frog, 2 hooks, 2 line ties, NOT MET	EX-	$635.00	00-04
Moonlight	Pikaroon	RH	EX-	$185.00	00-09
Moonlight	Pikaroon	4", bar perch, GE	EX-	$405.00	00-03

BRAND	MODEL	SERIES / MFG. CODE / DESCRIPTION	GRADE	PRICE	DATE yy/mm
Moonlight	Pikaroon	4⅛"	EX-	$164.00	02-02
Moonlight	Pikaroon	bar perch, single hook, Pikaroon	Mint	$2,500.00	01-04
Moonlight	Pikaroon	bar perch, 4"	EX	$352.00	00-04
Moonlight	Pikaroon	bar perch, GE, worm burn, NOT MET	avg	$51.00	00-02
Moonlight	Pikaroon	black, in box #1003	EXIB	$407.00	99-08
Moonlight	Pikaroon	blk/y belly, 5¼", 3 hooks	VG	$83.00	00-08
Moonlight	Pikaroon	blue scale	EX	$605.00	01-03
Moonlight	Pikaroon	bright yellow, single hook, minor nose chipping	EX	$1,595.00	05-04
Moonlight	Pikaroon	GE, black stripe & red top, cream-colored belly	VG+	$150.00	05-06
Moonlight	Pikaroon	green/black stripe	VG	$127.50	99-08
Moonlight	Pikaroon	green scale, decent box, NOT MET	VGIB	$232.50	00-02
Moonlight	Pikaroon	jointed, 4"	fair	$48.50	99-05
Moonlight	Pikaroon	orange/blk dots	EX	$628.00	02-02
Moonlight	Pikaroon	orange/blk spots, single hook	EX	$1,825.00	99-08
Moonlight	Pikaroon	perch, TE, NOT MET	VG-	$51.00	00-02
Moonlight	Pikaroon	RB, nice	EX-	$255.00	99-11
Moonlight	Pikaroon	RH, GE, NOT MET	VG	$79.00	00-02
Moonlight	Pikaroon	RH, GE, jointed, NOT MET	EX	$83.00	00-04
Moonlight	Pikaroon	single hook, red scale, orange belly	EX-	$790.00	03-07
Moonlight	Pikaroon	white (yellowed), black eyes	EX-	$281.10	00-03
Moonlight	Pikaroon	y/black eye shadow, GE	EX-	$228.60	00-02
Moonlight	Pikaroon	orange w/black spots	EX+	$850.00	01-04
Moonlight	Pikaroon 5¼"	bar perch, GE, nice	EX-	$356.00	00-11
Moonlight	Pikaroon	5" Pikaroon, in correct box	EX	$1,600.00	01-04
Moonlight	Pikaroon, jntd	gold scale over blk, poor box, NOT MET	VG+IB	$290.00	99-08
Moonlight	Pikaroon, jntd	shiner scale, sm chip by eye, SOLD	EX-	$275.00	00-05
Moonlight	Pikaroon, jntd	green scale, GE, NOT MET	avg	$54.00	00-02
Moonlight	Pikaroon, jntd	green scale, nice	VG+	$202.50	99-11
Moonlight	Pikaroon, jntd	r/w, GE, nice	EX-	$455.00	99-04
Moonlight	Pollywog	bar perch, GE	VG	$362.00	01-10
Moonlight	Pollywog	white/black tail & eye shadow, red chin	EX	$480.00	03-12
Moonlight	Polywog	green and black	EX	$425.00	01-04
Moonlight	Polywog	rainbow, in box	EX	$950.00	01-04
Moonlight	Spinning Bait	yellow, PE, POBW	EX-	$235.00	02-08
Moonlight	Surface Minnow	3-hooker, white, GE, NOT MET	avg	$100.00	99-08
Moonlight	Surf Oreno Type	gray crackle, un box, GE, nice	NIB	$481.00	00-05
Moonlight	Torpedo	green scale, GE	EX-	$219.00	00-05
Moonlight	Torpedo	2907, gold scale, GE, CR, age cracks, few light pntrs and few tiny flks	VG+	$115.00	05-05
Moonlight	Wobbler	LUM, nice un box	EXIB	$310.00	00-07
Moonlight	Woodpecker	LUM, ugly age line	EX-	$150.00	00-01
Moonlight	Woodpecker	luminous, 3-hooker side	EX-	$360.00	99-10
Moonlight	Zig Zag	3-pack, r/y, r/w, lum perch?	NIB	$2,358.33	99-03
Moonlight	Zipper Surface Lure	blue head/yellow body, yellow PE, SR	EX	$70.00	05-05
Mouse Co.	Mouse	Fort Worth, TX	VG	$68.00	99-06
Mueller-Perry	Crazy Legs	2 mint, one in box with papers	NIB	$36.76	99-03
Muskovie	Bomb	RH, spring loaded, plain box	NIB	$43.00	01-08
Musky Sucker	Flexie	7½", dirty box	NIB	$33.00	01-09

BRAND	MODEL	SERIES / MFG. CODE / DESCRIPTION	GRADE	PRICE	DATE yy/mm
Myers & Spellman		ugly, missing rear prop	avg	$123.00	03-02
Myers & Spellman	Minnow		EX	$380.00	99-10
Naturalure	Tropical Floater	RH	EX-	$19.00	04-07
Naturalure	Tropical Floater	goldish scale, injured minnow style	EX	$49.00	04-02
Nelson	Nature Lure		NIB	$86.51	99-01
Nemo	Bass Bait	yellow	EX	$850.00	99-10
Nemo	Bass Bait		EX	$600.00	01-04
Neon Mickey	Neon Mickey	red	NIB	$28.00	04-09
Ness	Nifty Minne	celluloid tube	VG	$1,025.00	02-02
Ness	Nifty Minnie	c. 1913, 5-hook, marked props, w/clear celluloid minnow tube	EX	$1,430.00	05-04
Ness	Nifty Minnie	celluloid tube, 5-hooker	EX-	$1,025.00	02-02
Ness	Nifty Minny	glass tube, marked prop	EX	$1,600.00	01-08
Nichols	Diving Shrimp	red/white	mint	$364.00	03-04
Nichols	Diving Zinger	yellow/black spots, 3"	VG	$30.00	05-07
Nichols	Fin Perch	carved tail, plastic? dorsal & anal fin, GE, 2BW	VG	$458.00	05-03
Nichols	Plunker	white scale, bead eyes	EX	$30.00	05-05
Nichols	Shrimp	nice box	NIB	$125.00	03-02
Nickel Tackle Co.	Mystic Minnow	with inserts & paper showing combos	EX	$30.00	04-09
Nixon	Aristocrat Minnow	Persian Ivory, 2¼", underwater minnow, unmarked props, flawless glass eyes, single belly weight, w/orig 2-piece cardboard box	EX	$4,290.00	05-04
Norman	Musky Humpback Rebel Type	FL, yellow/red dots, a big one	NIB	$44.00	04-02
North Channel	3-hook Minnow	2¾", GE (one broken), black back/whitebelly, 3 HPGM	VG	$99.00	04-11
North Channel	Minnow	5-hooker, touch-ups	VG	$800.00	05-02
North Channel	Minnow	black/white, NOT MET	EX	$867.00	01-03
Northwood Bait	Curve A Lure	blue back/white, fly rod size	EX	$5.00	05-03
NSH CO.	Daimond Fluted Spinner	St. Louis, MO, big #7, fluted blade, little wear	VG	$12.00	05-05
O Ridge	Crank Bait	Big O type, yellow	Mint	$8.06	05-07
Oceanic Tackle Shop	Leaping Lena	nice white 2PCCB box/blue printing, blue/white lure, flitter	NIB	$76.00	05-07
Ol Skipper	Chubby	black scale, age lines, nice box	EXIB	$49.00	05-07
Ol Skipper	Legs Wobbler	#1604 T, scale finish	NIB	$73.00	01-08
Ol Skipper	Spinna Tail	1401L bx EX, lure dirty but should clean up	EX-IB	$89.00	05-07
Old Dominion	Mr. Whiskers	wood plunker type, PTCB	NIB	$18.00	04-09
Oliver & Gruber	Glowurm	r & w	mint	$87.00	01-03
Oliver & Gruber	Glowurm	y/green, wood box nice	NIB	$344.00	01-09
Oliver & Gruber	Glowurm	crisp papers	EX	$81.00	02-08
Oliver & Gruber	Glowurm	green/yellow, jointed bait, w/wood box slightly faded	EX	$522.50	05-04
Oliver & Gruber	Glowurm	white/red stripes	EX	$115.00	03-02
Oliver & Gruber	Glowurm	w/red ribs, papers, NOT MET	EX	$90.00	00-04
Oliver & Gruber	Glowurm	r/w	EX+	$139.50	00-01
Olson	Salmon Plug		EXIB	$90.00	01-04
OPTIMUS	3-hk Minnow	EX box, South Bend hex lure	EXIB	$935.00	02-06
Orchard Ind.	Bottom Scratcher	red & yellow, by Orchard Ind., in plastic box VG+	EX-	$12.00	05-06
Orchard Ind.	Bottom Scratcher	red head/yellow	NIB	$48.00	05-04

BRAND	MODEL	SERIES / MFG. CODE / DESCRIPTION	GRADE	PRICE	DATE yy/mm
Orchard Ind.	Bottom Scratcher	RH, thick plastic box	NIB	$41.00	01-08
Orchard Ind.	Bottom Scratcher	spotted ape, papers	NIB	$16.00	01-04
Orchard Ind.	Bottom Scratcher	spotted ape, NOT MET	mint	$12.50	99-08
Orchard Ind.	Bottom Scratcher	WBH	NIB	$16.00	01-09
Oscar	The Frog	SOLD	NIB	$490.00	99-10
Oscar Meyer	Weiner	novelty, 3¼"	EX	$49.01	00-02
Outing	Bassy Getum	black bass finish	VG	$77.55	00-03
Outing	Du-Getum	grass frog	NIB	$430.75	99-05
Outing	Du-Getum	nice box, papers rough	NIB	$307.99	99-09
Outing	Du- Getum	white frogs, lg and small sizes, mint boxes	NIB	$715.00	99-12
Outing	Du-Getum	700, white/green, crisp box + papers	NIB	$285.00	02-11
Outing	Du-Getum	grass frog, rough box	NIB	$222.50	99-06
Outing	Du-Getum	frog, 2PCCB + papers	NIB	$400.00	98-12
Outing	Du-Getum	large	NIB	$380.00	99-10
Outing	Du-Getum	small	NIB	$355.00	99-10
Outing	Du-Getum	750, 2¾", white with green spots	VG+	$55.00	05-06
Outing	Getum	700 AR, NOT MET	NIB	$285.00	02-10
Outing	Pikey Getum	rainbow, 2 sm chips	EX-	$151.00	99-01
Outing	Porkey Getum	black double hook and weed guard	EX	$35.00	05-05
Outing	Bassy Getum	"Outing Elkhard" stamped, diving lip and gold trebles, some flaking at rear hook hanger, w/box aluminum + red Du-Getum nice, paperwork EX	EXIB	$550.00	05-04
Outing	Getum	pale frog, mint red/blue box, papers	NIB	$372.00	01-05
Ozarka	Talky Topper	red head/white	mint	$17.00	03-04
Ozarka	Talky Topper	white, crisp box	NIB	$54.00	04-07
Ozarka	Wee Gee	perch scale, Runt type crisp box	NIB	$32.00	04-07
P & K	Amazin Mazie	42P, nice box & papers	EXIB	$18.00	03-02
P & K	Amazin Mazie	42-RW, red & white	NIB	$32.00	99-03
P & K	Brite Eyes	2 diff, frog & shiner, NOT MET	NIB	$37.00	99-05
P & K	Brite Eyes	y/r	EXIB	$13.49	99-01
P & K	Crab	small lure and box nice, 2½"	NIB	$18.00	04-08
P & K	Cricket & Helgramite	2 lures on cards	NOC	$25.00	05-06
P & K	Fly Rod Mouse	light gray, very soft rubber, just a hint of wear	EX+	$22.00	05-05
P & K	Mouse	white, a little dirty	EXIB	$56.00	03-07
P & K	Redwing Blackbird	black/yellow wings, musky size, NOT MET	NIB	$76.00	99-04
P & K	Skip Jack Bass Bug	ribbed body w/8 hair legs, black body and legs, white belly	VG	$44.00	05-05
P & K	Softy, the Wonder Crab	fly size, tan, new and very soft in orig EX- cello window 2PCCB	NIB	$40.00	05-05
P & K	Spinning Minnie	fly rod size, silver, tiny 1" metal body, on card in cellophane	EX-OC	$24.00	05-05
P & K	Spinning Minnie Fly Rod	metal lure on nice card, tiny	EXOC	$10.00	05-06
P & K	Trap Lures	crab & frog, papers	NIB	$51.00	02-12
P & K	Walkie Talkie	43P, nice box & papers	EXIB	$29.00	03-02
P & K	Walkie Talkie	black w/white stripe down sides, PPE, 1 pointer on chin	EX	$19.00	05-05
P & K	Walkie Talkie	gold scale, pike, PPE, light edge wear and few minor nicks	VG	$10.00	05-05

BRAND	MODEL	SERIES / MFG. CODE / DESCRIPTION	GRADE	PRICE	DATE yy/mm
P & K	Walkie Talkie	perch, PPE, plastic, very light wear	EX-	$15.00	05-05
P & K	Whirl Away	30 GS, crisp box, black scale?	NIB	$43.00	01-03
P & K	Whirl Away	black, 2PCCB	EXIB	$49.00	02-07
P&V	Redwing Blackbird	musky size, yellow, crisp box	NIB	$97.00	05-07
Pal	Electro Lure	amber, like Bunyan, decent box, NOT MET	EXIB	$61.00	00-10
Pardee	3-hooker		mint	$8,000.00	01-12
Pardee	Musky 5-hk	box bottom only, paint on hubs	EXI½B	$10,000.00	01-06
Paulson	Combination Minnow	red/white, crisp paper & box	NIB	$510.00	01-05
Paulson	Combination Minnow	RH, great box	EXIB	$658.00	05-03
Paulson	Combination Minnow	RH, GE, papers	NIB	$1,165.00	00-10
Paulson	Wobbler	red & white	VG	$35.00	05-06
Paw Paw	#1 Fish Spoon	great picture box	NIB	$61.00	99-08
Paw Paw	3-hooker	RB, TE, Lucky Lure	NIB	$117.00	00-10
Paw Paw	3-hooker	rainbow	NIB	$102.50	98-12
Paw Paw	3-hooker	rainbow, TE	EX-	$47.00	99-06
Paw Paw	3-hooker	RB, TE	EX	$104.00	00-10
Paw Paw	301	perch, TE, y/blk, photo box nice	NIB	$153.00	01-09
Paw Paw	3200	3215 photo box, white, GE	NIB	$168.00	99-11
Paw Paw	3350 Minnow	green scale/gold dots, TE	mint	$255.00	00-04
Paw Paw	5 Lure Grab Bag	2 jntd pikies, 2 9300 and 1 9100, all VG to avg	group	$22.00	05-05
Paw Paw	9100	green back, gold scale, red ribs, blued lip	VG+	$12.00	05-06
Paw Paw	9100	splatter finish or Wotta Frog finish, PTE, light age lines, 1 pntr	EX	$38.00	05-05
Paw Paw	9300	splatter finish	EX	$10.00	04-11
Paw Paw	Amherst Bass Bug	Indian sign box & card EX-	EXIB	$331.00	03-01
Paw Paw	Aristocrat Minnow	#2400 floater, shiner	NIB	$25.75	99-01
Paw Paw	Bass Oreno	natural chub	EX	$26.00	01-08
Paw Paw	Bass Seeker	black/yellow, photo bx EX, bar perch, GE	EXIB	$117.00	05-07
Paw Paw	Bass Seeker	r/w, GE, great box	NIB	$153.70	99-09
Paw Paw	Bass Seeker	RH, c. 1927, crisp box	NIB	$291.00	00-09
Paw Paw	Bass Seeker	shiner scale, photo box	EXIB	$102.00	99-10
Paw Paw	Bone Head	Caster	mint	$142.00	03-04
Paw Paw	Bone Head	Petite Spin	mint	$33.00	03-04
Paw Paw	Bonehead	Caster, 12-G box	NIB	$129.00	05-02
Paw Paw	Bonehead	jntd pikie	mint	$71.00	03-04
Paw Paw	Bonehead	Swamp Minnow (pikie), rhinestone eyes	EX	$50.00	00-07
Paw Paw	Bonehead	Tiny Torpedo	mint	$68.00	03-04
Paw Paw	Bullfrog	red/white	EX	$645.00	00-08
Paw Paw	Bullhead	3504, orange/white dolphin box EX, Bullhead papers	EXIB	$500.00	05-03
Paw Paw	Bullhead	brown/black, TE, chip, NOT MET	VG	$102.50	00-02
Paw Paw	Bullhead	gold/black (pikie), TE, ugly	avg	$64.00	99-05
Paw Paw	Bullhead	green perch/gold belly, TE, orange/white unmarked box	EXIB	$381.00	05-07
Paw Paw	Bullhead	green/y, superb pic box, Bullhead papers	NIB	$535.00	01-05
Paw Paw	Bullhead	r/silver, #3505 avg box	VGIB	$128.00	99-03
Paw Paw	Bullhead	r/w, TE	EX	$182.50	99-06
Paw Paw	Bullhead	r/w, TE, NOT MET	EX	$157.50	99-08
Paw Paw	Bullhead	RH, TE	avg	$56.00	00-10

BRAND	MODEL	SERIES / MFG. CODE / DESCRIPTION	GRADE	PRICE	DATE yy/mm
Paw Paw	Caster	6800S, dbl cellophane window box EX	NIB	$335.00	04-02
Paw Paw	Caster	J.C. Higgins, perch color, box #3006	NIB	$44.00	05-02
Paw Paw	Caster	pike, #6400 dbl window silver bx EX	NIB	$427.00	05-02
Paw Paw	Caster	pike, 4½", chub scale	EX	$133.00	05-07
Paw Paw	Caster	rainbow trout	EX+	$493.00	04-11
Paw Paw	Caster	RT, 3½"	EX	$103.00	00-03
Paw Paw	Caster (pike shape)	5½", jntd, TE, huge touch-up, ugly	?	$76.00	00-01
Paw Paw	Caster 2"	green scale/copper back and sides	EX-	$86.00	99-10
Paw Paw	Caster Small	bass color	EX	$38.00	00-04
Paw Paw	Caster Trout	Mud Minnow, NOT MET	EX-	$79.00	00-11
Paw Paw	Casting Frog	75 PTCB	NIB	$227.50	00-01
Paw Paw	Crab	no feelers, orange box unmarked, TE	EXIB	$191.00	02-10
Paw Paw	Crawdad	brown & green full legs	EX	$150.00	05-07
Paw Paw	Crawdad	feelers and legs intact	mint	$162.50	99-08
Paw Paw	Crawdad	hanging belly weight, correct box and scarce paperwork	EXIB	$800.00	01-04
Paw Paw	Crawdad	pike scale, PE, Lucky Lure box	NIB	$204.52	00-01
Paw Paw	Crawfish	natural	EX-	$51.00	00-05
Paw Paw	Croaker Fly Rod	frog, brown, wood, TE, cute	EX	$661.00	03-02
Paw Paw	Croaker Frog	real skin, NOT MET	EX	$120.00	99-05
Paw Paw	Dreadnaught	rainbow trout, many pointers	VG-	$151.00	00-07
Paw Paw	Flapjack	32/135 Yel.- R.B., PTCB	NIB	$22.00	04-07
Paw Paw	Floater	803	NIB	$51.00	00-08
Paw Paw	Fly, 3 sm boxes	gold/black boxes with flies, nice	NIB	$197.50	99-05
Paw Paw	Go Getter	rainbow trout	VG	$57.00	99-01
Paw Paw	Great Injured Minnow	RH, TE, orange bx 3209 rough	EXIB	$256.00	04-02
Paw Paw	Great Injured Minnow	pikie, GE	EX	$372.00	01-04
Paw Paw	Great Injured Minnow	TE, red & white, 3⅞"	VG	$40.00	05-06
Paw Paw	Hair Mouse	nice box & card	EXIB	$455.00	03-09
Paw Paw	Hair Mouse	yellow HD/nat bucktail	EXIB	$265.00	99-06
Paw Paw	Hair Mouse Spinnered	RH, Lucky Lure box EX	NIB	$280.00	00-01
Paw Paw	Injured Minnow	frog, TE, box 4401	EX-IB	$50.00	99-02
Paw Paw	Jntd Dace Caster	dace scale, PTE, 3½", few light age lines and 1 tiny pntr	EX	$135.00	05-05
Paw Paw	Jntd Pike Caster	large 5¼" size, few minor pointers and nicks, age lines, paint off l-eye	VG	$55.00	05-05
Paw Paw	Jntd Pike Caster	large 5¼" size, few minor pointers and nicks	VG+	$88.00	05-05
Paw Paw	Jntd Chub Caster	green back, iridescent finish. 3½" long, light rust on hooks	VG	$43.60	05-07
Paw Paw	Junior Jntd Pikie	#1400, wood, pikie, GE, about 1940s	GD	$9.53	05-07
Paw Paw	Lippy Joe	frog	EX	$75.00	01-08
Paw Paw	Lippy Joe, jntd	Allen Stripey	EX	$50.00	01-08
Paw Paw	Lucky Lure	pikie, jointed, pike scale, 3⅞", tiny nose chip	EX-	$12.00	05-06
Paw Paw	Mouse	4741, PTCB, PE, yellow/blk stripe	NIB	$45.40	99-04
Paw Paw	Mouse	gray, black strip on back, 2½"; eyes, tail, and ears intact	VG+	$22.50	05-07
Paw Paw	Mouse	RH, G&O Lucky box	EX-IB	$102.00	00-11
Paw Paw	Mouse	RH, black back stripe	EX	$44.88	05-07

217

BRAND	MODEL	SERIES / MFG. CODE / DESCRIPTION	GRADE	PRICE	DATE yy/mm
Paw Paw	Mud Minnow	Caster? large TE, mottled	EX	$102.60	00-01
Paw Paw	Musky Hair Mouse	white head, sm nose chip, 5½"	EX-	$361.10	00-01
Paw Paw	Musky Minnow	shad scale	EX	$108.00	01-08
Paw Paw	Musky Mouse	silver, 4"	VG	$290.51	99-04
Paw Paw	Nikie	plastic! strawberry	mint	$154.00	01-08
Paw Paw	Old Flat Side	1506, TE, gold scale	VG+	$10.00	05-06
Paw Paw	Old Flat Side	2539, golden shiner scale, 3⅝"	EX-	$15.00	05-06
Paw Paw	Old Wounded Minnow	flat side, frog spot, PTE, CR, light age lines and few tiny pointers, in worn 2PSTB	EX-IB	$33.00	05-05
Paw Paw	Old Wounded Minoow	rainbow scale, blue back, silver scale and red sides, few light age lines	EX	$47.00	05-05
Paw Paw	Pencil Bait	black head/orange, PTE, 5", 2-hk, hint of age line	EX+	$32.00	05-05
Paw Paw	Pikie	pikie color, TE, groved head nice	EX	$18.00	01-07
Paw Paw	Pikie	pikie finish, nice wood lure	EX	$8.50	04-03
Paw Paw	Pikie	pikie, TE, great picture box	NIB	$153.60	99-08
Paw Paw	Pikie	RH/w pearl, orange & blk box crisp, TE	NIB	$378.58	99-12
Paw Paw	Pikie	silver flash, early lip, PTE, 2-hk, very light wear on this early pikie minnow	EX-	$18.00	05-05
Paw Paw	Pikie	perch, TE, r/w, Lucky Lure box crisp	NIB	$128.50	99-09
Paw Paw	Pikie	white/flitter, TE, 4¼"	EX	$25.12	99-02
Paw Paw	Pikie Getum	black/sparkles, rhinestone eyes	mint	$85.00	01-08
Paw Paw	Pikie Getum	perch, rhinestone eyes	mint	$44.00	01-08
Paw Paw	Pikie Getum	RH, rhinestone eyes	mint	$46.00	01-08
Paw Paw	Pikie Getum	shad, rhinestone eyes	mint	$75.00	01-08
Paw Paw	Pikie Jr.	TE, rainbow	EX-	$35.00	05-06
Paw Paw	Pikie Type	4", green, gold dots	mint	$26.00	05-02
Paw Paw	Pikie Type	pikie finish	EX	$9.00	04-03
Paw Paw	Pikie Type	Sears Meadowbrook box 3215	NIB	$34.00	05-03
Paw Paw	Pikie, Baby jntd	green pikie scale, PTE, brass cup, few light age lines and very light wear	EX-	$15.00	05-05
Paw Paw	Pikie, Baby jointed	2101TE, yellow, perch has couple pointers, 3⅝"	EX-	$12.00	05-06
Paw Paw	Pikie, fluted	Rainbow Fire	EX-	$48.50	00-04
Paw Paw	Pikie, Musky	RH	mint	$53.00	00-10
Paw Paw	Platypus	#3524, green scale	EX	$138.00	05-07
Paw Paw	Platypus	pikie, Flapjack hook hangers	EX	$226.00	00-04
Paw Paw	Platypus	rainbow trout	EX	$511.00	04-02
Paw Paw	Platypus	yellow/black spots	mint	$270.00	04-02
Paw Paw	Platypus	PTCB, plastic lure	NIB	$159.00	00-08
Paw Paw	Platypus	shad scale	EX-	$89.00	04-10
Paw Paw	Plenty Sparkle	gold scale, rhinestones on belly	EX	$131.00	01-08
Paw Paw	Plenty Sparkle	shiner scale?	EX	$118.00	02-11
Paw Paw	Plunker	flouescent red, TE	EX	$166.00	01-10
Paw Paw	Plunker	frog skin	EX	$103.00	04-11
Paw Paw	Plunker	Luny frog finish	EX	$51.00	04-07
Paw Paw	Plunker	perch, TE, B/Y pic box	NIB	$152.50	99-09
Paw Paw	Pumpkinseed	green shad scale, TE	VG+	$41.00	99-06
Paw Paw	River Chub	gold scale, PTE (nick on both), small flake at tail and dent on l-side	VG	$13.00	05-05

BRAND	MODEL	SERIES / MFG. CODE / DESCRIPTION	GRADE	PRICE	DATE yy/mm
Paw Paw	River Runt Type	904, narrow early lip, white & red, 2½", age lines	VG+	$8.00	05-06
Paw Paw	River Type	RB, tack	EX	$69.54	99-12
Paw Paw	River Type	RB, TE	EX	$66.00	00-01
Paw Paw	Saltwater Pier Bait	pearl	EX	$186.00	03-05
Paw Paw	Seagrams 7 Spoon	neat silver "7" w/red crown logo–shaped spoon	EX+	$34.00	05-05
Paw Paw	Slim Jim	pike scale, PTE, cup rig, POBW, very light wear, nice thin early body	EX-	$18.00	05-05
Paw Paw	Spinnered Hair Mouse	crisp orange bx with white fish border	NIB	$612.00	05-07
Paw Paw	Spoon	huge mother-of-pearl, W40 crisp blue box	NIB	$57.00	04-02
Paw Paw	Spoon Belly Wobbler/Pike	pike body, pearly side spinners	EX	$255.00	01-08
Paw Paw	Surf Oreno	r/w, TE, great picture box	NIB	$150.00	99-08
Paw Paw	Surf Oreno Type	RH, GE, b&y box	NIB	$177.50	99-10
Paw Paw	Surface Minnow	frog spot, 3¾", PTE, 2-hk	EX+	$30.00	05-05
Paw Paw	Surface Minnow	pikie, w/gold spots	EX	$108.00	00-05
Paw Paw	Torpedo	salesman sample, ring w/5 Torpedo bodies, never rigged	EX	$180.00	05-05
Paw Paw	Trout Caster	natural chub, TE, beauty!	EX+	$120.27	00-01
Paw Paw	Trout Caster	perch, TE, beauty!	EX+	$68.56	00-01
Paw Paw	War Horse	1100A, from Paw Paw factory archives, has little hangtag attached	NM	$68.00	05-05
Paw Paw	Weedless	Wotta Frog splatter	VG	$85.00	99-04
Paw Paw	Weedless Wow	frog splatter with papers	NIB	$225.00	02-01
Paw Paw	Weedless Wow	RH, GE, nice	VG+	$152.00	01-01
Paw Paw	Weedless Wow	silver flash, POBW, NOT MET	EX-	$76.55	00-02
Paw Paw	Wiggler	blk/yellow photo bx VG, yellow Bass Oreno type, TE	NIB	$80.00	05-07
Paw Paw	Wilson Wobbler	rainbow, chip on belly, otherwise nice	VG+	$76.00	05-07
Paw Paw	Wobbler	green	EX	$16.00	04-07
Paw Paw	Wobbler	rainbow, a beauty	mint	$21.00	05-02
Paw Paw	Wotta Frog	3¾"	EX	$81.00	99-03
Paw Paw	Wotta Frog	4", NOT MET	EX	$61.00	99-01
Paw Paw	Wotta Frog	large	EX	$65.00	99-08
Paw Paw	Wotta Frog	large, 3⅞"	EX	$103.00	04-11
Paw Paw	Wotta Frog	large	NIB	$82.00	99-09
Paw Paw	Wotta Frog	large size, PTCB, NOT MET	EX-IB	$66.00	00-11
Paw Paw	Wotta Frog	regular size	EX	$56.00	02-07
Paw Paw	Wotta Frog	small size in #72 bx EX	EXIB	$52.00	05-02
Paw Paw	Wotta Frog	TE, yellow splatter, eyes perfect	VG+	$55.00	05-06
Paw Paw	Wotta Frog	Victory finish, large size	EX	$130.13	99-12
Paw Paw	Wotta Frog	weedless, rubber legs, weed guard, NOT MET	VG+	$72.00	00-11
Paw Paw	Wotta Frog		VG	$27.00	99-01
Paw Paw	Wotta Frog	73, med size, tied hair legs, chips on inside edges of legs, few tiny pointers	EX-	$60.00	05-05
Paw Paw	Wotta Frog	74, large size, tied hair legs, small chip on r-eye and few age lines on belly, o/w new 2PSTB	EX-IB	$95.00	05-05
Peckinpaugh	Mouse Fly Rod	cutie in brown bead eyes	EX	$81.00	00-11
Peck's	Float-Rite Trout Bug	bee; black body, wings, and tail; w/yellow rings	Mint	$22.00	05-05

BRAND	MODEL	SERIES / MFG. CODE / DESCRIPTION	GRADE	PRICE	DATE yy/mm
Peck's	Float-Rite Trout Bug	brown hackle, black head, brown body and wings, red tail	Mint	$17.00	05-05
Peck's	Float-Rite Trout Bug	Cow Dung brown body, wings, and tail	mint	$17.00	05-05
Peck's	Float-Rite Trout Bug	Cricket Black body, wings, and tail	mint	$22.00	05-05
Peck's	Float-Rite Trout Bug	Gray Squirrel, black head, brown body, squirrel wings, red tail	mint	$20.00	05-05
Peck's	Float-Rite Trout Bug	Parma Bell, white head, yellow body, r and w wings and tail	near mint	$17.00	05-05
Peck's	Float-Rite Trout Bug	Silver Doctor, green head, glitter body, w/peacock wings and white tail	mint	$25.00	05-05
Peck's	Float-Rite Trout Bug	Yellow Sally, yellow body and wings, brown head, YPE	near mint	$17.00	05-05
Peck's	Hellgrammite	black rubber molded on single hook, rubber is soft, not brittle	EX	$12.00	05-05
Peck's	Kormish Frog	green frog, large 1½" size, rubber molded on long shank, treble, light wear	VG+	$39.00	05-05
Peck's	Taylor Popping Frog	WDLS, little chipping on lip edge	EX-	$22.00	05-05
Pecos River Tackle	Spinno Minno	nice box #507, shiner scale	EXIB	$158.00	05-02
Pemberton	Busy Baits	12-pk, 6 RH/white, 2 RH/green, 2 RH/silver, 2 RH/yellow	GD	$715.00	04-11
Pepper, Joe	3-hooker	green/yellow, GE, NOT MET	G	$164.00	01-03
Pepper, Joe	5-hook Minnow	GE, green, 3", round props	poor	$171.00	05-03
Pepper, Joe	5-hooker	green/w belly, heavy age lines ugly	VG-	$304.00	00-04
Pepper, Joe	Baby Roamer	1", GE, beautiful blended brown back, yellow belly, original string legs, extremely rare 2-piece picture box, light wear and corner seperation	EX+IB	$7,150.00	05-04
Pepper, Joe	Delta Wiggler	metallic green, YPE, 3-hk, weed guard, 4-blade prop, glass beads	EX	$125.00	05-05
Pepper, Joe	Fly Rod Mouse	on spinner, NOT MET	EX	$21.00	00-11
Pepper, Joe	Lake Delta Minnow	green and silver, w/red bars, composite 3" minnow body and unique blade	EX+	$65.00	05-05
Pepper, Joe	Metal Minnow	HPGM	EX	$141.50	99-06
Pepper, Joe	New Century Minnow	3-hook, silver	VG	$360.00	02-02
Pepper, Joe	New Century Minnow	silver, 3-hooker, no eyes	EX-	$365.00	02-02
Pepper, Joe	New Crown Spinner		EX	$455.00	99-06
Pepper, Joe	Revolving Minnow	box VG+, SOLD	NIB	$5,900.00	01-06
Pepper, Joe	Revolving Minnow	c. 1911, only age lines, some red paint missing from fins, wood box minor damage	EX+IB	$5,280.00	05-04
Pepper, Joe	Roamer	green/yellow, 3-hk, GE, screw eye hangers	VG	$154.00	02-09
Pepper, Joe	Roman Red Tail	wood box EX-	NIB	$3,500.00	01-12
Pepper, Joe	Roman Spider	sienna crackleback?	EX-	$338.00	04-04
Pepper, Joe	Spoon	brass, fish shaped, corrogated?	EX-	$20.00	04-03
Pepper, Joe	Spoon	NOT MET	NOC	$16.50	99-05
Pequea	Display	29 mother-of-pearl spinners in 13" x 21" wood box	EX	$1,100.00	04-11
Pequea	Display	40 Perfection lightweight spinners in 9" x 13" wood box	EX	$412.00	04-11
Perry, Buck	Spoonplug	5-pack kit with papers	NIB	$31.00	99-01
Perry, Buck	Spoonplug x 14	14 different, mostly mint	EX	$66.00	02-03
Pete's	Go-Gettum	display card, 12 assorted colors, neat	NOC	$85.00	04-02
Pfeffer	Darter	small, frog back/white belly, PE	EX	$383.00	05-07

BRAND	MODEL	SERIES / MFG. CODE / DESCRIPTION	GRADE	PRICE	DATE yy/mm
Pfeffer	Minnow	green/gold, open mouth, bag	NIbag	$114.49	99-05
Pfeffer	Shinner Minnow	pic box & papers EX, brown yellow scales	NIB	$510.00	04-11
Pfeffer	Single Hook Shiner	tarpon rig? green sunfish, weed guard, minor blems on r-side	VG+	$40.00	05-05
Pfeffer	Spin Dilly	br/o, flitter	EX	$100.00	99-02
Pfeffer	Spinning Dilly	silver scale, envelope "Famous Orlando Shiner Lures, P.O. Box 4164 Orando, Florida"	EXIE	$537.00	05-07
Pfeiffer	Glass Minnow Tube	nice paper, pic box VG+	EXIB	$4,900.00	01-06
Pfeiffer	Glass Minnow Tube	nice pic box & papers	NIB	$4,600.00	01-12
Pfeiffer	Minnow Tube	box EX- and papers	EXIB	$3,580.00	99-10
Pfeiffer	Pfeiffer Glass Minnow Tube	fly rod size, 3" long, celluloid cap and 2 double-sided hooks	unknown	$750.00	05-05
Pfiefer	Glass Minnow Tube	3" x ⅝"	EX	$385.00	04-11
Pfiefer	Minnow Tube		NIB	$3,400.00	00-02
Pflueger	Phantom Minnow	large	NIB	$200.00	01-04
Pflueger	#4	kidney blade spinner, small diagonal marking	EX+	$12.00	05-06
Pflueger	#5 and #6	tandem brass kidney trolling rig	EX-	$25.00	05-05
Pflueger	1/0	Diamond P, silver over brass, nice hair bucktail	EX	$15.00	05-06
Pflueger	3- hooker	Neverfail, strawberry, GE	avg	$31.99	05-07
Pflueger	3/0 Spinner	bi-color blade, LG, feathered dble hk, little wear to blade and feather	VG-	$12.00	05-05
Pflueger	3-hooker	3105, frog scale, blush, HOLD	EX-	$550.00	99-10
Pflueger	3-hooker	3165, frog, HOLD	mint	$525.00	99-10
Pflueger	3-hooker	3173, yellow perch, blue canoe	EXIB	$394.75	99-06
Pflueger	3-hooker	3195, red back stripe	EX	$490.00	99-10
Pflueger	3-hooker	3195, red back stripe, un, SOLD	EX+	$520.00	99-10
Pflueger	3-hooker	3196, RH	EX+	$350.00	99-10
Pflueger	3-hooker	4 Bros box 3169 EX-, SOLD	VGIB	$700.00	99-10
Pflueger	3-hooker	Argyle back, red/black side spots, box and papers	EXIB	$600.00	99-01
Pflueger	3-hooker	bar perch, GE, Neverfail hrdw	VG	$67.00	05-07
Pflueger	3-hooker	bar perch, bulldog props, GE	rough	$22.49	99-11
Pflueger	3-hooker	bar perch, GE	VG-	$72.00	00-04
Pflueger	3-hooker	bar perch, GE, Neverfail	EX	$209.49	99-12
Pflueger	3-hooker	bar perch, GE, Neverfail	EX	$430.00	00-03
Pflueger	3-hooker	broad green scale, fat body, GE	EX	$316.00	00-04
Pflueger	3-hooker	crackle, Neverfail, dog prop	VG+	$72.00	02-01
Pflueger	3-hooker	crackle, see through, pre-1910	VG+	$75.00	00-10
Pflueger	3-hooker	crackle, dog props, fat body, HPGM	VG+	$300.00	00-01
Pflueger	3-hooker	crackle, eyes cracked, nose chip	EX-	$150.00	00-04
Pflueger	3-hooker	crackle, flat plate, purty	EX	$318.77	99-08
Pflueger	3-hooker	crackle, GE	mint	$389.00	99-10
Pflueger	3-hooker	crackle, GE, Monarch fat body	VG+	$187.50	00-03
Pflueger	3-hooker	crackle, gem clip, HPGM, GE, gleamer	EX- – EX	$232.50	99-11
Pflueger	3-hooker	crackle, glass, HPGM, NOT MET	EX-	$81.25	99-11
Pflueger	3-hooker	crackle, NOT MET	EX	$178.56	99-06
Pflueger	3-hooker	crackle, split box	EXIB	$201.01	99-06
Pflueger	3-hooker	frog scale, GE	EX-	$356.00	00-04
Pflueger	3-hooker	frog, GE, Neverfail	VG	$59.00	03-02
Pflueger	3-hooker	frog, GE, NOT MET	EX-	$176.00	98-12

BRAND	MODEL	SERIES / MFG. CODE / DESCRIPTION	GRADE	PRICE	DATE yy/mm
Pflueger	3-hooker	frog scale, papers	NIB	$493.00	01-06
Pflueger	3-hooker	frog scale, GE	EX	$383.00	00-07
Pflueger	3-hooker	GE, w, maroon box VG, $450 NOT MET	EX-IB	$220.00	01-06
Pflueger	3-hooker	lum/gold spots, GE	EX-	$187.49	99-08
Pflueger	3-hooker	lum/gold spots, marked prop, SOLD	EX+	$325.00	99-12
Pflueger	3-hooker	metalized minnow, NOT MET	mint	$405.00	01-05
Pflueger	3-hooker	metalized, GE, NOT MET	EX-	$237.84	99-05
Pflueger	3-hooker	nat perch scale, GE	VG	$72.00	00-01
Pflueger	3-hooker	Neverfail, yellow/green back, GE	rough	$29.00	04-07
Pflueger	3-hooker	PE, argyle	EX-	$122.00	99-01
Pflueger	3-hooker	perch scale, GE, crisp box, NOT MET	NIB	$390.00	00-04
Pflueger	3-hooker	perch, TE	NIB	$103.49	99-04
Pflueger	3-hooker	r/w, GE, Neverfail	EX+	$361.00	99-12
Pflueger	3-hooker	r/w, GE, nice box	EX-IB	$206.49	99-09
Pflueger	3-hooker	r/w, worm burn, 1 side EX	fair/EX	$98.00	99-05
Pflueger	3-hooker	rainbow	EX-	$177.50	99-06
Pflueger	3-hooker	rainbow, GE	VG+	$80.00	00-06
Pflueger	3-hooker	rainbow, in canoe 2PCCB	EXIB	$385.00	98-12
Pflueger	3-hooker	rainbow, GE, Neverfail	EX	$212.50	99-06
Pflueger	3-hooker	rainbow, GE, Neverfail	EX	$242.50	99-03
Pflueger	3-hooker	RB, GE	EX	$157.00	02-03
Pflueger	3-hooker	RB, GE	VG+	$89.88	99-09
Pflueger	3-hooker	RB, GE, Neverfail	EX-	$102.00	00-05
Pflueger	3-hooker	RB, GE, bulldog OFP	EX-	$156.00	00-09
Pflueger	3-hooker	RB, PE, S-rig, POBW, NOT MET	EX	$52.00	99-06
Pflueger	3-hooker	RH, PE, PTCB	NIB	$181.19	00-03
Pflueger	3-hooker	sienna crackle, GE, HPGM	EX-	$410.50	00-03
Pflueger	3-hooker	silver, SOLD	EX+	$520.00	99-10
Pflueger	3-hooker	strawberry, GE, big chip on back	avg	$44.00	00-10
Pflueger	3-hooker	strawberry, GE, Neverfail	EX-	$240.50	00-03
Pflueger	3-hooker	strawberry, GE, Neverfail, repaint?	EX+	$383.58	00-02
Pflueger	3-hooker	white, gem clip, unmarked	EX	$366.01	99-10
Pflueger	3-hooker	white, Neverfail, GE, unmarked	EX-	$340.00	99-08
Pflueger	3-hooker Neverfail	Regal maroon box, red back/white blended	NIB	$808.00	99-04
Pflueger	3-hooker x 2	bulldog front props	VG-	$223.00	00-10
Pflueger	5-hooker Neverfail	sienna crackleback? a beauty	EX	$511.00	03-02
Pflueger	5-hooker	2195, red back stripe	EX-	$400.00	99-10
Pflueger	5-hooker	3104, nat pike, TE?	NIB	$431.00	99-12
Pflueger	5-hooker	3107, chub scale	EX+	$725.00	99-10
Pflueger	5-hooker	3169, spotted	VG	$250.00	99-10
Pflueger	5-hooker	3181, red, blue-rim canoe, papers	EX-IB	$500.55	00-02
Pflueger	5-hooker	3185, blush gills, crackle	EX+	$415.00	99-10
Pflueger	5-hooker	bar perch, Neverfail hrdw, PE, min $150, NO BIDS	EX+	no bids	05-07
Pflueger	5-hooker	bar perch, fat body, GE	VG	$249.40	99-05
Pflueger	5-hooker	bar perch, GE	VG+	$147.00	00-10
Pflueger	5-hooker	broad green scale	EX	$480.00	99-08
Pflueger	5-hooker	crackle, HPGM, chip at belly weight	EX-	$280.00	99-11

BRAND	MODEL	SERIES / MFG. CODE / DESCRIPTION	GRADE	PRICE	DATE yy/mm
Pflueger	5-hooker	crackle, Neverfail, GE, cpl pointers	EX-	$203.00	00-05
Pflueger	5-hooker	crackle, unmarked props	EX	$331.99	99-08
Pflueger	5-hooker	crackle? GE	EXIB	$275.00	99-09
Pflueger	5-hooker	crackleback, GE, POBW, ugly	NIB	$305.00	99-01
Pflueger	5-hooker	metalized minnow, Neverfail hrdw, GE nice	VG+	$167.00	05-07
Pflueger	5-hooker	metalized silver, big belly dent, dog props	VG+	$455.00	99-11
Pflueger	5-hooker	Neverfail, rainbow, GE	EX	$290.00	99-04
Pflueger	5-hooker	perch, GE, 3⅝"	mint	$570.65	99-03
Pflueger	5-hooker	perch, PE	VG	$91.00	99-04
Pflueger	5-hooker	Playfair wood box, white, see through	EX-IB	$1,724.00	00-05
Pflueger	5-hooker	rainbow, bulldog prop	VG-	$80.00	05-03
Pflueger	5-hooker	rainbow, GE, Neverfail	G	$92.00	99-02
Pflueger	5-hooker	rainbow, GE, Neverfail	VG	$242.50	99-03
Pflueger	5-hooker	RB, glass eye	EX+	$350.00	00-06
Pflueger	5-hooker	RB, GE	VG+	$97.00	00-07
Pflueger	5-hooker	RB, GE, NOT MET	EX	$380.00	99-09
Pflueger	5-hooker	RB, GE, NOT MET	EX	$401.99	99-08
Pflueger	5-hooker	RB, NOT MET	EX	$363.00	99-08
Pflueger	5-hooker	red/y, target maroon box crisp, see through	EX-IB	$1,200.00	01-08
Pflueger	5-hooker	spotted, gleamer but sm scruffy back	VG+	$360.00	00-01
Pflueger	5-hooker	3169 WH-GR-RED, strawberry	NIB	$767.00	99-01
Pflueger	5-hooker Competitor	green/y belly, metal TE	EX	$230.00	00-06
Pflueger	5-hooker Competitor	brass tack eye, green?	EX	$362.99	99-08
Pflueger	Admiral	embossed blade, rubber minnow, NOT MET	EX-	$343.00	04-02
Pflueger	American Ball Spinner	4½"	VG	$40.89	99-06
Pflueger	Armored	armored silver sparks lure w/correct box	GD	$25.00	05-07
Pflueger	Baby Scoop	later 60s version, RH/w w/glitter and black gills, PPE, SR, NSOP	EX	$18.00	05-05
Pflueger	Baby Surprise Minnow	WH/black body, GE, SR, lots of surface wear	F	$75.00	05-05
Pflueger	Ball Spinner	Alligator #7, marked	EX-	$104.00	99-02
Pflueger	Ball Spinner	glass bead	EX	$62.00	99-06
Pflueger	Ballerina	5439 Scramble finish, PE, ring around BW	NIB	$177.00	02-02
Pflueger	Bar Hook Minnow	gold, Ernest Pflueger, asking price	EX	$2,250.00	02-08
Pflueger	Breakless Devon Minnow	269NP, canoe box #3 VG	NIB	$61.00	02-01
Pflueger	Bulldog #5 Spinner	Brass heart-shaped blade, 5 red glass beads on shaft	EX+	$28.00	05-05
Pflueger	Catalina	canoe bx 5503, green mullet scale, silver flakes	NIB	$406.00	04-01
Pflueger	Catalina	crackleback, sm, oldest, HPGM, NOT MET	EX-	$400.00	02-09
Pflueger	Catalina	metalized, NOT MET	VG+	$330.00	04-02
Pflueger	Catalina	strawberry, POBW	EX	$660.00	04-03
Pflueger	Catalina	strawberry, lg, oldest, HPGM, NOT MET	EX-	$610.00	02-09
Pflueger	Catalina	y/g, GE, 5571 blue canoe VG+, NOT MET	NIB	$300.00	01-08
Pflueger	Catalina	5571	EX	$450.00	99-10
Pflueger	Catalina 2771	white/yellow/green mint box, nice, worm burn, GE	??IB	$785.00	03-02
Pflueger	Catalina Metalized	5", GE, NOT MET	EX-	$381.98	00-01
Pflueger	Catalina Musky	2787, metalized	EX	$680.00	99-10
Pflueger	Champion	brass eyes	EX+	$237.00	00-09
Pflueger	Champion	white, brass eye, shiney but plain	EX	$179.50	00-01

BRAND	MODEL	SERIES / MFG. CODE / DESCRIPTION	GRADE	PRICE	DATE yy/mm
Pflueger	Champion	white, brass, TE	EX+	$175.00	99-10
Pflueger	Chum Spoon 6-pak	big box nice, 6 mint smaller bxs, NOT MET	NIB	$177.00	02-01
Pflueger	Chum Spoon x 6	dealer 6-pack, lg canoe bx, 6 sm canoe bxs all crisp	NIB	$154.00	05-07
Pflueger	Competitor	5-hooker, tack eye, green back, blended y	EX+	$629.00	99-09
Pflueger	Conrad Frog	3", through-body hook rig, tie wraps intact, circa 1899	VG	$41.00	05-07
Pflueger	Conrad Frog	nice, NOT MET	EX-	$71.50	99-06
Pflueger	Conrad Frog	single weedless, NOT MET	EX	$70.00	02-01
Pflueger	Conrad Frog	sinker, NOT MET	EX-	$77.00	99-07
Pflueger	Crystal Minnow	chip on tail, NOT MET!	VG?	$820.00	00-07
Pflueger	Crystal Minnow	glass lure	EX-	$611.00	05-06
Pflueger	Delavon	#1 spinner, neat blade shape, red glass bead	EX+	$10.00	05-05
Pflueger	Delavon	#3 spinner, very unique blade shape	EX+	$10.00	05-05
Pflueger	Electric Minnow	RH, GE, Neverfail, Monarch props	EX-	$316.00	00-04
Pflueger	Floating Monarch	crackle, HPGM, cup, 2-hk	EX-	$510.00	01-11
Pflueger	Floating Monarch	lg, HPGM, gray/white belly chip	VG	$88.00	02-07
Pflueger	Floating Monarch	perch, HPGM, NOT MET	EX	$310.00	01-03
Pflueger	Floating Monarch	small white/red blush	avg	$77.00	02-07
Pflueger	Floating Monarch Minnow	yellow		$1,450.00	01-04
Pflueger	Fluted Spinner	fish design, NOT MET	EX	$102.00	00-11
Pflueger	Frug	yellow/gold dots, plastic box & papers	NIB	$22.00	04-07
Pflueger	Globe	2, one with Neverfail		$50.00	98-12
Pflueger	Globe	2 r/w, med, RH/pikie musky	VG	$35.00	99-01
Pflueger	Globe	3½", canoe box, NOT MET	EXIB	$34.00	99-01
Pflueger	Globe	3704, RH/pike, large size	NIB	$87.00	00-10
Pflueger	Globe	3704, red head/pikie	VGIB	$42.00	99-01
Pflueger	Globe	3750, blue crisp, side hooker, paper	NIB	$235.50	00-03
Pflueger	Globe	3750, canoe bx crisp, yellow/gold dots	NIB	$75.00	05-07
Pflueger	Globe	3750, yellow-gold, spring loaded	NIB	$130.00	04-11
Pflueger	Globe	3770LUM, 2¾", lum, Globe papers, canoe box crisp	EXIB	$117.00	05-07
Pflueger	Globe	3796, white/red head, papers, canoe box	NIB	$85.00	03-10
Pflueger	Globe	LUM	VG	$33.00	99-03
Pflueger	Globe	LUM, side hook, nice maroon box, paper!	NIB	$960.00	00-10
Pflueger	Globe	LUM, canoe box, papers	EXIB	$75.00	99-03
Pflueger	Globe	r/w, Canoe box, sm size	NIB	$102.50	99-08
Pflueger	Globe	side hooks, Otter box, cool	NIB	$811.51	99-02
Pflueger	Globe	sm side hooker, Neverfail, white	EX-	$61.50	99-11
Pflueger	Globe	sm y/gold dots, rough Canoe box	EX-IB	$40.00	99-10
Pflueger	Globe	y/gold spots, canoe box	NIB	$66.00	99-01
Pflueger	Globe 2¾"	LUM, papers, 3750, canoe box	NIB	$82.01	99-11
Pflueger	Globe 2¾"	r/w, papers, 3750, canoe box	NIB	$114.50	99-11
Pflueger	Globe 2¾"	yellow/gold, papers, 3750 canoe box	NIB	$87.00	99-11
Pflueger	Globe 3¾	lum/gold dots, papers	NIB	$85.00	02-01
Pflueger	Globe Bait	RH/w, 3⅝", Neverfail hdwr, in orig VG+ blue canoe 2PCCB w/papers	EX+IB	$125.00	05-05
Pflueger	Globe, Musky	# 3704, natural pike scale finish, RH, crisp canoe bx & papers	NIB	$100.00	05-07

BRAND	MODEL	SERIES / MFG. CODE / DESCRIPTION	GRADE	PRICE	DATE yy/mm
Pflueger	Gold Seal Wooden Minnow	wood box, paper label VG, 5-hook minnow, GE, gem clip hardware, white/red forehead finish	EX	$2,660.00	05-04
Pflueger	Grasshopper	maroon box, rubber lure	NOC	$168.49	99-12
Pflueger	Hellgramite	rubber, maroon un box, NOT MET	NOC-IB	$76.50	00-02
Pflueger	Hoptoit	hard rubber crawdad, 2", red bead eyes	VG+	$51.00	05-07
Pflueger	Indian Bead Spinner	#3 HMRD, kidney blade, 4 clay beads on wire feather, hk shy	VG	$30.00	05-05
Pflueger	Invincible Minnow	rubber? on bucktail, no spinner	VG+	$78.77	99-12
Pflueger	Jntd Palomine	pike scale, GE, blem on r-side, few pointers and light wear	VG	$19.00	05-05
Pflueger	Jntd Palomine	RH/glitter, GE, couple light pointers	EX-	$48.00	05-05
Pflueger	Kent Floater	frog, GE, nice but belly nick	VG+	$380.00	01-08
Pflueger	Kent Floater	maroon box #2	EXIB	$3,250.00	99-04
Pflueger	Kent Floater Frog	GE, diamond P, twisted wire	EX	$2,032.00	00-01
Pflueger	Kent Frog	2555, frog size 2, blue canoe box EX-, GE, HL cracks, bulldog props	NIB	$729.00	05-07
Pflueger	Kent Frog	bulldog props, GE	EX-	$372.00	04-12
Pflueger	Kent Frog	carved eye, huge touch-ups!	??	$275.00	02-08
Pflueger	Kent Frog	diamond P prop, NOT MET	poor	$118.00	01-09
Pflueger	Kent Frog	GE	VG-	$442.50	99-02
Pflueger	Kent Frog	GE, huge hook drag, chip	avg	$312.00	00-08
Pflueger	Kent Frog	GE, paint sliver, diamond P prop	VG	$636.00	04-02
Pflueger	Kent Frog	GE, shiney	EX-	$750.00	00-03
Pflueger	Kent Frog	glass eyes, L&R props, NOT MET	VG+	$611.00	04-12
Pflueger	Kent Frog	large tack eye	avg	$232.00	00-10
Pflueger	Kent Frog	modern 1999 version	NIB	$105.00	00-07
Pflueger	Kent Frog	modern, black frog	NIB	$118.00	00-11
Pflueger	Kent Frog	nice blue-border canoe box & paper, GE	NIB	$1,346.00	03-02
PFlueger	Kent Frog	Neverfail, red lateral line, GE, NOT MET	EX-	$755.00	02-01
Pflueger	Kent Frog 1999	set of 10 different, NOT MET	NIB	$232.00	04-11
Pflueger	Ketchum 5-hooker	Simmons Hardware, props marked	VG+	$576.99	99-06
Pflueger	Kidney Spinner	#5 silver with slant Pflueger logo	EX	$20.00	05-05
Pflueger	Kingfisher 3-hooker	crackleback, maroon 100 box	EXIB	$410.00	00-02
Pflueger	Kormish Frog	NO BIDS	NOC	$150.00	99-06
Pflueger	Kormish Frog	ugly, NOT MET	NOC	$62.00	99-07
Pflueger	Large Globe	yellow w/gold spots, 3" long, bulldog trademark	VG	$20.01	05-07
Pflueger	Livewire		EX	$33.50	99-01
Pflueger	Livewire	5474, PE, w/green & blk ribs, PTCB	NIB	$60.00	99-06
Pflueger	Livewire	mullet scale, red GE, lots of pointers and nicks, mostly on bell, in orig 2PCCB	VGIB	$195.00	05-05
Pflueger	Livewire	pikie, PE	EX	$109.29	00-02
Pflueger	Livewire	RH, PE, white/blue card no writing?!	NOC	$380.00	01-03
Pflueger	Livewire	w/blk ribs, 9453, PE, PTCB, 3¾"	NIB	$41.50	99-04
Pflueger	Luminous Crystal Minnow	still glows!	EX	$2,020.00	01-12
Pflueger	Magnet	bulldog label, maroon box 3697 VG+	EXIB	$164.00	05-03
Pflueger	Magnet	maroon bulldog nice, red/lum	EXIB	$850.00	01-08
Pflueger	Magnet	red & white	VG+	$25.00	05-06
Pflueger	Magnet	white, age lines, NOT MET	EX	$137.50	00-01

BRAND	MODEL	SERIES / MFG. CODE / DESCRIPTION	GRADE	PRICE	DATE yy/mm
Pflueger	Magnet/Merit Bait	RH/luminous, few scattered pntrs, varnish is tanning	VG	$52.00	05-05
Pflueger	Magnets x 2	RH/lum and lum	EX	$380.00	00-02
Pflueger	Marvelus Wooden Minnow	wood box, paper label EX-, white, 5-hook, Neverfail, minnow, GE, gem clip hardware, straight line marked prop, 2 HPGM	EXIB	$4,400.00	05-04
Pflueger	Marvelus Wooden Minnow	wood box, paper label EX-, yellow perch, 3-hook, Neverfail, minnow, GE, gem clip hardware, 2 HPGM	VG	$880.00	05-04
Pflueger	May Bug Spoon	glass beads	VG+	$1,525.00	99-05
Pflueger	May Bug Spoon	not much paint but nice	EX-	$1,594.00	05-02
Pflueger	Maybug	NOT MET	EX?	$1,593.00	01-06
Pflueger	McGinty	3511 canoe 2PCCB, skin? body	NIB	$32.00	03-01
Pflueger	Meadow Frog	cork or rubber, ugly	EX	$255.00	99-04
Pflueger	Merit	3697 LUM-RED, woodpecker type	EXIB	$188.20	99-10
Pflueger	Metal Minnow Flt	button tack eyes?	EX-	$137.50	99-04
Pflueger	Metalized Minnow	3-hooker	VG+	$299.00	02-08
Pflueger	Metalized Minnow	3-hooker, maroon bulldog box!	EXIB	$1,480.00	99-11
Pflueger	Metalized Minnow	cracks in metal, $450 NOT MET	G	$128.00	01-03
Pflueger	Metalized Monarch Minnow		EX	$1,250.00	01-04
Pflueger	Monarch	2185, slate, crack at tail, gem clip, c. 1910	VG?	$650.00	99-10
Pflueger	Monarch	3-hk, rainbow, bulldog prop	VG+	$600.00	99-10
Pflueger	Monarch	5-hk, crackle, HPGM, 1914, bulldog, SOLD	mint	$600.00	99-10
Pflueger	Monarch	3-hook, with marked front prop, chub scale	EX	$275.00	05-07
Pflueger	Monarch	white, HPGM, gem clip, dog Pflueger prop	EX++	$2,000.00	99-10
Pflueger	Monarch 3-hk	RB, fat, dog Monarch prop	EX-	$400.00	00-01
Pflueger	Monarch 3-hook	rainbow, bulldog props, GE	EX	$252.00	01-12
Pflueger	Monarch 5-hk	aluminum, round body, HPGM	EX-	$950.00	00-05
Pflueger	Monarch 5-hk	RB, fat body, nice	VG+	$725.00	00-05
Pflueger	Monarch 5-hooker	bar perch, crisp box, dog paper, NOT MET	NIB	$1,527.00	01-06
Pflueger	Monarch Minnow	Sienna Fire w/Monarch maroon box	EX	$3,500.00	01-04
Pflueger	Muskill	metal, gold/white with gold spots	EX	$7.00	05-07
Pflueger	Muskill	musky spinner	EX	$7.00	05-07
Pflueger	Muskollonge Minnow	7", rubber with metal fins, c. 1892	EX-	$627.00	05-02
Pflueger	Musky Minnow	5-hk, slate, HPGM	VG	$788.00	02-02
Pflueger	Musky Minnow	rubber, NOT MET	EX	$787.00	04-03
Pflueger	Musky Mustang	Red Squid, looks like goldfish scale, PPE, a hint of wear	EX-	$45.00	05-05
Pflueger	Musky Mustang	sunfish, PPE, new in orig VG large green canoe 2PCCB	NIB	$70.00	05-05
Pflueger	Mustang	9512, Reed Squid, canoe box & papers, PE	NIB	$113.00	03-05
Pflueger	Mustang	mullet scale, PE, 9512 canoe papers	NIB	$58.00	01-10
Pflueger	Mustang	PE, blue scale, plate on top and bottom, 5"	EX-	$18.00	05-06
Pflueger	Mustang	perch, plate, papers	NIB	$132.50	99-04
Pflueger	Mustang	red scale, 5", PE, nice	EX	$37.00	01-01
Pflueger	Mustang	saltwater version, sunfish scale, PE, canoe box crisp	NIB	$427.00	05-06
Pflueger	Mustang	strawberry, PE, PTCB	NIB	$52.00	00-08
Pflueger	Mustang	8903, sil/sparkle/green back, PE, PTCB	NIB	$31.51	99-06
Pflueger	Mustang	9509, blue mullet, paper, plate	NIB	$51.00	99-11

BRAND	MODEL	SERIES / MFG. CODE / DESCRIPTION	GRADE	PRICE	DATE yy/mm
Pflueger	Mustang	9540, sunfish scale, PE	NIB	$26.00	99-05
Pflueger	Mustang	9540, PE, sunfish color	NIB	$77.53	99-02
Pflueger	Mustang	r/w, PE, plates, canoe box	NIB	$135.00	99-02
Pflueger	Mustang Musky	blue scale, PE	NIB	$153.51	99-05
Pflueger	Mustang Musky	eel, PE	EXIB	$99.00	99-05
Pflueger	Mustang Musky	sunfish, PE	NIB	$172.50	99-05
Pflueger	Neverfail	rainbow, in correct box	NIB	$1,150.00	01-04
Pflueger	Neverfail	RB? blue canoe, purty lure	EXIB	$566.06	00-01
Pflueger	Neverfail	sienna	EX+	$850.00	01-04
Pflueger	Neverfail 3-hook	perch scale, GE, NOT MET	EX+	$280.00	00-08
Pflueger	O Boy	frog scale, GE, blue canoe, paper	NIB	$699.00	00-02
Pflueger	O Boy	peanut butter, GE	EX-	$140.25	00-02
Pflueger	O Boy	RH, 3½", GE, blue canoe, NOT MET	NIB	$202.50	00-02
Pflueger	O Boy	strawberry, NOT MET	EX-	$158.00	00-11
Pflueger	O Boy	strawberry, 3½", GE, blue canoe	NIB	$648.00	00-02
Pflueger	O Boy	strawberry, GE, marked lip	EX-	$200.00	99-08
Pflueger	O Boy	strawberry, GE, nice	EX	$205.00	99-10
Pflueger	Pakron	RH	EX-	$280.00	99-10
Pflueger	Palomine	5073, 3¼", rainbow, pressed eyes	NIB	$33.00	05-03
Pflueger	Palomine	4", GE, gr/silver scale	EX+	$64.50	99-01
Pflueger	Palomine	5006, pikie, GE, papers crisp box	NIB	$227.50	00-01
Pflueger	Palomine	5040SUN, PE, NOT MET	NIB	$44.00	99-02
Pflueger	Palomine	7604, nat pike, GE, blue, GE, NOT MET	NIB	$76.00	00-02
Pflueger	Palomine	9006, perch, PTCB, $35 reserve	NIB	$15.00	00-01
Pflueger	Palomine	blue scale, frog, PE, PTCB	NIB	$41.00	00-05
Pflueger	Palomine	blue scale, GE?	EX-	$43.99	99-02
Pflueger	Palomine	blue scale, pressed eye	NIB	$21.00	01-01
Pflueger	Palomine	crackle, GE	EX-	$54.00	00-10
Pflueger	Palomine	frog scale, GE	mint	$221.05	00-01
Pflueger	Palomine	frog scale, PE	EX-	$198.00	00-06
Pflueger	Palomine	frog scale, GE, 4⅜"	EX-	$68.00	05-07
Pflueger	Palomine	GE, swirl	EX	$110.00	05-06
Pflueger	Palomine	GE, red & white with silver specks on white, tough	EX	$60.00	05-06
Pflueger	Palomine	nat mullet, GE, blue canoe	NIB	$355.00	00-02
Pflueger	Palomine	peanut butter? PE	mint	$51.75	00-01
Pflueger	Palomine	perch, GE, small	EX	$45.00	00-10
Pflueger	Palomine	pike, shiner jntd, GE	avg	$26.00	99-01
Pflueger	Palomine	pikie scale, nice box, 4"?	NIB	$131.00	00-04
Pflueger	Palomine	pikie, PE	NIB	$76.00	99-11
Pflueger	Palomine	pikie, TE, modern, PTCB	NIB	$20.25	99-04
Pflueger	Palomine	rainbow, sm, PE, PTCB	NIB	$51.00	99-03
Pflueger	Palomine	RB, GE, NOT MET	EX	$46.00	00-04
Pflueger	Palomine	RB, PE	mint	$36.00	99-11
Pflueger	Palomine	RH/sparkles, lg, papers, PE	NIB	$46.00	00-02
Pflueger	Palomine	RH/w, GE, both crkd, early blunt nose, hks rusty and hdwr pitted	EX-	$29.00	05-05
Pflueger	Palomine	S-7033, plastic box, $35 reserve	NIB	$15.00	00-01

BRAND	MODEL	SERIES / MFG. CODE / DESCRIPTION	GRADE	PRICE	DATE yy/mm
Pflueger	Palomine	scale patterns, PE, PTCB	NIB	$47.00	00-05
Pflueger	Palomine	scramble finish, hooks rusty, paint great, 5080 PTCB	EXIB	$87.00	05-03
Pflueger	Palomine	scramble finish, PE	EX+	$77.00	05-07
Pflueger	Palomine	strawberry, PE, PTCB	NIB	$15.00	03-01
Pflueger	Palomine	strawberry, GE	EX-	$62.00	99-02
Pflueger	Palomine	sunfish PPE, light wear and hdwr pitted	VG+	$21.00	05-05
Pflueger	Palomine	swirl finish, 4½"	mint	$128.00	03-05
Pflueger	Palomine	white flash, GE, NOT MET	EXIB	$62.00	99-02
Pflueger	Palomine	y perch, PE	mint	$42.00	00-11
Pflueger	Palomine x 6	5078, rainbow, pressed eye, 6-pack	NIB	$184.00	00-07
Pflueger	Palomine x 6	silver sp/gr back, 6-pack, NOT MET	NIB	$102.50	99-06
Pflueger	Palomine, Baby	frog scale, GE, l-eye chip, SR, varn pntrs on belly and very light wear	VG	$19.00	05-05
Pflueger	Palomine, Baby	frog scale, GE, PPE, and some light wear	VG	$15.00	05-05
Pflueger	Palomine, Baby	perch scale, GE crkd, few tiny flakes and very light wear	VG	$18.00	05-05
Pflueger	Palomine, Baby	pike scale, GE, few light age lines and a hint of wear	EX	$30.00	05-05
Pflueger	Palomine, Baby	RH/w, l-eye crkd, light age lines and some very light wear	VG+	$21.00	05-05
Pflueger	Palomine, Baby	RH/w w/pearl sparkles, GE (actually ground mother-of-pearl), some pearls flaked off and pointer on nose	EX-	$59.00	05-05
Pflueger	Palomine, Baby	silver flash, GE, SR, tiny flake at r-eye, light age lines and nick on belly	EX-	$34.00	05-05
Pflueger	Palomine, Baby	white/red/yel/black spots, PPE, just a hint of wear	EX+	$25.00	05-05
Pflueger	Palomine, Baby jntd	GE, RH, glitter age lines and very light wear	EX-	$43.00	05-05
Pflueger	Palomine, Baby jntd	silver flash, GE, SR, very light wear	EX-	$42.00	05-05
Pflueger	Phantom	brown, canoe box VG	NIB	$39.00	05-02
Pflueger	Phantom	maroon box EX-	EXIB	$192.50	00-01
Pflueger	Phantom	musky size, new on card in box!	NIB	$62.00	00-01
Pflueger	Phantom	pic box VG	EX-IB	$225.00	99-10
Pflueger	Phantom Minnow	on card EX	EXOC	$125.00	01-04
Pflueger	Pilot Fly	1823 Royal Coachman #8	NOC	$25.00	02-02
Pflueger	Pippin Fly Rod Wobblers	12 diff sm metal, on nice card in EX box	NIB	$212.00	04-12
Pflueger	Pippin Spoon Fly Rod	card of 12 new in box	NIB	$150.00	04-03
Pflueger	Pirate	w/green, cheapie 3-hooker	VG	$32.00	00-01
Pflueger	Playfair 5-hooker	bar perch, GE, maroon Playfair box	NIB	$757.00	00-10
Pflueger	Pop Rite	black/silver, T-bolt, sparkle	EX	$41.00	00-05
Pflueger	Pop Rite	red side/silver scale, PE	mint	$60.00	05-03
Pflueger	Portage Peerless Minnow	3-hk, green/white, NE, screw eye, age lines and flakes	AVG	$12.00	05-05
Pflueger	Razem	6096, red/white, NOT MET	VGIB	$50.99	99-04
Pflueger	Red Devil	spinner, wood body	VG-	$32.00	03-02
Pflueger	Red Devil Spinner	#1 on card	NOC	$51.00	04-07
Pflueger	Scoop	9303, silver sparkle/green back, canoe, GE	EXIB	$122.51	99-06
Pflueger	Scoop	9355, Meadow Frog, GE, 2PCCB	EXIB	$125.49	99-11
Pflueger	Scoop	frog, injured minnow type, PE	EX-	$18.00	03-01
Pflueger	Scoop	silver flash and glass eyes, hint of wear, in orig 2PCCB, color insert	EX+IB	$210.00	05-05

BRAND	MODEL	SERIES / MFG. CODE / DESCRIPTION	GRADE	PRICE	DATE yy/mm
Pflueger	Spinner	#6 fish head design, glass beads	EX	$71.00	03-06
Pflueger	Spinner	c. 1880, scale textured, angle name	EX	$157.00	00-11
Pflueger	Spinner	scalloped, Abu Reflex, angled name	EX	$31.00	00-03
Pflueger	Spinner	textured scale, unmarked, brass	EX	$137.00	00-07
Pflueger	Spinner	textured, painted frog, musky size	avg	$41.00	01-03
Pflueger	Spinner	textured, lum moth pic, angled	EX-	$63.00	00-08
Pflueger	Surprise Minnow	golden shiner	EX+	$750.00	01-04
Pflueger	Surprise	hole eye, Neverfail, rigged bait, w/box rough but correct	EX	$220.00	05-04
Pflueger	Surprise	3980, white, hole eye	EX+	$500.00	99-10
Pflueger	Surprise	3985, crackle, lower lip chips, SOLD	EX-	$305.00	99-10
Pflueger	Surprise	golden shiner, GE	EX	$287.00	01-05
Pflueger	Surprise	golden shiner, GE	EX	$700.00	00-04
Pflueger	Surprise	hole eyes, white/red mouth	EX-	$112.00	03-02
Pflueger	Surprise	RB, GE, 2 hook, 4"	EX+	$393.88	00-02
Pflueger	Surprise	strawberry, hole eye, maroon bx 3969 crisp	NIB	$1,701.00	05-02
Pflueger	Surprise #4	RB, superb 3973 maroon box, hole eye	NIB	$1,053.00	01-09
Pflueger	Surprise 4 Bros	maroon box, with RB hole eye	VG-IB	$355.00	00-10
Pflueger	Surprise Minnow	4 Bros., white lure, maroon box crisp	NIB	$1,088.00	00-10
Pflueger	Surprise Minnow	4 Bros., maroon box, belly chip	VG+	$610.00	99-03
Pflueger	Surprise Minnow	canoe bx 3970 Luminous VG, GE, one eye chipped, dark paint	EX-IB	$178.00	05-07
Pflueger	Surprise Minnow	crackle, hole eye	EX	$525.00	00-05
Pflueger	Surprise Minnow	crackleback, hole eye	VG-	$127.53	00-02
Pflueger	Surprise Minnow	early hole eye, white w/black eyes, light age lines and few tiny pointers	EX-	$155.00	05-05
Pflueger	Surprise Minnow	white w/green and red spots, GE (r-eye crkd), lots of pointers and few small nicks	G+	$62.00	05-05
Pflueger	Surprise Minnow	lum, GE	EX	$256.00	00-10
Pflueger	Surprise Minnow	lum, hole eye, NOT MET	EX-	$257.52	00-01
Pflueger	Surprise Minnow	maroon box EX, age crack on belly, hole eye	EXIB	$709.00	04-03
Pflueger	Surprise Minnow	white, hole eye	EX-	$425.00	00-05
Pflueger	Tantrum x 6	PE, 6-pack, NOT MET	NIB	$122.50	99-05
Pflueger	TNT	metal, NOT MET	EX	$50.01	99-05
Pflueger	TNT	rainbow, metal	VG	$76.00	99-06
Pflueger	Wizard	3 hook, NOT MET	?	$156.00	00-03
Pflueger	Wizard	5-hooker, earliest model, right & left props	avg	$141.00	02-07
Pflueger	Wizard	frog, no eyes, 3½"	EX-	$42.00	03-01
Pflueger	Wizard	GE, perch with flap tail, 3⅛"	EX-	$65.00	05-06
Pflueger	Wizard	green crackleback, medium 3" size, NE, SR, few minor nicks and flakes	VG	$62.00	05-05
Pflueger	Wizard	gray mouse, GE, tail flasher, few tiny pointers and hint of age lines, in green canoe 2PCCB no #	EX-IB	$110.00	05-05
Pflueger	Wizard	LUM/gold dots, GE, 3¼", still glows great	mint	$53.00	04-12
Pflueger	Wizard	perch scale, GE, 3½"	EX	$61.00	05-07
Pflueger	Wizard	RB, PE, chip by eye	VG+	$57.00	00-10
Pflueger	Wizard	RH/w, 2¼" size, NE, varn bead off tail	EX-	$30.00	05-05
Pflueger	Wizard	scale pattern, no eyes	EX-	$22.00	02-12
Pflueger	Wizard	wood box VG+, yellow side lable, 2BW, c. 1903	VGIB	$1,850.00	05-06

BRAND	MODEL	SERIES / MFG. CODE / DESCRIPTION	GRADE	PRICE	DATE yy/mm
Pflueger	Wizard 3-hk	rainbow, screw eye hook hangers, HPGM	VG-	$325.00	02-10
Pflueger	Wizard 5-hk	c. 1903 silver, marked props, NOT MET	VG+	$157.00	01-01
Pflueger	Wizard Wiggler	fly rod, strawberry	EX	$41.99	00-03
Pflueger	Wizard	luminous paper, PTCB	NIB	$134.00	00-10
Pflueger	Woodpecker	lum/gold dots, collar rough, rest not bad	VG	$38.00	03-02
Pflueger	Zam	4854, PTCB	NIB	$32.00	03-02
Phillip Morris	#5	silver willow leaf/June bug, spinner type	EX	$6.00	04-03
Phillips	Frog	black/white PE, blem on each side	VG+	$38.00	05-05
Phillips	Frog	dark green frog w/thick tied hair legs, YPE, very minor nicks	EX	$85.00	05-05
Phillips	Frog	NE, RH/w, CR, light varnish wear	EX-	$12.00	05-05
Phillips	Frog	perch scale, PE, CR, very light wear	EX-	$17.00	05-05
Phillips	Frog	perch scale, PE, NSOB	NM	$16.00	05-05
Phillips	Frog	RH/w, GPE, pointers at l-eye and light age crackling	VG	$10.00	05-05
Pico	Peppy	brown scale	minty	$145.00	05-02
Pico	Perch	bead eye, clear/black CD/gold foil	EX	$82.00	00-04
Pico	Perch	green scale, yellow belly, 1st plastic model	EX	$90.00	05-03
Pico	Perch 12-pack	4 diff colors	NIB	$132.50	99-08
Pico	Pet	wood, glass eyes, pearly color	EX	$66.00	05-02
Pico	PICO Perch	perch, plastic, w/box and insert	EX	$12.50	05-07
Pico	Plunker	frog spot, ROBW	EX	$38.00	05-02
Pico	Pop	ad lure, 1 BID	NIB	$10.00	00-05
Pocono	Hair Frog	Popper type, hair legs, wood body, scale ribs	EX	$9.00	04-07
Poes	Jackpot Series	cedar wood, Jackpot series1300, white-gray	NIB	$3.24	05-07
Point Jude	6"	blue back/white, blister pack	NOC	$31.00	02-01
Point Jude	Stri-Pert	large striper crank, PE	NIB	$165.50	99-05
Pontiac	3-hook Pontiac Minnow	c. 1909, GE, green back/white	AVG	$49.50	04-11
Pontiac	Radiant 5-hk	pic box with half label missing, NOT MET	VG-IB	$480.00	03-08
Pontiac	Radiant Minnow	brass hardware, GE	avg	$134.00	02-08
Pontiac	Radium Minnow	5-hooker, water stained box w/papers	NIB sold	$6,060.00	99-10
Pontiac	Radium Minnow	box label half gone, ugly box, NOT MET	poorIB	$360.00	02-04
Pontiac	Radium Minnow	dark back/red, POBW, NOT MET	VG	$510.99	99-10
Pontiac Mfg. Co	Radium Minnow	5-hk, rainbow, wood box (lable ½ missing) VG?	EXIB	$5,000.00	05-07
Popps	Musky Lunch	black/white scale, extended hook hardware	EX	$20.00	04-03
Porter	Pop Stop	FL bait, plastic box	NIB	$10.00	00-07
Porter	Spin Hawk	3-pack, plastic box	NIB	$76.99	99-06
Powerpack	Big Frog	novelty fishing lure, dated 1991	GD	$7.35	05-07
Powerpack	Minnow	novelty wind-up lure, green	EX	$5.50	05-07
Pulver Lure	Pulver Riser	PL-408, orange/black spots	NIB	$37.00	04-08
R.K. Tackle	Hollowhead	4 diff, NOT MET	NIB	$102.50	99-05
R.K. Tackle	Hollowhead	mahogony, papers	NIB	$33.00	99-03
Rapala	Assorted	10 diff	NIB	$34.51	99-03
Rapala	Deep Diver 90	lg metal lip, like Fat Rap, 16 BIDS!	NIB	$27.00	00-11
Rapala	Fat Rap Shallow	8 diff, perch, chart, silver, gold x 2	NIB	$150.00	01-01
Reano Baits	Mouse	RH, knockoff of Abbey Imbrie, window bx	EX-IB	$47.00	04-01
Rebel	Pop R	P-70, TN shad, big one	NIB	$152.00	05-07
Red River	Top R	yellow/black head, LA item	NIB	$2.00	05-03

BRAND	MODEL	SERIES / MFG. CODE / DESCRIPTION	GRADE	PRICE	DATE yy/mm
Reds	Shur-Catch	12-pack display card, spring hook	NOC	$76.00	99-05
Research & Model Co.	Will-O-the-Wisp	y/blk box VG, electric lure, corroded inside	VGIB	$31.00	04-09
Reynold's	Temptor	white, painted tack eyes, tight age lines, side paint sliver	VG+	$55.00	05-04
Rhodes	3-hooker	blue/white, black ribs, 2 BW	EX	$638.00	03-04
Rhodes	3-hooker	green, through body wire, c. 1907	avg	$177.50	99-11
Rhodes	5-hooker	perch, see-through rig, GE	VG	$415.50	99-04
Rhodes	Kazoo Minnow	3-hooker, staple rig, metal eyes	EX-	$105.00	04-01
Rhodes	Mech Swimming Frog	rubber bait hand painted, picture box poor	EX	$874.50	04-11
Rhodes	Mechanical Frog	round belly weight, missing belly hook, frozen in-out position, wood picture box EX-	VG-	$2,750.00	05-04
Rhodes	Mechanical Frog		EX	$192.50	05-07
Rhodes	New Winner 3-hk	wood, A9059 EX-, Shakespeare hdwr, NOT MET	NIB	$2,400.00	00-11
Rhodes?	Musky Frog Bait	5½", large painted tack eyes, wood body with metal harness, holds spring-loaded rubber legs, side cup rig hardware, trailing tail treble, early frog paint finish	EX	$5,225.00	05-04
Rice Eng. Co.	Live Lure	plastic minnow tube, tiny cardboard fish, paper	NIB	$22.00	04-07
Rinehart	Jinx	35 diff, 3 boxes, display case	EX	$350.00	99-08
Rinehart	Jinx	4 diff musky, 2PCCB	NIB	$202.50	99-02
Rinehart	Jinx	5", r/w, 2PCCB, BBS, blue back shiner	EXIB	$37.17	99-06
Rinehart	Jinx	5", r/w, 2PCCB, LBR	EX-IB	$24.00	99-06
Rinehart	Jinx	5", r/w, 2PCCB, LBR, white shore	EXIB	$42.17	99-06
Rinehart	Jinx	BS, musky size, nice box	EXIB	$51.00	99-02
Rinehart	Jinx	PLT, small green scale, bx seams split	NIB	$37.00	03-06
Rinehart	Jinx	r/y, smaller size	EX	$34.91	99-12
Rinehart	Jinx	rainbow, early model, w/eye way up front and bar-rig style SR-hdwr, plastic, light varn wear	EX-	$22.00	05-05
Rinehart	Jinx	silver flash, plastic, SR, looks unfished in orig VG+ graphic 2PCCB w/catalog	EXIB	$35.00	05-05
Rinehart	Jinx	small, w/red ribs, crisp box	NIB	$27.00	00-08
Rinehart	Jinx	white shore, 2¼", 2PCCB	EXIB	$22.50	99-05
Rinehart	Jinx, Musky	black w/white ribs, black shore, few tiny nicks and very light wear	EX-	$44.00	05-05
Rinehart	Jinx, Musky	green perch? papers, nice box	NIB	$53.00	05-01
Rinehart	Jinx, Musky	green perch? hard plastic box	NIB	$42.00	02-08
Rinehart	Jinx, Musky	nice box	NIB	$36.50	99-02
Rinehart	Jinx, Musky	orange scale/green stripes	EX	$24.00	03-07
Rinehart	Jinx, Musky	perch scale	VG+	$18.00	01-03
Rinehart	Jinx, Musky	pikie?	EX	$35.57	99-06
Rinehart	Jinx, Musky	rainbow	EX-	$37.00	99-02
Rinehart	Jinx, Musky	RH/w, hint of age, in orig cool graphics 2PCCB w/catalog	EX+IB	$75.00	05-05
Rinehart	Jinx, Musky	silver head/blue	NIB	$43.00	99-09
Rinehart	Jinx, Musky	spotted flitter, papers	NIB	$65.00	00-09
Rinehart	Jinx, Musky	yellow w/red ribs, few tiny scratches and light wear	VG	$42.00	05-05

BRAND	MODEL	SERIES / MFG. CODE / DESCRIPTION	GRADE	PRICE	DATE yy/mm
Rinehart	Surfcaster	5", blue flash, musky jinx but 2-hk, few tiny pntrs	EX-	$75.00	05-05
Roberts C.C.	Mudpuppy	50/50, GE, natural finish, NOT MET	EX	$139.00	05-03
Roberts C.C.	Mudpuppy	50/50, GE, paint off tail, cartoon bx VG	EXIB	$255.00	05-07
Roberts C.C.	Mudpuppy	b/w, GE, cartoon special order	NIB	$117.00	00-09
Roberts C.C.	Mudpuppy	50/50, baby, GE, natural sucker, picture box EX & papers	EX-IB	$131.00	05-07
Roberts C.C.	Mudpuppy	2/3, GE, natural, cartoon box	NIB	$127.50	99-04
Roberts C.C.	Mudpuppy	2/3, nat, GE, cartoon	NIB	$85.00	99-05
Roberts C.C.	Mudpuppy	natural, lg, w/cat, GE	EXIB	$42.00	99-01
Roberts C.C.	Mudpuppy	natural, center cut, GE, cartoon box (wrong bx)	EX-	$289.00	02-10
Roberts C.C.	Mudpuppy	perch, musky size, slim head, one PE	VG+	$45.00	05-06
Roberts C.C.	Mudpuppy	perch, musky size, in cartoon box E- with paper, fat head	VG+IB	$60.00	05-06
Roberts C.C.	Mudpuppy	strawberry, newer in cartoon box, no eyes	NIB	$85.00	02-11
Roberts C.C.	Mudpuppy Little	GE, pic box, r/w, pic papers EX-	NIB	$205.00	01-06
Roberts C.C.	Mudpuppy Little	natural, decal eye, pic box, papers	EXIB	$58.00	00-03
Roberts C.C.	Pupette	y/b	NIB	$35.00	00-02
Robey	Fly Rod Popper	M234 window box, white/black feathers	EXIB	$130.00	04-05
Robfin	Fincheroo	white, red/blk spots, plastic box & insert	NIB	$57.00	05-07
Robinson	Mustached Torpedo	silver/green back, lg dent, nice otherwise	??	$178.00	04-10
Robinson Bait Co.	Popper	green/silver spots, PE, darter type, Florida item	EXIB	$126.00	05-02
Rochester	Spinner	on nice card, plain lure	NOC	$52.00	99-03
Ropher	Findingo	perch, "SINKER"	mint	$46.00	03-04
Ropher	Findingo	perch, in wrong 2PCCB	NIB	$92.50	98-12
Rosegard	Salmon	yellow/red gills, nice box	NIB	$27.00	02-02
Ross	Tumble Bug	red, weird old plastic	EX-	$44.00	06-05
Rush	SOS Tango	RH/w, 1 pointer on right side and hdwr rusty	EX-	$44.00	05-05
Rush	Swimming Minnow	5", yellow splatter back, $50 gold prize bx	EXIB	$70.00	05-02
Rush	Tango Jr.	silver victory finish, 4" long, light age lines and few minor pntrs	EX-	$55.00	05-05
Rush	Tango Jr.	y head/red, 3¾", skinny chip under tail, 2 pntrs on back and light varn loss	VG	$47.00	05-05
Rush	Tango Jr.	yellow, green and yellow mottled, 3¾", few light age lines on belly	EX	$60.00	05-05
Rush	Tangolure	RH/y, 3⅛", pnt flks off l side body, lip age cracks, blem on back	G	$39.00	05-05
Rush	Tiger Tango	gold victory finish, 5", light wear on lip edge and light pointers	VG+	$48.00	05-05
Rush	Tiger Tango	Radiant (luminous), 5", flakes and age lines, orig "No. 1 Radiant" 2PCCB EX	G+IB	$110.00	05-05
Rush	Tiger Tango	red face/y body, 5", small chip on tip of tail, few tiny nicks, hdwr a bit rusy	EX-	$62.00	05-05
Rush	Tiger Tango	RH/white, light age lines and hint of wear in VG+ y 2PCCB	EXIB	$165.00	05-05
Rush	Tiger Tango	y head/red body, 5", small chip on tip of tail	EX	$88.00	05-05
Rush	Trout Tango 6-pack	great pic 2PCCB EX, lures mint	NIB	$2,750.00	04-02
Rush	Trout Tango 6-pack	superb box with inside pic, 6 diff lures	NIB	$2,326.00	02-01
Russo C.	9" Chugger	goldfish scale, GE	EX	$284.99	00-03
Saf-T-Lure		green/white	EX	$43.00	00-10
Salmo	Bullhead	BD6FN, Poland	NIB	$21.00	04-07

BRAND	MODEL	SERIES / MFG. CODE / DESCRIPTION	GRADE	PRICE	DATE yy/mm
Salmo	Bullhead	wood, handmade, bullhead fishing lure w/box	VG+	$13.06	05-07
Sambo			NIB	$52.26	99-02
Sam-BO	Novelty Lure	black man in barrel; when lifted, exposes his privates	NIB	$50.00	05-05
San Luco	#151	wood, 3", 3 hooks, 2 props, GE? dace on one side, perch on other!	NIB	$53.00	05-07
San Luco	Injured Minnow	Christmas tree, nice box	NIB	$44.51	00-03
Sat-Kot	Spring-loaded Spoon	fish-shaped spoon	EX	$57.99	99-06
Schaefer	Turbulent	2 sections, white/multicolor dots	EX+	$116.00	01-08
Schaefer	Turbulent	green, red & white dots, 3 sections	EX-	$138.50	00-02
Schaefer	Turbulent	r/y, ugly dbl wood spinner	NIB	$293.88	99-11
Schaefer	Turbulent	red/yellow, 2 papers, $450 NOT MET	NIB	$305.00	02-06
Schilpp	Crawler #1	neat metal lure similar to Foss	EX	$15.00	05-03
Schilpp	Frog	similar to Foss	EX	$9.00	05-03
Schmelzer Arms	5-hooker	box VG-, red, HPGM, made by Heddon	EXIB	$935.00	04-03
Schröder	Big Pike	zinc eyes, yellow scale	NIB	$41.00	03-05
Schröder	Midget Baby Pikie	midget on back, zinc eyes	mint	$32.00	03-05
Schröder	Pikie, Baby jntd	perch scale, zinc eyes, Jenkki bx	NIB	$53.00	03-05
Schröder	Wiggler	zinc eyes, paint added, NOT MET	VG+	$18.00	03-05
Schroeders	Wonder Plug	dbl jointed, GE, basser type	EX	$215.00	99-01
Schuman	Big 3	real duckling — gross, crisp box	NIB	$55.00	05-03
Scooter Pooper	Scooter Pooper	box rough on end, paper	NIB	$153.00	04-02
Scooter Pooper	Scooter Pooper	metal	mint	$51.00	03-04
Scooter Pooper	Scooter Pooper	NOT MET	EX	$54.00	00-06
Scooter Pooper	Scooter Pooper	papers, NOT MET	NIB	$127.50	99-12
Scooter Pooper	Scooter Pooper		EX-	$52.99	99-05
Sea Gull	Polywog	pristine, in correctly marked and mint box	NIB	$2,000.00	01-04
Sea Gull Shoenfeld-Gutter	Fly Rod	504 box crisp, c. 1918	NIB	$710.00	04-07
Sears & Robuck	Winner Wood Minnow	9006, crackleback, box++	EXIB	$828.00	99-05
Selby	Flathead	red	EX	$12.00	04-02
Shadrac	Shadrac	perch scale, WB plastic box, Texas	EXIB	$13.00	05-05
Shadrac	Squaller	plastic, made in TX	EXIB	$15.00	03-02
Shaefer	Turbulent Lure	green polka dotted paint job, w/orig box and paperwork EX+/NM	NIB	$990.00	05-04
Shakespeare	#3 Submerged	perch, ring OBW, sm chips	VG+	$650.00	99-10
Shakespeare	#43 3-hooker	rainbow, gem clip, B prop	EX-	$700.00	01-12
Shakespeare	#6 Whirlwind	white, brass cup, flat plate	EX-	$510.00	00-01
Shakespeare	00 Like Artistic Minnow	sienna crackle, B, SOLD	EX+	$600.00	99-10
Shakespeare	00 Fancyback	twin props, 2-hk, crackle/green scale, GE	EX	$297.00	00-05
Shakespeare	03 Minnow		EX	$700.00	01-04
Shakespeare	03	crackle	EX	$394.00	01-05
Shakespeare	2-hooker	33SC, wood box EX, flat plate, B prop	EXIB	$2,850.00	99-10
Shakespeare	3-hooker	gem clip, brass cups, smooth props, missing hook	VG+	$79.00	03-02
Shakespeare	3-hook Floater	met red/sil, HPGM, B prop, flat, SOLD	EX	$2,050.00	99-10
Shakespeare	31 Floater	photo finish perch, GE, nice	EX	$137.00	03-08
Shakespeare	33 3-hooker	red/y, HPGM, gem clip, POBW	EX-	$650.00	99-10
Shakespeare	33 Gold Metalized	wood stamp/end label EX-, B prop, flat	EXIB	$4,050.00	01-06
Shakespeare	33 RB	wood box labeled EX, B prop, flat plate	NIB	$4,100.00	01-06

BRAND	MODEL	SERIES / MFG. CODE / DESCRIPTION	GRADE	PRICE	DATE yy/mm
Shakespeare	33GY	gray box EX-, flat plate	NIB	$2,450.00	01-06
Shakespeare	3-hooker	#33, crackle, GE	EX-	$155.00	99-06
Shakespeare	3-hooker	31YP, photo finish, red box, SOLD	EX-IB	$400.00	99-10
Shakespeare	3-hooker	33, copper, wood box EX	EXIB	$3,050.00	00-10
Shakespeare	3-hooker	33SR, solid red, SOLD	NIB	$1,550.00	99-10
Shakespeare	3-hooker	bar perch	VG+	$310.00	99-10
Shakespeare	3-hooker	brown sienna, y belly, SOLD	EX-	$525.00	00-05
Shakespeare	3-hooker	copper, see through, nice	VG+	$152.00	00-08
Shakespeare	3-hooker	crackle, in wood Sears Roebuck, NOT MET	EX-IB	$462.00	00-06
Shakespeare	3-hooker	crackle, plate, un props	VG+	$217.00	00-01
Shakespeare	3-hooker	g&y perch, sweeping HPGM, SOLD	EX	$600.00	99-10
Shakespeare	3-hooker	green/w, sweeping HPGM, flat, SOLD	EX-	$550.00	99-10
Shakespeare	3-hooker	green/white, pointed props	VG+	$100.00	00-04
Shakespeare	3-hooker	green/white, flat plate	VG+	$147.50	99-10
Shakespeare	3-hooker	metalized nickle, B props	EX-	$705.00	00-03
Shakespeare	3-hooker	RB, GE, HPGM, flat plate	EX	$247.00	00-06
Shakespeare	3-hooker	RB, wood box, faded top	EX-IB	$586.00	00-01
Shakespeare	3-hooker	sienna, CB, flat plate, PP	EX	$900.00	01-06
Shakespeare	3-hooker	sienna, flat plate, unmarked props	EX	$700.00	01-12
Shakespeare	3-hooker	white, E-, unmarked wood box EX	EX-IB	$1,324.00	99-01
Shakespeare	3-hooker	white, flat plate	VG+?	$90.00	99-05
Shakespeare	3-hooker	white, flat plate, SOLD	EX	$500.00	99-10
Shakespeare	3-hooker	white, high forehead, B, RABW, HPGM, NOT MET	EX-	$355.00	00-01
Shakespeare	3-hooker	white, HPGM, flat plate, wood box VG	EXIB	$1,260.00	00-02
Shakespeare	3-hooker	white, sweeping HPGM, gem clip	EX-	$570.00	99-10
Shakespeare	3-hooker	wood bx badly faded, GE, flat plate hook hangers, style B props, yellow, perch, tiny varnish flakes	EX-IB	$1,017.50	05-04
Shakespeare	42 Floater 3-hk (2-belly)	y/green back, high forehead, B props	EX-	$1,200.00	01-06
Shakespeare	43 3-hooker Long	red/silver, y/w, B props, gem clip, c. 1909	EX-	$800.00	01-06
Shakespeare	44 High Forehead	red bk/sil/w, B prop, back scratchs, c. 1909	VG+	$800.00	01-06
Shakespeare	44 High Forehead	y, gem clip, A prop, c. 1906	VG	$1,600.00	01-06
Shakespeare	44SY	gray box VG, flat plate, PP, sweeping HPGM	EX-IB	$1,900.00	01-06
Shakespeare	5-hooker	#44, bar perch, plate	EX-	$480.00	00-03
Shakespeare	5-hooker	alum/green, wood box rough, NOT MET	EX-	$355.00	03-11
Shakespeare	5-hooker	aluminum, unmarked wood box	NIB	$1,975.00	99-02
Shakespeare	5-hooker	bar perch, HPGM, plain prop	EX-	$695.00	99-10
Shakespeare	5-hooker	bar perch, plate, pointers	VG+	$537.50	00-01
Shakespeare	5-hooker	brown sienna, y belly, SOLD	EX-	$825.00	00-05
Shakespeare	5-hooker	crackle, flat plate, unmarked prop, pointed	mint	$380.00	01-12
Shakespeare	5-hooker	early green back, gem clip	EX-	$420.00	00-01
Shakespeare	5-hooker	fancy back, purty	EX-	$400.00	99-01
Shakespeare	5-hooker	frog, clip, HPGM	avg	$204.00	00-10
Shakespeare	5-hooker	g/w, HPGM, bad wood box, NOT MET	VGIB	$935.51	00-03
Shakespeare	5-hooker	green bar perch, HPGM, wood bx, no end label	EXIB	$910.00	03-08
Shakespeare	5-hooker	green/copper belly, missing 2 hks, plate, HPGM	EX-	$385.00	02-04
Shakespeare	5-hooker	green/w, sweeping HPGM, flat, SOLD	VG	$625.00	99-10
Shakespeare	5-hooker	green/white, un wood box VG	VG+IB	$1,055.00	00-01
Shakespeare	5-hooker	green scale, photo, cup, pressed eyes	VG-	$240.00	01-03

BRAND	MODEL	SERIES / MFG. CODE / DESCRIPTION	GRADE	PRICE	DATE yy/mm
Shakespeare	5-hooker	green back, RB	VG-	$325.00	00-05
Shakespeare	5-hooker	high forehead, green/y belly, touched up	R	$500.00	00-08
Shakespeare	5-hooker	maroon pic bx badly faded, #44 box, green back/aluminum belly	VGIB	$860.00	04-03
Shakespeare	5-hooker	metalized minnow, GE	EX-	$415.00	00-06
Shakespeare	5-hooker	musky minnow, B-notch props, gem clip hardware, r/w, wear to primer	VG+/EX-	$660.00	05-04
Shakespeare	5-hooker	nice wood box, NOT MET	VG-IB	$860.00	99-09
Shakespeare	5-hooker	notched props, gem clip, 50% repaint	poor	$67.00	05-05
Shakespeare	5-hooker	RB, flat plate, HPGM	EX-	$456.00	00-10
Shakespeare	5-hooker	RB, oldest style? ugly	poor	$148.00	99-03
Shakespeare	5-hooker	RB, plate hdwr, scratches but decent	VG-	$179.01	00-01
Shakespeare	5-hooker	RB, plate, HPGM	VG-	$217.49	00-02
Shakespeare	5-hooker	red, see through, nasty chin	?	$162.00	99-01
Shakespeare	5-hooker	RH, see through, checked paint	odd	$47.00	00-05
Shakespeare	5-hooker	sienna CB, flat plate, PP	EX-	$1,000.00	01-06
Shakespeare	5-hooker	sienna crackle, HPGM, see through plate	EX-	$455.00	04-02
Shakespeare	5-hooker	sienna, flat plate, unmarked props	EX-	$900.00	01-12
Shakespeare	5-hooker	white, HPGM, 1 BW, gem clip	VG	$225.01	99-06
Shakespeare	5-hooker	y perch, high forehead, pic box G, paper EX	EX-IB	$4,250.00	01-12
Shakespeare	5-hooker	yellow, flat plate, un props, gray box EX-	NIB	$1,600.00	01-12
Shakespeare	5-hooker #44	perch? gem clip, POBW, B props	EX-	$636.61	99-04
Shakespeare	5-hooker, 44W	poor pic box	poorIB	$405.00	00-10
Shakespeare	61 Musky 2-hk Floater	red/y gills, gem clip, chip belly, c. 1907	EX-?	$5,600.00	01-06
Shakespeare	64 Musky 5-hook	CB/sil back/red side, flat plate, 3 HPGM, PP, c. 1916	EX-	$5,100.00	01-06
Shakespeare	64 Musky 5-hook	white, flat plate, 3 HPGM, PP, c. 1916	VG+/EX-	$3,800.00	01-06
Shakespeare	Baby Paddler	RH, sm chip, SOLD	EX-	$30.00	99-10
Shakespeare	Baby Pikie Kazoo	RH, GE, SOLD	EX	$150.00	99-10
Shakespeare	Baby Pikie Kazoo	637, r/w, GE	EX	$58.00	99-01
Shakespeare	Baby Revolution	black pic box VG-, SOLD	EXIB	$2,450.00	99-10
Shakespeare	Baby Revolution	sm dent	EX	$300.00	00-04
Shakespeare	Baby Size Revolution	3"?	EX	$357.50	05-04
Shakespeare	Barnacle Bill	green back/silver flitter, GE, SOLD	EX	$750.00	99-10
Shakespeare	Barnacle Bill	white	VG	$483.00	02-07
Shakespeare	Barnacle Bill	white/black tail, flitter, GE	EX	$309.00	01-03
Shakespeare	Bass A Lure	CCBC, NRA box, SOLD	NIB	$275.00	99-10
Shakespeare	Bass A Lure	RH, GE, age lines a mite ugly	EX-	$48.00	04-07
Shakespeare	Bass A Lure	3 hooks, red & white	VG+	$45.00	05-06
Shakespeare	Bass Kazoo	NE, red & white	VG+	$35.00	05-06
Shakespeare	Bright Shiny Musky-size Revolution	Mickey Mouse–style props, earliest version, c. 1902	EX	$1,100.00	05-04
Shakespeare	Bucktail Jr.	4", aluminum hollow body	EX-	$237.00	04-02
Shakespeare	Bucktail Revolution	brown bucktail	EX	$501.00	05-06
Shakespeare	Buddy	6568	NIB	$107.50	00-03
Shakespeare	Darter	4", RH, ball-type rear hook hanger	mint	$65.00	05-02
Shakespeare	Darting Shrimp	br back/copper, GE, very nice	EX	$175.00	99-11
Shakespeare	Darting Shrimp	copper, GE, small joint chip	EX-	$250.00	99-12
Shakespeare	Darting Shrimp	gold, GE, 2 BW	VG+	$136.00	05-07

LURES

BRAND	MODEL	SERIES / MFG. CODE / DESCRIPTION	GRADE	PRICE	DATE yy/mm
Shakespeare	Darting Shrimp	silver, GE nice	EX-	$224.50	99-08
Shakespeare	Dopey	6603, black body/white head	NIB	$77.00	01-05
Shakespeare	Dopey	6603, YP, nice box, papers	NIB	$53.99	99-03
Shakespeare	Dopey	frog	EXIB	$30.00	03-02
Shakespeare	Egyptian Wobbler	6636, RH, GE	EXIB	$148.00	01-02
Shakespeare	Evolution	4", perch finish, box swivel, very nice overall	VG+	$67.00	05-07
Shakespeare	Evolution	gray box EX, SOLD	VGIB	$500.00	99-10
Shakespeare	Evolution	gray oval box EX	EX-IB	$644.00	01-03
Shakespeare	Evolution	pic box faded avg, NOT MET	EXIB	$510.00	03-02
Shakespeare	Evolution	sm chips	EX-	$300.00	02-10
Shakespeare	Evolution Minnow	4GAEA, gray oval box crisp	EXIB	$621.00	00-10
Shakespeare	Favorite	strawberry, GE, Zara type	VG+	$305.00	99-08
Shakespeare	Favorite Floater	red, GE, screw eyes, plain	EX-	$432.51	00-01
Shakespeare	Favorite Floater	triangle body, screw, no eyes, SOLD	EX	$150.00	99-10
Shakespeare	Favorite Floating Bait	red, chipping around eyes, repaint?	EX-	$800.00	00-10
Shakespeare	First Version Revolution	Mickey Mouse–style props	EX	$258.50	05-04
Shakespeare	Fisher Bait	bar perch, PE, SOLD	EX	$155.00	99-10
Shakespeare	Fishey	hard rubber, sm tail chip, SOLD	EXOC	$325.00	99-10
Shakespeare	Floater	high forehead, yellow	VG+/EX-	$3,550.00	01-12
Shakespeare	Floater 2-hk	red back/white, c. 1906, A props	EX	$3,000.00	01-06
Shakespeare	Floater 3-hk	y perch, flat plate, c. 1916	EX	$780.00	01-06
Shakespeare	Floating Minnow	B-style prop	VG+	$495.00	05-07
Shakespeare	Floating Minnow	SB, triangle body (J. Dandy?)	EX-	$666.00	01-03
Shakespeare	Fly Rod Bait	w/red eyes	EX	$250.00	01-04
Shakespeare	Fly Rod Bug	metal lip, marked "Skakespeare," SB	EX-	$77.00	02-01
Shakespeare	Fly Rod Mouse	RH, PE	VG	$130.00	00-07
Shakespeare	Frog Skin	Eger? GE	EX-	$200.00	99-10
Shakespeare	Frog Skin Fishing Darter	white eyes	EX	$165.00	05-07
Shakespeare	Glo-Lite Mouse	6570T, tiger, PTCB	NIB	$42.00	04-02
Shakespeare	Glo-Lite Pup	frog spot, PE, little wear on r-edge of lip	EX-	$20.00	05-05
Shakespeare	Grumpy	6602S; white/red, black, and yellow spots; PPE, light pointers on nose	EX-	$15.00	05-05
Shakespeare	Hard Rubber Frog	3rd leg still there, ugly, SOLD	VG	$1,360.00	99-10
Shakespeare	Hydroplane	709, crackle, photo sides	EX-?	$91.00	00-05
Shakespeare	Hydroplane	early version	mint	$210.00	01-12
Shakespeare	Hydroplane	green scale	EX-	$205.00	00-03
Shakespeare	Hydroplane	rainbow, no eyes	EX	$405.00	03-02
Shakespeare	Hydroplane	RB, NOT MET	EX	$187.50	00-01
Shakespeare	Hydroplane	RB scale, photo finish	VG+	$95.00	00-10
Shakespeare	Hydroplane	red/y, no washer	mint	$355.00	99-10
Shakespeare	Injun Joe	frog, GE, decent	VG+	$48.00	00-01
Shakespeare	Injun Joe	RH	EX+	$87.86	00-01
Shakespeare	Injun Joe	sil flitter, GE	EX	$250.00	99-10
Shakespeare	Jacksmith	crackleback, photo finish, perch, ball post hdwr, GE	EX	$147.00	05-07
Shakespeare	Jim Dandy Floater	green scale	VG+	$70.00	99-10
Shakespeare	Jim Dandy Kazoo Chub	RH/black, tiny GE (1 chipped), age cracking and tiny flakes	VG-	$17.00	05-05

BRAND	MODEL	SERIES / MFG. CODE / DESCRIPTION	GRADE	PRICE	DATE yy/mm
Shakespeare	Jim Dandy Punkinseed	RH, no eyes, POBW, SOLD	EX-	$60.00	99-10
Shakespeare	Kazoo	rainbow, glass eye, plain bx stamped "2017"	EX-	$165.00	05-07
Shakespeare	Kazoo Bug	SOLD	near mint	$300.00	99-10
Shakespeare	Kazoo Chub	638, GE	EX	$300.00	99-10
Shakespeare	Kazoo	6637, photo, PE, ball hook, SOLD	EX	$135.00	99-10
Shakespeare	Kazoo	6637, green scale photo, GE	mint	$184.50	00-01
Shakespeare	Kazoo	green, photo (orig), GE	EX	$235.00	99-10
Shakespeare	Kazoo	RH, GE, ball hook hanger, gleamer	EX	$112.50	00-01
Shakespeare	Kazoo, jntd	photo perch, PE, SOLD	EX-	$124.00	99-10
Shakespeare	Kazoo Bug	straw, feathers, GE	VG	$45.98	99-04
Shakespeare	King Wobbler	white, GE, one side EX, other worm burn	?	$45.99	00-03
Shakespeare	Mermaid	RH, SOLD	EX	$125.00	99-10
Shakespeare	Metalized Minnow	3-hook, nickle, SOLD	EX	$1,020.00	99-10
Shakespeare	Midget Spinner	6301WR	NIB	$12.84	05-07
Shakespeare	Midget Spinner	6601GP, photo perch, pressed eye	NIB	$52.00	00-10
Shakespeare	Midget Spinner	red/green scale, PE	mint	$100.00	99-10
Shakespeare	Midget Underwater	gold crackle/y scale	EX-	$380.00	99-10
Shakespeare	Midget Underwater 6600	sienna back, photo side, GE	VG+	$266.00	00-01
Shakespeare	Midget Metalized Minnow	copper, B prop, c. 1909	EX	$2,500.00	01-06
Shakespeare	Mouse	copper or gold/green back, GE	EX	$73.00	03-08
Shakespeare	Mouse	g&y, GE	EX	$110.00	99-10
Shakespeare	Mouse	green, GE	EX	$38.00	04-07
Shakespeare	Mouse	green, GE, tail, tiny lip chip	EX	$56.00	00-01
Shakespeare	Musky 51 Floater	high forehead (1 of 3 known), clip, B prop, y gills	EX-/VG+	$5,200.00	01-12
Shakespeare	Musky 5-hooker	5½", big GE, 2 BW, 3 HPGM, green back/white, 2 hooks	VG	$2,392.00	00-04
Shakespeare	Musky 5-hooker	o/y, sweeping HPGM, sm chips	EX-	$2,600.00	99-10
Shakespeare	Musky 5-hooker	white, flat plate, NOT MET	EX-	$510.00	02-10
Shakespeare	Musky 5-hooker	white, sweeping HPGM, HOLD	EX-	$4,000.00	99-10
Shakespeare	Musky 64	green/red/silver, plate, unmarked props, c. 1916	EX-	$5,000.00	01-12
Shakespeare	Musky 64	white, flat plate, unmarked props, c. 1916	EX-/VG+	$3,500.00	01-12
Shakespeare	Musky Minnow	5⅜", no hooks or rear prop!	VG-	$645.57	00-03
Shakespeare	Musky Minnow	5-hook, green back/white smooth props	EX	$3,079.00	02-08
Shakespeare	Musky Minnow	Shakespeare Musky Minnow, early rainbow	EX-	$3,350.00	01-04
Shakespeare	Musky Paddler	frog	VG+	$125.00	00-09
Shakespeare	Musky Revolution	bow tie props	EX-	$313.00	02-03
Shakespeare	Musky Revolution	pointed props, 1 hook tip miss, SOLD	EX	$1,280.00	99-10
Shakespeare	Musky Revolution	r/w, some lg chips, still nice	VG	$1,750.00	99-08
Shakespeare	New Shiner Minnow	slate, wood label dirty avg	EXIB	$2,850.00	01-06
Shakespeare	New Shinner Minnow #23	wood box VG, paper label poor	EX-IB	$1,500.00	01-12
Shakespeare	No 53 Musky Minnow	3-hook, GE, B-notch props, gem clip hardware, HPGM	VG+	$550.00	05-04
Shakespeare	Paddler	frog	EX	$100.00	00-07
Shakespeare	Paddler	frog, pressed eye	EX	$158.00	00-04
Shakespeare	Paddler	gray mouse	VG	$58.00	99-02
Shakespeare	Paddler	r/w, 3¼"	mint	$267.50	00-01
Shakespeare	Paddler	RH	EX	$210.00	99-10

BRAND	MODEL	SERIES / MFG. CODE / DESCRIPTION	GRADE	PRICE	DATE yy/mm
Shakespeare	Panatella 3-hk	green scale, w eye, HPGM, shallow cup	mint	$1,250.00	00-05
Shakespeare	Plopper	RH, GE	EX-	$56.00	04-07
Shakespeare	Pop Eye	6575 SF	NIB	$40.00	05-03
Shakespeare	Pumpkinseed	red back/alum, B prop, SOLD	EX-	$1,320.00	99-10
Shakespeare	Pumpkinseed	red back/silver, HPGN, varnish ugly	EX-	$411.98	00-03
Shakespeare	Pumpkinseed	paper EX, green?/silver	EX-	$1,700.00	01-12
Shakespeare	Pumpkinseed Sinker	slate, nice papers! no box	EX-	$2,000.00	01-06
Shakespeare	Rainey's Secret	made for Florida company, RH/w and black back, PPE, unique	VG	$35.00	05-05
Shakespeare	Revolution	2 prop, egg-shaped tail, nice bucktail patina	EX	$392.00	01-09
Shakespeare	Revolution	2 prop, round, NOT MET	EX	$281.00	01-05
Shakespeare	Revolution	2nd style, acorn rear, Micky Mouse props	EX	$300.00	99-08
Shakespeare	Revolution	3¼", egg-shaped rear section, marked props	VG+	$405.00	03-06
Shakespeare	Revolution	4SAR, wood box EX	EXIB	$2,000.00	99-10
Shakespeare	Revolution	Acorn-style body, unmarked Rhodes-style props	EX	$220.00	05-04
Shakespeare	Revolution	acorn style, 3⅜"	EX-	$216.00	05-07
Shakespeare	Revolution	baby size, RH, no dents but some missing paint	EX-	$433.00	04-03
Shakespeare	Revolution	early model	EX-	$350.00	00-05
Shakespeare	Revolution	marked rear prop, 1st model	EX-	$214.50	99-09
Shakespeare	Revolution	MM props, SOLD	EX-	$350.00	99-10
Shakespeare	Revolution	oldest 1899 model	EX	$483.00	00-08
Shakespeare	Revolution	round ball	EX-	$160.00	04-07
Shakespeare	Revolution	rounded rear section, 2 props, older type	VG	$150.00	05-07
Shakespeare	Revolution	y, in blk/sil VG+	VGIB	$3,650.00	01-06
Shakespeare	Revolution	reg size, Mickey props, round ball	EX	$300.00	00-03
Shakespeare	Revolution, Musky	B-style props, ball	EX-	$610.00	05-07
Shakespeare	Revolution, Musky	no dents, "unused"	EX	$521.00	04-02
Shakespeare	Revolution x 4	4 diff, 2 Wordens + 2 Revs (1 dent)	EX	$1,176.00	00-01
Shakespeare	Rhodes	yellow, gem clip	EX+	$1,080.00	01-12
Shakespeare	Rhodes 3-hook	y, gem clip, c. 1906	EX	$1,080.00	01-06
Shakespeare	Rhodes 3-hooker	green-blue/w, flat, Rhodes props, SOLD	EX-	$950.00	99-10
Shakespeare	Rhodes 5 hooker	green stripes, gem clip	EX-	$358.00	00-03
Shakespeare	Rhodes 5-hooker	green/w, flat plate, 2HPGM, SOLD	EX-	$350.00	99-10
Shakespeare	Rhodes 5-hooker	red/y, flat, pointed prop	VG+	$370.00	99-10
Shakespeare	Rhodes Fancyback Minnow	2¾", GE, gem clip, tapered body	VG+	$225.00	05-06
Shakespeare	Rhodes Frog	Kalamazoo 2PCCB G, SOLD	EXIB	$2,900.00	99-10
Shakespeare	Rhodes Frog	wood box EX	NIB	$5,000.00	01-12
Shakespeare	Rhodes Mechanical Frog	one leg repaired, still nice	EX-	$160.00	03-02
Shakespeare	Rhodes Minnow	3-hk, notched props, white label box fixable	VGIB	$580.00	05-07
Shakespeare	Rhodes Minnow	3-hooker, early box EX+, yellow	NIB	$4,800.00	01-12
Shakespeare	Rhodes Minnow	white label box EX-, rainbow stripes, 5-hk	EXIB	$4,100.00	04-09
Shakespeare	Saltwater Minnow	721, POBW, PE, SOLD	VG+	$250.00	99-10
Shakespeare	Sardinia	261, PE, rough box, 1 bidder	NIB	$250.00	00-07
Shakespeare	Sardinia	GE, POBW, SOLD	VG	$650.00	99-10
Shakespeare	Sea Witch	goldfish, nice box 6534 GF	NIB	$53.00	04-09
Shakespeare	Sea Witch	pearl, POBW	VG	$21.00	05-03
Shakespeare	Sea Witch	strawberry, crack on belly	VG+	$37.33	99-08

BRAND	MODEL	SERIES / MFG. CODE / DESCRIPTION	GRADE	PRICE	DATE yy/mm
Shakespeare	Second Style Shakespeare Revolution	Patent dated props, acorn-style body	EX	$275.00	05-04
Shakespeare	Shinner Minnow 3-hooker	43, wood box EX-, SOLD	EXIB	$2,900.00	99-10
Shakespeare	Slim Jim	3-hk, tiny glass eyes	VG+	$331.00	02-03
Shakespeare	Slim Jim	5 hook, sm eye, gray box, NOT MET	VGIB	$350.00	01-03
Shakespeare	Slim Jim	5-hooker, yellow perch	VG+	$350.00	99-10
Shakespeare	Slim Jim	6541, PE, green scale	NIB	$57.01	99-11
Shakespeare	Slim Jim	blue back & ribs/white, sm GE	VG+	$100.00	05-07
Shakespeare	Slim Jim	GE, green/white belly, Rhodes?	VG	$110.00	04-03
Shakespeare	Slim Jim	gray/pink belly, tiny GE, green stripes	EX-	$233.00	00-06
Shakespeare	Slim Jim	43GWJ, label box G, SOLD	EXIB	$550.00	99-10
Shakespeare	Slim Jim	perch photo, GE, 3-hk, decent	EX-	$86.01	00-03
Shakespeare	Slim Jim	rainbow, pressed eye	EX	$37.00	03-02
Shakespeare	Slim Jim	white intro box EX, c. 1908	NIB	$2,850.00	01-06
Shakespeare	Slim Jim	wood, brown with gold scales	avg	$6.80	05-07
Shakespeare	Slim Jim	yellow GE, black back & stripes, white bottom	EX-	$140.00	05-07
Shakespeare	Slim Jim 2-hk	RH, small eye	EX-	$70.99	00-01
Shakespeare	Slim Jim 3-hk	red scale photo, sm eye, big belly chip	VG	$96.00	00-01
Shakespeare	Slim Jim 5-hk	perch, tiny eye, plate	VG	$305.00	00-01
Shakespeare	Slim Jim Floater	red/green, GE	EX-	$350.00	99-10
Shakespeare	Slim Jim	6541YP, nice box, pressed eye	NIB	$154.00	00-11
Shakespeare	Special x 2	6546 & 6547, frog & photo finish perch	EX	$41.00	04-07
Shakespeare	Spin Lure Assortment	lg 2PCCB, 6 PE lures	NIB	$213.01	00-01
Shakespeare	Spinner	correct wood box EX	EXIB	$1,420.00	99-10
Shakespeare	Spinner	wood box EX? part label	EXIB	$800.00	01-12
Shakespeare	Spinner Floating	4 SYs, 2PCCB oval EX	EXIB	$745.00	00-02
Shakespeare	Spinning Mouse	wood, 03 80 G	NIB	$16.13	05-07
Shakespeare	Spoonbill Wobbler	blkH/r&y, GE, SOLD	EX	$190.00	99-10
Shakespeare	Stand-size Revolution	3¼" bait	EX	$247.50	05-04
Shakespeare	Strike It	photo reddish-brown scale, GE, fin chip	EX-	$125.00	00-11
Shakespeare	Submarine Floating	perch, red box, TE, SOLD	EXIB	$380.00	99-10
Shakespeare	Submarine Floating	photo perch, red box, TE, SOLD	EXIB	$350.00	99-10
Shakespeare	Sure Lure	black pic box EX-, SOLD	EXIB	$2,750.00	99-10
Shakespeare	Surface Spinner	y/gold dots, wood label/stamp VG+	EXIB	$1,200.00	01-06
Shakespeare	Surface Wonder	red & white early style	VG	$60.00	05-06
Shakespeare	Swimming Mouse	black, PE, in box VG+	VG+IB	$25.00	05-06
Shakespeare	Swimming Mouse	black/white head, pressed eyes, crisp box	NIB	$89.00	05-07
Shakespeare	Swimming Mouse	r/w in plastic top box	NIB	$32.00	99-01
Shakespeare	Swimming Mouse	yellow/RH, GE	VG	$22.00	05-05
Shakespeare	Swimming Mouse Jr.	6580B, black mouse, PPE, hint of wear	EX	$26.00	05-05
Shakespeare	Tantalizer	nat pike, missing 1 eye	EX-	$96.00	00-11
Shakespeare	Tantalizer	photo perch, GE	EX	$159.00	00-06
Shakespeare	Tantalizer	RH, GE	EX-	$160.00	00-06
Shakespeare	Tantalizer	photo, big joint chip on belly, gleamer	VG	$87.00	00-01
Shakespeare	Tantalizer	ball hook, GE	EX	$290.00	99-10
Shakespeare	Tantalizer	g&y photo, GE	EX-	$140.00	99-10
Shakespeare	Tantalizer	photo perch, pressed eye, ball hanger	EX	$224.00	00-10
Shakespeare	Tantalizer	RH/w, GE	EX-	$152.50	00-01

BRAND	MODEL	SERIES / MFG. CODE / DESCRIPTION	GRADE	PRICE	DATE yy/mm
Shakespeare	Tantilizer jntd	photo pikie, GE, knob hk, sm tail chip	EX-	$178.55	00-01
Shakespeare	Tarpalunge	#6640, natural scale	NIB	$810.00	99-03
Shakespeare	Waukazoo	frog, lots of age cracks	VG+	$120.00	05-06
Shakespeare	Waukazoo	frog, ball hook hanger	EX+	$382.00	04-02
Shakespeare	Waukazoo	red head, blended white	EX-	$144.00	04-02
Shakespeare	Waukazoo		avg	$90.00	00-11
Shakespeare	Waukazoo Surface	white	EX-	$79.00	02-01
Shakespeare	Whirlwind	red	EX	$330.00	01-03
Shakespeare	Whirlwind	red, hump props	VG+	$360.00	02-02
Shakespeare	Whirlwind	red, plain props	EX	$670.00	01-06
Shakespeare	Whirlwind	red, gem clip	EX	$604.64	99-12
Shakespeare	Worden Bucktail	acorn nose, capped tail	EX-	$368.00	05-07
Shakespeare	Worden Bucktail	alum, b/s pic box EX-, crisp paper	EXIB	$3,650.00	01-06
Shakespeare	Worden Bucktail	B props, SOLD	EX	$250.00	99-10
Shakespeare	Worden Bucktail	pat appl, props, one ding	EX-	$250.00	99-10
Shakespeare	Worden Bucktail	pat appl, props, replaced tail	EX	$200.00	99-10
Shakespeare	Worden Bucktail	pat appl, props, SOLD	EX	$250.00	99-10
Shakespeare	Worden Bucktail	yellow spotted	EX-	$429.00	00-03
Shakespeare	Worden Bucktail Spinner	intro black/silver pic bx VG-, NOT MET	EXIB	$2,370.00	05-07
Shakespeare	Worden Bucktail	2¼", silver, hook missing	EX	$188.88	00-02
Shannon	Twin Spin	Smiling Bill card, square swivel	NOC	$5.00	05-03
Shimano	CALCUTTA 400	with box	EXIB	$173.50	99-01
Shur Katch	Inj. Minnow	shiner scale, TE, nice 1PCCB	NIB	$40.00	00-01
Shur Strike	3 hooker	chain pickeral	EX	$316.00	02-02
Shur Strike	3-hooker	golden shiner	VG	$249.99	99-01
Shur Strike	3-hooker	green/rainbow, GE	VG+	$406.51	99-06
Shur Strike	3-hooker	green scale, GE (repaint? odd)	NIB	$431.00	00-11
Shur Strike	3-hooker	pikeral scale, GE	EXIB	$394.00	00-10
Shur Strike	3-hooker	pikie scale, GE	EXIB	$302.00	00-10
Shur Strike	3-hooker	pikie scale, GE, rd body, side hooker	EX-	$410.00	00-02
Shur Strike	3-hooker	pikie, TE, nice box	NIB	$156.00	00-11
Shur Strike	3-hooker	pikie, GE, not awful	G	$112.50	99-03
Shur Strike	3-hooker	RB, GE, not awful	VG-	$176.00	00-05
Shur Strike	3-hooker	RB, GE	poor	$12.60	99-08
Shur Strike	3-hooker	RH, TE	EX-	$77.10	99-10
Shur Strike	3-hooker	underwater	VG+	$204.00	00-07
Shur Strike	Anteater	peanut butter, GE	EX-	$82.00	01-10
Shur Strike	Babe Oreno Type	frog, GE, repaint?	EX	$100.00	01-05
Shur Strike	Baby Surface Spinner	yellow scale, GE, wrong box	NIB	$127.00	00-08
Shur Strike	Bass Oreno	dace? silver scale over red, dark head	EX	$55.00	00-04
Shur Strike	Bass Oreno	peanut butter, notch head, NRA	EXIB	$227.00	00-08
Shur Strike	Bass Oreno	peanut butter, GE, sm lip chip	EX-	$116.00	00-05
Shur Strike	Bass Oreno	RB, GE	VG-	$13.00	01-01
Shur Strike	Bass Oreno	red side? GE	EX	$76.00	00-12
Shur Strike	Bass Oreno	silver flash, GE	EX	$31.30	00-04
Shur Strike	Bass Oreno	silver flash, GE	EX	$41.00	01-01
Shur Strike	Bass Oreno	sm size, y shiner, GE	EX	$46.50	99-11
Shur Strike	Bass Oreno	yellow scale, GE	VG+	$22.30	00-05

BRAND	MODEL	SERIES / MFG. CODE / DESCRIPTION	GRADE	PRICE	DATE yy/mm
Shur Strike	Bass Oreno Groove Head	pikie, GE	EX-	$53.00	02-02
Shur Strike	Bass Oreno Small	BOT-2, GE	EXIB	$32.00	00-04
Shur Strike	Bass Oreno Type	black scale, TE, ugly	avg	$51.00	01-05
Shur Strike	Bass Oreno Type	GE, Bass Oreno style, chain pickeral	EX-	$25.00	05-06
Shur Strike	Bass Oreno Type	NE, Bass Oreno style, 2⅞", rainbow	VG+	$45.00	05-06
Shur Strike	Bass Oreno Type	red side, GE, purty	EX	$43.00	02-03
Shur Strike	Bass Oreno Type	shiner scale, GE	mint	$99.00	02-03
Shur Strike	Bass Oreno, Baby	BBOT-2 box, TE	NIB	$31.50	03-01
Shur Strike	Bass Oreno, Baby	peanut butter, GE	EX	$68.95	00-01
Shur Strike	Bass Oreno, Baby	shiner scale, GE	EX-	$22.00	02-08
Shur Strike	Bass Oreno	perch? TE	EX	$22.50	99-01
Shur Strike	Bass Oreno	V-notch, pikie, GE, nice	EX-	$103.51	00-01
Shur Strike	Bass Oreno Baby	silver scale, 2PCCB nice	NIB	$32.22	99-05
Shur Strike	Concave Belly Darter	RH, GE	EX	$103.00	00-04
Shur Strike	Crab	strawberry, GE, full feelers	EX	$292.00	03-09
Shur Strike	Crawdad	yellow/red & blk stripes, GE, Gateway	EX	$610.00	01-09
Shur Strike	Darter	concave belly, orange scale	VG+	$118.00	99-08
Shur Strike	Darter	PB, GE, 2 sm chips, lt drag	VG	$230.50	99-03
Shur Strike	Dolphin Nose Vamp	pikie scale, GE, top nose tie	EX-	$53.00	00-12
Shur Strike	Flatface	pikie type but with flat wood head	EX-	$102.00	03-02
Shur Strike	Flatface	orange scale, GE	EX-	$87.55	99-10
Shur Strike	Flatface	pike scale, $100 NOT MET	EX-	$15.00	00-10
Shur Strike	Floating Spinner	black head/yellow, GE	EX	$86.00	02-01
Shur Strike	Floating Tom	pikie, back stencil, GE	EX	$36.00	01-03
Shur Strike	Gar	#31 FL Special, white/black stripes, TE	EX	$136.00	05-01
Shur Strike	Gar	pikie finish (like Torpedo), NOT MET	VG+	$72.00	01-06
Shur Strike	Gar	Western Auto ghost color, white/wavy black lines, TE	VG	$81.00	05-07
Shur Strike	Gar, Baby	Torpedo type, pikie	VG	$136.00	01-04
Shur Strike	Grovehead Bass Oreno	pikie, GE	EX-	$47.00	00-12
Shur Strike	Husky Musky	white fish, GE, unmarked, CCBC?	EX	$517.03	99-06
Shur Strike	Injured Minnow	2, reg & petite, TE, nice	EX	$34.00	99-03
Shur Strike	Injured Minnow	IM2, RH, NRA, yellow/red box nice	NIB	$103.00	01-08
Shur Strike	Injured Minnow	red side, "Injured Tom," GE	EX	$85.00	99-12
Shur Strike	Injured Minnow	yellow/red box IM4 EX	NIB	$170.00	04-11
Shur Strike	Kingfish	yellow scale, GE	VG	$32.00	01-01
Shur Strike	Kingfisher	r/w, GE	EX	$87.55	99-10
Shur Strike	Lipped Minnow Fly Rod	like Heddon Runtie, wood, PE, red/white	EX-	$228.00	03-01
Shur Strike	Mouse	b/w, GE, tail decent	VG	$31.00	00-05
Shur Strike	Mouse	b/w, TE	EX	$33.50	99-10
Shur Strike	Mouse	black w/red bead eyes, weedless hook	VG+	$25.00	05-06
Shur Strike	Mouse	frog, GE, smaller one nice	EX	$57.00	02-02
Shur Strike	Mouse	frog, GE, tail decent	EX-	$40.00	00-05
Shur Strike	Mouse	gray, BE, bigger than usual, gleamer	EX+	$154.00	00-04
Shur Strike	Petite Spinner	peanut butter, GE	EX	$283.00	05-07
Shur Strike	Pikie	3-hooks, peanut butter, GE	EX	$181.00	02-07
Shur Strike	Pikie	3-hooks, shiner scale/blk eye shade	NIB	$64.00	99-10
Shur Strike	Pikie	4¼", chain pike, GE, insert lip	EX	$41.01	99-10

BRAND	MODEL	SERIES / MFG. CODE / DESCRIPTION	GRADE	PRICE	DATE yy/mm
Shur Strike	Pikie	BH, 3-hooks, GE, decent	VG+	$61.00	01-01
Shur Strike	Pikie	blue head/white, GE, unmarked box	NIB	$348.00	03-04
Shur Strike	Pikie	dace, TE	EX	$29.00	01-09
Shur Strike	Pikie	green scale, GE	EX-	$55.00	01-10
Shur Strike	Pikie	green scale, 2-hooks	EX-	$56.00	03-01
Shur Strike	Pikie	orange scale, GE, 2-hooks	EX-	$53.00	05-07
Shur Strike	Pikie	peanut butter, 1 eye cracked, GE	EX	$51.00	00-12
Shur Strike	Pikie	peanut butter, 3-hooks, GE	EX-	$139.00	01-01
Shur Strike	Pikie	perch, GE, sliver by eye, green box	EX-IB	$32.00	00-02
Shur Strike	Pikie	pikie scale, GE, 2PCCB	NIB	$61.75	99-06
Shur Strike	Pikie	pikie, GE	EXIB	$34.10	00-02
Shur Strike	Pikie	r/w, GE, O7B box crisp	NIB	$57.27	99-08
Shur Strike	Pikie	rainbow, GE, 3 hooks nice!	EX	$57.00	04-01
Shur Strike	Pikie	redfish? shiner scale, GE, 3-hooks	EX	$130.00	03-01
Shur Strike	Pikie	shiner scale, GE	EX	$43.00	00-08
Shur Strike	Pikie	silver flash, GE, round nose	EX	$79.00	01-10
Shur Strike	Pikie	sm, GE, yellow chain pike	EX	$52.50	99-11
Shur Strike	Pikie	Western Auto chain pikeral	EX-IB	$71.00	00-04
Shur Strike	Pikie	yellow scale, GE	VG	$23.50	99-01
Shur Strike	Pikie	yellow scale, GE, large size	EX	$61.00	02-01
Shur Strike	Pikie 700	peanut butter, 2-hook, GE nice	EX-	$104.00	01-01
Shur Strike	Pikie, Baby	round nose, silver flash, TE	mint	$15.00	01-01
Shur Strike	Pikie, jntd	lg size, chain pike, GE	EX	$31.03	99-11
Shur Strike	Pikie, jntd	pike scale, GE	EX	$33.00	00-08
Shur Strike	Pikie, jntd	silver flash, GE	EX	$24.89	00-01
Shur Strike	Pikie, jntd	yellow pikie, GE	EX	$47.00	00-05
Shur Strike	Pikie, jntd	peanut butter, GE	EX-	$100.89	99-12
Shur Strike	Pikie, jntd	RW, GE nice	EX	$22.50	02-11
Shur Strike	Pikie, jntd x 2	pike, TE; perch 3⅜"	EX-	$15.00	05-06
Shur Strike	Pikie Midget	red side scale, GE	EX	$132.00	00-07
Shur Strike	Pikie Small	peanut butter, GE	EX	$130.50	99-11
Shur Strike	Pikie Type	orange scale, GE, NOT MET	EX	$81.00	04-12
Shur Strike	Pikie Type	perch, TE, blue/orange box HR-0	EXIB	$46.00	99-08
Shur Strike	Pikie Type	TE, blue/orange box PT-14	EXIB	$45.00	99-08
Shur Strike	River Master	2 diff, GE, box RR2	VG	$19.49	99-04
Shur Strike	River Master	b/w, GE, ugly	VG-	$35.00	99-05
Shur Strike	River Master	black scale, TE	EX	$14.00	03-01
Shur Strike	River Master	black, GE	EX	$50.00	01-01
Shur Strike	River Master	black, GE, "Gateway," bad age lines	avg	$9.00	99-12
Shur Strike	River Master	black, GE, floater, NOT MET	EX-	$32.50	00-03
Shur Strike	River Master	blue scale over black, TE	EX	$28.00	01-09
Shur Strike	River Master	chain pikeral, GE	EX	$24.38	99-11
Shur Strike	River Master	D943RH, b&o box, GE	NIB	$57.00	00-10
Shur Strike	River Master	floater, GE, rainbow	EX	$85.00	00-05
Shur Strike	River Master	floater, green scale, TE, g/w box	EXIB	$91.00	00-08
Shur Strike	River Master	floater, yellow scale, GE	EX-	$20.00	02-01
Shur Strike	River Master	floater, pikie, GE	EX	$23.00	00-02
Shur Strike	River Master	Floating Tom, pikie scale, GE	VG+	$20.00	03-05

BRAND	MODEL	SERIES / MFG. CODE / DESCRIPTION	GRADE	PRICE	DATE yy/mm
Shur Strike	River Master	Floating Tom, TE, pikie	EX-	$11.00	00-01
Shur Strike	River Master	frog, GE, floater	VG+	$30.00	03-11
Shur Strike	River Master	frog, TE	EX	$34.00	02-01
Shur Strike	River Master	frog, TE, RR-5 box, NOT MET	EXIB	$20.00	01-01
Shur Strike	River Master	frog, GE, my max bid $179	EX-	$107.50	00-05
Shur Strike	River Master	frog, TE	EX	$16.50	00-02
Shur Strike	River Master	Gateway, black floater	EX-	$61.08	00-01
Shur Strike	River Master	Gateway, rainbow floater	EX-	$106.05	00-01
Shur Strike	River Master	J. C. Higgins, RH, TE	EX-	$15.50	00-02
Shur Strike	River Master	jointed sinker, RH/shiner scale, GE	EX-	$22.00	02-10
Shur Strike	River Master	pearl, GE	VG+	$62.00	01-03
Shur Strike	River Master	pearl, GE, NOT MET	EX	$38.00	00-11
Shur Strike	River Master	pearl, GE, NOT MET	EX	$56.00	03-11
Shur Strike	River Master	pearl, GE	VG	$41.00	99-04
Shur Strike	River Master	pearl/pink dots, GE	EX	$92.00	02-07
Shur Strike	River Master	perch? GE	EX	$36.00	99-04
Shur Strike	River Master	pike scale, GE, NO BIDS	EX	$19.00	01-01
Shur Strike	River Master	pike scale, GE	EX	$28.89	00-02
Shur Strike	River Master	pike scale, GE, poor box	VG+	$19.99	99-05
Shur Strike	River Master	RB, GE, in Gateway box	EXIB	$177.50	99-10
Shur Strike	River Master	RB, GE	VG	$12.00	01-01
Shur Strike	River Master	RB, GE, un box	EXIB	$31.00	00-02
Shur Strike	River Master	RH, floater, un box	EXIB	$42.00	01-11
Shur Strike	River Master	RH, GE	EX-	$14.00	00-05
Shur Strike	River Master	RH/shiner scale, GE, floater	EX	$52.77	99-08
Shur Strike	River Master	RH/shiner scale, GE, ugly g&w box	VG+IB	$40.00	99-10
Shur Strike	River Master	RH/w, TE	EX	$12.51	99-12
Shur Strike	River Master	RR8, rainbow, GE	EXIB	$56.99	99-04
Shur Strike	River Master	SB, TE	EX	$40.00	01-03
Shur Strike	River Master	SB, TE	EX	$45.00	01-01
Shur Strike	River Master	silver flash, TE, NO BIDS	EX	$10.00	00-12
Shur Strike	River Master	silver flash, GE	EX	$36.00	00-03
Shur Strike	River Master	sinker, pikie, TE	EX	$15.00	00-08
Shur Strike	River Master	sm, pearl, GE	EX	$49.76	99-11
Shur Strike	River Master	strawberry, TE	EX	$56.00	00-08
Shur Strike	River Master	strawberry, TE	EX	$33.00	01-09
Shur Strike	River Master	strawberry, GE	VG+	$46.00	99-09
Shur Strike	River Master	yellow flash, TE	EX	$26.00	00-10
Shur Strike	River Master	yellow scale, green box	EXIB	$37.50	00-04
Shur Strike	River Master Floater	brown, flitter, GE	EX-	$46.00	02-01
Shur Strike	River Master Floater	pike scale, GE	EX-	$16.00	00-02
Shur Strike	River Master Floater	yellow scale, GE	EX-	$74.00	01-01
Shur Strike	River Master Floater, jntd	green perch, GE	EX-	$46.00	01-01
Shur Strike	River Master Floater, jntd	green perch, GE, rough box	EX-IN	$36.00	01-04
Shur Strike	River Master Floater, jntd	silver flash, GE	EX-	$26.00	01-01
Shur Strike	River Master Fly Rod	shiner scale	EX	$200.00	99-10
Shur Strike	River Master Sinker, jntd	BWH, GE, chip but not awful	VG	$41.00	01-01
Shur Strike	River Master x 2	g box, r/b box, pike scale, dace? GE	EXIB	$150.45	00-03

BRAND	MODEL	SERIES / MFG. CODE / DESCRIPTION	GRADE	PRICE	DATE yy/mm
Shur Strike	River Master, jntd	blk head/white scale? TE	EX	$43.75	00-04
Shur Strike	River Master, jntd	Gateway, pearl, nice box	EXIB	$190.00	00-12
Shur Strike	River Master, jntd	green chain perch, box #4307, GE	EX-IB	$47.99	02-04
Shur Strike	River Master, jntd	pearl, "Andy Anderson," paper	mint	$232.27	99-03
Shur Strike	River Master, jntd	shiner scale, GE, "Gateway"	EX-	$19.00	02-11
Shur Strike	River Master, jntd	yellow flash, TE	EX-	$20.00	01-08
Shur Strike	River Master, jntd	yellow flash, red scale stripe, TE	VG+	$49.00	01-05
Shur Strike	River Master, jntd	yellow flash, TE, NOT MET	EX-	$33.00	01-04
Shur Strike	River Master x 2	RH, and shiner scale, GE decent	EX-	$18.10	00-03
Shur Strike	River Master Sinker	frog, GE, HR-19 box nice	VGIB	$78.00	01-06
Shur Strike	River Master Floater, jntd	Gateway, black GE	VG+	$52.00	03-11
Shur Strike	Slant Nose	yellow scale, GE	EX	$52.00	00-05
Shur Strike	Slope Nose	peanut butter, GE	EX	$102.00	01-01
Shur Strike	Slope Nose	shiner scale	EX-	$130.00	00-10
Shur Strike	Slope Nose	pikie scale, like Magnet, NOT MET	EX	$89.00	00-04
Shur Strike	Slope Nose	shiner scale, no eyes	VG+	$100.00	00-09
Shur Strike	Surface Glider	black & gold	EX	$450.00	01-04
Shur Strike	Surface Minnie	yellow scale, GE, NOT MET	EX	$51.00	00-06
Shur Strike	Surface Minnow	BH/y, GE	mint	$128.05	99-08
Shur Strike	Surface Minnow	scale, red stripe, GE nice	EX	$129.00	00-12
Shur Strike	Surface Spinner	blk/yellow, GE	EX-	$77.00	00-09
Shur Strike	Surface Spinner	peanut butter, GE	EX-	$114.00	00-12
Shur Strike	Surface Spinner	r/w, GE	EX-	$42.00	99-01
Shur Strike	Surface Spinner	shiner scale, GE	VG++	$66.00	00-06
Shur Strike	SurfaceSpinner	peanut butter, GE, NRA red/y box	EX-IB	$168.00	00-03
Shur Strike	Torpedo	GE, NOT MET	EX-	$56.55	99-05
Shur Strike	Torpedo GM Series	white/black stripes, GE	EX-	$81.00	01-10
Shur Strike	Underwater? Minnow?	peanut butter, 2-hook, front spinner, GE	EX-	$83.00	01-06
Shur Strike	Unique Crab Surface Spinner	crab color and body, 2 prop, NO BID	EX-	$100.00	02-03
Shur Strike	Wounded Minnow	peanut butter, GE	EX-	$48.00	02-02
Shurebite	Frog	plastic	NIB	$127.50	99-01
Shurebite	She Devil	white, nice box	NIB	$42.00	01-01
Shurebite	She Devil	red/white, picture box	NIB	$20.00	04-11
Shurebite	She Devil	r/y, nice pic box	NIB	$19.99	99-02
Shurkatch	Bassoreno	gold/blk bars, TE, great box	NIB	$52.00	00-09
Shurkatch	Runt Type	RH, wood in decent box	EXIB	$18.00	05-03
Silver Baits	AllPur	multibody lure, plastic box rough, paper	EXIB	$38.00	04-09
Silver Creek	Pikaroon	#909, 5¼", w/orig box, very minor wear on box	NIB	$3,300.00	05-04
Silver Creek	Pikaroon	rainbow, 5½", box rough	VG-IB	$179.00	04-04
Silver Creek	Pikeroon	RH, nice box!	EXIB	$1,630.00	00-05
Silver Creek	Pollywog	green back/white, 1010 box	EXIB	$886.00	03-11
Silver Creek	Polywog	box avg, lure huge, chips, shiny	fairIB	$202.50	00-04
Silver Creek Novelty	Pikaroon	5", green/white belly, decent box	NIB	$960.00	01-05
Silver Creek Novelty	Pollywog	Moonlight? perch GE	EX-	$421.00	02-08
Simmons Hrdw	Keetch-em 5-hooker	red/black gills, GE, Neverfail, box VG	EX-IB	$457.00	01-11
Skilton	Spinner	in neat box, with hangtag, glass beads, old	NIB	$34.00	04-12

BRAND	MODEL	SERIES / MFG. CODE / DESCRIPTION	GRADE	PRICE	DATE yy/mm
Skilton	Spinner x 2	2 pearl, new on cards in nice box	NIB	$16.00	04-12
Skinner	#7	#7, all brass fluted spinner	NM	$25.00	05-05
Skinner	#9	fat willow leaf, musky spinner, name stamped in center of blade	VG+	$14.00	05-05
Skinner	Spinner	5 assorted	VG+	$27.01	99-05
Skinner	Turkey Wing	spinner blade only, 1874 pat	EX	$240.00	02-08
Skinner	Turkey Wing #15	2¼"	EX	$280.00	99-11
Smallwood	Darter	orange spot	VG	$29.00	05-01
Smith & Yelton	Craw Pappy	brown, a beauty	mint	$56.00	05-02
Smithwick	Devil Horse Butterfly	1972, white lure	EX	$15.50	05-07
Smithwick	Devil Horse Rouge	wood, white silver scale, red under head and tail	EX	$2.43	05-07
Smithwick	Devil Horse	#216, 2PCCB EX, perch scale? color	NIB	$59.00	05-07
Smithwick	Devil Horse	black, bubble pack	NOC	$31.00	00-10
Smithwick	Devil Horse Musky	A-105, yellow/black ribs, crisp box	NIB	$152.00	04-07
Smithwick	Ma-Scooter	greenish yellow/black ribs	NIB	$13.00	05-02
Smithwick	Scooter	RH/sparkles	EX	$102.00	03-02
Smithwick	Tootsie Bug	peanut shape, dual spinners surface	EX	$152.00	04-11
Smithwick	Top N Bottom Stud Duck	yellow/white ribs	poor	$36.00	02-10
Snod-Lo	Musky Flaptail	green, PE, c. 1980	EX	$150.00	02-01
Snook Bait Co	Giant Weasel	silver flash, 7½"	EX	$611.00	05-03
Snook Bait Co.	Big Snook	blue herring, white/blue spots/flitter	NIB	$548.00	04-02
Snook Bait Co.	Flaptail Musky Type	perch scale? company name on belly	mint	$608.00	04-02
Snook Bait Co.	Flaptail Musky Type	silver flash, company name on belly	mint	$590.00	04-02
Snook Bait Co.	Striped Bass Lure	pikie type, GE, belly stenciled "NY," NOT MET	EX-	$61.00	03-04
Sockdolager	Spring Hook	4½", uncocked	mint	$332.00	00-07
South Bend	3-hook midget	brown stripe, SOLD	EX	$330.00	99-10
South Bend	3-hooker	901, green scale, GE, chip under eye	VG	$76.00	00-10
South Bend	3-hooker	901YP, name on prop	EX+	$178.00	04-02
South Bend	3-hooker	903GCB, green crackleback, GE, NSOP, ring on BW and hint of wear	EX	$145.00	05-05
South Bend	3-hooker	903GCB, green crackleback, GE, NSOP, varn loss along the AL on belly, in VG- 2PCCB	EX-IB	$160.00	05-05
South Bend	3-hooker	903YP, yellow perch, GE, CR, NSOP, 1 tiny flake at BW and light AL in VG+ 2PCCB	EX-IB	$135.00	05-05
South Bend	3-hooker	903RAIN, intro box, NOT MET	NIB	$960.00	01-05
South Bend	3-hooker	904, crackle, GE, nice	EX	$152.00	01-08
South Bend	3-hooker	904, intro box VG+, hex pattern	EX-IB	$149.00	04-12
South Bend	3-hooker	bar perch, GE	avg	$81.00	98-12
South Bend	3-hooker	chain pikeral, TE	VG+	$43.00	01-04
South Bend	3-hooker	crackle, GE	VG	$87.00	00-05
South Bend	3-hooker	crackleback, unmarked props	avg	$67.00	03-11
South Bend	3-hooker	frog, GE, belly chips	G	$60.23	99-04
South Bend	3-hooker	GE, hex	VG+	$65.00	05-06
South Bend	3-hooker	gold/RH, GE (1 missing)	EX	$109.00	05-01
South Bend	3-hooker	green back stripe, SOLD	EX	$415.00	99-10
South Bend	3-hooker	hex pattern, SOLD	EX	$450.00	99-10
South Bend	3-hooker	hex pattern, GE	EX-	$156.00	04-11
South Bend	3-hooker	perch	EX	$275.00	99-10

BRAND	MODEL	SERIES / MFG. CODE / DESCRIPTION	GRADE	PRICE	DATE yy/mm
South Bend	3-hooker	perch scale, GE, thin age lines	EX	$88.00	05-04
South Bend	3-hooker	r/w, TE, decent	VG+	$36.81	99-11
South Bend	3-hooker	r/w/r, black eye shadow, GE	EX-	$157.00	01-03
South Bend	3-hooker	rainbow, GE, decent	VG+	$47.00	03-02
South Bend	3-hooker	RB, GE	EX-	$200.00	99-06
South Bend	3-hooker	RB, GE	VG	$62.00	00-11
South Bend	3-hooker	RB, HPGM, NOT MET	EX-	$188.00	00-10
South Bend	3-hooker	RB, GE, HPGM, NOT MET	EX-	$140.50	00-03
South Bend	3-hooker	red/black dots	VG	$221.00	01-04
South Bend	3-hooker	scale "SF," GE, nice box, NOT MET	EXIB	$157.00	01-08
South Bend	3-hooker	strawberry, 952YP, nice old box	ugly	$66.87	99-06
South Bend	3-hooker	strawberry, un, cup, HPGM, GE	EX-	$182.50	00-02
South Bend	3-hooker	white/dark green stripe	EX	$291.00	00-01
South Bend	3-hooker	white/red stripe	EX-	$355.00	00-01
South Bend	3-hooker	yellow perch, SOLD	EX	$380.00	99-10
South Bend	3-hooker	yellow spotted, GE, cup	EX	$223.50	00-02
South Bend	3-hooker	yellow, perch, GE, shiny!	EX	$233.00	01-03
South Bend	3-hooker	yellow, hex, GE (crack)	EX-	$317.00	00-08
South Bend	3-hooker midget	strawberry, SOLD	EX	$585.00	99-10
South Bend	5-hooker	905GCB, green crackleback, GE, CR, NSOP, POBW and very light wear, early hardware	EX-	$180.00	05-05
South Bend	5-hooker	905RCBY, red crackleback on yellow, GE, CR NNOP, light varn loss on belly and tiny flake	EX-	$385.00	05-05
South Bend	5-hooker	905RH, "Minnow" box VG-, GE	EXIB	$207.00	04-01
South Bend	5-hooker	905W, hex pattern, yellow box	EX-IB	$335.00	01-01
South Bend	5-hooker	905YP, GE, nice box, NOT MET	EXIB	$280.00	01-11
South Bend	5-hooker	913RB, GE, brass tail cap, box rough	EX-IB	$240.00	00-06
South Bend	5-hooker	915RSB, red scale blend	NIB	$515.00	99-05
South Bend	5-hooker	bar perch, GE, HPGM	EX+	$313.00	05-07
South Bend	5-hooker	crackle, GE	EX+	$400.00	00-03
South Bend	5-hooker	crackleback nice	EX-EX	$296.00	99-03
South Bend	5-hooker	GE, brown back, cream colored sides & belly	VG	$45.00	05-06
South Bend	5-hooker	perch	VG+	$176.00	00-08
South Bend	5-hooker	perch	NIB	$665.00	99-10
South Bend	5-hooker	RB, HPGM	VG	$163.00	00-09
South Bend	5-hooker	RB, SOLD	EX	$375.00	99-10
South Bend	5-hooker	RB, some sm chips	VG-	$101.75	00-03
South Bend	5-hooker	sienna, unmarked, SOLD	EX	$710.00	99-10
South Bend	5-hooker	slate?	avg	$69.00	98-12
South Bend	5-hooker	white hex	EX-	$363.00	00-08
South Bend	5-hooker	white/red stripe, chip but otherwise EX	nice	$212.50	00-01
South Bend	5-hooker	yellow/green back	mint	$510.00	00-05
South Bend	5-hooker x 2	ugly	poor	$90.00	00-10
South Bend	903 3-hooker	903GCB, age lines	EXIB	$325.00	01-01
South Bend	920	luminous marked prop, NOT MET	EX	$334.00	01-11
South Bend	921 Floater Minnow	red mask/white, GE, old box	EXIB	$460.55	99-09
South Bend	956 Musky Minnow	5-hook, crackleback, 4 BW, GE, aluminum cups, c. 1915, sweet!	EX-	$921.00	05-07

BRAND	MODEL	SERIES / MFG. CODE / DESCRIPTION	GRADE	PRICE	DATE yy/mm
South Bend	Babe Oreno	972BH, early box EX, no eyes	EX-IB	$380.00	00-11
South Bend	Babe Oreno	972F, TE, crisp box & perfect catalog	NIB	$29.00	04-03
South Bend	Babe Oreno	972RH, script box, GE	NIB	$41.00	03-07
South Bend	Babe Oreno	972SP, PE, PTCB	NIB	$30.00	99-01
South Bend	Babe Oreno	973LUM, intro box	EXIB	$62.51	99-02
South Bend	Babe Oreno	973RH, GE, intro? box	NIB	$73.00	99-08
South Bend	Babe Oreno	973RS, stars box, GE, red stripe	EXIB	$187.00	00-06
South Bend	Babe Oreno	973YP, intro box, no eyes	NIB	$200.00	00-06
South Bend	Babe Oreno	BH/red body, GE	EX-	$42.00	99-10
South Bend	Babe Oreno	GE, green scale, "Babe Oreno" double stamped on back, unique, in orig 2PCCB	VG+IB	$44.00	05-05
South Bend	Babe Oreno	GE, perch, pointers on back, small flake on lip, in orig 2PCCB w/papers	EX-IB	$58.00	05-05
South Bend	Babe Oreno	GE, rainbow, 2 teeny pointers, few light age lines	EX	$70.00	05-05
South Bend	Babe Oreno	GE, rainbow, light pointers and age lines, in worn intro 2PCCB baint	VG+IB	$39.00	05-05
South Bend	Babe Oreno	GE, shiner scale, RSF, few light pointers	VG++	$45.00	05-05
South Bend	Babe Oreno	gold/red, NE, old style box	EXIB	$52.00	99-01
South Bend	Babe Oreno	green scale, GE	NIB	$168.09	99-03
South Bend	Babe Oreno	green scale, TE, box 910YP	EX+	$46.50	99-02
South Bend	Babe Oreno	moon & stars box	EXIB	$152.00	00-05
South Bend	Babe Oreno	NE, green scale, very early, w/silver scales all around body, very light varnish wear	EX-	$33.00	05-05
South Bend	Babe Oreno	NE, rainbow, small flake at cup and very light varn wear, in G- intro 2PCCB	EX-IB	$48.00	05-05
South Bend	Babe Oreno	NE, shiner, RSF, light age lines, in orig VG intro 2PCCB	Ex-IB	$55.00	05-05
South Bend	Babe Oreno	Nite-Luming, intro box, papers	EXIB	$182.50	00-02
South Bend	Babe Oreno	Nite-Luming, NE, in c. 1920 box E with paper	EX+IB	$250.00	05-06
South Bend	Babe Oreno	Pagin scale, long sliver of missing paint	??	$18.00	04-03
South Bend	Babe Oreno	r/w, arrowhead, GE	VG-	$30.00	99-05
South Bend	Babe Oreno	r/w, no eyes, old box, papers	NIB	$64.09	99-05
South Bend	Babe Oreno	RH sparkle, GE	EX	$62.00	00-05
South Bend	Babe Oreno	RH, GE, cartoon box	NIB	$132.50	00-02
South Bend	Babe Oreno	RH/aluminum, GE	EX-IB	$52.50	00-02
South Bend	Babe Oreno	RS (red stripe), GE	EXIB	$275.00	99-09
South Bend	Babe Oreno	strawberry, GE, lip chips	VG	$27.00	99-05
South Bend	Bass Bug x 6	on card in cellophane	NOC	$305.00	01-06
South Bend	Bass Obite	frog spot	EX	$25.00	05-03
South Bend	Bass Oreno	12-pack, Luhr Jensen special edition, RH	NIB	$71.00	04-01
South Bend	Bass Oreno	973FW, frog, tack, cat	NIB	$56.00	99-07
South Bend	Bass Oreno	973PL, GE	NIB	$472.00	04-11
South Bend	Bass Oreno	973RAIN, no eyes, nice early box	NIB	$104.00	00-11
South Bend	Bass Oreno	973YP, TE, crisp box & perfect catalog	NIB	$26.00	04-03
South Bend	Bass Oreno	B.A.S.S. limited edition, r/w/b, modern	NIB	$60.00	00-05
South Bend	Bass Oreno	better type, lum	NIB	$125.00	03-01
South Bend	Bass Oreno	black/red eye shadow, GE	VG++	$91.00	00-06
South Bend	Bass Oreno	copper, GE	EX-	$70.00	99-03
South Bend	Bass Oreno	copper/black back stripe, GE	VG+	$54.00	00-11

BRAND	MODEL	SERIES / MFG. CODE / DESCRIPTION	GRADE	PRICE	DATE yy/mm
South Bend	Bass Oreno	G973FO, PE, hangtag, NOT MET	NIB	$53.00	01-04
South Bend	Bass Oreno	G973FO, orange firelaquer	NIB	$59.00	99-09
South Bend	Bass Oreno	G973NR, red firelaquer, PE, NOT MET	NIB	$42.00	99-09
South Bend	Bass Oreno	GE, red & white, in red sky/pine tree box E+	NIB	$90.00	05-06
South Bend	Bass Oreno	GE, red head/black body	EX-	$65.00	05-06
South Bend	Bass Oreno	GE, frog spot, 2 tiny flakes on belly and very light wear	EX-	$40.00	05-05
South Bend	Bass Oreno	GE, luminous, NSOB, few light varnish pointers, in orig 2PCCB w/catalog	EX-IB	$95.00	05-05
South Bend	Bass Oreno	GE, rainbow, light age lines on belly and 2 tiny flakes on belly	EX	$50.00	05-05
South Bend	Bass Oreno	GE, shiner, RSF, few small varnish pointers and very light wear	EX-	$35.00	05-05
South Bend	Bass Oreno	GE, white w/red and blk spots, little yellowed, light age lines and few pointers	VG	$42.00	05-05
South Bend	Bass Oreno	GE, yellow, perch, just a hint of wear	EX	$65.00	05-05
South Bend	Bass Oreno	moon & stars box crisp, GE	NIB	$230.00	01-07
South Bend	Bass Oreno	NE, red head & aluminum	EX+	$50.00	05-06
South Bend	Bass Oreno	NE, RH/gold, light on varnish, few tiny flakes and pointers on belly, light lip edge wear	VG	$35.00	05-05
South Bend	Bass Oreno	NE, RH/w, clean lure but has a hook drag under chin, in very early yellow-base intro box	EX-IB	$38.00	05-05
South Bend	Bass Oreno	NE, yellow perch, some light age lines in varnish, very light wear	EX-	$40.00	05-05
South Bend	Bass Oreno	Nite-Luming, intro box VG+	EX+IB	$228.50	00-01
South Bend	Bass Oreno	olive scale, no eyes, lt hook drag	EX-	$41.00	00-04
South Bend	Bass Oreno	Pagin scale, GE, orange/gold, beauty	EX	$391.00	01-06
South Bend	Bass Oreno	Pagin scale, shiner, natural scale, GE	EX	$103.00	05-07
South Bend	Bass Oreno	RB, no eyes, Jersey Q single hooks, early box	NIB	$350.00	01-09
South Bend	Bass Oreno	red scale, no eyes, intro box	EXIB	$98.50	99-09
South Bend	Bass Oreno	red sky box VG, RH, GE	EXIB	$113.00	05-07
South Bend	Bass Oreno	red, no eyes, no washer line tie, shallow cups	EX	$90.00	02-09
South Bend	Bass Oreno	RH arrow, TE, cat, crisp box	NIB	$41.00	99-09
South Bend	Bass Oreno	RH/gold sparkle, GE	EX	$62.00	00-06
South Bend	Bass Oreno	RH/sparkle, TE, nice box	NIB	$83.00	00-10
South Bend	Bass Oreno	RH/w, GE	VG+	$20.00	99-03
South Bend	Bass Oreno	RH/w, GE	EX	$50.00	99-03
South Bend	Bass Oreno	RSF, GE, general wear	VG+	$25.00	99-03
South Bend	Bass Oreno	SRW, TE, nice box	VG+IB	$34.00	05-02
South Bend	Bass Oreno	TE, r&w, shadow wave, very light age lines and few tiny pointers, in orig VG 2PCCB	EX-IB	$55.00	05-05
South Bend	Bass Oreno	TE, RH/yellow, light age crackling, hook drag on chin and belly, few tiny flakes	VG	$30.00	05-05
South Bend	Bass Oreno	white/red side & back stripe, GE	VG+	$54.00	00-11
South Bend	Bass Oreno	yellow spotted, no eyes	NIB	$112.51	00-03
South Bend	Bass Oreno	yellow/red stripe, GE	EXIB	$130.22	99-09
South Bend	Bass Oreno, Baby	BH, no eyes	VG	$129.00	01-01
South Bend	Bass Oreno, King	G977FO, with "S" stamped on box	EXIB	$157.00	04-11
South Bend	Bass Oreno x 39	8 boxes, mostly NE or TE	avg – VG	$414.00	00-09
South Bend	BassO, TeaseO	RH, GE, w/flitter/blk wave, TE	NIB	$149.00	99-05

BRAND	MODEL	SERIES / MFG. CODE / DESCRIPTION	GRADE	PRICE	DATE yy/mm
South Bend	Be Bop	902SSY	EXIB	$22.00	03-02
South Bend	Be Bop	blue mullet scale	mint	$22.00	03-01
South Bend	Better Bass Oreno	2-hook saltwater, SZ, white/blue shadow wave	EX-	$715.00	04-11
South Bend	Better Bass Oreno	rainbow, in cellophane!	NIB	$152.50	99-01
South Bend	Better Fly Oreno	pike scale, PE, 1 pointer on l-side	EX	$32.00	05-05
South Bend	Bug Oreno	#820, black, white glass eyes	EX	$209.00	00-11
South Bend	Callmac Bass Bug	#13, "Brann's Ranger," PE, silver body and pheasant wings, w/red and yellow tail	EX	$25.00	05-05
South Bend	Callmac Bass Bug	#9, "Bob Davis," PE, new on Fish and Feel Fit card, in orig EX- bull's-eye 2PCCB	NOCIB	$170.00	05-05
South Bend	Callmac Bass Bug	#9, "Bob Davis," PE, wings a tad dirty, rest is clean	EX-	$19.00	05-05
South Bend	Callmac Bass Bug	Peet's Choice, chip on face and light wear, very early Callmac card	VGOC	$29.00	05-05
South Bend	Callmac Bass Bug	uncataloged color — white body, blue wings, red tail — red, white, and blue	EX-	$34.00	05-05
South Bend	Callmac Bug	#9, Bob Davis	NIB	$82.00	00-09
South Bend	Callmac Bug	Bob Davis, NOC, window box	NIB	$117.00	00-10
South Bend	Calmac Bug	Zane Grey model, lg box	EXIB	$41.00	00-10
South Bend	Calmac Bug #25	fly rod, on NRA card	NOC	$127.50	99-06
South Bend	Calmac Bug Fly Rod	#7, great intro box	NIB	$363.88	99-04
South Bend	Coast Oreno	985, TE	NIB	$520.00	00-01
South Bend	Coast Oreno	intro box, RH	EXIB	$650.00	03-07
South Bend	Coast Oreno	y/red/brown (RB?)	EX	$308.00	00-07
South Bend	Combination Minnow	hex finish, hackle VG	EX	$475.00	00-05
South Bend	Combination Minnow	red/black hex finish, orig tail	EX	$400.00	99-08
South Bend	Combination Minnow	w/blk stripe, GE	EX	$310.00	99-10
South Bend	Combo Minnow	perch, hook drags but nice	VG	$127.00	01-03
South Bend	Crippled Minnow	965RB, script box	EXIB	$488.00	04-03
South Bend	Crippled Minnow	rainbow, GE, 965RB	NIB	$488.00	04-03
South Bend	Crippled Minnow	silver flash, GE, a beauty!	EX	$71.00	05-07
South Bend	Dart Oreno	super graphic intro box, lure is just a hook!	NIB	$113.00	01-05
South Bend	Dive Oreno	952RW, TE, crisp box	NIB	$27.00	01-08
South Bend	Dive Oreno	953RH, TE, "obsolete"	NIB	$33.76	99-02
South Bend	Dive Oreno x 12	nice 2PCCB, 12-pack, RH arrow	NIB	$255.00	00-08
South Bend	Dragon Oreno	fly rod, yellow	EX	$55.00	00-11
South Bend	Findingo	red/white, NO BIDS	VG	$19.99	99-05
South Bend	Findingo	sunfish?	VG	$30.01	99-04
South Bend	Findingo	Up, yellow, perch, plastic, a unique self-standing lure, very light wear	EX-	$33.00	05-05
South Bend	Fish O Bite	1991RW, plastic lure	NIB	$23.00	01-08
South Bend	Fish O Bite	red/black squiggle, plastic	EX-	$42.00	00-09
South Bend	Fish O Bite	1991RW	NIB	$15.00	05-03
South Bend	Fish O Bite	r&w shadow wave, plastic, Entice Oreno, very light wear	EX-	$12.00	05-05
South Bend	Fish O Bite	WAH, white arrowhead, black plastic, Entice Oreno, very light wear	EX-	$19.00	05-05
South Bend	Fish Oreno	953P, box EX, GE	NIB	$79.00	05-07
South Bend	Fish Oreno	953RH, RH/w, GE, few tiny pointers and light age lines, in yellow intro box w/hangtag and catalog	EX-IB	$150.00	05-05

249

BRAND	MODEL	SERIES / MFG. CODE / DESCRIPTION	GRADE	PRICE	DATE yy/mm
South Bend	Fish Oreno	953SSY, yellow w/black shadow wave and glitter, TE, light age lines and shows light use	VG	$35.00	05-05
South Bend	Fish Oreno	953P, guarantee box crisp, GE, wow	NIB	$199.50	00-01
South Bend	Fish Oreno	953S, silver, GE, intro box	NIB	$191.00	99-07
South Bend	Fish Oreno	953YP, TE	NIB	$72.00	01-01
South Bend	Fish Oreno	959RH, intro box, GE	EX-IB	$57.00	00-03
South Bend	Fish Oreno	copper, GE	EX-	$77.25	99-05
South Bend	Fish Oreno	frog, glass eyes	EX-	$55.00	04-03
South Bend	Fish Oreno	frog, GE, intro box, tag, papers mint	NIB	$545.00	00-01
South Bend	Fish Oreno	GE, copper	EX-	$70.00	05-06
South Bend	Fish Oreno	guarantee box, hangtag, cat, paper	NIB	$406.00	01-05
South Bend	Fish Oreno	pike scale, hangtag, mint intro box	NIB	$483.00	00-03
South Bend	Fish Oreno	pikie, GE, intro box, hangtag!	EX-IB	$141.50	99-07
South Bend	Fish Oreno	r/w, intro box, papers	NIB	$77.00	99-02
South Bend	Fish Oreno	RH, GE, intro box, cat, hangtag	NIB	$203.00	00-11
South Bend	Fish Oreno	RH, intro box	EXIB	$76.00	00-03
South Bend	Fish Oreno	RH, GE, insurance, old box	EXIB	$93.00	99-05
South Bend	Fish Oreno	RH, GE, intro, tag, cat, "Guarantee"	NIB	$188.50	99-08
South Bend	Fish Oreno	RH/orange and black spots, GE	EX-	$189.00	00-04
South bend	Fish Oreno	wood, GE, leopard frog	VG	$21.00	05-07
South Bend	Fish Oreno	yellow spotted, GE	EX-	$67.00	00-09
South Bend	Floating Minnow	red mask, GE	EXIB	$460.55	99-09
South Bend	Fly-Oreno	perch scale, PE, early wire through, very light wear	EX-	$15.00	05-05
South Bend	Fly-Oreno	RH/w, PE, early wire through, just a hint of wear	EX	$10.00	05-05
South Bend	Fly Rod Bait		EX	$125.00	01-04
South Bend	Frog Fly Rod	bucktail, curved legs, NOT MET	EX	$21.00	00-11
South Bend	Frog Oreno	nice hair legs	EX-	$52.00	04-02
South Bend	Hop Oreno	yellow, #816 PTCB	EX-IB	$76.00	02-02
South Bend	Injured Minnow	RB? GE nice	VG+	$53.00	00-02
South Bend	Injured Minnow	silver flake, GE	EX	$45.44	99-10
South Bend	Jersey Spinner	365, ½ oz., red, nice red hair bucktail	EX-	$20.00	05-06
South Bend	Ketch Minnow	fly rod	mint	$300.00	02-02
South Bend	Ketch Oreno	fly rod, green scale?	mint	$300.00	02-02
South Bend	King Bass Oreno	997-SFS, PTCB, silver scale, PE	NIB	$42.99	00-01
South Bend	King Oreno	green scale finish, w/orig box, cat, and tissue EX	EX+	$687.50	05-04
South Bend	Large Trolling spinner	pearl, pntd blade, 7" long, w/3" fluted blade, varnish flakes	VG+	$20.00	05-05
South Bend	Lunge Oreno	966RH, 6", hangtag!	EXIB	$261.10	99-11
South Bend	Lunge Oreno	yellow spotted, two big props, box VG+	VG+IB	$220.00	05-07
South Bend	Lunge Oreno	966RH	VG++IB	$210.00	00-08
South Bend	Midget Minnow	901RAIN, intro box, crisp	NIB	$761.00	02-06
South Bend	Midget Minnow	intro box, rainbow black eye shadow, nice	NIB	$280.00	02-06
South Bend	Min Buck	945, 2 diff, 3-hk, aluminum, OS, nice	VG+	$434.00	99-04
South Bend	Min Buck	5-hkr, 4 belly weights, HPGM	VG+	$1,180.00	99-03
South Bend	Min Buck	5-hooker, red/black stripe, hex? GE, decent	avg	$100.00	00-11
South Bend	Min Buck	yellow hex, 5-hook, HPGM, POBW	EX-	$575.00	02-08
South Bend	Min Buck	943, 3-hooker, NOT MET	VG+	$91.00	00-07
South Bend	Min Buck? 3-hooker	red/black dots hex? GE, HPGM	VG+	$238.00	01-01

BRAND	MODEL	SERIES / MFG. CODE / DESCRIPTION	GRADE	PRICE	DATE yy/mm
South Bend	Min Oreno	RH/y, token paperwork, nice box	NIB	$263.00	01-05
South Bend	Minnow	RB, GE, crack BW	NIB	$355.00	00-04
South Bend	Monster Musky Min-Buck	fancy back finish, chipping to wood on belly	VG	$1,017.50	05-04
South Bend	Mouse	949BLK, POBW, very nice box	EXIB	$119.38	99-03
South Bend	Mouse Oreno	fly rod, gray, bead eye	EX	$61.00	99-02
South Bend	Mouse Oreno	gray, large size	VG	$12.00	05-06
South Bend	Mouse Oreno	gray	EX	$30.00	04-11
South Bend	Mouse Oreno, fly rod	948GM, script box dirty	EX-IB	$57.00	04-03
South Bend	Mouse Oreno, fly rod	gray, white eyes	EX	$40.00	05-02
South Bend	Mouse-Oreno, fly rod	black, PE, tiny flake at tail and few age lines	VG+	$50.00	05-05
South Bend	Mouse-Oreno, fly rod	white w/black back, very light age lines, very light wear	EX	$100.00	05-05
South Bend	Musk Oreno	976RW, GE	EX-IB	$36.00	04-11
South Bend	Musk Oreno	GE, RH/w, light wear along front lip edge, in unmarked bull's-eye 2PCCB	EXIB	$75.00	05-05
South Bend	Musk Oreno	green scale, GE, Musk Oreno box	NIB	$400.00	00-06
South Bend	Musk Oreno	NE, blk head/red, flakes down belly, chin light varnish wear	G+	$32.00	05-05
South Bend	Musk Oreno	NE, frog spot, few small flakes and varnish wear	G+	$20.00	05-05
South Bend	Musk Oreno	RH, intro box	VG+IB	$97.00	01-06
South Bend	Musk Oreno	RW, intro box decent, GE	NIB	$57.00	02-11
South Bend	Muskie Wiggins Oreno	huge 12" multiblade spinner	EX	$35.00	05-05
South Bend	Musky 5-hook	yellow, 4 staggered belly weights, fake?	avg	$300.00	00-07
South Bend	Musky Lunge Oreno	936RH, GE, plain box	VG+IB	$407.00	99-10
South Bend	Musky Min-Buck	5-hook, crackle, NOT MET	EX-	$1,285.00	00-09
South Bend	Musky Min-Buck	rainbow finish, unmarked pointed props, nice full bucktail, general wear and rubs	VG	$550.00	05-04
South Bend	Musky Minnow	shallow cup hardware, 5¾", bait, yellow perch finish, rough chipping to wood	G	$220.00	05-04
South Bend	Musky Minnow	spotted, 4 BW, ugly, NOT MET	VG	$417.00	00-04
South Bend	Musky Minnow 5-hk	brown back, RB, cup, marked, nice	VG+	$860.00	99-08
South Bend	Musky Minnow Trolling	GE, 4 belly weights, unmarked blunt props	G	$220.00	05-04
South Bend	Musky Surf Oreno	green scale, NOT MET	VG	$206.49	99-05
South Bend	Musky Surf Oreno	RH, GE, 6", NOT MET	VG	$66.00	00-11
South Bend	Musky x 2 GE	MuskO & underwater minnow, NOT MET	repaint	$152.00	00-05
South Bend	Musky x 2 GE	Pikeo & MuskO, copper/blk back, NOT MET	repaint	$36.00	00-05
South Bend	Nip-I-Diddee	12-pack Luhr Jensen special edition, green scale	NIB	$54.00	04-01
South Bend	Nip-I-Diddee	12-pack Luhr Jensen special edition, RH	NIB	$43.00	04-01
South Bend	Nip-I-Diddee	910RY, crisp box with papers, red/yellow, obsolete, TE super	NIB	$31.00	05-07
South Bend	Nip-I-Diddee	alum, painted eye, PTCB	NIB	$16.00	04-03
South Bend	Nip-I-Diddee	black, painted eye, PTCB	NIB	$16.00	04-03
South Bend	Nip-I-Diddee	Fireplug	NIB	$36.00	99-02
South Bend	Nip-I-Diddee	Luhr Jenson special edition, wood 2PCCB	NIB	$18.00	03-01
South Bend	Nip-I-Diddee	SM, painted eye, PTCB	NIB	$23.00	04-03
South Bend	Optic	677GX, green, new in orig 2PPB, on card	NIB	$20.00	05-05
South Bend	Optic	677YX, yellow, a hint of wear	EX	$13.00	05-05
South Bend	Optic	12-pack, dealer display box	NIB	$300.00	99-03
South Bend	Oreno Bass Bug	850-1, golden, cellophane over card minty	NOC	$105.00	01-10

BRAND	MODEL	SERIES / MFG. CODE / DESCRIPTION	GRADE	PRICE	DATE yy/mm
South Bend	Oreno Bass Bug	850-6, yellow Sally, cellophane over card minty	NOC	$169.00	01-10
South Bend	Oreno Display	37 lures, salesman sample	EX	$2,751.00	99-05
South Bend	Oreno Popper x 2	yellow, white, 2 different	EX	$158.25	00-02
South Bend	Panatella	3-hook, GE, red side	VG	$173.00	00-10
South Bend	Panatella	5-hook, green scale, end cap, GE	EX	$351.01	00-01
South Bend	Panatella	crackle, GE, tail chip but nice	EX-	$103.00	00-10
South Bend	Panatella	crackle, TE, 5 hooks	EX	$153.00	00-10
South Bend	Panatella	crackle, 3-hooker side, HPGM, RE?	EX+	$472.00	00-02
South Bend	Panatella	crackle, tail cup	EX-	$375.00	99-10
South Bend	Panatella	GE, 5-hook, red & white	VG+	$65.00	05-06
South Bend	Panatella	intro box EX-, crackleback tail cap, 3-hk	EXIB	$500.00	03-07
South Bend	Panatella	minnow, intro box 913 Special RSF, rough	EXIB	$220.00	04-03
South Bend	Panatella	r/w, GE	EX-	$177.00	99-07
South Bend	Panatella	rainbow, GE, 5-hooker, chips but not awful	avg	$41.00	03-07
South Bend	Panatella	RSF, blended red scale	EX-	$162.00	00-08
South Bend	Panatella	RW/r, GE, 5 hooks	VG-	$83.00	00-10
South Bend	Panatella	scale pattern, 3 hooks belly	EX-	$125.00	03-07
South Bend	Panatella	y/brown stripe, no cup, SOLD	EX	$440.00	99-10
South Bend	Panatella 5-hooker	915RSF, GE, nice box, mint lure	NIB	$565.00	00-01
South Bend	Panatella 915	RH/gold, 5-hk, GE, full tail cap paint	EX	$268.00	02-03
South Bend	Pike Oreno	958SPLGS, 5⅜", TE, green scale	NIB	$254.00	00-05
South Bend	Pike Oreno	956P, TE, NOT MET	NIB	$31.00	01-04
South Bend	Pike Oreno	956RW, TE, NOT MET	NIB	$36.00	01-04
South Bend	Pike Oreno	957PL, GE, box EX-	VG+IB	$37.00	04-02
South Bend	Pike Oreno	957RH, GE, pointed nose, chip on nose	VGIB	$21.00	04-07
South Bend	Pike Oreno	957SSY, box & catalog, pressed eye	NIB	$26.00	04-11
South Bend	Pike Oreno	975YP, yellow perch, TE, very light age lines and very light wear	EX-	$17.00	05-05
South Bend	Pike Oreno	green scale, GE, pointed nose, some chips, NO BIDS	?	$10.00	04-12
South Bend	Pike Oreno	green scale, thin, no eyes, early model	VG+	$16.00	02-08
South Bend	Pike Oreno	intro box 975RH nice, green scale, early cup face, GE	EXIB	$70.00	04-03
South Bend	Pike Oreno	intro box MM (mud minnow) EX-, no eyes	EXIB	$650.00	03-07
South Bend	Pike Oreno	pike, GE, NO BIDS	EX	$50.00	04-12
South Bend	Pike Oreno	r/w, arrowhead, TE	EXIB	$41.00	99-05
South Bend	Pike Oreno	RH, tack, papers, mint box	NIB	$49.99	99-12
South Bend	Pike Oreno, Baby	strawberry, TE	VG	$10.00	05-04
South Bend	Pike Oreno, Baby	yellow sine wave/glitter, TE	mint	$36.00	04-04
South Bend	Pike Oreno, Baby	956RW, red, AH/w, TE, light age lines and little yellow, in orig 2PCCB w/catalog	EX-IB	$38.00	05-05
South Bend	Pike Oreno, Baby	956S, silver flash, TE, looks unfinished but has very light box wear, in VG+ orig 2PCCB w/catalog	EXIB	$42.00	05-05
South Bend	Pike Oreno, Baby	956SF, green scale, GE, very light age lines and few light pointers	EX-	$30.00	05-05
South Bend	Pike Oreno, jntd	2956S, crisp box, TE	NIB	$56.00	04-11
South Bend	Pike Oreno, jntd	2956YP, crisp box, TE	NIB	$27.00	04-11

BRAND	MODEL	SERIES / MFG. CODE / DESCRIPTION	GRADE	PRICE	DATE yy/mm
South Bend	Pike Oreno, jntd	960, 8", green scale? TE	mint	$93.00	00-05
South Bend	Pike Oreno, jntd giant	Allen Stripey color, TE	EX	$69.00	04-04
South Bend	Pike Oreno, midget	GE, pointed nose, rainbow	EX	$49.00	04-07
South Bend	Pike Oreno, Musky	958RH, tack eye, NOT MET	EX	$47.00	05-07
South Bend	Pike Oreno, Musky	958SF, lg box EX-, green scale, GE	EXIB	$700.00	05-07
South Bend	Pike Oreno, Musky	973RH, jointed, TE, nice box 960RW	EXIB	$92.00	04-11
South Bend	Pippin	fly rod, new in tube	NIT	$50.00	02-03
South Bend	Plug Oreno	frog, TE	EX	$305.00	02-02
South Bend	Plug Oreno	frog, TE, small chip	EX-	$384.00	00-05
South Bend	Plug Oreno	GE, r&w	VG	$65.00	05-06
South Bend	Plug Oreno	RH, TE, ring around BW	mint	$350.00	00-10
South Bend	Plug Oreno	TE, frog, top ½ VG+, bottom ½ VG	VG	$120.00	05-06
South Bend	Plug Oreno	TE, frog, top ½ VG+, bottom ½ VG	VG	$120.00	05-06
South Bend	Plug Oreno	yellow spotted, GE	VG+	$378.00	00-02
South Bend	Plug Oreno	yellow spotted, GE, nice	VG+	$358.00	02-03
South Bend	Plunk Oreno	929SF, green scale, GE, earliest body style, small flake on face, in orig 2PCCB	EX-IB	$110.00	05-05
South Bend	Plunk Oreno	929F, fly type, lip chips	VG+IB	$76.00	00-02
South Bend	Plunk Oreno	929RB, TE, red fly	NIB	$452.00	02-12
South Bend	Plunk Oreno	black, later type TE, 2 hooks	EX	$86.00	01-01
South Bend	Plunk Oreno	frog splotch, TE, 2-hooks	EX-	$61.00	02-11
South Bend	Plunk Oreno	frog, TE, 1 hook, in 929-3YP box	NIb	$204.00	05-03
South Bend	Plunk Oreno	frog, TE	VG+/EX-	$50.00	99-12
South Bend	Plunk Oreno	rainbow, TE, 2 hooks, slant face	VG+	$122.00	02-07
South Bend	Plunk Oreno	RB, TE, with fly (rough)	EX	$285.00	01-01
South Bend	Plunk Oreno	RH, TE, 2 hooks	EX	$87.00	02-01
South Bend	Plunk Oreno	RH, TE, great fly	EX-	$54.99	99-09
South Bend	Plunk Oreno	RW, 2 hooks, slant face	EX	$125.00	02-07
South Bend	Plunk Oreno	YP, TE, 1 hook	EX-	$57.00	01-08
South Bend	Plunk Oreno, fly rod	light frog, scratch	VG	$90.00	02-03
South Bend	Plunk Oreno, fly rod	RB, varnish, 1 ding, lousy pics	??	$77.00	01-03
South Bend	Plunk Oreno, fly rod	light frog, white fly	EX	$225.00	02-05
South Bend	Spin-I-Diddee x 6	1917YP, PTCB, nice display, 6-pack	NIB	$237.00	00-11
South Bend	Spin-I-Diddee	alum, painted eye, PTCB	NIB	$16.00	04-03
South Bend	Strike Oreno	The Oriole, black body, yellow and black feathered tail, light age cracks	EX-	$60.00	05-05
South Bend	Sun Spot Spoon	525CR, nice yellow jumping fish box	NIB	$78.00	02-01
South Bend	Sun Spot Spoon	red/chrome, 1 oz., 3½"	EX	$26.00	03-01
South Bend	Sun Spot Spoon	red/silver, musky size, 4¾"	EX	$31.00	04-09
South Bend	Sunspot Spoon, Musky	5", red	EX	$57.00	04-03
South Bend	Super Snooper	G1960FG, Firelacquer finish	NIB	$61.00	00-11
South Bend	Surf Oreno	963RAIN	EXIB	$177.39	99-03
South Bend	Surf Oreno	963RAIN, box EX, GE	NIB	$236.00	05-07
South Bend	Surf Oreno	963RH, TE, RH/w, wire through chip on 1 eye, age lines and very minor wear	VG+	$20.00	05-05
South Bend	Surf Oreno	963RHA, RH/aluminum, GE, wire through, hook drag on belly, varn flakes at l-eye, light wear	VG	$44.00	05-05

BRAND	MODEL	SERIES / MFG. CODE / DESCRIPTION	GRADE	PRICE	DATE yy/mm
South Bend	Surf Oreno	963RJ, early RH/w, no eyes	EX-IB	$70.00	05-05
South Bend	Surf Oreno	963RH	NIB	$79.00	00-05
South Bend	Surf Oreno	963SF, green scale, GE	NIB	$280.00	00-10
South Bend	Surf Oreno	973RH, pressed eye, arrow, papers	NIB	$38.00	99-08
South Bend	Surf Oreno	BH/white, GE	EX-/EX	$406.12	00-01
South Bend	Surf Oreno	black forehead, red, SOLD	EX-	$305.00	99-10
South Bend	Surf Oreno	chub? GE, tube props	EX-	$121.00	99-06
South Bend	Surf Oreno	crackle	EX	$200.00	99-10
South Bend	Surf Oreno	crackle, reinforced prop, GE, varnish	EX-?	$125.00	01-08
South Bend	Surf Oreno	crackleback, GE	VG+	$87.00	99-06
South Bend	Surf Oreno	frog, GE, beauty	EX	$192.00	00-09
South Bend	Surf Oreno	frog, old type, 1 loose prop, old poor box	EX	$123.00	99-01
South Bend	Surf Oreno	GE, yellow with red & black spots, slim body style	VG+	$55.00	05-06
South Bend	Surf Oreno	gold scale, red bars, TE	EX-	$37.55	99-01
South Bend	Surf Oreno	green scale, GE	EX-	$83.59	00-01
South Bend	Surf Oreno	luminous, TE, new in box, few age lines	NIB	$57.00	01-08
South Bend	Surf Oreno	luminous, TE, nice box	NIB	$95.00	01-05
South Bend	Surf Oreno	luminous, TE	EX	$76.00	00-04
South Bend	Surf Oreno	one GE & one lead eye, blue & white, 2-hook, Bing hooks	VG+	$85.00	05-06
South Bend	Surf Oreno	r/w, reinforced, GE	NIB	$129.01	99-12
South Bend	Surf Oreno	RB, GE, regular box	NIB	$255.00	00-10
South Bend	Surf Oreno	RB, GE	VG+	$83.00	00-03
South Bend	Surf Oreno	RB, GE, older, NOT MET	EX	$154.75	99-06
South Bend	Surf Oreno	red head/gold flitter, GE	EX	$128.00	02-09
South Bend	Surf Oreno	red, blk eye shadow, stencil back	EX	$209.00	00-10
South Bend	Surf Oreno	RFS, red scale, GE, reinforced hardware	EX+	$209.00	00-10
South Bend	Surf Oreno	RH, GE	EXIB	$66.88	00-03
South Bend	Surf Oreno	RH/alum, reinforced hardware, big dent on side	VG+??	$81.00	04-02
South Bend	Surf Oreno	spotted, reinforced hardware, GE, nice	EX	$202.00	01-01
South Bend	Surf Oreno	strawberry, old 903GCBW box	EXIB	$185.00	99-06
South Bend	Surf Oreno	strawberry, GE	EX-	$178.49	99-03
South Bend	Surf Oreno	TE, red & white	VG+	$30.00	05-06
South Bend	Surf Oreno	TE, perch scale	VG+	$35.00	05-06
South Bend	Surf Oreno	yellow/strawberry, GE	EX	$176.00	01-03
South Bend	Surf Oreno	yellow spot, GE	EX-	$101.00	05-07
South Bend	Surf Oreno, Baby	copper, GE, reinforced nose	EX-	$202.50	99-08
South Bend	Surf Oreno, Baby	962RH, GE	NIB	$76.00	00-10
South Bend	Surf Oreno, Baby	BH/white, GE	EX	$255.00	00-03
South Bend	Surf Oreno, Baby	frog, pressed eye	VG+	$20.00	00-04
South Bend	Surf Oreno, fly rod	brown back, scale	VG+	$43.00	00-08
South Bend	Surf Oreno, fly rod	frog spot	VG	$19.00	05-03
South Bend	Surf Oreno, fly rod	green scale, PE, beauty	EX+	$87.00	00-04
South Bend	Surf Oreno, Midget	962, orange/blk spots, GE	EX-	$141.38	99-10
South Bend	Surf Oreno, Midget	962, red/silver, GE	EX-	$129.52	99-10
South Bend	Surf Oreno, Midget	orange/blk dots, GE	VG	$113.62	99-08
South Bend	Surf Oreno, Midget	red/black, skull cap nice, GE	EX	$210.00	05-07

BRAND	MODEL	SERIES / MFG. CODE / DESCRIPTION	GRADE	PRICE	DATE yy/mm
South Bend	Surface Minnow	3-hooks, old style, GE, hex pattern	EX	$848.00	00-03
South Bend	Surface Minnow	920MS, mullet scale, GE, NSOP, light general wear	VG	$165.00	05-05
South Bend	Surface Minnow	intro minnow 921 box VG, RH, GE, Bing hooks, unmarked front prop	VG+IB	$204.00	05-07
South Bend	Surface Minnow	white/red face mask, GE	EX	$278.00	02-09
South Bend	Surf-Oreno, fly rod	green scale, PE, couple tiny pointers and light age lines in varnish	EX-	$45.00	05-05
South Bend	Surf-Oreno, fly rod	red scale	EX	$65.00	99-01
South Bend	Surf-Oreno, Midget	962RH, GE, RH/w, reinforced hardware, age lines and light varn flakes	VG-	$25.00	05-05
South Bend	Surf-Oreno, Midget	962SG, green scale, GE, CR, light varnish wear and loss, skinny body, in intro label 2PCCB	EX-IB	$45.00	05-05
South Bend	Surf-Oreno, Midget	green scale, with intro box VG	EX-IB	$88.00	05-07
South Bend	Surf-Oreno, Midget	green scale, GE, intro box VG	NIB	$415.00	00-02
South Bend	Surf-Oreno, Midget	rainbow, GE, reinfored	mint	$367.88	99-05
South Bend	Surf-Oreno, Midget	special box, r/w, GE	EXIB	$52.02	98-12
South Bend	Tarp Oreno	blue mullet scale, carved eye, intro box 979MS EX-	EX-IB	$450.00	02-06
South Bend	Tarp Oreno	blue scale, PE	EX	$174.01	99-07
South Bend	Tarp Oreno	green mullet scale, TE	VG+	$225.00	02-06
South Bend	Tarp Oreno	mint box, blue scale, 8", 2 single hooks, carved eye	NIB	$220.00	04-11
South Bend	Tarp Oreno	pearl, TE	VG+	$325.00	02-06
South Bend	Tarp Oreno	red head, carved eye, 979RW box EX-	EX-IB	$400.00	02-06
South Bend	Tarp Oreno	RH/aluminum, GE, double hooks	VG-	$200.00	02-06
South Bend	Tarp Oreno	RH, GE	VG	$175.00	02-06
South Bend	Tarp Oreno	RH/gold, GE, 2 single hks, bottom of box	EX	$305.00	01-04
South Bend	Tarp Oreno	Tarpon Special, carved eye, 979RW box EX-	EXIB	$450.00	02-06
South Bend	Tarp Oreno	yellow spotted, TE	VG	$225.00	02-06
South Bend	Tease Oreno	939RH, script box, GE	EXIB	$37.00	03-07
South Bend	Tease Oreno	940YP, yellow perch, GE, CR, 3 tiny flakes, 1 pointer, age lines, in orig EX- 2PCCB	VG+IB	$55.00	05-05
South Bend	Tease Oreno	940YP, crisp box, GE	EX-IB	$47.00	02-03
South Bend	Tease Oreno	frog, GE, NOT MET	EXIB	$76.05	99-04
South Bend	Tease Oreno	r/w, TE	NIB	$77.00	99-12
South Bend	Tease Oreno	RH, GE	VG+	$17.38	05-07
South Bend	Teaser	11", EX, RH, edge of lip chipped	EX-IB	$100.00	05-07
South Bend	Teaser	11", white/sine wave, 2PCCB	EXIB	$218.49	99-02
South Bend	Teaser	r/w, PE	NIB	$331.00	99-01
South Bend	Teaser	RH, 11", PE	NIB	$203.50	00-02
South Bend	Teaser	RH/gold, 11", no hardware	VG+	$56.00	99-05
South Bend	Teaser	TE, box rough, RH, NOT MET	EX-IB	$129.00	00-05
South Bend	Teaser Zane Grey	blue/black water waves, 11"	EX	$109.00	01-05
South Bend	Tex Oreno	RB, weedless	EX-	$62.00	00-11
South Bend	Trix Oreno	959PL, pearl, medium sized, one in orig tiny bull's-eye 2PCCB	EX-IB	$25.00	05-05
South Bend	Troll Oreno	978, intro box EX-, no eyes, scale pattern, wowser combo	EXIB	$203.00	05-07
South Bend	Troll Oreno	green scale, GE	EX-	$58.00	02-06

BRAND	MODEL	SERIES / MFG. CODE / DESCRIPTION	GRADE	PRICE	DATE yy/mm
South Bend	Trout Oreno	12-pack, intro box EX-, all different colors	NIB	$3,482.00	05-02
South Bend	Trout Oreno	971BH, NOT MET!	EXIB	$290.00	99-10
South Bend	Trout Oreno	intro box repaired VG-, green scale	VGIB	$200.00	03-07
South Bend	Trout Oreno	RH/alum, tiny intro box crisp	NIB	$394.00	01-05
South Bend	Truck Oreno	fake, yellow spotted color, total reproduction	EX	$199.00	99-06
South Bend	Truck Oreno	red/white, nice box	NIB	$7,500.00	02-04
South Bend	Truck Oreno	RH, TE, lots of pointers and rubs	G	$578.00	03-07
South Bend	Two Obite	frog spot	EX-	$60.00	05-07
South Bend	Two Oreno	r/w, window box, NOT MET	NIB	$77.53	99-03
South Bend	Two Oreno	974LUM, TE, luminous, age cracks and 2 small flks on lip, in rare EX- cello window 2PCCB	VG+IB	$75.00	05-05
South Bend	Vacuum	#21, white/red ribs, nice bx, hg eye chip, NOT MET		$305.00	00-02
South Bend	Vacuum	dragonfly, papers, SOLD	NIB	$2,305.00	99-10
South Bend	Vacuum	dragonfly, papers, crisp box	NIB	$2,500.00	04-04
South Bend	Vacuum	frog spot, intro box EX & papers, NOT MET	NIB	$710.00	05-06
South Bend	Vacuum	GE, white with red stripes, ½ paint chipped off face	VG	$120.00	05-06
South Bend	Vacuum	intro box & papers crisp, stamped "R," red frog spot color! NOT MET	EXIB	$710.00	05-07
South Bend	Vacuum	red/blk spots, varnish flaking	VG	$416.00	99-03
South Bend	Vacuum	white, paint off cups, #1 box EX	NIB	$813.00	02-03
South Bend	Vacuum	white/red gills?	VG	$70.00	00-11
South Bend	Vacuum	yellow spotted	EX-	$180.00	05-07
South Bend	Weedless Bucktail		EX	$100.00	01-04
South Bend	Weedless Floater	Bing hooks	EX	$275.00	99-10
South Bend	Whirl Oreno	butterfly, NOT MET	EX	$283.00	01-03
South Bend	Whirl Oreno	butterfly, 935 box	VGIB	$300.00	00-02
South Bend	Whirl Oreno	frog	VG	$142.50	99-05
South Bend	Whirl Oreno	frog	VG+	$157.00	00-08
South Bend	Whirl Oreno	frog, nice hair	EX-	$100.00	99-08
South Bend	Whirl Oreno	r/w	VG-	$66.01	99-12
South Bend	Whirl Oreno	r/w, decent	VG	$93.00	00-10
South Bend	Whirl Oreno	r/w, nice	VG+	$129.50	99-01
South Bend	Whirl Oreno	r/w, NOT MET	EX+	$153.49	99-06
South Bend	Whirl Oreno	r/w, 20% paint loss one side	avg	$48.77	99-07
South Bend	Whirl Oreno	red & white	VG+	$165.00	05-06
South Bend	Whirl Oreno	red & white	EX-	$195.00	05-06
South Bend	Whirl Oreno	RH	EX-	$223.71	00-03
South Bend	Whirl Oreno	RH, poor pictures, NOT MET	VG+	$77.00	04-01
South Bend	Whisker	fly new on card, unmarked, yellow window box	NIB	$96.00	02-09
South Bend	Wiz Oreno	967C, copper black hackle, GE, lots age lines in varnish and very light wear	VG	$68.00	05-05
South Bend	Wiz Oreno	967RH, RH/w, red hackle, GE, light age lines and eyes crkd, in orig VG+ y intro 2PCCB	EX-IB	$130.00	05-05
South Bend	Wiz Oreno	967RH, crisp intro box	NIB	$255.00	99-08
South Bend	Wiz Oreno	GE, red & aluminum	EX	$100.00	05-06
South Bend	Wobbler	pre–Bass Oreno, NE, rainbow, no washer tail or screw	EX	$70.00	05-06

BRAND	MODEL	SERIES / MFG. CODE / DESCRIPTION	GRADE	PRICE	DATE yy/mm
South Bend	Wobbler	pre–Bass Oreno, NE, white w/red and green spots, no washer	EX	$75.00	05-06
South Bend	Wobbler	RH, rare intro box EX	NIB	$2,500.00	03-07
South Bend	Woodpecker	2-hk, Bings, red & white, some varnish flaking	EX	$85.00	05-06
South Bend	Woodpecker	923MS-LUM, RH/lum, 3-hk, CR, hk-chatter on belly and few small flakes, in orig VG+ 2PCCB	VG+IB	$85.00	05-05
South Bend	Woodpecker Midget	926LUM, red head luminous, correct box EX-, 2 Bing hooks	EX+IB	$135.00	05-06
South Bend	Woodpecker Weedless	RH	EX-	$229.17	00-01
South Bend	Zane Grey Teaser	TE, silver/blue back, NOT MET	VG	$123.00	00-05
South Coast	Minnow	3 BW, heavy age lines on belly	VG	$88.00	05-07
South Coast	Minnow		EX	$420.00	99-10
Southern Bait Co.	Stick	perch, PTCB	NIB	$48.00	01-04
Sparks, Jack	Hair Mouse	jointed, spinner, NOT MET	EX	$37.00	01-05
Spider	Lure	multispring loaded	NIB	$100.00	99-06
Spinno Minnow	509	perch scale, blue sides, brown back and ribs, gold scale and yellow belly	EX+	$60.00	05-05
Spinno Minnow	509	perch scale, blue sides, brown back and ribs, gold scale and yellow belly, EX 2PCCB	EX+IB	$65.00	05-05
Sportsland MFG Co.	Shimmy Shiner	605, RH, clear plastic box, worm burn	NIB	$20.00	04-09
Sportsman	Texas Shorty Shrimp	clear amber? 2 BW	EX	$51.00	05-07
Springfield	2" Revolving Body Bait "Reel"	silver/green stripe, box EX+	VG	$137.50	04-11
Springfield Novelty	Reel Lure	barber pole style	NIB	$204.40	99-03
Springfield Novelty	Reel Lure	gold/black, lg dealer poster	NIB	$547.99	00-01
Springfield Novelty	Reel Lure	silver/red stripe	NIB	$281.50	00-02
Springfield Novelty	Reel Lure	white/blk stripe	NIB	$383.00	00-01
Springfield Novelty	Reel Lure	white/blk stripe, crisp box	VG+IB	$155.00	03-02
Springfield Novelty	Reel Lure		NIB	$185.00	99-10
Staley Johnson	Honey	green perch scale	EX	$106.00	05-03
Staley Johnson	Twin Minn	one lg chip, nice box	VGIB	$105.00	00-10
Staley Johnson	Twin Minn	golden shiner	VG+	$60.00	05-06
Staley Johnson	Twin Minn	nice 2PCCB	NIB	$149.00	98-12
Staley Johnson	Twin Minn	papers, mint box	NIB	$332.52	99-06
Staley Johnson	Twin Minn	red & white, box VG+	EX-IB	$125.00	05-06
Staley Johnson	Twin Minn	red head/white, crisp box, NOT MET	NIB	$66.00	05-05
Staley-Johnson	Twin Minn	brown scale? box VG & papers	NIB	$165.00	02-03
Staley-Johnson	Twin Minn Minnow	gold shimmer scale, plate patent pending, box EX marked "S-105"	EX	$66.00	04-11
Steeles	Wigglefrog	in tube	NIT	$165.00	99-03
Sterling	3-hooker	Pflueger hardware, Reese	EXIB	$333.00	00-08
Sterling	3-hooker Neverfail	bar perch, maroon box	EX-IB(VG-)	$569.00	99-09
Stevens, Carrie	fly, Royal Tiger	autographed on card	EX	$256.00	99-05
Stewart, Bud	5 different	decent shape	VG-EX	$153.00	01-04
Stewart, Bud	Crippled Frog	spinnered foot, Creation signed	NM	$137.50	05-04
Stewart, Bud	Frog Plunker	frog finish	EX	$43.00	05-02
Stewart, Bud	Hammer-handle Pike Lure	10", Bud's green scale finish	EX-?	$77.00	04-11
Stewart, Bud	One-eye PollyWog	hand-painted bait, spotted pattern	EX	$99.00	05-04
Stewart, Bud	Pad Hopper	light frog	EX-	$67.00	99-08

BRAND	MODEL	SERIES / MFG. CODE / DESCRIPTION	GRADE	PRICE	DATE yy/mm
Stewart, Bud	Pad Hopper	small lip chip	VG	$32.00	99-03
Stewart, Bud	Pad Hopper	300	NIB	$177.00	98-12
Stewart, Bud	Pad Hopper		NIB	$125.00	99-01
Stewart, Bud	Spoon	fancy paint job, autographed	EX	$31.00	02-12
Storm	Glop	black, weird	EX	$52.00	99-08
Storm	Glop	coach dog	EX	$25.00	03-02
Storm	Glop	coach dog	EX	$72.00	02-02
Storm	Glop	golden shiner?	EX	$37.00	99-12
Storm	Glop	yellow/white, red spots, plastic box	NIB	$96.00	04-09
Storm	Hot-N-Tot x 2	2 lures, Patriot & Desert Storm	NOC	$38.00	03-01
Storm	Pee Wee Wart	YV66, fluorescent orange scale, Mini Deep Diver	EX	$22.50	05-07
Storm	Thin Fin	green back, white belly, 2½", black around painted eye	EX	$6.50	05-07
Storm	Thin Fin	silver shad, T-3 floater, circa 1967, ⅛ oz., w/box	NIB	$13.50	05-07
Storm	Thin Fin	TF08-060, natural perch, ½ oz., 3" long	NIB	$9.00	05-07
Storm	Wiggle Wart	V183, Prizm Flash, gold shiner	EX	$18.50	05-07
Stormy	Petrel	frog color, nice box, NOT MET	NIB	$431.00	02-01
Stormy	Petrel	frog, large size, nice box, only 1 bid	NIB	$430.00	02-02
Stormy Petrel	Frog	box VG	VG+IB	$121.00	00-10
Stormy Petrel	Fly Rod	black	EX	$222.00	00-11
Stream Eze	Mermaid	gold/gold, PTCB	NIB	$36.00	99-06
Stream Eze	Mermaid Fly Rod	silver/brown hair/green tail	mint	$51.00	00-05
Stream Eze	Virgin Mermaid	black/black	EX-	$25.00	99-10
Stream Eze	Virgin Mermaid	NOT MET	EX	$34.00	99-07
Stream Eze	Virgin Mermaid	with box, NOT MET	EX-	$20.00	99-01
Stream Eze	Virgin Mermaid, fly rod	red/green, tiny box	NIB	$70.00	99-08
Streich	Flex-O-Minno	box faded & soiled	EXIB	$36.00	03-02
Strike King	Bass King	RH, no eyes, nice 8546 box	NIB	$123.00	00-09
Strike Master	Surface Glidder Minnow	RH/silver, GE, nice	EX	$308.33	00-01
Strike Master	Surface Killer	RH, GE, NOT MET	EX-	$105.50	00-03
Strikee	Minnow	3½"	mint	$32.80	99-06
Strikemaster	Hellgramite	RH/red dots, rubber legs	EX	$225.00	05-07
Strikemaster	Killer	white, GE, brass cups	EX	$128.00	00-06
Strike-Master	Water Waltzer	black/white head	VGIB	$90.00	02-01
Success	Surface Spinner	yellow w/gold spots, rare 2-hk model, very light pointers	EX	$110.00	05-05
Summer Moth	Fly Rod Bug	plastic box, gray, 6 blk legs	NIB	$13.00	04-07
Surebite	She Devil	Al Sisco box, r/y	EXIB	$37.50	00-03
Survivor	Bleeder Type	r/w, SOLD	NIB	$575.00	99-10
Swedberg	Vamp type	25", crackleback, modern display item	EX	$99.00	05-04
Sylvester	Jerry's Blue Mullet #61	Surf lure, plain 2PCCB, no eyes, wood, RI	EXIB	$351.00	03-10
Szabo	Cree Duk	2½", brown/white, NOT MET	NOC	$42.99	99-06
Szabo	Cree Duk	brown/white	EX	$33.23	98-12
Szabo	Cree Duk	white/black	VG	$38.73	99-01
T & M	Darby's Spin-head Weedless	green back/white belly/red and white head, w/crisp box and instuction sheet	NIB	$495.00	05-04
T & W	Flutter Jack Jr.	nickle/blk hair, pic box	NIB	$34.77	99-01
Talbot	Niangua	serial no. 1094	EX-	$750.00	04-01

BRAND	MODEL	SERIES / MFG. CODE / DESCRIPTION	GRADE	PRICE	DATE yy/mm
Tango, Rush	Midget	Victory finish	mint	$355.00	00-01
Tango, Rush	SOS	yellow Victory finish	EX-	$100.00	99-08
Tango, Rush	Swiming Minnow	RH/w, prize box #8	NIB	$182.50	99-04
Tango, Rush	Swiming Minnow	RH/y, prize box	NIB	$197.50	99-04
Tango, Rush		mottled, nice box	NIB	$139.00	00-11
Tango, Rush		mottled, $50 box	NIB	$176.89	99-08
Tango, Rush		w/red & green mottling	EX	$70.00	00-04
Ted Smallwoods	Plug	darter type, decal eyes ugly	EX	$109.00	02-04
Tempter	Frog	box rough, paper VG	EXIB	$760.00	05-02
Tempter	Frog	with legs	EX	$182.50	99-06
Tempter	Frog		EX	$150.00	00-10
Tempter	Frog		EX	$82.50	05-07
Thompson	Doll Fish	V/85, hard plastic box with insert, gold chrome finish	NIB	$6.49	05-07
Thompson	Doll Top Secret	shad	NIB	$18.39	99-12
Thompson Metal	Silver Demon	nice graphic 2PCCB	NIB	$11.00	04-07
Thoren	Minnow Chaser	new but rear lure, 1 med chip	?	$180.00	01-06
Thoren	Minnow Chaser	pikie scale, GE, great box & papers	NIB	$760.00	05-02
Thoren	Minnow Chaser	r/w, NOT MET	EX	$380.08	99-06
Thoren	Minnow Chaser	RH with pearl? sm minnow	mint	$378.00	04-03
Thoren	Minnow Chaser	RH/Y with pearl? sm minnow	mint	$517.00	04-03
Thoren	Minnow Chaser	w/box, RH/silver	NIB	$440.00	05-07
Tiderunner	Popping Plug	red/white, GE, handmade end label box	EXIB	$854.00	05-01
Tiede	Doodler		NIB	$15.50	99-01
Tillicum	Salmon Plug	pearl, 5"	EX	$35.00	01-04
Tillicum	Tyee	7", salmon plug, PE, RB, no hooks	mint	$305.00	01-01
Tom Bait Co.	Gizmo	RH, Illinois lure	EX	$30.00	04-03
Tooley's	Spinnered Bunty Bait	c. 1913, tight age lines, repaired paint, silver on belly and tail	F	$412.50	05-04
Top Notch Tackle Co.	Water Lou	4 different, all in crisp boxes	NIB	$37.00	04-01
Trenton	Spin Diver	scale pattern, KY lure	EX	$24.00	00-06
Tropical Bait Co.	Bug-eyed Babbler x 2	frog, black yellow spots	EX	$220.00	04-11
Tropical Bait Co.	Stormy Petrel	yellow/black spots, box VG- (minor stain)	EX	$275.00	04-11
True Temper	Bass Pop	frog, GE	EX	$222.50	99-01
True Temper	Crippled Shad	chub, 1 age line on the left side	EX	$17.00	05-05
True Temper	Crippled Shad	orange/blk spots (Speed Shad?)	mint	$125.00	99-06
True Temper	Crippled Shad	perch, little yellowing to varnish	EX-	$15.00	05-05
True Temper	Crippled Shad	RH/pearl white, 1 small chip under tail and few light age lines	VG-	$10.00	05-05
True Temper	Crippled Shad	shad, NOT MET	EX	$14.00	00-11
True Temper	Crippled Shad	silver shad, hdwr little pitted, very light wear	EX-	$12.00	05-05
True Temper	Crippled Shad	Speed Shad, window box	NIB	$18.05	99-06
True Temper	Crippled Shad		VG	$11.50	99-01
True Temper	Speed Shad	Chub	EX+	$20.00	05-05
True Temper	Speed Shad	103, pearl	NIB	$16.50	99-01
True Temper	Speed Shad	r/w	NIB	$26.29	99-02
True Temper	Speed Shad	RH/pearl, just a hint of wear on the hdwr	EX+	$22.00	05-05
Tubby Tackle	Good Buddy	made by Storm, later "Flat Wart," bar perch color	NOC	$203.00	05-07

BRAND	MODEL	SERIES / MFG. CODE / DESCRIPTION	GRADE	PRICE	DATE yy/mm
Turbulent	Excitor	white with black dots	EX	$283.00	05-02
Turner	Spider	multispring hook	NIB	$77.00	00-09
Turner	Spider Lure	multispring hook	NIB	$113.50	99-01
Turner	Spider Lure	multispring hook, c. 1949	NIB	$104.00	00-04
Turner	Spider Lure	multispring hook, papers	NIB	$159.15	99-08
Turner, Zachary	Casting Bait	removable belly weight, 4¼", 5 hooks, bait orange/white, chipping around 2 cups	EX-	$495.00	05-04
Tuttle	Bass Devil Bug	nice box	EXIB	$64.79	99-07
Tuttle	Devil Bug	mouse, raggedy box, NOT MET	VG-IB	$27.00	99-06
Tuttle	Devil Bug	nice pic box	NIB	$127.50	99-02
Tuttle	Devil Bug	red box	EX-IB	$135.83	00-02
Tuttle	Devil Bug Mouse	pic intro box VG-	EX-IB	$55.55	99-08
Tuttle	Sea Devil Bug	6", deer hair	EX	$357.50	05-04
Tuttle	Trout Devil Bug	12, smallest one, made yellow	EX	$25.00	05-05
U.S.Speciality	Rush Tango	mottled, 1PCCB	NIB	$179.50	99-11
U-get-em	3-hooker	crackle, by Pflueger, maroon box, NOT MET	NIB	$1,228.00	99-06
Uniline	Spinno Minno	506, lt green scale	NIB	$199.99	99-04
Uniline	Spinno Minno	507, blue bugger	NIB	$213.50	99-04
Uniline	Spinno Minno	508, goldfish	NIB	$126.50	99-04
Uniline	Spinno Minno	508, goldfish scale	NIB	$127.50	99-09
Uniline	Spinno Minno	504, shinner scale, NOT MET	NIB	$68.77	99-05
Uniline	Spinno Minno	505, b/w	NIB	$117.51	99-05
Uniline	Spinno Minno	514, pike scale	NIB	$83.00	00-09
Uniline	Spinno Minno	blue/yellow, silver scale	VG	$58.00	99-04
Uniline	Spinno Minno	frog	NIB	$75.00	99-11
Uniline	Spinno Minno	frog, great pic box	NIB	$113.41	99-04
Uniline	Spinno Minno	501, gold scale, very nice box	NIB	$81.00	99-03
Uniline	Spinno Minno	green/white? RB?	VG	$36.00	99-04
Uniline	Spinno Minno	nice box, shiner scale	NIB	$81.05	99-03
Uniline	Spinno Minno	5, charcoal & gold	NIB	$159.00	01-03
Uniline	Spinno Minno	r/w, decent box	VGIB	$52.00	99-03
Uniline	Spinno Minno	rainbow	EX	$86.55	99-04
Uniline	Spinno Minno	RB, fair box	EXIB	$104.00	00-04
Uniline	Spinno Minno	white/yellow	EXIB	$53.00	99-06
Uniline	Spinno Minno	511, yellow scale	NIB	$96.50	99-06
Uniline	Spinno Minno #4	shiner, crisp box	NIB	$95.00	00-02
Uniline	Spinno Minnow	red head, black back & sides, tan ribs, tail hook	EX-	$35.00	05-06
Uniline	Spinno Minnow	yellow with white ribs	EX+	$50.00	05-06
Unknown	Bite 'Em All Bait	RH, revolving body bait	VG+	$121.00	04-11
Unknown	Rotating Winged Bait	fins appear celluloid, flat rimmed cups, GE, eggshell-type finish with age cracks	EX	$880.00	05-04
Utility Mfg. Co.	Rinehart Master-Kaster #2	pump, built-in reel & rod & pouch, NOT MET	EX	$230.00	03-08
Val-Lure	Val-Lure	RH/w, PTE, neat Chicago lure and has all components for creating 10 lures	EX+	$120.00	05-05
Van Clay	Zaragossa	perch	EX	$1,250.00	99-10
Vann Clay	Retrievable Minnow	rainbow finish, GE, marked, lip rigged injured minnow style, spring-loaded line tie, 4¼"	EX+	$1,320.00	05-04
Vann-Clay	Minnow	spring-loaded, head, c. 1920s	VG	$860.00	02-02

BRAND	MODEL	SERIES / MFG. CODE / DESCRIPTION	GRADE	PRICE	DATE yy/mm
Vann-Clay	Retrievable Minnow	red side hook (unique?)	G	$975.00	00-05
Vaughn	Vaughn's Lure	black, rainbow head, tail chip, c. 1946	NIB	$356.00	00-09
Vaughn	Vaughn's Lure	black, pic box nice	NIB	$326.00	00-05
Vaughn	Vaughn's Lure	SOLD	NIB	$320.00	99-10
Vaughn	Vaughn's Lure	minnow body, twirly head, black	EX	$200.00	00-10
Vaughn	Vaughn's Lure	r/w, nice box	EX-IB	$295.00	00-02
Vaughn's Tackle	Vaughn's Lure	super nice box, yellow/red gills	NIB	$505.00	05-07
Viking	Christensen Frog	crisp box, NOT MET	NIB	$1,525.00	03-02
Viking	Frog	crisp box, 3-hooker, NOT MET	NIB	$1,350.00	04-11
Vom Hofe, Ed.	423, 3/0 Fly Reel	Restigouche + case	EX	$2,680.00	05-05
Vom Hofe, Ed.	Perfection Fly Reel	#2, Jan. 23, '83, g. sil/rubber, 2" x ⅞", nice case	EXIC	$4,255.00	02-05
Vom Hofe, Ed.	Perfection Fly Reel	Jan. 23, '83, g. sil/rubber, 3"x 2"x ⅞", torn case	EXIC	$4,600.00	02-05
Vom Hofe, J.	Raised Pillar Fly	brass? 1903 pat, l nice	EX-	$511.50	00-02
Wadham	Phantom	2½", blue back/gold	NIB	$15.00	05-02
Wallace	Highline	salmon plug, 2PCCB EX, white lure/red gills, 3½"	NIB	$52.00	05-07
Wallsten	Cisco Kid	2PCCB, yellow/red taped, 3½", silver scale, green head, unmarked lip	NIB	$217.00	04-02
Walton	Speed Bait	12 props! weird	EX	$210.00	01-06
Ward's	Bass Katcher	RH, TE, Bass Oreno type, EX 2PCCB #7980	NIB	$51.00	05-02
Water Scouts B.C.	Little Eddie	b/w, like Clark's Scout, plastic box	NIB	$44.00	99-06
Weber	Al Foss Shimmy Wiggler	r/w	NIB	$25.00	99-09
Weber	Beetle x 22	nice assortment, Lur All	EX	$103.00	00-10
Weber	Beetle x 4	4 fly rod lures in round plastic container	EX	$20.00	05-06
Weber	Big Burp	BT5, orange spot	NIB	$16.00	04-07
Weber	Big Burp	orange w/black and red spots, YPE, plastic	Nw	$13.00	05-05
Weber	Dive-N-Wobble	4", frog spot	mint	$81.00	04-02
Weber	Dive-N-Wobble	orange/spotted	NIB	$65.50	00-04
Weber	Dive-N-Wobble	RPE, 3½", wood, string through and single tail hk, brown scale on green	EX	$75.00	05-05
Weber	Dive-N-Wobble	white w/glitter, RPE, string through to belly, tail hooks, age crackling and paint very light wear	VG-	$35.00	05-05
Weber	Dive-N-Wobble	DFR21 No. D, sm, white/sparkle	NIB	$105.00	01-03
Weber	Dr. Henshall	hairy bass fly on great card	NOC	$23.00	00-09
Weber	Dr. Henshall Bass Bug	spider box, gray	EXIB	$43.55	99-06
Weber	Dr. Henshall Bass Bug	spider box, white/red	EXIB	$52.55	99-06
Weber	Flip Frog		NIB	$15.00	99-06
Weber	Lifelike Beetle x 3	3 diff, new on round card, plastic box	NIB	$33.00	01-08
Weber	Little Sam	gray scale, plastic, very light wear	EX	$10.00	05-05
Weber	Pop Wobble	mouse	EX-	$26.00	98-12
Weber	Popperakle	fire in rough box, NOT MET	NIB	$12.00	00-07
Weber	Streamer Fly x 20	display, styrofoam, looks like frame	EX	$15.00	99-09
Weber	Swim King	black frog	NIB	$81.00	00-11
Weber	Swim King	yellow frog	EX	$32.00	99-03
Weed King	Weedless Plug	hiden hooks	NIB	$170.01	98-12
Weed Queen	Weed Queen	pike scale, GE, wood, 1 crack in left eye	EX+	$77.00	05-05
Weed Spliter	Weedless Spoon	plain marked box	NIB	$11.00	04-09
Weezel	Casting Feathered Minnow	yellow, on card in original cellophane mint	NOC	$16.00	04-07

BRAND	MODEL	SERIES / MFG. CODE / DESCRIPTION	GRADE	PRICE	DATE yy/mm
Weezel	Minnow	yellow body w/red and yellow feathers, new on large EX- card	NOC	$20.00	05-05
Weezel	Sparrow		NIB	$103.00	00-09
Weezel	Sparrow	nice pic box	NIB	$129.00	99-07
Weezel	Sparrow	nice pic box, 2PCCB & papers	NIB	$113.00	04-02
Welch & Grave	Minnow Tube	trout size, 3⅛", odd rigging	EX	$1,913.00	05-03
Welch & Graves	Glass Minnow Tube	wood box!	NIB	$1,775.00	99-05
Welch & Graves	Glass Minnow Tube	NOT MET	EX	$810.00	99-09
Weller	3-jointed	143, chub, nice box with paper	NIB	$207.00	00-04
Weller	Professor	lousy spoon in pic box	NIB	$41.00	02-01
Western Auto	Pikie (Shur Strike)	perch scale, nice box	NIB	$62.25	99-06
Whopper Stopper	2-Hellraisers		NOC	$67.00	99-02
Whopper Stopper	2-Hellraisers		EX+	$108.50	99-01
Whopper Stopper	Bayou Boogee Top	funny little prop bait	EX	$24.00	99-02
Whopper Stopper	Bayou Boogee	5 diff, in boxes	NIB	$66.25	99-03
Whopper Stopper	Crap Shooter	novelty lure	NIB	$12.00	05-05
Whopper Stopper	Dirt Bird	1402, ½ oz., black, w/papers	Mint	$15.26	05-07
Whopper Stopper	Dog Walker	frog, like Zara Spook	EX	$21.50	99-01
Whopper Stopper	Dog Walker	perch	NOC	$20.50	99-01
Whopper Stopper	Fly Rod	Tadpolly type, white/black spots	EX	$30.00	05-02
Whopper Stopper	Hellbender	2PCCB tan/black printing EX+, paper, black shore lure	EXIB	$51.00	05-07
Whopper Stopper	Hellbender	yellow cd, plastic, YPE, new in early yellow 2PCCB stamped "#03"	NIB	$27.00	05-05
Whopper Stopper	Hellbender	yellow with black ribs	EX	$7.52	05-07
Whopper Stopper	Hellraiser	RH/w	NIB	$11.00	00-01
Whopper Stopper	Hellraiser	#365, round props	NOC	$7.00	99-03
Whopper Stopper	Hellraiser	10 (XBW), lr 500 size	NOC	$26.00	99-04
Whopper Stopper	Hellraiser	304S, silver scale	NIB	$21.00	99-02
Whopper Stopper	Hellraiser	365, yellow/green stripes	NOC	$7.00	99-02
Whopper Stopper	Hellraiser	5G, round props, 300 sm size	NOC	$19.80	99-04
Whopper Stopper	Hellraiser	clear, screw-in line tie	EX	$19.99	99-06
Whopper Stopper	Hellraiser	lg, frog	NOC	$33.00	99-11
Whopper Stopper	Hellraiser	r/w, beater	EX-	$19.99	99-02
Whopper Stopper	Hellraiser	r/w, plastic box	NIB	$10.50	99-06
Whopper Stopper	Hellraiser	Series 500, black and white coach dog with yellow belly and eyes	VG+	$14.02	05-07
Whopper Stopper	Hellraiser	white shore	NOC	$9.00	99-02
Whopper Stopper	Hellraiser		NIB	$19.99	99-02
Whopper Stopper	Jointed	y/black ribs, NOT MET	mint	$25.00	99-11
Whopper Stopper	Lizard	eel-looking lure, hard plastic box	NIB	$32.50	99-11
Whopper Stopper	Scrambler	pikie, Zara, with props	NOC	$21.50	99-03
Whopper Stopper	Topper	coach dog	EX	$24.00	03-05
Whopper Stopper	Whopper-Stopper	#100, white/RH with glitter, 2¾"	GD	$3.80	05-07
Wilcox	Wiggler	brown mottled pattern, one broken side treble, two small chips on belly at joint	VG+	$3,080.00	05-04
Wilcox	Wiggler	maroon/red, very nice, NOT MET	EX-	$3,201.00	02-09
Wilcox	Wiggler	NO BIDS	avg	$1,800.00	00-02
Wilcox	Wiggler	rainbow!	EX	$3,000.00	05-06

BRAND	MODEL	SERIES / MFG. CODE / DESCRIPTION	GRADE	PRICE	DATE yy/mm
Wilcox	Wiggler	type 2, frog, NOT MET	VG	$1,750.00	99-06
Wilcox	Wiggler	ugly, NOT MET	fair	$760.00	99-03
Wilcox	Wiggler Type 2, 3-hk	ugly color, SOLD	EX	$4,880.00	01-06
Wilford	Croaker Bass Bait	white, jointed woodpecker type, bad pics	??	$300.00	01-08
Wilford	Croaker Bass Bait	brass crew eye, hardware primitive, white paint job, 4¼" bait	EX	$88.00	05-04
Wilford & Co.	Croaker	white	VG+	$201.00	05-07
Williams, Ted	Ny Buck (jigs!)	counter display, Miami, FL, ugly	poor	$721.00	00-05
Wilmer	No Follin	salmon plug, NOT MET	EX	$327.00	03-06
Wilson	6 in 1	bar perch	EX	$550.00	00-05
Wilson	Bassmerizer	r/w	EX	$360.00	99-04
Wilson	Bassmerizer	blended RH	EX	$550.00	00-05
Wilson	Bassmerizer	r/w, NOT MET	EX+	$370.00	99-06
Wilson	Cupped Wobbler	RH/w, CR flakes under tail and chin, light age lines and few pointers	VG	$68.00	05-05
Wilson	Early Winged Wobbler	c. 1914, RH	VG	$66.00	04-11
Wilson	Fluted Wobbler	bar perch!	EX	$128.50	99-04
Wilson	Grass Widow	white, red spots, ¼", round flake on chin	VG+	$50.00	05-05
Wilson	Six-in-One Wobbler	white/red chin, box faded avg	EXIB	$429.00	05-02
Wilson	Six-in-One Wobbler	white spotted, green back, c. 1917	GD	$137.50	04-11
Wilson	Winged Wobbler	white	EX	$85.00	00-05
Wilson	Winged Woggler	all red, brass crew eyes only intro, c. 1912, lots of wear	g-	$29.00	05-05
Wilson	Wobbler Fluted	pic 2PCCB, neat	EXIB	$132.50	99-03
Winchester	3-hook Underwater Minnow	GE, green crackleback, "9015" marked lip	AVG+	$110.00	04-11
Winchester	3-hooker	9012, green back/gold	VG+	$383.00	00-04
Winchester	3-hooker	9015, crackleback	VG-IB	$810.00	99-04
Winchester	3-hooker	9016, crackle, sm chip	VG+	$406.00	00-11
Winchester	3-hooker	9014, blended red, original, GE	EX	$250.00	05-07
Winchester	3-hooker	blood red, box EX	NIB	$2,400.00	01-12
Winchester	3-hooker	crackle, papers, box missing end flap	NIB	$1,000.00	00-07
Winchester	3-hooker	dark red	EX	$1,350.00	99-10
Winchester	3-hooker	dark red, unmarked box EX-	EXIB	$2,500.00	01-06
Winchester	3-hooker	green	poor	$90.98	99-05
Winchester	3-hooker	9015, nice box & papers, crackleback, nose chip, NOT MET	EX-IB	$430.00	05-06
Winchester	3-hooker	no eyes, cheapie, prop marked, NOT MET	EX	$153.50	00-03
Winchester	3-hooker	r/w, cheap line, lg body	poor	$74.00	99-01
Winchester	3-hooker	RB (repaint?), Mahinski sell	EX	$810.00	00-03
Winchester	3-hooker	RB, marked prop	EX	$688.00	00-10
Winchester	3-hooker	red	mint	$650.00	01-12
Winchester	3-hooker	red, 3-hk	EX-	$1,200.00	00-05
Winchester	3-hooker	white/brown back stripe, red chin	EX-	$431.00	00-10
Winchester	5-hook Minnow	replica, classic Winchester minnow No. 2001	NIB	$55.00	04-11
Winchester	5-hooker	awful, chips, no hooks, "#9215" on prop	poor	$204.00	00-04
Winchester	5-hooker	crackle, big chip by eye	avg	$305.00	03-02
Winchester	5-hooker	mint repaint	REPAINT	$325.00	99-12
Winchester	5-hooker	parrot finish	EX	$1,150.00	02-08

LURES

BRAND	MODEL	SERIES / MFG. CODE / DESCRIPTION	GRADE	PRICE	DATE yy/mm
Winchester	5-hooker	rainbow, underwater minnow	EX	$1,000.00	01-12
Winchester	5-hooker	RB, ROBW	EX-	$1,650.00	99-10
Winchester	5-hooker	RB, tiny tail chip	EX	$1,400.00	01-06
Winchester	5-hooker		EX-	$1,500.00	99-04
Winchester	Bass Fly	on card	NOC	$172.00	99-04
Winchester	Crusader 9482	spinner, lg willow leaf	EX-	$36.00	05-02
Winchester	Diving Beauty	3¾", GE, RH/silver	VG	$181.50	04-11
Winchester	Multi-Wobbler	9202, green, NOT MET	EX	$277.00	00-03
Winchester	Multi-Wobbler	crackleback	EX-	$316.00	99-03
Winchester	Multi-Wobbler	gold/brown back stripe	EX	$400.00	00-10
Winchester	Multi-Wobbler	green/gold side, NOT MET	EX-	$304.89	99-05
Winchester	Multi-Wobbler	rainbow	VG	$158.00	02-11
Winchester	Multi-Wobbler	rainbow, crisp box, packer's slip	NIB	$1,277.00	02-06
Winchester	Multi-Wobbler	RH, looks decent	VG+	$233.00	00-04
Winchester	Multi-Wobbler 9200	RB? GE, decent, NOT MET	VG	$180.50	99-09
Winchester	Multi-Wobbler	9201, green/gold back, YB, papers	NIB	$793.00	00-09
Winchester	Multi-Wobbler	9206 RB, crisp box and paper, NOT MET	NIB	$1,675.00	00-10
Winchester	Multi-Wobbler	GE, green crackleback, "9205" marked lip	EX	$165.00	04-11
Winchester	Multi-Wobbler	green parrot in nice box	EXIB	$776.00	99-02
Winchester	Multi-Wobbler	RB, several sm chips, NOT MET	avg	$179.00	00-10
Winchester	Multi-Wobbler	white/red eyes	EX	$376.10	99-11
Winchester	Spinner	9611	EX-	$41.00	02-06
Winchester	Spinner	9623	EX	$66.00	00-03
Winchester	Spinner	9639, 3", kidney	EX-	$66.00	05-02
Winchester	Superior Bass Fly	corner missing on card	EXOC	$113.00	05-03
Winchester	Wobbler	9201, green	VG	$275.00	99-01
Winchester	Wobbler	9204, red	avg	$202.50	99-01
Winchester	2001	5-hk minnow, GE, gold scale, reproduction that sold out quickly	NIB	$65.00	05-05
Winnie	Michigan Stump Dodger	perch, metal eyes, nice pic box	EXIB	$1,300.00	02-04
Winnie	Michigan Stump Dodger	red/white, metal eyes, age lines, nice pic box	EX-IB	$1,176.00	02-04
Winter	Weedless Surface Bait	1¾", red/white finish, hand-painted celluloid wings	EX	$357.50	05-04
Winters	Bass Bait		EX	$650.00	01-04
Wise, Leo	Jim Dandy	frog spot, unique hdwr, very minor defects	EX+	$57.00	05-05
Wise, Leo	Jim Dandy	solid white, very skinny body style, varnish a bit tan	EX+	$50.00	05-05
Wise, Leo	Mouse	1⅝", white with tiny spots	EX	$428.00	04-02
Wise, Leo	Mouse	gray speckled, drilled-out belly weight	EX	$247.00	05-04
Wise, Leo	Mouse	gray hair, bead eyes, sponge tail	EX	$410.00	99-11
Wise, Leo	Mouse Bait	gray speckled paint, drilled-out belly weight	EX	$247.50	05-04
Wise, Leo	Twin Spin Frog	black BE, hardware rigging, speckled paint finish, 2¼", some chipping	VG+	$247.50	05-04
Wise/Schillinger	Jim Dandy	circa 1917, r and w, scramble and sharp edges	VG+	$50.00	05-05
Wood	Deep-R-Doddle	1800, blue, 5½" long, w/correct light blue/cream box	EX	$60.13	05-07
Wood, Ed	Crab Crawler	PTCB	NIB	$26.00	03-10
Woods Mfg. Co.	2 Diff	005, Doodler perch, Deep-R-Doodle 1001	NIB x 2	$310.00	99-04

BRAND	MODEL	SERIES / MFG. CODE / DESCRIPTION	GRADE	PRICE	DATE yy/mm
Woods Mfg. Co.	4 Diff	common, one box and cat	EX	$52.86	99-01
Woods Mfg. Co.	6 Diff	6-pack, nice display, PTCB	NIB	$102.50	99-04
Woods Mfg. Co.	Arkansas Wiggler	nice pic box, like Spoonplug metal	NIB	$61.00	00-05
Woods Mfg. Co.	Dipsy Doodle	perch	NIB	$15.50	99-01
Woods Mfg. Co.	Dipsy Doodle	yellow scale like one on box	NIB	$80.00	99-01
Woods Mfg. Co.	Doodler	#616, pic box, black, cat	NIB	$51.00	00-05
Woods Mfg. Co.	Doodler	shad scale, #604 box VG+, plastic lure!	NIB	$100.00	01-08
Woods Mfg. Co.	Doodler	YSB1215, y/silver bars, cat nice	NIB	$88.00	00-09
Woods Mfg. Co.	Mixed	3 diff	EX	$17.45	99-03
Woods Mfg. Co.	Poppa Doodle	1997 reissue	NIB	$15.00	01-04
Woods Mfg. Co.	Spot Tail	703, RH, papers, pic 2PCCB	NIB	$203.00	00-01
Woods Mfg. Co.	Spot Tail Minnow	silver scales and black back, YPE, hint of wear	EX	$14.00	05-05
Woods Mfg. Co.	Spot Tail	black in box, one more nice	EXIB	$20.25	99-01
Woods, F.C.	5-hook Expert Minnow	3¼", yellow, GE, 3 HPGM	Poor	$82.50	04-11
Woods, F.C.	5-hook Expert Minnow	3⅝", white, GE, 3 HPGM, olive green back/white	AVG	$82.50	04-11
Woods, F.C.	5-hook Expert Minnow	3⅝", yellow, GE, olive green back/pinkish tan	VG	$176.00	04-11
Woods, F.C.	Early 5-hook Expert Minnow	4⅝", yellow, GE, gold, 3 red HPGM	VG-	$302.50	04-11
Woods, F.C.	Expert	3-hooker, green/white, "EXPERT"	EX	$1,200.00	01-12
Woods, F.C.	Expert	5-hooker, aluminum, wood box EX-	EXIB	$4,000.00	01-12
Woods, F.C.	Expert	5-hk, yellow GE, large font pre-1905 Holzworth? green back	EX	$455.00	05-07
Woods, F.C.	Expert	5-hk, yellow GE, floppy, no hole props, blk back/silver	EX	$505.00	05-07
Woods, F.C.	Expert	5-hooker, 3¾", 2 BW, wood box, about ⅓ lettering missing	EXIB	$830.00	05-06
Woods, F.C.	Expert	5-hooker	VG-	$515.00	99-05
Woods, F.C.	Expert	alum, HPGM, NOT MET	VG	$257.00	01-05
Woods, F.C.	Expert	gold! round body, #1 removable hooks	EX-	$800.00	99-01
Woods, F.C.	Expert	maroon box VG, round, NOT MET	EXIB	$1,484.00	04-03
Woods, F.C.	Expert	pre-1904, 2½", green/white, NOT MET	EX-?	$511.00	02-09
Woods, F.C.	Expert	wood bx, label rough, gold 5-hk, detach hooks	EX-IB	$2,650.00	02-11
Woods, F.C.	Expert 5-hooker	green/white, #1 detachable hooks	EX-	$1,500.00	01-06
Woods, F.C.	Expert 5-hooker	wood box label EX-, alum	EXIB	$4,000.00	01-06
Woods, F.C.	Expert 5-hooker	The Expert, brown? back	EX	$1,300.00	01-12
Woods, F.C.	Expert 5-hooker	green, hole props, 2 BW, re-hooks	VG	$391.00	01-05
Woods, F.C.	Expert Minnow	2½", baby-size blunt end props with large holes, twisted wire hook hangers, yellow GE, 3 HPGM, retains paint and belly weights as well as "The Expert" written on left side	EX	$2,090.00	05-04
Woods, F.C.	Expert 3-hooker	green/white, #1 hooks	EX	$1,500.00	01-06
Woods, F.C.	3-hook Expert Minnow	3", yellow, GE, 3 HPGM, olive green back/white	AVG	$220.00	04-11
Worden	3-hooker	green, purty, 1 chip, NOT MET	EX-	$464.00	99-11
Worden	5-hooker	ugly, screw hook holders, awful	poor	$160.50	99-10
Worden	Combination Minnow	aluminum, w/box EX, orig string tie	EXIB	$4,600.00	01-06
Worden	Combination Minnow	white box EX, aluminum, line tie	EXIB	$4,500.00	01-12
Worth	Flutter Fin	6 different colors	NIB	$202.85	99-03
Worth	Flutter Fin	black/white scales	mint	$19.50	99-01
Worth	Flutter Fin	newest box, NOT MET! (wishful thinking)	NIB	$32.00	04-02

BRAND	MODEL	SERIES / MFG. CODE / DESCRIPTION	GRADE	PRICE	DATE yy/mm
Worth	Flutter Fin	orange body, black spots w/orange and black tail feathers, circa 1960s	EX	$22.03	05-07
Worth	Flutter Fin	orange/black scales, PTCB	NIB	$33.00	04-07
Worth	Flutter Fin	orange/black scales	EX	$17.77	99-07
Worth	Flutter Fin	yellow/black spots	AVG	$11.00	05-07
Worth	Flutter Fin	black/white scales, older and nearly square PTCB	NIB	$31.00	04-03
Worth	Flutter Fin	white/red scales, older and nearly square PTCB	NIB	$30.00	04-03
Worth	Flutter Fin x 2	2 diff	VG	$26.00	99-06
Wright McGill	Fly x 24	salesman display, NO BIDS	EX	$200.00	99-06
Wright McGill	7-11 Lucky Spinner Fly	glass beads and leader, new on graphic EX- fold-open card	NOC	$20.00	05-05
Wright McGill	Baby Mouse	ugly, lint covered, NOT MET	EX?	$189.50	00-01
Wright McGill	Bass Big	blk head, yellow body, white wings and tail, l wing bit shy, tiny GE	VG+	$27.00	05-05
Wright McGill	Bass Nabber	b/w, GE, NOT MET	VG+	$76.00	00-03
Wright McGill	Bass Nabber	brown/black ribs, GE, hair legs	EX-	$64.00	05-01
Wright McGill	Bass O Gram	g/y, GE, 2½"	EX-	$370.00	00-02
Wright McGill	Bass O Gram	RH	EX-	$199.00	00-09
Wright McGill	Bass O Gram	read head & tail, GE, belly crk	nice	$300.00	99-03
Wright McGill	Bass-Zoo-Ka	RH on card, crisp box 301-0S	NIB	$23.00	04-11
Wright McGill	Bug-A-Boo	b/w, 1½"	EX-	$17.00	99-01
Wright McGill	Bug-A-Boo	#303, w/box	AVG	$9.53	05-07
Wright McGill	Crawdad	gold, brown	EX	$86.00	99-08
Wright McGill	Crawfish	green, BE	EX	$96.00	00-01
Wright McGill	Crawfish	softshell, rough box #551	EXIB	$76.00	00-03
Wright McGill	Flapper Crab	2", no legs	EX	$86.00	00-01
Wright McGill	Flapper Crab	gray, 1¾", no legs	EX	$132.50	00-01
Wright McGill	Flapper Crab	legs gone	EXIB	$165.00	99-09
Wright McGill	Flapper Crab	missing legs	EXIB	$103.00	99-01
Wright McGill	Flapper Crab	yellow, 2", nice!	mint	$170.50	00-01
Wright McGill	Flapper Crab		EX	$75.00	99-04
Wright McGill	Fly Naturefaker	BB eyes	VG	$28.00	99-01
Wright McGill	Fly Rod Bait		EX	$100.00	01-04
Wright McGill	Frog Fly Rod	supernice	EX	$155.00	00-11
Wright McGill	Hijacker	gold scale, nice box	EXIB	$13.50	00-04
Wright McGill	Hijacker	r/w	NIB	$24.99	99-06
Wright McGill	Horsefly	fly rod, GE, ugly	poor	$20.00	99-06
Wright McGill	Miracle Minnow	472-J18	NIB	$15.50	99-05
Wright McGill	Miracle Minnow	452J-C (jointed chrome), on correct card	NIB	$25.00	03-01
Wright McGill	Miracle Minnow	470W	NIB	$25.99	00-02
Wright McGill	Miracle Minnow	471W, on card in crisp box, gold hardware	NIB	$30.00	04-09
Wright McGill	Miracle Minnow	472J7	NIB	$27.00	99-05
Wright McGill	Mouse	fly rod size, black/white head, wowser	EX+	$255.00	05-07
Wright McGill	Nicky Mouse	black and gray, a beauty	EX	$164.00	05-01
Wright McGill	Nicky Mouse	gray, nice whiskers and eyes	EX-	$291.00	00-02
Wright McGill	Nicky Mouse	I sniped $103.79! but "problem"	EX	$103.50	99-09
Wright McGill	Open Mouth Shiner	r/w, ugly	avg	$62.00	99-12
Wright McGill	Skipper, fly rod	y/blk stripe, GE	EX+	$109.01	99-05

BRAND	MODEL	SERIES / MFG. CODE / DESCRIPTION	GRADE	PRICE	DATE yy/mm
Wright McGill	Skippy Minnow	black w/red stripe down sides, tiny GE, flasher tail	EX	$90.00	05-05
Wright McGill	Swim Mouse	ugly, NOT MET	avg	$30.50	99-08
Wright McGill	Whirlwind Spinner	neat 4-bladed propeller spinner, nickel and copper, w/red feather treble	EX-	$25.00	05-05
Wyers	Devon	3 cm, c. 1910, safety box	NIB	$100.00	00-07
Wynne	Ol' Skipper	Lucky Tail Wobbler, box top EX-	EXIB	$49.00	02-08
Wynne	Ol' Skipper	r/w, 1603 box	NIB	$46.00	99-02
Yawman & Erbe	Auto Flyreel	great picture bx VG+, H&I logo on reel	EX-IB	$137.00	03-08
Young Lures Inc.	Boiling Big Y	chartreuse, with packs of tablets	NIB	$22.00	04-09
Young, Fred	Big O	original, hand carved & signed	mint	$455.00	05-02
Ypsilanti	Ypsilanti Minnow	3¾", RH, painted eye	VG	$77.00	04-11
Zane Grey	South Bend King Oreno	crisp intro box, 6¼", standard red and white finish, GE, single hook bait, one blemish on left side	EXIB	$687.50	05-04
Zane Grey	Tarp Oreno	red head, aluminum, glass eyes, intro box crisp	EX+IB	$935.00	05-04
Zimmy	Plastic Plug	S5-5, Brass Flash, nice box	NIB	$17.00	05-01
Zink	Screwtail	b/w	EX	$77.76	00-01
Zink	Screwtail	box nice	EXIB	$176.00	05-07
Zink	Screwtail	green/yellow	EX-	$99.00	00-07
Zink	Screwtail	r/w	VG+	$66.50	99-01
Zink	Screwtail	r/w	EX-	$76.00	99-04
Zink	Screwtail	r/w	EX	$84.00	99-04
Zink	Screwtail	red head/white	EX	$80.00	05-02
Zink	Screwtail	RH, papers	NIB	$255.00	00-01
Zink	Screwtail	white/black	NIB	$211.00	05-02
Zink	Screwtail	yellow/blk stripe	NIB	$190.00	99-07
Zumski	Whiptail Sucker	GE, gray, NOT MET!	VG+	$103.50	99-01

Lure Retrievers

BRAND	MODEL	SERIES / MFG. CODE / DESCRIPTION	GRADE	PRICE	DATE
Hound Dog	Lure Retriever	lead shaped like sleeping dog, paper	mint	$26.00	03-02

Photo Gallery

Abbey & Imbrie Crawdad, $21.00.

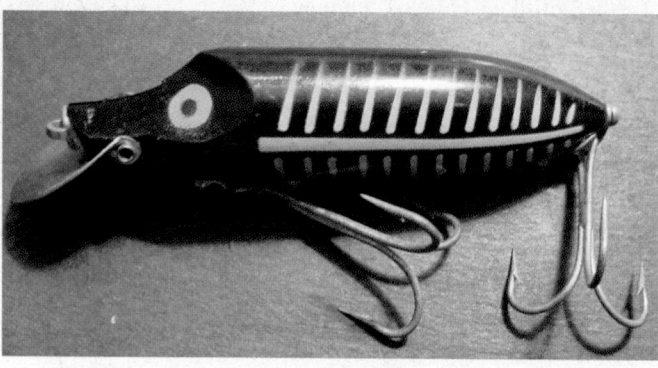

Abu, Hi-Lo, $12.00.

Accepted Lures, Dozy Boy, $76.00.

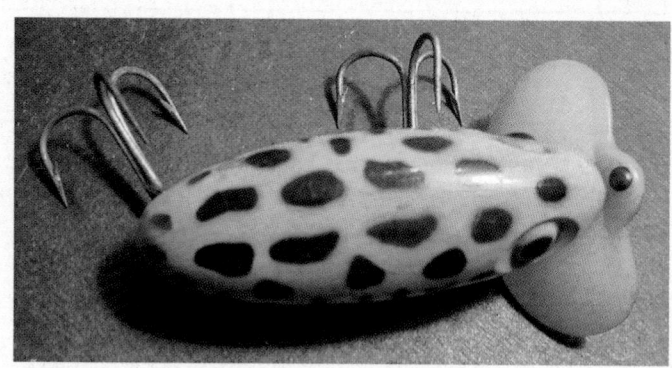

Arbogast, Jitterbug, $26.00.

Barber, Reel Shad, $26.00.

Bauman Bait, bait cage, $5,500.00. Photo courtesy of Lang's.

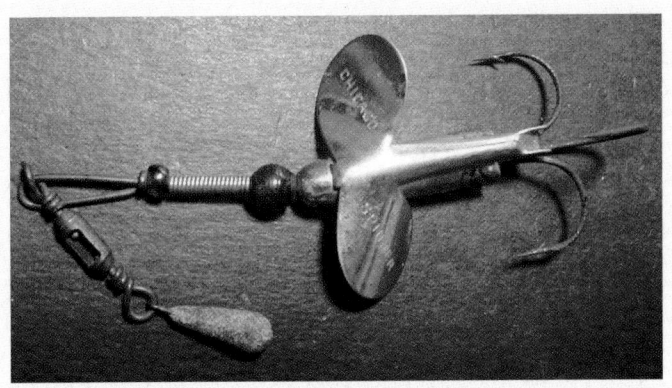

Bew, Charles; Chicago Spinner, $282.00.

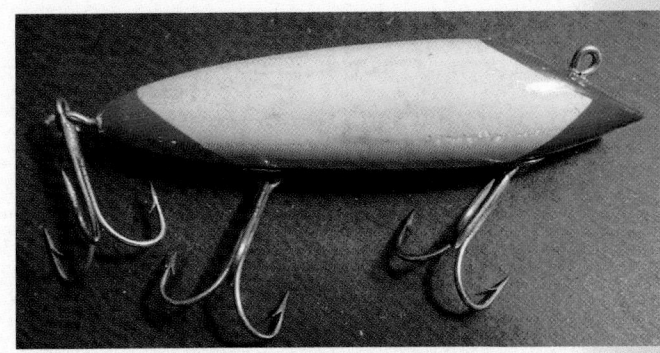

Wobbler, Bite'Em Bait, $93.90

Buckeye Bait Co., Bug-N-Bass, $52.00.

Burke, Big Dig, $6.05

Clark, Make 'Em Bite, $3,795.00.
Photo courtesy of Lang's.

Clewell, Snakebait, $1,540.00. Photo courtesy of Lang's.

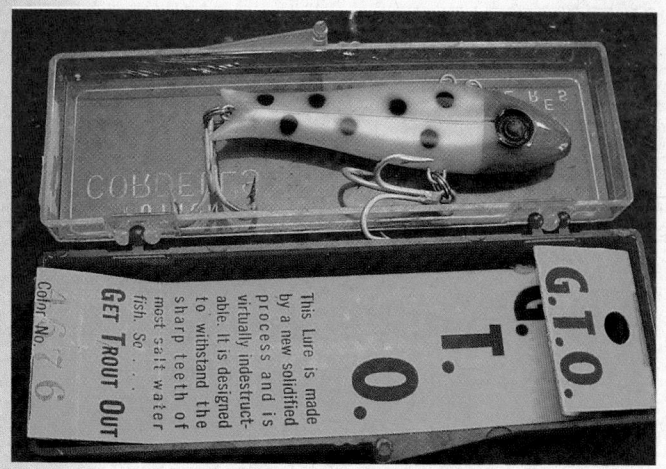

Cordell, GTO, $7.00.

CCBC, Dingbat, $47.00.

934 CCBC, Pikie, Baby, $189.00.

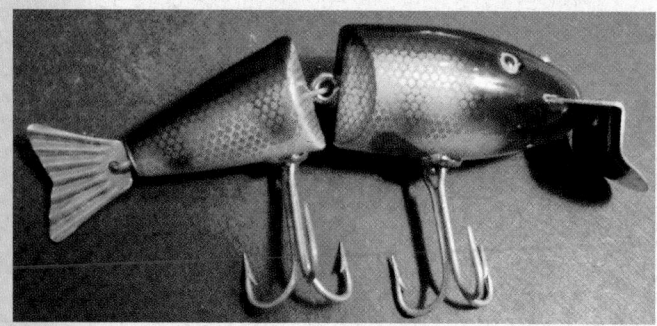

CCBC, Wiggle Fish, $64.00.

CCBC, Cray-Z Fish, $11.00.

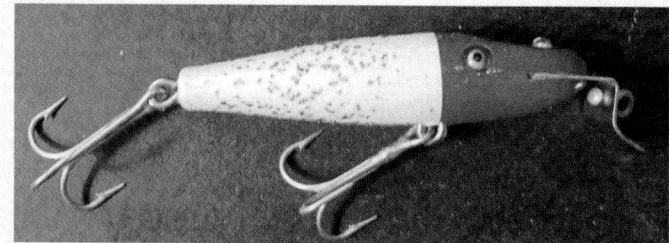

2222 CCBC, Pikie Midget, $321.00.

CCBC, Wiggle Diver, $32.00.

CCBC, Wiggler 100, $16.00.

Conroy/J. Vom, Silver King 2/00, $310.00.

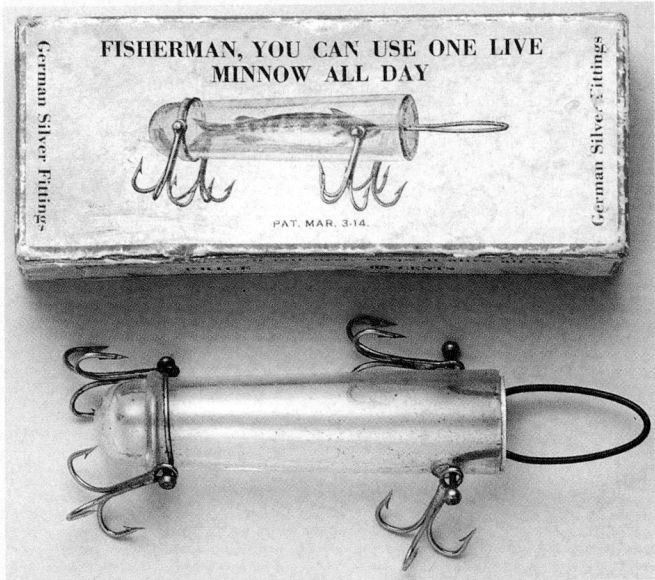

Detroit, Glass Minnow Tube, $1,760.00. Photo courtesy of Lang's.

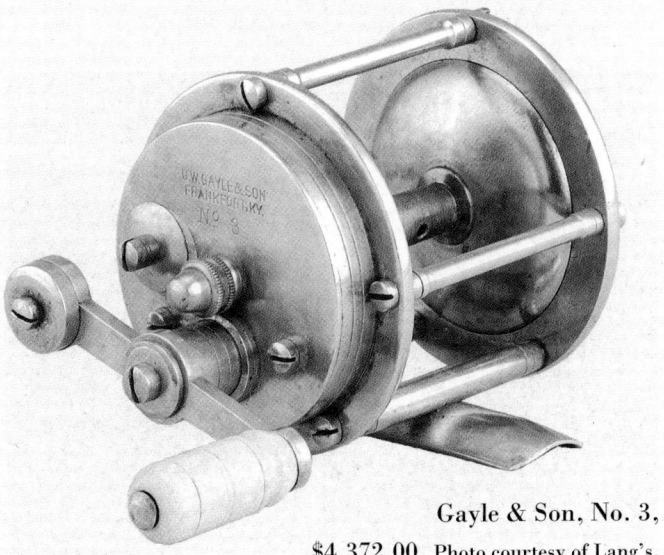

Gayle & Son, No. 3, $4,372.00. Photo courtesy of Lang's.

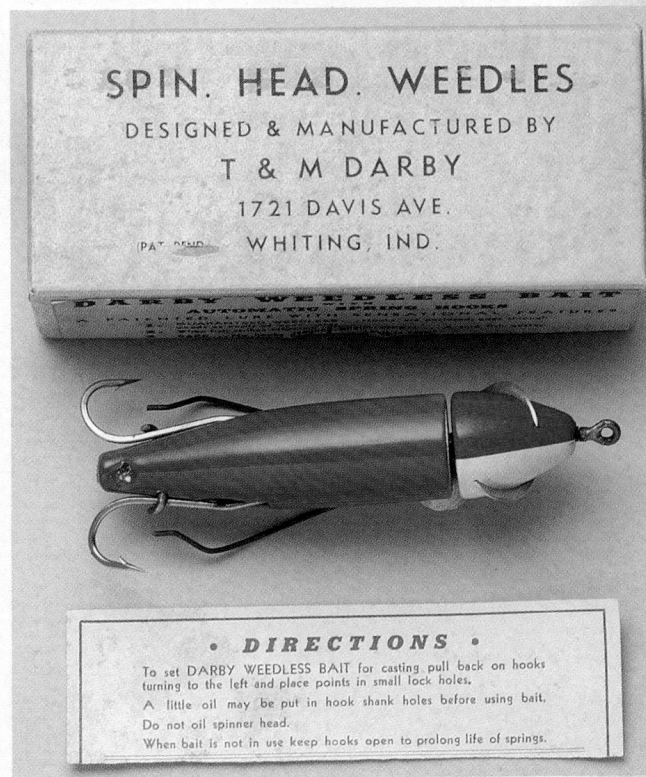

Darby, Spin Head, $495.00. Photo courtesy of Lang's.

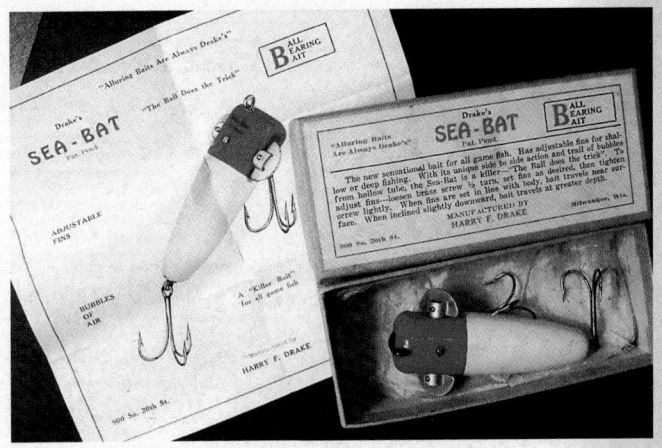

Drake's, Sea Bat, $432.00.

271

Harrison Inds., Vibra Bat, $32.00.

Haskell, Minnow, $101,200.00. Photo courtesy of Lang's.

Hawk, Walleye, $36.00.

1411 Heddon, Slopenose, $11,110.00. Photo courtesy of Lang's.

H210SD Heddon, 210 Spook, $43.00.

Heddon, Go-Deeper Crab, $36.00.

380SUN Heddon, Punkinseed, Tiny, $41.00.

119P Heddon, River Runt, $77.65.

9430XRS Heddon, River Runt Jointed Sinker, $31.00.

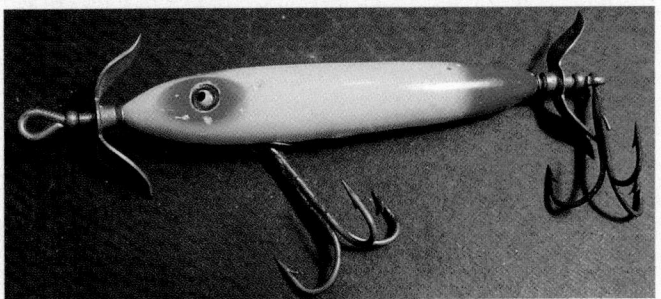

120RET Heddon, Torpedo, $109.00.

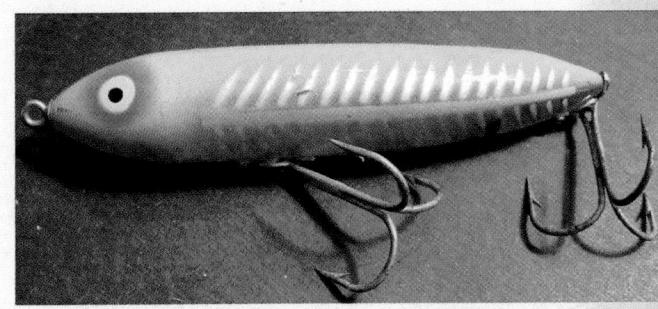

XRY Heddon, Zara Spook, $4.00.

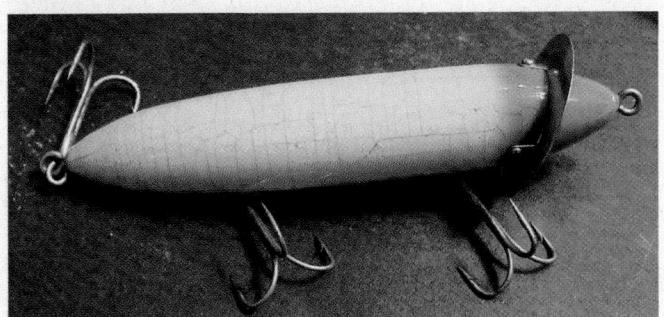

Heddon, 200, $105.00.

Heddon, 300, $181.00.

Henshall, G.S. Bait casting reel, $5,060.00. Photo courtesy of Lang's.

Hosmer, J.D., mechanical frog, $5,170.00. Photo courtesy of Lang's.

Immel, Chippewa, Musky, $2,810.00. Photo courtesy of Lang's.

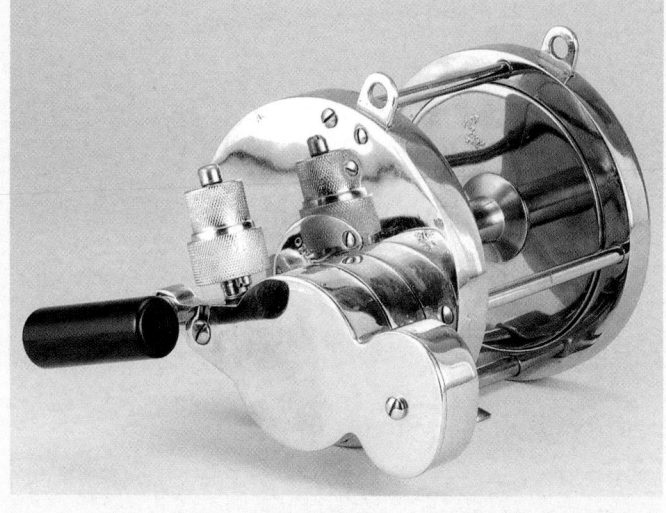

Kovalovsky, Big Game Reel, $1,980.00. Photo courtesy of Lang's.

Lawrence, Tillamook Creel, $1,100.00. Photo courtesy of Lang's.

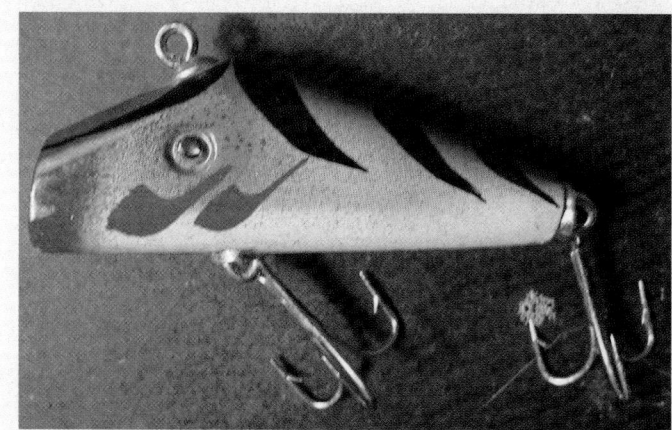

Lex Baits, Kentucky Leader, $18.00.

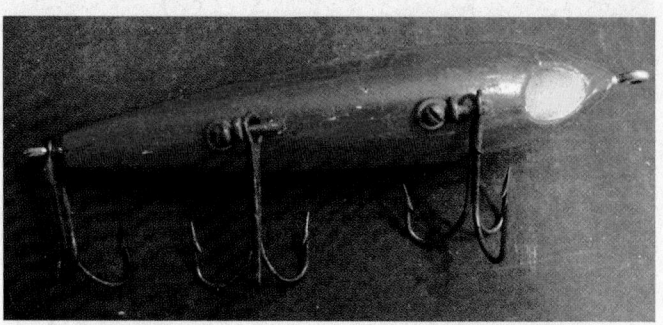

WaterWitch Lockhart, Wagtail Witch, $83.00.

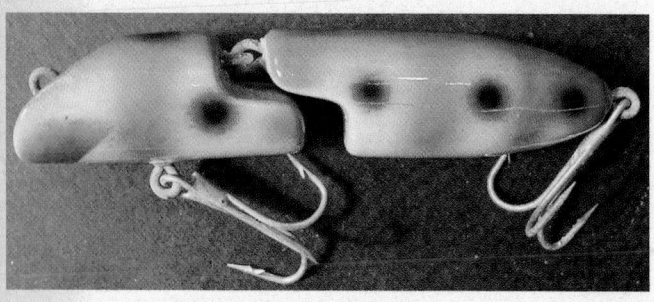

Makinen, Merry Widow, $13.00.

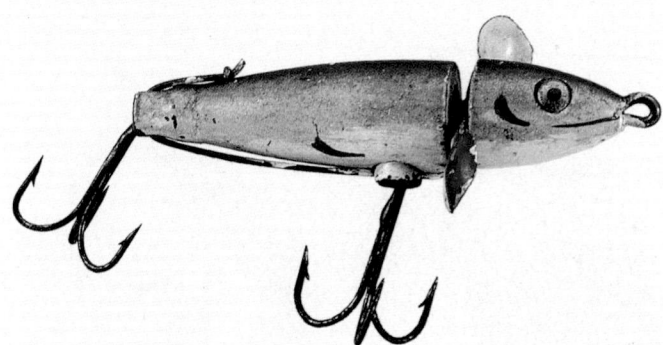

Manistee, Minnow, $3,080.00. Photo courtesy of Lang's.

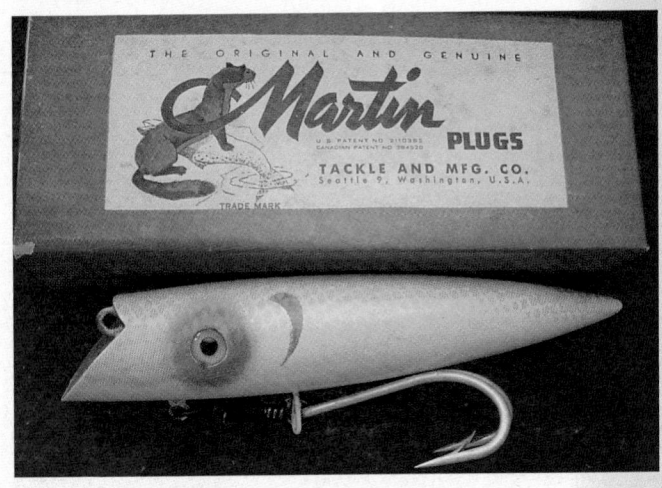

7KS Martin, Salmon lure, $43.00.

Meek, #3, $316.00.

Meek & Milam, No. 6 casting reel, $6,345.00. Photo courtesy of Lang's.

Meek & Milam, marked "Ky No. 5," $3,630.00. Photo courtesy of Lang's.

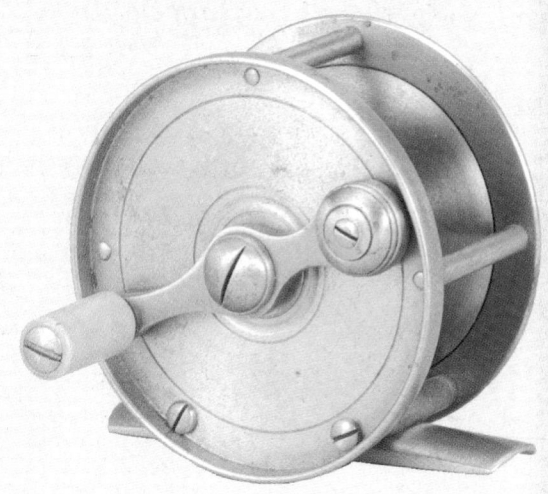

Meek & Sons, No. 44, $9,020.00. Photo courtesy of Lang's.

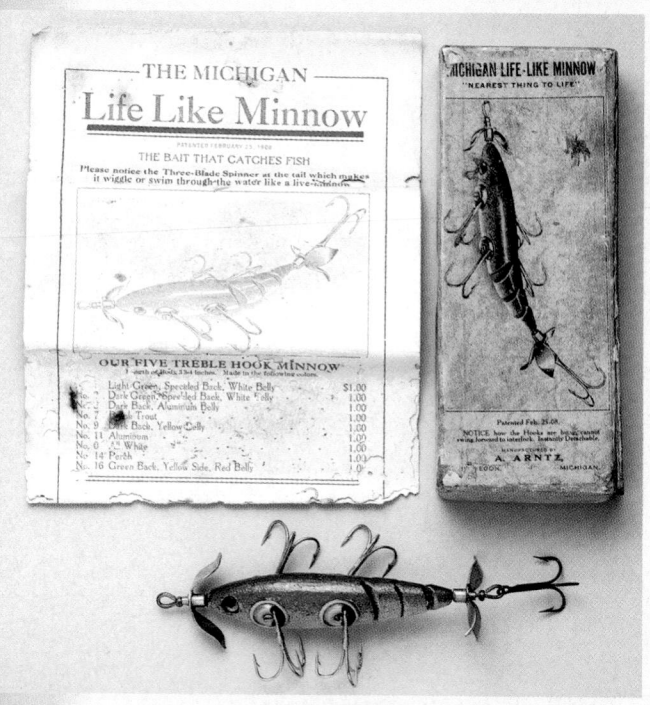

Michigan, Life Like Minnow, $6,270.00. Photo courtesy of Lang's.

Milam, B.C., No. 5, $3,190.00. Photo courtesy of Lang's.

Milam, B.C., No. 2, $1,980.00. Photo courtesy of Lang's.

Miller, Reversible Minnow, $6,875.00. Photo courtesy of Lang's.

Ness, Nifty Minne. Box and paper only, no lure. $3,742.00.

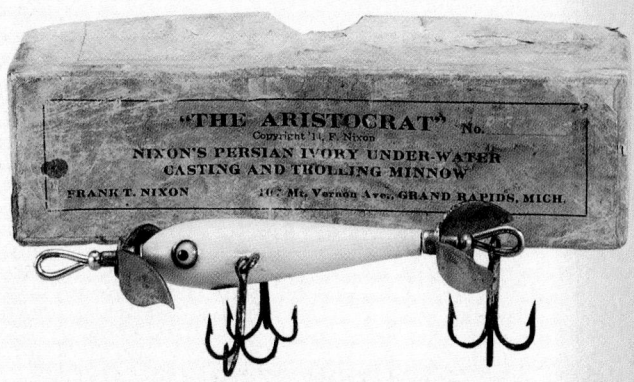

Nixon, Aristocrat Minnow, $4,290.00. Photo courtesy of Lang's.

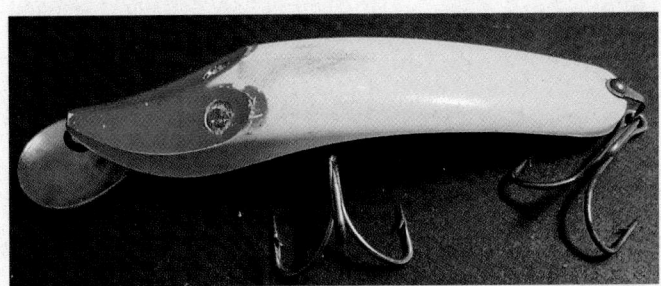

Paul Bunyan, Dodger, $14.00.

Sears Paw Paw, Pikie type, $34.00.

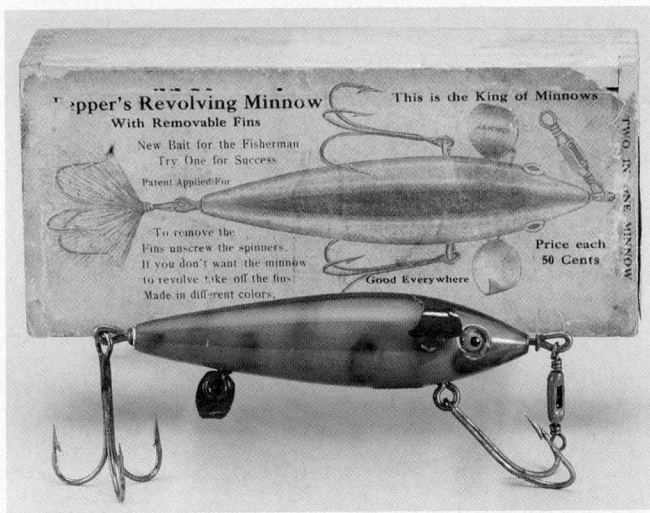

Pepper, Revolving Minnow, $5,280.00. Photo courtesy of Lang's.

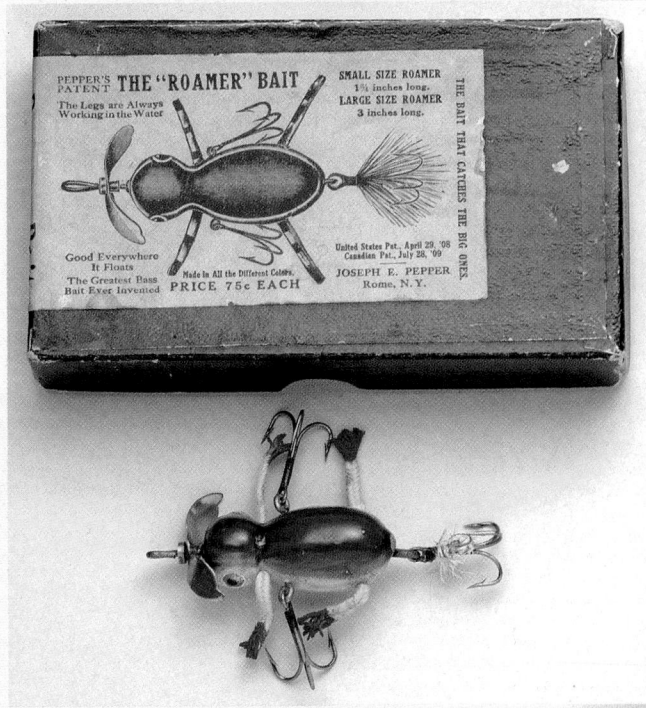

Pepper, Roamer, $7,150.00. Photo courtesy of Lang's.

Pflueger, Magnet, $164.00.

Pflueger, Muskill, $7.00.

Pico, Peppy, $145.00.

Red River, Top R, $2.00.

Rhodes? Musky Frog Bait, $5,225.00. Photo courtesy of Lang's.

Rhodes, Roy; Rhodes Minnow, $64.00.

Rinehart, Musky Jinx, $53.00.

Shurkatch, Runt type, $18.00.

Silver Creek, Pikaroon, $3,300.00. Photo courtesy of Lang's.

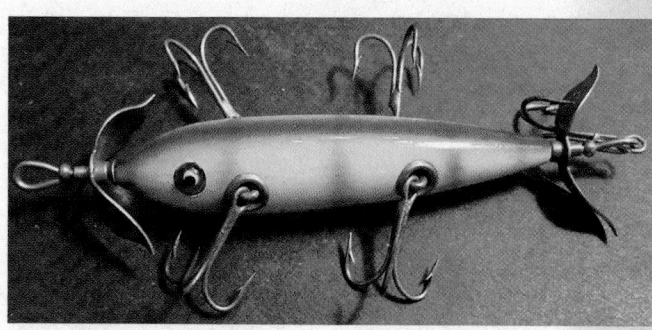

South Bend, 5-hooker, $313.00.

South Bend, Bass Obite, $25.00.

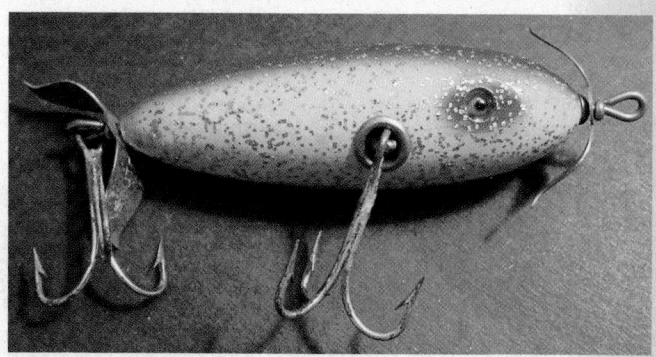

South Bend, Crippled Minnow, $71.00.

South Bend, Nip-I-Diddee, $27.00.

Turbulent, Excitor, $283.00.

Vom Hofe, E., Model 355 Perfection, $6,710.00. Photo courtesy of Lang's.

Vom Hofe, E., Perfection Model 360, $6,050.00. Photo courtesy of Lang's.

Zinc, Screwtail, $80.00.

Magazines

BRAND	MODEL	SERIES / MFG. CODE / DESCRIPTION	GRADE	PRICE	DATE yy/mm
Field & Stream	1906		fair	$48.77	99-02
Outdoor Life	1930, March	great color cover	EX	$26.00	99-02

Match Safes

BRAND	MODEL	SERIES / MFG. CODE / DESCRIPTION	GRADE	PRICE	DATE yy/mm
sterling silver	Fancy Scroll	fly fisherman, marked "STERLING"	EX	$209.00	01-01

Matchbooks

BRAND	MODEL	SERIES / MFG. CODE / DESCRIPTION	GRADE	PRICE	DATE yy/mm
Heddon	O. and O. Sporting Goods	Rochester, MN, ad on book of matches	VG	$27.00	02-09

Minnow Buckets

BRAND	MODEL	SERIES / MFG. CODE / DESCRIPTION	GRADE	PRICE	DATE yy/mm
Arrow	Minnow Bucket	oval, weak printing	VG	$82.00	04-11
Banta	Aerating Minnow Pail	oval, 8" x 12" x 6", denim cover, air pump, some rust	VG	$302.00	04-11
Climax	Lifesaver 100	green, floating	EX+	$43.00	01-10
Cream City	Good Luck	blue/silver & gold lettering, only two known	VG	$522.00	04-11
Deshler Mail Box Co.	Jones Minnow Pail	oval, 6" x 16" x 10", green, fish on side	VG	$192.00	04-11
Eclipse	No. 12	7½" tall, 9" diameter, green/gold lettering	EX-	$385.00	04-11
Eclipse	No. 2	8' tall, 8" wide, black/silver lettering, round	EX-	$467.00	04-11
Expert	Oval	green, cool stencil of fish	EX-	$395.00	02-08
Falls City	10 qt.	9' tall, 9½" dia., "Magic," green/gold lettering	VG	$192.00	04-11
Falls City	Expert	fish "614," no handle	rough	$137.00	04-11
Falls City	Wade In #1	writing still bold, but many scrapes	avg	$167.00	05-02
Falls City	Winner No. 110	large size, green/silver lettering	VG	$192.00	04-11
Hartford	Float	Buy it Now $1,000! NOT MET	EX	$112.00	02-05
Joy	½ gallon	glass, corrogated cardboard box VG, metal lid rusty	EXIB	$485.00	05-07
Keen Kutter	2-piece Metal	galvanized	mint	$120.00	99-04
Lucas		c. 1917, nice graphics	VG+	$228.00	01-01
Midget	No. 2	oval, 4½" tall, 6", "Minnow & Frog"	EX-	$1,100.00	04-11
Min-O-Life	Minnow Bucked	excellent paint, Kansas City, MO	EX	$66.00	05-07
Old Pal	Hand Aerator	red/blue logo neat	EX-	$150.00	02-08
Witherspoon Simpson Glass Co.	Joy	glass, c. 1935	EX	$87.00	00-05

Minnow Traps

BRAND	MODEL	SERIES / MFG. CODE / DESCRIPTION	GRADE	PRICE	DATE yy/mm
Orvis	Glass Minnow	wood box	NIB	$380.00	99-05
Shakespeare	Pig	Hawco lid, wood box no lid	EXIB	$1,026.00	03-11

Model Airplanes

BRAND	MODEL	SERIES / MFG. CODE / DESCRIPTION	GRADE	PRICE	DATE yy/mm
Heddon	Jenny	model plane and picture	EX	$192.50	05-07

Nets

BRAND	MODEL	SERIES / MFG. CODE / DESCRIPTION	GRADE	PRICE	DATE yy/mm
Weber	Small	trout stream size, 2 colors wood, nice decal	EX	$77.00	05-07

Outboard Motors

BRAND	MODEL	SERIES / MFG. CODE / DESCRIPTION	GRADE	PRICE	DATE yy/mm
Montgomery Ward	Sea King 2.8 hp	1936 vintage, still runs well!	VG+	$158.00	05-07

Paint Sticks

BRAND	MODEL	SERIES / MFG. CODE / DESCRIPTION	GRADE	PRICE	DATE yy/mm
Heddon	Dummy Double	crackleback, HPGM, no hardware	EX	$2,607.00	05-03

Paperwork

BRAND	MODEL	SERIES / MFG. CODE / DESCRIPTION	GRADE	PRICE	DATE yy/mm
Heddon	Dummy Double Intro	New 1500, "Most valuable invention"	EX-	$210.00	04-11
CCBC	c. 1920s	pocket catalog, 1920s Chub Wiggler shown first	EX-	$90.00	05-06
CCBC	c. 1927	pocket catalog, boy fishing, new Weed Bug	VG+	$40.00	05-06
CCBC	c. 1930 – 50	all white	VG+	$12.00	05-06
CCBC	c. 1931	pocket catalog, boy fishing, new fly rod mouse	VG+	$25.00	05-06
CCBC	1924	pocket catalog, c. 1924, new Fintail Shiner	VG+	$65.00	05-06
CCBC	1924	pocket catalog, c. 1924, new Fintail Shiner	EX	$100.00	05-06
Enterprise Mfg. Co.	1885	4 page brochure, *Luminous Fish Baits*	VG+	$357.00	04-11

BRAND	MODEL	SERIES / MFG. CODE / DESCRIPTION	GRADE	PRICE	DATE yy/mm
Heddon	Crazy Crawler	green insert	EX	$25.00	05-06
Heddon	Dummy Double	box insert, line drawing of L-rig 1500	EX	$461.00	02-02
Heddon	O and Slopenose	bamboo rods on rev, c. 1912	EX	$382.00	01-01
Heddon	The Why of It!	for wood box lures	EX	$494.00	03-04

Pork Rinds

BRAND	MODEL	SERIES / MFG. CODE / DESCRIPTION	GRADE	PRICE	DATE yy/mm
Foss, Al	Glass Jar	real nice, never opened	EX	$76.00	01-08

Postcards

BRAND	MODEL	SERIES / MFG. CODE / DESCRIPTION	GRADE	PRICE	DATE yy/mm
Abbey & Imbrie	1886	neat postcard with stamp from 1886	EX	$38.00	03-10

Practice Plugs

BRAND	MODEL	SERIES / MFG. CODE / DESCRIPTION	GRADE	PRICE	DATE yy/mm
AL&W	2½"	wood, white/red paint, gold decal	EX	$179.00	03-08
ShakeSpeare	⅝ oz.	white w/red "Shakespeare ⅝ oz." stamped on side, 1 small flake	EX-	$42.00	05-05

Printing Blocks

BRAND	MODEL	SERIES / MFG. CODE / DESCRIPTION	GRADE	PRICE	DATE yy/mm
Coxe	Coxe 320	Bronson 2800 reels (2 blocks)	EX	$64.00	03-12

Racks

BRAND	MODEL	SERIES / MFG. CODE / DESCRIPTION	GRADE	PRICE	DATE yy/mm
Heddon	Store Rack	store rack, c. 1950s?	EX	$148.50	05-07

Reels

BRAND	MODEL	SERIES / MFG. CODE / DESCRIPTION	GRADE	PRICE	DATE yy/mm
Unknown	2:1, ball handle	1871, Terry patent reel seat	VG	$215.00	99-04
Unknown	Neptune	gs, 60 yd., front-mounted click, inoperable drag button	VG	$220.00	05-0
4 Brothers	De Lite	fly, 80, g. silver/hard rubber	EX-	$330.00	00-05
4 Brothers	Sumco 2257	brass, nice	EX	$55.00	01-10
4 Brothers	Sumco 2258		G	$35.00	99-01
Abbey & Imbrie	Ball Casting	no mention of condition!	VG?	$157.00	00-10
Abbey & Imbrie	Fly Reel	2' x 1" wood handle	VG	$115.50	04-11
Abbey & Imbrie	Silver King #82	nice box, 300 yd.	EXIB	$51.00	00-02
Abbey & Imbrie	Vom Hofe Compensating	wood box EX with interior label, NOT MET	EX-IB	$405.00	02-06
Abbey & Imbrie		2/00, raised pillar, foot filed	VG	$132.00	00-10
Abel	#1	in pouch, NOT MET	mint	$257.00	99-01
Abel	TR-1	high quality, USA fly reel, smaller size	EX-	$100.00	03-08
Abel	TR-2	extra spool	EX	$271.01	99-03
Abel	TR-Light	high quality, USA fly reel, UL size	NIB	$187.00	03-08
ABU	5000DLX	level wind worn, looks decent	VG?	$169.50	99-07
ABU	10000C		NIB	$197.00	01-08
ABU	10000CDL	goodies	NIB	$400.00	01-03
ABU	1000C	black, modern	EX-	$47.00	99-01
ABU	1044 Spincast	underslung	EX-	$54.00	99-01
ABU	1075 Abumatic		EX-	$31.00	99-04
ABU	1500(C?)	silver	EX-	$125.00	99-03
ABU	1500C	all goodies	NIB	$193.50	99-06
ABU	1500C	case	EX	$192.45	99-03
ABU	1500C	NOT MET	EX-	$85.00	00-01
ABU	1500C	NOT MET	EX	$113.00	99-07
ABU	1500C	serial no. 771200 & goodies	NIB	$293.00	02-06
ABU	1500C	silver	EX	$125.00	05-07
ABU	1500C		EX	$114.50	99-08
ABU	1500C		NIB	$232.00	99-05
ABU	1500C DLX	black/gold, wood box, NOT MET	NIB	$860.00	01-03
ABU	1750 Freespool	red	EX-	$50.00	99-06
ABU	1750A	free spool	EX+	$91.00	02-08
ABU	1750A	red/white spacers	mint	$102.00	05-07
ABU	1750A		VG	$51.00	99-05
ABU	1750A		EX	$97.00	99-09
ABU	1750A		mint	$165.83	99-05
ABU	2100 Sport		EXIB	$311.99	99-06
ABU	2500 (C?)	short twin handles	EX-	$147.50	99-11
ABU	2500 C	all goodies	NIB	$305.00	98-12
ABU	2500C	2 pearl	EX	$135.00	98-12
ABU	2500C	770100, silver	EX-	$73.00	05-07
ABU	2500C	all goodies	NIB	$276.01	99-02
ABU	2500C	box, case, parts	EXIB	$172.00	99-09

BRAND	MODEL	SERIES / MFG. CODE / DESCRIPTION	GRADE	PRICE	DATE yy/mm
ABU	2500C	near mint	EX+	$152.50	99-01
ABU	2500C	NOT MET	EX	$71.00	00-04
ABU	2500C	NOT MET	EX-	$114.00	00-09
ABU	2500C	pouch	mint	$256.80	00-01
ABU	2500C	silver	EX	$83.00	99-03
ABU	2500C		EX-	$67.00	00-07
ABU	2500C		EX	$83.00	99-03
ABU	2500C		EX	$102.50	99-01
ABU	2500C		VG	$102.50	99-03
ABU	2500C		EX-	$105.49	99-06
ABU	2500C		EX	$110.00	99-05
ABU	2500C		mint	$122.50	99-02
ABU	2500C		VG	$127.50	98-12
ABU	2500C		NIB	$171.00	99-07
ABU	2500C		NIB	$183.55	99-03
ABU	33 DeLuxe	gold/black, wood box, NOT MET	NIB	$358.00	99-03
ABU	3500C	modern	NIB	$150.00	99-01
ABU	3500C	modern, no knob	EX	$92.00	98-12
ABU	3500C	modern, no knob, silver	EX	$107.49	99-02
ABU	4000D	bad rash	avg	$162.50	99-02
ABU	4000D	bad rash, NOT MET	VG-	$152.00	99-04
ABU	4000D	boat rash	VG-	$112.50	99-05
ABU	4000D	bronze	EX-	$192.00	00-08
ABU	4000D	brown	VG+	$107.00	01-05
ABU	4000D	copper	EX-	$152.00	00-04
ABU	4000D	copper	EX-	$165.00	99-10
ABU	4000D	crisp box	NIB	$504.00	03-04
ABU	4000D	dbl black handle	mint	$436.00	99-01
ABU	4000D	gold? not really	VG+	$183.00	02-02
ABU	4000D	NOT MET	G	$77.00	00-05
ABU	4000D	papers	EX+IB	$520.00	00-01
ABU	4000D	741000	EX-	$237.00	04-03
ABU	4000D		VG	$45.00	99-04
ABU	4000D		VG	$91.00	99-07
ABU	4000D		VG	$138.50	99-04
ABU	4000D		VG	$150.01	99-08
ABU	4000D		VG+	$167.00	00-10
ABU	4000D		VG+	$169.50	99-04
ABU	4000D		EX-	$193.00	99-01
ABU	4000D		VG+	$200.00	01-11
ABU	4000D		EX	$222.00	00-09
ABU	4000D		EX	$234.00	99-03
ABU	4000D		VG	$242.50	99-01
ABU	4000D		EX+	$261.00	00-10
ABU	4000D		mint	$285.00	00-04
ABU	4000D		EX	$325.00	99-11
ABU	444A	Service	EX	$204.00	00-08
ABU	444A	spinning, looks like Cardinal	EX-	$202.00	98-12

BRAND	MODEL	SERIES / MFG. CODE / DESCRIPTION	GRADE	PRICE	DATE yy/mm
ABU	4500C	2, both with extra spools	EX	$255.00	99-03
ABU	4500C	extra spool	EX-	$127.50	99-06
ABU	4500C	modern	EX	$45.95	99-02
ABU	4500C		VG-	$71.00	99-06
ABU	4500C		EX	$105.00	00-03
ABU	4500C		VG+	$125.50	99-03
ABU	4500C		NIB	$280.00	99-03
ABU	4500C		NIB	$371.00	99-11
ABU	4500CB	box	EXIB	$76.53	99-02
ABU	4500CS	modern	NIB	$136.60	99-03
ABU	4500D	green, NOT MET	mint	$510.00	02-02
ABU	4600C	black/red thumb bar	EX	$303.00	99-01
ABU	4600C	newer type	NIB	$41.01	98-12
ABU	4600C	red thumb bar	EX	$204.50	99-11
ABU	4600C	red thumb bar, box, papers	VG+IB	$255.50	99-02
ABU	4600C	red thumb bar, goodies	EXIB	$132.50	99-07
ABU	4600C	red thumb bar, black finish, 780200	EX	$125.00	05-07
ABU	4600CB	red, smooth side, NOT MET	EX	$43.00	00-10
ABU	4600CS	red, NOT MET	EX	$102.50	99-01
ABU	5000	pouch	EX-IP	$80.00	00-08
ABU	5000 CDL	wood box & goodies	NIB	$355.00	02-06
ABU	5000 Handles	2 red, 2 pearl, 1 black	VG	$82.00	98-12
ABU	5000A	3-screw	NIB	$285.01	99-05
ABU	5000A	4-screw, all goodies	NIB	$380.00	99-06
ABU	5000A	box and goodies, 2 pearl	EXIB	$212.00	99-01
ABU	5000B	3-screw	EX-	$96.00	00-08
ABU	5000B	3-screw, counterbalance	VG+	$132.00	99-01
ABU	5000B	nice display box, 3-screw	NIB	$255.00	01-08
ABU	5000C	#047200, near mint	EXIB	$152.50	00-02
ABU	5000C	3-screw	VG+	$96.00	98-12
ABU	5000C	4-screw, alum arbor, no ABU pouch	EX+IP	$522.00	01-04
ABU	5000C	4-screw, case & papers	near mint	$360.00	99-03
ABU	5000C	75th anniversary, NOT MET	NIB	$153.03	99-03
ABU	5000C	75th anniversary, polished chrome	NIB	$250.00	99-03
ABU	5000C	75th anniversary, stainless steel	NIB	$225.00	98-12
ABU	5000C	black	EX	$202.50	99-09
ABU	5000C	black case only with parts	EX	$25.00	99-02
ABU	5000C	serial no. 010102, black finish	NM	$27.50	04-11
ABU	5000C	black, works good	avg	$33.00	99-01
ABU	5000C	black, wrong handle	VG-	$62.00	99-01
ABU	5000C	black, wrong handle	VG+	$85.00	99-01
ABU	5000C	box and goodies	EXIB	$212.50	99-05
ABU	5000C	box and goodies	NIB	$355.00	99-07
ABU	5000C	box and goodies, sm edge rub	EXIB	$261.00	99-02
ABU	5000C	case and goodies	mint	$345.00	99-11
ABU	5000C	counterbalance handle	EX-	$112.50	98-12
ABU	5000C	leather case included	VG	$132.00	99-01
ABU	5000C	leather pouch	mint	$355.00	99-03

BRAND	MODEL	SERIES / MFG. CODE / DESCRIPTION	GRADE	PRICE	DATE yy/mm
ABU	5000C	serial no. 730402, nice	mint	$142.00	02-06
ABU	5000C	no goodies	mint	$313.00	99-02
ABU	5000C	papers	EXIB	$232.50	99-07
ABU	5000C	pouch, box, goodies	EXIB	$179.51	99-01
ABU	5000C	serial no. 83983, papers	EX	$158.50	99-01
ABU	5000C	wrong handle	EX	$128.50	98-12
ABU	5000C		VG	$78.02	99-02
ABU	5000C		VG	$86.00	99-01
ABU	5000C		EX-	$222.50	99-02
ABU	5000CDL	no box, boat rash	VG	$445.00	99-02
ABU	5000CDLX	black/gold trim	EX-	$330.00	05-07
ABU	5000CDLX	wood box, T9, 1969	NIB	$885.00	03-08
ABU	5000CDL	1996 version, wood box and goodies	NIB	$355.00	99-03
ABU	5000CDL	box and goodies	NIB	$910.00	99-04
ABU	5000CDL	serial no. 86-0 89-90, wood box, goodies	NIB	$406.60	00-02
ABU	5000CDL	teak box, goodies, c. 1990	NIB	$510.00	00-02
ABU	5000CDL	wood box	EXIB	$380.00	01-01
ABU	5000CDL	wood box	NIB	$520.00	99-02
ABU	5000CDL	wood box	NIB	$570.00	99-01
ABU	5000CDL	wood box	NIB	$620.00	99-12
ABU	5000CDL	wood box	NIB	$950.00	00-08
ABU	5000CDL	wood box, all goodies	NIB	$710.00	99-05
ABU	5000D	3 handles only	VG	$38.50	99-01
ABU	5000D	all goodies	NIB	$305.00	99-08
ABU	5000D	blue teal	VG+	$273.45	99-11
ABU	5000D	box and goodies	NIB	$356.00	00-04
ABU	5000D	case and parts	VG	$87.50	98-12
ABU	5000D	champaign color	EX-	$710.00	02-07
ABU	5000D	dbl pearl, click	VG	$81.00	99-01
ABU	5000D	gold, papers	NIB	$2,850.00	99-11
ABU	5000D	741100, gold	EX-	$644.00	05-06
ABU	5000D	green	EX-	$136.00	01-01
ABU	5000D	green, NOT MET	NIB	$178.00	02-09
ABU	5000D	750200, green	EX+	$205.00	05-07
ABU	5000D	minor rash	VG+	$66.00	99-04
ABU	5000D	NOT MET	EX	$139.00	99-04
ABU	5000D	pouch and box	NIB	$187.00	01-03
ABU	5000D	ragged box	EXIB	$130.00	99-06
ABU	5000D		VG+	$41.00	00-08
ABU	5000D		VG	$55.00	98-12
ABU	5000D		avg	$56.00	98-12
ABU	5000D		VG-	$58.00	99-01
ABU	5000D		VG	$66.50	99-01
ABU	5000D		VG	$67.00	99-01
ABU	5000D		VG	$70.00	99-03
ABU	5000D		VG	$76.00	99-01
ABU	5000D		EX-	$91.00	98-12
ABU	5000D		EX-	$103.50	99-08

BRAND	MODEL	SERIES / MFG. CODE / DESCRIPTION	GRADE	PRICE	DATE yy/mm
ABU	5000D		mint	$244.85	99-11
ABU	5000D		NIB	$256.00	00-11
ABU	5000D		NIB	$305.00	99-03
ABU	5000DLX	4-screw, black/gold, wood box, c. 1962	NIB	$1,313.00	04-03
ABU	5000DLX	a little ugly	VG-	$330.00	99-03
ABU	5000DLX	all goodies, but reel rough	avgIB	$255.00	99-06
ABU	5000DLX	black/gold trim, light boat rash, replaced handle?	EX-	$396.00	05-06
ABU	5000DLX	black/gold, boat rash	VG	$197.00	00-10
ABU	5000DLX	in box, goodies	EXIB	$711.00	99-05
ABU	5000DLX	some roughness	EX	$601.00	99-01
ABU	5000DLX	wood box, goodies, NOT MET	EXIB	$810.00	00-04
ABU	5000DLX	wood box, all goodies	NIB	$910.00	00-11
ABU	5000DLX	wood box, extra side plate, "John Lee," NOT MET	NIB	$899.00	05-07
ABU	5001C	3-screw	EXIB	$125.00	00-08
ABU	5001C	4 used reels	VG	$455.00	99-02
ABU	5001C	black	EX-	$84.00	01-06
ABU	5001C	goodies	EXIP	$368.50	00-01
ABU	5001C	new in box, with mint goodies	NIB	$372.00	04-12
ABU	5001C	pouch	EX	$162.00	00-07
ABU	5001C		EX	$96.00	99-03
ABU	5001C		EX-	$104.00	01-03
ABU	5001C		VG	$120.00	00-10
ABU	5001C		VG	$152.50	99-01
ABU	5001C		NIB	$315.00	99-05
ABU	5001C, 6001C	two diff, NOT MET	EX-	$1,625.00	99-08
ABU	500DLX	wood box, NOT MET	EXIB	$738.00	99-03
ABU	503 Spincast	underslung, black/gold	mint	$147.50	99-01
ABU	505 Spincast	underslung, black/red	EX-	$130.00	99-01
ABU	506M	underslung closed face	EXIB	$179.00	00-04
ABU	506M	underslung	mint	$202.50	99-01
ABU	507 Spincast	oiler and goodies	VGIB	$154.50	99-06
ABU	507 Spincast	underslung, black/silver?	EX-	$126.00	99-01
ABU	5500C	2, both steel, blue	EX	$800.00	99-02
ABU	5500C	Abu Garcia box, no goodies	NIB	$518.99	99-04
ABU	5500C	black	EX-	$89.00	99-02
ABU	5500C	black	EX-	$207.50	99-02
ABU	5500C	serial no. 800804, black, goodies	NIB	$380.00	02-06
ABU	5500C	blue-gray color	NIB	$820.00	99-12
ABU	5500C	case, and goodies	EX-	$168.50	99-04
ABU	5500C	gold plated, wood box, c. 1972	NIB	$3,800.00	05-01
ABU	5500C	green? nice box, pouch & goodies	EXIB	$542.00	05-07
ABU	5500C	power handle	EX-	$95.99	99-02
ABU	5500C	rough	avg.	$46.01	99-03
ABU	5500C	serial no. 771103, goodies	NIB	$338.00	02-06
ABU	5500C	serial no. 790303, goodies	NIB	$283.00	02-06
ABU	5500C	serial no. 730401	EX-	$154.00	01-02
ABU	5500C	silver	rough	$61.00	98-12
ABU	5500C		EX-	$56.00	99-06

BRAND	MODEL	SERIES / MFG. CODE / DESCRIPTION	GRADE	PRICE	DATE yy/mm
ABU	5500C		VG	$103.38	98-12
ABU	5500C		EX-	$160.00	00-07
ABU	5500C		VG+	$162.50	99-04
ABU	5500C		mint	$182.00	01-08
ABU	5500CDL	teak box	NIB	$4,000.00	02-02
ABU	5500D	green	EX	$225.00	02-10
ABU	5500D	NOT MET	EX-IB	$212.50	99-08
ABU	5500D	serial no. 771100	EX	$202.52	99-01
ABU	5600C	red thumb bar	VG	$71.00	99-07
ABU	5600C	red thumb bar	EX	$96.00	99-04
ABU	5600C	red thumb bar	VG-	$103.49	99-03
ABU	5600C	red thumb bar	VG+	$112.50	99-04
ABU	5600C	red thumb bar	EX-	$115.00	04-12
ABU	5600C	red thumb bar	EX	$127.50	99-03
ABU	5600C	red thumb bar, rebuilt	VG	$135.00	98-12
ABU	5600CDL	662/1000, fancy box	NIB	$350.00	99-04
ABU	5600CDL	795/1000, modern fancy box	NIB	$197.50	99-04
ABU	6000C	3-screw, NOT MET	EX	$61.00	01-10
ABU	6000C	black	VG+	$61.00	00-09
ABU	6000C	black	mint	$225.35	99-02
ABU	6000C	serial no. 7301010, black finish, tiny nick on rim	EX	$55.00	04-11
ABU	6000C	box and all goodies	NIB	$268.00	00-03
ABU	6000C	case only with goodies	mint	$50.00	99-03
ABU	6000C		EX+	$182.50	99-03
ABU	6000C		NIB	$328.00	99-03
ABU	6000C (red?)	4-screw, DP & CB handles	EX	$107.49	99-02
ABU	6001C	1987 model	NIB	$142.79	99-04
ABU	6001C	serial no. 87	NIB	$129.50	00-01
ABU	6001C		VG	$102.51	99-05
ABU	6500A	high speed, smooth side plates, newer model	EX+	$168.00	05-07
ABU	6500C	No. 750902, pouch & goodies	EXIP	$310.00	00-09
ABU	6500C	black?	NIB	$366.00	98-12
ABU	6500C	box, goodies silver?	NIB	$416.50	99-02
ABU	6500C	box, pouch & all goodies	NIB	$357.00	01-03
ABU	6500C	purple silver	EX-	$330.00	00-02
ABU	6500C	serial no. 730801	EX	$229.00	02-06
ABU	6500C	silver	EX-	$144.50	99-01
ABU	6500C	with pouch	EX	$168.30	99-02
ABU	6500C		EXIB	$107.50	99-03
ABU	6500C		EX	$168.00	98-12
ABU	6500C3	bubble pack	NOC	$65.00	99-01
ABU	6500C3	CT, Mag Elite	NIB	$130.50	99-01
ABU	6500C3	left handed	EX	$63.51	99-01
ABU	6600C	red thumb bar	VG+	$285.00	01-01
ABU	6600CL	click	EX	$71.00	99-01
ABU	7000C	black, NOT MET	NIB	$96.00	00-09
ABU	7000C	Synchro, modern	NIB	$134.24	99-03
ABU	Abu-matic 120	NOT MET	EX	$18.00	99-01

BRAND	MODEL	SERIES / MFG. CODE / DESCRIPTION	GRADE	PRICE	DATE yy/mm
ABU	Abu-Matic 170	NOT MET	EX	$20.50	99-01
ABU	Abu-Matic 80	sm dent, box	VGIB	$51.00	99-03
ABU	Ambassadeur	anniversary reel w/presentation wood box, issued 1995, limited edition, 1000 issued, silver and black finish, reel no. 798 engraved on back plate	NEW	$220.00	05-04
ABU	Ambassadeur	anniversary, chrome, NOT MET	NIB	$256.00	00-08
ABU	Ambassadeur 30	leather case, papers	NIB	$158.05	99-07
ABU	Ambassaduer Black 5000 C	made in Sweden, never used, in leather box, contents	NIB	$300.00	05-05
ABU	Cardinal	880/1000, wood box, gold plate, NOT MET	NIB	$555.00	03-11
ABU	Cardinal 154	spin	mint	$61.00	99-05
ABU	Cardinal 154	Spincast		$38.50	99-01
ABU	Cardinal 157	Garcia	EX	$61.50	99-04
ABU	Cardinal 222	green, spinning	VG	$217.50	99-06
ABU	Cardinal 3	beige/black, all goodies, spool	NIB	$215.00	99-04
ABU	Cardinal 3	brown	EX	$190.00	99-07
ABU	Cardinal 3	crisp box & extra spool	NIB	$180.00	05-07
ABU	Cardinal 3	crisp box & goodies	NIB	$180.00	05-07
ABU	Cardinal 3	crisp box, NOT MET	NIB	$177.00	04-12
ABU	Cardinal 3	extra spool, box and goodies	EXIB	$187.50	99-08
ABU	Cardinal 3	gray/blk spool	EX	$224.50	99-01
ABU	Cardinal 3		mint	$224.00	99-01
ABU	Cardinal 33	1 type #750100	EX	$202.50	99-08
ABU	Cardinal 33	2 type #750600	NIB	$180.50	99-08
ABU	Cardinal 33	3 type #761000	NIB	$204.50	99-08
ABU	Cardinal 33	rough box, NOT MET	mint	$151.00	00-04
ABU	Cardinal 33	spare spool	NIB	$94.00	00-09
ABU	Cardinal 33	spinning, like Zebco	EX	$89.55	99-05
ABU	Cardinal 33	with oiler, spool, goodies	EXIB	$100.00	00-04
ABU	Cardinal 4	beige frame/blk rotor	EX+	$204.49	99-06
ABU	Cardinal 4	black rotor/beige frame	EX-	$122.50	99-06
ABU	Cardinal 4	crisp box & goodies	NIB	$97.00	01-06
ABU	Cardinal 4		avg	$71.00	99-09
ABU	Cardinal 4		EXIB	$152.50	99-10
ABU	Cardinal 4		mint	$157.50	00-01
ABU	Cardinal 40	blue/white	EX	$67.00	00-07
ABU	Cardinal 40		VGIB	$81.00	00-11
ABU	Cardinal 40		NIB	$155.40	00-02
ABU	Cardinal 44	Express, rare UK tourney special	NIB	$467.00	00-11
ABU	Cardinal 44	serial no. 37200	EX	$168.50	99-09
ABU	Cardinal 44	spinning	VG+	$93.00	99-05
ABU	Cardinal 4X	beige/dark brown	VG	$195.00	99-04
ABU	Cardinal 4X	extra spool & goodies, crisp box	NIB	$311.00	01-05
ABU	Cardinal 4X	gray/maroon rotor	EX	$198.00	01-03
ABU	Cardinal 4X	nice box	EXIB	$167.00	03-08
ABU	Cardinal 4X	rare	EX	$132.51	99-08
ABU	Cardinal 52	Sweden, black	EX-	$85.00	04-11
ABU	Cardinal 54	nice box & goodies	NIB	$107.00	00-04

BRAND	MODEL	SERIES / MFG. CODE / DESCRIPTION	GRADE	PRICE	DATE yy/mm
ABU	Cardinal 55	skirted spool	EX	$49.50	99-08
ABU	Cardinal 6	similar to Zebco, papers	NIB	$250.00	01-10
ABU	Cardinal 6		VG	$76.00	99-01
ABU	Cardinal 60		NIB	$191.40	00-01
ABU	Cardinal 60A	brown/black	EX	$116.50	99-01
ABU	Cardinal 66	extra spool	NIB	$135.05	99-08
ABU	Cardinal 66	nice box & extra spool + goodies	NIB	$272.00	04-11
ABU	Cardinal 753		NIB	$32.00	99-01
ABU	Cardinal 77	cream/green, NOT MET	mint	$66.00	00-10
ABU	Cardinal 77	extra spool	NIB	$142.50	99-08
ABU	Cardinal 77		EXIB	$102.50	99-10
ABU	Cardinal 77X	goodies	NIB	$152.00	00-02
ABU	Cardinal 77X	NOT MET	EX-	$77.00	99-01
ABU	Cardinal 77X		VG	$57.99	99-06
ABU	Cardinal C4X	extra spool	NIB	$101.00	01-08
ABU	Cardinal C4X	extra spool, nice box & goodies	NIB	$125.00	05-07
ABU	Cardinal C4X		EX	$86.02	99-03
ABU	Diplomat 178		VG	$76.00	99-06
ABU	Diplomat 601M	Spincast	NIB	$36.00	99-05
ABU	Fast Cast 1	spinning	NIB	$52.99	99-05
ABU	Morrum MM	wood box & goodies	NIB	$310.00	02-06
ABU	Record 1800A	NOT MET	VG	$91.00	99-01
ABU	Record 1800C	bag and box	EX-IB	$93.00	99-08
ABU	Record 2100 Sport	leather-soft pouch included	EX-	$225.00	05-07
ABU	Record 600	spinning	VG	$192.50	99-07
ABU	Record Flyer 3000	box, great access, spool in tube, etc.	NIB	$736.00	00-09
ABU	Record Sport 2100	narrow spool	VG+	$237.50	99-06
ABU	Record Standard	fly reel	EX-	$100.00	05-07
ABU	Spin	similar to Cardinal, name on side	EX-	$142.50	99-02
ABU	T6600CL	tournament	NIB	$91.00	99-01
ABU	Tournament Reel	No. 2100, narrow spool reel, thumb activated, free spool lever, knurled thumb rest, black plates	EX	$522.50	05-04
ABU	Ultra Mag XL 1V	serial no. 850100	mint	$151.00	02-06
ABU	Ultra Mag XL II	nice box	EXIB	$168.00	05-07
ABU	75	75th anniversary, wood box, goodies, NOT MET	NIB	$243.00	00-05
ABU	136	Spincast	EX	$20.00	99-01
ABU	170	Abu Matic	NIB	$102.50	99-03
ABU	170		NIB	$89.00	01-08
ABU	222	spinning, ugly green, rinky-dink	NIB	$212.50	99-12
ABU	222		VG	$200.00	99-04
ABU	225	spinning	mint	$290.00	98-12
ABU	290		NIB	$56.00	99-03
ABU	333	spinning	EX-	$107.50	99-05
ABU	444	black/gray	EXIB	$207.50	99-03
ABU	444	looks similar to Zebco Cardinal 4	EX	$76.00	00-10
ABU	444	spinning	EX-	$90.00	98-12
ABU	501	nice box	NIB	$152.00	00-09
ABU	501	underslung, Spincast	EXIB	$177.50	99-03

BRAND	MODEL	SERIES / MFG. CODE / DESCRIPTION	GRADE	PRICE	DATE yy/mm
ABU	503	Spincast	EX	$73.00	99-05
ABU	503	underslung, closed face	NIB	$405.00	00-01
ABU	505	black/red, Spincast	EX-	$122.50	99-01
ABU	505	underslung, closed face	EX-	$213.50	99-03
ABU	505	underslung, Spincast	near mint	$190.00	98-12
ABU	505		EX	$79.00	00-07
ABU	505		EX	$112.50	99-03
ABU	505		VG	$153.50	99-03
ABU	505		EX+	$202.50	99-03
ABU	506	Spincast	EX-	$52.00	99-05
ABU	506	underslung, Spincast, in nice custom wood box	EX	$88.00	05-07
ABU	506	underslung, Spincast	EX	$76.00	99-08
ABU	506		EX	$83.00	00-07
ABU	506		VG	$86.00	00-05
ABU	506		EX	$128.50	99-03
ABU	507	blue box	NIB	$190.00	99-09
ABU	507		EX	$183.50	99-04
ABU	520	closed faced, spinning	EX-	$79.00	99-08
ABU	520	underslung, Spincast	EX	$66.00	04-02
ABU	1000	stainless, modern	EX	$102.50	99-01
ABU	1000	white, 1 knob	NIB	$108.00	00-09
ABU	1044	closed face spinning, x spool, goodies	NIB	$123.50	99-06
ABU	1750	clicker broke	EX	$151.50	99-09
ABU	2000	direct drive	EX-	$114.00	01-09
ABU	2000	red, white spacers	EX	$153.00	05-07
ABU	2000		EX	$150.00	99-09
ABU	2000		mint	$187.50	99-05
ABU	2050	great box, goodies	NIB	$521.00	05-06
ABU	2050	nice box, goodies	NMIB	$333.00	99-06
ABU	2050	pouch	EX	$117.56	99-02
ABU	2050	pouch, narrow spool	VG	$150.00	99-01
ABU	2500	direct drive	EX-	$277.00	01-09
ABU	2600	FS, SD, red/white spacers	EX-	$140.00	99-01
ABU	2650		EX	$177.50	99-08
ABU	3000	brown	EX	$222.50	99-06
ABU	3000	casting, FS, SD	VG+	$41.00	04-12
ABU	3000		VG+	$35.00	01-08
ABU	4000	red	EX	$138.50	99-06
ABU	4000	suede pouch, goodies, nice	EX	$157.50	99-01
ABU	4500	NOT MET	mint	$212.00	01-11
ABU	4500	red	EX-	$200.00	00-09
ABU	4500	red	EX-	$206.00	00-09
ABU	4500	red	EX	$225.01	99-08
ABU	4500	red	mint	$263.00	99-10
ABU	4500	red	EX+	$356.02	99-06
ABU	4500	No. 780100, red	EX	$208.00	05-07
ABU	4500	red, pouch, 3-screw	EX	$228.00	00-08
ABU	4500	red, power handle	EX	$261.99	99-11

BRAND	MODEL	SERIES / MFG. CODE / DESCRIPTION	GRADE	PRICE	DATE yy/mm
ABU	4500		VG	$172.51	99-07
ABU	5000	3-screw	VG	$67.00	99-01
ABU	5000	3-screw, case and goodies, mint	NIC	$212.50	99-02
ABU	5000	3-screw, case, dbl	VG	$115.50	99-02
ABU	5000	3-screw, dbl pearl, all accessories	near mint	$200.75	99-01
ABU	5000	3-screw, double	VG+	$81.00	99-01
ABU	5000	3-screw, all accessories	near mint	$176.00	99-01
ABU	5000	3-screw, case and goodies	VG	$55.55	99-01
ABU	5000	3-screw, purty	EX	$43.50	99-11
ABU	5000	3-screw, rash, 2 blk handles	VG	$95.00	98-12
ABU	5000	4-screw	mint	$129.00	00-10
ABU	5000	4-screw, in pouch	EX	$348.00	00-07
ABU	5000	4-screw, case	EX	$168.51	98-12
ABU	5000	4-screw, smooth sides	avg	$42.00	99-01
ABU	5000	4-screw, broken handle	EX	$46.00	99-01
ABU	5000	4-screw, case, parts, oiler	mint	$182.50	99-03
ABU	5000	4-screw, dbl pearl, goodies & case	NIC	$167.50	99-03
ABU	5000	4-screw, dbl pearl, accessories	EX	$187.00	99-01
ABU	5000	4-screw, double pearl, goodies	EX	$197.00	99-01
ABU	5000	4-screw, oil holes, goodies	EXIP	$184.50	99-05
ABU	5000	4-screw	VG	$81.05	99-02
ABU	5000	4-screw, dbl, pearl, pouch, accessories	EXIP	$128.00	00-10
ABU	5000	4-screw, goodies, pouch	NIP	$158.00	00-10
ABU	5000	4-screw, case, 2 pearl	VG	$60.00	98-12
ABU	5000	4-screw, case, oil hole, nice	EXIB	$50.00	99-08
ABU	5000	4-screw, dbl pearl, goodies	VG	$115.00	99-01
ABU	5000	4-screw, goodies	NIB	$456.00	99-07
ABU	5000	4-screw, NOT MET	EXIB	$230.00	99-06
ABU	5000	No. 800900, 3-screw	EX+	$119.00	05-07
ABU	5000	case and all goodies, mint	NIB	$231.49	99-04
ABU	5000	case and goodies only	EX	$51.00	99-02
ABU	5000	case and parts tube	EX	$143.00	01-01
ABU	5000	case, catalog, 4-screw, dbl pearl	EX+	$165.50	99-11
ABU	5000	dbl pearl, 3-screw, case & goodies	mint	$201.00	99-12
ABU	5000	dbl pearl, 3-screw, goodies, NOT MET	NIP	$95.00	00-04
ABU	5000	double knob handle	VG	$87.00	98-12
ABU	5000	Garcia, black label, no goodies	NIB	$150.00	99-04
ABU	5000	record paperwork, goodies, wowser	NIB	$548.00	99-11
ABU	5000	single handle	VG	$41.00	98-12
ABU	5000	with case	EX	$75.00	99-01
ABU	5000	with case	VG	$62.00	99-01
ABU	5000	wrong handle	VG	$51.00	99-01
ABU	5000		VG	$44.52	98-12
ABU	5000		VG	$50.00	99-01
ABU	5500	bronze	EX-	$172.00	01-08
ABU	5500	bronze	VG+	$307.50	99-06
ABU	5500	bronze, goodies	EXIB	$395.00	01-08
ABU	5500	brown	VG	$127.50	99-04

BRAND	MODEL	SERIES / MFG. CODE / DESCRIPTION	GRADE	PRICE	DATE yy/mm
ABU	5500	brown	EX-	$222.50	00-03
ABU	5500	brown	VG-	$242.49	00-01
ABU	5500	brown	EX	$255.00	00-10
ABU	5500	brown	EX-	$268.00	01-04
ABU	5500	brown	EX-	$275.00	03-08
ABU	5500	brown	near mint	$341.66	99-03
ABU	5500	brown	NIB	$610.00	00-04
ABU	5500	brown, pouch, papers	mint	$405.00	00-09
ABU	5500	brown, with case	EX-	$370.00	99-10
ABU	5500	brown, much rash	fair	$81.00	99-01
ABU	5500	gold, NOT MET	EX	$1,274.99	98-12
ABU	5500	maroon	VG+	$204.00	01-11
ABU	5500	No. 760301, maroon	EX	$376.00	99-09
ABU	5500	red	EX	$167.50	99-03
ABU	5500	red	VG	$202.49	99-06
ABU	5500	red	EX	$233.50	99-03
ABU	5500	red	EX	$256.00	99-11
ABU	5500	red	EXIB	$371.00	01-08
ABU	5500	red	EX	$415.00	99-11
ABU	5500	red	NIB	$700.00	02-02
ABU	5500	"800800" on foot, not a 5500C, red	mint	$407.00	05-02
ABU	6000	3-screw, case	EX	$191.00	99-01
ABU	6000	3-screw	EX	$90.99	99-09
ABU	6000	4-screw	EX	$80.00	98-12
ABU	6000	4-screw	EX	$95.00	98-12
ABU	6000	4-screw, counterbalance, goodies	NIP	$302.00	01-03
ABU	6000	4-screw, box and pouch	EXIB	$97.50	99-01
ABU	6000	4-screw, case	EX	$150.00	99-03
ABU	6000	4-screw, CB handle, case & goodies	EXIB	$150.00	99-03
ABU	6000	4-screw, old CB handle #020902	EX	$96.00	99-02
ABU	6000	4-screw, papers, mint goodies	NIB	$346.00	00-10
ABU	6000	4-screw, leather case, box	EXIB	$91.00	98-12
ABU	6000	case, part, box	EX	$66.00	98-12
ABU	6000	CB	EX-	$80.00	99-01
ABU	6000	much rubs	G	$37.00	99-02
ABU	6000	no serial #	VG-	$58.00	99-03
ABU	6000	Service	EX	$315.00	00-08
ABU	6000		VG	$51.00	98-12
ABU	6500	brown in nice box	NIB	$670.00	02-09
ABU	6500	No. 761100, brown, high speed, boat rash	VG+	$294.00	05-07
ABU	6500	red	NIB	$355.00	99-07
ABU	6500	No. 700201, red, high speed	EX-	$265.00	01-12
ABU	6500	red, CB, handle, 3-screw	mint	$455.00	99-02
ABU	7000	box, papers	VG	$118.49	99-01
ABU	7000	disassembled! parts only	VG	$76.98	99-02
ABU	7000	green, "Pro Shop"	NIB	$177.50	99-03
ABU	7000	maroon	mint	$93.79	99-01
ABU	7000	NOT MET	NIB	$132.00	01-08

BRAND	MODEL	SERIES / MFG. CODE / DESCRIPTION	GRADE	PRICE	DATE yy/mm
ABU	7000	red	EX-	$87.00	99-01
ABU	7000		VG+	$91.00	99-02
ABU	7000		EX	$98.00	99-02
ABU	7000		NIB	$207.50	99-05
ABU	7000		near mint	$271.00	99-01
ABU	8000	3 speed, red	EX	$227.00	01-08
ABU	8600	Ambassadeur	VG+	$152.00	01-03
ABU	8600	deep sea	EX	$136.00	00-10
ABU	8600		EX	$122.00	01-08
ABU	9000	box & goodies EX	EXIB	$360.00	05-07
ABU	9000	red	EX	$222.00	05-04
ABU Record	Standard	nice box	NIB	$228.50	99-08
ABU-Garcia	Ambassadeur 30	salt water, goodies	EXIB	$158.05	99-07
Adams, Bill	Tiny Trout Reel	2¾" dia., 1" wide spool reel, w/Adam reels, marked case	EX	$192.50	04-11
Adcock	Stanton	centerpin, 4¾"	EX-	$134.00	05-07
Aero Products	Aerocast	3-knob handle, plastic or Bakelite	EX-	$77.00	05-03
Aero Products	Aerocast 329	triple handle, LW casting, crisp box	NIB	$152.00	05-07
Airex	2A	in box, works OK but lots of wear	VGIB	$10.00	04-12
Airex	Larchmont	by Lionel, pouch and goodies	NIB	$141.50	00-03
Airex	Larchmont	parts, all goodies, mint box	NIB	$107.00	98-12
Airex	Larchmont	spinning	EX-	$15.00	01-08
Airex	spool x 12	nice box, 12-pack, Lionel	NIB	$212.00	00-08
Airex	Vagabond	Lionel, pouch and goodies	EXIB	$44.00	01-08
Alcedo	2C		avg	$36.00	98-12
Alcedo	2CS	spinning, Italy	EX-	$50.00	01-08
Alcedo	Micron	1946 bent-leg version, extra spool	EX	$320.00	02-02
Alcedo	Micron	blue?	EX	$197.00	02-01
Alcedo	Micron	box and goodies	EXIB	$202.50	99-05
Alcedo	Micron	brown with lg-capacity spool	VG+	$428.00	03-04
Alcedo	Micron	C4	EX-	$143.00	99-01
Alcedo	Micron	extra spool, pouch	EX	$175.00	00-10
Alcedo	Micron	nice box	EXIB	$157.50	00-02
Alcedo	Micron	nice box and papers	EX+IB	$168.00	00-04
Alcedo	Micron	nice box, papers, spare spool	NIB	$185.00	00-10
Alcedo	Micron		VG	$63.75	99-01
Alcedo	Micron		EX	$90.00	99-02
Alcedo	Micron		EX-	$92.00	00-04
Alcedo	Micron		NIB	$155.00	99-11
Alcock-Stanley	Spin	early, ugly, NOT MET	VG+	$77.00	00-04
Alfred & Sons	Brass Handle Plate Trout Reel	engraved "Alfred & Sons — makers — 20 Moorgate St. London" on front plate, 2⅞" dia.	EX	$181.50	05-04
Allcock	Aerial	3½", works perfectly	EX-	$365.00	05-07
Allcock	Aerial	4", not marked, open spokes/cage type	VG+	$1,280.00	05-07
Allcock	Aerial	Ebonite, works okay but has repairs	avg	$421.00	05-07
Allcock	Aerial	3" ventilated spool, c. 1910	EX-	$550.00	02-08
Allcock	Aerial	4" ventilated narrow spool, trademark, c. 1920	EX	$610.00	02-08
Allcock	Aerial	4" ventilated wide spool, no trademark, c. 1920	EX-	$545.00	02-08

BRAND	MODEL	SERIES / MFG. CODE / DESCRIPTION	GRADE	PRICE	DATE yy/mm
Allcock	Aerial-Match	made only in 1939, box VG+	EX-IB	$2,706.00	03-12
Allcock	Stanley	1930s spinning reel, works fine but ugly paint	avg	$61.00	05-07
Allcock	Viking	4½", Bickerdyke line guide, scratches	VG	$61.00	04-01
Allcocks	Black Knight		EXIB	$102.50	99-01
Allcocks	Felton	spinning, crosswind, missing much paint	avg	$65.00	05-07
Allcocks	Match Aerial	red box, black reel, 4½"	NIB	$433.00	03-12
Allcocks	Pattern 9 Centrepin	made only in 1939	EX-	$484.00	01-09
Allen	Spinet	spinning, c. 1925, exposed gears, England	EX-	$175.00	03-07
Am. Display Co.	Stubby	rod & reel combo	VG	$17.00	04-12
America	No. 2	gs, 1902 pat, quick takedown	EX-	$260.00	02-12
Ari't Hart	F4	2 extra spools, pouches, NOT MET	mint	$365.00	00-09
Arjon	600 Spincast	goodies, $200 NOT MET	NIB	$76.00	01-04
Arjon	Champion	red, Swedish, leather pouch, purty	NIP	$830.00	00-10
Arjon	Commander	gold	EX	$400.00	00-10
Arjon	Commander	leather pouch, parts tubes, papers	NIP	$355.00	02-08
Arjon	Commander	pouch & goodies	NIP	$1,093.00	01-04
Arjon	Commander	silver-gray, nice pouch & goodies	NIP	$695.00	05-07
Arjon	Commander	Sweden	EX-	$338.00	03-12
Armax	Baitcasting	plain	VG	$63.00	99-01
Art Fargo	Spinning	rotate spool type	EX	$107.00	04-01
Ayers & Son	St. Johns	fly, brass or g. silver, purty	EX	$77.00	02-01
Bache Brown	Spinster Mark VI	spinning	EX-	$69.00	99-01
Beetzsel	Bait Casting Reel	jeweled bearing caps, level wind mechanism, falling line guide, rare spool attachment	EX	$220.00	05-04
Beetzsel	Casting	level wind, German, case, nice	EX	$385.00	00-03
Billinghurst	Fly	folding handle, c. 1859	EX	$2,782.00	04-11
Blue Grass	No. 3	serial no. 11262, marked "G.S.," handmade bait casting reel, 2" dia., 1⅝" wide, replaced handle	VG-	$137.50	04-11
Blue Grass	No. 4	serial no. 14584, jeweled end cap, front click and drag switches	EX	$385.00	05-04
Blue Grass	No. 3	serial no. 801, gs, c. 1898, 2" dia., 1⅝" wide spool reel, jeweled	EX	$660.00	05-04
Blue Grass	Simplex No. 25	gs, bait casting reel, rear click switch and crew off, markings, marked "E" on foot	EX	$220.00	05-04
Blue Grass	Simplex No. 25	gs, bait casting reel, 1⅞" dia. and 1½" wide spool, take-apart reel, rear click switch	G	$55.00	04-11
Blue Grass Reel Works	No. 3	missing one screw, "589" on foot	VG	$344.00	05-07
Blue Grass Reel works	No. 3	serial no. 8620, gs, click and drag switches, inoperable	VG	$203.50	05-04
Blue Grass Reel works	No. 3	gs, handmade bait casting reel, 2" dia., 1⅝" wide, smooth click, replaced handle grasp	VG	$220.00	04-11
Blue Grass Reel works	No. 3	serial no. 1727, marked "G.S.," bait casting reel, circa 1898, 2" dia., 1⅝" wide	VG	$660.00	04-11
Blue Grass Reel works	No. 3	serial no. 846, name engraved, NOT MET	EX-	$604.00	02-08
Bogdan	No. 1 Salmon	c. 1977, NOT MET	EX-	$1,326.00	99-06
Bogdan	3¾"	3/0?	EX-	$921.00	01-02
Bogdan	No. 50?	3⅛" x 1⅛"	mint	$1,725.00	00-09

BRAND	MODEL	SERIES / MFG. CODE / DESCRIPTION	GRADE	PRICE	DATE yy/mm
Bogdan	Handmade Baby Trout Reel w/Pouch	2⅝" dia., ⅝" wide spool, silver anodized, with black plates	NM	$1,595.00	04-11
Bogdan	No. 1 Salmon Multiplier	NOT MET	EX	$1,225.00	01-04
Bourne & Bond	Kentucky	nice	EX	$147.50	00-02
Bradford	Fly	Boston, decent, NOT MET	VG+	$1,225.00	01-08
Bradford & Anthony	Ball Handle Reel	40 yd., 1⅞" dia., 1¼" wide spool reel, rim mounted, pull drag works fine, removable rear oil cap, walnut handle grasp	EX	$495.00	05-04
Bradford & Anthony	Brass Multiplying Ball Handle Reel	300 yd., 3¼" dia., 2⅛" wide, slightly damaged, walnut handle grasp, altered foot, removable rear bearing, minor rim rash	VG	$192.50	05-04
Bradford & Anthony		2⅞" dia., 1⅞" wide spool brass reel, walnut grasp, no. 1 size marking on unfiled foot		$440.00	05-04
Bradford & Anthony	250 yd.	g. silver, 3½", S-handle	VG	$731.00	00-04
Bradford & Anthony	Brass Ball Handle Reel	all brass, 3⅝" dia., 2¼" wide spool reel, front rim, drag switch, marked "OO" on foot	EX-	$275.00	04-11
Bradley, W.H.	Single Action Casting	only known example	EX-	$9,350.00	04-11
Bronson	Coronet 25N	nice	EX	$62.00	99-07
Bronson	Invader 26	asking price	EX	$350.00	01-01
Bronson	Invader 26	box VG, papers & pouch, missing one screw	EX-IB	$413.00	05-02
Bronson	Invader 26		EX	$303.00	04-11
Bronson	Lion	No. 1800, unused in orig and colorful 2PCCB w/paperwork, M-10/C-9.5	EX+IB	$75.00	05-05
Bronson	Lion 1800	nice red box	NIB	$43.00	03-12
Bronson	Lion 2900	LW-ABL, casting reel	VG+	$11.00	04-12
Bronson	Royalist Fly Reel	No. 570, burgandy and silver aluminum, single action, very light wear, M-9.5/C-9.5	EX	$30.00	05-05
Bronson	Spinit 400	crisp box & papers	NIB	$152.00	04-01
Car Gem	17	sealed bag!	NIB	$45.00	99-08
Carlton Mfg.	GEM	fly reel, nickle plated	EX-	$109.00	05-07
Carpenter, Walt	Trout	2⅝" x 1⁄12" beauty	EX	$665.00	02-02
Centaure	Caribe	lg spinning reel, France	EX	$125.00	04-07
Centaure	Pacific	red, ½ bail, France	VG+	$22.00	04-07
Centaure	Spinning	large	EX-	$85.00	99-08
Chamberlin Cartridge & Target Co.	Hunter	c. 1910, free spool tournament, NOT MET	EX-	$306.00	05-01
Chamberlin Cartridge & Target Co.	Hunter		VG	$310.00	99-03
Chicago	Streamliner	metal side plate, case nice, NOT MET	EXIC	$175.00	99-06
Chicago	Streamliner	with rod	VG	$115.00	99-04
Chicago	Streamliner		EX	$100.00	99-06
Chicago	Streamliner 1788	Gentleman, no tip	VG	$200.00	99-04
Chicago Fishing	Streamliner 1086	reel only	EX	$224.72	99-03
Chubb, T. M.	Small Fly	raised pillar, g. silver, 1886 patent	VG+	$1,782.00	02-09
Clerk	Round Ball Handle	nice toning	VG+	$381.00	00-05
Clerk	4	nickel silver, 2¼", foot filed slightly	VG+	$760.00	02-08
Climax	Raised Pillar Reel	tiny 40 yd., light use, needs cleaning	VG+	$22.00	05-05

BRAND	MODEL	SERIES / MFG. CODE / DESCRIPTION	GRADE	PRICE	DATE yy/mm
Coit	Reel	3 colors, your choice, crisp boxes	NIB	$199.00	02-03
Conroy	2¾"	counterbalance handle	VG	$155.00	01-04
Conroy	Baitcaster	extended seat, simple, NOT MET	EX-	$351.00	01-01
Conroy	Brass Ball Handle	2" dia., 1⅜" wide spool, full length offset foot reel, early low dome rear, with oil hole	EX	$137.50	05-04
Conroy	Brass Bell Handle Reel	2⅞" dia., 1⅞" wide, marked "1" on foot brace, walnut handle, low rear bearing dome, lacking an oil hole	EX-	$247.50	05-04
Conroy	Brass Casting	lots of honest wear, looks okay	G (6/7)	$410.00	01-08
Conroy	Marked Brass Multiplying Reel	2¾" dia., 2" wide spool reel, unusual screw drag that is not operable mounted on front plate	EX	$385.00	05-04
Conroy	Salmon Fly Reel	3½", gs & Bakelite, alloy spool, raised pillar	EX	$1,303.00	05-07
Conroy Bissett & Malleson	Fly	4½", brown color	VG	$449.00	00-03
Conroy, Bissett & Malleson	Brass Ball Handle Reel	2⅞" dia., 1⅜" wide spool, full length offset foot reel, early low dome rear plating bearing with an oil hole	EX	$660.00	05-04
Conroy, Bissett & Malleson	Brass Ball Handle Reel	c. 1875, 2⅞" dia., 1⅞" wide spool reel, walnut handle, smooth operation, foot marked "150," marked leather case	VG	$660.00	05-04
Conroy, Thos. J.	Kentucky	2⅛" dia., 1¼" wide narrow spool reel, fixed oil caps are tapped, with removable screws, 6 o'clock counterbalanced handle and ivory grasp	EX	$1,237.50	05-04
Conroy/ J.Vom Hofe	Silver King 2/00	in rough Conroy leather pouch, works fine	VG+IP	$310.00	05-01
Coptes	Mousquito Kid	spinning	EX	$153.50	99-06
Coxe	10C	Bronson papers & goodies	NIB	$53.00	01-11
Coxe	14/0	cradle, NOT MET	EX-	$761.00	99-10
Coxe	1470-C	by Bronson, huge saltwater	EX	$2,660.00	05-02
Coxe	25-2	Bakelite/German silver	EX-	$98.00	99-02
Coxe	25-2	tiny knob chip	EX	$104.38	99-02
Coxe	25-23	silver/black	VG+	$183.00	99-01
Coxe	25-3	gs, marked pouch, nice	EXIP	$90.00	02-02
Coxe	25-3	wood arbor	EX-	$57.00	99-07
Coxe	25C	leather pouch, correct 2PCCB VG+	EXIB	$77.00	02-02
Coxe	25N	pouch, box, narrow spool, NOT MET	NIB	$250.00	99-05
Coxe	25N	purty	EX	$57.00	01-03
Coxe	25N	purty	EX	$74.73	99-10
Coxe	25N-2	German silver, nice case	EX	$214.50	99-01
Coxe	30C	nice box, more modern style	NIB	$66.00	99-05
Coxe	315L		VG	$53.88	99-01
Coxe	Apr-00	Zane Gray	EX	$1,481.00	04-03
Coxe	9/0	Bakelite/gs, pat 5-27-24, spool light pitting	EX-	$1,176.00	05-07
Coxe	Coronet 25	Bronson, case	EXIC	$40.00	99-08
Coxe	Coronet 25	case	EXIC	$47.76	99-07
Coxe	Coronet 25	marked pouch EX	EXIP	$60.00	02-08
Coxe	Coronet 25	oiler, papers, leather pouch	EXIP	$63.00	99-07
Coxe	Expert Twenty-20	No. 3129000, gs, knurled pillars, jeweled end caps, screw-type drag adjuster, small chips from one handle grasp	EX	$220.00	05-04

BRAND	MODEL	SERIES / MFG. CODE / DESCRIPTION	GRADE	PRICE	DATE yy/mm
Coxe	Free Spool Bait	No. 25N-2, gs, black plates, narrow spool reel, 2⅛" dia., 1⅜" wide, with click	EX	$110.00	05-04
Coxe	Invader	missing end cap	EX	$228.00	01-04
Coxe	Invader 26	FS, red/white	mint	$409.00	00-09
Coxe	Invader 26	FS, SD, red/white spacers	EX	$339.00	01-03
Coxe	15	serial no. 36, pouch, paper	EXIB	$360.00	00-09
Coxe	15	gs, with aluminum spool and level wind housing, knurled rims	EX-	$154.00	04-11
Coxe	950	500 yd., crisp box & papers, NOT MET	NIB	$102.00	02-08
Coxe	36861	silver/rubber, a beauty, NOT MET	EX+	$611.02	00-03
Coxon	Aerial	3½", 4 spokes, NOT MET	EX	$870.00	02-08
Cozzone	150 yd.	German silver	9-Aug	$70.00	99-12
Cozzone	Deep Sea	German silver	VG+	$99.00	99-06
Cozzone	Fly Reel	gs & hard rubber, 2½" x 1", box VG	EXIB	$880.00	04-11
Cozzone	Multiplying Saltwater Reel	3¼" dia., 2⅛" wide spool reel, click switch, Vom Hofe–style rear bearing cap, free spool lever, replaced handle	G	$225.50	05-04
Cozzone	Saltwater Reel	2⅞" dia., 1½" wide spool reel, Julius Vom Hofe–style wear compensating rear bearing cap, free spool lever, star drag marked "150"	EX	$220.00	05-04
Cozzone	Saltwater Reel	low profile 100 yd. reel, front-mounted free spool, Ever and Vom Hofe–style wear compensating rear bearing	VG	$143.00	05-04
Cozzone	Squidder	gs, 3¼" dia., 2¼" wide spool reel, features star drag and 7 o'clock mounted free spool lever, 4" handle complete with pawl	G	$66.00	05-04
Cozzone	Saltwater	3", g. silver/rubber	EX-	$73.00	00-08
Cozzone	Sidewinder Reel	early walnut and brass, 4" dia., knurled drag adjuster, S-handle and bulbous wood knobs	VG	$165.00	04-11
Crack	300	nice box	NIB	$299.00	01-05
Crack	700	fly reel, bronze nice box	NIB	$81.00	04-11
Crescent	Kentucky Style	O9ON, mark on reel foot, click & drag	EX-	$77.00	05-07
Crook, J.B.	Brass Multiplying Reel	c. 1870, 2⅞" dia., 2⅛" wide, walnut grasp with smooth-action rim-mounted drag works	EX	$330.00	05-04
Crook, J.B.	German Silver NY-style Reel	unique free spool mech, 3⅛" dia., 1¹⁵⁄₁₆" wide spool, reel features a unique free spool button mounted on front rim, counterbalanced S-handle is moved away from main gear, single knurled center screw, rim-mounted drag	VG	$852.50	05-04
D.A.M.	250L	papers and box	EXIB	$140.00	00-07
D.A.M.	256 Auto	Spincast, 10 bids	NIB	$776.00	00-03
D.A.M.	330?	220?	NIB	$80.00	01-01
D.A.M.	330N	box and papers	EXIB	$45.50	99-02
D.A.M.	700B		NIB	$152.00	99-03
D.A.M.	800B		EX	$83.00	00-09
D.A.M.	Effzet 495	brass fly, NOT MET	EX-	$67.00	99-10
D.A.M.	Fly Reel	2", no writing, goat emblem, polished brass, fake?	EX-	$405.00	04-02
D.A.M.	Quick 110	box & goodies	NIB	$65.00	05-07

BRAND	MODEL	SERIES / MFG. CODE / DESCRIPTION	GRADE	PRICE	DATE yy/mm
D.A.M.	Quick 330		VG	$19.00	99-01
D.A.M.	Quick 331	nice box	NIB	$114.00	04-11
D.A.M.	Quick Super 2 Speed	gear shift	EX-	$79.00	01-11
D.A.M.	Stationary Drum Baitcasting	no antireverse, black & silver, extra spool	EXIB	$1,325.00	03-08
D.A.M.	Super	larger spinning, two-toned beauty!	EX	$40.00	03-06
D.A.M.	SW68	Berlin ½ bail, no antireverse, c. 1938	avg	$632.00	03-04
D.A.M.	110	nice box	NIB	$71.00	04-12
D.A.M.	220		VG-	$29.50	99-02
D.A.M.	238	spinning	EX	$78.75	99-02
D.A.M.	270	rough box and goodies	NIB	$80.00	99-01
D.A.M.	270		NIB	$100.00	99-03
D.A.M.	330	papers	EX	$27.00	00-10
D.A.M.	550		EX	$58.00	99-02
D.A.M.	1001	extra spool, spring, goodies	EXIB	$76.01	99-06
D.A.M.	1401	extra spool, spring, goodies	EXIB	$71.01	99-06
D.A.M.	4000	spinning	EX-	$56.00	00-09
Dame Stoddard & Kendall	Kendall	RP, pat June 15, '86, 1¾" dia., 1⅛" wide spool reel, click switch	EX	$148.50	04-11
Deb Manufacturing Co.	Thunderbird	nice 2PCCB, "Keahoni"	EXIB	$57.00	05-07
Diawa	Millionaire	5HS, Met-Brown, 2 BB, high speed, light rash on edges, in bag, M-10/C-9	EX	$70.00	05-05
Diawa	Millionaire 3RM	box and papers	EXIB	$43.50	99-01
Diawa	Millionaire 5HS	box and goodies	EXIB	$83.00	00-05
Diawa	Millionaire II	500M, 5.2:1	EX	$41.00	99-05
Diawa	TD1Hi	bait casting	EX	$81.00	99-01
Dingley	Fly	3", with silk line	mint	$260.00	02-08
Dingley	Fly 3"	similar to Hardy Uniqua	EX-	$138.00	01-08
Dove	Fly Reel	2⅜" dia.	VG	$66.00	05-07
Dreiser	1850 Dated	built into wood handle, nice	EX-	$710.00	99-05
Dukehart	Vom Hoff #3½	raised pillar, nice case	VG+	$211.50	99-06
Eagle Claw	ECQ	spin, made in Italy	mint	$56.00	02-12
Eagle Claw	Spinning	fair box	VGIB	$56.00	99-02
Emery	Tarpon	fly reel, 3.85" in diameter and 1.15" wide, weighs 14.5 oz., NOT MET		$504.00	05-07
Emery John	Tarpon Fly	like Fin Nor	EX+	$279.00	00-11
Empire City	60 yd.	nice nickle plated, sm casting? reel	EX-	$25.00	04-03
Empire City	Raised Pillar	60 yd.	EX-	$25.00	05-03
English	Mahogony Trolling	wide casting reel, iron & wood, c. 1770	EX-	$1,205.00	02-08
English	Nottingham	Ebonite and brass, Nottingham-style salmon reel, nickle-plated rims, 4½" dia., 1¼" wide spool reel, slater latch, rear sliding click	VG	$192.50	05-04
Eppinger	Baitcaster	NOT MET	EX	$54.00	00-04
Eppinger	No Tangle #25	spool control on right upper side plate	EX	$331.00	05-07
Farlow	Cobra	3½", nice box, NOT MET	EXIB	$60.00	05-07
Farlow	Platewind Winch	brass, 6.5 cm diameter x 3.2 cm wide, nice patina	VG+	$110.00	05-07
Farlow	Wood & Brass	5½", reel seat signed	EX-	$130.00	00-07

BRAND	MODEL	SERIES / MFG. CODE / DESCRIPTION	GRADE	PRICE	DATE yy/mm
Farlow & Co. Ltd.	Malloch's Patent	c. 1900, 3¼" dia. back plate reel, early version, rim control click, large line guide	EX	$154.00	05-04
Farlow & Co. Ltd.	Malloch's Patent	spinning reel, 4" dia., 1¾" wide spool reel, fitted leather case	EX	$187.00	05-04
Farlow, C.	Fly Reel	all brass plate wind reel, 2¼", c. 1885 – 94	EX-	$135.00	05-07
Farshure	Spinning	weird looking	EX	$1,137.00	01-11
FB	202	flip reel, big 1½ lb.	EX	$130.00	04-03
Feurer Bros	480 Taurus	papers, 1975 receipt	NIB	$189.00	00-11
Fin Nor	#2 Fly Reel	wedding cake–style, engraved "J. Rutzky"	EX	$2,125.00	05-06
Fin Nor	#3	wedding cake, NOT MET	EX	$860.00	00-10
Fin Nor	#4 Fly	extra spool, goodies	NIB	$465.00	99-06
Fin Nor	15/0	c. 1938, g. silver? NOT MET	EX-	$2,750.00	00-11
Fin Nor	2.5/0	retails for $1669	EX	$405.00	99-01
Fin Nor	2.5/0		EX-	$466.01	99-03
Fin Nor	4"	gold	EX-	$325.00	99-11
Fin Nor	4.5/0	gold	EX-	$638.00	99-01
Fin Nor	4C651	gold finish	mint	$503.00	01-04
Fin Nor	Ahab #8		EX	$124.17	99-01
Fin Nor	CR 45	fly, for 4, 5, 6 lines	mint	$152.00	99-01
Fin Nor	Estima E.S.200		new	$39.00	01-05
Fin Nor	FR10		mint	$300.00	00-05
Fin Nor	FR8		mint	$311.00	00-05
Fin Nor	Lite S200	with rod	EX	$86.00	01-05
Fin Nor	No. 3	spinning reel, black die-cast body, large gold anodized spool	VG	$121.00	04-11
Fin Nor	No. 3 Wedding Cake Fly Reel	serial no. 3-265, 4" dia., 1" wide spool reel, set for left hand wind, slight boat rash around gold anodized rim	VG+	$1,155.00	05-04
Fin Nor	No. 7 Big Game Reel	serial no. 546, #50 and #80 class reel, gold anodized finish, lever-operated drag system, furnished with line	EX	$357.50	05-04
Fin Nor	No. 1 Wedding Cake Fly Reel	left-hand wind, 3" dia., 1" wide spool reel, marked "serial 1-243," name plate inscribed "Ken Mead," gold anodized finish, scratch free	EX+	$1,182.50	05-04
Fin Nor	No. 2 Wedding Cake Fly Reel	right hand wind, 3½" dia., 1" wide spool reel, marked "serial 2-292"	EX	$1,017.50	05-04
Fin Nor	No. 3 Saltwater Fly Reel	3¼" dia., 1" wide spool reel, gold anodized finish, left-hand wind	EX	$220.00	05-04
Fin Nor	No. 3 Saltwater Fly Reel	3⅞" dia., 1" wide spool reel, gold anodized finish, left-hand wind	EX	$385.00	05-04
Fin Nor	No. 4 Saltwater Fly Reel	3⅞" dia., 1½" wide spool reel, gold anodized finish, left-hand wind	EX	$247.50	05-04
Fin Nor	No. 4.5 Saltwater Fly Reel	Mass., 4½" dia., 1" wide spool, gold anodized finish, left-hand wind	EX	$330.00	05-04
Fin Nor	No.3	spinning reel, black die-cast body, large gold anodized spool, c. 1958, click antireverse lever behind spool	VG+	$330.00	04-11
Fin Nor	No. 3	designed by Gar Wood Jr., spinning reel, black and gold, little usage	EX	$236.50	05-04
Fin Nor	No. 4	designed by Gar Wood Jr., black and gold, little usage	EX	$82.50	05-04

BRAND	MODEL	SERIES / MFG. CODE / DESCRIPTION	GRADE	PRICE	DATE yy/mm
Fin Nor	Saltwater Reel	marked on side "M 301 4" pat number, black insert with early Miami address, 4½" dia., 2¼" wide, gold anodized reel, earlier elaborate drag lever, large black handle	EX	$357.50	05-04
Fin Nor	Viscount	4" dia., 2¼" wide spool, plated reel, white plastic side plates, lever-activated free spool, missing rod attaching clamp, some corrosion	G	$22.00	05-04
Fin Nor	3	salmon reel, 3¾" dia., 1" wide spool, gold anodized, with line	EX	$247.50	04-11
Fin Nor	3	spinning, NOT MET	EX	$207.00	99-01
Fin Nor	245		EX	$795.00	99-01
Fin Nor	336		VG	$650.00	99-02
Firestone	Casting	c. 1950, yellow spacer & handles	EX	$77.00	05-01
Firestone	S-5642-3	bait caster, made by Shakespeare? bx VG+	EXIB	$65.00	03-07
Flo Line	Pencil Sharpener	looks new	mint	$203.00	02-03
Flo Line	Spinning Reel	stationary reel with swiveling base, green finish, chrome-plated spool	G	$82.50	04-11
Follett	Fly	open birdcage design, 3¾"	EX	$965.00	00-03
Follett	Fly	open Indiana style, ugly	VG+	$300.00	99-04
Foss, Al	25-Mar	NOT MET	EX	$406.00	00-10
Foster's Ashbourne	D1 Dingley	3¾", NOT MET	VG	$157.00	02-09
Fowlers	Fly Reel	c.1875, one of earliest hard rubber reels, 2⅛" diameter, locking screw	EX	$6,270.00	04-11
Fullilove, Frank	Crown	KY style, c. 1903, NOT MET	mint	$3,550.00	02-02
G Little Makers	Old English	brass handle, plate, salmon reel, 3½" dia., engraved "G Little Makers to H.R.H. Prince of Wales Hnymurket"	VG	$220.00	05-04
Garcia	Abu 444	open face, spinning	EX	$143.01	99-01
Garcia	Abu Matic 40	nice box	EXIB	$46.60	99-01
Garcia	Abu Matic 501	closed face, spinning	NIB	$208.50	99-01
Garcia	Cardinal 3	spool only	EX	$14.50	99-01
Garcia	Mitchell 300	all goodies	NIB	$155.00	00-10
Garcia	408	in box	near mint	$139.50	98-12
Gates, Geo.	Salmon Fly Reel	3½" x 1¼", tiny pictures, NOT MET	EX-	$1,058.00	02-02
Gayle & Son	No. 3	2" x 1½", 6 o'clock, front click	EX	$4,372.00	05-04
Gayle & Sons	#3 Tournament	screw head, broken off	VG	$1,335.00	99-11
Gayle & Son	No. 3	aluminum pitted, NOT MET	VG	$810.00	98-12
Goite	5"	agate, rough box and papers	EXIB	$46.00	99-06
Goite	Indiana	metal eye	EX-	$51.00	00-05
Goite	Indiana Style	nice pic box	EXIB	$129.01	99-05
Goite	Indiana Style		EX	$66.00	99-02
Goite	Indiana Style	lg size in VG orig 2PCCB, box has hole in top	NIB	$95.00	05-05
Goite	Indiana Style	lg size, reel is dirty and box is darkned a little bit	VG+IB	$60.00	05-05
Great Lakes	Whirlaway		EX	$66.00	99-06
Great Lakes	Whirlaway 75	papers	NIB	$66.00	02-09
Grice & Young	Avon	fly reel, center pin	EX	$53.00	05-07

BRAND	MODEL	SERIES / MFG. CODE / DESCRIPTION	GRADE	PRICE	DATE yy/mm
Grice & Young	Fly Reel	center pin	NIB	$104.00	05-07
Grice & Young	Orlando Minor	manual side caster	EXIB	$237.50	99-06
Grice & Young	Golden Eagle	4½"	EX	$74.00	01-11
Gulf	Casting	light saltwater, made in Dallas, TX	VG+	$51.00	04-12
Handmade	Big Game Reel	4⅝" dia., 2" wide, all brass dual grasp, 4½" long handle, knurled click switch mounted 12 o'clock, also antireverse lever	VG	$330.00	05-04
Handmade	Big Game Reel	4⅝" dia., 4⅛" wide spool reel, brass construction star drag, 5½" handle with wooden hand grip	VG	$440.00	05-04
Hardy	3½" Salmon Reel	early, smooth brass foot unmarked, set for right hand	VG+	$220.00	05-04
Hardy	Altex	No. 2, MK5, spinning reel	VGIB	$100.00	05-07
Hardy	Altex #2	MK V, spinning	EX	$240.00	01-09
Hardy	Birmingham	2½", nice patina	EX-	$682.00	05-07
Hardy	Bougle	1998 reissue, NOT MET	NIC	$306.75	99-06
Hardy	Bougle	Bougle Lightweight I, one of only 50 made, 2½"	NIB	$295.00	05-07
Hardy	Bougle	3", aluminum	EX-	$2,000.00	01-06
Hardy	Bougle Perfect	3¼", c. 1921 – 23	VG	$2,300.00	00-03
Hardy	Cascapedia	4/0, salmon, limited edition, NOT MET	NIB	$1,300.00	02-08
Hardy	Cascapedia 4/0	marked case	EXIC	$10,000.00	01-06
Hardy	Cascapedia 4/0	304/500, modern repro, in pouch	NIP	$921.00	03-11
Hardy	Conquest	4¼" x ⅝", internal width, aluminum	EX	$369.00	05-07
Hardy	Conquest	free spool reel, 4⅜" dia., alloy reel, brass foot, heavy wire line guide	VG	$82.50	05-04
Hardy	Duplicate Mark 1	2⅞", well used		$278.00	99-01
Hardy	Elarex	level wind bait casting reel, original hard fiber case, click and drag controls lever, oil hole covers, knurled thumb rest, grooved foot	EX	$192.50	05-04
Hardy	Elarex	level wind bait caster, NOT MET	VG+	$114.00	01-06
Hardy	Exalta	box and goodies	NIB	$224.50	99-01
Hardy	Exalta	spinning, nice bx & extra spool	EXIB	$263.00	05-07
Hardy	Featherweight	small	VG+	$471.00	03-10
Hardy	Featherweight Trout Reel	2⅞" dia., 11/16" wide, small chip on foot	G	$275.00	04-11
Hardy	Featherweight Trout Reel	2⅞" dia., 11/16" wide, small chip on foot, spare spool	G	$275.00	04-11
Hardy	Featherweight Trout Reel	2⅞" dia., 11/16" wide spool reel, spare spool	G	$269.50	04-11
Hardy	Featherweight Trout Reel	2⅞" dia., comes with spare spool	EX-	$137.50	04-11
Hardy	Filey	c. 1925 – 31, rust	VG-	$668.00	04-03
Hardy	fly (Pf. Medalist type)	brass (dark), ivory hand, hand-on-rod trademark	VG-	$1,651.00	01-04
Hardy	Flyweight	in case	EX	$102.50	99-01
Hardy	Hardex	No. 1 Mk1, spinning, half bail, paint rough, works fine	VG	$53.00	05-07
Hardy	Hardex Spinning Reel	marked "No. 1-MK1," early half bail design, w/original box with bag, spare spool, and wrench	VG	$176.00	05-04
Hardy	Hercules	c. 1896, brass salmon reel, 4" dia., 15/16" wide	EX	$330.00	05-04
Hardy	Husky Salmon Reel	3⅜" dia., 1⅛" wide spool reel, marked "hardy case"	EX	$82.50	04-11
Hardy	Hydra	fly reel, 3½"	VG+IB	$116.00	05-07

BRAND	MODEL	SERIES / MFG. CODE / DESCRIPTION	GRADE	PRICE	DATE yy/mm
Hardy	Lightweight	LHR, 3³⁄₁₆"	EX-	$154.00	05-07
Hardy	Longstone	"Longstone" Dural, 3½", 1938, rubber foot, box VG+	NIB	$530.00	05-07
Hardy	Longstone	3½", rubber foot, 2PCCB VG+, c. 1938, NOT MET	NIB	$455.00	05-07
Hardy	Longstone	3½", nice box, NOT MET	EX-IB	$318.00	05-07
Hardy	Marquis	No. 2, salmon reel, 4⅛" dia., 1⅛" wide spool reel	EX	$82.50	04-11
Hardy	Marquis #5	Allcocks leather pouch	EXIP	$107.00	05-07
Hardy	Marquis #2	#10 line, pouch & spare spool	EX-IP	$213.00	05-07
Hardy	Marquis #1	comes with #10 line, modern box & goodies	NIB	$258.00	05-07
Hardy	Monogram 3½"	pat no. 272408	VG+	$435.00	05-07
Hardy	Ocean Prince	antireverse salmon reel, with 2 extra spools, left-hand wind, 3¾" dia., 1¼" wide spool reel	EX	$104.50	05-04
Hardy	Orvis CFO V	trout reel, marked "Made in England," 3⅜" dia., 1" wide spool reel, comes with line	EX	$357.50	05-04
Hardy	Perfect	marked only "Hardys Alnwick-patent," smooth brass foot, white handle, and no line guides	VG	$770.00	04-11
Hardy	Perfect	¼", circa 1912, white ivory handle, strap over tension adjustment, with turk head, long smooth brass foot, 4 cus	EX-	$805.00	05-07
Hardy	Perfect	2¾", c. 1911	VG	$1,131.00	04-01
Hardy	Perfect	2⅞", agate line guide	VG+	$610.00	02-09
Hardy	Perfect	3¼" wide spool, "JS" inside, NOT MET	VG+	$255.00	05-07
Hardy	Perfect	3⅜", older box EX-, engraved "Mathew Haeney"	VG+IB	$363.00	05-07
Hardy	Perfect	3⅝"	NIB	$530.00	99-08
Hardy	Perfect	50% loss of bluing	VG	$265.02	99-01
Hardy	Perfect	brass faced, c. 1906, 3½"	EX-	$1,181.00	04-01
Hardy	Perfect	missing agate line guide	VG	$588.00	01-04
Hardy	Perfect	salmon reel, with extra spool, 3⅝" dia., ⅞" wide, late version with gray enamel, white agate line guide, right-hand wind	EX	$220.00	05-04
Hardy	Perfect	Spitfire, 2⅞", crisp box & papers	NIB	$1,190.00	05-07
Hardy	Perfect	trout reel, 3⅝" dia., ⅞" wide spool, late version w/gray enamel finish, white agate line guide	VG	$165.00	05-04
Hardy	Perfect	Walter Dingley, 3"	EX-	$396.00	05-07
Hardy	Perfect #4	USA, duplicated mark II	EX	$330.00	99-03
Hardy	Perfect 2⅞"	owned by "famous" people, c. 1923 – 26	VG	$698.75	99-08
Hardy	Perfect 2⅞"	box with plain paper label, ugly	EX-	$456.00	99-08
Hardy	Perfect 3⅛"	duplicated mark II, pat no. 24245 & 9261, agate guide	VG+	$409.00	05-05
Hardy	Perfect 4"	very nice box	EXIB	$427.00	00-05
Hardy	Perfect Fly	2⅞", A&F, agate guide, spare pawl	EX-	$830.00	00-10
Hardy	Perfect MKII	Duralumin, 3¾", duplicated, no black finish original	EX	$715.00	05-07
Hardy	Perfect MKII	wide spool, c. 1950, NOT MET	EX-	$242.50	99-05
Hardy	Perfect Salmon	4¼", wide spool	EX-	$560.00	05-06

BRAND	MODEL	SERIES / MFG. CODE / DESCRIPTION	GRADE	PRICE	DATE yy/mm
Hardy	Perfect Salmon Reel	3½" dia., 1⅛" wide spool, grooved brass foot, old line wear around handle	VG	$275.00	04-11
Hardy	Perfect Salmon Reel	3⅝" dia., 1¼" wide, ribbed brass foot, gs line guard	VG	$495.00	05-04
Hardy	Perfect Trout Reel	2⅞" dia., ⅝" wide, agate line guide, smooth brass foot, original fitted leather case	VG	$660.00	04-11
Hardy	Perfect Trout Reel	2⅞", with duplicated mark II stamp, ⅝" wide spool reel	VG	$495.00	05-04
Hardy	Perfect Trout Reel	2⅞", with duplicated mark II stamp, ⅝" wide spool reel	VG	$495.00	05-04
Hardy	Perfect Trout Reel	3⅛", with duplicated mark II stamp, ⅝" wide spool reel	VG	$385.00	05-04
Hardy	Perfect Trout Reel	3⅛", with duplicated mark II stamp, ⅝" wide spool reel	VG	$385.00	05-04
Hardy	Perfect Trout Reel	3⅜" dia., late version, gray enamel, extra spool in pouch	EX	$192.50	04-11
Hardy	Perfect Trout Reel	gs, 3¼" dia., 1" wide, grooved brass unaltered foot, most finish worn	VG-	$533.50	04-11
Hardy	Perfect Trout Reel	late version with gray enamel, 3⅝" dia., 13/16" wide spool reel	NM	$247.50	04-11
Hardy	Perfect 3⅛"	paint loss	VG	$319.00	99-01
Hardy	Prince Salmon Reel	3¾" dia., 1¼" wide antireverse reel	VG	$385.00	04-11
Hardy	Prince Trout Reel	3¼" dia., ⅞" wide spool reel, Hardy pouch	EX	$93.50	05-04
Hardy	Princess	3½", papers	mint	$247.50	99-05
Hardy	Princess Trout Reel	2 spare spools, 3½" dia., gs dual prong line guide and rim check	VG+	$148.50	04-11
Hardy	Princess Trout Reel	3½" dia., ⅝" wide spool reel, gs reversible line guide, some rim scratches	EX-	$137.50	04-11
Hardy	Princess Trout Reel	reversible line guide, 3½" dia., ⅝" wide spool reel	EX	$137.50	05-04
Hardy	Sage 509	salmon reel inscribed "DEMO," 3⅞" dia., ⅞" wide spool reel, comes with line	EX	$181.50	05-04
Hardy	Scientific Angler System 5	50th anniversary trout reel, 3" dia., 11/16" wide spool reel, comes in fitted walnut box no. 0362	EX	$220.00	05-04
Hardy	Scientific Anglers "One Fifty"	salmon reel, 4" dia., ⅞" wide spool reel	G	$88.00	04-11
Hardy	Scientific Anglers System 9	salmon reel, 4" dia., ⅝" wide spool reel, 2 spare spools	G	$137.50	04-11
Hardy	Silex	4", rubber/brass foot, blue pouch	NIB	$452.00	05-07
Hardy	Silex Major	3½", alloy drum	VG+	$255.00	05-07
Hardy	Silex Major	4"	EX-	$384.00	99-12
Hardy	Silex Multiplier	much loss of finish, pat no. 2206 & 9788/15	VG	$1,227.00	04-02
Hardy	Spinning	pouch, well used	VG-	$162.50	00-03
Hardy	Spitfire	St. John, 3⅞", NOT MET	VG+IB	$307.00	99-01
Hardy	Spitfire Uniqua	dup MK2, 2⅝", check, white handle, ribbed brass foot, telephone drum latch, rim tension regulator	EX	$810.00	05-07
Hardy	St. Aidan	salmon reel, 3¾" dia., ⅞" wide spool reel	VG	$104.50	05-04
Hardy	St. Aidan	salmon reel, with extra spool, 2" screw model, reversible line guide, 3¾" dia., ⅞" wide with line	G	$104.50	05-04

BRAND	MODEL	SERIES / MFG. CODE / DESCRIPTION	GRADE	PRICE	DATE yy/mm
Hardy	St. George	2⁹⁄₁₆", ribbed foot	VG	$677.00	05-07
Hardy	St. George	3", trout reel, with brass foot, brown agate line guide, ¹³⁄₁₆" spool	VG	$632.50	05-04
Hardy	St. George Fly Reel	3" dia., with metal ring line guide, (thin crack) ribbed brass foot	VG	$385.00	04-11
Hardy	St. George Trout Reel	3⅜" dia., 3-screw latch hub, agate line guide, ridged brass foot, some wear to pewter finish	EX-	$412.50	04-11
Hardy	St. John	salmon reel, 3⅞" dia., ⅞" wide spool reel ,most finish worn off, ribbed brass foot altered	G	$66.00	05-04
Hardy	St. John	salmon reel 3⅞ " dia., ⅞" wide spool reel, ribbed foot with line	VG	$104.50	05-04
Hardy	St. George	3", 2-screw Drun latch, agate eye	EX	$265.00	05-07
Hardy	St. George	multiplier, 3⅜", agate line guide, neat!	EX-	$2,381.00	05-07
Hardy	St. George	salmon reel, 5⅜ " dia., ¹³⁄₁₆" wide spool reel, rim wear, owner name engraved on front	VG-	$148.50	04-11
Hardy	St. George Jr.	Abercrombie and Fitch, fancy case	EX	$1,032.00	01-10
Hardy	St. George Jr.	IWE 145, heavy leather pouch, crisp box	NIB	$469.00	05-07
Hardy	St. John MK2	fly reel	VG+	$92.00	05-01
Hardy	Sunbeam	3", blue/cream box	NIB	$326.00	00-09
Hardy	Sunbeam	lots of wear, NOT MET	VG	$177.00	01-08
Hardy	Super Silex	4½", c. 1930, works okay but lots of corrosion	avg	$455.00	05-07
Hardy	The Lightweight Trout Reel	3³⁄₁₆" dia., 60% finish aluminum foot unaltered	VG-	$434.00	04-11
Hardy	The Ocean Prince One	serial no. 411, salmon reel, 3¾" dia., 1" wide, first edition	NM	$302.50	04-11
Hardy	The Perfect Trout Reel	3⅜" dia., ¾" wide spool reel, early corrugated brass foot attached with pins, plating missing	G	$220.00	05-04
Hardy	The Zenith	salmon reel with extra spool, 3⅝" dia., 1⅛" wide, old style, gs, reversible line guide, past owner's name on foot	VG	$126.50	05-04
Hardy	Uniqua	3⅛", pre-1912	avg	$305.00	00-02
Hardy	Uniqua 2⅝"	slight filing on foot, 1923	EX-	$260.00	99-02
Hardy	Uniqua Fly Reel	marked with duplicated mark II and patent nos. 24245 and 926, fine knurled rims, 3¾" dia., 1¼" wide	VG	$220.00	05-04
Hardy	Uniqua Salmon Reel	3⅞" dia., 1¼" wide, marked "Hardy Bros Ltd. Alnwick," plain foot (trimmed), gs, telephone latch	VG	$104.50	05-04
Hardy	Uniqua Trout Reel	2⅝", with duplicated mark II stamp, ⁹⁄₁₆" wide, narrow plain foot, brass telephone latch	VG	$412.00	05-04
Hardy	Uniqua	patent with duplicated mark 1 and telephone-style latch, 2⅞", minimal brassing	VG	$330.00	05-04
Hardy	Uniqua Patent with Duplicated Mark 1 and Telephone-style Latch Reel	2⅞", minimal brassing	VG	$330.00	05-04
Hardy	Unique Trout Reel	2⅞", with duplicated mark II stamp, ⅝" wide spool reel, worn finish	VG	$302.00	05-04
Hardy	Unique Trout Reel	2⅞", with duplicated mark II stamp, ⅝" wide spool reel, worn finish	VG	$302.00	05-04
Hardy	Wallis	3½", ribbed foot, free spool lever	EX-	$767.00	05-07
Hardy	Zeneth	3⅝" x ⅝"	NIB	$127.50	99-08
Hardy	Zenith Salmon Reel	3⅜" dia., 1⅛" wide spool reel, slight rim wear	EX-	$192.50	04-11

BRAND	MODEL	SERIES / MFG. CODE / DESCRIPTION	GRADE	PRICE	DATE yy/mm
Harrington	350	modern design, NOT MET	EX	$51.00	00-10
Hastine & Co	Umpqua 721	casting reel, in round tin box EX	EX-IT	$520.00	05-07
Heddon	105SS		EX	$100.00	00-08
Heddon	125 Imperial	fly reel, agate line guide	VG+	$125.00	04-11
Heddon	125 Imperial	fly reel, nice, NOT MET	EX	$179.00	00-07
Heddon	152 Spincast		EXIB	$20.50	99-01
Heddon	206 Lone Eagle	Down Bass	NIB	$360.00	00-09
Heddon	206 Lone Eagle	nice box	EXIB	$255.00	00-08
Heddon	215 Whitehouse	rough Up Bass box	VGIB	$86.00	00-11
Heddon	236 Spinning	box and papers	NIB	$37.00	98-12
Heddon	236 Spinning	box, papers	EXIB	$37.17	98-12
Heddon	15-Mar	dull finish, SOLD	EX	$180.00	99-10
Heddon	15-Mar	German silver	EX	$270.00	99-10
Heddon	15-Mar	gold plated, engraved at factory "BILL LOGAN DALLAS"	EX-	$3,552.00	05-01
Heddon	15-Mar	Kentucky style, gs	EX	$315.00	02-03
Heddon	15-Mar	leather un pouch	EX	$225.00	00-04
Heddon	15-Mar	perfect mechanically	EX	$190.00	05-07
Heddon	15-Mar	unmarked case	VG+	$163.00	03-11
Heddon	31AB Waltonian		EX	$344.00	00-04
Heddon	3200 Mark IV	nice pouch	EXIB	$76.00	02-08
Heddon	25-Mar	bag	VG+	$220.02	99-03
Heddon	25-Mar	German silver	EX	$275.00	99-10
Heddon	25-Mar	LW	EX	$291.00	01-04
Heddon	25-Mar	marked leather pouch, very nice	EXIP	$350.00	02-01
Heddon	25-Mar	No. 915, level wind, NOT MET	EX	$202.00	04-12
Heddon	25-Mar		EX-	$240.00	99-05
Heddon	30-Mar	magnesium spool, alum handle, white sapphire	EX+	$2,025.00	01-11
Heddon	30-Mar	serial no. 891	EX	$650.00	03-02
Heddon	30-Mar	tournament, NOT MET	EX	$765.00	02-02
Heddon	30-Mar	unpolished gs nice, jeweled	EX	$750.00	02-03
Heddon	3-30 ST	tourney handle	EX	$1,350.00	99-10
Heddon	Mar-35	broken screw head	EX-	$155.00	99-07
Heddon	Mar-35	dull finish, SOLD	EX	$315.00	99-10
Heddon	Mar-35	serial no. B207, gs, ivory handle grasps and cork spool arbor	EX	$159.50	05-04
Heddon	Mar-35	serial no. 3445, gs, level wind bait casting reel, stamped on foot "pat app for"	VG	$154.00	05-04
Heddon	Mar-35	German silver	EX	$350.00	03-11
Heddon	Mar-35	marked leather pouch	EX-IP	$169.00	05-07
Heddon	Mar-35	nice, NOT MET	EX	$227.50	99-05
Heddon	Mar-35	NO BIDS	mint	$222.22	99-10
Heddon	Mar-35	satin	EX+	$307.00	99-07
Heddon	Mar-35	Up Bass box!	EXIB	$511.00	00-02
Heddon	3-35 Prototype	extra bail & adj nut, NOT MET	EX	$505.00	01-08
Heddon	18-Apr	click bad, replaced washer under screw	SOLD	$2,450.00	99-10
Heddon	18-Apr	rubber ball arbor, windshield wiper guide	EX	$2,995.00	03-01
Heddon	18-Apr	windshield wiper guide, 3 o'clock, unpolished, nice	EX	$3,050.00	04-07

BRAND	MODEL	SERIES / MFG. CODE / DESCRIPTION	GRADE	PRICE	DATE yy/mm
Heddon	420 Dominator	Daisy, deep sea	NIB	$367.00	99-08
Heddon	45 Reel	with brown box	EXIB	$550.00	05-07
Heddon	57 Auto Fly	great Banner box	NIB	$87.00	00-10
Heddon	9-41N	narrow spool, black frame	EX	$41.05	99-08
Heddon	Baitcasting	no model number, level wind	EX-	$510.00	02-08
Heddon	Casting Reel	serial no. 6736, gs, front-mounted click switch, dual grasp handle, marked on foot	EX	$192.50	05-04
Heddon	Chief Do-wa-giac	nice box, great papers	EX-IB	$224.00	99-03
Heddon	Chief Do-wa-giac #4	nice box, papers	EXIB	$335.00	02-03
Heddon	Chief Do-wa-giac #4	nut buggered	VG+	$54.00	01-03
Heddon	Fly Auto	rim rash, Banner box	EX-IB	$95.00	99-10
Heddon	Heritage 30	2 hangtags, pouch	NIB	$310.00	01-11
Heddon	Heritage 30	mark III, pouch goodies, rubs	avg	$86.00	99-01
Heddon	Heritage 30	nice marked pouch	NIP	$139.00	03-11
Heddon	Heritage 30	pouch	EX	$102.50	99-11
Heddon	Heritage 35	pouch, goodies, paper	EX	$150.00	99-01
Heddon	Heritage 40	EX pouch	EXIP	$163.00	04-01
Heddon	Heritage 45	great box	NIB	$153.00	00-10
Heddon	Indian Chief #3	missing level wind & screw	?	$302.00	99-07
Heddon	Lone Eagle 206	ratty box	EXIB	$71.00	01-05
Heddon	Mark IV		EX	$75.00	01-04
Heddon	Mark IV 3200	box and all goodies	NIB	$265.00	99-01
Heddon	Mark IV 3200		VG	$89.00	98-12
Heddon	No 35	gs, bait casting reel, 2" dia., 1⅝" wide, teardrop-shaped oil port on head plate, sliding click bottom, dual grasp handle	EX	$1,870.00	05-04
Heddon	No 45	marked on rear plate "Carter's Pat Jul 5 04 Nov 28 05"	VG	$154.00	05-04
Heddon	No. 45	nonlevel winding, German silver, bait casting, click switch, dual ivory grasp handle, knurled thumb rest	EX-	$247.50	05-04
Heddon	P-41	bag and box	EXIB	$86.00	00-03
Heddon	P-41	black plate, removable ring, NOT MET	NIB	$154.00	02-08
Heddon	P-41	black sides, pouch, crisp box	EXIB	$86.00	00-03
Heddon	P-41	black, nice box & goodies	NIB	$162.00	04-11
Heddon	P-41	black, papers	NIB	$77.00	00-09
Heddon	P-41	gold	EX-	$56.00	99-05
Heddon	P-41	gold, nice box	EXIB	$178.00	01-01
Heddon	P-41	silver, quick take down, crisp box, papers	NIB	$157.00	03-08
Heddon	P-41	silver, missing 2 screws	EX	$41.27	00-03
Heddon	Pal 25	Proweight, gold!	minty	$86.00	00-09
Heddon	Pal P-41	black, jeweled end caps	EX	$46.02	99-01
Heddon	Pal Pro Weight 26	level wind, NOT MET	EX-	$54.00	00-04
Heddon	Silver Level Casting Reel	front-mounted click switch, dual grasp handle, marked foot, gs	EX	$165.00	05-04
Heddon	White House	Angler	EX	$250.00	99-01
Heddon	White House Angler	avg box, NOT MET	VG+IB	$157.00	00-10
Heddon	White House Angler	decent box	EX+IB	$306.00	01-03
Heddon	Winona 108-48	picture box little rough	EXIB	$50.00	00-03

BRAND	MODEL	SERIES / MFG. CODE / DESCRIPTION	GRADE	PRICE	DATE yy/mm
Heddon	Winona	1929 patent, Indiana style	VG+	$29.00	04-12
Heddon	Winona 105 FF		VG	$40.00	99-09
Heddon	Winona 105SS	nice box & papers, extension piece	NIB	$256.00	02-04
Heddon	35	NOT MET	EX	$382.00	99-12
Heddon	40	Carter pats	EX	$950.00	99-10
Heddon	45	Carter '04 & '05 pats, nice	EX	$336.00	01-11
Heddon	45	Carter pat '04, NOT MET	VG	$212.00	00-06
Heddon	45	Carter pat '04 & '05	EX	$580.00	99-10
Heddon	45	NOT MET	EX	$237.50	00-02
Heddon	45	NOT MET	EX	$282.88	99-06
Heddon	45	take apart, Carter pat	EX-	$232.50	99-10
Heddon	45	unmarked case, polished, gs, non-level wind	EX	$286.00	05-07
Heddon	45		EX	$257.00	01-04
Heddon	87	auto fly reel	VG+IB	$31.00	04-12
Heddon	100	spincast	mint	$86.00	98-12
Heddon	262	spinning	NIB	$17.00	04-12
Heddon	320	fly, papers	NIB	$43.00	01-01
Heddon	415	windshield wiper, SOLD	EX	$2,680.00	99-10
Heddon	450	trolling		$41.00	99-01
Heddon	3200	box and all goodies	NIB	$202.50	99-05
Heddon	25-Mar	serial no. 1597, click switch on front plate, dual ivory grasps on handle, and "pat's appd for" on foot	EX	$165.00	04-11
Helical	Helical Casting Reel	tiny reel, early half bail, comes in case with full label, brass alloy construction, w/very good box, leather strap	VG	$159.50	05-04
Hendryx	150 Raised Pillar	1876, 1888, brass, silver gone	VG+	$100.00	00-04
Hendryx	250 Yard Bay Reel	hard rubber and nickel plate reel, 3½" dia., 1⅞" wide spool, 1 missing screw	VG+	$110.00	05-04
Hendryx	Brass	60 yd., embossed rope design on one side plate	VG+	$305.00	05-07
Hendryx	4907	80 yd., raised pillar	EX	$97.00	00-05
Henshall	Bass Reel	gs, click on back plate, counterbalanced handle, covered with verdigris, no damage to reel	VG+	$2,365.00	05-04
Henshall	German Silver Bait Casting Reel	first Henshall–Van Antwerp, 2⅜" dia., 1⅜" wide, front rim click switch	EX	$5,060.00	05-04
Henshall	Van Antwerp	bait/fly, ugly design	EX-	$1,580.00	01-06
Henshall & Van Antwerp	Kentucky	g. silver, '83 & '87 patents, "99" on foot	EX	$2,247.00	05-03
Hermos	250 yd.	German silver	9-Aug	$38.88	99-12
Herters	709 Fly	box and goodies	NIB	$36.00	01-06
Herters	Fly	unmarked, single action	EX	$97.00	00-06
Herters	11	bay reel, lt saltwater size, nonlevel wind	EX	$41.00	04-01
Herters	703	fly	NIB	$227.50	00-02
Holzman	Saltwater	g. silver/rubber	EX	$3,050.00	00-10
Holzman	Wolf	c. 1892, 1¾" spool #54, NOT MET	EX	$3,150.00	03-04
Horrock-Ibbotson	Utica Auto Fly	little Finger, c. 1912	VG	$162.50	99-10
Horrock-Ibbotson	Vernely	fly, Bakelite	NIB	$26.00	99-04
Horton	#25 Bluegrass	Simplex	EX	$460.00	99-04
Horton	#3 Bluegrass	15059, nice	EX	$183.00	05-07

BRAND	MODEL	SERIES / MFG. CODE / DESCRIPTION	GRADE	PRICE	DATE yy/mm
Horton	#3 Bluegrass	NOT MET	EX-	$255.00	99-06
Horton	Bluegrass	No. 3, serial no. 15742, gs, 2" dia., 1⅝" wide, jeweled end caps	EX	$440.00	05-04
Horton	Bristol 65	fly reel	NIB	$47.00	03-11
Horton	Meek 3	free spool, original patina	EX	$449.00	05-02
Horton	Meek 30	LW, pear shape side plates, #271 parts	EX	$565.00	05-02
Horton	Meek No. 3	serial no. 8916, correctly marked box, 2" dia., 1⅝" wide spool, gs, with click and drag, 3JM box	EX	$660.00	05-04
Horton	Meek No. 30	gs, level wind bait casting reel, front-mounted rotary drag control, rear click switch	VG+	$247.50	05-04
Horton	No. 3 Bluegrass	serial no. 5105, gs, bait casting reel, click and drag, jeweled and ivory grasp handle	EX	$143.00	05-04
Horton	No. 34 Bluegrass	gs, Simplex free spool, take-apart style, bait casting reel, with side plates	VG	$82.50	05-04
Horton	No. 3	serial no. 11394, Bluegrass, minus jeweled end caps	VG	$1,265.00	05-04
Horton Meek	#3		NIB	$499.00	01-06
Horton-Bristol	#10	level wind, German silver, gleamer	EX+	$391.00	00-05
Humpal	66	Spincast, + Johnson #40	NIB	$164.00	98-12
Hurd	Supercaster	2 stripped screws	VG	$75.00	01-01
Hurd	Supercaster	missing 2 screws, broken tip, case	avgIC	$100.00	01-03
Hurd	Supercaster	case	VG	$255.00	99-03
Hurd	Supercaster	in pouch	EX	$197.00	01-08
Hurd	Supercaster	no case, NOT MET	EX	$129.00	00-08
Hurd	Supercaster	normal type?	EX	$305.00	00-04
Hurd	Supercaster	pouch	NIP	$290.01	99-06
Hurd	Supercaster	pouch & paperwork	EXIP	$155.00	03-01
Hurd	Supercaster	serial no. 25224, 5½", walnut grip, case EX	EXIC	$172.00	05-07
Hurd	Supercaster	walnut, no rod tip	VG?	$193.38	99-04
Hurd	Supercaster	with case	EXIC	$150.00	00-02
Hurd	Supercaster	with tip and case	EX-IC	$150.00	01-07
Hurd	Supercaster	wood	VG+	$119.00	99-10
Hurd	Supercaster	wood, case	EXIC	$202.50	99-05
Hurd	Supercaster	wood, case, box VG	NIB	$405.00	99-05
Hurd	Supercaster	wood, NOT MET	EX	$178.00	99-02
Hurd	Supercaster	wood, wrong handle	VG	$119.52	99-03
J.B. Cook and Co.	40 yd.	1⅞" dia., 1" wide, click switch inoperable, missing rear end cap	G-	$275.00	04-11
J.T. Crouch & Sons	Tournament	beauty, NOT MET	EX	$105.00	01-03
Johnson	Fiskar	nice display box & papers, underslung SC	NIB	$139.00	02-03
Johnson	Pink Princess	by Denison-Johnson Inc.	EX-IB	$129.00	04-11
Julius Vom Hofe	Size 1 Trout Reel	2⅞" dia., 1" wide spool, German silver and hard rubber reel	EX-	$605.00	05-04
Katchem	Ice Fishing	built in reel, cool! NOT MET	EX-	$101.00	00-10
Kiest	Aluminum Casting Reel	w/orig tin container, small 16-page brochure, 99% of label	EX+	$275.00	05-04
Kiest	Indiana Aluminum Casting	round tin & pic box & 3 papers, all mint	NIB	$511.00	05-07
Kiest	Reel Red Tin	has paperwork inside and label outside	EX	$75.00	05-05
Kiffe	350 yd.	hard rubber side plates	VG+	$67.00	04-01

BRAND	MODEL	SERIES / MFG. CODE / DESCRIPTION	GRADE	PRICE	DATE yy/mm
Kiffe	Brass Multiplying Reel	3¼" dia., 2⅛" wide spool reel, S-handle, repair to reel foot	VG	$93.50	05-04
Kiffe Co	Small Raised Pillar Trout	1⅝" dia., 1" wide, ivory grasp, NP, drag switch	EX-	$82.00	04-11
Kilian	Neo Caster	crisp box and papers	NIB	$114.00	00-09
Klondike	Cozzone Bank Reel	5" dia., w/box	EXIB	$132.00	05-07
Kopf	Mills #3	Dec. 16, '81 pat., embossed, foot sides one piece	EX	$2,500.00	01-06
Kosmic	300 yd.	g. sil/rubber nice	EX	$121.50	00-03
Kosmic	Baitcasting	serial no. 946, c. 1895, purty! g. silver/rubber	EX	$1,028.00	03-11
Kosmic		missing 2 screws	VG	$152.50	99-01
Kovalovsky	Dec-00	unused	EX	$2,293.00	05-02
Kovalovsky	16/0, type 2	NOT MET	EX+	$3,500.00	99-08
Kovalovsky	6/0	patent 1, 958, 919 3-7, 8" x 2⅜"	EX	$2,420.00	04-11
Kovalovsky	9/0 Standard	#24 D6, NOT MET	EX	$2,550.00	03-04
Kovalovsky	9/0	from the Granville Island Sportfishing Museum	EX	$3,250.00	05-06
Kovalovsky	9/0		EX?	$1,799.00	05-02
Kovalovsky	Big Game Reel	5¾" dia., "3" marked in small foot, handle house, free spool mechanism, rear mounted click	EX	$1,980.00	05-04
Kovalovsky	Model C	Tuna Club decal, NOT MET	mint	$1,875.00	01-06
Kovalovsky	Type 1 Micarda	14/0, some pitting on spool, otherwise nice, NOT MET	VG+	$2,600.00	05-07
Kovalovsky	245	type 2, gray	VG	$910.00	99-01
Kovalovsky	36861	gold, some repairs, NOT MET	VG+	$1,805.00	01-03
Kovalovsky-Zane Gray	Cradle Big Game Reel	7½" dia., 4¾" wide spool reel, weight is nearly 15 lb., 3-tier, 1½", knurled drag adjusting knob	G	$2,970.00	04-11
L & S	4610	weird plastic, maybe spinning? + goodies	NIB	$535.00	00-12
Lampson	LP1.5	fly, spare spool	mint	$142.50	99-03
Langley	820GB	spinning	VG	$17.00	05-05
Langley	Plugcast	#360 NAR-SP	9-Sep	$120.00	05-06
Langley	Target 340	decent box	NIB	$210.00	01-03
Langley	Target 340	green	VG+	$82.00	02-01
Langley	Target 340	nice 2PCCB + papers	EX-IB	$59.00	05-07
Langley	Whitecap	LW, in EX marked box, 9-Sep		$100.00	05-06
Lasso	Spin	old, ugly, France	VG-	$74.00	00-04
Lectro-matic		Spincast, battery operated	EX	$75.00	99-01
Lenz Machine Works	Plastic & Aluminum	weird, with clear windows to view bearings	VG+	$315.00	02-02
Leonard	4" Fly Salmon Raised Pillar	patent no. 18183, bimetal alloy	EX	$1,695.00	05-05
Leonard Mills	Marked Raised Pillar	gs, hard rubber and aluminum trout reel, 3" dia., 1" wide spool, brass arbor, aluminum spool	EX	$1,430.00	05-04
Leonard Mills	44	raised pillar fly, g. silver, beauty	EX	$1,260.00	01-08
Leonard, H. L.	Bimetal Fly	g. silver and brass	EX	$2,550.00	00-03
Leonard, H. L.	Handmade	hard rubber, aluminum, gs, 3¾" dia., 1⅛" wide, patent no. 191813, marking	VG	$660.00	05-04
Leonard, H. L.	Lenoard Mills	3¾" dia. and 1⅜" wide spool of aluminum	EX	$1,155.00	05-04
Leonard, H. L.	Raised Pillar Fly	rubber/German silver, NOT MET	EX	$1,025.00	99-08
Leonard-Mills	44	raised pillar trout, click reel, 2⅝" dia., ¾" wide spool reel, alum front and rear rims, hard rubber, gs, foot unmarked	EX	$1,430.00	04-11

BRAND	MODEL	SERIES / MFG. CODE / DESCRIPTION	GRADE	PRICE	DATE yy/mm
Lexington	Kentucky Type		EX-	$330.59	99-06
Lexington Mfg.	Kentucky	end cap soldered down	VG-	$2,025.00	02-11
Luxor	#2	France	EX-	$112.00	01-08
Luxor	#2	P-No.2, R50 skeleton handle	VG+	$81.00	04-07
Luxor	#3	spinning, papers	EXIB	$152.50	99-07
Luxor	Moulinet No. 3	nice box	NIB	$126.00	05-07
Luxor	Spin		EX	$142.50	99-03
Luxor	Spinning	gray, initials scratched	VG-	$56.55	99-02
Luxor	Spinning	nice	EX-	$71.00	99-06
Luxor	Spinning		VG	$106.66	99-03
Makoora	Big Game	Australia, 500 made	EX	$1,625.00	00-04
Malleson	RP Casting	bimetal, brass frame/aluminum sides, interior light pitting, 1¼" wide	EX-	$2,764.00	05-07
Malleson, Frederick	Brass Salmon Reel	c. 1860, brass, 3½" dia., 1⅝" wide, roller pillers, half handle, 3-screw raised hosing on rear plate	EX	$770.00	05-04
Malloch	Brass Trout Reel	¾" wide, 2½" dia., horn handle, unfiled foot	VG	$148.00	04-11
Malloch	Circa 1920	fixed spool spinning reel, 3¼" dia. spool, click switch	G	$110.00	04-11
Malloch	Fly	ebonite, g. silver, NOT MET	EX	$318.00	00-11
Malloch	Fly Reel	4", alloy plate, lead finish, nice pouch	EX-	$455.00	05-07
Malloch	Marked Side Cast Reel	3¼" dia., 1⅜" wide spool reel	VG	$137.50	05-04
Malloch	Sidecaster	2⅞", leather pouch	EX-IP	$555.00	04-03
Malloch	Sidecaster	Scottish, 100 mm x 50 mm	EX-	$132.00	05-07
Malloch	Spinning	brass, rotating head, c. 1884	EX-	$158.00	01-08
Malte Blohm	River Royal	casting, blue, similar to ABU, c. 1954, pouch & goodies, NOT MET	NIP	$406.00	05-07
Marine Record	Spinning	Swiss	EX	$103.00	00-09
Marryat	MR8	lightweight, Japan, high quality	mint	$101.00	04-11
Martin	67A	fly reel	EXIB	$20.00	04-07
Martin	72	fancy big drag fly reel, papers	NIB	$75.00	01-06
Martin Novelty Works	Fly Auto	1892, 1895 patent dates	VG+	$255.00	99-11
Martin, Alex	Marked Trout Reel	3" dia., ½" wide spool reel, missing most of blued finish, repair to handle	??	$27.50	04-11
Mascotte	Spinning	blue/black	EX	$203.50	99-06
Masters	Ball Type	c. 1860s? brass, Brooklyn, NY	VG	$237.50	99-06
Masters, E.	Brass Ball Handled Reel	3" dia., 2" wide spool, "2" stamped on foot, tarnished finish is in good condition	G	$415.50	05-04
Meek	#2 Tournament	alum tiny handle, Max Hartstall, 1910	EX	$1,375.00	02-06
Meek	#3	free spool, aluminum spool, cork arbor	EX	$561.00	04-11
Meek	2 Horton	jeweled end caps	EX	$685.00	99-09
Meek	25 Bluegrass		EX-	$350.00	01-05
Meek	3	cork arbor, 2" x 1¹³⁄₁₆"	EX	$455.00	99-07
Meek	3	jeweled, click, drag	EX	$605.00	99-04
Meek	3" Light Saltwater?	No. 1385, hard rubber/g. silver, nice! NOT MET	EX	$2,610.00	04-01
Meek	Bluegrass 34	Horton Simplex, free spool	VG	$180.00	00-08
Meek	34 Freespool	polished but decent	VG+	$202.00	01-10
Meek	44 Fly		avg	$187.50	99-02

BRAND	MODEL	SERIES / MFG. CODE / DESCRIPTION	GRADE	PRICE	DATE yy/mm
Meek	Bluegrass #5	No. 8074, newer style	EX-	$1,530.00	04-11
Meek	Bluegrass #3	nice	EX-	$316.00	05-03
Meek	Bluegrass #4	serial no. 8406, gs, front-mounted click, drag switches counterbalanced, handle jeweled end caps	EX	$825.00	05-04
Meek	No. 3	serial no. 11914, bait casting reel, 2" dia., 1½" wide spool, gs, click switch (NW), one screw on front soldered	VG-	$192.50	04-11
Meek	No. 5 Casting Reel	gs, 2½" dia., 1¾" wide, strong drag, loud click switches mounted on face plate; 4 o'clock straight counterbalanced handle turns smoothly, operating reel effortlessly; small hole drilled in foot, jeweled end caps	EX	$2,200.00	05-04
Meek	No. 2	serial no. 8886, gs, tiny tournament handle, cork arbor, free spool tournament reel, small amount of line and inoperable drag switch, action stiff	EX	$990.00	05-04
Meek	3	beauty	EX	$361.00	00-04
Meek	3	Horton Mfg., balsa spool	EX	$325.51	00-02
Meek	3	tri-handled tournament	EX-	$430.76	99-02
Meek	7		EX-	$661.00	99-03
Meek	25	Horton	EX	$250.00	00-08
Meek	33	pat 1905, Carter's, Bluegrass, $600 NOT MET	EX	$340.00	01-03
Meek	55	fly, NOT MET	VG	$124.00	00-11
Meek & Milam	No. 4	c. 1870s, no serial #, NOT MET	EX	$1,059.00	04-02
Meek & Milam	1	foot filed	EX-	$3,412.00	00-10
Meek & Milam	4	brass	VG	$2,025.00	00-04
Meek & Milam	No. 4	2⅛" x 1⅞", 12 o'clock half handle, foot filed	EX-	$2,805.00	05-04
Meek & Milam	No. 6 Casting Reel	gs, three numbered screws, 2¾" dia., 2⅛" wide, foot filed	EX	$6,435.00	05-04
Meek & Milam	2	handmade brass bait casting reel, 3 numbered screws, full brass foot, pre-serial num, 1¾" dia., 1⁹⁄₁₆" wide, stroke click, handle replaced	G	$605.00	04-11
Meek & Milam	2	Lawrence Jones, NOT MET	EX	$3,000.00	02-01
Meek & Milam	3	12 o'clock, 2 clicks, one replaced screw	EX-	$2,214.00	01-08
Meek & Milam	Ky No. 5 Marked	handmade, gs, bait casting reel, 2½" dia., 2⅛" wide spool, highly polished reel, 12 o'clock dog leg	EX	$3,630.00	05-04
Meek & Son	Bluegrass 33	purty	EX	$142.00	05-07
Meek & Son	2	original patina	EX	$1,576.00	01-02
Meek & Son	Bluegrass 33	NOT MET	VG	$177.50	99-06
Meek & Son	4	toned, looks nice	EX-	$701.00	02-08
Meek & Sons	2	serial no. 4245, marked, jeweled, gs, tournament casting reel, click, no drag, 1¾" dia., 1⅝" wide, all aluminum handle, tiny grasp	EX-	$1,210.00	04-11
Meek & Sons	Bluegrass 25	"C" on foot	EX-	$350.00	99-05
Meek & Sons	Bluegrass 25		VG+	$358.00	99-01
Meek & Sons	Bluegrass 3	3 o'clock	EX	$285.00	02-02
Meek & Sons	4	filed seat, bent spool, NOT MET	OK	$310.00	00-02

BRAND	MODEL	SERIES / MFG. CODE / DESCRIPTION	GRADE	PRICE	DATE yy/mm
Meek & Sons	Bluegrass	marked, bait casting reel, replaced handle, spool and repaired click switch	G-	$55.00	04-11
Meek & Sons	Bluegrass 3	serial no. 4865	EX	$385.00	05-04
Meek & Sons	Bluegrass 33	Carter pat	EX	$267.00	99-04
Meek & Sons	Direct Drive Glaskyd	No. 2060 Mod-FF LW, green plastic, drag, M-0/C-8.5	VG+	$40.00	05-05
Meek & Sons	Free Spool No. 3	serial no. 11917, aluminum spool, cork arbor	EX	$275.00	05-04
Meek & Sons	44	No. 3271, fly reel, 2¼" x 1"	EX+	$9,020.00	05-04
Meek & Sons	Nobby	No.1963, satin finish, very light wear, in orig g and w 2PCCB w/papers, reel stiff	EXIB	$60.00	05-05
Meek & Sons	Redifor	serial no. 10992, 60 yd., KY-style cast reel, very light wear, M-9.5/C	EX	$320.00	05-05
Meek & Sons	VL&A Club Special 60 Yard	Kentucky-style bait casting, rear jeweled bearing caps, 2" dia., 1⅞" wide spool reel, both click and drag switch	VG+	$137.50	04-11
Meek & Sons	2	serial no. 4312, marked, gs, bait casting reel, 1¾" dia., 1⅝" wide spool, strong click	EX	$1,045.00	04-11
Meek & Sons	5	unmarked, case unpolished!	EX	$1,100.00	02-09
Meek & Sons	33	Bluegrass	VG	$200.00	99-02
Meek & Sons	33	marked, take-apart-type reel, click switch, thumb rest, gs, plate EX-	EX	$110.00	04-11
Meek Horton	3 Tournament	1" spool, tiny handle, alum spool, NOT MET	EX-	$621.00	02-01
Meek Horton	3 Tournament	narrow spool, sm handle, NOT MET	EX	$355.00	01-01
Meek Horton	Bluegrass 3	g. silver, ivory handle	mint	$381.00	02-11
Meek Horton	4	jeweled	EX	$405.00	99-06
Meek JF & BF	Casting	7 numbered screws EX, Rice collection 8/9	EX-	$15,877.00	05-01
Meek, B.F.	6	c. 1884	VG	$5,111.00	02-02
Meek, B.F.	Bluegrass 3	serial no. 3409, gs, bait casting reel, dog leg counterbalanced handle, click and drag, missing rear end cap, minor screw head use	G	$165.00	05-04
Meek, B.F.	Bluegrass 3	serial no. 11580, gs, bait casting reel, jeweled end caps, fancy click and drag switches, counterbalanced handle example	EX	$412.50	05-04
Meek, B.F.	Bluegrass 33	little brassing and wear from use	G	$82.50	05-04
Meek-Horton	Bluegrass 3	2 clicks, NOT MET	EX	$306.00	99-07
Meek-Horton	Bluegrass 3	NOT MET	EX	$295.00	00-02
Meek-Horton	4		EX	$382.88	99-07
Meek-Horton	30	level wind, g. silver, missing 1 screw	EX-	$158.00	01-05
Meisselbach	Large	rubber/g. silver?	EX-	$76.00	99-01
Meisselbach	105 Target	ratty box, cheap plastic bait caster	EXIB	$21.00	00-10
Meisselbach	2½"	unmarked, g. silver/Bakelite, pretty	EX	$167.50	99-06
Meisselbach	280 Featherlight	open spool	VG+	$58.00	01-01
Meisselbach	580 Tripart	80 yd., patents '04, '05, '07 & '09, purty	EX	$80.00	05-07
Meisselbach	620 Okeh		EX-	$73.00	05-07
Meisselbach	685 Freespool	sapphire bearings, gs, NOT MET	EX	$359.00	02-02
Meisselbach	780 Tri-Part	German silver	EX	$381.00	00-01
Meisselbach	Auto Fly	1914 pat	VG	$68.00	00-08
Meisselbach	Casting	round posts, c. 1903, no model no., beauty	EX+	$310.00	04-11

BRAND	MODEL	SERIES / MFG. CODE / DESCRIPTION	GRADE	PRICE	DATE yy/mm
Meisselbach	D48	saltwater, gs, hard rubber	VG+	$246.00	05-07
Meisselbach	Expert Fly	plating loss, open design	VG	$157.00	00-07
Meisselbach	Featherlight No. 260	fly	VG+	$53.00	00-08
Meisselbach	Featherlight No. 260	nice box!	NIB	$246.00	01-11
Meisselbach	Flyer 645		EX	$148.45	99-08
Meisselbach	Neptune	silver/Bakelite	VG	$66.51	99-01
Meisselbach	Neptune Reel	3¼" dia., 1⅞" wide spool, gs, hard rubber construction, features unique free spool, knurled wheel with arrowhead pointer with lock button, on/off indicators	EX	$165.00	05-04
Meisselbach	Okeh 600	polished, some brassing, works fine	VG+	$304.00	05-07
Meisselbach	Okeh 625		EX	$100.00	01-04
Meisselbach	Rainbow 731 Fly	all finish rubbed off	VG	$137.00	00-04
Meisselbach	Rainbow 627 Fly	nice box + paper	EXIB	$322.00	00-08
Meisselbach	Rainbow 631	fly, closed sides	VG+	$165.00	00-10
Meisselbach	Ranger No. 130	in box	NIB	$227.75	99-03
Meisselbach	Symploreel 254	free spool	VG+	$200.00	05-01
Meisselbach	Tripart	Heddon Dowagiac	EX	$431.00	01-06
Meisselbach	Tripart 580	1909 patent	EX	$20.00	04-07
Meisselbach	Tripart 580	1909 patent	EX	$61.00	99-01
Meisselbach	Tripart 581	box, pocket cat nice	EXIB	$141.00	99-02
Meisselbach	Tripart 581	decent box	EXIB	$87.00	01-03
Meisselbach	Triton	2621-T, picture box poor	EX-IB	$53.00	05-07
Meisselbach	22	pat, thumb brake	VG	$160.00	02-01
Meisselbach	205	level wind, newer	NIB	$73.03	00-02
Meisselbach	580	nice, NOT MET	EX+	$42.00	99-06
Meisselbach	645	nice box	EX-IB	$178.00	01-01
Meisselbach	660	auto fly reel	EXIB	$183.50	99-06
Meisselbach?	No. 50 Alround	fly, 2" dia., ⅞" wide spool reel, tiny handle grasp fastened to the outer rim	VG	$440.00	05-04
Meisselbach?	Tiny Marked "No 50 Alround" Fly Reel	2" dia., ⅞" wide spool reel, tiny handle grasp fastened to the outer rim	VG	$440.00	05-04
Mepps	Super Meca	box & all goodies, NOT MET	EXIB	$214.00	04-01
Mepps	Super Meca	box, papers, extra spool	EXIB	$221.00	00-04
Mepps	Super Meca	spinning, France	EX-	$51.00	05-07
Mepps	Super Meca		VG+	$91.00	01-01
Mepps	Super Meca		EX	$143.65	99-04
Meyer	Flo Line	pencil sharpener type, crisp box & papers	NIB	$120.00	05-07
Meyer, Lou	Flo Line	pencil sharpener, paint rough	VG	$35.00	01-08
Milac, B.C.	#3	looks well used from pic	VG	$849.00	99-06
Milam	#2	wrong handle, toned nicely	EX	$1,225.00	00-04
Milam	#3	No. 6291, 2" x 1⅝"	EX	$990.00	05-04
Milam	Multiplier #3	NOT MET	VG+	$1,282.00	04-03
Milam	Rustic #3	drag not working	VG	$416.88	99-04
Milam & Son	No. 5 Frankfort Kentucky Reel		VG+	$1,476.00	99-03
Milam & Son	No. 2 Frankfort Kentucky Reel	No. 9494, gs, 12 o'clock counterbalanced handle, click and drag switch, fixed jeweled end caps	EX	$1,210.00	05-04

BRAND	MODEL	SERIES / MFG. CODE / DESCRIPTION	GRADE	PRICE	DATE yy/mm
Milam & Son	No. 3 Frankfort Kentucky Reel	No. 11549, 12 o'clock counterbalanced handle, click, fixed jeweled end caps, minor foot alterations	EX	$990.00	05-04
Milam & Son	No. 5 Large	NOT MET	EX-	$911.00	98-12
Milam & Sons	No. 5	ivory handle cracked, sm nicks left side	EX-	$1,380.00	02-05
Milam, B.C.	No. 2	No. 6352, 12 o'clock handle	EX	$1,200.00	04-01
Milam, B.C.	No. 2	serial no. 6339, gs, bait casting reel, ivory handle grasp, 10 o'clock handle, click and drag switches	EX	$1,980.00	05-04
Milam, B.C.	No. 3	6 o'clock, 2 clicks, NOT MET	EX-	$895.00	01-08
Milam, B.C.	No. 3	gs, marked with "3" on foot and "J.U.W." on back plate, 6 o'clock handle, reel equiped with click and drag, minor damage from pliers	VG+	$715.00	05-04
Milam, B.C.	No. 3	serial no. 3079, gs, bait casting reel, marked "Dj. J.O. Stillson," "Indianapolis Ind." engraved on back, 2" dia., 1⅝" wide spool reel, 10 o'clock ivory grasp		$1,210.00	05-04
Milam, B.C.	No. 4	"J.M. BUFORD," meek handle, NOT MET	VG+	$510.00	04-01
Milam, B. C.	No. 5	12 o'clock counterbalanced handle, 2⅜" x 1¾", foot trimmed	EX-	$3,190.00	05-04
Milam, B.C.		serial no. 6652, click and drag, fixed bearing cap, 6 o'clock mounted handle, full unalterd foot, replaced handle	EX-	$1,375.00	04-11
Mills	50N Trout Reel	2⅜" dia., ⅝" wide spool reel, hardly any scratches and foot bent on one side	VG	$1,210.00	04-11
Mills, William & Son	No. 3	c. 1890, gs and hard rubber, raised pillar reel, 2" dia., 1⁵⁄₁₆" wide, S-handle, foot marked "80," handle at 1 o'clock	EX	$687.50	05-04
Mills, Wm.	#2 Saltwater	by Vom Hofe, g. sil, end cap gone	VG	$230.00	01-01
Minnetonka	Casting	60 yd., jeweled end caps	EX-	$77.00	05-07
Mitchell	300 DL	lots of wear, still works fine	VG	$158.00	04-12
Mitchell	300 Tournament	long distance spool, NOT MET	EX-	$455.00	04-01
Mitchell	300S	skirted, papers	NIB	$102.50	99-05
Mitchell	302 Albatros	made special for the Netherlands	EX	$71.00	05-07
Mitchell	306 Albatros Combi	rare, produced for the Netherlands	EX	$73.00	05-07
Mitchell	402 PUM	mint	mint	$137.00	05-05
Mitchell	408 DL	lots of wear, still works fine	VG	$277.00	04-12
Mitchell	408G	gold plated, wood box, extra spool, no papers or goodies	NIB	$649.00	05-07
MItchell	498 Pro	crisp box	NIB	$177.00	05-07
Mitchell	CAP		VG	$26.00	99-02
Mitchell	Prince 358	box & goodies, rare model	EXIB	$255.00	05-07
Mitchell	Tournament	spinning, with huge extended cone, spool & a similar spare spool	EX	$685.00	05-07
Mitchell	Tournament	spinning, stacked spool, weird	mint	$1,075.00	99-12
Mitchell	300	2PCCB, SN 1101, extra spool & goodies, very early model	NIB	$127.00	05-07
Mitchell	300	blue box, papers	EXIB	$81.00	99-03
Mitchell	300	box and ad	NIB	$43.00	99-01
Mitchell	300	box and all goodies	NIB	$35.00	99-01
Mitchell	300	box, goodies, mint	NIB	$80.00	99-02
Mitchell	300	clam box, no sleeve, all goodies	NIB	$78.00	02-06

BRAND	MODEL	SERIES / MFG. CODE / DESCRIPTION	GRADE	PRICE	DATE yy/mm
Mitchell	300	clam shell box, papers	NIB	$167.00	02-11
Mitchell	300	nice box	NIB	$42.50	98-12
Mitchell	300	no bail spring	VG+	$23.50	98-12
Mitchell	300	plastic box	NIB	$51.01	99-02
Mitchell	300		EX-	$22.50	99-01
Mitchell	300		VG	$23.00	99-01
Mitchell	300		EX-	$28.77	99-01
Mitchell	300		NIB	$67.00	99-02
Mitchell	301		VGIB	$39.00	99-07
Mitchell	302		VG	$32.02	99-01
Mitchell	302		EX-	$33.60	98-12
Mitchell	304	display box, papers crisp	NIB	$242.00	01-08
Mitchell	304	manual	mint	$82.00	99-04
Mitchell	304	nice box & goodies, NOT MET	NIB	$97.00	04-12
Mitchell	304	with goodies	NIB	$113.00	03-12
Mitchell	306		EX	$39.00	99-01
Mitchell	308	box, goodies, mint	NIB	$122.50	99-02
Mitchell	308	E007101, c. 1975, total package including sleeve	NIB	$291.00	05-07
Mitchell	308	extra spool	EX-	$31.00	99-02
Mitchell	308	NOT MET	EX	$52.55	00-02
Mitchell	308	NOT MET	EX	$58.00	98-12
Mitchell	308		VG	$38.00	99-02
Mitchell	308		EX-	$49.99	99-02
Mitchell	308		mint	$56.00	99-05
Mitchell	308		EX-	$58.00	98-12
Mitchell	308		EX	$58.00	99-02
Mitchell	309	France, left hand	EX-	$18.00	04-07
Mitchell	330	old 2PCCB VG+, extra spool	NIB	$53.00	05-07
Mitchell	330		EX-	$32.00	99-01
Mitchell	340	Garcia, nice box & goodies	NIB	$162.00	03-06
Mitchell	350	old blue box, extra spool	NIB	$174.00	05-07
Mitchell	386		EX-	$50.00	98-12
Mitchell	400		VG	$14.50	99-01
Mitchell	402	box and goodies	NIB	$169.50	99-01
Mitchell	406	no goodies	NIB	$56.00	01-08
Mitchell	408	early model, extra spool	EX	$53.00	05-07
Mitchell	408	extra spool	VG+	$66.00	00-04
Mitchell	408	extra spool	EX	$85.00	99-02
Mitchell	408	in 308 box, papers	NIB	$122.51	99-05
Mitchell	408	plastic clam box, extra spool	NIB	$147.00	01-10
Mitchell	408		NIB	$83.00	00-03
Mitchell	408		EX	$84.77	99-04
Mitchell	408		near mint	$113.50	98-12
Mitchell	408		mint	$118.00	01-02
Mitchell	409		EX	$65.00	99-01
Mitchell	410	extra spool	EX	$46.00	99-01
Mitchell	486	spin XL	EX	$100.00	99-01
Mitchell	489	near mint with goodies, NOT MET	EX+IB	$118.00	05-02

BRAND	MODEL	SERIES / MFG. CODE / DESCRIPTION	GRADE	PRICE	DATE yy/mm
Mitchell	498	crisp box & goodies, NOT MET	NIB	$213.00	05-07
Mitchell	510	special rod needed	mint	$61.00	99-03
Mitchell	510	with special rod, reel only fits this rod	EX	$153.00	01-06
Mitchell	811	1975 model, 6:1 retrieve	EX	$131.00	05-07
Mitchell	900	nice box & papers, spinning reel	NIB	$76.00	05-07
Mitchell	908	bronze, c. 1980, foot #01G1	EX	$155.00	05-07
Mitchell	908	spinning, crisp box & papers	NIB	$104.00	01-01
Mitchell	7130	fly	NIB	$41.00	99-01
Montague	Casting Reel	gs, 2½" dia., 1⅞" wide, marked on counter-balanced handle "Sold by E. Vom Hofe & Co. NY"	EX	$132.00	05-04
Montague	Jupiter	No. 100, 60 yd., steel axle, nonlevel wind, jeweled end caps, drag switches, ivory grasp handle	EX	$467.50	05-04
Montague	Neversink	fly reel, hard rubber & gs, 100 yd.	EX-	$504.00	05-07
N.Z. Sports Mfg.	Wilhous Brand	brass telephone latch, purty	EX	$250.00	01-03
National Specialties Co.	Indian Style	some wires on guides missing	VG	$137.00	03-12
National Specialities	Indiana Type	wire broken	EX-	$137.50	99-08
Neptune	Tournament	GS, NS, FS, 9-Sep		$350.00	05-06
Newport	350	rubber/g. silver, thumb brake, grubby	VG	$47.00	01-03
Nordic	45 Supreme		NIB	$222.00	00-08
North Fork	Trout Reel	3⅝" dia., reel with spare spool	EX	$330.00	04-11
Nottingham	Nottingham	large, walnut and brass, 6" dia., star back brace rear spool end, strong click	VG	$385.00	05-04
Ny-O-Lite	White/Brown		EX	$16.25	99-10
Ocean City	77	single action fly reel, nicely made	EX-	$15.00	04-03
Ocean City	109	narrow 1" spool, great box, NOT MET	NIB	$190.00	00-11
Ocean City	245	609	EX-	$202.50	99-02
Ocean City	981	box, papers	VGIB	$31.00	99-01
Ocean City	Ike Walton	300 yd., surf casting, box rough, gs & hard rubber	EX-	$60.00	05-07
Old Pal	Electric	tackle box case, charger, battery nice	EXIB	$178.00	02-09
Onion, Haigh & Cornwall	Nickel Plated Ball Handle Reel	2" dia., 1¼" wide spool reel, nearly 100% of plating intact, features rim pull drag system, hard rubber handle grasp, full-length foot, removable rare end cap	EX+	$605.00	05-04
Orvis	1874 Fly Reel	second version fly reel, inoperable click, 2¾" dia., ½" wide spool, riveted construction reel, removable handle, fitted walnut box, old line	?	$605.00	05-04
Orvis	100A		EX	$56.00	99-02
Orvis	1874 Imitation	125th anniversary reissue, walnut box	NIB	$192.50	05-04
Orvis	300 Spin		mint	$113.00	01-01
Orvis	50A	spinning Ultralite, goodies	NIB	$200.00	01-06
Orvis	50A	spinning, pouch, manual	EX+	$213.50	99-01
Orvis	50A		NIB	$272.00	99-08
Orvis	Battenkill 5/6	fly	VG	$76.00	99-02
Orvis	Battenkill 5/6	made in England, nice pouch	NIP	$117.00	03-08
Orvis	Battenkill Mark IV	trout reel, with adjustable drag, 3½" dia., ¾" wide spool reel	EX	$55.00	04-11

BRAND	MODEL	SERIES / MFG. CODE / DESCRIPTION	GRADE	PRICE	DATE yy/mm
Orvis	DXR 9/10	salmon reel, 3¾" dia., 1⅛" wide spool reel, with line	EX	$115.50	05-04
Orvis	EXR V Salmon Reel	3¾" dia., ¾" wide spool reel	VG	$11.00	04-11
Orvis	Fly	patented May 12, 1874, second version fly reel, inoperable click, 2¾" x ½" spool, riveted construction, removable handle, fitted walnut box, old line		$605.00	05-04
Orvis	Lord II	salmon reel, 4" dia., 1" wide, "Made in Sweden," comes with line	EX	$165.00	05-04
Orvis	Madison	3, 4, 5 line with bag	mint	$45.01	99-01
Orvis	Madison II	made in England, nice pouch	NIP	$71.00	03-08
Orvis	Madison Model 8	3½" dia., ¾" wide spool reel, WF9F line	EX	$82.50	04-11
Orvis	Model 51A	Ultralight spinning reel with extra spool, marked "Made in Italy," for right-hand wind	EX	$60.50	04-11
Orvis	Perf. Fly Reel	S-handle, CB, marked "Manch.VT"	VG	$836.26	99-06
Orvis	Presentation EXR III Trout Reel	3¼" dia., ¾" wide spool reel	NM	$110.00	04-11
Orvis	101	spinning, lefty, made in Italy	VG	$34.00	01-08
Orvis	1874	fly reel, not 125th anniversary repro, wood box, filed foot	VG+IB	$360.00	05-07
Pate, Billy	Antireverse Fly Reel	serial no. R79, 3½" dia., ¾" wide spool reel, under handle drag, light wear to black finish	EX-	$165.00	05-04
Paton of Perth	Salmon Fly Reel	rosewood & brass, leather case	EX-IP	$690.00	04-03
Peen	Sailfisher 130	works fine	VG+	$57.00	05-07
Peerless	2	3⅛", g. silver, purty	EXIC	$350.00	00-11
Peetz	Mahogany	nice decal, Canada	EX	$47.00	01-03
Peetz	Salmon	mahogany and brass, 65th anniversary	EX	$86.00	99-01
Peetz	1500	crisp 1PCCB & paper, purty wood reel, 5"	NIB	$56.00	05-07
Peetz & Son	Wood	nice	EX	$50.00	01-03
Penn	Senator 114H	4/0 or 6/0	EX	$48.00	00-04
Penn	# 716	UL spinning	MINT	$151.51	99-02
Penn	112H Special Senator	red 3/0	NIB	$61.00	00-09
Penn	12LT		mint	$285.00	99-01
Penn	140 Squidder	extra spool, nice box	NIB	$98.00	04-11
Penn	25GLS	black	EX-	$65.00	00-10
Penn	26M	green Monofil, box	EX	$102.50	99-01
Penn	40 GLS	graphite	EX	$102.98	99-01
Penn	420 SS	spinning, black & gold finish	EX+	$112.00	05-07
Penn	450SS	spinning, NOT MET	NIB	$76.00	99-05
Penn	49M	Super Mariner, box VG	NIB	$56.00	05-07
Penn	49M	Super Mariner, great box & goodies	NIB	$73.00	05-07
Penn	501M	nice box, NOT MET	NIB	$44.00	04-12
Penn	5500SS	modern, spinning, BB, SS	mint	$68.00	99-01
Penn	706 Spin	bailless, box and papers	EXIB	$265.00	99-06
Penn	712 Spin	green/white drag & knob	EX	$51.00	00-04
Penn	716 Spinfisher	green	VG	$44.00	01-03
Penn	80W	brass, NOT MET	EX	$340.00	00-11
Penn	8500 SS	gold and black, spinning	mint	$84.50	99-01
Penn	930 Levelmatic		EX	$58.00	99-01

BRAND	MODEL	SERIES / MFG. CODE / DESCRIPTION	GRADE	PRICE	DATE yy/mm
Penn	International 50 Deep Sea Tournament Reel	gold anodized finish, 4-slide-operated free spool, yellow "torpedo" shaped handle	VG+	$192.50	05-04
Penn	International 50	special edition, wood box	NIB	$611.00	05-07
Penn	International 50W	ding on left side	EX-	$370.00	99-02
Penn	International 80TX		mint	$550.00	99-02
Penn	International 12H	NOT MET	NIB	$250.00	99-03
Penn	International 12T	modern	mint	$285.00	00-11
Penn	International 20		VG	$140.25	99-02
Penn	International 30	650 yd., line	EX	$242.50	99-05
Penn	International 30 Big Game Fish Reel	gold anodized reel, slide-operated free spool lever, presented in wood box; wrenches, lube, and spare parts	NM	$302.50	05-04
Penn	International 50	gold	EX-	$300.00	01-04
Penn	International 50	50th anniversary #241	mint	$850.00	02-01
Penn	International 50		EX-	$280.00	99-01
Penn	International 50W		EX-	$290.00	99-03
Penn	International 6	gold, "only 6 known," NOT MET	NIB	$1,075.00	02-11
Penn	International 80W		EX-	$380.00	99-03
Penn	International 80W		EX	$416.00	99-01
Penn	International II 130ST	box & all goodies, NOT MET	NIB	$925.00	99-08
Penn	Levelmatic #940	box and papers	EXIB	$96.07	99-01
Penn	Peer N209		VG	$21.00	99-01
Penn	Peerless #9	box and goodies	EXIB	$24.50	99-02
Penn	Sea-Boy 85	in nice box + catalog	EX-IB	$22.00	05-03
Penn	Senator	114 HL	EX	$74.00	00-09
Penn	Senator	14/0, 7" dia., 4" wide spool reel, brown torpedo handle, front rim free spool lever, click switch	VG	$192.50	05-04
Penn	Senator	16/0	EX-	$511.00	00-10
Penn	Senator	9/0, big game reel, 4⅝" dia., 3¼" wide spool reel, front plate free spool lever, click switch	VG+	$71.50	05-04
Penn	Senator 1/0	blue box with metal corners, goodies	NIB	$79.00	03-11
Penn	Senator 1/0	superb, with goodies	NIB	$150.00	04-11
Penn	Senator 1/0		EX	$90.00	99-06
Penn	Senator 10/0	light corrosion	VG	$102.00	04-11
Penn	Senator 10/0		VG	$124.00	99-01
Penn	Senator 111-2/0	box with papers	NIB	$127.50	99-01
Penn	Senator 112 3/0		EXIB	$52.00	99-01
Penn	Senator 113S	4/0, nice box and goodies, c. 1950s	NIB	$149.00	03-06
Penn	Senator 115 9/0		EXIB	$201.00	99-01
Penn	Senator 12/0	silver/black, NOT MET	EX	$128.00	99-01
Penn	Senator 12/0	with Star roller rod, NOT MET	EX-	$257.00	01-05
Penn	Senator 14/0	light corrosion	VG	$153.00	04-11
Penn	Senator 14/0	silver/black	EX	$227.00	99-01
Penn	Senator 14/0 Big Game Fish Reel	free spool lever click, yellow torpedo handle; wrenches, lube, catalog, and extra parts	EX+	$247.50	05-04
Penn	Senator 16/0		EX	$405.00	99-10
Penn	Senator 16/0		EX-	$538.00	00-05
Penn	Senator 2/0	superb, with goodies	NIB	$165.00	04-11

BRAND	MODEL	SERIES / MFG. CODE / DESCRIPTION	GRADE	PRICE	DATE yy/mm
Penn	Senator 3/0	112H	EX	$69.00	99-01
Penn	Senator 3/0	blue box, c. 1960	NIB	$146.00	00-01
Penn	Senator 3/0	superb, with goodies	NIB	$103.00	04-11
Penn	Senator 3/0	worn box	VGIB	$46.00	99-01
Penn	Senator 3/0		VG	$38.00	99-01
Penn	Senator 3/0 112H	gold/red, pretty	EX-	$57.00	99-01
Penn	Senator 4/0	113H	NIB	$84.00	99-02
Penn	Senator 4/0	maroon box with papers	EXIB	$66.00	99-01
Penn	Senator 4/0	nice	EX	$62.00	05-07
Penn	Senator 4/0		EX	$53.00	99-01
Penn	Senator 4/0		VG	$57.00	99-01
Penn	Senator 6/0	Black Beauty	EX	$54.00	99-02
Penn	Senator 9/0		EX	$89.00	99-04
Penn	Senator 9/0 big game fish reel	front rim, free spool lever, click, yellow torpedo handle	EX+	$77.00	05-04
Penn	Senator 115	9/0, box EX	EXIB	$202.00	02-08
Penn	Spinfisher 704	green	EX	$53.00	01-10
Penn	Squidder 140		EX-	$35.00	99-01
Penn	Squider	box, goodies	NIB	$49.10	99-02
Penn	Squider 140		EXIB	$68.00	99-02
Penn	10	level wind	EX	$46.99	99-01
Penn	115	9/0, nice box	NIB	$164.00	02-08
Penn	275	NOT MET	VG	$70.00	99-06
Penn	706	greenie, manual bail	EX	$117.00	05-07
Penn	706	lg spinning, green/w handle & drag	EX	$148.00	00-04
Penn	706	manual bail	EX-	$204.00	00-04
Penn	706	spinning, manual bail, nice bx & goodies	EXIB	$510.00	04-12
Penn	710	black	EX	$76.00	03-05
Penn	710	spinning, greenie, goodies	NIB	$152.00	01-08
Penn	710	spinning, green/white drag knob	mint	$49.00	00-10
Penn	712	spinning	EX-	$33.95	99-01
Penn	714	greenie, spinning, nice box	EXIB	$139.00	02-12
Penn	930	Levelmatic, wide spool, bx & manual	EXIB	$114.00	05-07
Penzon & Michel	Luxor	spinning	EX	$50.00	00-04
Perez	No. 1 Surf Casting Reel	serial no. 9081, gs and hard rubber, reel worn but correct box	EX+	$286.00	05-04
Perez	Surf Casting Reel	serial no. 8051, identical to Perez No. 1 reel	VG+	$247.50	05-04
Peters	Indiana		EX-	$160.00	01-04
Peters Bait Co.	Indiana Style	9-Sep		$175.00	05-06
Pflueger	#88	spinning reel in EX marked box, 9-Sep		$40.00	05-06
Pflueger	1495 Fly	old style, box	VGIB	$121.50	99-04
Pflueger	1576 Supreme	leaping bass emblem, super nice box & goodies	NIB	$168.00	05-07
Pflueger	1576 Supreme	leaping bass, wide spool, pouch	EX-IB	$81.00	99-12
Pflueger	1775?	FS, leaping bass, narrow spool	mint	$87.50	00-03
Pflueger	1784 Progress Fly	nice box & paper	VG+IB	$91.60	00-03
Pflueger	1788 Capitol	red end plate, purty, big	EX	$77.00	00-09
Pflueger	1943, 1944	2, Trumph, 1944 brass	NIB	$167.50	99-03

BRAND	MODEL	SERIES / MFG. CODE / DESCRIPTION	GRADE	PRICE	DATE yy/mm
Pflueger	4 Brothers Delite	g. silver/rubber, 60 yd.	EX	$480.00	00-09
Pflueger	400 Templar		VG+	$96.00	00-05
Pflueger	4-Bros	Sentrie, 60 yd., 9-Aug, NOT MET		$35.00	05-06
Pflueger	611B	bronze color, mint	mint	$142.50	99-02
Pflueger	611B	brown, FS, SD	EX	$112.50	98-12
Pflueger	8053x Raised Pillar	brass reel, diamond P, "Kentucky"	NIB	$404.50	99-01
Pflueger	Akerite 2068	nice box, lt saltwater type	EXIB	$61.00	01-03
Pflueger	Akron	1893, great box & goodies, jeweled end caps	NIB	$66.00	05-07
Pflueger	Akron	papers	NIB	$46.00	99-05
Pflueger	Akron 1893L		EX	$24.50	99-01
Pflueger	Atlapac	very cool tin box & bag	EXIT	$420.00	02-01
Pflueger	Atlapac 6/0	4½"	VG	$130.00	05-07
Pflueger	Atlas Portage Fly	raised pillar, looks g. silver, nice	EX-	$91.00	00-04
Pflueger	Avalon	1909 pat	VG	$300.00	00-10
Pflueger	Avalon 350	bulldog emblem, 1909 pat	VG-	$300.00	00-10
Pflueger	Buckeye	lt boat rash	VG+	$51.00	01-05
Pflueger	Buckeye	replaced handle, for parts	fair	$37.00	99-01
Pflueger	Buckeye		VG	$64.00	99-04
Pflueger	Buckeye		EX-	$141.38	99-08
Pflueger	Buckeye		EX-	$153.50	99-09
Pflueger	Buckeye 80		VG+	$71.50	99-03
Pflueger	Capitol 605J	tall maroon box	NIB	$160.50	99-04
Pflueger	Captain	line guide + brake	9-Sep	$45.00	05-06
Pflueger	Delite Fly 80 yd.	g. silver/rubber	EX-	$300.00	00-04
Pflueger	Diamond P	KY-style crosshatch, brass	NIB	$404.50	99-01
Pflueger	Golden West	60 yd., gs, sandwiched hard rubber and aluminum plates, 2½" dia., ⅞" wide, slotted bearing cap, excellent gold on black bulldog medallion	EX	$577.50	04-11
Pflueger	Golden West	60 yd.	EX	$635.00	01-06
Pflueger	Golden West	fly	VG	$326.00	00-09
Pflueger	Golden West	patented Feb. 10, 1903, and Jan. 23, 1907, marked, 60 yd., gs, trout reel, 2½" dia., ⅞" wide	EX-	$550.00	04-11
Pflueger	Golden West 7095	"60" on foot, bulldog emblem, 2½"	EX	$662.00	02-08
Pflueger	Golden West Fly	2½", smallest size	EX+	$600.00	99-11
Pflueger	Golden West Fly	2½", big gouge from handle wear	VG	$380.00	99-08
Pflueger	Hawkeye	80 yd., fly, rubber & g. silver	EX-	$461.00	02-11
Pflueger	Hawkeye	German silver and hard rubber, size 60, 2½" dia., ⅞" wide spool, very weak logo, strike pair	G	$302.50	05-04
Pflueger	Hawkeye	2½", silver/rubber, missing end cap	EX-	$350.00	00-04
Pflueger	Kentucky	click, drag, similar to a Meek Bluegrass	EX	$1,614.00	04-11
Pflueger	Knobby 1963	FS, SD, red	EX	$93.00	99-01
Pflueger	Knobby 1963		NIB	$52.50	00-04
Pflueger	Knobby 1965	FS, SD, red	EX+IB	$138.50	99-06
Pflueger	Knobby Delux	hangtag, papers, wrench, red color	NIB	$203.00	01-10
Pflueger	Medalist	#1494 DA, drag and plastic center, 9-Aug		$30.00	05-06
Pflueger	Medalist	agate, metal name tag	VG-	$284.00	00-08

BRAND	MODEL	SERIES / MFG. CODE / DESCRIPTION	GRADE	PRICE	DATE yy/mm
Pflueger	Medalist	#1495, fly reel, metal center and guide, in good box with paper	8/9IB	$195.00	05-06
Pflueger	Medalist	#1496, fly reel, ½ drag, plastic center, 9-Aug		$30.00	05-06
Pflueger	Medalist	#1492, 9-Aug		$20.00	05-06
Pflueger	Medalist 1492	Agate line guide, sculpted pillars	VG-	$65.60	99-08
Pflueger	Medalist 1492	extra spool, NOT MET	EX	$33.00	99-08
Pflueger	Medalist 1492	metal center, ID button, missing much paint	avg	$152.00	04-02
Pflueger	Medalist 1494	round line guide, amber handle	EX	$137.00	01-04
Pflueger	Medalist 1494	silver? Diamolite line guide	EX	$128.00	01-03
Pflueger	Medalist 1495	nice box	NIB	$46.00	99-01
Pflueger	Medalist 1495		NIB	$86.00	99-11
Pflueger	Medalist 1394	fly reel, reel seat filed, ugly	poor	$66.76	99-01
Pflueger	Model 1573	c. 1920 – 23, bulldog trademark, level wind mechanism, early model	EX	$407.00	05-04
Pflueger	Monarch	top mount, bulldog logo, 9-Aug		$50.00	05-06
Pflueger	Nobby	#1963, silver, nice box & goodies	NIB	$51.00	05-07
Pflueger	Nobby 1960	FS, SD, red	mint	$200.00	99-01
Pflueger	Nobby 1965	free spool	NIB	$208.00	03-01
Pflueger	Norka	#1335, 300 yd., FS, LW, CBH, in EX maroon marked box, 9-Sep		$145.00	05-06
Pflueger	Norka	40 yd., c. 1911, jeweled	EX	$1,225.00	02-02
Pflueger	Oceanic Casting Reel	gs, 350 yd. size, saltwater reel, Williams drag	VG	$55.00	05-04
Pflueger	Oceanic Free Spool Surf Casting Reel	4¼" dia., 2⅛" wide spool reel, marked "patent pending" on face plate, large wooden handle grasp sits at end of a 4" S-handle of gs	VG	$55.00	05-04
Pflueger	Ohio 1978	250 yd., nice box	EX+IB	$91.00	00-04
Pflueger	Pakron 3178	wire, line type	EX	$37.00	00-11
Pflueger	Pakron 3178	NOT MET	EXIB	$44.83	00-05
Pflueger	Pelican 1020	nice box & papers	NIB	$75.00	04-11
Pflueger	Pontiac	1907 & '23 patents, light saltwater size	VG	$29.00	04-12
Pflueger	Portage	Medina, 60 yd., NOB, CBH, 9-Aug		$35.00	05-06
Pflueger	President LP	newer model, crisp box	NIB	$100.00	05-07
Pflueger	Progress	brass fly reel	VG	$80.75	99-02
Pflueger	Progress	fly, brass	VG+	$101.00	99-06
Pflueger	Progress	raised pillar fly, dog on foot	EX	$152.00	00-10
Pflueger	Progress 1783	nice box	NIB	$181.94	00-03
Pflueger	Progress 1783	raised pillar fly, maroon box	EXIB	$114.00	00-09
Pflueger	Progress 1923	fly reel skeleton	EX-?	$107.50	99-04
Pflueger	Progress	60 yd., bulldog logo, gunmetal/silver	EX	$163.00	00-08
Pflueger	Quadruple	small end cap, 80 yd., CBH, white grip, NOB, 9-Aug		$100.00	05-06
Pflueger	Redifor	g. silver, jeweled, 1907 & '14 pats	EX	$176.60	99-10
Pflueger	Redifor	gs, jewels, bulldog logo	VG+	$177.50	99-01
Pflueger	Redifor	jeweled, Kentucky style	EX	$251.38	00-01
Pflueger	Redifor	NOT MET	EX	$128.50	99-08
Pflueger	Redifor		VG	$224.50	99-01
Pflueger	Rocket	#1335, with good box, 9-Aug		$50.00	05-06
Pflueger	Rocket	1345, box & papers crisp, all minty	NIB	$58.00	05-07
Pflueger	Rocket	Bakelite spacer	EX	$122.50	99-06

323

BRAND	MODEL	SERIES / MFG. CODE / DESCRIPTION	GRADE	PRICE	DATE yy/mm
Pflueger	Rocket 1365-F		EXIB	$66.00	99-06
Pflueger	Rocket 1375		NIB	$69.75	99-04
Pflueger	Skillcast 1953	hangtag	NIB	$97.66	99-06
Pflueger	Summit	#1995 LW JW FS, 9-Sep		$45.00	05-06
Pflueger	Summit	first model, level line, GS, drag button, JW, 9-Sep		$115.00	05-06
Pflueger	Summit	goodies	NIB	$81.00	00-10
Pflueger	Summit	maroon box G, goodies, 1926 patent	EXIB	$224.00	01-11
Pflueger	Summit	mint pouch (leather bag)	EX	$41.00	00-05
Pflueger	Summit	raised pillar, first model, replaced screws	EX	$878.00	04-11
Pflueger	Summit		mint	$55.00	00-10
Pflueger	Summit 1993L	crisp box and all goodies	NIB	$306.00	00-04
Pflueger	Summit 1993L	nice box, L=light spool	EXIB	$347.00	00-04
Pflueger	Summit 1993L	pouch	EX+	$102.00	00-04
Pflueger	Summit 1993L		EX-	$25.00	99-08
Pflueger	Suprem 611B	ball bearing	EX	$127.50	99-10
Pflueger	Supreme	1st Model, Pat. 1907 – 08, 9-Sep		$350.00	05-06
Pflueger	Supreme	1st model #11634, bulldog logo, unique level wind, NOT MET	VG	$106.00	05-07
Pflueger	Supreme	1st model, windshield wiper	EX-	$300.00	99-08
Pflueger	Supreme	bass emblem, FS, SD, wide spool	EX-	$28.00	04-12
Pflueger	Supreme	box, papers	VGIB	$47.00	99-01
Pflueger	Supreme	brown/gold, "Last one made"	EX-	$626.00	02-09
Pflueger	Supreme	Douglas pat, old type, free spool	EX-	$250.00	99-04
Pflueger	Supreme	FS NAR-SP LW, fish model, 9-Sep		$75.00	05-06
Pflueger	Supreme	FS, hex drag	EX	$61.00	99-08
Pflueger	Supreme	model CK, high speed type, DL	EX	$1,036.00	01-05
Pflueger	Supreme	high speed, metallic brown, wrong bx	NIB	$860.00	03-02
Pflueger	Supreme	leather bag, ex-Cub handle, goodies	NIB	$159.10	99-06
Pflueger	Supreme	missing part, level wind, replaced nut	avg	$150.00	99-09
Pflueger	Supreme	model CK, brown, high speed, BB, SD	EX	$505.00	01-06
Pflueger	Supreme	SDFS, gray wide spool, pouch	NIP	$55.00	00-11
Pflueger	Supreme 1573	box and all goodie, beauty	NIB	$206.40	99-02
Pflueger	Supreme 1573	comfort grip, ring papers, Cub, bass logo	NIB	$112.00	00-08
Pflueger	Supreme 1573	FS, goodies, 2PCCB	NIB	$73.00	99-01
Pflueger	Supreme 1573	gold/blk box, papers	VGIB	$24.15	99-01
Pflueger	Supreme 1573	mint in gold/blk box, goodies	NIB	$280.00	99-01
Pflueger	Supreme 1573		VG	$17.50	98-12
Pflueger	Supreme 1577	leaping bass, narrow spool	EX	$152.50	99-08
Pflueger	Supreme 1577	narrow spool, leaping bass	NIB	$148.00	00-05
Pflueger	Supreme 1577	narrow spool, FS, plastic box	NIB	$114.00	01-03
Pflueger	Supreme 1793	all goodies minty	NIB	$333.00	01-09
Pflueger	Supreme 1973	all goodies, box little rough	EX-IB	$35.00	00-04
Pflueger	Supreme 1973?	Cub handle, great box and goodies	NIB	$162.00	00-04
Pflueger	Supreme 510	box, goodies	NIB	$135.83	99-05
Pflueger	Supreme 510	pouch, tool, oil, NOT MET	EX	$52.50	99-08
Pflueger	Supreme 511		EX+	$66.00	99-06
Pflueger	Supreme 578	salmon reel, 4" dia., 1" wide adjustable drag, switchable, antireverse feature	VG	$137.50	04-11

BRAND	MODEL	SERIES / MFG. CODE / DESCRIPTION	GRADE	PRICE	DATE yy/mm
Pflueger	Supreme 1575	FS, SD	EX	$56.00	00-02
Pflueger	Templar	pat Nov. 18, 1909	EX	$152.50	00-03
Pflueger	Templer	350 1419½, silver/rubber, bulldog	EX	$199.00	00-04
Pflueger	Templer	g. silver/rubber, Williams drag	EX	$172.00	00-10
Pflueger	Templer	gs/hard rubber, lt saltwater	EX-	$125.00	00-08
Pflueger	Trump	c. 1974, AK, NOT MET	NIB	$33.78	99-05
Pflueger	Trump 1942		NIB	$57.00	99-04
Pflueger	Trump 1943	cat	NIB	$36.51	00-01
Pflueger	Trumph 1943		NIB	$52.55	99-01
Pflueger	Trumph 1943	crisp box & papers, celo still on reel	NIB	$125.00	02-01
Pflueger	Trusty 1933	newer box, cellophane on reel	NIB	$78.00	00-04
Pflueger	Worth	Jan. 22, 1907 and Dec. 29, 1914	EX-	$261.00	01-03
Pflueger	Worth	jeweled	EX	$150.00	01-06
Pflueger	Worth 2963		EX-	$130.00	02-01
Pflueger	40	maroon box	EX	$123.00	99-01
Pflueger	511	papers, NOT MET	EX+	$34.40	99-10
Pflueger	511		VG-	$56.00	99-01
Pflueger	1394	first model, Medalist	VG	$205.00	02-08
Pflueger	1494	box	VG-	$115.00	99-02
Pflueger	1494	oldest, maroon box, papers	NIB	$258.50	99-04
Pflueger	1510	Fas Kast, casting reel	VG+	$51.00	05-05
Pflueger	1576	leaping bass	EX-	$76.00	99-09
Pflueger	1878	Golden West, bait caster	VG+	$50.00	99-12
Pflueger	1895	jewels, very nice	EX	$24.00	00-05
Pflueger	1964	100th anniversary	EX	$43.00	99-06
Pflueger	2016	150 yd., maroon box EX-, pre-bulldog	EXIB	$500.00	05-02
Pflueger	2600	all accessories	NIB	$1,202.00	99-10
Pflueger	2600	nice	EX	$566.00	99-03
Pflueger	2800	goodies	NIB	$690.00	99-11
Pflueger	2800	leaping bass emblem	EX-	$193.00	02-02
Pflueger	2800	model DF	mint	$588.00	99-06
Pflueger	2800	name scratched on rim	VG	$294.00	04-12
Pflueger	2800	no handle, release not working	EX-?	$222.00	01-08
Pflueger	2800	noisy, release doesn't work!	broken	$405.00	99-08
Pflueger	2800		EX-	$635.00	99-10
Pflueger	2800		NIB	$709.00	00-11
Pflueger	2859	GS, leather brake	VG	$51.01	99-01
Pflueger	Hawkeye	Jan. 23, 1907 – Apr. 3, 1923, market yard size, German silver trout reel, 2½" dia.	EX-	$385.00	05-04
Pflueger	Raised Pill Fly	40 yd., unmarked Pflueger? nice	EX	$92.00	00-05
Pflueger	Templar	500 yd., saltwater reel, Williams drag	VG	$110.00	04-11
Pflueger	Templar Ocean Reel	4½" dia., 3¼" wide spool reel, star drag, front plate, free spool lever click switch, black torpedo-shaped handle, leather thumb break	EX-	$88.00	05-04
Philbrook & Payne	Fly Reel	GS & orange & blk marblized hard rubber, 1⅞" x ¾"	EX	$12,100.00	04-11
Precisionbilt	Marquette	Mar 100	EX-	$52.00	05-07

BRAND	MODEL	SERIES / MFG. CODE / DESCRIPTION	GRADE	PRICE	DATE yy/mm
Precisionbilt	Mosquito		EX	$40.77	99-07
Quick-O-Mat	Spin	neat	EX	$109.00	00-11
Rainbow	888	Sweden, bait casting, NOT MET	EXIB	$163.00	00-10
Record	1500C		EXIB	$90.10	99-11
Record	1600		EXIB	$232.51	99-10
Record	1600C		EXIB	$80.00	99-11
Record	1600C		EXIB	$135.30	99-10
Record	1700C		EX+IB	$96.10	99-11
Record	1800C	nice box, goodies	NIB	$142.50	99-11
Record	1800C		NIB	$255.00	00-02
Record	5000 Ambassadeur	pre-ABU	EX-	$520.00	99-01
Record	5000 SG	pouch and goodies	EX-	$960.00	00-05
Record	Ambassadeur 5000	box and all goodies	NIB	$660.00	03-11
Record	Ambassadeur 5000	model SG, goodies	EXIP	$1,572.00	01-04
Record	Ambassadeur 5000	nice	EX	$688.00	00-07
Record	Ambassadeur 5000	no serial #	EX	$599.00	99-06
Record	Ambassadeur 5000	rubs	VG-	$320.00	99-06
Record	Ambassadeur 5000	SG, case and parts	EX-	$1,075.00	01-05
Record	Ambassadeur 5000		VG+	$535.00	99-09
Record	Clipper 2300C	NLW, competition, purty	EX	$227.50	99-09
Record	Fly	solid aluminum sides	EX-	$107.50	99-09
Record	Rullen	parts, all goodies, mint box	NIB	$612.00	98-12
Record	Spinning	Swiss, old ½-bail type	VG+	$11.00	04-07
Record	Standard	fly, pewter, nice	EX-	$76.00	00-08
Record	1700	all goodies	EXIB	$172.55	99-10
Record	1800	all goodies	EXIB	$153.50	99-10
Record	1800	engraved end plates, leather case	VG	$355.00	99-09
Record	1800	white agate bearing, nice	EX	$206.00	00-03
REcord	1900	in pouch	EX	$320.00	00-08
Record	1900	nice box	NIB	$256.00	00-01
Record	2000	c. 1942, box & goodies	VG	$1,728.00	02-02
Record	2000		EX-	$178.50	99-03
Record	5000	Ambassadeur	VG	$520.50	99-01
Record	5000	case, papers, goodies	EX-	$405.99	99-02
Record	5000	goodies	EXIP	$428.00	00-02
Record	5000	model SG, first model, pouch + goodies	EXIP	$1,825.00	01-04
Record	5000	no serial number, goodies	EXIP	$787.00	00-02
Record	5000	pouch	EXIP	$455.00	00-02
Record	5000	pouch and goodies	NIP	$610.00	00-01
Record	5000	pouch and goodies	EX+	$660.00	00-01
Record	5000	pouch, alum parts tube	EXIP	$510.00	00-10
Record	5000	pouch, rash	VG+	$404.99	99-11
Record	5000	pouch, goodies	EX	$660.00	00-03
Record	5000	with goodies	EX	$424.00	99-03
Record	5000		VG+	$255.00	00-03
Record	5000		EX	$1,001.55	99-11
Record	6000	pouch and goodies	EXIP	$300.00	00-10

BRAND	MODEL	SERIES / MFG. CODE / DESCRIPTION	GRADE	PRICE	DATE yy/mm
Record	6000	pouch, papers & goodies	EXIP	$611.00	05-07
Record Abu	6000	pouch, parts, gray spool	EX	$670.00	98-12
Redifor	Beetzel	jewel caps, NOT MET	VG+	$177.50	99-06
Redifor		jeweled, NOT MET	VG	$179.00	00-04
Reuben	Centerpin	4", wood & brass, twin horn handles on brass receiver plates, brass-lined back plate with brass drum back	EX-	$58.00	
Rider	Indiana Style		EX	$204.00	05-07
Rinehart	Master Pumper	case, NOT MET	EXIC	$260.00	99-11
Rivers	500 Tournament	similar to ABU, NOT MET	VG+	$49.00	01-09
Rivers Expert	Tourney	Sweden, 2 star drags	EX-	$320.00	00-07
Rochester	#1 Ideal	fly reel, 1910 patent, sticky	EX-	$42.00	04-08
Rock RIver	Fly	Rockford, IL	NIB	$102.50	00-03
Rocket	1355	NO BIDS	NIB	$175.00	00-03
Rogers Bros.	Ebro Simplex	Australia, brass, 2" fly reel	VG+	$128.00	03-02
Ross	Cimmarron C2		EX	$103.50	99-03
Ross	No. 2-1058	3" dia., ⅝" wide spool reel, has spare spool	EX	$194.00	04-11
Ross	The Ross Reel	No. S 1-0104, trout reel with extra spool, in orig pouch, 3¼" dia., 1⅛" wide	EX	$165.00	05-04
S. Allcock & Co.	Easicast	salmon reel, 4" dia., 1" wide spool, alloy reel, click lever mounted on back rim	VG	$82.50	05-04
Sage	508 Fly	pouch	mint	$156.00	99-01
Saracione	Deluxe Salmon Reel	serial no. 291, Delrin side plates, 3½" dia., 1½" wide spool reel	EX	$1,870.00	05-04
Saracione	Deluxe Trout Reel	serial no. 291, Delrin side plates, 3¼" dia., 1½" wide spool reel, drag adjusting lever on back plate	NM	$1,210.00	05-04
Saracione	Deluxe Trout Reel	serial no. 291 NM 1210, Delrin side plates, 3¼" dia., 1½" wide spool reel, drag adjusting lever on back plate	NM	$1,210.00	05-04
Saracione, Joe	25	presentation reel, 3" dia., 1" wide spool, features fine scrollwork along handle, w/box, 1 broken hinge	EX	$1,100.00	04-11
Schaller	Automatic Trolling	Detroit River hand lining style	EX-	$56.00	05-07
Schmelzer	Tournament	NOT MET	EX	$28.00	99-04
Seamaster	Fly Reel	Miami, FL, made	EX	$1,426.00	05-01
Seamaster	Mark III	fly reel, 4" x 1¾"	EX	$3,250.00	05-02
Seamaster	Mark III	saltwater fly, SS pillar, c. 1981	EX	$3,200.00	01-06
Sears	Hydro Sheer	casting reel	NIB	$22.00	04-07
Shakespeare	#3	serial no. 3151, style B, LW, NOT MET	EX-	$306.00	05-07
Shakespeare	#3 Model B	twin screw	VG+	$265.28	99-10
Shakespeare	1740 Tournament "HE"	free spool, balsa arbor, beauty!	MINT!	$129.00	99-08
Shakespeare	1740 Tournament Reel	nice box	NIB	$220.00	05-07
Shakespeare	1795 Wondercast	Spincast	VG-	$52.50	99-04
Shakespeare	1810 FC	Spincast, underslung	EXIB	$56.00	05-07
Shakespeare	1909 Black Knight	cheaper model, black rubber side plates	EX	$38.00	01-08
Shakespeare	1980 Pres. II		mint	$247.00	98-12
Shakespeare	1980 President II	black, NOT MET	VG+	$66.00	00-09
Shakespeare	1981 DC		EX	$222.50	99-10

BRAND	MODEL	SERIES / MFG. CODE / DESCRIPTION	GRADE	PRICE	DATE yy/mm
Shakespeare	1982 Sportcast	free spool	EX	$50.00	99-03
Shakespeare	3M		VG-	$164.00	00-08
Shakespeare	B	parts only (most missing!)	poor	$143.00	00-08
Shakespeare	Beetzsel	falling line guide, g. silver	EX-	$159.00	05-01
Shakespeare	Criterion	1960 model, FA, left hand	EX	$51.00	99-03
Shakespeare	Executive 1992	model QU MK-1, FS, SD, box VG+	EXIB	$71.00	03-09
Shakespeare	Favorite #2	nonlevel wind, 1910, decent	VG+	$52.00	01-10
Shakespeare	Favorite 60 yd.	g. silver? c. 1910, decent	VG+	$52.00	01-10
Shakespeare	Featherweight	small fly reel	EX-	$42.00	04-03
Shakespeare	Free Spool Tournament Reel	small level wind reel, jeweled bearings, click aluminum handle	NM	$220.00	05-04
Shakespeare	Glaykyd	Service 2030	EX-	$10.00	04-12
Shakespeare	Hercules 1966	200 yd., g. silver/rubber, purty	EX	$103.00	00-05
Shakespeare	Hoosier	Indiana style, aluminum	VG+	$378.00	03-01
Shakespeare	Intrinsic 22650	nonlevel wind bait casting reel, knurled rear plate and straight counterbalanced handle, 1910 model, 80 yd.	EX	$132.00	05-04
Shakespeare	Kazoo	fly reel, works good, missing finish	VG	$33.00	04-03
Shakespeare	Level Winding Reel	No. 1862-A, gs, bait casting reel, in 60 yd. size, 1⁹⁄₁₆" dia., 1¼" wide, style A reel, c. 1919	EX	$2,090.00	05-04
Shakespeare	Marhoff	German silver, goodies	EXIB	$60.00	00-08
Shakespeare	Marhoff	hard plastic box	NIB	$205.00	01-02
Shakespeare	Marhoff	model 26, light pitting, works fine	VG	$18.00	04-12
Shakespeare	Marhoff 1964	hinged plastic case	EXIB	$51.00	00-08
Shakespeare	Model 1965 Professional	Presentation Day 1922 – 23, "First Prize Shakespeare Display Contest 1922 – 23" on front plate, rear plate engraved with fishing scene, includes leaping bass hard rubber spacers, rim control click & drag	EX	$121.00	05-04
Shakespeare	Model 26 Tournament		EX	$86.00	00-05
Shakespeare	President	#1970, model FK LW, white spacers	9-Sep	$55.00	05-06
Shakespeare	President 1970	nice box and goodies	EXIB	$51.00	05-05
Shakespeare	President 1970A		NIB	$197.50	00-01
Shakespeare	President 1970GE	SS, g. silver? pillars, no raindrop, purty	EX	$162.50	99-09
Shakespeare	President 1980HB	model DF, FS, SD, engraving	EX-	$152.50	99-04
Shakespeare	President II	1982, DB	VG	$89.00	99-04
Shakespeare	President II	1984, black/white scroll, box, rim rash	VG+IB	$73.00	05-07
Shakespeare	President II	fancy scroll	EX	$294.01	98-12
Shakespeare	President II	HB, eagle emblem	EX	$169.50	99-10
Shakespeare	President II	model DB, lots of rash	VG?	$91.00	01-08
Shakespeare	President II	model DF, black/white scroll, high speed, 2 ball bearings	EX-	$138.00	05-07
Shakespeare	President II	US eagle, nice box & goodies	NIB	$179.00	02-08
Shakespeare	President II	1980	EX-	$122.50	99-06
Shakespeare	President II	1982	VG+	$82.00	99-01
Shakespeare	President II	1982	VG	$142.50	99-04
Shakespeare	President II #1981	blue oval, engraved	EX-	$181.50	99-09
Shakespeare	President II 1980	black, silver eagle, NOT MET	EX-	$117.50	00-04
Shakespeare	President II 1981	crisp box and goodies	NIB	$187.00	00-04

BRAND	MODEL	SERIES / MFG. CODE / DESCRIPTION	GRADE	PRICE	DATE yy/mm
Shakespeare	President II 2800DE	spining reel, blue	EX-	$89.00	02-11
Shakespeare	President II Spin	2810, DE	EX	$67.00	01-03
Shakespeare	President II 1982	fancy scroll	VG	$89.00	99-04
Shakespeare	President II 1984B	fancy scroll, eagle	mint	$116.50	99-04
Shakespeare	Professional #3	100 yd., uad, nonlevel wind	EX-	$305.00	03-11
Shakespeare	Service	#1944, KB, gray marbled spacer, star drag, 9-Sep		$95.00	05-06
Shakespeare	Service No. 2	narrow spool, 60 yd.	VG	$81.00	99-04
Shakespeare	Shakespeare Jr.	level winding reel No. 3, 60 yd., style B, twin screw level wind and rim, controlled drag and click, nickel-plated brass	EX	$440.00	05-04
Shakespeare	Silver Swan	dark color, ugly, runs good	VG+	$41.00	01-08
Shakespeare	Standard 2L	pat applied for, L&R adjustment knobs on rim	VG+	$70.00	04-12
Shakespeare	Style C		VG	$810.00	02-02
Shakespeare	Tournament	model 1924, NOT MET, AL finish, tiny handle	EX-	$247.00	02-01
Shakespeare	Tournament 1914		EX	$155.00	99-01
Shakespeare	Tourney 1910	g. silver, 50 yd., tiny handle	EX	$338.00	00-07
Shakespeare	Type B	double worm gear, pitting	VG	$206.00	02-02
Shakespeare	Wm. Shakespeare Jr.	Vom Hofe patent, 80 yd., 6 o'clock positioned handle, eared plates, fancy click on rim, small crack to rear plate	EX	$467.50	05-04
Shakespeare	Wm. Shakespeare Jr. Kalamazoo	serial no. 2278, 60 yd., style B, screw off bearing caps, level wind cover is upside down, replaced screw on tail plate	VG	$220.00	05-04
Shakespeare	Wondereel 1870	closed face, spinning	VG	$36.00	05-05
Shakespeare	3	type B, NOT MET	VG+	$250.00	01-01
Shakespeare	26	tournament, aluminum	EX	$69.00	01-02
Shakespeare	1740	model FK, free spool tournament reel, jeweled nickel silver reel	EX	$93.50	05-04
Shakespeare	1740	model HE, free spool tournament reel, with correct marked box, 60 yd.	EX+	$126.50	05-04
Shakespeare	1740	model FK, tournament free spool, some brassing	EX-	$77.00	05-07
Shakespeare	1740	tournament free spool	EX-	$125.00	05-01
Shakespeare	1798	Spincast	EXIB	$29.71	99-05
Shakespeare	1810	Spincast, underslung	NIB	$76.00	05-07
Shakespeare	1850	Spincast	EXIB	$127.50	99-12
Shakespeare	1920	nice box and all goodies	NIB	$126.99	99-03
Shakespeare	1924	sm handle, arbor, pouch	EX	$150.00	99-10
Shakespeare	1924		NIB	$43.00	00-03
Shakespeare	1930	nice box, goodies	NIB	$48.00	00-10
Shakespeare	1960	Criterion	NIB	$50.00	00-07
Shakespeare	1975	red/white/blue BC, FS, SD, missing 1 emblem	EX	$48.00	02-08
Shakespeare	1975	red/white/blue casting, FS, SD	EX	$94.00	05-07
Shakespeare	2052		mint	$41.50	99-05
Shakespeare	2052		EX	$57.00	99-08
Shakespeare	2062	spinning	NIB	$53.00	00-08
Shakespeare	2062		VG	$28.50	99-02
Shakespeare	2091	spinning, large	NIB	$60.00	99-02
Shakespeare	2502	nice box & goodies, spinning reel	NIB	$77.00	05-07

BRAND	MODEL	SERIES / MFG. CODE / DESCRIPTION	GRADE	PRICE	DATE yy/mm
Shimano	100 Bantam	spare spool & handle	mint	$155.00	00-08
Shimano	100X	Bantampro Mag	EX	$44.00	01-03
Shimano	250 Calcutta		EX-	$127.50	99-02
Shimano	Bantam	CITICA 200	EX	$66.00	99-01
Shimano	Bantam 10	black	EX	$32.00	99-01
Shimano	Bantam 100	silver	EX	$69.00	99-06
Shimano	Bantam 100	silver	EX	$86.03	99-06
Shimano	Bantam 100		EX-	$51.00	99-03
Shimano	Bantam 100		EX	$80.50	99-01
Shimano	Bantam 1000		NIB	$100.00	99-06
Shimano	Bantam 100EX	gray	mint	$286.00	04-02
Shimano	Bantam 100EX	wood handle	VG+	$121.00	99-01
Shimano	Bantam 100EX		NIB	$227.52	99-09
Shimano	Bantam 200	wood handles	EX	$101.99	99-03
Shimano	Bantam 300		mint	$180.00	00-07
Shimano	Bantam 400		mint	$152.00	00-07
Shimano	Bantam 500		mint	$152.00	00-07
Shimano	BantamMag 50SG	hvy, freshwater	EX	$42.50	99-03
Shimano	Bantum 100		VG+	$53.50	99-04
Shimano	Bantum 100EX	box and goodies	EXIB	$152.50	99-04
Shimano	BB1	Lews Speed Spool, fish emblem	mint	$127.00	02-08
Shimano	Calcutta 100		mint	$110.00	99-01
Shimano	Calcutta 100		NIB	$140.50	99-03
Shimano	Calcutta 200	bag, papers	mint	$132.50	99-02
Shimano	Calcutta 400		EXIB	$152.50	99-03
Shimano	Calcutta 700	gold, pretty	EX	$182.00	99-01
Shimano	Coriolis		mint	$51.00	99-01
Shimano	Curado 201		EX	$93.00	99-03
Shimano	Curado CU-201		EX	$75.50	99-03
Shimano	Spirex 1000		EX	$42.00	99-01
Shimano	Stella	1000F	NIB	$386.00	01-05
Shimano	Stella	2500F	NIB	$402.00	01-05
Shimano	Stradic	2000FG	EX	$52.00	01-05
Shimano	Synetre	2000FH	NIB	$63.00	01-05
Shimano	TLD 10	nice box	NIB	$280.00	02-03
Shimano	Triton TLD 25 L		EX-	$162.50	99-03
Shimano	4500	spinning, Baitrunner	EX	$77.50	99-02
Silas Terry	Brass Trout Click Reel	pat Nov. 14, 1871, bend in foot, 2" dia., 1" wide	EX	$302.00	05-04
Smith, Ogden	Fly	3¼", c. 1917 – 20, red agate line guide	EX-	$177.00	03-11
Smith, Ogden	Fly Reel	3¼", London	VG+	$143.00	05-07
Solite	Fly Reel	raised pillar, skeleton, foot drilled	VG+	$46.00	03-02
South Bend	1131A	intro box, papers, tag, reel used	avg	$92.53	99-11
South Bend	1131B	serial no. 30041, pat 1907	EX-	$82.67	00-01
South Bend	1155 Oreno	fly	EXIB	$67.00	00-02
South Bend	1196 Oreno	single action fly	EX	$46.00	01-04
South Bend	750 Perfectoreno	crisp box & papers	NIB	$80.00	01-08
South Bend	900 ABL	box	EX-IB	$204.00	00-05

BRAND	MODEL	SERIES / MFG. CODE / DESCRIPTION	GRADE	PRICE	DATE yy/mm
South Bend	Kentucky Left Handed	horseshoe marking, nonlevel, pouch	EX-	$717.67	00-01
South Bend	No. 1000 Model E	LW, ABL, very light use, in orig EX-2PCCB, papers, M-9.5/C9.5+	EXIB	$45.00	05-05
South Bend	No. 75	model C, saltwater reel, some use wear, no box	G+	$18.00	05-05
South Bend	Perfectoreno	No. 850, model C, saltwater reel, LW, light use, in orig VG 2PCCB, M9/C8.5	EX-IB	$47.00	05-05
South Bend	St. Joe 1170	fly reel, raised pillar	VG+	$48.00	00-08
South Bend	St. Joe 1170	fly	EX-	$47.00	00-05
South Bend	400		EXIB	$37.00	00-10
South Bend	450	in cool tin can, "Our Hardware"	VGIC	$66.05	99-04
South Bend	750	NOT MET	NIB	$61.00	99-04
South Bend	1000	gs, nice leather pouch	EX-IP	$34.00	01-08
South Bend	1126	Oreno Matic, VG box	EXIB	$39.00	99-02
South Bend	1250	arbor, pouch, goodies	NIB	$100.00	01-09
South Bend	1250	model E, red marble grip & spacer	mint	$70.00	00-05
South Bend	2500	stainless, neat box	NIB	$373.00	00-10
Speedia	Fly Reel	center pin, 4", black, c. 1960s	EX	$81.00	05-07
Stadler	Merit	casting/spin casting, weird, looks like casting reel with Spincast sideways?	EX	$336.00	05-07
Staro	4758	Swiss made, spinning reel	VG+	$20.50	04-03
Stead	36770	g. silver/rubber back, plate cracked	EX-?	$1,791.00	02-08
Stevens	16/0	7½", "86-16-0"	EX	$3,550.00	00-03
Stockford			VG	$200.00	99-06
Stork	Fly		VG-	$153.00	99-02
Talbot	Ben Hur	Nevada, MO	EX	$3,975.00	99-11
Talbot	Club Special	Nevada, MO, probably #2, no markings	EX	$1,000.00	03-05
Talbot	Comet	serial no. 5194, gs, 1⅞" dia., 1⅝" wide, click switch, ivory handle grasp	EX	$506.00	05-04
Talbot	Comet	serial no. 6936, gs, bait casting reel, no. 2 size, removable oil caps	EX	$302.50	05-04
Talbot	Comet	serial 5464, gs, bait casting reel, no. 2 size, 6 o'clock counterbalanced handle	EX	$550.00	05-04
Talbot	Eli	Abercrombie & Fitch	EX	$871.00	99-10
Talbot	Eli	CBH, black grip, small no. 2 size, 9-Sep		$1,550.00	05-06
Talbot	Eli	Nevada, MO, seat rough	VG+	$810.00	05-03
Talbot	Eli Marked	serial no. 5244, gs, 1⅞" dia., front click on 2-piece head plate	EX	$770.00	05-04
Talbot	Mars	gs, aluminum dual grasp tournment-type handle, 2" dia., 1⅝" wide spool reel, click and drag switch	EX	$632.50	05-04
Talbot	Mars	K.C., MO, pouch, handle a modern reproduction	EX	$450.00	02-01
Talbot	Mars	serial no. 6154, 1¾" dia., 1⅝" wide, click switch, counterbalanced handle	EX	$1,347.50	05-04
Talbot	Meteor	K.C ., MO		$448.33	99-03
Talbot	Meteor	K.C., 3 o'clock	EX	$513.00	00-02
Talbot	Meteor	K.C., MO, 1901 patent, NOT MET	EX-	$360.00	05-01
Talbot	Meteor	Nevada, MO	EX	$640.00	01-05
Talbot	Meteor	Schmetzler Arms	EX	$811.00	99-09
Talbot	Niangia	gs, K.C., has white sapphire jewels, 9-Sep		$765.00	05-06

BRAND	MODEL	SERIES / MFG. CODE / DESCRIPTION	GRADE	PRICE	DATE yy/mm
Talbot	Niangua	serial no. 5248, g.s., bait casting reel, removable knurled end caps, 1⅞" dia., 1⅝" wide, foot filed	VG+	$467.50	05-04
Talbot	Niangua	gs, front mounted click switch, counterbalanced handle	VG	$165.00	05-04
Talbot	#41	serial no. 3439, bait casting reel, gs, 2" dia., 1⅝" wide spool, c. 1907; click, drag, and removable oil caps; finely knurled	EX	$1,787.50	05-04
Talbot	Premier #3	"George P. Doane Washington D.C."	EX	$900.00	03-05
Talbot	Premier #3	#417, Nevada, MO, patent 1901	EX-	$1,225.00	05-07
Talbot	Star	serial no. 12024, gs, bait casting reel, ivory handle grasp example, slight screw head damage	VG	$192.50	05-04
Talbot	Star	GS, K.C., 9-Sep		$450.00	05-06
Talbot	Star	K.C., MO, 3 o'clock	EX-	$346.00	03-04
Talbot	Star	K.C., MO, filed reel, seat nice	EX-	$330.50	99-05
Talbot	Star	Marshall Fields, not graded, looks OK	EX-?	$395.00	02-08
Talbot	Star	Schmelzer Arms, K.C., MO	8.5/9	$425.00	99-06
Talbot	Tomahawk	K.C., MO, 3 o'clock, 1 click polished	EX	$1,539.00	01-08
Talbot	Tomahawk	Chicago, NOT MET	EX	$635.00	00-07
Talbot	Tournament #2	looks like chrome plated? K.C., MO	EX	$487.00	04-02
Talbot	3	outside jeweled caps	EX	$1,680.00	00-09
Talbot	33	Nevada, MO, NOT MET	EX?	$1,302.00	02-02
Talbot	35	as found, looks OK	EX	$1,452.00	99-12
Talbot	50	#4 size, Nevada, MO	EX-	$3,000.00	02-08
Tatman	500	spinning reel, from Pentwater, MI	EX	$141.00	04-01
Thommen	Record	spinning, Swiss, pouch & paper	VG+	$26.00	04-07
Thommen	Record 400	spinning	VG	$25.00	99-01
Thommen	Record 400	spinning, papers, nice box	NIB	$81.00	98-12
Thommen	Record 50B	spinning, papers, nice box	NIB	$147.50	98-12
Thos J Conroy NY	"The Wells"	marked, raised pillar, trout reel, made by Julius Vom Hofe, 3½" pillar to pillar dia., 1" wide spool reel; aluminum with German silver handle, foot, and pillars; brass spool shaft	G-	$2,200.00	04-11
Tidemaster	Three	salmon reel from LLBean, 3⅞" dia., ¾" wide spool reel	VG	$220.00	04-11
Timson	Side Cast	brass & alloy, weird looking, c. 1920s	EX-	$945.00	05-06
Tioga	Salmon Reel	3⅝" dia., ⅞" wide, w/two spools with line	EX	$115.50	05-04
Topper	Spin		NIB	$78.00	01-01
Torino	II Spinning	Italy, plain old spinning reel, bull emblem, works OK	VG	$183.00	03-06
True Temper	No. 1000	black, aluminum side plates and stainless steel LW, new in gold 1PCCB	NIB	$20.00	05-05
Turnbull	Fly	4½", heavy brass	EX	$361.00	99-06
Union Hardware	Sampson	hinged side plate! neat	EX-	$45.00	03-06
Union Jack	2000	fly reel, yellow box	NIB	$21.00	03-12
Unknown	Brass New York Multiplying Reel	S-handle, marked "250" on foot, 3" dia., 2⅛" wide spool reel	VG	$99.00	05-04
Unknown	Salmon Reel	gs, hard rubber reel, fixed click, counterbalanced handle with shaped grasp	VG	$302.50	05-04
Utility Mfg. Co.	Rinehart Master-Kaster #3	pump, built-in reel & rod, NOT MET	EX	$338.00	03-08
Val-Craft	350 Fly	gold anodized aluminum, nice	EX	$137.50	99-01

BRAND	MODEL	SERIES / MFG. CODE / DESCRIPTION	GRADE	PRICE	DATE yy/mm
Vetco	Pioneer Model B	#0001, crisp box & papers, NOT MET	NIB	$137.00	02-08
VL&A	Club Special	60 yd., Kentucky style, bait cast reel, 2" dia., 1⅞" wide spool reel, both click and drag switches	VG+	$137.50	04-11
Vom Hofe	521 6-0	silver/black, pretty	EX	$621.00	99-01
Vom Hofe	621 3	1¾" x 3", purty, bass fishing size	EX	$479.00	02-11
Vom Hofe	621 4/0	needs cleaning, looks nice	EX?	$350.00	01-08
Vom Hofe	Dame Stoddard & Co.	box little rough, bay reel	EX-IB	$650.00	99-08
Vom Hofe	Peerless #3	2½" x ¾", fly reel, NOT MET	EX+	$2,851.00	03-07
Vom Hofe	Sam #7		EX-	$56.00	99-08
Vom Hofe	Universal Star 6/0	pat July 14, 1896 & 1902	EX	$350.00	99-03
Vom Hofe	36617	1896 pats, original case	VG+IC	$305.00	00-05
Vom Hofe, Ed	Apr-00	model 521, gs and hard rubber, 3⅞" dia., 2⅛" wide spool reel, Pflueger bulldog, leather drag, front mounted click and throw-offs, HR free crack	VG	$275.00	04-11
Vom Hofe, Ed	Apr-00	Model 491 Universe, gs and hard rubber saltwater reel, intro 1970, 3⅞" dia., 1⅝" wide spool reel, 1902 pat, rear rim throw-off drag, leather thumb drag	VG	$440.00	04-11
Vom Hofe, Ed	Jun-00	521, gs and hard rubber saltwater reel, 4¼" dia., 2⅜" wide spool reel, leather thumb drag, universal, adjustable, star drag system, filed foot	G	$302.50	04-11
Vom Hofe, Ed	Marked Perfection Model 360 Size 1	handmade, German silver and hard rubber trout reel, 3" dia., ⅞" wide spool, rear click, slightly faded rubber	EX+	$6,050.00	05-04
Vom Hofe, Ed	Model 355 Perfection	small size 3, handmade, German silver and hard rubber trout reel	EX+	$6,710.00	05-04
Vom Hofe, Ed	Size 1	gs and hard rubber bass reel, 2⅞" dia., 1⅜" wide spool reel, top pillar in	EX	$506.00	04-11
Vom Hofe, Ed.	#1 Fly	#504	EX	$3,000.00	00-10
Vom Hofe, Ed.	#2	2¾" x 1¼", c. 1894 – 1896, a beauty!	EX	$910.00	03-05
Vom Hofe, Ed.	#4	fly reel, NOT MET	EX-	$1,525.00	03-04
Vom Hofe, Ed.	#501 6/0	name engraved, silver/rubber	EX-	$500.00	01-05
Vom Hofe, Ed.	16/0	original case, SD	EX-	$11,500.00	02-08
Vom Hofe, Ed.	4/0 Fly	salmon reel	EX-	$1,550.00	99-02
Vom Hofe, Ed.	423 3/0	fly, $2250 reserve MET LATER	mint	$1,825.00	99-04
Vom Hofe, Ed.	464 Regal		VG	$710.00	99-04
Vom Hofe, Ed.	491 Regal	#1, box, hangtag, NOT MET	EX+IB	$898.00	99-08
Vom Hofe, Ed.	504 Model Tobique	2/0, with un case, NOT MET	EX	$2,640.00	00-01
Vom Hofe, Ed.	504 Tobique	4/0, salmon, "RNB" engraved reel & pouch	EX-IP	$1,677.00	03-08
Vom Hofe, Ed.	6/0 EVH	perforated star drag	EX-	$370.00	99-02
Vom Hofe, Ed.	621 1/0	foot ground down, NOT MET	EX	$584.00	00-11
Vom Hofe, Ed.	Bay Reel	1902 pat	VG+	$282.88	99-04
Vom Hofe, Ed.	Celebrated	model 481, striped bass and tarpoon reel, 3/0 size, 3⅝" dia., 1¾" wide	EX	$495.00	05-04
Vom Hofe, Ed.	Commander Ross 10/0	#712, purty	EX-	$2,025.00	00-04
Vom Hofe, Ed.	Model 355 Perfection	small size 3, gs, 2½" dia., ⅞" wide spool reel	EX+	$6,710.00	05-04
Vom Hofe, Ed.	Model 423	restigouche, gs and hard rubber salmon reel, 4/0 size, 3⅞" dia., 1¾" wide	EX	$1,870.00	05-04

BRAND	MODEL	SERIES / MFG. CODE / DESCRIPTION	GRADE	PRICE	DATE yy/mm
Vom Hofe, Ed.	Model 481	gs, hard rubber reel, unmarked, 3/0 size, 3⅝" dia., 2" wide, presentation date of 1881 and name, front oil cap, early star logo, rear drag switch not functional	VG	$467.50	05-04
Vom Hofe, Ed.	Model 491	gs and hard rubber, Celebrated bass tarpon tuna reel, 3" dia., 1⅜" wide spool reel, marked "491" on base, size 1	EX	$440.00	05-04
Vom Hofe, Ed.	Model 491	gs and hard rubber reel, c. 1907, 3⅛" dia., 1⅜" wide spool reel, marked on foot "491," size 1/0	EX	$440.00	05-04
Vom Hofe, Ed.	Model 501	4/0 size, 3⅞" dia., 2" wide spool reel, leather thumb drag, nice dark side plates	EX	$412.50	05-04
Vom Hofe, Ed.	Model 501 "Special Celebrated"	bass tarpon and tuna reel, 4/0 size, 3⅞" dia., 2" wide spool reel, offered in 1907 cat, nice dark hard rubber sides, terrific knurling on front rim	EX	$495.00	05-04
Vom Hofe, Ed.	Model 504	Edward Vom Hofe, 2/0 size, Tobique, gs and hard rubber multiplying reel, 3⅝" dia., 1⅛" wide, pat 1902	EX	$2,090.00	05-04
Vom Hofe, Ed.	Model 550	star size 2/0, gs and hard rubber surf reel, 3⅜" dia., 1½" wide, oil caps, front-mounted throw-off lever and rear mounted click and drag lever	EX+	$605.00	05-04
Vom Hofe, Ed.	Model 560	Matecombe, gs, no. 1 size, c. 1929, 3" dia., 2¼" wide	VG+	$533.50	05-04
Vom Hofe, Ed.	Model 621	2/0 size, 3½" dia., 1¾" wide spool reel, front and rear throw-offs, early star drag oil caps, both marked with patent date, foot offset, all original, with "k99" markings	EX	$412.50	05-04
Vom Hofe, Ed.	Model 621	gs and hard rubber reel, 1902 pat date, 3⅞" dia., 2⅛" wide, front and back rim throw-offs, side plates polished, very light scratching	EX	$302.50	05-04
Vom Hofe, Ed.	Model 800 Long Key	gs and hard rubber, 2¾"dia., 1⅝" wide, no. 2 size reel	EX	$907.50	05-04
Vom Hofe, Ed.	Multiplying Reel	4/0 size, 3⅞" dia., 1¾" wide spool, star logo, oil caps, 1867 pat date, no model or size marking anywhere, reverse handle screws off, polished hard rubber face plate, leather thumb drag	EX	$412.50	05-04
Vom Hofe, Ed.	Multiplier Fly #2	2¼ ratio	EX	$450.00	00-03
Vom Hofe, Ed.	Perfection Model 360	size 1, German silver and hard rubber, 3" dia., ⅞" wide spool, rear click, slightly faded rubber	EX+	$6,050.00	05-04
Vom Hofe, Ed.	Restigouche 2/0	nice factory leather pouch	NIP	$2,425.00	03-08
Vom Hofe, Ed.	Restigouche 6/0	#423, fly, purty, NOT MET	EXIC	$2,125.00	99-11
Vom Hofe, Ed.	Restigue 4/0 fly	replaced seat screws, clicker	EX?	$1,725.00	99-07
Vom Hofe, Ed.	Saltwater Big Game Reel	5" dia., 3⅛" wide, 8/0 size, front rear rim throw-off, past owner's name on back	VG	$550.00	05-04
Vom Hofe, Ed.	Sam's Spoon	#5 & #6, 2 diff	EX	$125.00	99-06
Vom Hofe, Ed.	Sam's Spoon	3 different	EX	$80.00	00-04
Vom Hofe, Ed.	92	1902	EX	$510.00	99-01
Vom Hofe, Ed.	200	decent, NOT MET	EX-	$127.00	01-10
Vom Hofe, Ed.	423	4/0, fly reel, NOT MET	EX	$2,500.00	99-02
Vom Hofe, Ed.	491	1.0, leather case missing snap	EX-IC	$517.00	02-05

BRAND	MODEL	SERIES / MFG. CODE / DESCRIPTION	GRADE	PRICE	DATE yy/mm
Vom Hofe, Ed.	504	gs and hard rubber, size 3, salmon reel, 3⅝" dia., 1¼" wide spool, handmade reel click switch, 1902 pat date, marked rear cap	EX	$1,980.00	04-11
Vom Hofe, Ed.	504	#1, fly reel, g. silver/rubber	EX-	$3,000.00	00-10
Vom Hofe, Ed.	504	4/0, spool corroded	EX-	$1,500.00	02-02
Vom Hofe, Ed.	521	6/0, beauty, g. silver/rubber	EX	$355.00	00-08
Vom Hofe, Ed.	521	wrong handle, cracked side	VG+IC	$287.00	02-05
Vom Hofe, Ed.	521	wrong handle, marked leather case rough	VG-	$144.00	02-05
Vom Hofe, Ed.	521	wrong handle, marked leather case rough	VG-	$287.00	02-05
Vom Hofe, Ed.	591	size 1, 3" diameter, 1⅜" wide, NOT MET	EX	$516.00	05-07
Vom Hofe, Ed.	621	2/0, '96 patent	EX-	$455.00	02-09
Vom Hofe, Ed.	621	6/0, ugly	avg	$168.00	00-10
Vom Hofe, Ed.	621	61	EX	$350.00	99-06
Vom Hofe, Ed.	621	36617	EX	$284.00	00-11
Vom Hofe, Ed.	992	bass reel, 3", leather case poor	EX-IC	$575.00	02-05
Vom Hofe, Ed.	36678	1902 pat	EX	$550.00	00-03
Vom Hofe, F	Ball Handle	brass, stamped	?	$1,380.00	00-10
Vom Hofe, F	Black Bass	hard rubber, g. silver	EX	$987.00	00-04
Vom Hofe, F.	Multiplying G.S. Reel	4" dia., 2" wide spool, S-handle reel, c. 1870, large walnut grasp, sliding oil caps both front & back, Vom Hofe, leather drag added by fisherman	VG+/EX-	$495.00	05-04
Vom Hofe, J.	#3	raised pillar, Oct. 08, 1989, NOT MET	VG	$99.02	99-06
Vom Hofe, J.	#3 Baitcaster	J.P. Lovell Arms Co., '86 & '89 pats, raised pillar	EX	$290.00	00-03
Vom Hofe, J.	#4 Fly	2⅛", Abbie & Imbrie imprint	VG+	$475.00	99-04
Vom Hofe, J.	1/0 Fly	flat top raised pillar, S-handle nice	EX-	$3,158.00	04-11
Vom Hofe, J.	1/0	'85, '89 pats, some screw bug	EX-	$465.00	99-04
Vom Hofe, J.	6/0	pre–B Ocean stamping, 4½" x 2⅜", SD, GS & HR	VG+	$550.00	04-11
Vom Hofe, J.	9/0	1911 pat	EX	$402.00	00-10
Vom Hofe, J.	B 4/0	George Eastman, purty	EX	$510.00	99-09
Vom Hofe, J.	Bay Reel	gs and hard rubber, with sliding oil cap, 2⅞" dia., 1¾" wide, front mouthed, free spool lever, size no. 1, marked foot	EX	$159.50	05-04
Vom Hofe, J.	Brass RP	solid brass, 4" x 2", 1889 patent	VG+	$100.00	05-07
Vom Hofe, J.	Casting	all metal	VG+	$91.00	00-03
Vom Hofe, J.	Casting RP	Abbey & Imbrie, pat Jan. 17, '82, pat Oct. 8, '89, 1¾" x 2⅛"	EX	$112.00	05-07
Vom Hofe, J.	Early Brass	cloverleaf, 2", rubber, ugly	avg	$148.00	00-09
Vom Hofe, J.	Fly	g. silver/rubber, very nice patina, smaller 1889	EX	$961.00	02-01
Vom Hofe, J.	Fly #3	Dame-Stoddard Co., Boston, outer rim perforated	VG+	$2,275.00	01-04
Vom Hofe, J.	Fly Reel	2" x 1", hard rubber/gs, light filing on foot	VG+	$471.00	05-07
Vom Hofe, J.	Fly Reel	Bakelite, 2¼", nice, unpolished	EX-	$283.00	01-10
Vom Hofe, J.	Kentucky	gs/rubber, click button, '89 pat	EX-	$450.00	01-06
Vom Hofe, J.	Large Fly Reel	Folsom Arms	EX-	$516.00	99-07
Vom Hofe, J.	Locking Reel	3" dia., 2" wide, gs, free spool lever on replaced screw and slightly damaged screw heads	VG	$93.50	05-04
Vom Hofe, J.	Light Saltwater	1885 pat, missing end cap	avg	$51.00	00-09
Vom Hofe, J.	Pre B-Ocean Reel	3/0 size, 3⅞" dia., 2⅛" wide, nicely inset front throw-off lever, click very strong	EX	$275.00	05-04

BRAND	MODEL	SERIES / MFG. CODE / DESCRIPTION	GRADE	PRICE	DATE yy/mm
Vom Hofe, J.	Raised Pillar	JVH, 1886 pat	avg	$133.50	99-04
Vom Hofe, J.	Raised Pillar	unmarked, c. 1890	VG-	$210.00	99-04
Vom Hofe, J.	Raised Pillar Fly	2¼", rubber, 1889 pat	EX	$675.00	99-08
Vom Hofe, J.	Size 3½ Handle Plate Type Trout Click Reel	2¼" dia., 1" wide spool reel, very good clicker, one tiny chip from front rim	VG-	$137.00	04-11
Vom Hofe, J.	Size 3½ Trout Reel	2¼" dia., 1" wide spool reel, strong click, 90% plating intact, 23-Sep		$632.00	04-11
Vom Hofe, J.	Surf Casting Reel	pat Nov. 17, '85, Oct. 8, 1889, pat Mar. 21, Brooklyn, NY, 2/00 size, gs and hard rubber, 3¼" dia., 1⅞" wide	G-	$126.50	05-04
Vom Hofe, J.	Thos. J. Conroy	foot damage, not awful	avg	$152.51	99-01
Vom Hofe, J.	Trout 1¾" x 2"	pat Oct. 8, '89	EX+	$372.00	01-03
Vom Hofe, J.	92		VG	$227.50	99-01
Vom Hofe, J.	153	1911 pat	EX-	$310.00	99-06
Vom Hofe, J.	36557	raised pillar, spool corr but otherwise nice	VG+	$108.00	01-08
Vom Hofe, J.		2", cloverleaf logo, g. silver/rubber	EX	$1,436.00	00-10
Vom Hofe, J.		serial no. B299, gs and hard rubber, handmade ocean reel, 4" dia., 2" wide, leather thumb drag, universal and adjustable star drag system, sliding click switch on back plate	EX	$330.00	05-04
Wakeman	Skeleton	pat 1886	EX	$744.00	00-04
Walker	2/0 Salmon	NOT MET	restored!	$1,280.00	00-01
Waltco	Ny-O-Lyte	red/white	NIB	$70.00	99-08
Warren	Casting	brass, round ball	VG+	$255.65	00-03
Waterwitch	Casting	nice box VG	EXIB	$128.00	05-01
Weber	Futurist	fly, sm chip, replaced screw	fair	$26.00	99-01
Welch, Jack	Casting	Kentucky style, "Hand Made"	EX	$1,000.00	04-11
Welch, JAck		handmade	EX	$1,015.00	01-06
Wildon, D.D.	Kentucky	DDS, one of 4 known	EX	$3,350.00	01-04
William Mills and Son	#3	marked "Julius Vom Hofe," 2½" dia., 1" wide spool reel	EX-	$275.00	04-11
Williams, Ted	440 Spin	nice Sears box	EXIB	$32.00	01-03
Williams, Ted	450 Spin	made by Alcedo? VG box & paper	EX-IB	$66.00	00-04
Williams, Ted	450 Spin		VGIB	$51.00	01-05
Williams, Ted	550 Spin	Italy, papers and soft pouch nice	NIP	$103.00	01-08
Williams, Ted	Baitcasting	FS, SD, Shk President II?	EX	$232.00	00-04
Williams, Ted	IV Spinning		EX-IB	$65.00	99-05
Williams, Ted	312.3114	single action fly reel, brown-bronze color	EX	$56.00	02-09
Williams, Ted	430	casting	EX+	$97.00	00-04
Williams, Ted	470	fly, case, nice	EXIC	$153.50	99-05
Williams, Ted	535.3849	casting, SD, Sears & Roebuck	EX-	$89.00	01-11
Williams, Ted	540	Spincast	EX+	$50.00	00-10
Williams, Ted	31231552	fly single action, pouch + papers	NIP	$76.00	00-09
Winchester	1236 Fly	NOT MET	EX	$104.49	99-07
Winchester	1236 Fly	raised pillar, cheapie, knob missing	EX-	$90.00	00-05
Winchester	1336 Fly	alum? ugly, NOT MET	VG	$76.00	00-03
Winchester	Fly	small, punch pressed, poorly made	EX	$132.00	00-08
Winchester	Fly Reel	single action, poor pictures	VG?	$163.00	04-11

BRAND	MODEL	SERIES / MFG. CODE / DESCRIPTION	GRADE	PRICE	DATE yy/mm
Winchester	Marked Bait Casting Reel	2" dia., nonlevel wind reel, nickel plating, marked "60" on foot, one jeweled bearing	VG	$82.50	04-11
Winchester	No. 2236	nonlevel wind casting reel, click and drag switches, 60 yd., nickel plated reel, counterbalanced handle	G	$66.00	05-04
Winchester	No. 2230	1¾" dia., nickel plated, on level wind reel, raised pillars, marked "60" on foot	VG	$110.00	05-04
Winchester	1119	raised pillar, 25 yd., gold? plated	VG+	$112.00	00-11
Winchester	1212	screw frame, better quality than usual	EX	$202.00	02-01
Winchester	1236	fly reel	EX	$202.00	99-06
Winchester	1312	raised pillar, 60 yd, German silver, wowser	EX+	$184.00	05-07
Winchester	2230	60 yd., raised pillers, 9-Aug, NOT MET		$175.00	05-06
Winchester	2236		VG	$104.50	99-01
Winchester	2644	poorly made box, poorly made reel, NOT MET	VGIB	$660.50	00-02
Winchester	4246	80 yd., jeweled, non-LW, nicer than usual Winchester	EX	$140.00	05-07
Winchester	4350	nice casting, g. silver (Meisselbach)	EX-	$178.00	04-03
Winchester	4391	100 yd., 9-Sep, NOT MET		$180.00	05-06
Wisner	fly	German silver, C.H.Wisner, Flint, Mich.	EX	$1,526.00	04-11
Wood	English	brass, nice	EX	$103.00	01-01
Wright McGill	Free-Line	like Whirl Away, built-in bulb at base of rod	EX-	$86.00	01-08
Yankee	269	RP, nickle plated, 300 yd., great 2PCCB	EXIB	$59.00	05-07
Yawman & Erbe	Fly, auto	pat 1891	avg	$67.51	99-11
Yawman & Erbe	Fly, auto			$112.30	99-02
Young	Beaudex	3½", with line, used but works fine	VG	$41.00	05-03
Young	Landex	fly reel, lg capacity wide spool, foot lightly filed	EXIB	$107.00	03-06
Young, J.W.	Freedex	4", combined fly spin, center pin, free spool	EX	$109.00	05-07
Young, J.W.	Trudex Reel	5½" dia., ½" wide spool, click lever, drag adjusting thumb screw, reversible wire line guide	VG	$55.00	05-04
Young, J.W.	Valdex	fly, 3⅛"	EX-	$109.00	05-07
Young, J.W.	Landex	fly, 3½"	G	$77.00	99-01
Zangi	3V	3-speed, spinning reel, Italy	VG	$200.00	04-07
Zangi	3V	spinning, honest wear but runs well	VG+	$286.00	01-08
Zebco	#44	#44, below-handle mount, pitching reel, 9-Sep		$35.00	05-06
Zebco	33 Black	y/black box, 1955 papers	NIB	$56.00	99-07
Zebco	33XBL	gold-plated hardware	EX-	$61.00	05-07
Zebco	Cardinal 3	no bail!	VG+	$66.50	99-05
Zebco	Cardinal 3	2 extra spools	EX-	$133.00	00-04
Zebco	Cardinal 3	box EX & goodies	EXIB	$203.00	05-07
Zebco	Cardinal 3	crisp box & goodies	EXIB	$203.00	05-07
Zebco	Cardinal 3	crisp box & goodies, extra spool	NIB	$244.00	04-02
Zebco	Cardinal 3	extra spool	EX	$125.50	99-08
Zebco	Cardinal 3	green/white	EX	$60.00	02-08
Zebco	Cardinal 3	nice box + goodies & extra spool	NIB	$269.00	05-07
Zebco	Cardinal 3	wear on reel foot	EX-	$150.00	99-02
Zebco	Cardinal 3		EX	$76.00	00-10
Zebco	Cardinal 3		EX-	$91.00	99-10
Zebco	Cardinal 3		VG	$91.01	99-01

BRAND	MODEL	SERIES / MFG. CODE / DESCRIPTION	GRADE	PRICE	DATE yy/mm
Zebco	Cardinal 3		EX-	$116.05	99-03
Zebco	Cardinal 3		VG	$117.50	99-03
Zebco	Cardinal 3		EX	$132.00	01-04
Zebco	Cardinal 3		EX	$165.33	99-08
Zebco	Cardinal 3		EX-	$170.00	99-03
Zebco	Cardinal 3		NIB	$194.00	00-07
Zebco	Cardinal 3		NIB	$270.00	99-03
Zebco	Cardinal 3 &4	2 diff, 1 extra spool	VG	$172.28	99-05
Zebco	Cardinal 33	modern	NIB	$202.50	99-04
Zebco	Cardinal 4	bail doesn't work, turns rough	poor	$67.00	01-08
Zebco	Cardinal 4	box and papers	EXIB	$167.50	99-02
Zebco	Cardinal 4	by ABU, dark green/lt green	VG	$81.00	99-01
Zebco	Cardinal 4	extra spool, papers	EX	$100.00	00-11
Zebco	Cardinal 4	extra spool, foam box, parts	EX	$141.63	99-05
Zebco	Cardinal 4	green box	NIB	$153.50	99-04
Zebco	Cardinal 4	NOT MET	EX-	$81.00	99-05
Zebco	Cardinal 4	NOT MET	NIB	$120.15	99-05
Zebco	Cardinal 4	papers	mint	$118.00	00-11
Zebco	Cardinal 4	rod & reel blister pack!	NOC	$255.00	00-01
Zebco	Cardinal 4	spare spool	EX	$150.00	99-03
Zebco	Cardinal 4	spool only, reproduction aluminum	EX	$31.00	99-08
Zebco	Cardinal 554	papers	NIB	$87.00	01-06
Zebco	Cardinal 557	in Cardinal 57 box	NIB	$50.00	99-02
Zebco	Cardinal 6	extra spool	EX-	$76.00	99-04
Zebco	Cardinal 6	NOT MET	NIB	$75.00	99-05
Zebco	Cardinal 6	NOT MET	NIB	$91.00	99-03
Zebco	Cardinal 6		VG	$70.00	99-01
Zebco	Cardinal 6		EX	$75.00	99-01
Zebco	Cardinal 6		EX+	$76.00	99-03
Zebco	Cardinal 6		VG	$83.00	99-09
Zebco	Cardinal 6X	rough box, NOT MET	EX	$127.50	00-03
Zebco	Cardinal 7	2 extra spools	EX	$109.00	01-08
Zebco	Cardinal 7	by ABU, NOT MET	EX	$100.50	99-04
Zebco	Cardinal 7	spare spool	mint	$125.00	99-03
Zebco	Cardinal 7		VG	$48.99	99-06
Zebco	Cardinal 7		avg	$51.00	99-03
Zebco	Cardinal 7		EX-	$68.57	99-03
Zebco	Cardinal 7		EXIB	$72.55	99-04
Zebco	Cardinal 7		EX	$75.00	01-04
Zebco	Cardinal 7		NIB	$94.00	00-07
Zebco	Cardinal 7X	brown/white	VG-	$77.00	99-03
Zebco	Classic	#444, below handle mount, large hole, 9-Sep		$35.00	05-06
Zebco	11	two VG and EX		$40.00	99-01
Zebco	22	nice box	EXIB	$51.00	00-11
Zebco	44	underslung, Spincast	NIB	$76.00	99-08
Zebco	55	y/red box	EXIB	$59.00	01-08
Zebco	55		NIB	$136.00	00-10
Zebco	204	blue box EX, blue Zee Bee reel	EX-IB	$82.00	05-07

BRAND	MODEL	SERIES / MFG. CODE / DESCRIPTION	GRADE	PRICE	DATE yy/mm
Zero Hour Bomb Co.	Zebco	black manual, spinning, ball drag	VG	$11.00	05-03
Zwarg	2/0	600 yd.	EX-	$610.00	05-06
Zwarg	2/0	leather case, never used	mint	$237.00	05-07
Zwarg	4/0	400 yd., plain unmarked box, "from factory"	NIB	$2,036.00	05-07
Zwarg	4/0	unmarked plain box, printer block, "Otto Zwarg"	NIB	$2,325.00	05-07
Zwarg	Maximo	2/0 size, gs, hard rubber, front and rear rim throw-offs, star drag	EX	$550.00	05-04
Zwarg	Model 600	size 4/0, 3⅞" dia., 2" wide, star drag front rim, free spool, sliding oil caps, wire line on spool	VG	$385.00	05-04
Zwarg	Saugenay 2/0	fly	near mint	$2,651.00	00-05
Zwarg	36557	g. silver/rubber, NOT MET	EX	$499.00	00-10
Zwarg	36770	g. silver, never polished, NOT MET	EX	$935.00	00-03
Zwarg, Otto	4/0 Salmon Reel	g. silver and hard rubber	VG+	$1,650.00	04-11
Zwarg, Otto	600, 4/0	serial no. E-327	mint	$338.00	03-04

Rods

BRAND	MODEL	SERIES / MFG. CODE / DESCRIPTION	GRADE	PRICE	DATE yy/mm
Unknown	Kosmic	8', 3/1, detachable handle, with all nickel silver reel, seat stamped "No 318," ⅛" cork rings, ferrules are waisted and have witness marks, guides English twist wrapped in red silk, full intermediates	F-/P	$440.00	05-04
Unknown	Little Divine Fairy Rod	7½', 3/2, decal 100%, "H 4638" stamped on butt cap, w/orig bag hanging tag and tube	EX	$825.00	05-04
Abercrombie & Fitch	Fly Rod	7', 2/2, round decal, butt section A & F markings, green-tipped black wraps, cork reel, seat sanded in middle	EX	$330.00	05-04
Abercrombie & Fitch	Nickle Silver Reel Seat	9', 3/1, 1 tip ¾ short, none serrated, nickel silver ferrules	G	$82.50	05-04
Abercrombie & Fitch	Trout Reel	7', 2/1, tiny 3¾" cork grip, diminutive reel seat stepped up to meet cork grip with tiny sliding band and butt cap, c. 1920, English guides graduating down to tiniest size on tip, agate stripping guide is replacement, 3" repair wrap between top snake guide tip-top and rod refinished	VG	$522.50	05-04
ABU	Suecia 321	glass, spinning, 2pc	mint	$81.00	00-10
ABU	Tournament II	6' baitcast, 2pc, pouch, nice	EX	$167.50	00-03
Andrews, Tim	Fly Rod	7'9", 2/2, tips ¼" longer, 5 wt. red wraps, tipped black cigar handle, sliding band reel, snake guides, chrome stripper red glass insert	VG	$176.00	05-04
Armax	7286	3/2, fly rod	EX	$133.81	99-01
Bean, L.L.	Featherweight	8', 3/2, nickel silver fittings, cork reel, seat with sliding band, slight ridging to grip, grip ferrules	VG	$352.00	05-04

BRAND	MODEL	SERIES / MFG. CODE / DESCRIPTION	GRADE	PRICE	DATE yy/mm
		cleaned, w/Thomas bag and capless tube			
Bernard & Sons	Fly Rod	6½', 2/1, bamboo, purty!	EX	$110.00	05-07
Blue Blood	Trout Rod	7½', 3/2, resorcinol glue lines, red wraps, glass stripper guide, rust stains on bamboo, redone earlier manufactured rod, older bag, new tube	VG?	$82.50	05-04
Browness & Browness	Marked Salmon Rod	13', 3/2, wood fly rod guides, older floppy ring type, mid to but sect reversed, screw-on brass	EX	$550.00	04-11
Browning	Boron	model #132915, 2pc, 6'6", spinning	EX	$62.00	04-12
Browning	Dave Fritts	E-glass, 6'	mint	$41.00	99-03
Browning	Silaflex	bait caster, custom case	EX	$312.00	99-11
Browning	Silaflex	casting, 6'6", 2-piece	EX+	$201.50	99-12
Browning	Silaflex 122910	dual fly rod, 6'4" or 8'9" length	NIT	$100.00	04-02
Browning	Silaflex 312920	2-piece, bait casting	EX	$134.00	02-06
Browning	312910	casting, tube and pouch	EXIT	$395.00	00-02
Browning Silaflex	Medallion 23965	bag & tube, NOT MET	NIT	$110.07	99-11
Carlson, Sam	Carlson Four	7½', 2/2, w/original bag/tube	EX	$3,630.00	04-11
Carlson, Sam	Quadrate Bait Casting Rod	6'4", 2/1, w/bag/tube	EX	$797.50	04-11
Carlson, Sam	Quadrate Salmon Rod	9½', 3/2, w/5" extension butt marked "Bill Rosgen" in black ink, w/orig bag/tube	EX	$1,100.00	04-11
Carlson, Sam	"The Thomas Rod Co." H	cane trout rod, 5', 1-piece rod w/orig bag/tube	EX	$1,430.00	04-11
Carpenter, Walt	7 ft.	trout rod, 2/2, flamed rod ferrules and hardware, blued varnish glass like	MINT	$4,180.00	05-04
Carpenter, Walt	Browntone	8', 2/2, checking tapers	EX	$3,080.00	04-11
Cortland	444 LTD	6½', trout rod, 2/1, butt 1⅛" short, impregnated rod, flamed cane, 4¼" handle, brass ferrules	VG	$220.00	05-04
Cortland	444 Trout Rod	impregnated, 2/1, 8-weight line, w/orig bag/tube	EX+	$115.50	05-04
Cortland	Trout Rod	impregnated, 8', 2/2, 4¼ oz., no. 8 line, red wraps, chrome guides, brass ferrules, w/orig bag/tube	EX	$110.00	05-04
Coulson & lyon	Trout Rod	9', 3/2, HCH or D line, marked "Imperial No. 215" on shaft, both tips slight, sets and varnish somewhat wrinkled, w/marked bag and tube	G+	$77.00	05-04
Crocker, K.C.	Me 332	7', 2/2, all cork sliding band, skeletal reel, seat oxidized, super Z ferrules	EX	$495.00	05-04
Crocker, Ken	Trout Rod	8', 2/2, darkly flamed cane, medium brown wraps, agate stripper guide, oxidized nickel silver ferrules, tips ³⁄₁₆" and ⅜" shorter than butt, made that way	EX	$192.50	05-04
Davis	Special	9'	mint	$310.00	99-09
Dickerson	7'4"	2/1, no tube, no bag, ferrule lose, c. 1962	EX	$900.00	99-12
Dickerson	8015 Special	8', 2/2, tube & sock, 1 of 16 ever made	EXIT	$4,076.00	01-04
Dickerson	90182	9', 3/2, bag and tube	EXIT	$2,275.78	99-08
Edwards	Quadrate	model 40, 7', 2/2, blued hardware, brown wraps tipped black, w/orig tube and replacement bag	VG	$687.50	05-04
Edwards	Quadrate	No. 50, 8½', 3/2, with one tip differing slightly from other in color of wraps and profile on snake guides, w/orig bag and leather tube	EX	$605.00	05-04
Edwards E.	Bamboo Fly Rod	8½', 3/2, bag and tube	VG+	$465.65	99-06
Edwards, Bill	Model 33 Quadrate	7½', 3/2, w/orig bag and tube	EX	$1,155.00	04-11

BRAND	MODEL	SERIES / MFG. CODE / DESCRIPTION	GRADE	PRICE	DATE yy/mm
Edwards, Bill	Model 35 Quadrate Trout Rod	8½', 3/2, restored, w/orig bag and tube	EX	$577.50	04-11
Edwards, Bill	Model 40 Trout Rod	7', 2/2, 1 tip short 4" and missing ferrule	VG	$770.00	04-11
Edwards, Bill	Model 425 Spinning Rod	7', 2/1, w/orig bag and peerless tube	EX	$220.00	04-11
Edwards, Bill	Model 56 Quadrate	9', 3/2, sticky varnish on both tips, trout rod, butt cap, plug loose, w/orig bag tube	VG+	$220.00	04-11
Edwards, Bill	One Piece Bait Casting Rod	5'11", rod needs wrap repairs and guide replaced, w/orig bag tube	G	$137.50	04-11
Edwards, Bill	Quadrate Model 54	8½', 3/2, restored reel seat, w/bag tube	EX	$385.00	04-11
Edwards, Gene	Brown Spinning Rod	7', 2/1, rodent damage on cork handle	VG-	$82.50	05-04
Edwards, W.E.	Deluxe	No. 25, 5½', 2/2, staggered ferrule rod, aluminum downlocking reel seat, ridging to cork	VG	$275.00	05-04
Edwards, W.E.	Fly Rod	9', mid has clear 1' wrap, 3/3, 1 tip ½" short, another 7" short, rod restored as indicated	G	$110.00	05-04
Edwards, W.E.	Quadrate	6½', 2/2, 4½ oz., w/orig signature wraps and ferrule wraps, ferrules nicely blued, varnish is VG	VG	$137.50	05-04
Edwards, W.E.	Quadrate	No. 300, 7', 2/1, 4⅞ oz., varnish glass like, w/orig bag/tube, nearly perfect label	EX	$550.00	05-04
Edwards, W.E.	Special	8½', 3/1, Bristol-era guide wraps on mid, reel seat replaced with Heddon, may have overvarnish	G	$110.00	05-04
Edwards, W.E.	Spinning Rod	fiberglass, 7', 2/1, marked "No. 208," c. 1950, dual aluminum siding	EX	$55.00	05-04
Farlow	The Dream Series	6', 3 – 4 oz. weight, 2/1, w/orig bag/tube	mint	$275.00	05-04
Fenwick	#FF807	8', #7 line, bag & tube mint	NIT	$126.50	99-08
Fenwick	5½" medium	Featherweight All-Angle grip	EX-	$141.50	99-08
Fenwick	Custom Baitcaster	All-Angle grip, nice	EX	$152.52	99-08
Fenwick	FC60	Ferilite, 6', 2/1, tobacco glass, handwritten model, 8¼ oz.	EXIT	$660.00	05-07
Fenwick	FC60	serial no. J106880	EXIT	$404.00	05-07
Fenwick	FC65	2/1, tobacco glass, Feralite, 6½', All-Angle grip, hand lettering	EX-	$404.00	05-07
Fenwick	FF60	6', 2pc, 5-6 line, bag & tube	EX	$213.36	99-03
Fenwick	FF756-4	fly, backpack, tube & case	NIT	$180.00	99-05
Fenwick	FF807	8', 3⅜ oz., #7 line, bag & tube, NOT MET	NIT	$77.00	99-06
Fenwick	FS55	serial no. I26808, Feralite, 5½', 2⅜ oz., bag & tube	EXIT	$125.00	05-07
Fenwick	FS55	ultralight spinning, Feralite, with pouch	EXIT	$76.00	05-07
Fenwick	Lunkerstick	1260, 5'	EX-	$93.00	04-11
Fenwick	Lunkerstick	PLC60, 6', 2pc, rod w/Champion handle	EX	$33.00	05-07
Fenwick	Lunkerstick	#207446, 6'	EX	$200.00	99-02
Fenwick	Lunkerstick	1155, 5'6", 2¼ oz., shaft, ⅜ – ¾ oz.	EX	$305.00	00-08
Fenwick	Lunkerstick	1460, 6'8", ⅜ oz., 10 – 20 lb.	EX	$200.00	99-02
Fenwick	Lunkerstick	PLC55, 5½', ½ – 1 oz.	EXIC	$411.00	00-02
Fenwick	Lunkerstick	bag, 1255	EXIB	$144.50	99-08
Fenwick	Lunkerstick	1461, Champion grip, ceramic eyes	EX-	$75.00	99-12
Fenwick	Lunkerstick	2000BC	EX	$127.00	00-04
Fenwick	Lunkerstick	newer 2056, 5½', ½ – 1 oz.	EX	$134.50	99-03
Fenwick	Lunkerstick	PLC, 5½', 11" rubber handle	mint	$232.50	99-04
Fenwick	Lunkerstick	PLC60, 2pc, reg grip	mint	$260.00	99-04

BRAND	MODEL	SERIES / MFG. CODE / DESCRIPTION	GRADE	PRICE	DATE yy/mm
Fenwick	Lunkerstick	PLC65, 6½'	EX	$303.50	99-03
Fenwick	Lunkerstick 1256	5½', reg grip, ⅝ – 1¼ oz., 15 – 25 lb.	EX	$213.50	99-03
Fenwick	Lunkerstick 1261	⅝ – 1¼ oz., 6', NOT MET	EX	$51.00	99-08
Fenwick	Lunkerstick 1361		EX	$61.00	99-12
Fenwick	Lunkerstick 2000	#2053, 5½', pistol grip, wow	EX	$510.00	99-10
Fenwick	Lunkerstick 2000	#2054, serial no. P233839, 5½', 1/1	EX-	$390.00	05-07
Fenwick	Lunkerstick 2000	#2060, 6', medium	mint	$510.00	99-11
Fenwick	Lunkerstick 2000	2050, 5 power, 8 – 20 lb. line	mint	$556.00	04-11
Fenwick	Lunkerstick 2000	2056, newer grip, 10 – 20 lb. line, 6 power	EX	$206.00	01-06
Fenwick	Lunkerstick 2000	2057, 1pc, molded plastic grip	EX	$79.00	04-02
Fenwick	Lunkerstick 2000	2057, 5½'	EX	$104.00	04-07
Fenwick	PLC 65	2-piece	EX	$232.50	99-10
Fenwick	PLS 65	spinning, with bag and tube	VG	$53.00	99-01
Fenwick	1255	5½'	EX	$150.00	00-10
Fenwick	1256	Lunker Stick	EX-	$81.00	99-08
Fenwick	1456	Lunker Stick, Fenwick grip	EX	$162.50	99-04
French, P.	Fly Rod	7', 2-2, bag and case, NOT MET!	mint	$820.00	99-01
Garcia	#2102	Conlon, five star, 7', M, agate eyes	NIbag	$67.00	00-04
Garcia	Conolon Companion	2621, 2pc, casting light, blue	EX	$74.00	99-07
Gephart	700	4'6", casting, NOT MET	NIC	$51.00	00-10
Gillum, H.S.	Salmon Rod	2/2, medium colored cane glue lines, aluminun uplocking seat hook, ding butt section	EX	$2,200.00	05-04
Goodwin	Deluxe	9½', trout rod, 3/2, one tip 2¾" short, other 3½" short, c. 1930, 2 factory mids and bag marks to varnish, 1 guide wrap needs replacing, thumb depression added to earlier grip, w/orig 5-compartment bag, earlier tube replacement cap	VG	$126.50	05-04
Goodwin	Granger	7', 2/2, "Victory," tube & bag	EXIT	$725.00	99-06
Goodwin Granger	Favorite	9', trout rod, 3/2, 1 tip 1½" short, with a loose ferrule, chrome-plated brass reel seat, possible refinish, guide wrapped with white and black jasper tipped black, w/orig bag and later tube	EX+?	$220.00	05-04
Goodwin Granger	Fly	8½', 3/2, bag & tube, "Victory," NOT MET	EX-	$305.75	99-08
Goodwin Granger	Special	9', trout rod, 3/2, few areas of rough varnish, w/orginal bag tube	EX+	$165.00	05-04
Goodwin Granger	Trout Rod	7½', 3/2, few areas rough varnish, original bag/tube	NM	$990.00	05-04
Goodwin Granger	Trout Rod	7½', 3/2, w/bag and tube	NM	$715.00	05-04
Granger	Deluxe	8½', 3/2, bag and tube, needs work	??IT	$410.00	99-09
Granger	Special	8½', 3/2, one tip ⅜" short, goldfish wraps	VG+	$368.00	05-07
Handmade	Sage	9½', graphite rod, 4-piece, marked "The Anglers Club of New York 1990," packs into tube with Angler Club logo	EX+	$385.00	05-04
Hardy	Banty	serial no. H40813C, 4'4", trout rod, 2/1, all cork reel seat, with aluminum cap	?	$632.00	05-04
Hardy	Fairchild	No. H 8670, 8', 3/2, museum quality	NIT	$1,000.00	05-07

BRAND	MODEL	SERIES / MFG. CODE / DESCRIPTION	GRADE	PRICE	DATE yy/mm
Hardy	Fly Rod	serial no. 4014, 11', 3/2, floppy ring guides, "pool cue" type grip, alternating cane and wood ferrules, locking type	VG	$440.00	04-11
Hardy	Light Salmon Rod	8'9", 2/2, English rod, new and unused, plastic still on handle, black wraps, green tipping, chrome snake guides, blued ferrules	EX+	$302.50	05-04
Hardy	Marvel	7½', trout rod, 3/2, tip rod is in near new condition, w/orig bag/tube	EX+	$1,100.00	04-11
Hardy	Palakona	7½', 2/1, 6 weight, w/bag and tube	EX	$330.00	05-04
Hardy	Palakona	7½', 2/1, all original varnish showing moderate signs of use, red wraps, tipped green, marked "for No. 6 line," w/orig bag and standard tube	VG	$330.00	05-04
Hardy	Palakona	7½', 3/2, w/orig marked bag/tube (no cap)	EX+	$275.00	04-11
Hardy	Palakona	Halford Knockabout, salmon rod, 9½', 2/1, w/extension butt, original bag/tube	EX+	$220.00	04-11
Hardy	Palakona	trout rod, 8½', 3/2, tip rod, w/bag, hanging tag, replacement tube	EX+	$550.00	04-11
Hardy	Palakona Regal	serial no. 17578B, 10', trout rod, 3/2, both tips short 2", marked "Palakona Regal No. 246936 the deluxe rod," stamped serial no., very good condition, full intermediates, some areas of varnish roughness, original labeled bag and tube, no cap	VG	$110.00	05-04
Hardy	Palokona H24442	Gold Medal, 10½', 2/2, missing an eye	EX-	$114.00	05-07
Hardy	Phantom	6', trout rod, 2/1, pleasing dry fly action, no. 5 line, w/orig dark blue bag and replacement tube	EX+	$385.00	05-04
Hardy	Salmon Deluxe	9½', 3/2, 7 wt. line rod, original bag, tube, extension butt	NIT	$495.00	04-11
Hardy	Salmon Deluxe Palakona	9½', 3/2, both tips 1" short, made that way, 6¾ oz., detachable extension butt, ferrule plugs, original labeled bag, no tube	EX	$110.00	05-04
Hardy	Salmon Rod	14½', 3/2, floppy ring guides, one missing, locking ferrules with plugs	VG	$165.00	05-04
Hardy	Trout Rod	6', 2/1, ½" short, plastic wrap on handle, w/ferrule plug, in labeled bag	MINT	$330.00	05-04
Harvey	Trout Rod	9½', 3/1, 1½" short, "J.Harvey" engraved on reel seat, plated ferrules, refinished ghosting where original wraps were, w/replacement bag and tube	VG	$55.00	05-04
Heddon	#10	8', 3/2, 4 weight, 1½ ferrule	EX	$400.00	02-02
Heddon	#10 8½	3/2, tube and bag, NOT MET	EXIT	$178.50	00-01
Heddon	#14	8½'	EXR	$244.50	99-01
Heddon	#17	7½', 3/2, bag, Sci Ang tube	NIT	$525.00	00-09
Heddon	#17	8', 3/2, tube and bag	EXIT	$673.87	00-01
Heddon	#17	Black Beauty, bag, tube 8½'	EX	$425.99	99-01
Heddon	#17 Black Beauty	8½', 3/2, pouch, tube, mint	NIT	$465.00	00-08
Heddon	#17 Black Beauty	8½', 3/2, very minty bag and tube	NIT	$434.00	00-07
Heddon	#17 Black Beauty	9', 3/2, sack, poor tube, refinished, nice	EX	$300.00	01-12

BRAND	MODEL	SERIES / MFG. CODE / DESCRIPTION	GRADE	PRICE	DATE yy/mm
Heddon	#211-6' L	bait casting, newer hollow glass	mint	$108.51	99-05
Heddon	#261	casting, tube glass, pouch 5½'	EXIP	$170.00	02-04
Heddon	#35	9', 3/2, restored	EX-rest.	$267.00	02-03
Heddon	#35 Deluxe Peerless	8½', #2 ferrule, 3/2	EX-	$565.00	99-04
Heddon	#60 9'	3/2, NOT MET	restored!	$500.00	00-01
Heddon	#9	bait casting, 2/1, bag and brass top tube	NIT	$332.00	99-08
Heddon	14 Thoroughbred	3/1	VG+	$207.50	99-07
Heddon	31 Featherlite	7'2", overvarnish, NOT MET	EXIT	$560.00	01-03
Heddon	3151 L	5', bamboo steel, nice pouch	NIP	$151.00	01-08
Heddon	3151L	steel, bamboo color, walnut grip, case	NIC	$242.00	00-03
Heddon	35 DeLuxe	9', 3/2, 6 – 7 lb. line, revarnished	EXRe	$350.00	01-09
Heddon	4451 Pal Spook	4½', with case	mint	$192.50	99-01
Heddon	6783-6'	brown glass	EX	$31.00	00-07
Heddon	75 Black Beauty	8½', fly line, C-HCH, fiberglass	EXIT	$50.00	00-09
Heddon	8457 Mark IV	8½', 2/1, nice tube, plastic on cork	NIT	$150.00	02-03
Heddon	Black Beauty	17'8", 1¾, F- HD	NIS	$544.00	01-04
Heddon	Black Beauty No. 17	8½', trout rod, 3/2, original plastic wrap on handle cracked, w/labeled bag and tube	EX+	$412.50	05-04
Heddon	Black Beauty No. 17	8½', 3/2, #2F, HDH, pouch & tube	EXIT	$400.00	05-07
Heddon	Black Pal	708, newer fiberglass	mint	$137.50	99-05
Heddon	Casting Bamboo	#400-5'-4F, 2pc, revarnished	EX-IT	$152.00	01-03
Heddon	Casting Rod	6', 2/1, detachable handle, checkered walnut foregrip stamped "Heddon Pal," nicely swelled butt says "Heddon Jim Heddons Favorite No. 851-6'XL," varnish EX	EX	$550.00	05-04
Heddon	Exclusive Rod	stainless steel wraps, new in tube, spinning	NIB	$77.00	05-07
Heddon	Expert #125	9', 3F, GBG or C, 3/2, c. 1950s	EXIT	$251.00	05-07
Heddon	Expert 125	8½', 3/2, 2½', F-HCH or D, nice pouch	NIT	$400.00	02-03
Heddon	Expert 125	8½', 3/2, center 2" short	VG	$302.77	99-04
Heddon	Expert 125	9', 3/2, tube & bag, NOT MET	mint	$257.00	99-06
Heddon	Featherweight #14	7½', 2/2, tube & bag	NIT	$690.00	00-02
Heddon	Fly Rod	metal bamboo, 8½', 3/2, bag	EXIT	$255.00	00-03
Heddon	Golden Mark 50 Fly	6½', #5 line	mint	$208.50	99-12
Heddon	Mark IV	6905, Power Plus	EX	$74.00	02-02
Heddon	Mark IV #6903	6', 2pc	EX	$76.00	00-02
Heddon	Mark IV 6903	2pc	EX	$81.00	99-04
Heddon	Mark IV Fly Rod	#8457, 8½', pouch	NIT	$71.00	00-04
Heddon	Mark V	6'6", Spincast, walnut SS wraps, tube	EXIC	$255.00	99-12
Heddon	Mark-2	fly rod, 9', new in tube	NIB	$88.00	05-07
Heddon	Mark-2	spinning rod, new in tube	NIB	$77.00	05-07
Heddon	Mark-3	spinning rod, 7', new in tube	NIB	$55.00	05-07
Heddon	Mark-4	fly rod, 8', new in tube	NIB	$88.00	05-07
Heddon	Model 13	8½', trout rod, 3/2, for HDH or E line, minor varnish roughness, guide on butt section off but present, w/labeled bag	EX-	$192.50	05-04

BRAND	MODEL	SERIES / MFG. CODE / DESCRIPTION	GRADE	PRICE	DATE yy/mm
Heddon	Model 14	early version, 8½', trout rod, 3/2, refinished, some ghosting is evident where guides were on tips, 1 tip heavier replacement, both tip ferrules pinched out of round in attempt to tighten fit, tiny crack at node on one tip, should have repair wrap applied, cork grip, some ridging, thumb depression added	VG	$82.50	05-04
Heddon	Musky Pal	#5123-5', Spook	EX	$41.00	00-01
Heddon	Musky Special 6276	5½', yellow, fiberglass	EX	$6.00	02-03
Heddon	No. 10	7½', 3¼ oz., 2/2, nice pouch, no tube, wowser	NIP	$458.00	05-07
Heddon	Pal	5'1", tobacco hollow glass	EX-	$64.00	02-03
Heddon	Pal	8½', fly rod, wire wrap, in bag & marked tube	EX	$95.00	05-06
Heddon	Pal # 3/5 - 5'L.	Pal p-41 reel	EX	$150.00	99-01
Heddon	Pal #130	6½', M, spinning	NIT	$82.75	99-04
Heddon	Pal #5551-5½' L	case	EXIC	$87.00	99-08
Heddon	Pal #718	spinning, 71	mint	$20.50	99-05
Heddon	Pal #816	6', 2pc	EX	$67.12	99-05
Heddon	Pal Mark 3	#8407, 8½', tube	nice	$46.00	99-01
Heddon	PAL mark II 6'	#6803, 2pc	NIT	$198.50	99-06
Heddon	Pal Mark IV	6'	EX	$76.50	99-04
Heddon	Pal Spook	#3351, 5½', L, bag	NIB	$191.72	99-04
Heddon	Pal Spook	in bag, tube	NIT	$213.50	99-04
Heddon	Pal Spook 6651L	case, 5½', light	EXIC	$202.50	99-09
Heddon	Pal Superlative	glass, with pouch #1-L, 5½'	VG+	$38.00	04-11
Heddon	Pal V	6918, 2pc, 6½'	EX	$58.00	00-02
Heddon	Premier	9', 3/2, HGH, alum tube, sock	EXIT	$330.00	00-11
Heddon	Premier #115	fly rod, 7½', 3/2, tube and bag	EXIT	$678.00	01-08
Heddon	President #150	7-6', wraps poor, uneven sections	VG?	$496.06	99-01
Heddon	President #50	8', 2F, HDH or E, 3/2, one tip 1½" short	EX-	$485.00	05-07
Heddon	President Deluxe 50	50-9'-2F-HDH or E, 4¾ oz., NOT MET	EX	$404.00	03-02
Heddon	Roto Tip	ice fishing rod	EX	$82.00	99-11
Heddon	Spook	5551, 4', L	EX-	$127.50	00-04
Heddon	Superlative	#2270 L, hollow glass, vinyl case	EXIP	$359.00	03-11
Heddon	Superlative	1170-7'-L, spinning, 2pc	NIT	$156.01	00-02
Heddon	Superlative	No. 2270 M, 5½', repaired?	EX-	$152.00	04-04
Heddon	Superlative	T2270 XL, pouch, beauty	NIP	$256.00	00-04
Heddon	Superlative	T2270, 24K eyes	EX-	$345.47	99-04
Heddon	Superlative 2270L	5½', tube and papers	EXIT	$325.00	99-11
Heddon	Superlative 2270M	5½', medium, nice case	EXIC	$283.00	99-11
Heddon	10	8½'-2F-HDH or E, plastic still on grip! bag	NIT	$500.00	02-01
Heddon	14	2½F-HEH or D, 3/2, 9' tube & bag	NIT	$165.00	03-08
Heddon	20	2/3, tips! 7'-0½F-HEH or F, 1 tip short	EX-?	$756.00	01-12
Heddon	20	2½F, 9'	EXR	$200.00	99-01
Heddon	35	9½', 3/2, restored	mint R	$660.00	02-11
Heddon	50	8'-3/2, 1½F, 4 wt., 1 tip repaired, NOT MET	EX-IT	$516.00	02-01
Heddon	75	glass, 9', Black Beauty	mint	$217.50	99-01

BRAND	MODEL	SERIES / MFG. CODE / DESCRIPTION	GRADE	PRICE	DATE yy/mm
Heddon	400	6' med bag, tag still on	mint	$275.00	99-02
Heddon	1000	9', 3/1, refinished	REX	$361.00	01-10
Heddon	#35	Deluxe, 3/2, 9', 5-6 wt. lines	EX	$566.00	02-05
Heddon	Mark IV	6', 2-piece, medium action, nice pouch & tube	NIT	$122.00	02-05
Heddon	President #50	9', 3/2, 6 wt., overvarnish, bag & tube	EX_R	$643.00	02-05
Heddon	Musky Special	6276, tobacco glass	mint	$100.00	01-10
Herters	Fly	8', bamboo	EX	$138.00	99-03
Hexagraph	Graphite Rod	9½', 2/2, 7-8 wt. line, imitation bamboo appearance, uplocking aluminum reel seat	EX	$165.00	05-04
Hildabrand, N.W.	Trout Rod	7', 2/2, 3 wt., lightly flamed cane, red wraps tipped black, uplocking reel seat, wood spacer	G	$137.50	05-04
Horrock - Ibbotson	Chancellor	8½', 3/2, case, NOT MET	NIT	$416.00	00-03
Horrock - Ibbotson	fly 2411	7¾', bag, very nice	EX+IB	$46.00	99-11
Horrock - Ibbotson	Spinner	9', 3/1, tip short, wrong eye, bag	EX?	$100.00	00-08
Horrock - Ibbotson	Tonka Queen	7¾', 4 wt., 2/2, marked pouch	NIP	$465.00	05-02
Horrock - Ibbotson	Tonka Queen	7¾', 2/2, tube and bag	NIT	$360.00	00-02
Horrock - Ibbotson	Tonkin Prince	7', 2/1	EX	$212.00	01-09
Houston, Ed	Salmon Rod	9', 3/2, 4½" butt extension, w/original bag and tube, no cap	EX	$412.50	04-11
Howells	Marked 9 ft. Rod	serial no. 4126, 9', 2/2, uplocking aluminum reel seat, Circassian walnut spacer, modified wells, grip stainless guides and tip tops	EX+	$1,705.00	05-04
Howells	Marked Trout Rod	serial no. 4125, 7½', 2/2, 3⅛ oz., mortised cork reel seat, hooded butt cap, black Bakelite bottom slightly soiled, modified wells grip, stainless guides and tip tops	EX+	$3,080.00	05-04
Howells, Gary	No. 4012	8½', 2/2, marked rod shart medium flamed can snake guide, mildrm style stripper	EX+	$2,090.00	05-04
Howells, G.H	#4438, 8 ft.	2/2, 6 weight, tube and sock	NIT	$1,825.00	00-11
Howes	9 ft. Trout Rod	3/3, 1" repair wrap on butt section; ridging to cork reel seat on tip 1¼" short, 3½" short; 2" repair wrap full tip, lighter color replacement, w/replacement bag and tube	FAIR	$385.00	05-04
Hull	Trout Rod	8½', 2/2, impregnated rod, Super Z ferrules wells grip, marked 2 flaps above grip, but 1 tip wrapped red	G-	$192.50	05-04
Hull	Trout Rod	9', 2/2, 6¼ oz., all sections marked "No. 168"	VG	$302.50	05-04
Hurd	Spuercaster	wood, case	EXIC	$308.00	99-08
Hurd	Supercaster	in correct pouch, wood handle, user's manual	EX+IP	$275.00	04-02
Hurd	Supercaster	walnut handle	VG	$155.25	99-01
Hurd	Tip Only	2 great pamphlets, tube	EX	$405.00	99-04
James, B.	Avocet	split bamboo, 3/1, length unknown, pouch	EXIP	$393.00	03-02
Jenkins	GA 652-1	6½', 2/2, c. 1991, Tonkin cane	NIT	$1,570.00	05-02
Jenkins	GA-70L	2/2, plugs, bag, tube, NOT MET	NIT	$811.00	99-11
Jenkins, C.W.	Bamboo Fly	2/2, plastic on grip, NOT MET	mint	$835.00	99-10
Johnson	Profile	Uniglass 800 8C64, Phillipson?	EX	$610.00	01-06
Johnson	Profile 600	6C60, by Phillipson, in orig pouch	EXIP	$725.00	04-12

BRAND	MODEL	SERIES / MFG. CODE / DESCRIPTION	GRADE	PRICE	DATE yy/mm
Johnson	Profile 800	8C60, by Phillipson, 2-piece, labels + pouch	mint	$1,135.00	04-11
Johnson	Sagamore	9', 3/2, c. 1906, locking nut on reel seat, nickel silver hardware, ferrules on butt	VG	$104.50	05-04
Kade, Art	FlyCraft Rod	8½', 3/2, 6 wt., downlocking reel seat, walnut spacer, polished to yield standard varnish look, w/orig bag and tube	EX	$165.00	05-04
Kusse Ron	Fly Rod	8', 2/2, mint bag, tube, #6 or #7 line, beauty	NIT	$1,500.00	01-08
Lancaster	The Indianapolis Fly Caster V Trout Rod	7'9", 2/2, based on Garrison 209E taper	EX+	$192.50	04-11
Leonard	39DF-4	#472P, 2/2, 7½', #4 line, bag and tube	EXIT	$2,225.00	99-04
Leonard	51S. D.F	9', 3/2, fighting grip, all goodies mint	NIT	$896.00	01-09
Leonard	7', 2/2	Maxwell era	mint	$2,425.00	00-04
Leonard	Baby Catskill	6', 2/2, one tip1" short, bag	EXIT	$1,275.00	00-08
Leonard	Fly	7½', 2/1, marked reel seat, couple loose wraps but nice	EX-	$277.00	05-07
Leonard	Model 50	8½', 3/2, one tip 4" short, missing 1 guide, patent dates on ferrule; orig bag, tag, tube	F	$660.00	05-04
Leonard, H. L.	65L	7½', 2/1, pouch & tube	EXIT	$2,300.00	05-07
Leonard, H. L.	Fairy Catskill Trout Rod	8', 3/2, restored	EX	$2,200.00	04-11
Leonard, H. L.	Fly	8'8", 3/2, wood reel seat, brass cap tube	EXIT	$430.00	05-03
Leonard, H. L.	Hunt Model 69	salmon rod, 10½', 3/3, 6" butt ext, blue wear	VG	$220.00	04-11
Leonard, H. L.	Hunt Series	8', trout rod, 3/2, 4.5 oz., 5 wt., prefire rod, blackened screw, uplocking reel seat, silk wraps translucent gold	EX	$3,080.00	05-04
Leonard, H. L.	Light Line Trout Rod	9', 3/2, full intermediate guides, w/orig sack and tip, tube no cap	VG	$880.00	04-11
Leonard, H. L.	Model 38	7', 2/3, light trout rod, refinished, small repair wrap at butt section, w/orig bag/tube	VG+	$660.00	04-11
Leonard, H. L.	Model 41	serial no. 1562, red wrapped, 8½', 2/2, NS butt cap, 6⅝" cigar grip	MINT	$1,375.00	05-04
Leonard, H. L.	Model 50	8½', 3/2, light line, w/orig bag/tube	EX	$1,210.00	04-11
Leonard, H. L.	Model 50 Trout Rod	early model, 8', 3/2, needs restoration, w/orig bag/tube	G-	$742.50	04-11
Leonard, H. L.	No. 51	tournament salmon rod, prefire, 9', 3/2, gs reel seat, gold wraps tipped with black	NM	$440.00	05-04
Leonard, H. L.	Salmon Rod	11', 3/2, several replaced guide wraps, grips on butt and removal, fighting butt wrapped in rattan	VG	$220.00	05-04
Leonard, H. L.	Salmon Rod	11', 3/2, several replaced guide wraps, grips on butt and removal, fighting butt wrapped in rattan	G	$220.00	05-04
Leonard, H. L.	Salmon Rod	12', 3/2, all cork reel seat, knurled sliding band, one guide butt missing	EX	$220.00	05-04
Leonard, H. L.	Salmon Rod	14', 3/2, damage to varnish	G-	$357.00	05-04
Leonard, H. L.	Salmon Rod	9½', 3/2, detachable 6" butt, w/orig sack/tip tube	VG+	$247.00	04-11
Leonard, H. L.	Special Tournament	9½', 3/2, 1 tip fractured, full nickle silver downlocking reel seat, English guides, agate stripper, agate tip tops, 1 guide off butt section	VG	$220.00	05-04
Leonard, H. L.	Special Tournament	9', 3/2, 6¾ oz., dark tea-colored bamboo, downlocking, gs, single rail notched out, heavy double knurled locking nut, two guides knocked off the mid	G	$220.00	05-04

BRAND	MODEL	SERIES / MFG. CODE / DESCRIPTION	GRADE	PRICE	DATE yy/mm
Leonard, H. L.	Tournament Trout Rod	8', 3/3; tips 2" short, 3" short, 4¼" short; 3½" repair wrap	F	$165.00	05-04
Leonard, H. L.	Trout Fly Rod	8', 3/2, prefire model 50, overvarnish, lip short ¾" at ferrule end	VG	$495.00	05-04
Leonard, H. L.	Trout Rod	11½', trout rod, 3/1, prior to Bangor markings, owner name engraved on nickle silver grip check 4 strip, turned down cane	VG	$330.00	05-04
Leonard, H. L.	Trout Rod	serial no. 430, 8', 3/2, 1 tip 1½" short, model 50 rod, aluminum downlocking reel seat, butternut spacer, nickel silver butt cap, large bright stainless guides	VG	$385.00	05-04
Leonard, H. L.	Two-handed Salmon Rod	12', 3/2, rod revarnished, missing rubber butt cap	VG-	$220.00	04-11
Leonard, H. L.	53	10', 7¾ oz., 3/2, bag & tube	NIT	$600.00	99-08
Leonard, H. L.	136	6', 2/2, #3 line, bag & tube	EXIT	$1,550.00	99-04
Little Usla	Harrisburg Caster	6'7", 2/1, 4 oz., Nat Uslan's 5-sided rod, marked with serial 40151 F	VG	$104.50	05-04
Marshall Fields	Carlisle Special	9½', trout rod, 3/2, one tip 1" short, other short ½", gs fittings, intermediate wraps, original finish VG	VG++	$104.50	05-04
Maxwell, Tom	Trout Rod	7', 2/2	EX+	$2,970.00	04-11
Maxwell, Tom	Trout Rod	7½', 3/2, flamed hand-drawn fisherman, plastic still on handle	EX+	$3,300.00	04-11
Mills	Standard	7½', trout rod, 3/1, English twist, nickel silver guides and nonserrated nickel ferrules over varn	VG	$522.50	05-04
Mills	Tarpon Rod	7'3", 2/2, c. 1910 – 1920, Hl Leonard rod with rattan-wrapped grips, several guides off (included), fraying wraps, loose reel seat, varnish roughness w/orig bag	G-	$115.50	05-04
Montague	Clipper	3/1, tube	EX	$79.00	99-08
Montague	Flash	9', 3/1	EX	$230.50	99-01
Montague	Rapidian	7½', 2/1	EX	$180.00	00-02
Montague	Rapidian	8½', 3/2, goodies	NIT	$290.00	99-05
Montague	Redwing	7½', 3/2, bag & tube	EX	$640.00	99-06
Montague	Somers Point	5½', 2pc, saltwater, extra hvy duty	EXIT	$128.50	99-07
Montigue	Manitou	9', 3/2, nice decal	EX	$333.00	01-08
Nevros, Gus	Custom Trout Rod	8½', 3/2, 5-sided rod, burled ferrule plugs, winding check, reel seat insert	EX	$550.00	05-04
Nova	West Branch Trout Rod	6½', 3/2, w/spare section to make it 7½', w/orig bag and tube	EX	$385.00	04-11
Orchard Ind.	Action	burgandy/white grip	EX	$190.00	03-08
Orchard Ind.	Action	metal 61", white/maroon grip	EX	$124.00	04-01
Orchard Ind.	Action	square, maroon/white	EX	$20.50	00-05
Orchard Ind.	Action Rod	5", white/red stripes	EX	$65.00	00-10
Orchard Ind.	Action Rod	fancy grip, maroon/white, 4½'	EX	$63.00	02-01
Orchard Ind.	Action Rod	green/white Bakelite handle, round shaft	EX	$215.00	01-11
Orchard Ind.	Action Rod	maroon Bakelite handle	EX	$55.00	04-02
Orchard Ind.	Action Rod	metal, red/white grip	EX	$104.00	00-10
Orchard Ind.	Action Rod AS-47	with case, NOT MET	NIC	$86.00	00-03
Orchard Ind.	Action Rod 1680	8', 2/1, glass, pouch, NOT MET	NIP	$53.00	00-07
Orchard Ind.	Metal	white/maroon Bakelite grip, hex metal tip, 5'	EX	$63.00	05-07

BRAND	MODEL	SERIES / MFG. CODE / DESCRIPTION	GRADE	PRICE	DATE yy/mm
Orchard Ind.	51	casting, cork grip, blue/orange wraps	EX-	$67.00	05-01
Orivs	Model "99"	serial no. 397XX, 7½', trout rod, 2/1, w/original bag, labeled tube	VG	$385.00	05-04
Orvis	9 wt. Salmon Rod	10', 3/1, 3" butt extension, w/labeled bag and tube	NM	$126.50	05-04
Orvis	All Rounder	graphite, 8'3", 7 wt., nice tube	EXIT	$99.00	05-02
Orvis	Battenkill	2/2, 4 oz., impregnated rod, HDG, 6-line, light soiling of cork handle	EX	$467.50	05-04
Orvis	Battenkill	6½', 3/2, bag & tube	EX	$807.50	99-03
Orvis	Battenkill	serial no. 44XXX, 7½', 2/2, w/orig bag and tube	EX	$467.50	05-04
Orvis	Battenkill	7½', 2/2, dent in tube, otherwise nice, c. 1970	EXIT	$528.00	01-10
Orvis	Battenkill	7½', 2/2, tube and bag	EX+IT	$600.00	00-02
Orvis	Battenkill	7½', 2/2, 4¼ oz., bag & tube	EXIT	$585.00	99-06
Orvis	Battenkill	7½', 2/2, HDH, bag & tube, NOT MET		$480.00	99-04
Orvis	Battenkill	serial no. 43XXX, 8½', trout rod, 2/2, fractured several inches from top of one tip, butt section has a set, w/original bag, labeled case	G	$115.50	05-04
Orvis	Battenkill	8'6", bag and tube	EX+	$515.96	99-01
Orvis	Battenkill	serial no. 29XXX, 8', trout rod, 2/2, 4¼ oz., c. 1961 w/original bag, labeled tube	EX	$335.50	05-04
Orvis	Battenkill	8½', 3/2, tube cap damaged	EX	$400.00	99-03
Orvis	Battenkill	serial no. 21XXX, 9', impregnated, 3/2, some replaced wraps	VG	$330.00	05-04
Orvis	Battenkill	9', 3/2, 8-9 line, "Impregnated" dark, bag	EXIB	$405.00	01-09
Orvis	Battenkill	serial no. 38XXX, impregnated, 7½', 2/2, w/orig bag and tube, no cap	EX	$440.00	04-11
Orvis	Battenkill	serial no. 47XXX, 8', 2/2, light damage 1" long on corner of cane below stripper guide, one snake guide	VG	$181.50	05-04
Orvis	Battenkill	spinning, #21151-7½', 2/1, nice metal Orvis nonoriginal tube	EXIT	$306.00	05-07
Orvis	Battenkill #99	8', 2/1, 8 wt., impregnated, nice tube & pouch	EXIT	$315.00	05-07
Orvis	Battenkill Midge	7½', 2/2, 3⅝ oz., H.E.G. (5)	EXIT	$635.00	05-02
Orvis	Deluxe	serial no. 27XXX, 6½', trout rod, 2/2, 2 oz., cork reel seat, two delicate sliding bands, tiny 4" grip, very light wear to oxidizing on ferrules	EX	$605.00	05-04
Orvis	Deluxe	serial no. 34XXX, 7', fly rod, 2/2, 2⅝ oz., nickel silver ferrules and small 4½" grip, Aetna foul proof guides, w/original bag and gold-labeled case	EX+	$412.50	05-04
Orvis	Fly Rod	serial no. 47XXX, impregnated, 8', 2/1, w/orig bag/tube	EX	$385.00	05-04
Orvis	Fly Rod	fiberglass, 8½', 2/1, alum tube (dent) GBF-8	NIT	$90.00	03-06
Orvis	Golden Eagle	glass, 7½', 6 wt., tube & tube	EX+	$301.10	99-03
Orvis	Graphite	7'9", tube & bag, NOT MET	EX	$190.00	99-07
Orvis	HLS 2	9', 7 wt., 2pc	mint	$167.00	99-01
Orvis	Impregnated Special	6½', 2/1, tube and bag	EXIT	$566.00	00-08
Orvis	Kit	8', 2/1, tip 1" longer than butt, w/bag and tube	VG	$55.00	05-04
Orvis	Kit	8', 2/2, inked "Orvis Battenkill," 4⅜ oz., 1968, on 2 flats of rod shaft above grip	EX	$137.50	05-04
Orvis	Kit	9', 2/3, two tips ¼" longer than butt section, w/bag and tube	VG	$148.50	05-04

BRAND	MODEL	SERIES / MFG. CODE / DESCRIPTION	GRADE	PRICE	DATE yy/mm
Orvis	Kit Rod	9'8", 2/1, with bag and tube	EX	$82.50	04-11
Orvis	Limestone Special	8½', 2/2, tube and sock	NIT	$709.00	01-04
Orvis	Madison	serial no. 78XXX, 7½', trout rod, 2/1, 3¼" short, HCF 7 line grip, slight soiling stripper guide, carbide ring seperated from frame	EX-	$126.50	05-04
Orvis	Madison	8½', 4¾ oz., 2/1, tube & bag	NIT	$612.00	00-02
Orvis	Madison	8', 2/1, 4⅜ oz., factory tube	EXIT	$414.00	04-11
Orvis	MCL Flea	fly rod, 6½', 2/1, 2⅜ oz.	EX	$440.00	04-11
Orvis	Midge	7½', #5 line, 2/2, sock & tube crisp	NIT	$600.00	02-01
Orvis	Midge Light Trout Rod	serial no. 45XXX, 7½', 2/2, drying out of the guide wraps, w/orig bag/tube	EX	$495.00	04-11
Orvis	Mitey Mite	5', 2/1, bag & tube	EXIT	$947.00	99-04
Orvis	Model 99	serial no. 27XXX, 7', impregnated, fly rod, 2/1	EX	$357.50	04-11
Orvis	Penn's Creek	7', 2/2, 3⅝ oz., #4 line, sock	NIT	$895.00	01-10
Orvis	Salmon Rod	Aetna foul proof guides, 11', 3/2, some wraps replaced, butt extension measures 5", w/orig bag/tube	EX-	$220.00	04-11
Orvis	Silver Label	Full Flex 5.5, 7'9", 2 wt.	EXIT	$138.00	05-02
Orvis	Superfine	serial no. 24XXX, 1-piece, trout rod, 5½', one of 125 made by Orvis	EX	$605.00	04-11
Orvis	Superlight	5', spinning rod, 2-piece, 1 tip, 2¼ oz., impregnated, w/orig bag, marked tube, owner's manual	EX	$357.50	05-04
Orvis	Wes Jordan Fly	8', 4¾ oz., for a GBF, NOT MET	MIT	$890.00	99-08
Orvis	Wes Jordan	serial no. 62XXX, 8½', trout rod, 2/2, impregnated rod, right hand grip, w/Orvis leather tube VG	EX+	$550.00	04-11
Orvis	Wes Jordan	serial no. 45XXX, 8', 2/2, grip shaped, right handed caster, w/orig bag/alum tube	EX+	$660.00	04-11
Patridge	The Arnold	7'9", fly rod, 2/2, original wrap on handle, 6 wt., comes with original bag/tube, and ferrule plug	NM	$385.00	05-04
Patridge	The Mosquito	8'9", fly rod, 2/2, original wrap on handle, 5 wt., w/original bag/tube, ferrule plug	NM	$275.00	05-04
Paul H. Young	Special	8½', 3/2, w/bag and tube	EX	$467.50	04-11
Payne	Dry Fly Salmon Rod	model 400, 9', 3/2, one tip short 1⅝", other 3¾", light salmon rod, detachable 6¾" fighting butt, ferrule plugs, restored	EX	$275.00	05-04
Payne	Fly Rod	7½', 3/2, neat bamboo tube, one tip an inch short	EXIT	$1,220.00	05-07
Payne	Model 202	8', trout rod, 3/1, loop on one tip is broken, case crossout, two tips added	EX	$2,750.00	05-04
Payne	Model 98 Trout Rod	serial no. 48610, 7', 2/2, 3 oz., original tissue paper from maker wrapped over cork handle	EX+	$4,620.00	05-04
Payne	Salmon Rod	11', 3/1, marked "E.F. Payne Rod Company Makers" on nickel silver sliding band reel seat, male ferrule on midsection missing water stop, bag marks in varnish, line residue under guides			
Payne	Trout Rod	8', 3/2, 1 tip 2" short, c. 1930, walnut reel seat, sliding band missing 60% blueing, stripper guide missing	VG	$2,200.00	05-04

BRAND	MODEL	SERIES / MFG. CODE / DESCRIPTION	GRADE	PRICE	DATE yy/mm
Payne	Wet Fly Salmon Rod	11½', 3/3, 12⅞ oz., "Payne" and original owner name engraved on locking nut of reel seat, chestnut-toned cane, original ferrule plugs, 3 tips but 1 replacement, splinter of cane missing below stripper guide on butt section, hook keeper is missing	EX	$330.00	05-04
Payne	98	7', 2/2, 2¹³⁄₁₆ oz., bag	EXIT	$3,000.00	02-10
Payne		7½', 3/2, varnish a little rough	EX-?	$600.00	02-01
Payne, E.F.	Abercrombie & Fitch	9', 3/2, replacement tip, c. 1920s, NOT MET	EXIT	$1,025.00	01-10
Payne, Jim	200	8', 3/2, restored	MR	$2,426.00	00-04
Payne, Jim	208	9', 3/2, 5-6 line, restored	EXrestored	$1,502.50	99-08
Payne, Jim	Banty	4'4", 2/2, 1½ oz., sliding band, downlocking over cork reel seat	EX+	$3,300.00	04-11
Payne, Kim	209	9', 3/2, restored by George Guba, 7 wt.	EXrestored	$936.00	05-07
Peak, Russ	#51	C170L-424L, glass, 2/2, 6', 1¾ oz.	EXIT	$1,445.00	04-12
Pezon et Michel	Baby Zephyr	7'9", 2/2, 5-6 line, removeable grip handle, lightly used, ferrule plugs for butt grip sections	EX	$825.00	05-04
Pezon et Michel	Fario Club	marked, 8½', trout rod, 2/2, 5¼ oz., one tip section 1" fracture lifting 28" from ferrule, small piece of cane missing result of cracked node, original 8" ferrule plug, comes in original bag	G-	$286.00	05-04
Pezon et Michel	Fario Club Super Parabolic	8'6", 2/2, staggered ferrule design rod, w/original warranty card still attached to grip, w/orig bag, labeled tube, labeled canvas bag	NM	$412.50	05-04
Pezon et Michel	Le Petite Fario Club	7'2", trout rod, 2/2, staggered ferrule rod	EX	$550.00	04-11
Pezon et Michel	Model A 263 Colorado	7'7", 2/2, 5-6 wt. line, original warrant card still attached, w/orig drawstring bag, case, canvas bag	MINT	$797.50	05-04
Pezon et Michel	Ritz Super Parabolic	staggered ferrule trout rod, 7'3", 2/2, 3¾ oz., rod copper colored, aluminum downlocking reel seat, corked filler	EX	$330.00	05-04
Pezon et Michel	Royal	staggered ferrule trout rod, 6'10", 2/1, wrapper still on handle	EX	$330.00	04-11
Pezon et Michel	Super Parabolic	featherweight trout rod, 6'4", 2/2, each tip missing 2 guides, staggered ferrule rod	G	$220.00	04-11
Pezon et Michel	Telebolic	5'7", light spinning rod, 2/1, staggered ferrule rod, 2' long butt section with ferrule plug, 43⅓" long tip, minor grip soiling, original bag	EX	$220.00	05-04
Pflueger	Steel Casting		mint	$56.26	99-08
Pflueger	Supreme Glass	No.121P-6'0" M, EEM	NIC	$206.00	00-05
Philipson	Pacemaker 18	bamboo, 6', 2pc, bend	VG	$470.00	99-02
Philipson	Pacemaker 18	bamboo, 6', 2pc, bend	VG	$560.00	99-02
Philipson	76" Eponite	custom built for Furrs	VG+	$730.00	99-10
Philipson	8C64	6'4", glass, bag, 2pc	EX	$1,325.00	99-03
Philipson	Bamboo Fly Rod	8½', 3/1, tube and bag	EX-	$178.50	99-08
Philipson	DC60B	Dlx Swamp Fox, NOT MET	EXIC	$1,200.00	01-04
Philipson	Fly Rod	P86F HDH, 4¾ oz.	EX	$169.16	99-02
Philipson	Fly Rod	fiberglass, tube and bag, NOT MET	EX	$34.00	99-08

BRAND	MODEL	SERIES / MFG. CODE / DESCRIPTION	GRADE	PRICE	DATE yy/mm
Philipson	Haywood Zephyr	modern, made with old blank, 7½'	NIT	$395.00	00-11
Philipson	Johnson Profile	6C64, 2pc, 6'4", bait caster	EX	$910.00	01-03
Philipson	Master G-M0652	5'5", spinning	EX	$172.50	98-12
Philipson	P76F	5 wt., 7½', sack, no tube	mint	$193.05	99-04
Philipson	P7OL	spinning	mint	$257.00	99-03
Philipson	Pacemaker	8½', 3/2, cardboard tube	NIT	$510.00	99-12
Philipson	Paragon Bamboo	79 9-578 HCH, 9', 3/2	EX-	$200.00	99-08
Philipson	PH60	modern repro, NOT MET	mint	$417.66	00-02
Philipson	Phillipson Peerless "5"	8', 3/2, bag and tube, #5 line	EXIT	$892.00	00-04
Philipson	Power-Kast	6'3", 2/1, writing on handle? on rod?	EX-	$425.00	01-10
Philipson	SK 64	Stream Knight, spinning, 2pc	NIT	$103.00	01-04
Philipson	Smuggler	fly rod, 4/1, 7'8", unmarked tube 24"	EXIT	$477.00	04-02
Philipson	Uniglas 800	3/2, #8, bag, tube	EX	$128.51	99-01
Phillipson	BC50	3M, Basstamer, 5', 7½ to ⅝ oz. lures	mint	$2,035.00	02-09
Phillipson	BC56	3M, Basstamer, 5'6", 1 oz., missing reel lock	mint	$1,705.00	02-09
Phillipson	Johnson Profile	8F76LC, 3⅛ oz., line #6, 7½', 2/1, fiberglass	EX	$115.00	05-07
Phillipson	Mity Lite	62 HDH or HCF, fly rod, 68", 2/1	mint	$46.00	05-03
Phillipson	Pacemaker	8½', trout rod, 3/2, HDH line, few spots of rough varnish, w/orig bag and tube	EX-	$275.00	05-04
Phillipson	Pacemaker	8½', 3/2, tube & sock	EX-IT	$373.00	01-08
Phillipson	Pacemaker	9', 3/2, sock & tube	EXIT	$250.00	02-08
Phillipson	Paramount	6', 2/1, white/black jasper wraps, chrome casting guides	EX+	$330.00	05-04
Phillipson	Paramount	8½', 3/2, HDH line, w/orig bag and tube	EX	$330.00	05-04
Phillipson	Phillipson Peerless	7', 2/2, small repair wrap on 1 tip, w/bag and tube	EX	$440.00	04-11
Phillipson	Royale RC64	2/1, 6'4", spincast, light action, odd color	VG+	$436.00	05-05
Powell, E.C.	Salmon Rod	"Hollow Built," 9½', 2/2, both tip tops broken off	G	$220.00	04-11
Powell, Walton	Golden Signature	length unknown, fly rod, 2 butts & 2 tips, 2/2	EX	$1,111.00	05-07
Powell, Walton	Graphite Fly Rod	9', 2/1, 6-7 weight line, w/orig bag/tube	EX+	$137.50	05-04
Prichard	Lemonwood	1881 & 1889 pats, wood case	avg	$206.14	99-06
Record	Corona	5½', 2-piece, sack, nice	EX	$187.00	00-08
Record	49	bait casting, 5', med, cheapie	NIbag	$66.00	01-04
Reddich, Falcon	The Merlin	5', 2/1, intermediate wraps, tip top rest	EX	$104.50	05-04
Sans Pariel	5 wt.	2/2, tube	NIT	$1,700.00	00-10
Schaff	Dickerson 7012	7', 2pc, 4 wt., fancy bag & tube, 1994	NIT	$1,575.00	00-05
Shakespeare	Fly	Wonderrod, 3/1, bag and alum tube	NIT	$69.00	00-08
Shakespeare	Fly	7¾', bag and tube	EXIT	$41.00	99-11
Sharp	Avon	2/1, bamboo, surf rod	EX	$201.00	04-03
Shimano	Speed Master	SM-2062, 6'2", spinning, 2pc	EX	$37.00	04-02
Shimano	Speedmaster	SM-2602, 2pc, spinning	mint	$177.00	03-07
Shimano	Speedmaster #30	SM1753, 7½', heavy flippin	EX	$108.00	01-05
Silaflex	ASP65RL-2	casting, 6½', All Angle Grip, NOT MET	EX	$32.00	03-02
Silaflex	Perfexion 201	fly, 7½', pre-Browning, tube, sack	EX	$330.00	99-07
South Bend	#13	9½', 3/2, overvarnish, NOT MET	EX??	$104.00	02-02
South Bend	#290	#290, 7½', 2/2, bag and tube	EXIT	$275.00	00-02
South Bend	166-9	9', 3/2, HDH, tube, bag	EXIT	$250.00	99-06

BRAND	MODEL	SERIES / MFG. CODE / DESCRIPTION	GRADE	PRICE	DATE yy/mm
South Bend	Casting Rod	5½', 2/1, red glass guides, varnish slight bag marks	G	$77.00	05-04
South Bend	Model 1500	7½', 2/2, varnish roughness	EX	$209.00	05-04
South Bend	No. 290-7½	bamboo, 3/2	VG+	$305.00	99-03
South Bend	24	some problems, 3/2, ferrule crack	VGIT	$54.00	01-04
South Bend	26	7½', 2/1, refinished	EXIT	$285.00	01-09
South Bend	290	7½', 2/2, one tip top missing, bag	EXIT	$190.00	00-10
South Bend	290	7½', 2/2	EX	$255.00	00-07
South Bend	291	7½', 3/2, sock	NIT	$360.00	00-11
South Bend	359	9', 3/2, dry fly action	NIT	$150.00	00-10
South Bend	359	9', 3/2, bag	mint	$127.50	99-08
Spalding	Fly Rod	6½', 2/1, fiberglass, bag & tube	EXIT	$103.00	05-07
Sprite, AKF	Trout Rod	7½', 2/2, tips ⅝" short, possible redo of production rod, with replacement reel seat, both tips different, snake guides, w/bag, old fiber tube missing cap	VG	$82.50	05-04
St. Albans	Trout Rod	7', 2/2, 1 tip marked "⅞ oz.," other marked "¾ oz.," both short ¾", replacement bag and tube	EX	$165.00	05-04
Summers, R.W.	735	7'3", 2/2, #4-5 line, c. 1984, bag & tube	EXIT	$2,075.00	01-09
Thomas	Browntone	serial no. E4, 9', 3/2, 1 tip replacement heavier at top, loose pocketed butt cap, cracked node 9" from grip, w/original labeled case	VG	$165.00	05-04
Thomas	Dirigo	8½', 3/2, 1½" short tip, w/original bag tube	EX	$330.00	05-04
Thomas	Special	9', 3/2, "30" stamped on bottom, agate stripper guide tip tops, honey colored cane	EX+	$770.00	05-04
Thomas	Special	serial no. 120, marked, 8', butt cap, 2/3, 1 tip short 1¼", 1 tip short ⅛", repair wrap, agate stripper guide	VG	$852.50	05-04
Thomas	Special 9 ft. Trout Rod	3/2, "4" stamped on butt cap, red windings accented with gold trip, three groups of closely spaced signature wraps above grip, three narrow trip wraps above each ferrule tip, top wraps fraying — need replacing, overcoat of varnish	VG?	$275.00	05-04
Thomas & Thomas	Classic Bait Cast	No. 4416, 6', 2/2, impregnated rod, nickel silver downlocking reel seat, gold/bronze wraps with agate/agatine guides and dark flame finish	NM	$990.00	05-04
Thomas & Thomas	Midge	serial no. 2795, 7', 2/2, no. 4 line rod, plastic wrap protecting handle, showing slight wear on butt cap	EX+	$1,980.00	05-04
Thomas & Thomas	Paradigm	serial no. 37XX, 8', trout rod, 2/2, wraps honey gold tipped, brown T and T screw uplocking reel seat, walnut spacer	EX+	$1,375.00	05-04
Thomas & Thomas	Paradigm	No. 3968, 8', 2/2, 5-wt. line, dramatic swelled butt, burled walnut seat, with n/s fittings, translucent wraps tipped with cinnamon	EX+	$2,255.00	05-04
Thomas & Thomas	Special Trouter	No. 3600, 8', 2/2, no. 6 line, impregnated rod, w/bag and tube	EX	$797.50	05-04
Thomas & Thomas	The Midge	serial no. 24XX, 7½', 2/2, rated no. 5 line, impregnated, red wraps, screw uplocking reel seat, walnut spacer	EX+	$1,375.00	05-04
Thomas, F.E.	Bangor 214	8½', 3/2, 5½ oz., unmarked tube	EX	$656.00	03-02
Thomas, F.E.	Special Browntone	8', bag and tube	EX	$1,825.00	99-04

BRAND	MODEL	SERIES / MFG. CODE / DESCRIPTION	GRADE	PRICE	DATE yy/mm
Thomas, F.E.	Browntone	9', 3/2, 1 tip is ¼" short, appears to be Thomas replacement, agate stripper, downlocking aluminum reel seat	VG	$247.50	05-04
Thomas, F.E.	Dirigo	9', 3/2, 3 pieces broken off of top of 1 tip, included composite cork grips; nickel silver bell, trumpet guides, and hardware	G	$110.00	05-04
Thomas, F.E.	Dirigo	9', 3/2, composite cork grips, nickel silver hardware bell guides, plier marks on several ferrules, both tips short	G	$192.50	05-04
Thomas, F.E.	Dirigo	9', 3/3, one tip short 4", red silk wraps, English twist guides, clamed can, some nicks in varnish	G	$247.50	05-04
Thomas, F.E.	Special	serial no. 502, 8½', 3/2, mid section short 1¾", ridge cork grip wrap on but needs replacing, varnish overcoat	CG	$440.00	05-04
Thomas, F.E.	Special	8', c. 1920, 3/2, patented downlocking reel seat, pat June 1913	VG	$115.00	05-04
Thomas, F.E.	Special	serial no. E-30, 9½', 3/1, 2½" short at ferrrule end, 7⅛ oz., minor chip in cork grip	G	$110.00	05-04
Thomas, F.E.	Dirigo Trout Rod	8½', 3/2, 1 tip short 1½", other tip 3" short, 3¾" extension butt	EX-	$110.00	04-11
Thomas, F.E.	Salmon Rod	special two-handed, 12', 3/2, 1 tip 5" short, rod shows some bad glue lines, w/orig sack and tip tube	G-	$110.00	04-11
True Temper		5'7", yellow steel	NIC	$112.00	00-10
Tycoon	Deep Sea Trolling	81", x-heavy duty bamboo	EX	$1,855.00	99-05
Tycoon Tackle	Scion	6'10", over 5 lbs., 1938	EX	$1,626.00	99-10
Uslan	Fly Rod	8', 2/2, w/orig bag and tube	EX	$440.00	04-11
Vom Hofe, Ed.	Casting	5', 2/2, probably Heddon?	VG+	$87.00	04-11
Vom Hofe, J.	#2 Fly	seat bent	VG-	$406.00	99-01
Von Hofe & Co	Trout Rod	8½', 3/2, c. 1900, plated brass fittings, ferrules	VG-	$302.50	05-04
Walker, Richard	Mark IV	carp rod, revarnished, NOT MET	EX	$1,900.00	02-08
Walton	Trout Rod	8½', 2/2, "The Walton Powell Rod" and original owner's name under varnish above hook keeper, marked "74-30" on sections, tips ¼" longer than butt	EX+	$797.50	05-04
Weber	Henshall	8½', 3/2, orig bag, no tube	VG	$228.00	99-06
Weber	Mastercraft 3500	8½', Heddon made 35, NOT MET	EXres	$170.00	01-01
Weir John	9'	2/2, custom, $5,000 NOT MET!	NIT	$500.00	01-04
Williams, Ted	Spincast	reel, pouches	NIC	$127.50	00-03
Winchester	Bait Casting	5', 2-piece, staggered ferrule, rod decal on shaft with agate guides	VG	$214.50	05-04
Winchester	Fly Rod	3/1, steel, wood grip, NO BIDS	EX	$100.00	00-03
Winchester	Fly Rod	9', 3/2, 1 tip short 2½", Winchester stamping "no. 6086," orginal ferrule, plugs missing, hook keeper	VG	$247.50	05-04
Winchester	Model No. 6163 Fly Rod	made by Eustis Edwards, 7', 2/2, one tip fracture, orig bag	EX-	$715.00	04-11
Windson	Light Steelhead Fly Rod	serial no. 9126, 9', 2/2, 5⅛ oz., original owner's name inked on rod shaft, putty-colored thread wraps, bright guides and small stripper guides used in place of first three snake guides above main stripping guide	near mint	$715.00	05-04

BRAND	MODEL	SERIES / MFG. CODE / DESCRIPTION	GRADE	PRICE	DATE yy/mm
Winston	#IM6 8½' #6	2/1, pouch and tube	EXIT	$304.00	00-10
Winston	Fly Rod	serial no. 2022, 8½', 2/2, w/original bag and tube	EX+	$1,100.00	05-04
Winston	Fly Rod	serial no. 2022, 8½', 2/2, w/original bag and tube	EX+	$1,100.00	05-04
Winston	Fly Rod	mint bag, tube, 7'	NIT	$406.53	99-03
Winston	Graphite Fly Rod	2⅛ oz., 2/1, 8½', w/marked bag/tube	mint	$302.50	05-04
Winston	Light Steelhead Fly Rod	serial no. 9126, 9', 2/2, 5⅛ oz., hollow-built rod, original owner's name inked on rod shaft, putty-colored thread wraps, bright guides and small stripper guides used in place of first three snake guides above the main stripping guide	near mint	$715.00	05-04
Winston	Trout Rod	serial no. 1082, 2/1, 8½', hollow-built rod, slight soiling of Wells-style grip	EX+	$770.00	05-04
Winston, R.L.	Graphite Fly Rod	7½', 1⅞ oz., 2/1, w/marked tube bag	near mint	$302.50	05-04
Winston, R.L.	Graphite Fly Rod	2½ oz., 2/1, 9', w/marked bag and tube	EX	$165.00	05-04
Wright McGill	Granger	9', 3/2, bag & tube	EXIT	$373.00	02-08
Wright McGill	Granger	GS 9050, 9', 3/2, 5 oz., EX tube	NIT	$456.00	05-07
Wright McGill	Granger Favorite	3-1, bag and tube, 9'	VG+	$210.00	99-01
Wright McGill	Granger Favorite	9', 3/2, wrap still on grip, tube, sack	NIT	$1,000.00	99-09
Wright McGill	Granger Favorite	8½', 3/2	EX	$495.00	01-05
Wright Mcgill	Granger No. GS 8040	special, 3/2, 4 oz., #5 line, butt ¾" short	refinished	$660.00	01-09
Wright McGill	Granger Victory	8', 3/2, restored	REX	$650.00	99-03
Wright McGill	Special	8½', trout rod, 3/2, plastic on grip, w/original bag/tube	NM	$522.50	05-04
Wright McGill	Special	8½', trout rod, c. 1950s, 3/2, replaced tip lighter in color, wrapped in lime green with gold tipping, measurement increments applied in fingernail polish, hook keeper added	EX	$165.00	05-04
Wright McGill	Trailmaster	4TMU 7½', spin/fly combo, 4-piece, pouch & tube	EXIT	$76.00	05-07
Wright McGill	Victory	8½', 3/2, lightly used, little white residue under guides, w/orig bag, labeled tube	EX	$330.00	05-04
Young, Paul	7½'	2/1, dated June '53, bag and tube	mint	$1,275.00	99-08
Young, Paul	Fly Rod	8', 2/2, #6 line, possible overvarnish nice	EXIT	$810.00	01-08
Young, Paul	Ace	8', 2/2, 1 tip 2" short, 1940, downlocking skel reel seat	VG	$660.00	05-04
Young, Paul	Perfectionist	7½', 2.2, restored	MR	$2,700.00	00-04
Young, Paul	Spinmaster	6½', 2/1	EX	$482.00	02-02
Young, Paul	The Texan	serial no. 4609, 8½', trout rod, tiger flamed, 2/1, 4⅞ oz., owner's name on grip	EX+	$990.00	05-04

Rod Handles

BRAND	MODEL	SERIES / MFG. CODE / DESCRIPTION	GRADE	PRICE	DATE yy/mm
Champion	All Angle		EX-	$50.00	02-01
Champion	All Angle		EX	$44.00	04-03
Champion	Featherweight	walnut checkered grip, NOT MET	EX	$81.00	04-03
Champion	Featherweight Fat Boy	black/yellow/green swirl	EX	$200.00	04-03
Champion	Pistol Grip	green	EX	$135.00	05-07
Champion	Pistol Grip	Fat Boy? bluish white	EX	$432.00	02-09
Featherweight	All Angle	cork dirty, no end cap	avg	$108.50	00-01
Featherweight	All Angle	foam, NOT MET	VG+	$51.00	00-03
Featherweight	All Angle	plastic still on cork	mint	$222.50	99-12
Featherweight	All Angle	repro? color odd	mint	$125.00	99-11
Featherweight	All Angle	small repair	VG+	$125.00	00-03
Featherweight	All Angle		VG+	$62.00	99-09
Featherweight	All Angle		EX	$113.49	00-03
Featherweight	All Angle		EX	$122.50	99-06
Featherweight	All Angle		EX-	$125.00	00-03
Featherweight	All Angle		EX	$152.50	00-03
Featherweight	All Angle		EX	$155.50	99-08
Featherweight	Blue	fat, pistol grip	EX	$850.00	04-11
Featherweight	Champion	6AP30, plastic bag	NIB	$78.00	00-09
Featherweight	Champion	black pistol	EX	$222.50	99-06
Featherweight	Champion	brown pistol	EX-	$152.50	00-03
Featherweight	Champion	cork	VG	$49.99	99-05
Featherweight	Champion	cork	EX	$69.00	00-06
Featherweight	Champion	foam	EX	$58.00	01-04
Featherweight	Champion	foam handle	EX	$46.00	00-10
Featherweight	Champion	green pistol grip	EX	$350.00	99-08
Featherweight	Champion	pistol grip	VG-	$78.00	99-05
Featherweight	Champion	black pistol grip, spacers	EX	$367.00	99-05
Featherweight	Champion	pistol, black	EX	$301.15	99-08
Featherweight	Champion	pistol, black, spacers	EX	$376.00	99-05
Featherweight	Champion	plastic still on cork	mint	$151.00	99-12
Featherweight	Champion	purple pistol grip	EX	$227.50	99-10
Featherweight	Champion	walnut	EX	$90.00	00-06
Featherweight	Champion	wood, probably not factory	EX	$103.50	99-08
Featherweight	Champion	wrong Garcia endcap, NOT MET	VG	$51.22	99-06
Featherweight	Champion		EX	$112.52	99-08
Featherweight	Pistol	brown	EX	$124.00	00-06
Featherweight	Pistol	burgandy, 11"	EX	$287.50	99-10
Featherweight	Spinchucker 22A	rough box	NIB	$102.50	99-08
Orchard Ind.	Action Rod	black & white Bakelite, lg double screw	VG+	$61.00	05-07

Rod Holders

BRAND	MODEL	SERIES / MFG. CODE / DESCRIPTION	GRADE	PRICE	DATE yy/mm
Hold Rite	Holdrite	nice 2PCCB graphics	NIB	$4.00	04-12

Sample Boards

BRAND	MODEL	SERIES / MFG. CODE / DESCRIPTION	GRADE	PRICE	DATE yy/mm
Snude	Snelled Hooks	folding, many hooks	EX	$165.00	05-07

Signs

BRAND	MODEL	SERIES / MFG. CODE / DESCRIPTION	GRADE	PRICE	DATE yy/mm
CCBC	Tri-fold	25" x 37"	VG	$2,625.00	98-12
Heddon	Shore Minnow River Runts	4 Stooges, transparent panel, NOT MET	EX	$1,158.00	02-02
Milwards	High/Low Tide Clock	tin, c. 1910, neat but NOT MET	VG+	$455.00	04-12
Sealand	Rainbeau Lines	electric sign & clock, 18" x 33", c. 1950	EX	$472.00	05-02

Sonars

BRAND	MODEL	SERIES / MFG. CODE / DESCRIPTION	GRADE	PRICE	DATE yy/mm
Lawrence	LFP 300	green box no. 762358, papers	mint	$400.00	00-06

Spears

BRAND	MODEL	SERIES / MFG. CODE / DESCRIPTION	GRADE	PRICE	DATE yy/mm
Forged	6 Tines	7½", plain	EX	$62.00	99-04
Pflueger	Ecko Frog Spear	7 spears, Zebra box	NIB	$57.00	01-08

Split Shots

BRAND	MODEL	SERIES / MFG. CODE / DESCRIPTION	GRADE	PRICE	DATE yy/mm
Abbey & Imbrie	Round	white, bluish-black writing	EX	$158.00	04-02
Abbey & Imbrie	Split Shot	round	EX-	$81.00	99-12
Abbey & Imbrie		x 2, celluloid	EX-	$160.00	00-10
Abbey & Imbrie		round	EX	$142.00	02-11
Abercrombie & Fitch	Round	white, bluish-black writing	EX	$151.00	04-02

BRAND	MODEL	SERIES / MFG. CODE / DESCRIPTION	GRADE	PRICE	DATE yy/mm
Best Little Sinkers	Dealer Box Brown Wood Grain		VG+	$22.00	05-06
Burkhard	Duck Head	round, slide hole	EX	$306.02	00-02
Clean Cut	Tin		EX	$80.00	05-06
Houston	Split Shot 3/0	yellow/red letters	EX	$20.51	99-12
Kingfisher	BB	1½" x 1", paper label, white/red picture and printing	EX	$53.00	05-07
Koon Kreek	BB	neat picture of coon on tin	EX	$48.00	04-01
Pflueger	BB	36 tins in display box, cool	NIB	$102.50	99-04
Selby	Round	"AMERICAN ART WORKS COSMOCTON O."	EX	$57.00	04-02
Shurkatch	36-pack	nice 3-dozen box	NIB	$115.00	00-10
Winchester	12-shot Paper Pouch	123A, paper	EX	$39.00	03-05
Winchester	Round	shot tin, rotating hole, NOT MET	VG-	$178.00	99-03
Winchester	9114	NOT MET	EX	$157.50	99-04
Winchester	9114	round, some staining	VG	$101.00	05-02

Spools

BRAND	MODEL	SERIES / MFG. CODE / DESCRIPTION	GRADE	PRICE	DATE yy/mm
Zebco	Cardinal 4	spool only	EX	$22.51	00-01
Zebco	Cardinal 4	with case	NIC	$27.00	00-01
Zebco	Cardinal 4 x 5	5 spools, NOT MET	new	$75.75	00-03

Spring Hook

BRAND	MODEL	SERIES / MFG. CODE / DESCRIPTION	GRADE	PRICE	DATE yy/mm
Evans & Son	Eagleclaw	8-hook spring trap	EX-	$455.00	05-02
Unknown	Spring Hook	patent 1846	EX	$987.00	03-07

Tackle Boxes

BRAND	MODEL	SERIES / MFG. CODE / DESCRIPTION	GRADE	PRICE	DATE yy/mm
Airex	730	Lionel Train Corp.	VG	$96.00	99-01
Crossman-Brinkman	Floating Pal	11 lb., Bakelite? neat looking	EX-	$100.00	03-06
Hardy	Vest Pocket	leather fly case, 7" x 5½", embossed	EX	$345.00	01-06
Heddon	Outing	r/b, crackleback, bass logo	VG	$202.50	99-01
Heddon	Outing		VG	$78.00	01-01
Kennedy	CO-155-AL	med AL newer	EX	$32.00	99-04
Kennedy	Hip Roof Great Lakes	gray liner, 6 trays, lg compartments	mint	$82.00	01-05
Kennedy	Large	brass hardware, AL trays	mint	$262.00	99-06
Tronick	Wood	no medallion	EX	$200.00	00-09
UMCO	1000A		mint	$511.00	99-08

BRAND	MODEL	SERIES / MFG. CODE / DESCRIPTION	GRADE	PRICE	DATE yy/mm
UMCO	1000A	clean	EX	$67.66	99-08
UMCO	1000A	sm dent, clean trays	EX-	$76.00	99-01
UMCO	1000A		VG	$132.50	99-01
UMCO	1000U	green	EX-	$94.00	99-05
UMCO	1000U	green	VG+	$108.05	99-04
UMCO	1000U	musky, with 5 decent lures	EX	$76.00	98-12
UMCO	1000US	2 worm burns	EX-	$142.50	99-04
UMCO	1000W	brown	VG+	$100.99	99-07
UMCO	1000W		EX	$100.00	99-10
UMCO	10B	14 compartments	EX	$16.50	99-01
UMCO	10B		mint	$11.49	99-08
UMCO	1133P	red 7½" x 13½" plastic trays	EX	$375.00	03-06
UMCO	131AS		mint	$48.00	99-01
UMCO	133AS		EX-	$51.00	99-01
UMCO	173A		EX	$62.00	99-01
UMCO	175U	worm burn	G	$53.50	99-03
UMCO	2000U	5 worm burns	VG	$131.50	99-04
UMCO	204A	correct shipping cardboard box	NIB	$240.00	01-09
UMCO	204r	large lure compartments	EX-	$123.49	00-03
UMCO	205A	aluminum, 3 trays, no burns	EX+	$74.00	00-11
UMCO	2080U	green, hard white plastic trays, NOT MET	mint	$152.00	02-08
UMCO	2080U	hard plastic trays, brown wood finish outer	EX	$132.00	01-10
UMCO	3080-UPB	with cheap lures	EX	$680.00	99-02
UMCO	3500U	Possum Belly	EX	$222.00	00-10
UMCO	3500U	worm burns	VG	$270.00	99-04
UMCO	3500UPB	double belly, NOT MET	EX	$202.00	00-06
UMCO	3500US	missing 2 trays	EX	$214.50	99-03
UMCO	4' x 9'	pocket size	EX	$34.33	99-01
UMCO	4500U	brown	EX	$216.00	00-11
UMCO	4500UPB	no "UMCO," just code made for Bass Pro Shops	mint	$173.00	02-01
UMCO	4500UPR	plastic trays	EX	$160.00	99-04
UMCO	900W		mint	$182.50	99-10
UMCO	P9		mint	$18.00	99-01
UMCO	U2000	few worm burns, crack, NOT MET	VG	$58.77	99-07
UMCO	Vest Pocket	2 round compartments, 1 oval compartment	EX	$45.00	99-01
UMCO	204	aluminum	EX	$82.00	99-07
UMCO	803	dirty trays	EX-	$69.00	00-03
UMCO	1000	bigger trays	EX-	$62.00	00-07
UMCO	1000	silver latches	EX	$178.05	00-03
UMCO	3060	green, Umcolite, big	EX-	$248.00	01-11
UMCO	4500	80 good modern lures included	EX	$251.00	99-03
Wheatley	Small Fly	6 compartments	EX	$69.00	00-11
Winchester	Metal	inside lid stencil, simple small box	VG	$95.00	04-11

Tin Cans

BRAND	MODEL	SERIES / MFG. CODE / DESCRIPTION	GRADE	PRICE	DATE yy/mm
Creel	Creamed Corn	can with paper label showing creel, 1906 date	VG-	$56.00	05-07

Tobacco Tins

BRAND	MODEL	SERIES / MFG. CODE / DESCRIPTION	GRADE	PRICE	DATE yy/mm
Trout Line	Tobacco	fishing sceen	VG+	$616.00	00-10

Toy Motors

BRAND	MODEL	SERIES / MFG. CODE / DESCRIPTION	GRADE	PRICE	DATE yy/mm
Atwater, Scott	40HP	red/white toy motor, box missing top, some tears	EX	$275.00	05-04
Evinrude	Big Twin	w/box missing top, motor, metallic blue	EX	$385.00	05-04
Evinrude	Electric Outboard Motor	metal, Japan, runs	VG	$160.00	03-02
Evinrude	Star Flighte	motor, complete with all orig parts w/box	EX+	$467.50	05-04
Evinrude	1911	decent looking, stored since 1935	EX-	$985.00	00-02
Johnson	30 HP	motor, with brown and white finish, nice and crisp, w/box missing two flaps	EX	$357.50	05-04
Johnson	Seahorse 25 HP	green finish w/nice decals, w/box	EX	$412.50	05-04
Mercury	Mark 55 Thunderbolt	green/silver finish, w/box -lid	EX	$357.50	05-04

Toys

BRAND	MODEL	SERIES / MFG. CODE / DESCRIPTION	GRADE	PRICE	DATE yy/mm
Lakeside Toys Co.	Aquaphibian Terror Fish	# 8607, c. 1960	NIB	$431.00	01-06

Trays

BRAND	MODEL	SERIES / MFG. CODE / DESCRIPTION	GRADE	PRICE	DATE yy/mm
Heddon	Lure-drying Tray	factory lure, drying tray marked "HEDDON"	EX	$165.00	05-07

Weather Vanes

BRAND	MODEL	SERIES / MFG. CODE / DESCRIPTION	GRADE	PRICE	DATE yy/mm
Cast Iron	Fish	early 1900s	EX	$13,100.00	02-04

Worm Prods

BRAND	MODEL	SERIES / MFG. CODE / DESCRIPTION	GRADE	PRICE	DATE yy/mm
Unknown	Electric	stick-in-ground, plug-in, cord frayed	VG	$1.00	04-12

Pirate stuff.

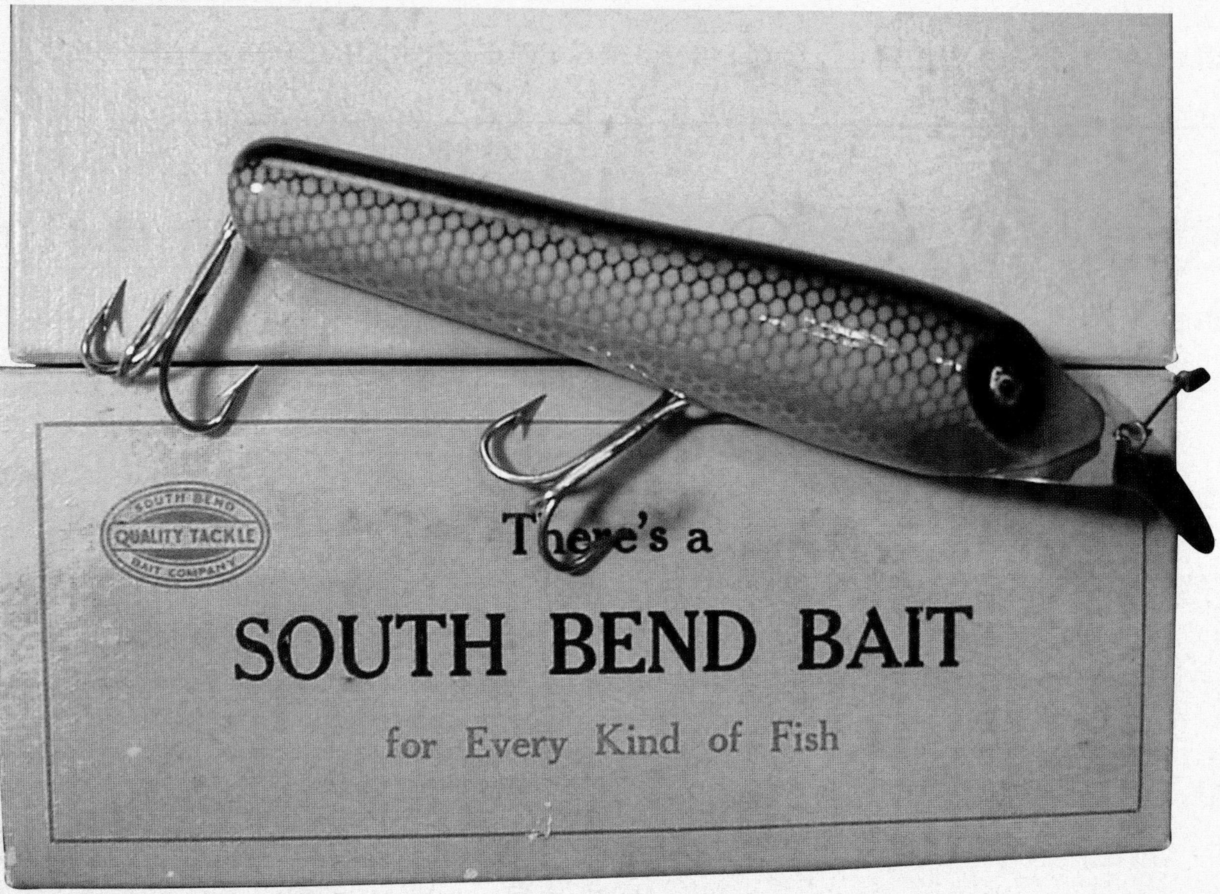

South Bend Musky Pike Oreno, $700.00 NIB.

South Bend New Pike Oreno, die-cut counter display, $650.00.

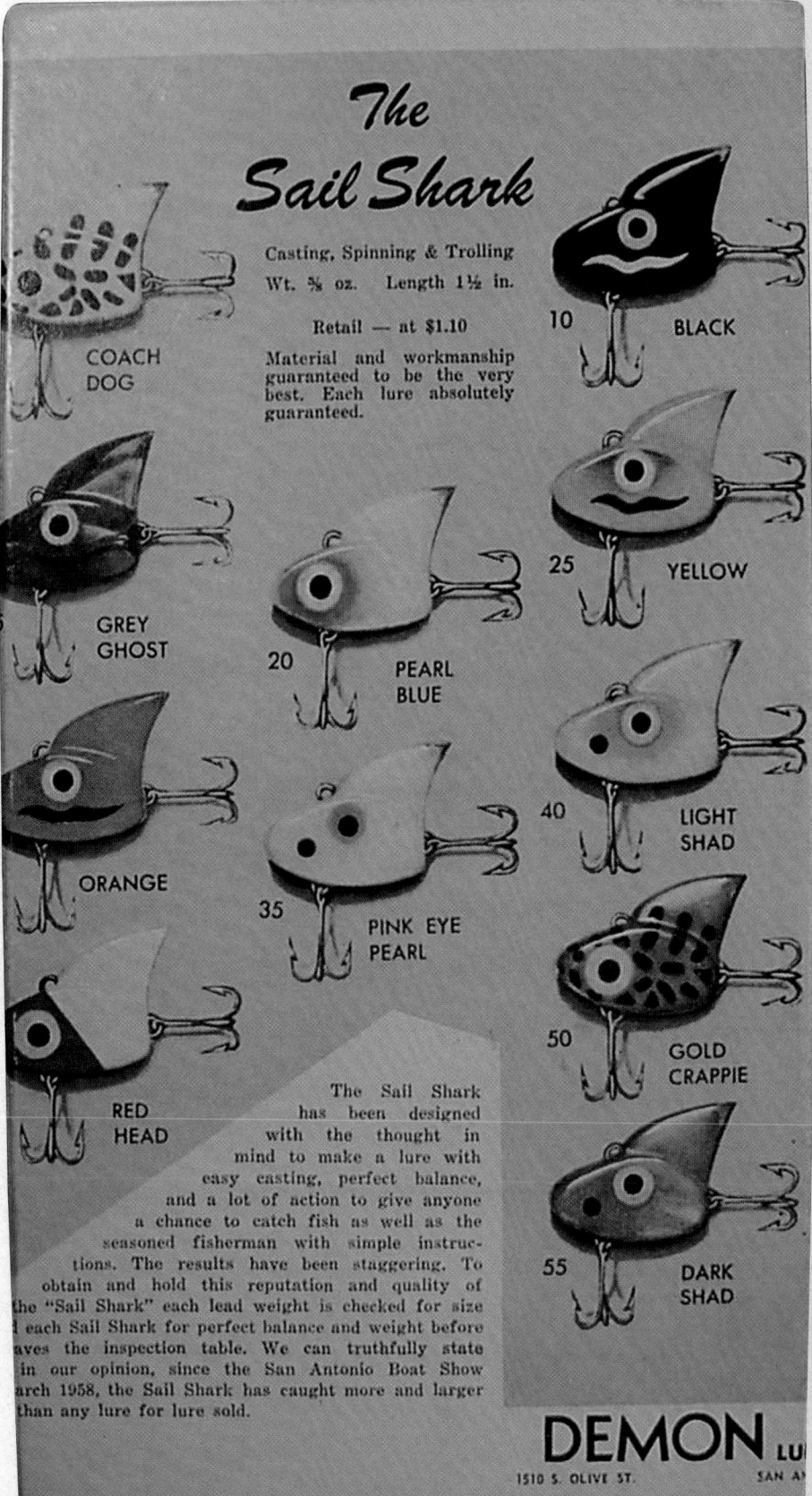

Demon Sail Shark picture box, $500.00.

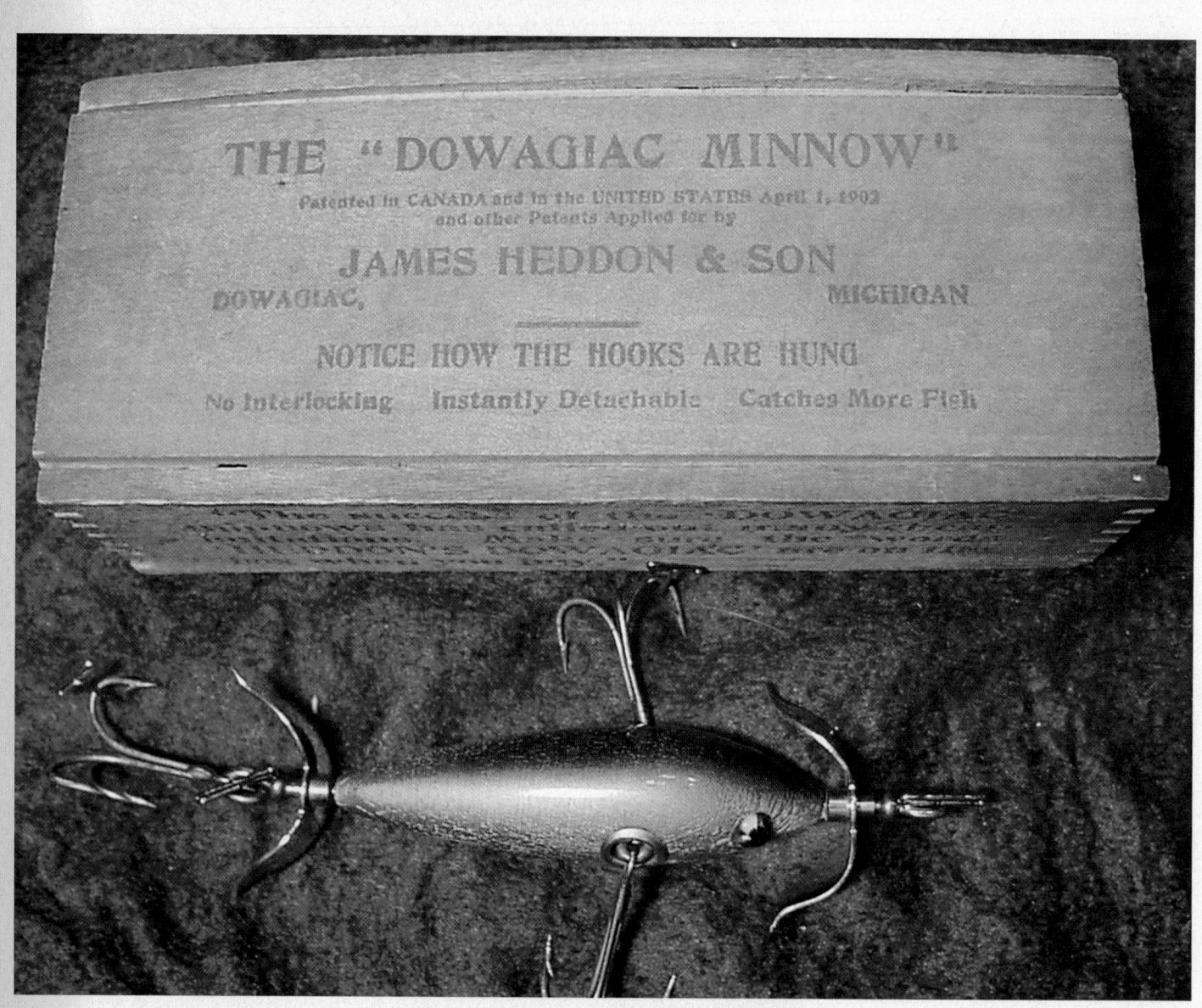

Heddon Gold 100 in wooden box, $2,500.00.

About the Author

An avid angler for over 50 years, I only started collecting antique tackle about 10 years ago. I thought I had a lot of tackle before I started collecting! Now it seems every room in our house has something in it connected to fishing.

For 10 years, I was a fulltime guide on the Wisconsin River. Since then I have made my living as an antique tackle dealer. "Capt. John" is one of the most recognized names on eBay, where I sell over 5,000 lots every year. Many of these items are consigned to me by fellow collectors and dealers.

I am always looking for items to add to my collection. Please contact me if you have a big collection or just one nice item for sale. I will also try to answer questions you might have about old tackle.

John A. Kolbeck
a.k.a. Capt. John
1610 Michigan Ave.
Stevens Point, WI 54481
Telephone (715) 341-5687
Email jakolbeck@charter.net
Member of NFLCC

Captain John

COLLECTOR BOOKS
informing today's collector

www.collectorbooks.com

For over two decades we have been keeping collectors informed on trends and values
in all fields of antiques and collectibles.

OTHER COLLECTIBLES

This is only a partial listing of the books on antiques that are available from Collector Books. All books are well illustrated and contain current values. Most of these books are available from your local bookseller, antique dealer, or public library. If you are unable to locate certain titles in your area, you may order by mail from **COLLECTOR BOOKS**, P.O. Box 3009, Paducah, KY 42002-3009. Customers with Visa, MasterCard, or Discover may phone in orders from 7:00 a.m. to 5:00 p.m. CT, Monday – Friday, toll free **1-800-626-5420**, or online at **www.collectorbooks.com**. Add $4.00 for postage for the first book ordered and 50¢ for each additional book. Include item number, title, and price when ordering. Allow 14 to 21 days for delivery.

www.collectorbooks.com

1-800-626-5420
Fax: 1-270-898-8890